Economic Innovations and Technological Developments in HRM

Salim Kurnaz
Kazimiero Simonaviciaus University, Lithuania

Jolanta Bieliauskaitė
Kazimiera Simonaviciaus University, Lithuania

IGI Global
Publishing Tomorrow's Research Today

Published in the United States of America by
    IGI Global
    701 E. Chocolate Avenue
    Hershey PA, USA 17033
    Tel: 717-533-8845
    Fax: 717-533-8661
    E-mail: cust@igi-global.com
    Web site: https://www.igi-global.com

Library of Congress Cataloging-in-Publication Data

CIP Pending
ISBN: 979-8-3693-4412-5
EISBN: 979-8-3693-4413-2

British Cataloguing in Publication Data
A Cataloguing in Publication record for this book is available from the British Library.

All work contributed to this book is new, previously-unpublished material.
The views expressed in this book are those of the authors, but not necessarily of the publisher.

Table of Contents

Detailed Table of Contents

Chapter 1

Serap Türkyilmaz, Beykent Üniversitesi, Turkey

Nowadays, digital transformation is evident in all aspects of life as processes are being replaced with smart systems, enhancing satisfaction levels with increased online services.By converting traditional programs into modern digital programs, it facilitates the work of human resource managers. Along the way, in addition to having a specific goal, all ideas must be prioritized. To prevent any disruptions to work, everyone should have a comprehensive partnership in this system, along with the organization's culture. This section discusses the benefits, disadvantages, and key factors that lead to digital transformation in the organization, reducing time, error percentage, and costs separately.In addition to reducing risk, this strategic model also leads to learning new capabilities for sustainable feedback.

Chapter 2

Fatma Gül Karaçelebi, Niğde Ömer Halisdemir Üniversitesi, Turkey

This study focuses on the relationship between digital transformation and green human resources management in businesses. In this context, first of all, the historical development of human resources management is mentioned, and the change in management's perspective on human resources is explained. At the same time, information about the transition to the human resources management process is included. It has been attempted to explain why digital transformation applications are necessary in businesses, especially in the human resources unit. The concept of Green Human Resource Management (HRM) is explained, and Green HRM practices in businesses are elucidated with the help of a model.

This study examined the impact of flexible work arrangements on work-family balance among bank workers in India, based on interviews with 10 employees from various private banks. Using the Interpretative Phenomenological Analysis method, employees' experiences before the adoption of flexible schedules and their expectations and impacts afterward were explored. While there is hope for the benefits of flexible schedules, a smooth transition is crucial. Key success factors include effective monitoring systems for accountability and productivity, role-specific flexibility models to meet diverse needs, technology integration for smooth operations, and employee well-being initiatives to address burnout, isolation, and work-life imbalance, along with clear communication. The study highlights the importance of these elements in fostering a supportive and adaptable work culture in the Indian banking sector. By prioritizing these success factors, organizations can overcome implementation challenges and promote work-family balance among bank employees.

The COVID-19 pandemic has had a major effect on the field of Human Resource Management HRM, prompting quick adaptation and innovation by organizations around the world. This chapter examines the pandemic's multifaceted effects on HRM practices, highlighting both the challenges that were encountered and the innovative measures implemented in response. The pandemic has hastened the adoption of digital technology, resulting in a considerable increase in remote work habits and digital transformation within organizations. While these developments have increased operational efficiency, they have also raised worries about employees' digital abilities, privacy, and the blurring of work-life boundaries. The epidemic has highlighted the significance of strategic workforce planning, with HRM practitioners focusing on improving employee skills, well-being, and engagement. This chapter will provide an in-depth overview of these changes, exploring the evolution of HRM practices and identifying the most effective ways for navigating the challenges created by the pandemic.

Deeksha Gupta Ganguly, Christ University, India
Deepti Sinha, Christ University, India
Vandita Bhaumik, Christ University, India
Ronit Varghese, Christ University, India

Job satisfaction and Employee engagement are critical to the success of any business, particularly in the education sector. This study examines the relationship between job satisfaction and employee engagement in the education sector, focusing on Delhi NCR. The research uses collection of data from 16 educators through semi structured interviews. It is based on Interpretative Phenomenological Analysis (IPA) tool to examine the factors affecting employee engagement and job satisfaction. The findings aim to improve teaching quality, student outcomes, and institutional effectiveness. However, the study has limitations, including subjectivity, risk of bias, and being limited to the educational sector. Despite these limitations, the study contributes to the existing knowledge by revealing the dynamics of work satisfaction and employee engagement in the education sector, providing valuable insights for organizational management and policy formation.

S. Raksithaa, Christ University, India
Ginu George, Westford University College, India

This paper aims to explore and understand employees' subjective experiences and perceptions regarding work-life balance in the context of evolving leadership styles post-COVID-19. It also examines the coping mechanisms and strategies employees and organizations employ to navigate work-life balance challenges in the changed work landscape. Finally, this paper examines the changes in remote work in the context of WLB and various types of leadership in the post-pandemic scenario. The Boolean search was employed, and. keywords relevant to Work-life Balance and Leadership were utilized to find the papers for further analysis. The results state that leaders understand and cooperate with employees during this transition period. They prioritize employees' well-being and flexibility in the work schedule. Leaders follow a mix of servant and transformational leadership styles to lead the employees. The study also highlights the coping mechanisms and the workplace changes that navigate the employees' work-life balance.

GHRM or Green Human Resource Management refers to the use of environmentally friendly as well as environmentally conscious practices across the whole Human Resource Management function. Policies, practices, and systems that encourage green and environmentally sound resource implementation among an organization's staff are called green as well as sustainable practices, respectively. The goal of this work is to show how Human Resource Management can go green without sacrificing effectiveness. The United States, China, and the United Kingdom are among the fastest-developing countries in terms of Green HR laws and practices. The rest of the emerging world is right behind them. Today, sustainable fashion is at the forefront of the textile industry. . McDonagh drafted a green management plan in 1997, but it's unclear when GHRM was first developed. Human resource activities including hiring, orientation, training, promoting, assessing performance, and setting salaries are all part of the plan.

This chapter examines the legal challenges facing the public sector in managing human resources, which can hinder excellent and efficient public administration. The chapter examines the legal challenges most encountered in the public sector due to its specific working conditions and legislative and regulatory requirements, such as ensuring equal opportunities, conflicts of interest, ensuring privacy and confidentiality of public servants, and other legally relevant aspects of human resource management in the civil service.

Cem Angin, Ordu University, Turkey

Human resources management refers to the organizational and managerial activities covering the processes of recruitment, training, development and adaptation of personnel, which is one of the most basic needs of an organization, to the objectives of the organization. Human resources management, which symbolizes a break from the classical understanding of personnel management, first emerged in the private sector and then spread to public administration. For both the private and public sectors, the human element is now of "strategic" importance. This importance has been a development that has brought human resource management to the forefront today. This study focuses on the bibliometric analysis of studies in the field of human resource management. The study will present a multidimensional analysis of the studies conducted in the field of human resource management in the world. In this context, the study aims both to guide academics and researchers who will work in this field and to open the door to new studies by revealing the shortcomings and gaps in this field.

Sunil Kumar, Shoolini University, India
Dushyanth Kumar, Lovely Professional University, India

E-training refers to virtual, web-based training programs. Organizations are increasingly adopting e-training tools and methods for human resource management (HRM). This study aims to describe the role of e-training and its tools in the learning and development of employees across organizations. Data were collected from the SCOPUS database, identifying 80 publications on e-training through keyword searches. Performance analysis was conducted using bibliometric methods, identifying relevant sources, authors, and countries, along with thematic and factorial evolution. Various problems, challenges, tools, and technologies were identified based on the literature. This study aims to guide and assist learning and development practitioners, scholars, and HR managers in understanding the significance of e-training methods and tools in HRM.

Kübra Nur Cingöz, Gaziantep University, Turkey
Vildan Durmaz, Eskisehir Technical University, Turkey

The surge in airline transportation since the early 2000s, buoyed by incentives like fuel discounts and landing-stopover benefits, has necessitated the expansion of existing airports for sustainable growth. Sabiha Gökçen Airport, experiencing rapid air traffic escalation since 2014, grapples with substantial waiting queues for both aircraft and passengers. Addressing these challenges requires effective stakeholder communication and collaboration. This study underscores the pivotal role of communication in mitigating issues arising from escalating aircraft traffic at Sabiha Gökçen Airport, emphasizing that sustainable growth cannot be attained amidst prolonged waiting times. The study interrogates the extent to which increased capacity influences operational productivity and explores strategies for leveraging enhanced capacity through effective stakeholder collaboration

B. Anthony Brown, Walden University, USA
Keri L. Heitner, Walden University, USA

The theories and practices comprising modern human resource management (HRM) boast an extensive evolution and continue to evolve. Fayolism by Henri Fayol (1841-1925), Taylorism by Frederic Winslow Taylor (1857-1915), bureaucracy by Maximilian Weber (1864-1920), leadership styles and change management by Kurt Lewin (1890-1947), theory X and theory Y by Douglas McGregor (1906-1964), the hierarchy of needs by Abraham Maslow (1908-1970), need theory by David Clarence McClelland (1917- 1988), and motivation-hygiene theory by Frederick Herzberg (1923-2000) precipitated and consolidated HRM as known today. Although fundamental to present-day HRM, globally, the HRM tenets hewed in the three previous industrial revolutions remain largely misaligned with sustainable human asset management (sHAM). Given the preceding, the question is whether organizational leaders can use disruptive innovation to (a) enable sustainable human asset management while (b) maximizing efficiency and production to achieve organizational sustainability in the impending fourth industrial revolution.

This study investigates how human resource employees experience the big data phenomenon in the recruitment function of human resource management and how their perceptions of the phenomenon have evolved. This study also examines how big data will affect organizational and human resource management and how it can be improved in other functions of human resources. In this exploratory study, which comprehensively addresses the big data phenomenon in human resources management, the phenomenological design approach, one of the qualitative research methods, was applied to test the research questions and a semi-structured interview form was used for research data.

The burgeoning adoption of robotics in Human Resource Management (HRM) offers a double-edged sword. Automation by robots unlocks a plethora of opportunities, streamlining HR processes and enabling strategic pursuits. However, this integration presents significant challenges that demand attention. Job displacement due to automation, the emergence of skill gaps, ethical concerns surrounding data privacy and algorithmic bias, and potential employee resistance all pose hurdles to successful implementation. This study delves into these challenges and proposes solutions for a smooth transition towards a robotics-infused HRM framework, ensuring organizations reap the benefits of this technological revolution.

Chapter 15

Mohammad Badruddoza Talukder, International University of Business
Agriculture and Technology, Bangladesh
Sharmin Akter Chowdhury, International University of Business
Agriculture and Technology, Bangladesh
Musfiqur Rahoman Khan, Daffodil Institute of IT, Bangladesh

Technological developments and economic breakthroughs are propelling the gig economy, revolutionizing human resource management. Significant economic shifts include decentralized workplaces, flexible work arrangements, freelancing, and dynamic pricing patterns. The administration of gig workers is made more accessible by technological improvements, including digital HR tools, AI-driven recruitment, and virtual collaboration platforms. Considering these shifts, strategic workforce planning, regulatory compliance, and initiatives to engage and retain gig workers are imperative. HR departments must adjust to a diverse workforce by promoting inclusivity striking a balance between stability and flexibility. Technology-enabled integration of gig workers improves productivity and job satisfaction. To manage a diversified and regionally distributed workforce, businesses must adopt these advances to enhance their HR procedures. This flexibility is essential to keeping a competitive advantage in the changing labour market, where the gig economy is becoming increasingly important.

Chapter 16

Alev Orhan, Sivas Cumhuriyet Üniversitesi, Turkey
Salim Kurnaz, Kazimiera Simonaviaus University, Lithuania

The objective of this study is to conduct a bibliometric analysis of the keyword network, numerical distribution by years, citation network of the most frequently cited publications, most active researchers, most active journals, countries and institutions of the studies published in the field of human resource management education between 1990 and May 1, 2024 in the WOS database. Furthermore, the objectives of the studies examined in the research are analysed in order to identify the trends of research in the field of artificial intelligence in human resources management and the remaining gaps in the research area. In the study, the criterion sampling method, one of the purposive sampling methods, was selected. The research is a descriptive content analysis study employing qualitative research methods. The R Programming Language "biblioshiny" package program was employed in the analysis of the data collected for the initial objective of the study, while MAXQDA 2020 (20.4.0) was utilized in the second stage.

Preface

Human Resource Management (HRM), over the past two decades has ushered in transformative changes that have redefined how organizations approach their most valuable asset: their people. As the editors of this reference book, we, Assoc. Prof. Dr. Salim Kurnaz from Turkey and Prof. Dr. Jolanta Bieliauskaite from Lithuania, are thrilled to present "Economic Innovations and Technological Developments in HRM," a comprehensive exploration of contemporary HRM theory and practice in the twenty-first century.

The COVID-19 pandemic has served as a catalyst for significant shifts in HRM, challenging traditional methodologies and forcing organizations to adapt swiftly to new realities. As we navigate this post-pandemic era, it becomes imperative to reflect on the lessons learned and to analyze the innovative practices that have emerged. This book aims to serve as both a scholarly resource and a practical guide, offering insights into how HRM can evolve to meet future challenges.

In our first section, we delve into the foundational studies that have shaped HRM to date, establishing a theoretical framework that informs our understanding of current practices. This comprehensive review provides valuable context for researchers and practitioners alike.

The second part of our exploration focuses on the intersection of economic innovations and technological advancements with HRM. As digital transformation accelerates, we examine its impact on workplace culture and employee engagement, as well as the broader implications for social and economic life.

We then turn our attention to the effects of the COVID-19 pandemic, analyzing its profound impact on working life and the emergence of new management practices. Understanding these changes is crucial for developing a resilient and adaptable HRM framework that can thrive in an unpredictable world.

Finally, we look toward the future of HRM, evaluating different strategies employed across nations and sectors. By synthesizing these varied approaches, we aim to offer guidance that will not only inform academic discourse but also influence practical applications in the field.

This publication is designed for a diverse audience, including researchers, scholars, practitioners, and students across multiple disciplines. We invite you to engage with the empirical data, theoretical insights, and case studies presented herein, which collectively illuminate the dynamic and multifaceted nature of HRM.

As we embark on this journey through the evolving world of HRM, we hope this book will inspire further research, foster innovation, and contribute to the ongoing dialogue on the strategic importance of human resources in organizations today and in the future.

In "Economic Innovations and Technological Developments in HRM," each chapter contributes valuable insights into the evolving landscape of Human Resource Management. Below, we provide an overview of each chapter, emphasizing the critical themes and findings presented by our esteemed contributors.

Chapter 1: Digital Transformation In HRM

Serap Türkyilmaz explores the profound impact of digital transformation on HRM processes, emphasizing how transitioning from traditional systems to smart technologies enhances efficiency and employee satisfaction. The chapter discusses the essential elements for successful implementation, highlighting the need for organizational culture to support this shift. Türkyilmaz analyzes the benefits and potential drawbacks of digital systems, focusing on how they reduce errors and operational costs while fostering continuous learning.

Chapter 2: Digital Transformation in Human Resources Management - Green Human Resources Management

Fatma Karaçelebi investigates the synergy between digital transformation and Green Human Resource Management (GHRM). By tracing the historical evolution of HRM, this chapter articulates the necessity for digital applications within HR to foster sustainability. Karaçelebi elaborates on GHRM practices, offering a model that integrates environmental consciousness into HR functions, showcasing the potential for businesses to operate sustainably.

Chapter 3: The Role of Flexible Work Arrangements in Work-Life Balance

Vedika Pathania and colleagues provide an in-depth analysis of flexible work arrangements in the Indian banking sector. Through qualitative interviews, the authors uncover employees' experiences with these arrangements, emphasizing the critical success factors necessary for their effective implementation. This chapter underscores the importance of technology, accountability, and communication in promoting work-life balance and preventing burnout.

Chapter 4: Reshaping Human Resource Management Insights from the COVID-19 Pandemic

Ece Yilmaz examines the transformative effects of the COVID-19 pandemic on HRM practices. This chapter highlights the rapid adoption of digital tools and remote work, while also addressing challenges related to employee engagement and digital competency. Yilmaz discusses strategic workforce planning as a vital component for future HRM success, offering insights into how organizations can enhance employee well-being in this new landscape.

Chapter 5: Nurturing Excellence: The Influence of Employee Engagement on Job Satisfaction in the Educational Realm

Deeksha Ganguly and her team delve into the relationship between employee engagement and job satisfaction in the education sector. Through qualitative research, they reveal key factors that influence engagement and satisfaction among educators. The findings aim to enhance teaching quality and institutional effectiveness, contributing valuable insights for educational management.

Chapter 6: Navigating the New Norm: Exploring Work-Life Balance with Evolving Leadership Styles

Raksithaa S and Ginu George explore how leadership styles affect employees' work-life balance post-COVID-19. By analyzing coping strategies and leadership dynamics, the authors highlight the importance of flexibility and well-being initiatives in fostering a supportive work environment. This chapter emphasizes the role of empathetic leadership in navigating the challenges of modern work settings.

Chapter 7: Green Human Resource Management in the Textile Industry for Conflict Management

Tanushree Gupta and Hari Prapan Sharma present GHRM practices within the textile industry, advocating for environmentally sustainable HR policies. This chapter highlights the critical role of HRM in promoting green initiatives without compromising organizational efficiency, showcasing global examples of successful GHRM implementation.

Chapter 8: Legal Challenges in Managing Human Resources in the Public Sector

Laura Matjošaityte addresses the legal complexities that impact HRM in the public sector. This chapter discusses issues such as equal opportunity, privacy, and conflict of interest, providing a framework for understanding the regulatory landscape that shapes public HR practices.

Chapter 9: Examining Human Resource Management with the Bibliometric Analysis Method

Cem Angin conducts a bibliometric analysis to explore the evolution of HRM literature. By identifying key trends and gaps, this chapter serves as a guide for researchers, helping them navigate the vast field of HRM and identify future research opportunities.

Chapter 10: E-Training in HRM Context - A Bibliometric Approach

Sunil Kumar and Dushyanth Kumar investigate the role of e-training in employee development. Utilizing bibliometric methods, this chapter analyzes the growth of e-training literature, offering insights into its impact on HRM practices and identifying key challenges and tools in the field.

Chapter 11: Harmonizing Stakeholder Synergy for Operational Excellence

Kübra Cingöz and Vildan Durmaz analyze the operational challenges faced by Sabiha Gökçen Airport due to increased traffic. This chapter emphasizes the importance of stakeholder communication and collaboration in achieving operational excellence and sustainable growth.

Chapter 12: Disruptive Innovations in Human Resource Management

B. Anthony Brown and Keri Heitner discuss how disruptive innovations can reshape HRM practices in the context of the Fourth Industrial Revolution. This chapter addresses the need for organizations to align traditional HRM practices with emerging technologies and sustainability goals.

Chapter 13: Big Data Analytics in Human Resource Management with Qualitative Insights

Hüseyin Erol and Ahmet Yildirim explore the implications of big data in HRM, focusing on recruitment and organizational management. Through qualitative research, this chapter provides insights into how HR professionals can leverage big data for improved decision-making.

Chapter 14: Integrating Robotics into the HRM Framework

Jaspreet Kaur investigates the dual opportunities and challenges posed by the integration of robotics in HRM. This chapter addresses the potential for automation to enhance efficiency while also discussing the ethical and practical challenges that organizations must navigate.

Chapter 15: The Gig Economy: Economic Innovations and Technological Advancements in Human Resource Management

Mohammad Talukder and Musfiqur Khan examine the transformative effects of the gig economy on HRM. This chapter highlights how technology enables the management of gig workers and discusses strategies for inclusivity and engagement in a decentralized workforce.

Chapter 16: Artificial Intelligence in Human Resource Management Training

Alev Orhan and Salim Kurnaz conduct a bibliometric analysis of AI applications in HRM education, identifying trends and gaps in the research. This chapter offers a comprehensive overview of the evolving role of AI in HR training and highlights areas for future exploration.

In summary, this edited volume not only addresses the current trends and challenges within HRM but also provides a roadmap for future research and practice in a rapidly changing environment. We invite you to delve into these chapters and explore the innovative approaches shaping the future of HRM.

As we conclude this comprehensive exploration in "Economic Innovations and Technological Developments in HRM," we are reminded of the profound transformations that have reshaped Human Resource Management in recent years. The contributions from our esteemed authors illuminate the dynamic interplay between technological advancements, economic shifts, and the evolving needs of the workforce.

This volume has not only documented the lessons learned from the COVID-19 pandemic but has also highlighted the innovative practices that have emerged in response to unprecedented challenges. From digital transformation and green HR practices to the integration of robotics and big data, each chapter offers invaluable insights that reflect the current landscape of HRM.

As editors, we believe that understanding these changes is essential for researchers, practitioners, and educators alike. The diverse perspectives presented herein provide a robust framework for navigating the complexities of modern HRM, encouraging dialogue and collaboration across disciplines.

We hope that this book serves as both a scholarly resource and a practical guide, inspiring ongoing research and fostering innovative approaches in HRM. As we look to the future, the adaptability and strategic importance of human resources will be paramount in ensuring organizational success in an ever-evolving global context.

Thank you for engaging with this work, and we trust that it will contribute meaningfully to your understanding of the critical role HRM plays in shaping a sustainable and inclusive future.

Sincerely,

Dr. Salim Kurnaz, Turkey

Dr. Jolanta Bieliauskaite, Lithuania

Chapter 1
Digital Transformation in HRM

Serap Türkyilmaz

https://orcid.org/0000-0001-9847-4164

Beykent Üniversitesi, Turkey

ABSTRACT

Nowadays, digital transformation is evident in all aspects of life as processes are being replaced with smart systems, enhancing satisfaction levels with increased online services.By converting traditional programs into modern digital programs, it facilitates the work of human resource managers. Along the way, in addition to having a specific goal, all ideas must be prioritized. To prevent any disruptions to work, everyone should have a comprehensive partnership in this system, along with the organization's culture. This section discusses the benefits, disadvantages, and key factors that lead to digital transformation in the organization, reducing time, error percentage, and costs separately.In addition to reducing risk, this strategic model also leads to learning new capabilities for sustainable feedback.

INTRODUCTION

In the professional work environment, with the use of technology tools, the manager of human resources is also subject to various developments. With the modernization of human resources and the digitalization of the employment process, leadership decisions are evolving. In the digital age of analysis, communication, ideas, and the ability to understand human skills are of particular importance.

As you can see in the graphic below, a large gap can be seen in the rate of change with the passage of time. The rate of digital growth is growing exponentially and there is a big gap between business and technology change.

DOI: 10.4018/979-8-3693-4412-5.ch001

Figure 1. The connection between the time and digital changes leads to transformation

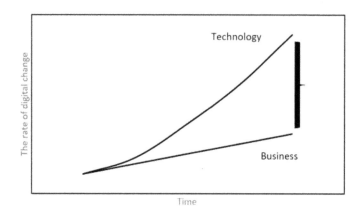

Digital transformation in the field of human resources is classified into three categories: targets, processes, and infrastructure. The targets mostly deal with workplace and work quality, digital processes, time improvement, cost reduction, and experience.

The process or the middle layer also points to the main activity for digital integration, support, development, and evaluation. In fact, ways to achieve goals are done with data-oriented processes and engineering processes.

The last layer of infrastructure deals with the discussion of new technologies in the fields of cultural, human, organizational, and management, which is the basis of this transformation. In the field of human resource management in digital transformation, the human aspect is more focused on the creation of digital culture (Kumar, 2016).

One of the benefits of digital human resources is the increase in digital skills and the release of time for specialists. The use of central data processes leads to increased organizational adaptation to the workforce. Other impacts of the process of digitalization of human resources lead to changes in business and community areas (Thite, 2019). Organizations integrate with digital elements, including tools and media, and adopt digital approaches. This process affects the entire organization in its own way, emphasizing the need for group participation.

One of the reasons for the intense competition in the digital transformation process is that it allows employees to work from anywhere, improving relationships. During the COVID-19 pandemic, most employees were forced to adapt and utilize digital tools. However, transformation is not an easy task, as many companies have failed on this path while others have successfully progressed by implementing effective strategies. It also necessitates changes in the skills required and guidance for employees to enhance organizational performance, led by HR managers. In studies, most researchers define digital transformation as a combination of advanced technology, changes based on data analytics, information technologies, and communication (Bharadwaj, 2013; Burchardt, 2019; Cichosz, 2020).

Due to the rapid changes of business models, organizations need to have well-designed human resource management processes (Bajer, 2017; Goetz et al., 2020). Digital transformation is particularly evident in the human and technological aspects. The blurring of boundaries between managers and employees during work hours, after work, or even after leaving the job has raised concerns and challenges related to privacy. This creates a foundation for privacy breaches. The benefits and drawbacks of the digital transformation process are discussed in this section, along with its role in leadership and management decisions, especially in the recruitment process and enhancing work quality.

1.THE ROLE OF DIGITAL TRANSFORMATION IN HRM

The concept of digitalization in human resource management (HR) is often referred to as "transformation," which involves fundamental changes in HR practices. With the evolving job market, organizations are facing challenges in finding and hiring suitable personnel. To address this, various tools are being utilized to identify and retain talented individuals. Technologies such as robotics, sensors, and artificial intelligence offer access to a global talent pool, but companies also need to consider the needs of their employees, including rewards and advancement opportunities.

To streamline the recruitment process and ensure the use of accurate data, HR professionals use Human Resource Information Systems (HRIS) and Applicant Tracking Systems (ATS) in tandem. HRIS helps man employee information such as benefits, salaries, performance evaluations, attendance, and absenteeism, while ATS leverages artificial intelligence to attract experienced candidates in a competitive market. Additionally, Learning Management Systems (LMS) software assists management in offering online courses, tracking employee progress, and evaluating performance.

With the development of software and automation systems, it is possible to facilitate interaction and collaboration between employees and organizations. For instance, Unilever's digital transformation of its human resources through online games and networking has helped attract skilled talent during the recruitment process. Similarly, IBM has leveraged digital platforms to enhance employee experiences. The COVID-19 pandemic has accelerated these digital transformations, leading companies to innovate further. One approach to digital transformation in recruitment involves inputting individual and organizational data into personal systems and platforms without direct employee involvement. This strategic method aims to streamline the recruitment process by filtering out unqualified candidates. One key advantage of these systems is the promotion of equal employment opportunities regardless of age, ethnicity, or gender. The concept of a digital HR matrix, which combines human resources technology and digital technologies, plays a significant role in categorizing candidates for job roles using artificial intelligence and Natural Language Processing (NLP) to identify the most suitable candidates.

In the past, before digitalization, the discussion of socialization was raised at the beginning of recruitment. Today, with the advent of digital recruitment processes, alignment and socialization are discussed. Unfortunately, authors often use these concepts with multiple interpretations, as noted by Platanus and Mäkelä (2016). Some advantages of digital recruitment include the ability to use digital signatures and provide conditions for job applications without physical presence, allowing candidates to submit their applications via mobile phones or computers.

Recruitment automation streamlines the process, saving time and money. Interviews can be conducted remotely. Implementing digital programs can motivate employees and help organizations achieve strategic goals.

Human Reliability Assessment (HRA) as a core human resources strategy relies on digital potentials (Bye, 2023). While its full impact may not be visible now, its potential for realization in the future is significant. In the digital era, the employment landscape has been greatly influenced by various technologies, leading to challenges and changes in the recruitment process. Today, the workforce is a valuable asset for any organization, making it crucial to hire talented individuals for organizational performance. The impact of these developments on employees should be considered, as it transforms their roles to be more analytical, active, and strategic.

Recruitment plays a vital role in strategic human resource management (SHRM), encompassing the organization's needs, developing strategies to attract and hire personnel, and aligning these efforts with specific goals to drive organizational success.

Figure 2. Main Factors Cause Digital Transformation in HRM

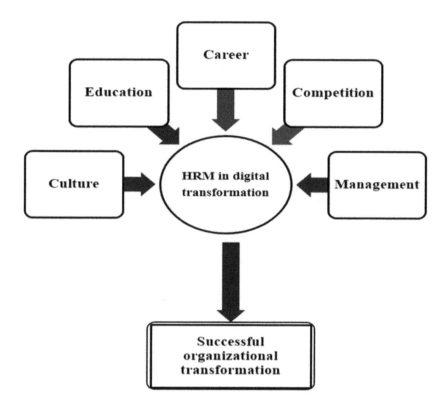

As shown in Figure 2, the basic and general factors affecting digital transformation can be categorized into 5 branches: culture, education, job, competition, and management. Each of these branches can be further divided into several sub-branches.

According to studies (Hoberg et al., 2017), digital transformation has been identified as a disruptive process that leads to changes in the competitive landscape, value proposition, and interactions of companies. According to Wright et al. (2001) and Biesalski (2003), organizations should recognize the importance of their human capital in the strategic and digital processes and strive to attract more talented employees. Organizations should understand that human resources (HR) are actually assets that do not incur costs.

The integration of humans with digital processes accelerates organizational growth, fosters new ways of working, and enhances innovation, making the recruitment of efficient and adaptable individuals crucial for achieving organizational objectives (Green, 2020). Additionally, the use of social networks, artificial intelligence (AI), digital assessments, and video interviews has streamlined the hiring process, emphasizing the significance of human capital in digital transformation and recruitment. Optimizing human capital through effective human resource management is essential for enhancing strategic performance and meeting future organizational needs.

Organizations should prioritize resource acquisition over focusing solely on the competitive business environment. Leading organizations like Apple, Google, and Microsoft recognize human capital as a fundamental resource that drives the development of effective recruitment processes and workforce a alignment with long-term organizational goals (Gifford, 2021). Recruitment practices have evolved over the years (Sekiguchi and Huber, 2011), with organizations now hiring employees based on organizational criteria to ensure survival and success, while also creating competitive advantages alongside profitability. According to Tabrizi et al. (2019), organizations must focus on changing employee mindsets and adapting organizational processes and culture to effectively leverage digital tools.

Human capital plays a critical role in achieving success in digital transformation and recruitment processes. Leveraging new digital tools to attract talented individuals can significantly enhance organizational performance and meet future needs. Recruiting digital talent drives organizational change in three ways: 1. Aligning recruiters' actions with the target group. 2. Enhancing recruiters' understanding of modern digital assessment conditions. 3. Employer support for digital transformation (Gilch and Sieweke, 2021).

The digital process is a significant revolution in business transformation that impacts organizational performance. Currently, digital organizations in industries like automotive, retail, and finance are competing with traditional or pre-digital organizations (Loebbecke and Picot, 2015). One of the key challenges for pre-digital companies is the lack of KSA (knowledge, skills, abilities) among their workforce, leading them to seek digital talent.

To achieve its goal of developing more than 60% of the operating system, the Volkswagen factory plans to increase its IT specialist employees from 2,000 in 2019 to over 10,000 by 2025 (Menzel, 2020). However, the demand for digital talent far exceeds the available supply.

Pre-digital organizations face challenges in recruiting digital talent due to: 1. Limited supply of digital talent and high demand, resulting in a "war for digital talent" (Edelman, 2012). 2. Lack of familiarity with the role and importance of digital talent, making it difficult to attract such talent. Companies are enhancing the integration of software and refining recruitment criteria to continuously improve the recruitment process.

The potential for market scalability is growing exponentially as digitization technology becomes more globally accessible. According to the analyses conducted, it is evident that human resource specialists are facing challenges in attracting labor, leading to a shift towards a public relations and marketing mentality. Additionally, there is a challenge related to the different positions of employment on social networks, which are often seen as marketing and public relations platforms rather than selection tools for candidates (King et al., 2014). Social networks are primarily used by job seekers, but recruiters also find them beneficial for viewing candidates' profiles for electronic recruitment.

The COVID-19 pandemic has brought significant changes to the recruitment process and work operations. The limitations imposed during this period have been mitigated by digital trends. Leaders in recruitment processes should avoid making hasty decisions and instead focus on organizing and planning meticulously to prevent disruptions in the system.

One of the objectives of digitizing the recruitment process is to understand the digital landscape in recruitment globally and assess the outcomes of remote work based on epidemiological standards. The interview department for employment is one of the most adaptable units in the online realm.

In this context, the following points should be considered:

1) Recruiters and employers must acknowledge that digitalization is inevitable and can lead to more efficient outcomes with proper management of programs.
2) Utilizing various online platforms streamlines the recruitment process, and allocating a budget for this purpose is essential.
3) The increased demand for working hours necessitates government support for concessions to some companies.

New technologies have transformed the HRM process through electronic recruitment methods, such as the integration of chatbots in the recruitment process. Technology-driven human resources have become more effective due to digitalization and the implementation of updated human resource strategies. E-HRM is tailored for human resource activities in the virtual realm. By gathering data from experts, informed decisions can be made in three key areas: salaries, selection and recruitment, and the transformation of processes into strategic functions, ultimately promoting fair employment.

2. ADVANTAGES OF HRM

Advantages of digital transformation in human resources:

- In the digital field, the possibility of human error is reduced in the process of recording information.
- The employee evaluation process is facilitated.

- The salary and reward system is easily controllable.
- Save time
- Increasing the speed of evaluation and organizational functions
- Facilitates the management process
- Ability to perform and control remote tasks
- Facilitate recruitment performance
- Checking the productivity of the organization
- Maintaining and easy access to data

Digital transformation, while leading to the facilitation of work, is a difficult and challenging process. According to the report by Deloitte, this development leads to a double challenge in the way of working and the workforce. Anyway, any change in human resources for business is logical to meet the needs. Among the problems created is trying to solve the problems of the new digital system and the work of the employees while using this technology.

Success stage of digital transformation:

- Carrying out experiments and various projects in the field of digital transformation throughout the organization
- Improving digital literacy and increasing creativity of employees
- Carrying out strategic plans and public participation in it
- Allocation of a specific operational team for the plans and programs of the organization to support the digital transformation
- Trying to create a new digital ecosystem for business promotion.

Another advantage of this evolution is the provision of universal programs such as HCM (Human Capital Management), self-service portals where employees and managers can access required information.

- Check the information related to NPS(Net Promoter Score), rating and customer satisfaction.
- Self-evaluation information, training, and organizational goals.
- Survey
- Job opportunity.
- Notification of meetings and company news.
- Informing employees about training courses to improve skills.

According to Deloitte, in 2021, the human resources manager must align all the talents of the organization's culture and structure to lead to transformation and increase the productivity of processes. Another topic is investigating transparency in digital human resource systems with the workforce, which leads to an increase in the sense of justice. Each organization should provide separate training channels and programs according to the needs and job position. Creating a digital workplace simultaneously with increasing employee motivation also leads to a reduction in infrastructure and operational costs.

Increasing feedback, reducing bribery in human functions, reducing work stress are among the benefits of digital transformation. One of the most important benefits of HRM is its role in long-term development and business operations.

The advantages of e-recruitment are:

- Low costs
- No intermediaries
- Reduction of time for recruitment
- Hiring the right people
- Efficiency of the recruitment process

Organizations are increasingly using artificial intelligence (AI) to support human resource (HR) management and decision-making processes. Although AI has the potential to fundamentally transform HR practices, there is little systematic research on how this transformation affects micro-level HR processes in organizations (recruitment, selection, training, evaluation of performance). Therefore, the primary objectives are (a) to examine how AI practices and processes are changing, (b) to examine the limited research on the effectiveness of AI in active HR processes, (c) present the advantages and disadvantages of using AI, and (d) provide directions for future practice and research on the use of AI in HR.

3. CHALLENGES IN DIGITAL TRANSFORMATION

Digital transformation was first proposed by Patel and McCarthy in 2000 and later by Roel and van der Kap in 2012 as a technology for radical change. In this context, the concept of digitalization and its impact on business are examined, focusing on converting analog data to digital and leading to quick and easier access to data (Parviainen et al., 2017).

Due to the constant change and adaptation of managers and organizations to environmental conditions, new learning models are considered an important challenge. According to these conditions, employees need to quickly acquire enough skills in different fields. Digital transformation, with the constant changes to digital technologies in the field of hardware and software, leads to social welfare. According to studies at the University of MIT, companies using digital technologies are almost

26% more profitable than other companies (Balakrishnan and Das, 2020). In the digital economy, workplace forces challenge the new generation of employment and traditional human values (Vardarlier, 2020). Today, artificial intelligence and robotics have replaced millions of jobs, but jobs related to this technology have also been created. Human resources managers must apply this digital transformation in their field of work and be accountable to improve the quality of service (Dahlbom et al., 2019). Reducing the boundaries between work and life and enhancing digital skills at work have led to organizational challenges. Every challenge brings a new opportunity and a new idea, but the lasting challenge is a new feature that has its own complexity.

However, most companies consider the categories of digital transformation and sustainability separately. Most investors in digital transformation believe that it makes them more flexible. The process of digitization, while increasing flexibility and reducing costs, leads to an increase in mass orders. Business models create new challenges by intertwining designers, suppliers, and customers, while renovating and changing the chain structure. Business competition, while eliminating industrial and non-industrial boundaries, leads to the provision of high-quality digital services.

Innovations in digital technologies, known as the fourth industrial revolution, lead to the creation of competitive and commercial conditions in the global market by making key changes in the industry sector. To continue this competition and support the growth of the national economy, companies must engage in digital transformation to communicate with all partners and customers. The challenges created by digital changes in domestic and foreign companies are clearly visible. New business models, opportunities, and rules in the global economy are evolving. With the creation of new opportunities, the flow of income and service provision increases. As digital transformation is closely related to technology, the presence of a digital leader is required to facilitate the rapid transformation of industries.

The digital paradigm brings relative benefits to people, changing lives and creating new opportunities. Companies should be aware of their digital assets and have a capable workforce. By providing employees with digital tools, organizations can increase productivity. Sometimes, hiring new staff can lead to a real increase in profits. The main advantage of the digital process is to meet customers' needs and create interaction. The concept of digital business requires technical and social skills, emphasizing the design process over production.

At the group level, approximately 40% of European companies do not utilize any technology related to digital entrepreneurship. These companies are typically small and medium-sized enterprises operating in sectors such as mining, construction, manufacturing, transportation, storage, and facilities (Marijana and Iva, 2017).

The challenges of digital business transformation regarding the possible risks that managers face can have adverse consequences. To address this issue, relevant algorithms in digital business transformation can provide support.

The challenges that company face in digital transformation include:

1) The fundamental nature of digital transformation and the factors that drive it
2) The necessary processes to address and implement these challenges
3) Algorithms required for digital business transformation

The primary issue for companies established before the digital age is to instigate change not just externally on the internet but also internally within the organization. According to researches in assessing organizations' readiness for digital transformation, conditions focusing on opportunities, resources, and management solutions to adapt to new realities are considered.

The stages of digital business transformation typically follow this sequence:

1) Identifying the digital position
2) Formulating a digital transformation strategy
3) Establishing measurable goals over time
4) Prioritizing goals based on importance.
5) Evaluating and reviewing results
6) Implementing necessary measures for improvement (Miroslava, 2018)

The results indicate that digitalization is a strategic, cultural, and organizational asset for companies, requiring effective management for commitment. Companies can adapt to market conditions by employing unique and personalized methods with customers, ensuring competitiveness. Concerns among business managers often revolve around new entrants disrupting business models and diminishing customer loyalty.

Companies must possess the ability to adapt and evolve with new business models; otherwise, the digital transformation process may become a disruptive or incremental change process for organizations. Typically, digital transformation commences with changes in the marketing function, leading to a demand for a skilled workforce and creating new job opportunities.

Managers seek ways to effectively manage remote teams, with process automation proving beneficial in this aspect. When initiating a digitization project, leaders must create conditions conducive to the company's digital transformation, as it impacts the organization's strategies (Henriette et al., 2016).

Digitization is a global phenomenon that fundamentally leads to changes and disruptions in assumptions related to life and work organization in the postmodern world. Therefore, proper and efficient planning for digital transformation, achieving flexible conditions, and creating competition is crucial for organizations. This process is lengthy, and its results have not yet been precisely determined. It requires significant resources for investment and competent labor. Unfortunately, an in-depth study on the effects and consequences of digitization in organizations has not been proposed. However, scientific knowledge should still prepare organizations for the risks and challenges arising from it. Simultaneously, long-term and sustainable planning should be undertaken to ensure the growth of the digital economy and its effects (Gorensek, 2018).

In many studies, a positive relationship between digital transformation and improving organizational performance is observed. According to the conducted research, integrating digital technologies into the overall infrastructure of the organization leads to profitability, and enhances communication among colleagues, suppliers, and partners, thereby improving added value. The increasing reliance on digital processes in all aspects has made organizations vulnerable to cyberattacks and security breaches. Addressing this issue requires significant financial costs, and technical solutions are necessary to tackle these challenges, including data loss prevention, data discovery and classification, backup and recovery, and environmental defense. Studies indicate that digital transformation plans are successful when organizations can address information security issues by taking appropriate measures.

4. MOVING TOWARDS DATA CENTRICITY

What Drives Human Resources Towards Digitization?

The transformation of human resources is necessary to reduce the gap between business productivity and technology growth and transformation in the field of human capital. In this direction, it is almost facing resistance from internal and old forces in digital businesses. Therefore, new digital technologies, cloud computing, artificial intelligence, etc., in the field of human capital should be utilized by reviewing organizational functions. One of the main reasons for the failure of these plans is the lack of using the proper method and roadmap for human resources. Using digital transformation in the roadmap is a method to improve these plans. The digital workforce analyzes their work processes with the help of internet-connected devices, including mobile phones, video, etc. Digital transformation is actually the conversion of traditional processes and work based on paper and filing to systems based on technology. This transformation starts with changing culture, management, and people's way of working. In fact, every time the employee clicks on the mouse, they have a digital experience. Digital transformation is a multi-step process and it cannot be done just because of competitors because this idea leads to costs for the organization. But transformation means talent management in the fields of recruitment, business, data management, etc. The Covid-19 crisis has clearly shown the effective role of digital transformation and data-based decision-making in all work areas. In the long term, by investing in digital transformation in human resources, organizations will see an increase in the efficiency of the organization and a reduction in cost and time.

Figure 3. Leading uses of AI to Assist Workers in their Organization According to Global Business and HR Leaders as of 2020 (Statista 2024)

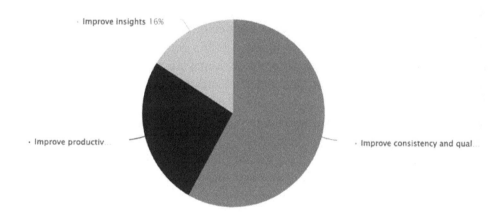

According to Statista website in 2020, business leaders and human resources used artificial intelligence (AI) during a study to help employees of their organization around the world. According to the results obtained in 58% of them, the main use of Artificial intelligence led to the improvement of the quality and stability of their work. In 26% of them, it improved productivity and 16% improved their insight.

5. STRENGTHENING THE WORKFORCE

Organizations have integrated digital elements such as tools and media and have turned to digital approaches (Maditheti, 2017). All employees involved in digital transformation must change and adjust their priorities by considering a series of options. Recently, the issue of reskilling has been raised by human resource managers in digital transformation, aiming to increase employees' literacy and promote them to higher levels.

The digital process is an integral part of human life. Changes in technology affect the communication process and the way of working, and these changes should have a positive impact on employees' work productivity and satisfaction. The digitalization process is aligned with the design and development of new professional roles in human resources. According to Wibowo et al. (2020) and Zhang et al. (2023), all professions must be prepared to strengthen themselves in the digital domain; otherwise, it may lead to collapse.

The Covid-19 pandemic has shown that digital transformation and the integration of online and offline technologies are essential for continued survival; otherwise, companies may not survive (Yu & Jinajun, 2020). Digital transformation enables quick access to information and better decision-making. In this regard, trust in organizations distinguishes them from others in attracting skilled talents.

Digitization has propelled organizations forward since the discovery of the Internet. Today, people cannot imagine their business or personal life without digital technologies. Digitalization has created many challenges as well as great opportunities for organizations. Most of the existing studies have investigated the role of digitalization on business performance and worker productivity. In most studies, job satisfaction, work/life balance, and worker autonomy have been favored as three areas of academic research in the field of digitalization. We suggest that digitization improves job satisfaction, disrupts work/life balance, and promotes greater worker autonomy.

The findings of this research can help managers better understand the importance and effects of digitalization. As digitalization in the workplace brings challenges as well as opportunities, it is important for managers to fully understand them to eliminate risks and increase the desired effects. Today, digital assets can be found in most organizations (Kuusisto, 2015). Labor markets have changed dramatically since the advent of digital and communication technologies (Castells, 2010). The effects of digital technologies have been studied since the 1960s. Fernandez-Macias (Eurofound, 2021) described the major consequences of digitalization on organizations. The changes that have occurred have affected all tasks and jobs and have brought new job roles. With the change in working conditions, the environmental, psychological, and physical needs have increased, while changes in industrial relations have altered the organization of employees and employers, and their work relations and disputes.

During the studies, some researchers are convinced that information and communication technology promotes autonomy, while others believe that it leads to increased monitoring of employees' performance, and also a group believes that digitalization can increase both autonomy and monitoring (Gerten, Beckmann & Bellmann, 2018).

With the replacement of machines with humans and the changes in the content of jobs, working relationships and working conditions have also changed. With the onset of COVID-19, the demand of employees for working hours increased and led to digital transformation in work environments. Algorithms based on artificial intelligence play an important role in the digital economy and manage all the employer's tasks from the interview stage for hiring to firing.

Digital technologies lead to the reduction of heavy, or dangerous workloads and improve working conditions. There are also concerns such as vague decision-making and intrusion into the privacy of people's lives (Eurofound, 2021). According to the report of the European Trade Union Institute, the use of artificial intelligence has negative effects on the work of workers (STOA, 2022). Of course, improving conditions is also possible in this way.

6. POSSIBLE PROBLEMS AND CONCERNS

Continuous socio-economic developments over time create competition, leading commercial and industrial institutions to focus on human resources for their survival and differentiation. This study addresses the human resource management problems faced by businesses and seeks solutions to these issues. Another aspect of digital transformation is how to store and archive employee information. In the past, human resource management used paper archives for information storage, but today all data is stored in computers and organizational servers for quick access.

Human resource management is systematically defined within the framework of policies and often encounters problems due to inefficient human resource policies. Digital psychology is another issue resulting from the blurring of boundaries between work and personal life, leading to psychological problems. Another problem with this system is that people from different cultures use different hand and face movements to perform certain tasks or understand issues, and digital systems make mistakes in interpreting these gestures. In fact, as technology advances, the capabilities of the applications should also increase. Another concern of people is that the use of digital systems in phones and laptops can lead to access to private systems and compromise people's privacy.

In Conclusion, as companies grow larger, there is a strong correlation between human capital and organizational performance, as well as the quality of life of employees. Hiring talented and skilled individuals leads to more efficient and better out comes. Employee trust contributes to increased job satisfaction and enhances their performance.

7. THE ROLE OF DIGITAL TRANSFORMATION IN LEADERSHIP AND MANAGEMENT DECISIONS

During the digital transformations, leadership should adapt to become a young and agile system, and employee performance should be evaluated based on data. In the Y generation, there is a focus on equality of rights between employees and employers, with connected networks being commonly used. The digital transformation of human resources involves changes in processes such as salaries, performance evaluation, development, recruitment, and rewards (Halid et al., 2020). This digitalization leads to faster processes and improved managerial performance by reducing costs and workforce (Micu et al., 2017). Strohmeier (2020) suggests that integrating digital strategies advances digital human resources management. Some researchers argue that digital human resource management can also be seen as green human resource management, benefiting the organization's environmental performance. It enhances and simplifies employees' work, and organizations must embrace digitalization to stay competitive.

All employees access their personal platform within the organization to retrieve relevant information from the portal. Managers can use the portal for group information, individual profiles, and conducting surveys to enhance organizational policies. The platform should be continuously updated to ensure employee satisfaction. By creating human resource chat bots, many questions from applicants can be answered online without wasting time and money. These bots are available 24 hours a day, throughout the week, to respond to everyone's messages at any time.

Older workers are less eager to accept this transformation; therefore, the human resources manager should implement a plan to convince and increase the understanding of this group within the organization's personnel and encourage them. Of course, if this transformation is done by surveying the employees, there is less possibility of resistance from the personnel.

The resource manager of the organization must first convince himself that the company needs transformation and that there is value in trying to improve and enhance the organizational benefits. In this area, by increasing the value of employees, it leads to the improvement of skills and job success.

By appointing people in each department, the human resources management must periodically evaluate the technologies and plans of each department to ensure that the plan used is effective in promoting the policy of organizational goals, or that the needs of employees and customers are met or not.

Digital human resources are actually an evolutionary path towards the conceptualization of human resources based on digital technology. As the intensity of digitization of human resources increases, the amount of relevant research in this field also increases. The digitalization of the workplace leads to changing demands and skills of employees, prompting a rethink in the way they are managed, which leads to career development. The effects of digitization directly and indirectly affect all the processes of the organization (Bajer, 2017; Kagermann, 2015; Schwanholz et al., 2018; Parida et al., 2019). To gain competitive advantages, it requires intellectual and human capital. In order to comprehensively analyze this development, the participation of managers and employees should be done to build relationships, and sufficient training should be provided.

According to the studies conducted, digitalization has a significant impact on all customer relations, marketing, purchasing behavior, and business relations, which has been relatively greater than its impact on the organization's internal behavior in human resource management (Burchardt et al., 2019). A new type of management process is proposed (Burchardt et al., 2019; Cortellazzo et al., 2019) with new conditions, it is accompanied by an increase in the efficiency of functions. This transformation is a flexible organizational process (Bajer, 2017).

Leadership involves one's ability to effectively direct, inspire, motivate, and organize the efforts of others in order to achieve a common goal (Cahyono et al., 2023). Meanwhile, there is a dynamic exchange between a leader and his followers in which the leader takes responsibility for providing direction, guidance, and support in order to facilitate.

The concept of leadership goes beyond an individual's position or organizational title and encompasses the characteristics and behaviors they exhibit. Leadership can be exercised by people who lack formal authority, as long as they have the ability to inspire and influence others through their vision, values, competencies, and positive behavior (Wang et al., 2022). There are different types of leadership approaches and theories developed by experts. Some common approaches include:

1. Transformational leadership: Inspirational leaders strive to achieve higher goals by motivating their followers to actively contribute to the success of the organization beyond their own expectations.
2. Interactive leadership: This approach involves organized exchange between employees and the leader. Leaders also offer rewards or incentives to those who achieve set goals.

3. Situational leadership: This approach shows that it is different depending on the specific situation and context. The demands and traits of the individuals or groups they are in charge of influence how a leader approaches their style of leadership.
4. Service leadership: As the main focus of service leadership, they dedicate themselves to helping and serving the needs of their followers with the goal of advancing the public good.

Effective leadership is a set of characteristics that include integrity, wisdom, reliability, compassion, communication skills, nurturing capacity, decision-making, and maintaining strong relationships with subordinates. The concept of digital transformation refers to the process by which organizations adopt and integrate digital technologies into their operations, strategies, and business models. Creating value in the organization, this concept includes integration (Sukenti, 2023). The digital transformation process goes beyond the adoption of new technologies. This includes changes in work culture, organizational structure, and cognitive frameworks in the organization.

This phenomenon involves applying innovative processes, understanding technological patterns, and organizational settings to effectively navigate an increasingly volatile and evolving environment.

Digital transformation management consists of several steps:

1. Implementation of digital technology, such as the introduction of new platforms, systems, or tools that suit the needs of organizations.
2. Analysis and planning to deeply understand the goals of digital transformation, identify areas that need improvement, and develop an overall strategic plan for the implementation of digital technologies.
3. Integration and optimization in the implementation phase, which integrates digital technologies into daily operations, ensuring their effective use.
4. Digital transformation also causes a change in organizational culture that supports and promotes collaboration and innovative thinking.

The importance of digital transformation management lies in recognizing the potential of digital technology to fundamentally change organizational processes, strengthen competitive advantage, and increase overall business performance (Kraus et al., 2021). However, the digital transformation process involves various obstacles, including the need for cultural changes, changes in work processes, and the adoption of complex technologies. Therefore, it becomes necessary to implement digital transformation management to effectively guide these changes in organizations and take full advantage of the wide capabilities offered by digital technology.

In addition to the roles mentioned, there are several other aspects that are important considerations in leadership positions in managing digital transformation in organizations. In our view, there are several additional aspects that can be considered:

1. By developing a culture of innovation, leaders create a new cultural environment that encourages innovation and a willingness to take risks, leading to the cultivation of creative thinking among employees. Leaders who create a favorable and safe space for experimentation can accelerate the digital transformation process.
2. A deep technological understanding of the technological aspects of digital transformation is essential for leaders. They should have a comprehensive understanding of inherent limitations and associated potential.
3. Changes brought about by digital transformation, including organizational frameworks, operational procedures, and cultural dynamics, must be effectively managed by leaders. In addition to management, they should also reduce resistance and improve the sense of dedication towards the changes. The psychological and social consequences of digital transformation should also be considered.
4. In the field of digital transformation, customer interaction is crucial. Leaders must have the ability to recognize and determine the needs of customers and their behavior patterns.
5. In digital transformation, the management and security of extensive and complex data are important. Leaders should have sufficient assurance to maintain procedures, policies, and overall infrastructure for effective data monitoring.
6. Leaders should strengthen the culture of cooperation and partnership and partner with external institutions.

8. IMPROVING THE QUALITY OF WORK LIFE

The most obvious impact of digital transformation on job search is that paper resumes are no longer used. Resumes are usually sent via email or online forms. Even today, artificial intelligence programs and performance evaluation algorithms are used to review and score applicants' resumes through systems like Hirevue. These systems assess people's reactions and actions by evaluating applicants' responses. However, a significant flaw of this system is its failure to consider individuals with mental and physical disabilities and their unique circumstances. When examining the disadvantages, solutions should be proposed to address each one of them. Ultimately, all processes should aim to enhance employee and customer satisfaction.

One of the key features of digital transformation is the connectivity it provides, enabling employees to work from anywhere and receive necessary support from the organization. Analytics is another crucial aspect of this development, allowing for data analysis through statistical data and modeling to assist managers. Recommendation systems powered by artificial intelligence are also a notable feature of this transformation, challenging traditional methods of operation.

In the past, all activities were confined to a physical location, but today they can be conducted in a virtual space, with work distributed among all employees. The role of leadership in managing digital transformation is paramount. Effective leadership implementation is essential for ensuring the success and efficiency of these changes. Leaders should consider several factors: understanding the organization's capacity in this area, anticipating changes and market trends, improving operational methods based on customer demands, and guiding the organization through the transformation process by fostering digital skills and comprehensive participation among employees. Leaders must stay informed about the latest digital technologies and provide relevant training for the organization, involving the entire workforce in this training and promoting active information exchange. By creating an innovative and supportive culture, leaders can mitigate risk factors and guide the organization towards success through effective change management and digital transformations.

CONCLUSION

After Covid-19, it has been observed that the amount of technical debt in companies has doubled. Therefore, it seems very logical to optimize digital transformation by investing in this sector. Digital transformation helps companies make better decisions, leading to better understanding and sustainable achievements. The digital process may be driven by customer expectations, competition pressure, new companies, regulations imposed by governments or organizations. The world is entering the fourth industrial revolution, which includes digital, biological, artificial intelligence, nano technologies, smart robots, virtual worlds, etc. Customer and organizational expectations will change accordingly.

Companies that embrace the comprehensive development of new platforms for digital human resource management improve the speed of organizational information construction. They also establish connections between internal and external information sources, enabling fast and scientific decision-making in a competitive environment.

A conceptual advance is made when HRM digitalization is combined with organizational digitization. Digital HRM then represents a future development in the idea of technology-based HRM. What is evident, though, is that innovation cannot be produced just by specific technical abilities. They should be combined with a variety of other abilities, including an understanding of organizations, entrepreneurship, and people, and cognitive skills. In addition, for innovation to be adopted and spread, people must possess a certain degree of general skills as both consumers and employees in order to fully capitalize on the advantages that innovation brings. It is also imperative that individuals adjust to the possible adverse effects.

REFERENCES

Bajer, J. (2017). Digital transformation needs the human touch. *Strategic HR Review*, 16(2), 91–92. DOI:10.1108/SHR-02-2017-0011

Balakrishnan, R., & Das, S. (2020). How do firms reorganize to implement digital transformation? *Strategic Change*, 29(5), 531–541. DOI:10.1002/jsc.2362

Bharadwaj, A., El Sawy, O., Pavlou, P., & Venkatraman, N. (2013). Digital business strategy: Toward the next generation of insights. *Management Information Systems Quarterly*, 37(2), 471–482. DOI:10.25300/MISQ/2013/37:2.3

Biesalski, E. (2003). Knowledge management and e-human resource management, Available at: https://www.kde.cs.uni-kassel.de/wpcontent/uploads/ws/LLWA03/fgwm/Resources/FGWM03_08_Ernst_Biesalski.pdf. [Accessed: 13 April 2024].

Burchardt, C., & Maisch, B. (2019). Digitalization needs a cultural change–examples of applying Agility and Open Innovation to drive the digital transformation. *Procedia CIRP*, 84, 112–117. DOI:10.1016/j.procir.2019.05.009

Bye, A. (2023). Future needs of human reliability analysis: The interaction between new technology, crew roles and performance. *Safety Science*, 158, 105962. DOI:10.1016/j.ssci.2022.105962

Cahyono, A. S., Tuhuteru, L., Julina, S., Suherlan, S., & Ausat, A. M. A. (2023). Building a Generation of Qualified Leaders: Leadership Education Strategies in Schools. *Journal of Education*, 5(4), 12974–12979. https://jonedu.org/index.php/joe/article/view/2289

Castells, M. (2010). *The rise of the network society. (Information age. economy, society and culture, 1.).* Wiley-Blackwell.

Cichosz, M., Wallenburg, C. M., & Knemeyer, A. M. (2020). Digital transformation at logistics service providers: Barriers, success factors and leading practices. *International Journal of Logistics Management*, 31(2), 209–238. DOI:10.1108/IJLM-08-2019-0229

Cortellazzo, L., Bruni, E., & Zampieri, R. (2019). The role of leadership in a digitalized world: A review. *Frontiers in Psychology*, 10, 1–21. DOI:10.3389/fpsyg.2019.01938 PMID:31507494

Dahlbom, P., Siikanen, N., Sajasalo, P., & Jarvenpää, M. (2019). Big data and HR analytics in the digital era. *Baltic Journal of Management*, 8(2), 221–234. DOI:10.1108/BJM-11-2018-0393

Deloitte. (2021). https://www2.deloitte.com/ua/en/pages/about-deloitte/press -releases/gx-2021-global-human-capital-trends-report.html.[Accessed: 13 April 2024].

Edelman, D. (2012). The war for digital talent is already here. Available at: https://www .forbes.com/sites/mckinsey/2012/01/23/the-war-for-digital-talent-is-alreadyhere/ #6c75189762cb, [Accessed: 14 April 2024).

Eurofound. (2021a). Digitisation in the workplace. Publications Office of the European Union, Luxembourg. Available at: https://www.eurofound.europa.eu/sites/ default/files/ef_publication/field_ef_document/ef21001en.pdf

Gerten, E., Beckmann, M., & Bellmann, L. (2018). Controlling working crowds: The impact of digitalization on worker autonomy and monitoring across hierarchical levels. Retrieved from: https://edoc.unibas.ch/61490/1/20180307130203 _5a9fd4bb4605b.pdf.

Gifford, J. (2021). Strategic human resource management. Available at: https:// www.cipd.co.uk/knowledge/strategy/hr/strategic-hrm-factsheet#gref [Accessed: 14 April 2024].

Gilch, P. M., & Sieweke, J. (2021). Recruiting digital talent: The strategic role of recruitment in organisations' digital transformation. *German Journal of Human Resource Management*, 35(1), 53–82. DOI:10.1177/2397002220952734

Göetz, M., & Jankowska, B. (2020). Adoption of Industry 4.0 Technologies and Company Competitiveness: Case Studies from a Post-Transition Economy. *National Research University Higher School of Economics*, 14(4), 61–78. DOI:10.17323/2500-2597.2020.4.61.78

Gorensek, T. & Kohont, A; (2018). Conceptualization of the Digitalization: Opportunities and Challenges for Organizations in the Euro- Meditteranean Area, 11(2). Pp. 94-115.

Green, M. (2020). Recruitment: an introduction Available at: https://www.cipd .ie/newsresources/practical-guidance/factsheets/recruitment#7034 [Accessed: 14 April 2024].

Halid, H., Yusoff, Y. M., & Somu, H. (2020). The relationship between digital human resource management and organizational performance, In First ASEAN Business, Environment, and Technology Symposium, Atlantis Press, pp: 96 -99.

Henriette, E., Feki, M., & Boughzala, I. (2016). Digital Transformation Challenges, *Tenth Mediterranean Conference on Information Systems (MCIS)*, Paphos, Cyprus, 33.pp 1-8.

Hoberg, P., Krcmar, H., & Welz, B. (2017). Skills for digital transformation Available at: http://www.corporateleaders.com/sitescene/custom/userfiles/file/Research/sapskillsfordigitaltransformation.pdf [Accessed: 10 April 2024].

Kagermann, H. (2015). Change through digitization - Value creation in the age of Industry 4.0. In *Management of permanent change* (pp. 23–45). Springer Gabler. DOI:10.1007/978-3-658-05014-6_2

King, D. B., O'Rourke, N., & DeLongis, A. (2014). Social media recruitment and online data collection: A beginner's guide and best practices for reaching low-prevalence and hard-to-reach populations. *Canadian Psychology*, 55(4), 240–248. DOI:10.1037/a0038087

Kraus, S., Mahto, R.V. & Walsh, S.T. (2021). "The importance of literature reviews in small business and entrepreneurship research", Journal of Small Business Management, Vol. ahead-of-print, .DOI:10.1080/00472778.2021.1955128

Kumar, B. N. (2016). Digital revolution in the mauritian public service: A human resource development perspective in two unrelated companies. *International Journal of Novel Research in Interdisciplinary Studies*, 3(5), 1–10.

Kuusisto, M. (2015). Effects of digitalization on organiza¬tions. Master of Science thesis. Tampere university of Technology.

Loebbecke, C., & Picot, A. (2015). Reflections on societal and business model transformation arising from digitization and big data analytics: A research agenda. *The Journal of Strategic Information Systems*, 24(3), 149–157. DOI:10.1016/j.jsis.2015.08.002

Menzel, S. (2020). *VW-Software-Einheit startet im Juli - Betriebssystem soll bis kommen*. Handelsblatt.

Micu, A., Capatina, A., Micu, A. E., & Schin, G. (2017). Exploring e -HCM Systems' benefits in organizations from private sector and public administration. *Journal of Promotion Management*, 23(3), 407–418. DOI:10.1080/10496491.2017.1294885

Miroslava, B. (2018). *Challenges Related To The Digital Transformation Of Business Companies*. Innovation Management, Entrepreneurship and Sustainability.

Nawaz, N. (2017). A comprehensive literature review of the digital HR research filed. In Information and Knowledge Management (Vol. 7, No. 4).

Parida, V., Sjödin, D., & Reim, W. (2019). Reviewing literature on digitalization, business model innovation, and sustainable industry: Past achievements and future promises. *Sustainability (Basel)*, 11(2), 391–410. DOI:10.3390/su11020391

Parviainen, P., Tihinen, M., Kääriäinen, J., & Teppola, S. (2017). Tackling the digitalization challenge: How to benefit from digitalization in practice. *International Journal of Information Systems and Project Management*, 5(1), 63–77. DOI:10.12821/ijispm050104

Platanou, K. & Mäkelä, K. (2016). HR function at the crossroads of digital disruption. Työn, 1, PP. 19–26.

Ruël, H., & Van der Kaap, H. (2012). E -HRM usage and value creation. Does a facilitating context matter? *German Journal of Human Resource Management*, 26(3), 260–281. DOI:10.1177/239700221202600304

Schwanholz, J., & Graham, T. (2018). Digital Transformation: New Opportunities and Challenges for Democracy? In Schwanholz J., Graham T., Stoll P. T. (Eds.), Managing Democracy in the Digital Age, pp. 1-7. Springer.

Strohmeier, , S. (2020), Digital human resource management: A conceptual clarification. *German Journal of Human Resource Management, 34*(3), pp. 345 -365.

Sekiguchi, T. & Huber, V. L. (2011). The use of person–organization fit and person–job fit information in making selection decisions', Organizational Behavior and Human Decision Processes, 116(2), pp. 203–216, ScienceDirect. .DOI:10.1016/j.obhdp.2011.04.001

STOA (Scientific Foresight Unit). (2022), AI and digital tools in workplace management and evaluation. An assessment of the EU's legal framework. Available at: https://www.europarl.europa.eu/RegData/etudes/STUD/2022/729516/EPRS _STU(2022)729516_EN.pdf

Sukenti, S. (2023). Financial Management Concepts: A Review. [ADMAN]. *Journal of Contemporary Administration and Management*, 1(1), 13–16. DOI:10.61100/ adman.v1i1.4

Tabrizi, B., Lam, E., Girard, K., & Irvin, V. (2019). Digital transformation is not about technology Available at: https://bluecirclemarketing.com/wpcontent/uploads/2019/ 07/Digital-Transformation-Is-Not-About-Technology.pdf [Accessed: 10 April 2024].

Thite, M. (2019). Electronic/digital HRM: a primer. In Thite, M. (Ed.), *e-HRM: Digital Approaches, Directions & Applications* (pp. 1–21). Routledge.

Vardarlier, P. (2020). Digital Transformation of Human Resource Management: Digital Applications and Strategic Tools in HRM. In *Digital Business Strategies in Blockchain Ecosystems* (pp. 239–264). Springer. DOI:10.1007/978-3-030-29739-8_11

Vidas, B. M., & Bubanja, I. (2017). The challenge of going digital. Journal of engineering management and competitiveness (jemc), 7(2), 126-136.

Wang, D., Cui, L., Vu, T., & Feng, T. (2022). Political capital and MNE responses to institutional voids: The case of Chinese state-owned enterprises in Africa. *Organization Studies*, 43(1), 105–126. DOI:10.1177/0170840620954011

Wibowo, A., Chen, S. C., Wiangin, U., Ma, Y., & Ruangkanjanases, A. (2020). Customer behavior as an outcome of social media marketing: The role of social media marketing activity and customer experience. *Sustainability (Basel)*, 13(1), 189. DOI:10.3390/su13010189

Wright, P. M., Dunford, B. B. & Snell, S. A. (2001). Human resources and the resourcebased view of the firm', Journal of Management, 27(6), pp. 701 - 721. Business Source Ultimate. .DOI:10.1177/014920630102700607

Yu, Z., & JInajun, N. (2020). How to achieve HRM digital transformation. available at: https://www.sohu.com/a/400600846_343325

Zhang, J., & Chen, Z. (2023). Exploring Human Resource Management Digital Transformation in the Digital Age. *Journal of the Knowledge Economy*, 1–17.

Chapter 2
Digital Transformation in Human Resources Management:
Green Human Resources Management

Fatma Gül Karaçelebi
https://orcid.org/0000-0001-8165-0491
Niğde Ömer Halisdemir Üniversitesi, Turkey

ABSTRACT

This study focuses on the relationship between digital transformation and green human resources management in businesses. In this context, first of all, the historical development of human resources management is mentioned, and the change in management's perspective on human resources is explained. At the same time, information about the transition to the human resources management process is included. It has been attempted to explain why digital transformation applications are necessary in businesses, especially in the human resources unit. The concept of Green Human Resource Management (HRM) is explained, and Green HRM practices in businesses are elucidated with the help of a model.

INTRODUCTION

The continuous development and transformation of technology is evident in every aspect of life. Keeping up with the emerging changes has become very important to stay current and understand the times. From a business perspective, the situation is equally important. The changes in technology after Industry 4.0 have significantly

DOI: 10.4018/979-8-3693-4412-5.ch002

affected businesses, as well as all areas of life (Munsamy & Telukdarie, 2019). Traditional methods of conducting business have been abandoned, and new methods have begun to be implemented under the guidance of technology (Chulanova, 2019; Rehman et al., 2023). Digital transformation, in a sense, involves investing in the labor market and businesses, challenging corporate culture by radically reconstructing business processes and practices (Mishra, Sarkar & Kiranmai, 2014; Manuti & De Palma, 2018).

This transformation in technology has brought about large-scale changes in all business processes. Factors such as conducting business transactions in a computerized environment and storing business data digitally now represent the new normal in the business world. Digitalization expands the utilization of digital technology in the production of goods and services by businesses. In this way, businesses can gain a competitive advantage over their competitors (Hrustek, Furjan, & Pihir, 2019; Kirilmaz, 2020). In addition to making a positive contribution to the efficiency and sustainability of businesses, digitalization also triggers changes in human resources processes. With the decrease in natural resources worldwide, businesses are now compelled by their stakeholders to adopt more sustainable and environmentally friendly practices (Rehman, Giordino, Zhang, & Alam, 2023). Digital transformation, which involves producing goods and services using environmentally friendly technologies, can facilitate businesses in achieving green transformation (Deniz & Büyük, 2023). It is stated that human resources play a key role in implementing successful environmental practices for businesses. The resource-based perspective also emphasizes the importance of businesses in achieving a competitive advantage due to reasons such as the rarity and non-recurrence of human resources (Tang, Chen, Jiang, Paillé, and Jia, 2018).

Digital transformation in business is compelling human resources management to make changes in this area. Now, all employee information in businesses is stored and tracked digitally. With this management style, known as digital human resources, human resources activities become more effective and efficient. With the understanding of the importance of human resources, there has been a transition from personnel management to human resources management. As strategy became a crucial element in managing human resources, the strategic human resources management approach has become dominant in the field. Today, the development of technology has created digital human resources, adding a new dimension to human resources management (Manuti & De Palma, 2018; Bayarçelik, 2020; Kirilmaz, 2020). Digital transformation not only facilitates the daily work of human resources but also contributes to the alignment with the requirements of the age in various areas such as human resources planning, recruitment, performance management, training and development, and employee relations (Fenech, Baguant, & Ivanov, 2019). Many businesses aiming to enhance their sustainability through digital transformation can bolster their environmental management and sustain their competitive advantage, particularly by implementing green human resources management (Tang, Chen, Jiang, Paillé, & Jia, 2018). Green human resources management refers to practices that encourage the increase of green initiatives by raising employees' awareness and commitment to environmental issues (Mishra, Sarkar & Kiranmai, 2014).

Although green human resources management (GHRM) includes human resources management practices, it differs in some aspects (Tang, et al., 2018).

- GHRM indicates the sensitivity of a business towards environmental protection.
- GHRM can provide more direct benefits to external stakeholders.
- It can be an incentive to increase employees' commitment to the environment and thus increase their work motivation and sense of belonging.
- Thanks to environmentally friendly practices, businesses can gain a position that will benefit them in the long term, such as reducing pressure from external stakeholders and gaining reputation.

GHRM includes technological developments such as job sharing, virtual meetings, recycling, energy efficient office spaces, and online education. It focuses on the greening of businesses through this type of human-related Technologies (Mishra, Sarkar & Kiranmai, 2014). Issues such as population growth and resource insufficiency in the world accelerate the awareness of the green human resources management approach. It is thought that with GHRM, organizations can develop more sustainable strategies and gain competitive advantage.

BACKGROUND

Human resources management (HRM) emerged with the Industrial Revolution that occurred in the second half of the 18th century and the rapid technological changes that followed. During this period, the perspective on the workforce was known to be quite strict. There was a process in which the workforce can be bought and sold like a commodity, and both they and the governments were not sufficient to protect their rights (Özgen & Yalçın, 2017; Şaşamaz, 2022). Later, Taylor and his friends brought new perspectives to HRM by conducting studies that focused on business efficiency issues in companies. Hawthorne research conducted by Elton Mayo and his friends in the 1920s highlighted the importance of human resources and human relations in businesses. Research results revealed that productivity is related to job satisfaction (Armstrong & Taylor, 2006). During this period, the emergence of groups that prioritized the economic well-being of the workforce introduced the concept of a "welfare secretariat," marking the initial stages of the personnel management approach (Armstrong & Taylor, 2006). Although the personnel management approach has changed the perspective on the workforce, it reveals a routine, document-collecting approach where efficiency and profit targets are at the forefront. It also demonstrates a rigid and one-sided approach in which the employees' opinions are not taken into account. However, many changes such as economic, social, and cultural transformations, the growth in manpower, increased participation of women in the workforce, advancements in technology, etc., have highlighted that personnel management is inadequate for effectively managing human resources. Since the middle of the 20th century, with the increase in technology and competition, it has been revealed that human resources should be managed with a holistic approach, leading to the emergence of the concept of HRM has emerged. In the post-1990 period, human beings have been positioned as a strategic resource for businesses. The understanding that it plays an important role in the implementation of the medium and long-term strategies of the business has become dominant. Generally speaking, HRM appears as a multidisciplinary function in businesses, where ideas and theories from various fields such as management, economics, sociology, and psychology are integrated (Chytiri, 2019). To briefly summarize the process, it covers the periods of personnel management (Industrial Revolution-1980), HRM (1980-1990), and Strategic HRM (1990 to present) (Turşucular, 2023).

Radical changes in technology are among the most important factors that accelerate the transition from an industrial society to an information society. The process reveals changes in business life as well as in many other aspects of life, such as economic, cultural, and social spheres. Industrial revolutions occurred with James Watt's invention of the steam engine.

- **Industry 1.0** (application of 18th-century mechanical production facilities): Invention of the steam engine
- **Industry 2.0** (transition to mass production based on electricity and division of labor in the 19th century): Invention of the telegraph and telephone in the 1800s, emergence of assembly lines
- **Industry 3.0** (automation of 20th-century production processes): Utilization of electronics and information technologies
- **Industry 4.0** (21st-century autonomous machines and virtual environments): Internet of Things

These changes, which affect all aspects of life and businesses, also manifest themselves in the field of HRM. Keeping up with digital transformation is now essential in the process of managing human resources. Considering that human resources are the key element that accelerates technological change in businesses, it is crucial for HRM to spearhead digital transformation. Digital transformation also leads to the development of employees' technical skills to establish an effective green management system (Cherian & Jacob, 2012). With Green HRM, more sustainable strategies can emerge in businesses. At the same time, it brings about the reorganization of HRM policies to utilize natural resources in the most efficient way. Green HRM (HRM) facilitates the adoption of environmentally friendly practices and supports green employees. It also promotes digital filing, waste control, fuel savings, and other eco-friendly initiatives. It helps employees in various fields adopt a lifestyle with a lower carbon footprint (Pandey, Viswanathan & Kamboj, 2016).

DIGITAL TRANSFORMATION IN HRM

Bringing together the resources necessary for the production of products and services is crucial for businesses to achieve their goals. The changes experienced since the Industrial Revolution (technological, social, cultural, demographic, etc.) have led to significant shifts in the way businesses view resources. During this process, the significance of human resources for businesses has increased significantly. As the importance of people for businesses is understood, it is evident that management processes are changing in this direction. The management process, which used to be based solely on efficiency and effectiveness, has now recognized the significance of taking into account the happiness and well-being of the individual.

Over the last 50 years, with increasing competition, it has been emphasized that businesses must develop multiple strategies to remain competitive. These strategies mainly encompassed traditional economic theories that focused on cost minimization and were geared towards the external environment (Srivastava, 2005). Later, with a shift in perspective on businesses, the concept that businesses are comprised of resources and capabilities, and that variances in these aspects can offer a competitive advantage, was proposed (Barney, 1991; Srivastava, 2005). The uniqueness of skill sets and emerging resource differences enable businesses to create significant distinctions in their strategies. As a result, this uniqueness was positioned as its inimitable elements by other businesses (Peteraf, 1993). The company's technology and products, etc. It may be possible to replicate resources over time. However, the fact that elements of human resources, such as talent and skill, are inimitable increases the importance of human resources. Today, human resources are viewed as essential talent for businesses to compete with their rivals. HRM practices in businesses are now developed from this perspective (Kirilmaz, 2020).

Industry 4.0 manifests itself in many areas of life. The emergence of technologies such as artificial intelligence (AI), Internet of Things (IoT), Internet of Services, and big data analysis reveals changes in the business models and operational methods of businesses. This enables businesses to develop new employee skills and competencies, thereby increasing their competitiveness (Mazurchenko & Marsikova, 2019). One of the areas where digitalization has the most impact is in business life. Digital business transformation plays a crucial role in enhancing effectiveness and efficiency through the implementation of new business models. It aims to eliminate barriers between individuals, businesses, and objects across various sectors (Schwertner, 2017). It is evident that digitalization, characterized by the advancement of communication and information technologies, impacts the way businesses operate (Barišić, Barišić & Miloloža, 2021). With digitalization, a transformation has occurred in the way businesses operate and in cost management. This situation offers businesses various ways to compete and brings along numerous opportunities (Ulatowska, Wainio & Pierzchala, 2023). Digitalization also paves the way for changing organizational culture and developing different types of leadership, such as open leadership or personal leadership, to help businesses maintain their performance (Burchardt & Maisch, 2019). Digital transformation creates value for businesses in many different aspects. Issues such as effectiveness and efficiency, cost control, superior customer experience, better stakeholder relations, and employee satisfaction can be given as examples (Schwertner, 2017). Digital transformation is often defined as a strategy or a business model. It is often defined as the utilization of new digital technologies to bring significant business enhancements (Fitzgerald, Kruschwitz, Bonet & Welch, 2014; Schwertner, 2017). What is important in digital transformation is not how much technology is used, but the use of technology that aligns with the company's strategies. Digital transformation, which supports business strategy, brings about radical change. From this perspective, each business's unique strategy supports digital transformation at various levels (Schwertner, 2017).

The area where digitalization has the most impact on businesses is HRM (Kirilmaz, 2020). Changing business models, along with technological developments in the modern digital world, cause radical changes in HRM (Fenech, 2022). HRM in organizations aims to ensure that employees utilize their skills, abilities, and behaviors in alignment with business goals. From this perspective, it can be seen that HRM is of critical importance for businesses. The digitalization of management processes in businesses, along with the adoption of new technologies, results in the development and implementation of new HR processes (Barišić, Barišić & Miloloža, 2021; Kagermann, 2014). Digital transformation and the impact of technology seem to bring about numerous changes in HRM. There is a transition of existing HR processes from manual to electronic, which also causes some processes to change, accelerate, or disappear (Ulatowska, Wainio & Pierzchala, 2023). Applications such as automatic scanning of manual CVs, which offer in-depth analysis and high performance in terms of speed and efficiency in recruitment, real-time monitoring of employees, and automation of transactional tasks, can be cited as examples of the impact of digital transformation on HRM (Fenech, 2022). It is observed that the recruitment process, which is one of the most crucial processes of HRM, is also influenced by digital transformation. Businesses now recruit through social media platforms such as Facebook and LinkedIn. This increases the efficiency and speed of businesses in processes through digitalization (Lumi, 2020). Lumi (2020) also emphasizes that there have been significant changes in HRM in the area of training and development. He states that, thanks to digital transformation, applications such as online courses, training videos, and computerized learning methods have made great progress for HRM. From this perspective, digital HRM focuses on the implementation of innovative solutions to increase workforce productivity and workforce development, unlike traditional personnel management (Molotkova, Makeeva & Khazanova, 2019).

Digital transformation paves the way for HRM to become more competitive. Halid, Yusoff, and Somu (2020) list the elements that should be included in a competitive HRM as follows:

- **Digital Workforce:** Current generations are considered part of the digital workforce. Individuals experience the Internet, its related services, and web-based applications throughout their daily lives. Businesses with this type of workforce also need to digitize their operations to effectively engage with their employees (Aggarwal & Sharon, 2017).
- **Digital Work and Tasks:** Digital elements need to be integrated into the business processes of companies. It is also necessary to have digital channels and media to communicate with employees (Aggarwal & Sharon, 2017).
- **Digital Support Management:** It includes the planning and implementing HRM processes (such as training and development, performance management) in businesses using digital technologies.
- **Updated HR Technology:** It includes the use of cloud-based system software instead of traditional methods and the activation of mobile HR applications (Nawaz, 2017).

DIGITAL TRANSFORMATION AND GREEN HRM

The depletion of natural resources worldwide is being increasingly felt across all aspects of life. Countries, and consequently governments, acknowledge that the environmental repercussions of businesses focusing solely on profitability and sales are becoming a growing concern. Social pressure is mounting on businesses, highlighting that their environmental footprint is unsustainable, contrary to previous beliefs (Rehman, Giordino, Zhang & Alam, 2023). Increasing environmental attitudes among consumers and their preference for environmentally friendly products require businesses to embrace a corporate environmental approach (Oncer, 2019). viewed through the lens of open system theory, it becomes evident that businesses are integral parts of society and are not separate entities from the environment (Uslu & Kedikli, 2017).

Businesses now have to take into account warnings about environmental policies from their stakeholders. Today, many companies adopt a proactive attitude towards environmental management rather than taking a reactive approach aimed mere compliance with environmental regulations. They implement various strategies to minimize environmental impacts, such as reducing energy consumption, preventing waste, and limiting consumption (O'Donohue & Torugsa, 2016). Environmental issues are becoming increasingly important in the strategic decision-making process of businesses. Strategic planning involves considering the environmental impacts of business functions such as production, marketing and human resources (Primc & Carter, 2015).

Human resources have the ability to reorganize employees' behaviors and motivations regarding sustainability in various areas. From this perspective, organizations can implement effective green HRM practices by incorporating policies related to environmental sustainability (Dumont, Shen, Deng, 2017).

Green Human Resource Management (Green HRM) is concerned with the systematic and planned alignment of typical human resource management practices with the environmental objectives of the business (Haddock-Millar, Sanyal & Müller-Carmen, 2016). Green HRM provides businesses with a holistic perspective on sustainability. Green HRM refers to human resources activities that focus on developing and implement a system to enhance employees' environmental awareness, thereby fostering an environmentally business. Green HRM involves the integration of the business's environmental management objectives into HRM processes, including the selection, recruitment, development, and training of human resources, performance management, and rewards for environmental sustainability (Das & Singh, 2016).

It is stated that this meticulous work carried out by the business, starting from the selection of human resources, will increase employees' awareness of environmental sustainability (Renwick, Redman, & Maguire, 2008). To achieve the company's goal and contribute to sustainability, the aim is to transform all employees into green employees (Das & Singh, 2016). With Green HRM, businesses implement environmentally friendly initiatives that lead to increased efficiency, reduced costs, and higher employee engagement, ultimately helping to decrease their carbon footprint (Sharma & Gupta, 2015). The goal of Green HRM is to position the business as environmentally conscious while also cultivating environmentally sensitive employees.

Green HRM, which focuses on environmental initiatives to preserve the environment and the planet, is a relatively recent concept with varying definitions according to different authors. Aksu & Doğan (2021) outlined various definitions of Green HRM provided by different authors in a table within their article.

Table 1. Green HRM Definitions (According to Various Authors)

Jabbour, 2013: 147- 148	Green HRM is the systematic and planned integration of typical HRM practices with the environmental objectives of the business.
Shen, Dumont ve Deng, 2018: 594; Jackson ve Seo, 2010	Green HRM refers to a set of HRM practices adopted by businesses to achieve their environmental goals and enhance the eco-friendly performance of their employees in the workplace.
Guerci and Carollo, 2016: 212	Green HRM refers to the relationship between a set of specific HRM practices (referred to as Green HRM) and environmental sustainability.
Zoogah, 2011: 118	Green HRM refers to the utilization of HRM policies, philosophies and practices to encourage the sustainable utilization of business resources and mitigate adverse impacts stemming from environmental issues within organizations.
Yusoff, vd., 2018: 4	Green HRM involves the utilization of human resources policies, philosophies and practices (such as recruitment and selection, training and development, performance management, and compensation) to foster sustainable business practices.
Mandip, 2012: 244	Green HRM involves implementing HRM policies in business organizations to encourage the sustainable use of resources and, more broadly, to guarantee ongoing environmental sustainability.
Ren, Tang ve Jackson, 2018: 778	Green HRM is a phenomenon aimed at understanding the relationships between organizational activities that affect the natural environment and the design, development, implementation, and impact of HRM systems.
Al-Romeedy, 2019: 529	Green HRM refers to the utilization of human resources policies to advocate for the sustainable use of business resources and ensure environmental sustainability.

Source: Aksu &Doğan (2021).

When Table 1 is examined, it can be seen that the concept of sustainability is included in most of the definitions related to Green HRM. This shows that the Green HRM process develops in parallel with sustainability. Generally speaking, sustainability appears as a strategic issue whose importance has been increasingly understood in both the public and private sectors since the beginning of the 21st century (Tüm, 2014). In 1987, the now-classic definition of sustainability was established in the report titled Our Common Future by the World Commission on Environment and Development, chaired by former Norwegian Prime Minister Gro Brundtland. According to the report, sustainability is defined as "Sustainable development is development that meets the needs of the present without compromising the ability of future generations to meet their own needs" (Scoones, 2007).

Studies sustainability in human resources have demonstrated that human resources play a crucial role in reducing environmental impacts within businesses. It has been observed that HRM plays a role in developing a culture of sustainability culture and spreading it to businesses. This highlights the significant role of human resources management in implementing sustainability strategies within businesses (Öncer, 2019).

Green HRM encompasses environmentally friendly initiatives that facilitate the development of HR strategies and processes aimed at enhancing productivity, reducing environmental impact, and cutting costs. Examples of Green HRM practices include electronic filing, job sharing, online training, recycling, remote work, teleconferencing, and energy-efficient office spaces (Sharma & Gupta, 2015). Furthermore, initiatives like promoting carpooling to save fuel and time, maximizing the use of natural light, recognizing employees who contribute sustainable ideas, and effective waste management are also considered part of Green HRM practices (Pandey, Viswanathan & Kamboj, 2016; Oncer, 2019).

GREEN HRM PRACTICES

Das and Singh (2016) in their study, Green HRM includes green job design and analysis, green human resources planning, green recruitment, green selection, green training and development, green performance, green reward management, green health and safety management, and green employee relations. They state that it is applicable to all traditional HRM processes, from discipline management to green employee relations, and aims to reduce the carbon footprint. Green HRM facilitates high levels of employee participation, cost-effective leadership, and supports environmentally friendly policies. In the same study, they illustrated the principles of Green HRM with the help of a figure

Figure 1. Dimensions of Green HRM

Jabbour, 2013: 147-148	Green HRM is the systematic and planned integration of typical HRM practices with the environmental objectives of the business.
Shen, Dumont ve Deng, 2018: 594; Jackson ve Seo, 2010	Green HRM refers to a set of HRM practices adopted by businesses to achieve their environmental goals and enhance the eco-friendly performance of their employees in the workplace.
Guerci and Carollo, 2016: 212	Green HRM refers to the relationship between a set of specific HRM practices (referred to as Green HRM) and environmental sustainability.
Zoogah, 2011: 118	Green HRM refers to the utilization of HRM policies, philosophies and practices to encourage the sustainable utilization of business resources and mitigate adverse impacts stemming from environmental issues within organizations.
Yusoff, vd., 2018: 4	Green HRM involves the utilization of human resources policies, philosophies and practices (such as recruitment and selection, training and development, performance management, and compensation) to foster sustainable business practices.
Mandip, 2012: 244	Green HRM involves implementing HRM policies in business organizations to encourage the sustainable use of resources and, more broadly, to guarantee ongoing environmental sustainability.
Ren, Tang ve Jackson, 2018: 778	Green HRM is a phenomenon aimed at understanding the relationships between organizational activities that affect the natural environment and the design, development, implementation, and impact of HRM systems.
Al-Romeedy, 2019: 529	Green HRM refers to the utilization of human resources policies to advocate for the sustainable use of business resources and ensure environmental sustainability.

Source: *(Das & Singh, 2016).*

When examining Figure 1, it is evident that there are five dimensions of Green HRM.

- **Job Description and Analysis**: In green HRM, job descriptions include duties and responsibilities, encompassing organizational and environmental sustainability (Das & Singh, 2016) and can be utilized to address various ecological concerns (Renwick, et al., 2008). Interactive scales can be used for job evaluation. Thanks to the developed software, managers and employees can determine the score and total score within the factors assigned to each job by answering questions via computer (Kiremitçi, 2023).
- **Recruitment and Selection:** Recruitment of talented personnel is key for human resources management. Many businesses now use Green HRM as an el-

ement of attraction for potential personnel to choose the business. Businesses try to include employees who are especially willing and knowledgeable about green practices (Renwick, et al., 2008; Öncer, 2019). Businesses can implement some green practices during the recruitment process. Examples of these include online application forms instead of paper, online interviews, or phone calls to save time and fuel. Using technological products, such as software or robots, saves time and reduces waste, leading to positive outcomes like quick analysis (Kiremitçi, 2023). At the same time, during the interview, it can convey that it attaches importance to green practices by choosing candidates who are environmentally sensitive and care about the protection of natural resources (Das & Singh, 2016)

- **Training and Development:** Training and development play a significant role in enhancing the competitive capacity of human resources in businesses. Providing training on environmental issues can help increase employees' environmental awareness and promote the proper use of natural resources. Green training and development are beneficial for educating employees about the company's environmental policies and enhancing their environmental consciousness. Orientation programs can be utilized to train new hires. Consider creating and editing training videos online and supplementing them with digital content instead of traditional printed materials. Employees can gain insights into environmental management, waste management, and energy management through training sessions (Renwick et al., 2008; Mandip, 2012; Öncer, 2019).

- **Performance Evaluation and Compensation:** Successful performance management in a business involves creating job descriptions that outline specific green targets and tasks for performance evaluations. Topics such as reducing carbon emissions and complying with environmental policies can be included in these job descriptions (Renwick, et al., 2008; Mandip, 2012). Green performance evaluation can serve as an incentive for employees to embrace and execute environmental policies.

- **Employee Participation in Green HR Initiatives:** It is crucial for businesses to ensure employees' involvement in green HR programs. This enhances employees' participatory actions such as generating eco-friendly ideas, implementing them, and engaging in environmental planning (Das & Singh, 2016). Human resources managers can take specific steps to conduct these initiatives effectively. These include hiring skilled staff, developing strategies to boost participation, offering Green HRM training, establishing assessments based on Green HR practices, and implementing a reward system linked to environmental performance (Öncer, 2019; Tariq, Jan, & Ahmad, 2016). In addition, the digital database allows tracking and controlling employee registration, debt, or payroll transactions from a single place. This allows employees to access their information whenever they want (Kiremitçi, 2023).

In another study, Sharma and Gupta (2015) developed the Green HRM model based on their examination of other studies. The model encompasses HR practices within the realm of green HRM. It consists of seven interconnected headings: *Green recruitment and retention, Measurement of green parameters and performance, Information sharing techniques and empowerment, Top manager following green modeling, Designing of green jobs, Talent development for green organization, and Desired green behavior from employees.*

In addition to the practices mentioned above, there are other Green HRM practices in businesses.

- **Career Management:** Career management in businesses mainly involves being promoted to a higher position and gaining the opportunity to take on more responsibilities in the current role. With the digitalization of career management, employees have the chance to explore new opportunities and career paths. When a position becomes available within the company, it offers a pathway for internal promotion rather than outsourcing. Additionally, enhancing employees' competence and skills can be achieved by enabling them to learn new technological programs (Kiremitçi, 2023).
- **Green Employee Relations:** Relations with human resources, which are an indispensable resource that will propel businesses forward, are crucial for businesses. Developing healthy and sustainable relationships will enhance engagement and willingness to adhere to the environmental policies of the business. Seeking and incorporating employees' feedback when formulating green policies can expedite the process. Establishing a common vision among all employees can foster a sense of collective effort. Additionally, endorsing employees' green citizenship initiatives can boost their involvement (Öncer, 2019).

When we examine green HRM practices, we observe their presence in all areas involving human resources. When a business's environmental policies and green initiatives are embraced by all staff members, they can transform the organizational culture and facilitate the adoption of a more sustainable outlook. The environmental consciousness cultivated among employees not only influences the business internally but also extends to their personal lives. This shift can lead to businesses, as integral parts of society, making a positive impact on both society and the environment.

FUTURE RESEARCH DIRECTIONS

The fact that natural resources are decreasing in the world manifests itself in every aspect of life. It is now recognized by all parties (society, consumers, stakeholders, states, etc.) that the profit-oriented aggressive production and sales policies of businesses have an impact on this process. Increasing sensitivity and awareness of environmental issues is prompting businesses to make radical changes in their operations. People now want to see businesses with environmental policies and green awareness. Thanks to the rapid development of technology and the production of goods and services that are more environmentally friendly, businesses can implement more sustainable policies. Businesses now operate using digital transformation applications. Thanks to innovative technologies such as artificial intelligence and the Internet of Things, business processes are accelerating, while efforts are being made to minimize environmental damage.

The most crucial element in driving digital transformation and sustainability for businesses is considered to be human resources management. Green transformation at every stage, from human resources planning to performance evaluation, from training development to career planning, supports the environmental policies of the entire enterprise. From this perspective, adapting this process, called Green HRM, within the business brings positive returns for both the business, the employees, and society.

This study is a theoretical examination of digital transformation and green Human Resource Management (HRM) practices in businesses. It is recommended that future studies investigate the effects of green Human Resource Management (HRM) practices on employees, businesses, and society. In this way, it is believed that the impacts of green transformation will be better comprehended, and awareness of green HRM practices will increase.

CONCLUSION

It has become necessary for businesses, which are integral parts of society, to collaborate as a team, especially given the decreasing availability of natural resources. Businesses are revising their environmental policies to enhance profitability and foster customer loyalty. Today, competition is achievable through effective environmental regulations and is applicable to any business anywhere in the world. Implementing practices and policies that minimize environmental damage has become a priority. Green management is a competitive advantage for businesses. This is essential for retaining customers and employees within the business and for attracting potential employees to the organization.

Being able to meet today's needs without depleting the resources that future generations require to sustain their lives is defined by sustainability. For businesses, sustainability has evolved into an obligation rather than a self-sacrificial behavior. Restructuring business models and processes around sustainability and creating green awareness has been the first priority for operations. To achieve this, businesses often choose to make changes in their products and services. However, it is not sufficient for sustainable development. Businesses should not only develop environmental policies at the point of product and service, but also give priority to the formation of an individual and holistic green awareness.

Human resources management is critical for businesses. The change that occurs especially after understanding that human resources are indispensable elements for businesses is quite significant. The contribution of HRM to the initiation of change in businesses, its spread throughout the business, and its adoption is obvious. This feature shows that HRM is a source of competitiveness rather than just a unit within the enterprise. When the issue is evaluated from this perspective, HRM's key role in changing the enterprise's environmental policies emerges. HRM "It's not the leaf that is only green—organization can also turn out to be green" (Tarig, Jan & Ahmad, 2016) represents the driving force for the formation of green organizations mentioned in the approach.

Human resources practices are needed to adapt human resources to sustainable environmental policies in processing. This process, called Green HRM, aims to ensure that employees reach and adopt environmental awareness. Green HRM aims to create a more sustainable development model, to spread environmental awareness, and to enable the production of goods and services with minimized damage to the environment. To initiate the green HRM process in businesses, traditional HRM practices need to be rearranged with green awareness. Preferring candidates with high environmental awareness when selecting personnel, explaining the environmental policies of the enterprise during the recruitment processes, and holding periodic briefings of the existing personnel on the subject are among the practices that can help raise the awareness of all employees. In addition, ensuring the participation of employees in environmental policies and implementing the ideas they develop will be beneficial in terms of green HRM.

It is thought that education and training activities will also have positive results on green HRM. With the training, the environmental policies of the company will be conveyed to the employees and the opportunity to develop the environmental awareness of the employees will be provided. Employees who increase their environmental awareness not only experience this awareness in their business life but also maintain this awareness in their non-work lives. This also provides great benefits in establishing the work-life balance of employees. Employees who change their lifestyle with environmental awareness can exhibit green behaviors. Thus, society will have more and more environmentally conscious individuals.

ACKNOWLEDGMENT

This research received no specific grant from any funding agency in the public, commercial, or not-forprofit sectors.

REFERENCES

Aggarwal, V., & Sharon, S. D. (2017). Digital human resource management. *Gyan Management Journal*, 11(2), 23–27.

Aksu, B. Ç., & Doğan, A. (2021). Çevresel sürdürülebilirlik ve insan kaynakları yönetimi fonksiyonlarının yeşil İKY bağlamında değerlendirilmesi. *Aksaray Üniversitesi İktisadi ve İdari Bilimler Fakültesi Dergisi*, 13(3), 137–148. DOI:10.52791/aksarayiibd.947200

Armstrong, M., & Taylor, S. (2006). *Human resource management practice* (10th ed.). Distributed Computing., DOI:10.1002/9781118802717

Barney, J. (1991). Firm Resources and Sustained Competitive Advantage. *Journal of Management*, 17(1), 99–121. DOI:10.1177/014920639101700108

Burchardt, C., & Maisch, B. (2019). Digitalization needs a cultural change–examples of applying Agility and Open Innovation to drive the digital transformation. *Procedia CIRP*, 84, 112–117. DOI:10.1016/j.procir.2019.05.009

Cherian, J., & Jacob, J. (2012). A study of green HR practices and its effective implementation in the organization: A review. *International Journal of Business and Management*, 7(21), 25–33. DOI:10.5539/ijbm.v7n21p25

Chytiri, A. P. (2019). Human resource managers' role in the digital era. *Journal of Economics and Business*, 69(1-2), 62–72.

Das, S. C., & Singh, R. K. (2016). Green HRM and organizational sustainability: An empirical review. *Kegees Journal of Social Science*, 8(1), 227–236.

Dumont, J., Shen, J., & Deng, X. (2017). Effects of green HRM practices on employee workplace green behavior: The role of psychological green climate and employee green values. *Human Resource Management*, 56(4), 613–627. DOI:10.1002/hrm.21792

Fenech, R. (2022). Human resource management in a digital era through the lens of next generation human resource managers. *Journal of Management Information and Decision Sciences*, 25(1), 1–10.

Fitzgerald, M., Kruschwitz, N., Bonnet, D., & Welch, M. (2014). Embracing digital technology: A new strategic imperative. *MIT Sloan Management Review*, 55(2), 1–16.

Florijan Barišić, A., Rybacka Barišić, J., & Miloloža, I. (2021). Digital transformation: Challenges for human resources management. [ENTRENOVA]. *ENTerprise REsearch InNOVAtion Conference*, 7(1), 377–387. DOI:10.54820/GTFN9743

Haddock-Millar, J., Sanyal, C., & Müller-Camen, M. (2016). Green human resource management: A comparative qualitative case study of a United States multinational corporation. *International Journal of Human Resource Management*, 27(2), 192–211. DOI:10.1080/09585192.2015.1052087

Halid, H., Yusoff, Y. M., & Somu, H. (2020). The relationship between digital human resource management and organizational performance. In *First ASEAN Business, Environment, and Technology Symposium (ABEATS 2019)*, 96-99. Atlantis Press. DOI:10.2991/aebmr.k.200514.022

Kagermann, H. (2014). Change through digitization—Value creation in the age of Industry 4.0. In *Management of permanent change* (pp. 23–45). Springer Fachmedien Wiesbaden.

Kiremitci, E. (2023). *İnsan kaynakları yönetiminde Dijital dönüşüm* (Doctoral dissertation, Dokuz Eylul Universitesi (Turkey).

Kirilmaz, S. K. (2020). Digital transformation in human resources management: Investigation of digital hrm practices of businesses. *Research Journal of Business and Management*, 7(3), 188–200. DOI:10.17261/Pressacademia.2020.1282

Kurnaz, S., Rodrigues, A., & Sunar, O. N. (2024). Digitalization in the Public Management: Turkish Public Institutions Example. In *Advancements in Socialized and Digital Media Communications* (pp. 135-150). IGI Global.

Lumi, A. (2020). The impact of digitalisation on human resources development. *Prizren Social Science Journal*, 4(3), 39–46. DOI:10.32936/pssj.v4i3.178

Mandip, G. (2012). Green HRM: People management commitment to environmental sustainability. *Research Journal of Recent Sciences, ISSN*, 2277, 2502.

Mazurchenko, A., & Maršíková, K. (2019). Digitally-powered human resource management: Skills and roles in the digital era. *Acta Informatica Pragensia*, 8(2), 72–87. DOI:10.18267/j.aip.125

Molotkova, N. V., Makeeva, M. N., & Khazanova, D. L. Digitalized Personnel Management. *European Proceedings of Social and Behavioural Sciences*. DOI:10.15405/epsbs.2019.03.75

Nawaz, N. (2017). A comprehensive literature review of the digital HR research filed. *Information and Knowledge Management 7*(4).

O'Donohue, W., & Torugsa, N. (2016). The moderating effect of 'Green' HRM on the association between proactive environmental management and financial performance in small firms. *International Journal of Human Resource Management*, 27(2), 239–261. DOI:10.1080/09585192.2015.1063078

Oncer, A. Z. (2019). Örgütlerde yeşil insan kaynakları yönetimi uygulamaları: Teorik bir inceleme. *İş ve İnsan Dergisi, 6*(2), 199-208, .DOI:10.18394/iid.552555

Özgen, H., & Yalçın, A. (2017). *İnsan kaynakları yönetimi stratejik bir yaklaşım.* Akademisyen Kitabevi.

Pandey, S., Viswanathan, V., & Kamboj, P. (2016). Sustainable green HRM – Importance and factors affecting successful implementation in organizations. *International Journal of Research in Management and Business*, 2(3), 11–29.

Peteraf, M. A. (1993). The Cornerstones of Competitive Advantage: A Resource Based–View. *Strategic Management Journal*, 14(3), 179–188. DOI:10.1002/smj.4250140303

Primc, K., & Čater, T. (2015). Environmental proactivity and firm performance: A fuzzy-set analysis. *Management Decision*, 53(3), 648–667. DOI:10.1108/MD-05-2014-0288

Rehman, S. U., Giordino, D., Zhang, Q., & Alam, G. M. (2023). Twin transitions & industry 4.0: Unpacking the relationship between digital and green factors to determine green competitive advantage. *Technology in Society*, 73, 102227. DOI:10.1016/j.techsoc.2023.102227

Renwick, D., Redman, T., & Maguire, S. (2008). Green HRM: A review, process model, and research agenda. *University of Sheffield Management School Discussion Paper, 1*(1), 1-46.

Şaşmaz, E. C. (2022). Dijital dönüşüm sürecinde insan kaynakları yönetimi. *Sosyal, beşeri ve idari bilimler alanında uluslararası araştırmalar VIII*, 239.

Schwertner, K. (2017). Digital transformation of business. *Trakia Journal of Sciences*, 15(1, Suppl.1), 388–393. DOI:10.15547/tjs.2017.s.01.065

Scoones, I. (2007). Sustainability. *Development in Practice*, 17(4-5), 589–596. DOI:10.1080/09614520701469609

Sharma, R., & Gupta, N. (2015). Green HRM: An innovative approach to environmental sustainability. In *Proceeding of the Twelfth AIMS International Conference on Management*, 2-5.

Srivastava, S. C. (2005). Managing core competence of the organization. *Vikalpa*, 30(4), 49–64. DOI:10.1177/0256090920050405

Tariq, S., Jan, F. A., & Ahmad, M. S. (2016). Green employee empowerment: A systematic literature review on state-of-art in green human resource management. *Quality & Quantity*, 50(1), 237–269. DOI:10.1007/s11135-014-0146-0

Tüm, K. (2014). Kurumsal sürdürülebilirlik ve muhasebeye yansımaları: Sürdürülebilirlik muhasebesi. *Akademik Yaklaşımlar Dergisi, 5*(1).

Turşucular, E. (2023). *Covid-19 salgın döneminde insan kaynakları yönetiminde meydana gelen değişimler ve dijital insan kaynakları yönetiminin artan önemi* (Master's thesis, Trakya Üniversitesi Sosyal Bilimler Enstitüsü).

Ulatowska, R., Wainio, E., & Pierzchała, M. (2023). Digital transformation in HRM of the modern business service sector in Finland and Poland. *Journal of Organizational Change Management*, 36(7), 1180–1192. DOI:10.1108/JOCM-11-2022-0339

Uslu, Y. D., & Kedikli, E. (2017). Sürdürülebilirlik kapsamında yeşil insan kaynakları yönetimine genel bir bakış. *Üçüncü Sektör Sosyal Ekonomi, 52*(3), 66-81, DOI:10.15659/3.sektor-sosyal-ekonomi.17.12.694

ADDITIONAL READING

Darvishmotevali, M., & Altinay, L. (2022). Green HRM, environmental awareness and green behaviors: The moderating role of servant leadership. *Tourism Management*, 88, 104401. DOI:10.1016/j.tourman.2021.104401

Islam, T., Khan, M. M., Ahmed, I., & Mahmood, K. (2021). Promoting in-role and extra-role green behavior through ethical leadership: Mediating role of green HRM and moderating role of individual green values. *International Journal of Manpower*, 42(6), 1102–1123. DOI:10.1108/IJM-01-2020-0036

Li, W., Abdalla, A. A., Mohammad, T., Khassawneh, O., & Parveen, M. (2023). Towards examining the link between green hrm practices and employee green in-role behavior: Spiritual leadership as a moderator. *Psychology Research and Behavior Management*, 16, 383–396. DOI:10.2147/PRBM.S396114 PMID:36798875

Muster, V., & Schrader, U. (2011). Green work-life balance: A new perspective for green HRM. *German Journal of Human Resource Management*, 25(2), 140–156. DOI:10.1177/239700221102500205

Paulet, R., Holland, P., & Morgan, D. (2021). A meta-review of 10 years of green human resource management: Is Green HRM headed towards a roadblock or a revitalisation? *Asia Pacific Journal of Human Resources*, 59(2), 159–183. DOI:10.1111/1744-7941.12285

Rubel, M. R. B., Kee, D. M. H., & Rimi, N. N. (2021). The influence of green HRM practices on green service behaviors: The mediating effect of green knowledge sharing. *Employee Relations*, 43(5), 996–1015. DOI:10.1108/ER-04-2020-0163

Vardarlier, P. (2020). Digital transformation of human resource management: digital applications and strategic tools in HRM. *Digital business strategies in blockchain ecosystems: Transformational design and future of global business*, 239-264.

Zhang, J., & Chen, Z. (2023). Exploring human resource management digital transformation in the digital age. *Journal of the Knowledge Economy*, 1–17.

KEY TERMS AND DEFINITIONS

Green HRM: Green HRM refers to the utilization of HRM policies, philosophies and practices to encourage the sustainable utilization of business resources and mitigate adverse impacts stemming from environmental issues within organizations.

Chapter 3
The Role of Flexible Work Arrangments in Work–Life Balance:
A Phenomenological Study on the Banking Sector of India

Vedika Pathania
Christ University, India

Deeksha Gupta Ganguly
https://orcid.org/0000-0002-5502-8276
Christ University, India

Deepti Sinha
Christ University, India

ABSTRACT

This study examined the impact of flexible work arrangements on work-family balance among bank workers in India, based on interviews with 10 employees from various private banks. Using the Interpretative Phenomenological Analysis method, employees' experiences before the adoption of flexible schedules and their expectations and impacts afterward were explored. While there is hope for the benefits of flexible schedules, a smooth transition is crucial. Key success factors include effective monitoring systems for accountability and productivity, role-specific flexibility models to meet diverse needs, technology integration for smooth operations, and employee well-being initiatives to address burnout, isolation, and work-life imbalance, along with clear communication. The study highlights the importance of these elements in fostering a supportive and adaptable work culture in the Indian banking sector.

DOI: 10.4018/979-8-3693-4412-5.ch003

By prioritizing these success factors, organizations can overcome implementation challenges and promote work-family balance among bank employees.

1. INTRODUCTION

In today's rapidly changing work landscape, the concept of flexible work arrangements has gained significant traction as a feasible strategy for improving work-life balance. Companies have recognized the importance of supporting their employees' efforts to manage their professional and personal responsibilities effectively, as the tremendous time constraints faced by many employees with significant family responsibilities have rendered current practices, schedules, and management philosophy inadequate, impeding their productivity (Rodgers, 1992) (Zülch et al., 2012).In the contemporary discourse on work-life balance, flexible work arrangements—like customized work schedules—have been given a lot of weight since they may have a big influence on employees' personal lives.

Best practice examples have shown that working-time arrangements can improve the situation of the employees, although it is important to note that there is no single perfect working-time model.

Work-life policies help employees better balance their personal and professional lives. They also help to enhance employee attitudes and behaviors, including loyalty, job satisfaction, and organizational attachment (Zainal et al., 2022).

Flexible work arrangements like remote work and flexible schedules have grown in popularity in recent years. Giving people the opportunity to work how best fits their lifestyle while also improving employee happiness, retention rates, and corporate efficiency are all benefits of providing flexible working options. Businesses can save time and money on hiring and training by using flexible work arrangements, which can also lower employee turnover and absenteeism. Nike continuously makes investments in its workers' health and financial security to support them in achieving excellence both within and beyond the workplace. Nike is one of the world's most flexible companies because it provides its workers with a plethora of benefits, such as access to insurance plans, fitness programs, and days off to encourage rest and recuperation. The overall goal of Nike's flexible working policy is to foster a more welcoming and encouraging work environment that prioritizes work-life balance and employee well-being. Microsoft is aware that there isn't a "one-size-fits-all" solution when it comes to flexible work arrangements. Because of this, the IT behemoth provides a variety of employment arrangements in three areas: workspace, location, and hours. Candidates can discuss flexibility with their recruiter and hiring manager during the recruiting process to discover the level of flexibility for a role. Job advertisements offer information about the hybrid workplace and these three dimensions. Another case is point is Delta Airlines. One of the biggest airlines in America, Delta, has made a significant effort to provide flexible work schedules that meet the constantly evolving needs of its staff. Apart from providing flexible work schedules, job-sharing options, and part-time work, the airline also makes investments in the professional growth of its staff members by giving leadership development, mentoring, and training.

India is also not far behind in introducing employee centric global practices. Accomplishing work-life balance, a concept that delves into how to prioritize between work and lifestyle has become a near-impossible goal for many people. As people find it challenging to maintain a balance in their personal and work spheres, there has been an increasing interest in the relationship and/or interface between the work and home domain which has been ongoing for decades (Kelliher et al., 2018). This paper examines the role that flexible work arrangements will play in improving work-life balance, with a focus on India's banking industry. A flexible work arrangement, hereinafter referred to as 'FWA', is any type of employment or managerial practice that gives a level of adjustment in when, where, and how long work is done (Brega et al., 2023). Flexible work arrangements can have positive effects on individual and family outcomes, minimizing work-family conflict and work-related stress and promoting employees' capacity to fulfill family responsibilities (Carlson et al., 2010).

The current study focuses on how flexible work schedules effectively achieve employee satisfaction and productivity in the banking industry. The paper aims to examine the key ideas and policies behind flexible work arrangements in the banking sector. Role of banking sector in contributing towards work life balance through flexible work arrangements has been explored. While examining flexi work arrangements, it is crucial to recognize that work-life balance policies alone cannot be effective unless they are supported by an organizational culture that emphasizes work, family, and personal life values, with managerial support. Employees may be reluctant to take advantage of these programs if they believe it might result in possible negative consequences for their work or even hostility from superiors and colleagues.

2. LITERATURE REVIEW

Flexible work arrangements have garnered significant attention as a means to enhance work-life balance, particularly in the last years. The research indicates that telecommuting, flextime, and job sharing, offer employees greater control over their work schedules and locations, potentially leading to improved job satisfaction and well-being. These arrangements have been linked to positive outcomes such as increased productivity, lower stress levels, and reduced rates. However, the literature also highlights some challenges associated with flexible working arrangements. For instance, there is a risk of increased isolation and difficulties in disconnecting from work, which may result in an unhealthy work-life balance.

Accomplishing work-life balance, a concept that delves into how to prioritize between work and lifestyle has become a near-impossible goal for many people. As people find it challenging to maintain a balance in their personal and work spheres, there has been an increasing interest in the relationship and/or interface between the work and home domain which has been ongoing for decades (Kelliher et al., 2018). This paper examines the role that flexible work arrangements will play in improving work-life balance, with a focus on India's banking industry. A flexible work arrangement, hereinafter referred to as 'FWA', is any type of employment or managerial practice that gives a level of adjustment in when, where, and how long work is done (Brega et al., 2023). Flexible work arrangements can have positive effects on individual and family outcomes, minimizing work-family conflict and work-related stress and promoting employees' capacity to fulfill family responsibilities (Carlson et al., 2010).

Over the past five years, flexible work arrangements and work-life balance policies have become increasingly prevalent and important in many industries. Several key trends and changes have emerged after COVID-19 pandemic accelerated the adoption of remote work. Many companies shifted to fully remote or hybrid models, allowing employees to work from home part or all of the time. Organizations have been more open to flexible working hours, enabling employees to start and finish their workdays at times that suit them better, as long as their core responsibilities are met. Some companies have introduced compressed workweeks, where employees work longer hours over fewer days (e.g., four 10-hour days instead of five 8-hour days).There has been an increase in part-time roles and job-sharing arrangements, where two or more employees share the responsibilities of a full-time position (Giannikis & Mihail, 2011).

There are various policies introduced by the organizations for improving work life balance such as mental health support, offering resources such as counseling services, mental health days, and wellness programs, Parental Leaves Flexible Leave Policies, including unlimited PTO (Paid Time Off), sabbaticals, and extended leave for personal reasons. Employee Assistance Programs (EAPs) including financial counseling, legal advice, and career coaching (Johanna Bath & Markulin, 2024). The impact on Employees and Organizations is also studied in detail by various authors such as productivity and job satisfaction, talent attraction and work-life integration. The boundaries between work and personal life have blurred, leading to a greater need for policies that support employees in managing their time effectively (Mgammal et al., 2022).

Work-life balance is considered as an individual's ability to balance between two different roles which are work and family and how such balance brings satisfaction to the life of the individual (Shaffer et al., 2015). Work-life balance as a phenomenon, connotes different things to different people depending on the context being used (Sirgy & Lee, 2017). Employees may consider work-life balance as the ability to successfully navigate and attain a balance between work engagements, family commitments, and other responsibilities that are non-work in nature and activities (Sirgy & Lee, 2017). This may not mean apportioning the same level of energy and time both to work and non-work demands but permitting employees some level of flexibility as to when, where, and how they work (Skinner et al., 2016) which may result in the absence of conflict between work, non-work activities, and caring duties or parental responsibilities.

Work-life balance has become a major factor for employee satisfaction and organizational growth. The implementation of flexible work arrangements has gained prominence in achieving work-life balance. This literature review explores the impact of flexible work arrangements on work-life balance. It examines various research findings that shed light on the factors that mediate the relationship between work-life balance and flexible work arrangements. Additionally, it also looks at the organizational outcomes resulting from work-life balance.

Job satisfaction is the pleasurable and emotional state arising from the appraisal of one's job or job experience (Dunnette, 1976). Job satisfaction depends upon the relaxation of working hours, payment for the work done, training given to the employees for enhancement of skills and off-the-job training, welfare benefits, and motivation (Mishra, 2013). The consequences of job satisfaction are crucial for both, employees and organizations. Employee's emotional attachment to their company determines how committed they are to it, i.e., the extent to which they are ready to partake in the aims and aspirations of their organization (Nwugballa, 2016). Employees who are satisfied with their jobs are less likely to quit, have lower absenteeism rates, and are more probable to perform well (TETT & MEYER, 1993). Positive outcomes such as job involvement, organizational commitment, and job performance have been linked to job satisfaction (Judge et al., 2001). On the organizational level, increased levels of job satisfaction are linked with increased productivity and better customer satisfaction. Organizational culture has been identified as a factor that affects job satisfaction. Work-life balance is an important determinant of job satisfaction, as employees who experience conflicts between work and family responsibilities often report lower levels of job satisfaction (Cheng et al., 2019).

A study by (Palumbo et al., 2020) explore the mediating factors that influence the relationship between work-life balance and flexible work arrangements. They found that organizational meaningfulness (OM) and work-related well-being (WB) mediate the relationship between working from home (HW) and work-life conflicts

(WLC), lessening the negative implications of working from home on work-life balance. This shows that soft tools, such as organizational meaningfulness and work-related well-being enhance work-life balance for employees.

Also, (Chaudhuri et al., 2020) explored the relationship between work-life balance and organizational outcomes in the banking sector which focused on two concepts: Organizational Commitment and Continuance Commitment. Whyte's 1956 work, The Organization Man, introduced the idea of organizational commitment to the public. It demonstrated the nature of the connections that exist between an organization's interests and its system, as well as how these connections influence employee behavior (Whyte, 1956). According to (Boje et al., 2012), continuation commitment is the extent to which a worker believes that it will be difficult to find meaningful work elsewhere and that quitting their company will result in significant unemployment costs. An employee's awareness of the repercussions of quitting the company makes their continued employment with it mandatory. Fear of not finding better job opportunities in the labor market, lack of relevant knowledge and skills that might be needed to work in a new organization, fear of not adjusting to a new organization with a different culture and value system, etc. are some of the reasons why an employee may feel compelled to stay with their current employer. From the research conducted, (Chaudhuri et al., 2020) found a positive association between work-life balance and organizational commitment (OC). However, it was observed that there is a negative relationship with continuance commitment. This reflects that employees who perceive a healthy work-life balance are more likely to have a normative and affective commitment toward the organization, while continuance commitment may affect other factors.

Perceived organizational support positively impacts work-life balance with organizational commitment as a mediator (Ugwu et al., 2017). This implies that organizations that provide support and resources to promote work-life balance are more likely to foster a positive work environment and enhance employee commitment. One study (Nawaz, 2016) identified several individual factors that have an impact on employee performance, including motivation, job satisfaction, and emotional intelligence. The study found that promoting these factors can enhance employee performance. A review by (Menges et al., 2017) discussed the role of intrinsic motivation in predicting employee performance. The review found that the employees who are intrinsically motivated, or motivated by the inherent enjoyment of the work, were more likely to perform well. The review also highlighted the importance of providing employees with autonomy, competence, and relatedness to enhance intrinsic motivation and performance. A review by (Saks, 2006) discussed the role of job demands and resources in predicting employee performance. The study found that high job demands, such as workload and time pressure, had a negative impact on employee performance. Employee performance was positively associated with job resources such as social support and autonomy. The review highlighted the importance of balancing job demands and resources to enhance employee performance. Furthermore, (Iddagoda et al., 2021) highlight the positive impact of work-life balance practices on employee performance. Their findings suggest that an appropriate association between various practices of work-life balance can result in a positive impact on the performance of an employee.

Flexible work arrangements have a major impact on work-life balance in the banking sector of India. It has a positive impact on certain aspects of an individual's job, i.e., having a positive sense of well-being at work and finding one's job meaningful, which reduces the stress of balancing both personal and professional life. Moreover, the ability to maintain this balance between work sphere and personal life can affect their commitment to their job and how productive they are.

Future studies should explore how flexible work arrangements affect work-life balance in the Indian banking sector through different mechanisms and outcomes. Furthermore, additional research is necessary to determine the effectiveness of flexible work arrangements, such as reduced workweeks and flextime, in promoting work-life balance. Additionally, research must be done on how organizational outcomes including productivity and employee engagement are affected by flexible work arrangements. Research should also explore strategies and interventions that can be implemented by organizations to promote work-life balance.

3. RESEARCH METHODOLOGY

3.1 Objective

Identify the influence of the implementation of flexible work arrangements to balance the work and family life of bank employees in India.

3.2 Research Design

The research will be descriptive in nature. Descriptive research involves observing, measuring, and analyzing data to describe a particular phenomenon. It provides a detailed and accurate account of a situation or phenomenon, without trying to establish cause-and-effect relationships.

3.3 Data Analysis Technique

This study applies to the employees of the banking sector (Private) of India. For this study, Interpretative Phenomenological Analysis (IPA) is conducted. Interpretative phenomenological analysis (IPA) is a qualitative research methodology used to explore individuals' personal and subjective experiences of a phenomenon. IPA is grounded in phenomenology, a philosophical approach that seeks to describe the essence of human experience through direct observation and reflection. The interpretative phenomenological analysis (IPA) aims to understand in detail how people make sense of their personal and social worlds.

Interpretative Phenomenological Analysis is chosen as the methodology of this study as it will provide us with a deep understanding of the experience of the employees without the implementation of the flexible work arrangements in the banking sector and their expectations and influence on the work-life balance after the implementation of the flexible work arrangements in the banking sector. Employees may experience flexible arrangements in different ways and may benefit from arrangements to different extents (Jeffrey Hill et al., 2008).

A purposive sample of 10 bank employees of India from the private sector is taken for this research. For this study, structured interviews were conducted which were recorded with the consent of the participants.

4. DATA ANALYSIS AND INTERPRETATION

The questions are analyzed based on themes created from respondents' opinions.

1. What are your initial thoughts and feelings about the potential implementation of flexible work arrangements within the banking sector in India?

Some of the excerpts from the interview are as follows:

"Flexible working hours are not possible in the Indian Banking System, keeping in consideration the large market segment handled by the existing banking staff. The sudden transformation would not be successful in its implementation."

"My initial thoughts about the potential implementation of flexible work arrangements would likely be a mix of excitement and apprehension. On one hand, the prospect of having more control over my work schedule and the possibility of a better work-life balance is appealing. On the other hand, concerns about how this might affect team collaboration, communication, and the traditional work structure could create some uncertainty."

"The flexible work model allows freedom to employees to conduct their work independently. It provides job autonomy which in turn provides a sense of owner-ship of work for the employees. This boosts their overall morale and productivity. In today's world, especially after Covid, flexibility has become an important factor in the success of the organization. The research has found that if flexibility is given to an employee, their overall performance goes up and the results of such a model are positive. Hence, we can say that it is the need of the hour."

"I think more digitalization in banking leads to more doubts in customers."

Table 1. Initial Thoughts and Feelings Towards Flexible Work Arrangements

Summary of Opinions	Themes	Iteration Keywords/Phrases
Mixed reactions exist toward flexible work in Indian banking. Some express skepticism, citing concerns about client interactions and the need for personal engagement. Others show a mix of excitement and apprehension, acknowledging potential benefits but expressing concerns about maintaining operations and team collaboration. However, some view flexible work positively, citing benefits like increased autonomy and better work-life balance. A concern is raised about digitalization impacting customer trust.	Feasibility and Resistance	Large market segment, Sudden transformation, Client engagements, Personal interaction.
	Mixed Feelings and Apprehension	Excitement, Apprehension, Work-life balance, Team collaboration, Communication gaps.
	Positive Outlook on Flexibility	Job autonomy, Ownership of work, Better work-life balance, Stress reduction, and Increased employee satisfaction.
	Digitalization Concerns	Digitalization, Doubts in customers.

Interpretation

The responses from table 1 reflect diverse opinions regarding the potential implementation of flexible work arrangements in the Indian banking sector. While some respondents express strong reservations about the feasibility of such arrangements due to the nature of banking operations and client interactions, others see the opportunity for positive outcomes, including improved work-life balance and increased job satisfaction. The mixed feelings and apprehensions center around concerns related to maintaining team cohesion, communication, and the traditional work structure in a flexible environment. The digitalization concern raises awareness of potential challenges associated with technological advancements in the sector.

2. How do you believe flexible work arrangements could impact your work-life balance, considering the demands of your role in the banking industry?

Some of the excerpts from the interview are as follows:

"This can definitely impact the work-life balance but as discussed above, it's difficult for the bankers to stay away from work for many days. If the shift system is applied here in India, then definitely the work-life balance can be improved."

"Flexible work arrangements have the potential to drastically improve my work-life balance. I could schedule doctor appointments, pick up kids from school, or even attend to aging parents without sacrificing work hours. This flexibility would reduce stress, improve mental well-being, and allow me to return to work with renewed energy and focus. Of course, finding the right balance and managing distractions while working remotely will be crucial. However, with proper planning and discipline, I believe the benefits for work-life harmony are immense."

"In banking, there are not 9 to 5 working jobs, in banking there are certain criteria like sale targets, etc. which need a lot of focus and dedication, ultimately such departments with targets can have a major impact through flexible work arrangements."

"Flexible work arrangements have the potential to positively impact my work-life balance. The banking industry is known for its demanding and sometimes unpredictable work hours. Having the flexibility to manage my work around personal commitments could lead to a more balanced and sustainable lifestyle. However, it would require effective time management and clear boundaries to avoid overworking."

"FWA will definitely have a great impact on my life. I will be able to look into my other life priorities and also will be able to maintain the balance. It might increase productivity as we will totally focus on work without thinking about other work as we will be getting time for it."

Table 2. Impact of Flexi Work Arrangements on Work Life Balance

Summary of Opinions	Themes	Iteration Keywords/Phrases
The responses from individuals in the banking industry reflect a consensus that flexible work arrangements (FWA) can positively impact work-life balance. Participants acknowledge the demanding nature of their roles in the banking sector, emphasizing the potential benefits of FWA in achieving a balance between professional obligations and personal life. Key points include improved well-being, increased productivity, reduced stress, and the ability to attend personal priorities.	Positive Impact Work & Life Spheres	Positive role, Maintain balance, Improve well-being, Reduce stress, Work-life harmony, Increase productivity, Focus on work.
	Challenges	Difficult for bankers, Stay away from work, Shift system, Juggling client calls and childcare, Challenging
	Impact on Banking Industry Dynamics	Banking not 9 to 5, Sale targets, Focus, and dedication, Flexible arrangements impact on targets.
	Time Management and Boundaries	Effective time management, Clear boundaries, Avoid Overworking, Manage distractions. Less commuting, More time for family, During school pick-ups, Remote work.
	Potential for Remote Work	

Interpretation

Most respondents see flexible work arrangements as a positive force for achieving a better work-life balance in the demanding banking industry (table 2). The potential benefits include increased productivity, improved well-being, and the ability to manage personal priorities. However, there are acknowledgments of challenges, including the difficulty of staying away from work for extended periods and the need for effective time management and boundaries. The impact on industry dynamics, such as meeting sales targets, is recognized. The potential for remote work is seen as beneficial, particularly in reducing commuting time. Overall, there is a recognition that finding the right balance and managing distractions will be crucial for the successful implementation of flexible work arrangements in the banking sector.

3. How do you think your colleagues and superiors within the banking sector would react to the introduction of flexible work arrangements, and how might this impact team dynamics?

Some of the excerpts from the interview are as follows:

"Introducing flexible work arrangements would receive a very positive response from my Colleagues and team due to the varied number of tasks they have. The need of the business requires the employees to conduct several tasks every single day including going on sales calls, processing transactions, handling the paperwork etc. To conduct these day-to-day activities, flexibility in work would act as a catalyst allowing them to be high on motivation and productivity. This would also help them find a new perspective towards their work. A task that needs to be completed in a certain manner and by a certain person only need not be the way of work anymore. There could be various other methods to accomplish the same in a faster and more efficient manner."

"Adapting to new communication channels and managing remote teams will be a challenge. Senior management needs to provide clear guidelines and ensure proper performance evaluation methods."

"I think it will be a mixed reaction of colleagues and superiors. There are always pros and cons to everything. There will be initial challenges in the beginning as superiors will think that the work might get delayed, and more staff need to be hired as the replacement will have to work. If the work has to be managed within the existing staff, then due to work pressure the chances of mistake will occur."

Table 3. Reaction of Colleagues and Superiors on Introduction of Flexi Work Arrangements

Summary of Opinions	Themes	Iteration Keywords/Phrases
While some express optimism and a positive outlook, others anticipate challenges and mixed reactions. The general sentiment is a recognition of the potential benefits, such as improved work-life balance, increased productivity, and positive impacts on motivation. However, concerns about challenges in communication, team dynamics, and potential resistance from superiors are also evident. The success of implementing flexible work arrangements is seen as contingent upon factors like clear communication, trust-building measures, and a supportive organizational culture.	Positive Outlook	Positive, Everyone needs change, Love it, Younger colleagues will love it, Autonomy, Increased control over work schedule, Life would be easy, High on motivation and productivity.
	Challenges and Mixed Reactions	Mixed reaction, Pros and cons, Initial challenges, Resistance, Fear of disruptions, Hesitant, Concerns about productivity and team dynamics, Clear guidelines, Proper performance evaluation, Communication channels, Managing remote teams, Clear communication, Transparency, and Virtual communication skills.
		Interested in flexible work arrangements in certain departments.
	Support for Flexibility in Certain Departments	

Interpretation

The data suggests a nuanced perspective within the banking sector regarding the introduction of flexible work arrangements. While a positive impact has been recognized on work-life balance, motivation, and productivity, there are also concerns about potential challenges, especially related to communication, team dynamics, and resistance from some senior members. Clear communication emerges as a recurring theme, indicating its critical role in addressing concerns and facilitating a smooth transition. The need for training and adaptation, particularly in virtual communication skills, is highlighted, emphasizing the importance of preparing employees and leaders for the changes. Overall, the responses underscore the complexity of implementing flexible work arrangements and the importance of a well-managed transition process.

4. In your opinion, what role do you think flexible work arrangements could play in enhancing overall job satisfaction and well-being among banking professionals?

Some of the excerpts from the interview are as follows:

"Flexible work arrangements have the potential to significantly enhance overall job satisfaction and well-being among banking professionals. By providing a better work-life balance, employees may experience reduced stress, increased job satisfaction, and improved mental health. This, in turn, can contribute to higher levels of engagement, retention, and overall well-being."

"Flexible work arrangements can significantly enhance job satisfaction and well-being. Feeling trusted and empowered to manage my time effectively would boost my morale and motivation. Less stress, better work-life balance, and increased control over my schedule would all contribute to improved mental and physical well-being. This, in turn, could lead to higher engagement, creativity, and productivity. A happier and healthier workforce is likely to translate into better customer service and overall positive organizational outcomes."

"It can be extremely satisfactory for the employees. They will get a lot of time to spend with family and friends. They can always be stress-free. Can utilize the time for the gym, exercises, dance, etc. This will always keep them motivated. But this should not be done at a cut in salary."

"Happy employees stay. Flexibility promotes well-being by reducing stress and improving work-life balance. Overall morale and engagement should rise."

Table 4. Role of Flexi Work Arrangements on Job Satisfaction and Well Being

Summary of Opinions	Themes	Iteration Keywords/Phrases
It reflects a generally positive sentiment towards the implementation of flexible work arrangements among banking professionals. Respondents believe that such arrangements could have a substantial impact on job satisfaction and overall well-being.	Work-Life Balance and Family Time	Family, work-life balance, personal life, time with family.
	Retention and Employee Morale	Retention, not leaving the organization, maintaining people, morale, and team spirit.
	Job Satisfaction and Psychological Well-being	Job satisfaction, happier workplace, overall well-being, reduced stress, mental health.
	Control and Empowerment	Feeling trusted, empowered, control over schedule, motivation.
	Health and Physical Well-being	Reduced stress, better work-life balance, increased physical activities, stress-free.

Interpretation

The overall sentiment is optimistic about the potential positive impact of flexible work arrangements on job satisfaction and well-being among banking professionals. The common themes revolve around achieving a better balance between work and personal life, improving psychological well-being, and fostering a positive workplace culture. Respondents believe that these benefits can lead to increased employee retention, higher morale, and improved overall organizational outcomes. It is noted that the trust and empowerment associated with flexible work arrangements are considered crucial factors in ensuring the success of such initiatives. Additionally, the emphasis on maintaining salary levels indicates that satisfaction is not solely derived from non-monetary benefits but requires a holistic approach to employee well-being.

5. How do you envision the potential impact of flexible work arrangements on productivity and efficiency in the banking sector, considering the nature of your job responsibilities?

Some of the excerpts from the interview are as follows:

"Flexible work schedule would have a positive impact on the productivity and efficiency of the company. These days, especially after COVID-19, companies are adopting flexible methods of work as they have witnessed the positive effects of the same during the pandemic. It is a win-win situation for both, the company, and the employee. The employee gets the freedom to choose the way they want to conduct their work. This enables them to be more productive as opposed to rigid working modules. Hence, this leads to increased efficiency for the organizations."

"The potential impact of flexible work arrangements on productivity and efficiency could be positive if managed effectively. The banking sector relies heavily on technology, and many tasks can be performed remotely. However, concerns about potential challenges in communication, collaboration, and maintaining a cohesive team may arise. Proper implementation of supportive technologies, clear guidelines, and regular communication channels can mitigate these concerns and contribute to sustained productivity."

"While the nature of some banking jobs requires physical presence, many tasks can be efficiently handled remotely. With technology available, I could process transactions, analyze data, or prepare reports from anywhere. This could improve efficiency and save time on commutes. However, concerns about communication and collaboration remain. Regular online meetings, clear communication channels, and well-defined project deadlines will be key to maintaining productivity and teamwork in a flexible environment."

"Productivity will surely improve. The motivation to work will also be improved. People will work with 100% efficiency and 0% mistakes. They will be enthusiastic about getting more work and of course more holidays."

"Depends on the role. Customer service relies on real-time interaction. Might need hybrid models to ensure client availability. However, focused work spirits from home could boost efficiency."

Table 5. Potential Impact of Flexible Work Arrangements on Productivity and Efficiency

Summary of Opinions	Themes	Iteration Keywords/Phrases
Most respondents in the banking sector express optimism about flexible work arrangements positively impacting productivity and efficiency. They believe that such flexibility enhances productivity by reducing stress and allowing focused task management. Striking a balance is crucial, especially for client-centric tasks. Post-COVID adoption is seen as beneficial for both organizations and employees, with technology playing a key role. Concerns about communication and team cohesion exist, but respondents emphasize the positive impact on motivation and efficiency, anticipating fewer mistakes and increased output.	Positive Impact Role Dependency Technology Facilitation Concerns and Mitigation Post-COVID Adoption	Positive impact, Enhanced productivity, Happy and calm mind, Improved motivation, 100% efficiency, and Enthusiasm for more work and holidays. Depends on the role and hybrid models for client availability. Relies on technology, Tasks handled remotely, and Supportive technologies. Concerns about communication, Collaboration, clear guidelines, Regular communication, Well-defined project deadlines. After COVID, Win-win situation, Increased efficiency.

Interpretation

The overall sentiment towards flexible work arrangements in the banking sector is positive. Respondents anticipate enhanced productivity, improved employee motivation, and positive outcomes for both the organization and clients. However, there is a recognition of the need for careful balance, especially considering the role-dependent nature of tasks. Technology is seen as a facilitator, but concerns about communication and collaboration require attention, emphasizing the importance of clear guidelines and supportive technologies. The post-COVID landscape has influenced the adoption of flexible methods, with an expectation of sustained efficiency when properly implemented.

5. IMPLICATIONS

To effectively execute flexible work arrangements within the banking industry, companies should provide top priority to clear and transparent communication tactics, as per the collected insights. Setting up policies, making sure there are frequent updates, and creating efficient virtual channels of communication are essential to controlling expectations and resolving issues. Organizations should implement customized flexibility models, particularly for tasks involving clients, considering the role-specific aspect of flexibility. These models could include hybrid approaches that strike a balance between remote work and in-person interactions. To reduce potential communication gaps, technology investment is essential. Tools for virtual collaboration, project management, and secure communication should be prioritized. The implementation of comprehensive employee well-being initiatives that include stress management techniques, mental health support, and work-life balance strategies ought to be essential elements to optimize the favorable effects on job satisfaction. Implementing robust monitoring and feedback mechanisms will enable organizations to adapt flexibly to evolving needs and challenges, ensuring a dynamic and responsive approach throughout the transition. By addressing these aspects, organizations can navigate the complexities of flexible work arrangements in the banking sector and cultivate a positive and adaptive work culture.

6. SCOPE FOR FUTURE RESEARCH

India, a rapidly developing country with significant population growth, faces challenges concerning work-life balance, particularly in the banking sector. While existing research has delved into the effects of flexible work arrangements on work-life balance, there remains considerable scope for future research to explore this topic comprehensively. Here are the potential avenues for further investigation to enrich our understanding of how flexible work arrangements influence work-life balance in the Indian banking sector.

1. Examination of Diverse Perspectives:

Future research could adopt a multi-dimensional approach to examine the impact of flexible work arrangements on work-life balance from various perspectives. This may include exploring the experiences of different demographic groups such as gender, age, hierarchical levels, and job roles within the banking sector.

2. Exploration of Organizational Culture and Policies:

A deeper exploration of organizational culture and policies is warranted to understand how they shape the implementation and effectiveness of flexible work arrangements. Investigating the attitudes of management towards flexibility, the presence of supportive policies, and the degree of organizational flexibility can offer valuable insights into the organizational factors that facilitate or hinder work-life balance initiatives in Indian banks.

3. Comparative Studies across Countries:

Given the global relevance of work-life balance issues, future research could extend beyond the confines of India and compare the impact of flexible work arrangements in the banking sector across different countries. By examining cultural differences, regulatory frameworks, and socio-economic contexts, comparative studies can highlight unique challenges and best practices in promoting work-life balance within diverse cultural and institutional settings.

4. Quantitative Analysis with Large Sample Sizes:

Addressing the limitation of small sample sizes, future research should prioritize quantitative studies with larger and more diverse samples drawn from multiple banks across India.

5. Examination of Technological Interventions:

With the increasing integration of technology in the workplace, future research could explore the role of technological interventions in facilitating flexible work arrangements and enhancing work-life balance. This may involve investigating the use of digital platforms, telecommuting technologies, and virtual collaboration tools in enabling remote work and flexible scheduling practices among bank employees.

7. CONCLUSION

The analysis of responses from individuals within the banking sector regarding the potential implementation of flexible work arrangements yields a complex picture. While there is evident optimism about the positive impact that such arrangements can have on various aspects of work, there are also concerns that need to be addressed for a successful transition.

The theme that emerges from the data is the importance of clear communication. Respondents consistently focus on the need for transparent guidelines, regular updates, and effective virtual communication channels. This implies that organizations looking to introduce flexible work arrangements should prioritize the development of robust communication strategies. Ensuring that all stakeholders are well-informed and engaged in the process is crucial for managing expectations and addressing concerns.

Another key consideration is the role-specific nature of flexibility within the banking sector. Recognizing that certain roles, especially those involving client interactions, may require a different approach, organizations are encouraged to adopt role-specific flexibility models. Hybrid models that balance remote work with in-person engagements for client-facing roles can be an effective strategy.

The reliance on technology is also a central theme. Respondents acknowledge the role of technology in facilitating remote work, and organizations are advised to invest in supportive technologies. This includes tools for virtual collaboration, project management, and secure communication. The successful integration of technology can alleviate concerns related to communication gaps and ensure a seamless transition to flexible work arrangements.

The emphasis on employee well-being is evident throughout the responses. Organizations are encouraged to develop holistic well-being programs that go beyond traditional benefits. Mental health support, stress management initiatives, and strategies for the maintenance of a healthy work-life balance should be integral components of such programs. This holistic approach is seen as essential for maximizing the positive impact of flexible work arrangements on job satisfaction and overall employee well-being.

Monitoring and feedback mechanisms are highlighted as crucial components of a successful transition. Regularly seeking feedback from employees and implementing adjustments based on evolving challenges and needs can contribute to a dynamic and responsive approach. Continuous evaluation ensures that the implementation of flexible work arrangements remains aligned with the changing dynamics of the banking sector.

In conclusion, the data suggests that while there is optimism about the potential benefits of flexible work arrangements, a well-managed transition is essential. Clear communication, role-specific flexibility models, technology integration, employee well-being programs, and effective monitoring mechanisms are key elements for success. By addressing these aspects, organizations can navigate the complexities of implementing flexible work arrangements in the banking sector and foster a positive and adaptive work culture.

REFERENCES

Boje, D., Burnes, B., & Hassard, J. (2012). *The Routledge companion to organizational change*. Routledge. DOI:10.4324/9780203810279

Brega, C., Briones, S., Javornik, J., León, M., & Yerkes, M. (2023). Flexible work arrangements for work-life balance: A cross-national policy evaluation from a capabilities perspective. *The International Journal of Sociology and Social Policy*, 43(13/14), 278–294. DOI:10.1108/IJSSP-03-2023-0077

Carlson, D. S., Grzywacz, J. G., & Michele Kacmar, K. (2010). The relationship of schedule flexibility and outcomes via the work-family interface. *Journal of Managerial Psychology*, 25(4), 330–355. DOI:10.1108/02683941011035278

Chaudhuri, S., Arora, R., & Roy, P. (2020). Work–life balance policies and organisational outcomes – a review of literature from the Indian context. *Industrial and Commercial Training*, 52(3), 155–170. DOI:10.1108/ICT-01-2019-0003

Cheng, Z., Nielsen, I., & Cutler, H. (2019). Perceived job quality, work-life interference and intention to stay. *International Journal of Manpower*, 40(1), 17–35. DOI:10.1108/IJM-08-2017-0208

Dunnette, M. D. (1976). *Handbook of industrial and organizational psychology*. Rand McNally College Publishing Company.

Giannikis, S. K., & Mihail, D. M. (2011). Flexible work arrangements in Greece: A study of employee perceptions. *International Journal of Human Resource Management*, 22(2), 417–432. DOI:10.1080/09585192.2011.540163

Iddagoda, A., Hysa, E., Bulińska-Stangrecka, H., & Manta, O. (2021). Green work-life balance and greenwashing the construct of work-life balance: Myth and reality. *Energies*, 14(15), 4556. DOI:10.3390/en14154556

Jeffrey Hill, E., Grzywacz, J. G., Allen, S., Blanchard, V. L., Matz-Costa, C., Shulkin, S., & Pitt-Catsouphes, M. (2008). Defining and conceptualizing workplace flexibility. *Community Work & Family*, 11(2), 149–163. DOI:10.1080/13668800802024678

Johanna Bath, J. X., & Markulin, V. (2024). Exploring the impact of work arrangements on employee well-being in the post-pandemic workplace: The role of perceived flexibility, work-life balance, and managerial support. International Journal of Business and Applied Social Science, 1-17. DOI:10.33642/ijbass.v10n1p1

Judge, T. A., Thoresen, C. J., Bono, J. E., & Patton, G. K. (2001). The job satisfaction-job performance relationship: A qualitative and quantitative review. *Psychological Bulletin*, 127(3), 376–407. DOI:10.1037/0033-2909.127.3.376 PMID:11393302

Kelliher, C., Richardson, J., & Boiarintseva, G. (2018). All of work? All of life? Reconceptualising work-life balance for the 21st century. *Human Resource Management Journal*, 29(2), 97–112. DOI:10.1111/1748-8583.12215

Khan, I., & Nawaz, A. (2016). The leadership styles and the employees performance: A review. *Gomal University Journal of Research*, 32(2), 144–150.

Menges, J. I., Tussing, D. V., Wihler, A., & Grant, A. M. (2017). When job performance is all relative: How family motivation energizes effort and compensates for intrinsic motivation. *Academy of Management Journal*, 60(2), 695–719. DOI:10.5465/amj.2014.0898

Mgammal, M. H., Mohammed Al-Matari, E., & Bardai, B. (2022). How coronavirus (COVID-19) pandemic thought concern affects employees' work performance: Evidence from real time survey. *Cogent Business & Management*, 9(1), 2064707. Advance online publication. DOI:10.1080/23311975.2022.2064707

Mishra, P. K. (2013). Job satisfaction. *IOSR Journal Of Humanities And Social Science*, 14(5), 45–54. DOI:10.9790/1959-1454554

Nidhi, B. S. (2023). The impact of flexible work arrangements on work-life balance. *International Journal For Multidisciplinary Research*, 5(3), 3144. Advance online publication. DOI:10.36948/ijfmr.2023.v05i03.3144

Nwugballa, E. A. (2016). Evaluating the relationship between work-family conflict and organisational commitment among rural women health workers in Ebonyi state, Nigeria. *International Journal of Academic Research in Business & Social Sciences*, 6(5). Advance online publication. DOI:10.6007/IJARBSS/v6-i5/2169

Palumbo, R., Manna, R., & Cavallone, M. (2020). Beware of side effects on quality! Investigating the implications of home working on work-life balance in educational services. *The TQM Journal*, 33(4), 915–929. DOI:10.1108/TQM-05-2020-0120

Rodgers, C. S. (1992). The flexible workplace: What have we learned? *Human Resource Management*, 31(3), 183–199. DOI:10.1002/hrm.3930310305

Saks, A. M. (2006). Antecedents and consequences of employee engagement. *Journal of Managerial Psychology*, 21(7), 600–619. DOI:10.1108/02683940610690169

Shaffer, M. A., Sebastian Reiche, B., Dimitrova, M., Lazarova, M., Chen, S., Westman, M., & Wurtz, O. (2015). Work- and family-role adjustment of different types of global professionals: Scale development and validation. *Journal of International Business Studies*, 47(2), 113–139. DOI:10.1057/jibs.2015.26

Sheikh, A. M. (2022). Impact of perceived organizational support on organizational commitment of banking employees: Role of work-life balance. *Journal of Asia Business Studies*, 17(1), 79–99. DOI:10.1108/JABS-02-2021-0071

Sirgy, M. J., & Lee, D. (2017). Work-life balance: An integrative review. *Applied Research in Quality of Life*, 13(1), 229–254. DOI:10.1007/s11482-017-9509-8

Skinner, N., Cathcart, A., & Pocock, B. (2016). To ask or not to ask? Investigating workers' flexibility requests and the phenomenon of discontented non-requesters. Labour & Industry: a journal of the social and economic relations of work, 26(2), 103-119. DOI:10.1080/10301763.2016.1157677

ten Brummelhuis, L. L., & Van der Lippe, T. (2010). Effective work-life balance support for various household structures. *Human Resource Management*, 49(2), 173–193. DOI:10.1002/hrm.20340

Tett, R. P., & Meyer, J. P.TETT. (1993). Job satisfaction, organizational commitment, turnover intention, and turnover: Path analyses based on meta-analytic findings. *Personnel Psychology*, 46(2), 259–293. DOI:10.1111/j.1744-6570.1993.tb00874.x

Ugwu, F. O., Amazue, L. O., & Onyedire, N. G. (2017). Work-family life balance in a Nigerian banking sector setting. *Cogent Psychology*, 4(1), 1290402. DOI:10.1080/23311908.2017.1290402

Whyte, W. H. (1956). *The organization man*. LaFarge Literary Agency.

Zainal, N. S., Wider, W., Lajuma, S., Ahmad Khadri, M. W., Taib, N. M., & Joseph, A. (2022). Employee retention in the service industry in Malaysia. *Frontiers in Sociology*, 7, 928951. Advance online publication. DOI:10.3389/fsoc.2022.928951 PMID:35880145

Zülch, G., Stock, P., & Schmidt, D. (2012). Analysis of the strain on employees in the retail sector considering work-life balance. *Work (Reading, Mass.)*, 41, 2675–2682. DOI:10.3233/WOR-2012-0510-2675 PMID:22317125

Chapter 4
Reshaping Human Resource Management:
Insights From the COVID–19 Pandemic

Sıdıka Ece Yılmaz
https://orcid.org/0000-0002-0375-3505
Adana Alparslan Türkeş Science and Technology University, Turkey

ABSTRACT

The COVID-19 pandemic has had a major effect on the field of Human Resource Management HRM, prompting quick adaptation and innovation by organizations around the world. This chapter examines the pandemic's multifaceted effects on HRM practices, highlighting both the challenges that were encountered and the innovative measures implemented in response. The pandemic has hastened the adoption of digital technology, resulting in a considerable increase in remote work habits and digital transformation within organizations. While these developments have increased operational efficiency, they have also raised worries about employees' digital abilities, privacy, and the blurring of work-life boundaries. The epidemic has highlighted the significance of strategic workforce planning, with HRM practitioners focusing on improving employee skills, well-being, and engagement. This chapter will provide an in-depth overview of these changes, exploring the evolution of HRM practices and identifying the most effective ways for navigating the challenges created by the pandemic.

DOI: 10.4018/979-8-3693-4412-5.ch004

1. INTRODUCTION

The coronavirus (COVID-19) began spreading in late 2019 and has since been marked a pandemic (Coronavirus Resource Center, 2020). The global outbreak of COVID-19 in Wuhan, China, followed by its rapid transmission worldwide, has resulted in numerous countries experiencing a pandemic and its multifaceted consequences (Plater, Frazier, Talbert, Davis, and Talbert, 2022). The pandemic's impact has necessitated quick adaptation by organizations and governments, leading to substantial transformations in individuals' personal, professional, and economic lives (Hamouche, 2023). During this time, issues such as the smooth operation of work organizations, restrictions on people gathering, the enforcement of social/ physical distances, commute restrictions, travel bans, and the cancellation or delay of business meetings arose (Dissanayake, 2020; KV and Walarine, 2021).

The COVID-19 pandemic has had extensive impacts on all facets of society, including the field of Human Resource Management (HRM). It has created a difficult challenge for organizations, especially in the field of HRM, as they are required to adjust and modify their workforce strategies (Carnevale and Hatak, 2020). The pandemic has significantly affected various organizations and prompted human resource managers to reconsider their responsibilities. Human resources managers have implemented a range of initiatives to ensure that individuals currently in the workforce remain productive, engaged, and dedicated, while also maintaining operational procedures (Draghici, 2020).

During this unprecedented coronavirus outbreak, HRM has played a vital role in enabling enterprises and their staff to adjust and thrive in the evolving work environment (Gigauri, 2020a). The pandemic has posed a variety of challenges for HRM professionals, who have had to manage disrupted workforces, agreements for remote employment, and economic uncertainties. These changes have had both immediate and enduring impacts on HRM practices and approaches (Azizi, Atlasi, Ziapour, Abbas, and Naemi, 2021). Additionally, the effectiveness of the human resources department has been crucial in efficiently managing this organizational process. The efficacy of human resources strategies has been particularly vital for businesses during times of crisis. Organizations have employed diverse techniques to handle the risks, challenges, and consequences effectively (Carnevale and Hatak 2020). For instance, many organizations have implemented different technical, physical, and socio-psychological strategies to downsize their staff to cope with the challenges posed by the ongoing pandemic (Barro and Weng, 2020). Most organizations applied digital communication solutions to oversee existing procedure. Amidst the growing global uncertainty caused by the absence of a vaccine or cure for the coronavirus, many organizations have endorsed and urged their employees to utilize online platforms or applications to carry out diverse HRM responsibilities (Kalogiannidis, 2021).

Scientific studies have been performed to provide support for human resources functions during this time. Aguinis and Burgi-Tian (2021) introduced the Performance Promoter Score (PPS) measure as a feasible and useful solution for addressing the performance management challenges arising from the COVID-19 pandemic. Li, Sun, Tao, and Lee (2021a) constructed a model that illustrates the significance of communication within organizations during the pandemic. They argued that implementing open internal communication within firms would have several benefits, including promoting problem-focused control, minimizing uncertainty, and enhancing relationships between employees and the organization.

In overall, the COVID-19 pandemic has significantly altered the HRM environment. Organizations have been forced to quickly adjust to new circumstances, requiring creative approaches to sustain production and keep employees engaged in the face of tremendous difficulties. This chapter will provide an in-depth overview of these changes, exploring the evolution of HRM practices and identifying the most effective ways for navigating the challenges created by the pandemic. The objective is to examine the diverse challenges and pioneering innovations that have emerged in response to the disruptions caused by the pandemic. In addition, the study aims to address the following Research Questions (RQ):

RQ1: What are innovative approaches that have arisen in HRM practices following the COVID-19 pandemic, and how have these approaches impacted organizations?

RQ2: What are the primary obstacles in implementing HRM practices during the pandemic and what are the most efficient strategies employed to address these obstacles?

2. LITERATURE REVIEW

Human resources managers have various responsibilities, including service providers, policy police, strategic partners, change agents, and welfare officers. These roles are considered the main components of an human resources managers' work (Welsh and Welch, 2012). Given these responsibilities, it is evident that human resources procedures have undergone substantial changes due to the impact of the epidemic.

Factors that need to be considered in human resources practices impacted by COVID-19 include work conditions, distance management and new competencies of managers, crisis management, new ways of human resources practices, training and education of employees using technologies, different approaches towards generations, lowering of salaries and wages, communication and building relationships, employer branding, safety and security, health protection, employee fluctuation and changes in structure of employees, psychological aspects (Vnoučková, 2020). Due to the impact of the pandemic, human resources and individuals faced many challenges and witnessed the emergence of innovations. This section addresses the HRM challenges that have emerged as a result of the COVID-19 pandemic, as well as the HRM innovations that have been introduced in response to it.

2.1. HRM Innovations through COVID 19

During the COVID-19 pandemic, numerous countries made substantial attempts to handle their workforce effectively, resulting in notable adjustments and advancements in the field of HRM. Also, various scientific investigations have been undertaken in many different countries to comprehend and improve the process. For instance, an analysis of 136 Portuguese businesses revealed substantial changes in the processes of work and safety, training, work organization, recruitment and selection, induction and onboarding, and communication. Furthermore, research has indicated that the magnitude of this transformation is correlated with the scale of the organization. Moreover, there has been an obvious increase in the adoption of remote working practices (Gonçalves, 2021).

The development of technology, digitalization, enhanced accessibility to technology and the internet, and the rise in technological literacy have inevitably impacted HRM. The HR field has experienced a considerable increase in the relevance of digitalization due to the accelerated pace of digitalization caused by the COVID-19 pandemic (Alkan, 2022). The COVID-19 pandemic has caused a significant increase in the utilization of digital technologies as a result of social distancing measures and widespread lockdowns (Pandey and Pal, 2020). A qualitative research study was undertaken in Georgia to assess the impact of Covid-19 on HRM. The results suggested that there was a growing trend towards digital transformation and remote work (Gigauri, 2020b). Thus, it is widely acknowledged that digital business operations are becoming increasingly significant. Another research was done with 554 employees on the Amazon Mechanical Turk platform to analyze the challenges of technological transformation and the readiness to embrace digital forms of work. The findings indicate that individuals perceive digital work forms to be considerably more reliable as a means of generating revenue compared to traditional jobs. Consequently, there has been an increase in the number of individuals working from home offices, and there has been a noticeable growth in digital transformation as a direct response to the COVID-19 pandemic (Nagel, 2020).

During the pandemic, studies implemented types of flexible working practices that permitted employees to work from home. The growing trend of digitalization has driven businesses to transition to a work-from-home (WFH) model (Pandey and Pal, 2020). Nevertheless, it is explicitly mentioned that this alternative working framework is better suited for service employees rather than employees in manufacturing (Koirala and Acharya, 2020). Due to the existence of COVID-19, remote work is becoming more common, and organizations are striving to offer increased flexibility to their employees. The ongoing topic of discussion revolves around the nature of the new normal. The current situation entails a shift towards remote working as the standard practice or an increase in the flexibility of working arrangements. Consequently, organizations are assessing the efficacy of remote work. However, numerous organizations are still unable to offer a broad understanding of the long-term implications of remote work (Aitken-Fox, et al., 2020).

Amidst the epidemic, the concept of organizational agility has gained significance as a crucial approach for successfully overcoming times of crisis. Organizations have implemented agile HRM strategies to swiftly and efficiently make choices during times of crisis. These strategies have facilitated organizations in promptly adjusting to evolving circumstances and acquiring adaptability (Acciarini, Boccardelli and Vitale, 2021). In times of crisis, leaders must embrace a flexible and agile mindset, demonstrate innovative thinking and creativity, and adjust to forthcoming obstacles (Dirani et al., 2020).

2.2. HRM challenges arising from Covid 19

The COVID-19 pandemic has brought forth a multitude of challenges for HRM practitioners worldwide. The COVID-19 pandemic has had a significant impact on various aspects that contribute to job satisfaction, including salary and wages, employment and promotion, the psychological and social well-being of employees, job security, and autonomy, etc. (Nyanga and Chindanya, 2020). During the pandemic, human resource managers especially had to deal with labor shortages and inefficiencies in their organizations (Dissanayake, 2020). On the other hand, there has been an increasing issue with the implementation of workforce reductions (Gonçalves, 2021). These circumstances posed substantial challenges for HRM methods. Conversely, a study found that the epidemic has a negative impact on the recruitment and retention of healthcare workers in rural areas of Australia (Jones, Versace, Lyle, and Walsh, 2021). This demonstrates that the pandemic has had a substantial impact on the recruitment process inside human resources functions. Furthermore, it indicates the presence of retention issues, a significant concern for organizations.

Employees who were primarily based within the physical facilities of their businesses must now rapidly adjust to remote work settings (Carnevale and Hatak, 2020). This posed a challenge for employees in terms of their digital skills (Gigauri, 2020b). A key point that HRM practitioners have learned during the COVID-19 epidemic is the necessity to improve the skills and knowledge of employees. Both human resources and senior leadership need to work together in strategic workforce planning, which includes digital transformation and workforce transformation (Plater et al., 2022).

The apprehension of the potential invasion of persons' privacy by computer technologies grows as technology advances (Best, Krueger, and Lad, 2006). The widespread usage of digital technology during this period has resulted in individuals experiencing significant privacy issues. The HR department should analyze the situation and determine that implementing a range of policies is necessary to enhance employees' sense of safety. A similar scenario arose during this time when governments began employing smartphone applications to track infected individuals and trace their contacts. Nongovernmental organizations have expressed worry over privacy and government surveillance (Pant and Lal, 2020).

As people in various industries learned to adjust to quickly changing circumstances, organizations also acquired new abilities and responsibilities in overseeing new forms of business models. The progression of artificial intelligence and the hastening of automation throughout this period have intensified the difficulty of this process. It is evident that HRM needed to establish a talent strategy that focuses on enhancing employees' essential digital and cognitive capabilities, social and emotional skills, adaptability, and resilience (Agrawal, De Smet, Lacroix and Reich, 2020). Additionally, HR managers were compelled to make pivotal decisions despite their lack of knowledge and comprehensive grasp of the pandemic and the significant uncertainties associated with it (Bratianu and Bejinaru, 2021). Due to the distinct nature of crisis situations, the skills required for crisis leadership differ from those needed for regular leadership. Guiding individuals during a crisis necessitates a distinct set of skills. During periods of crisis, a leader must possess the ability to promptly assess and analyze information, demonstrate strong resolve, establish a clear course of action, maintain composure, effectively handle fear, and exhibit proficiency in communication and empathy (Lagowska, Sobral and Furtado, 2020). The epidemic has exposed the necessity for organizations to possess specific talents and leadership traits. These abilities are essential at all levels of the workforce and workplace (Ibarra, 2020). As a result, several approaches to HRM have been assessed and put into action during the crisis time in terms of leadership.

During this time, there have been also challenges related to feelings of isolation, employee well-being, and job satisfaction (Gigauri, 2020b). The phenomenon of the "Great Resignation" caused by the COVID-19 pandemic. Amidst the situation, certain employees expressed discontent and contemplated resigning. Within this timeframe, a significant number of employees voluntarily terminated their employment (Xu, Dust and Liu, 2023). This scenario exemplifies the impact of the elevated stress and fear levels induced by the epidemic on daily life. It prompted employees to contemplate the significance and objective of life. A significant number of individuals have reached the conclusion that working long hours lacks rationality. Consequently, this resulted in job dissatisfaction and ultimately led to employee turnover. Accordingly, this resulted in substantial challenges in terms of HRM.

Employees may have experienced additional stressors that have negatively impacted their well-being throughout and following the COVID-19 pandemic (Plater et al., 2022). For example, within the healthcare profession, COVID-19 has resulted in sleep disruptions and suicidal ideation. The COVID-19 pandemic has resulted in a significant increase in stress, insomnia, substance abuse, and depression (Giorgi et al., 2020). A study conducted by Yu, Park and Hyun (2021) found that the characteristics of an epidemic induce stress for hotel employees, which in turn affects their overall performance. The HRM department has to address these concerns due to their potential impact on employee productivity and organizational results (Plater et al., 2022).

The COVID-19 epidemic has caused a blending of work and family responsibilities, making it increasingly challenging to establish clear boundaries between them (Giurge and Bohns, 2020). With the implementation of lockdowns and social distancing measures, remote work became imperative. Consequently, employees were compelled to work from home conditions that were frequently unsuitable for professional responsibilities. This abrupt change caused a merging of personal and professional life, resulting in a situation where the distinctions between work and home were less clear and more flexible. For several individuals, the home office serves as a multifunctional area where they handle chores at home, attend to childcare duties, and engage in personal endeavours. The convergence of these roles has given rise to a distinctive array of challenges.

3. METHODOLOGY

The chapter utilizes a qualitative research methodology by conducting a thorough examination and integration of current literature to investigate the effects of the COVID-19 pandemic on HRM practices. An extensive literature research was undertaken to gather relevant knowledge regarding the changes and challenges encountered by HRM amidst the COVID-19 pandemic. The sources utilized encompassed scholarly articles that underwent peer review, books, reports, and recognized online publications. The studies relevant to HRM practices, innovations, and difficulties in the context of the pandemic were identified using major databases including as Web of Science, SCOPUS, and Google Scholar. The literature selection criteria encompassed studies published from 2019 to 2023, with a specific focus on examining the influence of COVID-19 on HRM. Both empirical research and theoretical articles were incorporated to offer a comprehensive viewpoint on the topic. The search was guided by keywords such as "COVID-19," "epidemic," "pandemic," "HRM practices," "remote working," "digital transformation," and "flexible working". An extensive review of the literature was conducted to systematically identify recurring themes, trends, and notable results. The analysis centred on innovative HRM practices and challenges that arose as a result of the epidemic. Particular emphasis was placed on topics including remote working, digital transformation, flexible working, etc.

4. RESULTS AND DISCUSSION

Through the utilization of this qualitative methodology, the chapter presents a comprehensive examination of the changing HRM environment amongst the COVID-19 epidemic, delivering useful insights for both scholarly researchers and HR practitioners. The noticed themes were consolidated to offer a comprehension of how the pandemic has restructured HRM practices. Different studies were synthesized to emphasize the innovative ideas implemented by organizations and the challenges that they encountered. The discussion also encompassed theoretical viewpoints, such as the utilization of Contingency Theory, to place the findings within a wider context. The results on the future of HRM in a post-pandemic society were derived from the data in the literature. The practical implications for HRM practitioners were outlined, with a focus on the necessity of being flexible, resilient, and continuously innovative in HR processes.

The COVID-19 pandemic has resulted in major changes and challenges in the field of HRM. Organizations have been compelled to innovate and use novel approaches in order to efficiently manage employees due to the imperative of rapidly adapting to a changing circumstance. This discussion examines the theoretical perspective, innovations and challenges with HRM that arose during the epidemic and their consequences for the future.

In order to conceptualize the impact of a crisis, we might utilize Contingency Theory, which posits that there is no universally optimal approach to managing an organization. According to the theory, the optimal course of action is determined by the internal and external circumstances that the organization is now experiencing (Hofer, 1990). This theory is particularly pertinent for analyzing the impact of the pandemic on HRM practices and strategies, since it emphasizes the necessity of being flexible and adaptable in order to respond to evolving circumstances. Because, the fundamental principle of Contingency Theory is that management methods must be in accordance with the specific requirements and difficulties of the environment. The COVID-19 epidemic has necessitated HRM to swiftly adapt to a distinct set of circumstances.

For instance, HRM are increasingly adopting new technologies and providing support to organizations in order to pursue their aims and objectives in a more strategic manner (Rasskazova et al., 2019). Based on Contingency Theory, It can be asserted that by using cutting-edge technologies, HRM may provide organizations with enhanced and productive assistance, guaranteeing the accomplishment of their strategic objectives in spite of external pressures and challenges. Implementing new technology in HRM and offering strategic assistance to organizations are evident illustrations of the application of Contingency Theory. These practices demonstrate the necessity for HRM to consistently adjust to external circumstances and internal requirements in order to maintain effectiveness and alignment with its objectives.

Another example is that, prior to the epidemic, finding appropriate talent was already a challenge, and the epidemic has exacerbated this issue. The phenomenon has had a significant influence on the culture of organizations, undermined their competitive edge, posed threats to potential prospects, and necessitated frequent alterations and adjustments in regulations. Under these conditions, it has become evident that a new approach is necessary, which involves fostering internal talent, recognizing and attracting external talent, and ensuring ongoing opportunities for gaining experience within the business (Plater, Frazier, Talbert, Davis, and Talbert, 2022). Ultimately, the COVID-19 epidemic has underscored the importance of adopting a flexible approach to talent management. Organizations need to modify their HRM procedures to promote internal talent, recruit external talent, and offer ongoing growth opportunities. Contingency Theory elucidates the necessity of these adaptive strategies for upholding organizational resilience and competitiveness amidst continuous disruptions. By aligning talent management strategies with the specific challenges and circumstances arising from the pandemic, organizations can more efficiently handle the crisis and ultimately emerge with greater resilience.

Consequently, the COVID-19 epidemic has compelled some organizations to implement innovative approaches in the realm of HRM. The following innovations are outlined below, drawing from the studies mentioned in the literature:

Remote Working
Digital Transformation
Flexible Working
Health and Safety Precautions
Online Training and Development Programs
Agile HRM Practices

On the other hand, the COVID-19 epidemic has compelled many organizations to confront significant challenges in the realm of HRM Below are some of the challenges, as outlined from the mentioned studies in the literature:

Management of Remote Working
Management of New Forms of Business Model
Employee Health and Wellness
Recruitment and Retention Strategies
Layoffs
Turnover
Legal and Regulatory Issues
Shortage of Digital Skills

Upon examining RQ1, it becomes evident that novel methodologies have arisen in HR practices subsequent to the epidemic. These advances include remote working, digital transformation, flexible working hours, health and safety precautions, online training programs, and agile HR procedures. These improvements have enhanced the adaptability of organizations, resulting in cost efficiencies, increased employee engagement and commitment, and facilitated the acquisition of new skills. Remote working ensures organizational sustainability, while digital transformation enhances operational efficiency. Flexible working hours and health precautions are implemented to enhance job efficiency by promoting employee satisfaction and well-being. Furthermore, the objective is to facilitate the continuous development and adaptation of employees by means of online training programs and flexible HR regulations. Regarding RQ2, implementing HRM practices during the COVID-19 epidemic has been hindered by a multitude of challenging circumstances. Managing remote work can present challenges with concerns such as communication, maintaining business operations, and assessing employee productivity, particularly due to the quick nature of the move. Effectively managing emerging business models may include strategic planning to restructure current processes and optimize resource utilization. Ensuring the health and well-being of employees has become a top priority during the epidemic, and it is imperative to efficiently execute steps to protect their health and safety. Recruitment and retention tactics must to be reassessed and adjusted in light of evolving economic circumstances and employee requirements. Effective management of economic uncertainties and workforce planning strategies are necessary to address concerns such as layoffs and employee turnover. However, it is equally important to consider legal regulations and the lack of digital skills as crucial aspects in ensuring corporate compliance and facilitating digital transformation. For addressing these challenges, it is necessary to employ efficient communication and leadership, implement flexible policies, establish robust health and safety protocols to protect employee well-being, organize training programs to enhance digital skills, and comply with legal regulations.

5. CONCLUSION

The COVID-19 pandemic has undoubtedly reshaped the landscape of HRM, bringing up both unprecedented challenges and prospects for innovation. This chapter has delved into the multifaceted impacts of the pandemic on HRM practices and strategies. The study explores the extensive impact of the COVID-19 pandemic on HRM, shedding light on how organizations are adapting to these evolving circumstances and establishing plans for the future.

The global pandemic is a crisis that has impacted all aspects of the global economy, politics, and social structure. It has accelerated substantial growth and change in HRM practices. The swift implementation of remote work, digital transformation, and flexible working arrangements have fundamentally altered the HR field. Nevertheless, these advancements have presented a unique set of challenges, such as ensuring the welfare of employees, tackling privacy issues, and handling a scarcity of labour.

The global pandemic required businesses globally, especially in the field of HRM, to quickly change their workforce strategies to ensure productivity and engagement in a changing work environment. The global crisis caused by the pandemic led to the implementation of several creative solutions, including digital communication platforms, flexible work arrangements, and advanced performance management measures, to tackle the new challenges that arose. The shift to remote work has emerged as a prominent trend, as businesses increasingly depend on digital technologies to maintain business continuity and operational efficiency. Nevertheless, this transition also presented challenges with the digital skills of employees, potential invasion of privacy, and the merging of work and personal life borders.

The COVID-19 pandemic has emphasized the significance of strategic workforce planning and the imperative for HRM practitioners to set goals for the improvement of employees' skills and well-being. In the current period of change, HRM must maintain flexibility, remain agile, and innovative, and prioritize both the professional and personal development of their workforce. Organizations must persist in adjusting and improving their HRM strategies to effectively navigate the recurrent challenges and capitalize on the advancements introduced by the epidemic. To ensure long-term success in a post-pandemic environment, organizations should create resilience by adopting a comprehensive approach to employee well-being, investing in digital infrastructure, and embracing agile HRM practices. The knowledge gained during this period will be extremely significant for shaping the future of work and HRM.

This study enhances the existing body of knowledge by thoroughly investigating the innovative approaches that arose during and after the epidemic and impacted HRM practices. The strategies encompass remote working, digital transformation, flexible working, health and safety precautions, online training and development programs, and agile HRM practices. Furthermore, the study highlights the significance of strategic workforce planning and flexible HRM strategies during times of crisis. These strategies facilitate organizations in rapidly adjusting to evolving circumstances and ensuring their long-term sustainability, while also providing guidance on how to respond during times of crisis. The study also makes a theoretical contribution by elucidating the process via which HRM practices adjust to pandemic circumstances and proactively plan for the future. This is achieved by employing conceptual frameworks like Contingency Theory.

In conclusion, the COVID-19 pandemic has had a substantial effect on HRM practices, resulting in a profound change in how organizations handle their human resources. Although the challenges have been significant, they have also led to the development of novel ideas and initiatives that are likely to influence the future of HRM in a world after the epidemic. For efficiently manage the ever-changing global landscape, HRM must transform and adopt innovative approaches that promote adaptability, resilience, and sustainability in forthcoming uncertainty.

REFERENCES

Acciarini, C., Boccardelli, P., & Vitale, M. (2021). Resilient companies in the time of Covid-19 pandemic: A case study approach. *Journal of Entrepreneurship and Public Policy*, 10(3), 336–351. DOI:10.1108/JEPP-03-2021-0021

Agrawal, S., De Smet, A., Lacroix, S., & Reich, A. (2020). To emerge stronger from the COVID-19 crisis, companies should start reskilling their workforces now. *McKinsey Insights*, 2.

Aguinis, H., & Burgi-Tian, J. (2021). Measuring performance during crises and beyond: The Performance Promoter Score. *Business Horizons*, 64(1), 149–160. DOI:10.1016/j.bushor.2020.09.001 PMID:32981944

Aitken-Fox, E., Coffey, J., Dayaram, K., Fitzgerald, S., Gupta, C., McKenna, S., & Wei Tian, A. (2020). The impact of Covid-19 on human resource management: avoiding generalisations. *LSE Business Review*.

Alkan, A. D. (2022). The effects of COVID-19 on human resource management in aviation companies: the case of Europe. In *Digitalization and the Impacts of COVID-19 on the Aviation Industry* (pp. 225–242). IGI Global. DOI:10.4018/978-1-6684-2319-6.ch012

Azizi, M. R., Atlasi, R., Ziapour, A., Abbas, J., & Naemi, R. (2021). Innovative human resource management strategies during the COVID-19 pandemic: A systematic narrative review approach. *Heliyon*, 7(6), e07233. DOI:10.1016/j.heliyon.2021.e07233 PMID:34124399

Barro, R. J., Ursúa, J. F., & Weng, J. (2020). *The coronavirus and the great influenza pandemic: Lessons from the "Spanish flu" for the coronavirus's potential effects on mortality and economic activity* (No. w26866). National Bureau of Economic Research.

Best, S. J., Krueger, B. S., & Ladewig, J. (2006). Privacy in the information age. *Public Opinion Quarterly*, 70(3), 375–401. DOI:10.1093/poq/nfl018

Bratianu, C., & Bejinaru, R. (2021). COVID-19 induced emergent knowledge strategies. *Knowledge and Process Management*, 28(1), 11–17. DOI:10.1002/kpm.1656

Carnevale, J. B., & Hatak, I. (2020). Employee adjustment and well-being in the era of COVID-19: Implications for human resource management. *Journal of Business Research*, 116, 183–187. DOI:10.1016/j.jbusres.2020.05.037 PMID:32501303

Coronavirus Resource Center. (2020). Johns Hopkins University & Medicine. Retrieved on 22th March 2024 from https://coronavirus.jhu.edu/map.html

Dirani, K. M., Abadi, M., Alizadeh, A., Barhate, B., Garza, R. C., Gunasekara, N., Ibrahim, G., & Majzun, Z. (2020). Leadership competencies and the essential role of human resource development in times of crisis: A response to COVID-19 pandemic. *Human Resource Development International*, 23(4), 380–394. DOI:10.1080/13678868.2020.1780078

Dissanayake, K. (2020). Encountering COVID-19: Human resource management (HRM) practices in a pandemic crisis. *Colombo Journal of Multi-Disciplinary Research*, 5(1-2), 1–22. DOI:10.4038/cjmr.v5i1-2.52

Draghici, A. (2020). Changes and challenges of human systems management during and after the pandemic. *Human Systems Management*, 39(4), 469–472. DOI:10.3233/HSM-209001

Gigauri, I. (2020a). Implications of COVID-19 for human resource management. *International Journal of Economics and Management Studies*, 7(11), 25–33. DOI:10.14445/23939125/IJEMS-V7I11P104

Gigauri, I. (2020b). Effects of Covid-19 on Human Resource Management from the Perspective of Digitalization and Work-life-balance. *International Journal of Innovative Technologies in Economy*, 4(31). Advance online publication. DOI:10.31435/rsglobal_ijite/30092020/7148

Giorgi, G., Lecca, L. I., Alessa, F., Finstad, G. L., Bondanini, G., Lulli, L. G., & Mucci, N. (2020). COVID-19-related mental health effects in the workplace: A narrative review. *International Journal of Environmental Research and Public Health*, 17(21), 7857. DOI:10.3390/ijerph17217857 PMID:33120930

Giurge, L., & Bohns, V. K. (2020). 3 tips to avoid WFH burnout. *Harvard Business Review*.

Gonçalves, S. P., Santos, J. V. D., Silva, I. S., Veloso, A., Brandão, C., & Moura, R. (2021). COVID-19 and people management: The view of human resource managers. *Administrative Sciences*, 11(3), 69. DOI:10.3390/admsci11030069

Hamouche, S. (2023). Human resource management and the COVID-19 crisis: Implications, challenges, opportunities, and future organizational directions. *Journal of Management & Organization*, 29(5), 799–814. DOI:10.1017/jmo.2021.15

Hofer, C. W. (1990). *Toward a contingency theory of business strategy*. Physica-Verlag HD. DOI:10.1007/978-3-662-41484-2_7

Ibarra, P. (2020). "We've Always Done it that Way" Is Over—WHAT'S NEXT? Public Management, 6-9. Received from: https://gettingbetterallthetime.com/wp-content/uploads/2020/04/Ibarra-Bldg-a-Talent-Centric-Workforce.pdf

Jones, M., Versace, V., Lyle, D., & Walsh, S. (2021). Return of the unexpected: Rural workforce recruitment and retention in the era of COVID-19. *The Australian Journal of Rural Health*, 29(5), 612–616. DOI:10.1111/ajr.12817 PMID:34672056

Kalogiannidis, S. (2021). The Impact of COVID-19 on human resource management practices and future marketing. *International Journal of Industrial Marketing*, 6(1), 43–55. DOI:10.5296/ijim.v6i1.17994

Koirala, J., & Acharya, S. (2020). Dimensions of human resource management evolved with the outbreak of COVID-19. *Available at SSRN* 3584092. DOI:10.2139/ssrn.3584092

KV, B. M., & Walarine, M. T. (2021). Human Resource Management: Pre-pandemic, Pandemic and beyond. *Recoletos Multidisciplinary Research Journal*, 9(2), 103–114.

Lagowska, U., Sobral, F., & Furtado, L. M. G. P. (2020). Leadership under crises: A research agenda for the post-Covid-19 Era. *BAR - Brazilian Administration Review*, 17(2), e200062. DOI:10.1590/1807-7692bar2020200062

Li, J. Y., Sun, R., Tao, W., & Lee, Y. (2021). Employee coping with organizational change in the face of a pandemic: The role of transparent internal communication. *Public Relations Review*, 47(1), 101984. DOI:10.1016/j.pubrev.2020.101984 PMID:36568504

Nagel, L. (2020). The influence of the COVID-19 pandemic on the digital transformation of work. *The International Journal of Sociology and Social Policy*, 40(9/10), 861–875. DOI:10.1108/IJSSP-07-2020-0323

Nyanga, T., & Chindanya, A. (2020). Covid 19 pandemic shifting the job satisfaction landscape among employees. *Business Excellence and Management*, 10(5), 168–176. DOI:10.24818/beman/2020.S.I.1-14

Pandey, N., & Pal, A. (2020). Impact of digital surge during Covid-19 pandemic: A viewpoint on research and practice. *International Journal of Information Management*, 55, 102171. DOI:10.1016/j.ijinfomgt.2020.102171 PMID:32836633

Pant, B., & Lal, A. (2020). Aarogya Setu App: A tale of the complex challenges of a rights-based regime. May 13, Retrieved March 23, 2024, from https://thewire.in/tech/aarogya-setu-app-challenges-rights-based-regime

Plater, Q. C., Frazier, M. D., Talbert, P. Y., Davis, V. H., & Talbert, P. S. (2022). Human resources strategies & lessons learned during the COVID-19 pandemic: A literature review. *Management Dynamics in the Knowledge Economy*, 10(4), 330–342. DOI:10.2478/mdke-2022-0021

Rasskazova, A., Koroleva, E., & Rasskazov, S. (2019, March). Digital transformation: Statistical evaluation of success factors of an ICO-campaign. []. IOP Publishing.]. *IOP Conference Series. Materials Science and Engineering*, 497(1), 012087. DOI:10.1088/1757-899X/497/1/012087

Vnoučková, L. (2020). Impact of COVID-19 on human resource management. *RELAIS*, 3(1), 18–21.

Welch, C. L., & Welch, D. E. (2012). What do HR managers really do? HR roles on international projects. *MIR. Management International Review*, 52(4), 597–617. DOI:10.1007/s11575-011-0126-8

Xu, M., Dust, S. B., & Liu, S. (2023). COVID-19 and the great resignation: The role of death anxiety, need for meaningful work, and task significance. *The Journal of Applied Psychology*, 108(11), 1790–1811. DOI:10.1037/apl0001102 PMID:37261767

Yu, J., Park, J., & Hyun, S. S. (2021). Impacts of the COVID-19 pandemic on employees' work stress, well-being, mental health, organizational citizenship behavior, and employee-customer identification. *Journal of Hospitality Marketing & Management*, 30(5), 529–548. DOI:10.1080/19368623.2021.1867283

Chapter 5
Nurturing Excellence:
The Influence of Employee Engagement on Job Satisfaction in the Educational Realm

Deeksha Gupta Ganguly
https://orcid.org/0000-0002-5502-8276
Christ University, India

Deepti Sinha
Christ University, India

Vandita Bhaumik
Christ University, India

Ronit Varghese
https://orcid.org/0009-0004-4402-3877
Christ University, India

ABSTRACT

Job satisfaction and Employee engagement are critical to the success of any business, particularly in the education sector. This study examines the relationship between job satisfaction and employee engagement in the education sector, focusing on Delhi NCR. The research uses collection of data from 16 educators through semi structured interviews. It is based on Interpretative Phenomenological Analysis (IPA) tool to examine the factors affecting employee engagement and job satisfaction. The findings aim to improve teaching quality, student outcomes, and institutional effectiveness. However, the study has limitations, including subjectivity, risk of bias, and being limited to the educational sector. Despite these limitations, the study contributes to the existing knowledge by revealing the dynamics of work satisfaction and employee

DOI: 10.4018/979-8-3693-4412-5.ch005

engagement in the education sector, providing valuable insights for organizational management and policy formation.

1. INTRODUCTION

In the constantly changing landscape of modern organizations, where success is assessed not only in terms of profits/revenues but also in terms of employee satisfaction and engagement, the role of human beings emerges as the most reliable and precious resource. For years and years, they have been bringing their bundle of knowledge, expertise, and judgment along with themselves in the workplace, thereby, solidifying their position as the keystone of any successful organization. (Ugwu et al., 2014) put light on the significance of building a positive relationship between the employer and employees, based on the social exchange principle. He has well-stated the vital role of employees in organizational dynamics.

The foundation of these relationships is found to be the factor of trust. In today's fast-moving, global work environment, the engagement of employees increases when they perceive the organization to be trustworthy, igniting the engine of productivity. The long era of using job satisfaction as a factor solely for determining the impact of organizational practices on employee well-being is now gone. The spotlight has now shifted to a comprehensive concept of employee engagement.

As per the research carried out by Kahn (1990) the term employee engagement is used to describe how employees invest varying degrees of themselves physically, cognitively, and emotionally in their respective job roles. Salanova et al., (2005) have described employee engagement as individuals who exhibit motivation, enthusiasm, energy, and a steadfast passion for their work. This shift in focus highlights that engaged employees not only bring commitment but also increase satisfaction, organizational citizenship behaviour, and a desire to stick to their job role despite the challenges.

However, the concept of employee engagement differs from person to person as well as from organization to organization. Some of them compare it with job satisfaction, while others measure it by determining emotional commitment. The bedrock of this idea connects with other important additional factors such as employee commitment and organizational citizenship behaviour, creating a complex chain of relationships.

As per the Manager Director of Tower Perrins, higher employee engagement can lead to strong business performances and, thereby, create a loop of engagement and success. According to the report of the Global Workforce Study, it shows that organizations with high employee engagement led to significant improvements in net income while those with low engagement suffered through reductions.

On the other hand, Job Satisfaction means being attached as well as engaged in the job.

Employee engagement is not merely a trendy word, but it explains the alignment of job satisfaction and job contribution. A solid connection between the employees and their organizations, characterized by autonomy, commitment, growth, and impact is present there. Engaged employees go above and beyond as they possess a clear understanding of the organizational goals and an emotional attachment leading to employee loyalty towards it. It is noteworthy that an engaged employee is one who is passionate and dedicated to his or her work. They are willing to invest their efforts for the organization's success because they are concerned about the organization's future. This requires an organizational environment that is filled with positive emotions, involvement, and pride leading to improved performance and reduced turnover.

This study aims to shed light on the complexities of employee engagement and job satisfaction by exploring their interactions and impacts. This research will help to unravel the complex relationships between employee engagement and job satisfaction and the impact of job satisfaction on employee engagement.

1.1 Rationale

The choice of researching the influence of job satisfaction and employee engagement in the educational industry likely stems from the recognition of their pivotal roles in organizational success. Understanding how these factors impact educators can lead to insights on improving teaching quality, student outcomes, and overall institutional effectiveness.

1.2 Problem Statement

This research seeks to evaluate the relationship in understanding the intricate dynamics between job satisfaction and employee engagement in the educational industry in Delhi NCR.

1.3 Research Objectives

- To ascertain the relationship between Job Satisfaction and Employee engagement.
- To determine the effect of employee engagement on job satisfaction of an employee.

1.4 Research Gap

The existing body of literature on job satisfaction and employee engagement in the educational industry in Delhi NCR primarily focuses on full-time educators, leaving a notable research gap in the comprehensive assessment of part-time employees, whose unique roles and contributions remain understudied within the context of the specified research title.

2. LITERATURE REVIEW

This section provides an overview of the research about the constructs of employee engagement & job satisfaction and the relationship between both.

Employee Engagement: Employee engagement as "positive, fulfilling, work-related state of mind that is characterized by vigor, dedication, and absorption" by Rameshkumar (2020). Employee engagement is the sense of belonging that employees have to their jobs and organisations, which leads to increased levels of productivity, dedication, and loyalty (Saks, 2006). For the purpose of the study, following dimensions have also been explored:

Commitment

In organizational psychology and management literature, employee commitment is an intricate concept that has been thoroughly examined. Several dimensions and components have been identified in the literature to comprehend the nature and consequences of employee commitment. According to the study by scholars like (Muthuveloo & Rose, 2005) employee commitment is the capacity of workers to be faithful and identify with the organization about their roles and duties. (Yang, 2008) explains that there is a negative correlation between job satisfaction and employees' intention to quit, suggesting that more satisfied employees are more committed to their careers. (Aghdasi et al., 2011) stress that a cohesive relationship with the organization is the outcome of a strong attachment, which makes people enjoy working for the company. The three dimensions of employee commitment put out in the study of (Awais et al., 2015) are affective, normative, and continuance commitment.

In the research, defined by (Sow, 2015) affective commitment results from emotional attachment, identity, and connection with the organization that generates a need and want to stay there. This dimension shows how emotionally invested and connected the staff is to the company's objectives.

According to (Chung, 2013), employees experience continuity commitment when they believe they have few options for leaving their current position, such as unrivalled pay and benefits elsewhere. This type of commitment is influenced by non-transferable personal investments and the perceived high cost of quitting.

Normative Commitment refers to the sense of duty and devotion that employees have for their employers. It entails having an obligation to return the employer's kindness (Sow, 2015). This dedication is demonstrated by the worker's readiness to forego personal gain and refrain from criticizing the organization.

Positive organizational results are significantly influenced by employee commitment, which measures how much a worker identifies with the company and is dedicated to achieving its objectives. It includes being devoted, being willing to work hard, having goals and ideals that are in line, and wanting to continue working (Messner, 2013).

According to (Mowday et al., 1979) is the degree to which a person identifies and is involved with a specific organization. It is an organic, spontaneous process that arises when a person associates with an organization (Allen & Meyer, 1990).

Meyer & Allen (1991) proposed a model of organizational commitment, which consists of Affective, Continuance, and Normative commitment, serves as a foundational framework for understanding and analysing commitment. Continuance commitment is predicated on perceived expenses and investments, whereas affective commitment is characterized by emotional attachment and engagement. Normative commitment stems from emotions of obligations and faithfulness.

Organisational Identification

In organizational psychology, organizational identification is a key idea that affects many facets of employee performance and behaviour. The association between high organizational identification levels and employees' willingness to take chances to support their colleagues is one subject of particular attention.

According to (Edwards & Peccei, 2007) organizational identification is the psychological connection that exists between an individual and the organization, wherein the individual feels a strong emotional and cognitive affinity with the organization as a social entity. It entails people defining themselves in terms of the qualities of the organization, which promotes a sense of community. Research has demonstrated the significance of organizational identity in forecasting a range of work behaviours, including resistance to change (Van Dijk & Van Dick, 2009) cooperation (Tyler & Blader, 2001) commitment (Cole & Bruch, 2006), and turnover (Van Knippenberg et al., 2005). In examining the connection between employee risk-taking behaviour and organizational identification, (Bartels et al., 2006) suggested that higher organizational identification levels are linked to a higher propensity to take chances for the good of coworkers. Empirical research was done by (Bartels et al., 2006) investigate the suggested connection. According to their research, employee risk-taking and organizational identity were positively correlated. Workers who felt a strong sense of belonging to their company were more likely to take risks to help their colleagues. This shows the potential of organizational identity as a tool in addition to highlighting its significance.

Social identity theory and organizational identification are related, with the latter stressing the significance of status in shaping identification (Ashforth & Mael, 1989). Workers try to identify with companies they consider to be elite, which boosts their sense of value (Tyler & Blader, 2001b). One of the most important factors influencing organizational identification is this perceived external reputation (Dutton et al., 1994). It is crucial to consider the theoretical framework supporting the link between organizational identity and risk-taking to put these findings into context. Both social exchange theory and social identity theory provide insightful viewpoints. According to social exchange theory, which emphasizes the reciprocity of interactions inside businesses, employees may see taking risks to engage in social exchange that helps them build strong bonds with their coworkers (Karanika-Murray et al., 2015).

Work Motivation

Money was thought to be the main motive in the early 20th century, but the Hawthorne Studies shed question on this idea. Employee behaviour and attitudes were found to be related by Elton Mayo's research, which gave rise to the human relations approach in management (Kreitner, 1995).

A common definition of motivation is the process of decision-making that leads people to select goals and act toward achieving them. It entails putting in consistent, focused, and intense effort toward objectives. From a psychological standpoint, motivation is defined as a psychological process that gives conduct direction, intensity, and a goal. Organizational Perspective: (Robbins & Judge, 2007) characterizes motivation as the ability to meet individual needs influencing a willingness to put forth effort toward organizational goals.

According to (Baron & Greenberg, 1990) motivation is a collection of procedures pertaining to a force that energizes behaviour and guides it toward the accomplishment of objectives. Motivation is classified broadly into 2 types – Intrinsic Motivation and Extrinsic Motivation.

Work done for its own sake is referred to as intrinsic motivation, and it is linked to psychological advantages, self-actualization, and self-sustainability. Extrinsic Motivation involves outside rewards and is susceptible to the effects of a well-thought-out reward structure.

Early Theories (before 1960s): Among the fundamental theories were Skinner's Reinforcement Theory, Herzberg's Two-Factor Theory, and Maslow's Hierarchy of Needs.

The **instrumentality theory** postulates that people are driven by incentives that are closely related to their output. The theory first appeared in the latter part of the nineteenth century and placed a heavy focus on the necessity of rationalizing labour as well as economic results (Armstrong, 1999). Since incentives and punishments are directly linked to an individual's performance, it is assumed that people will be more motivated to work; so, rewards are conditional on effective performance, i.e., people only labour for financial gain.

The idea of instrumentality, which derives from (Skinner, 1974) theory of conditioning, holds that people can be "conditioned" to act in particular ways if they receive rewards for acting in a certain way. Reward or punishment are used to ensure that people behave or act in desired ways. One of the first management writers, F.W Taylor is credited with developing the notion when he stated that "workmen cannot be persuaded to work much harder than the average man around them over an extended period of time unless they are guaranteed a large and permanent increase in their pay."

Content (Needs) Theory focuses on needs that lead to conflict and a desire to accomplish objectives. The foundation of the content or needs theory is the idea that needs make up motivation's content. A goal that will satisfy the need is identified, and a behaviour pathway that will lead to the goal's achievement is chosen, to restore equilibrium when an unmet need leads to tension and a state of disequilibrium. (Armstrong, 2010)

Maslow proposed the idea of a hierarchy of needs in the development of the need's theory Alderfer's modified need hierarchy model, McClelland's achievement motivation model, and Herzberg's two-factor model are further ideas related to the requirements theory (Armstrong, 2010).

Herzberg's Two-Factor Theory: Job satisfaction is correlated with intrinsic variables (motivators), whereas unhappiness is correlated with external elements (hygiene factors). According to this notion, the job itself is more important than outside factors.

Extrinsic motivation depends on outside rewards, but intrinsic motivation views the activity itself as the reward. It was made clear by the Hawthorne Studies that financial incentives are not the only thing that drive workers. (Armstrong, 2010)

After looking into the causes of job satisfaction and discontent among engineers and accountants, (Giroux, 1960) created the two-factor model of satisfiers and dissatisfiers. People were thought to be able to accurately report the aspects of their occupations that made them happy or unhappy. (Herzberg, 2023) asserted that internal variables are linked to job satisfaction while extrinsic elements are associated to discontent based on the two types of motivators, that is, ones that result in contentment with one's job and those that result in displeasure for employees at work. The question "What do people want from their jobs?" served as the foundation for the idea. (Harpaz, 1990)

Based on the responses he received, Herzberg concluded that eliminating unsatisfactory aspects of a work does not guarantee job satisfaction (Armstrong, 2010). According to (Herzberg, 2023), there are two main variables that can contribute to job satisfaction: hygienic factors and motivators.

According to Herzberg, intrinsic elements like accomplishment, acknowledgment, accountability, advancement, challenges, and the work itself serve as motivators and allow for psychological growth and development at work (Ajila & Abiola, 2004) (Wilson, 2010; Ajila & Abiola, 2004). Conversely, hygiene elements are external and pertain to the workplace environment rather than the tasks performed (Armstrong, 2010). These include the following: administration, supervision, pay, work conditions, corporate policies, supervision, and relationships with supervisors and subordinates on a personal level.

Maslow's Hierarchy of Needs highlights the hierarchical model of needs from physiological to self-actualization, emphasizing that higher-order needs become motivators after lower-order needs are satisfied.

Job Satisfaction: Since its introduction in the middle of the 1970s, the idea of job satisfaction has attracted a lot of scholarly attention. It is defined as a pleasant or positive emotional state brought on by people's evaluation of their jobs or work-related activities. Subsequently, many interpretations have surfaced. (Brief & Weiss, 2002) provide a nuanced viewpoint, characterizing job satisfaction as an assessment of one's employment or work circumstances that is either good or negative. This study of the research delves into the complex relationship between job happiness and employee performance, as well as the reasons behind employee turnover intentions and its intrinsic and extrinsic factors. One of the main themes in the literature is the connection between individual performance and job satisfaction. (Judge et al., 2001) conducted a meta-analysis that verified a noteworthy correlation between job satisfaction and workplace performance.

Research on this relationship's direction of causality is still ongoing, indicating a complicated interaction between performance and job satisfaction. Numerous research (Price, 1977); (Mobley, 1982); (Choi, 2006) have shown that highly pleased workers have decreased turnover intentions and improved productivity, both of which are beneficial to the success of the business.

Herzberg's Motivation-Hygiene Theory makes a distinction between extrinsic and intrinsic elements that affect job satisfaction. Achievement and responsibility are examples of intrinsic variables that are connected to the work itself; on the other hand, extrinsic factors that are related to the work environment include things like pay, opportunities for advancement, and leadership. Academics like (Skaalvik & Skaalvik, 2011) stress the significance of a balanced approach to both components for overall job happiness, emphasizing the impact of extrinsic satisfaction on internal pleasure.

The effects of job satisfaction go beyond individual efficiency to include corporate goals. It increases the firm's competitiveness by fostering employee dedication, retention, and high-quality customer service (Lee et al., 2006). Furthermore, job satisfaction influences the success or failure of client experiences through favourable correlations with organizational dedication, productivity, and quality (Hsu & Wang, 2008) (De Menezes, 2012).

Numerous internal and external factors might impact an employee's level of job satisfaction. Extrinsic elements like fair treatment and supervision are also very important, but internal meaning, personal development, and accomplishment are linked to intrinsic job satisfaction.

2.1 Conceptual Framework

The framework illustrates the hypothesized connections between Job Satisfaction & Employee Engagement, forming the basis for our research hypotheses and guiding the analysis of their interdependencies.

Figure 1. Conceptual Framework

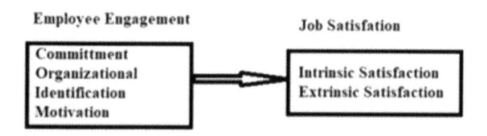

3. RESEARCH METHODOLOGY

Research design: The study will be descriptive in nature. Research that uses observation, measurement, and analysis of data to characterize a specific event is known as descriptive research. Without attempting to demonstrate cause-and-effect links, it is utilized to present a thorough and accurate explanation of a condition or occurrence.

Sampling: The research participants represent a sample. A sample is a subset of the population that serves as a representative sample. There are two kinds of sampling: non-probability sampling and probability sampling. The non-probability sampling method will be applied in this study.

a. **Sampling Frame-** The actual list of study respondents is referred to as the sampling frame. This research will include part-time employees working in educational sectors in Delhi NCR.

b. **Sampling Technique-** Purposive sampling is the method of sampling that will be applied in this study. This approach works well for qualitative research that aims to comprehend the causes and contributing elements of a given problem. "Purposive sampling" is a random sampling approach that tries to choose a sample group with characteristics. While this method can be used with many groups, its greatest results are obtained with smaller sample sizes and more homogeneous populations. A precise and cost-effective sample can be produced by the researcher by selecting people or points based on their knowledge.

c. **Sample Size-** The sample size for the research study would be 16 respondents for qualitative research.

Data collection method: Obtaining first-hand information is referred to as primary data collecting. The researcher conducts this through questionnaires, interviews, surveys, and other methods. Primary data collection for this study will involve a survey through questionnaire and interview schedule with follow-up questions. An interview schedule is a list of prearranged questions about a specific topic that the interviewer will pose to the interviewee. The respondents will be employees of the educational industry in Delhi NCR between the ages of 18-50 years.

Data analysis technique: Interpretative Phenomenological Analysis (IPA) has been used to analyse and better understand the outcome of the interactions with the respondents.

A qualitative research technique called interpretative phenomenological analysis (IPA) is used to investigate people's unique and subjective experiences with a phenomenon. The primary source of data for an interpretive phenomenological analysis (IPA) study is the meanings that individuals attach to certain experiences, events, and states. The goal of IPA is to investigate in depth how participants are making sense of their personal and social world. The greatest chance for researchers to comprehend the deepest thought processes behind the "lived experiences" of research participants is provided by IPA. Interpretative phenomenological analysis is a "participant-oriented" method that gives study participants, or interviewees, the freedom to tell their "lived experience" stories and express themselves in any way they choose without fear of retaliation or punishment. IPA involves a detailed analysis of the participants' narratives or interviews, paying close attention to the language and the specific words used by the participants to describe their experiences. Researchers who use IPA typically follow a structured analysis process, which involves reading and re-reading the data, identifying meaningful segments of the data, and analysing the data for themes and patterns.

4. ANALYSIS

Table 1. Demographic Profile of Respondents

Age	Gender	Marital Status	No. of Years of Service
37	Male	Single	2.5
44	Female	Married	22
43	Male	Married	2.7
40	Female	Married	17
45	Female	Married	20
34	Female	Married	1
52	Female	Married	15
52	Female	Married	29
37	Male	Married	16
37	Male	Married	20
28	Female	Unmarried	3+
48	Female	Married	24
50	Female	Married	24
39	Female	Married	10
43	Female	Married	15
43	Female	Married	15

The analysis of the questions is done based on the themes created based on the opinions of the respondents.

Analysis of questions on the basis of summary of opinions of respondents in a tabular form

Table 2. According to you, what is employee engagement?

Summary of Opinions	Theme	Iteration Keywords/ Phrases
The concept of employee engagement is complex and involves several elements, including emotional commitment, motivation, enthusiasm, and connection with company objectives. It includes individual willingness and organizational actions meant to promote employee engagement and satisfaction. Important components are a positive attitude toward work, alignment with the goals and objectives of the company, and promoting two-way communication. In general, it is believed that raising employee engagement is critical to developing a positive work environment, increasing productivity, and accomplishing organizational goals. .	• **Employee Engagement Factors**	Enthusiasm and Motivation Emotional Commitment Two-Way Communication Connection with company objectives
	• **Knowledge and understanding**	Lack of Understanding Lack of Knowledge
	• **Teamwork and Coordination**	Involvement in Activities Coordination Among Employees Team work enhancement
	• **Job Satisfaction and Enthusiasm**	Job Satisfaction Enthusiasm

Interpretation: The above question and results highlight the multifaceted nature of employee engagement, encompassing aspects such as motivation, commitment, communication, alignment with organizational goals, and satisfaction. Effective employee engagement strategies should address these various dimensions to foster a culture of engagement and maximize employee performance and well-being. Some responses suggest that employee engagement involves measures taken to motivate or retain talent within an organization. This indicates a focus on strategies aimed at keeping employees satisfied and committed to their roles. There is a consensus that employee engagement entails constructive and enthusiastic involvement in organizational activities. This suggests that engaged employees are actively partic-ipating in their work and are emotionally invested in the outcomes. Many responses highlight the emotional commitment that engaged employees have towards their organization and its goals. This emotional connection drives them to contribute positively and go the extra mile for the organization's success. Engaging employ-ees involves aligning their personal satisfaction and morale with the organization's mission and vision. This indicates the importance of ensuring that employees feel connected to the larger purpose of the organization. Employee engagement is seen as a two-way communication process aimed at achieving shared goals. This suggests that organizations should foster an environment where employees feel heard and valued. Engaged employees have both an emotional and professional connection to their organization, colleagues, and work. This implies that engagement goes beyond mere job satisfaction and encompasses a deeper sense of belonging and commitment. Employees engage in their work willingly and with enthusiasm. This highlights the importance of intrinsic motivation in driving employee engagement. Employee engagement is closely linked to job satisfaction and enthusiasm towards one's role. Satisfied employees are more likely to be engaged and committed to their work. Engaged employees participate in activities that promote teamwork and coordination within the organization. This suggests that engagement contributes to a positive work culture and effective collaboration.

Table 3. Do you find this kind of organization identification in your organizations? How?

Summary of Opinions	Theme	Iteration Keywords/ Phrases
Organization identification is influenced by a combination of individual experiences, organizational culture, and management practices. Some employees feel deeply connected to their organizations, others may require more support or opportunities for engagement to enhance their sense of identification and belonging. Efforts to promote a positive work environment, align organizational goals with individual values, and provide avenues for personal and professional growth may help strengthen organization identification among all employees.	• Sense of Belonging and Commitment	Employees feel proud to be part of the organization. Display high levels of commitment and loyalty. Feel connected with students or colleagues. Integral part of identity.
	• Supportive Environment and Employee-Centric Approach	Employees receive support when in need. Organization is described as employee-centric. Engagement and passion towards job responsibilities
	• Resilience and Adaptability	Resilient during changes. Adapt effectively to new circumstances.
	• Alignment with Organizational Goals and Values	Alignment with organizational goals and values. Participation in organizational activities and tasks with sincerity. Promoting cohesion and unity.

Interpretation: The above question and results highlight there are instances of strong organizational identification driven by pride, engagement, support, and passion, there are also challenges such as job dissatisfaction and inconsistency in engagement efforts. Some individuals express a strong sense of pride, engagement, and connection with the organization. They feel proud to be part of the organization, engage actively in activities, and demonstrate commitment, loyalty, and alignment with organizational goals and values. There is a recognition that a sense of belonging and alignment with organizational goals and values promotes commitment and loyalty among individuals. Others highlight resilience during changes and passion in work as factors contributing to organizational identification. They feel connected to their work and derive satisfaction from their responsibilities or interactions with students. Recognition and rewards for work are seen as occasions where individuals sometimes experience organizational identification. Resilience during change and passionate engagement with work are noted as factors contributing to organizational identification. Some respondents' express challenges or an absence of organizational identification within their organization, citing factors such as lack of job satisfaction or ineffective identification efforts.

Table 4. What is your opinion about commitment and employee engagement?

Summary of Opinions	Theme	Iteration Keywords/ Phrases
Commitment and employee engagement suggest a complex interplay between these two concepts in the workplace. Some view them as inherently linked, emphasizing that committed employees are more likely to be engaged, others argue that individual commitment and engagement may not always correlate. The alignment of organizational goals with individual interests is seen as crucial for fostering engagement. Excessive restrictive policies are recognized as potential barriers to job satisfaction and commitment, emphasizing the importance of creating a supportive and inclusive work environment. Overall, commitment is described as a personal perspective involving loyalty and responsibility, while employee engagement is viewed as a connection to the organization and colleagues.	• **Interconnection of Commitment and Engagement**	Only engaged employees are likely to be committed. Commitment and engagement are closely intertwined. Individual commitment is enhanced with employee engagement. A committed employee will be more engaged at the workplace.
	• **Alignment with Organizational Goals**	Organizational goals need to align with individual interests for engagement and commitment. Discussion of company goals and achievements to foster connection and commitment.
	• **Impact of Organizational Policies**	Excessive restrictive policies may hinder job satisfaction and commitment. Appreciation, relaxation, and freedom in the workplace contribute to engagement and commitment.
	• **Teamwork and Interpersonal Relationships**	Engagement and commitment involve teamwork between employee and employer. Builds interpersonal relationships within the organization

Interpretation: The question and results highlight the intricate relationship between commitment and employee engagement, influenced by organizational factors, personal perspectives, and collaborative efforts between employees and employers. Creating a supportive and inclusive workplace culture that prioritizes alignment of goals, appreciation, and effective communication is crucial for fostering commitment and engagement among employees, ultimately contributing to organizational success and employee well-being. The responses indicate a consensus that commitment and engagement are closely linked and mutually reinforce each other. Engaged employees tend to be more committed, and vice versa, contributing to overall productivity and retention within the organization. The analysis highlights the significance of aligning organizational goals with individual interests to foster employee engagement.

Excessive restrictive policies are identified as potential barriers that can negatively affect job satisfaction and commitment, leading to turnover. Conversely, creating an environment of appreciation, relaxation, and freedom in the workplace is deemed crucial for nurturing commitment and engagement. Respondents perceive commitment as a personal dedication to tasks and responsibilities, while engagement is seen as a deeper connection to the organization and colleagues. The ability to build interpersonal relationships and cultivate a supportive work environment is considered essential for enhancing both commitment and engagement among employees. The analysis underscores the importance of a collaborative effort between employees and employers in fostering commitment and engagement. Mutual support, effective communication, and feedback mechanisms are identified as key elements in facilitating a positive work environment conducive to commitment and engagement.

Table 5. Do you think when you are motivated, your dedication towards work increases?

Summary of Opinions	Theme	Iteration Keywords/Phrases
The opinions collectively underscore the profound impact of motivation on work dedication. Respondents consistently affirm that heightened motivation correlates with increased dedication and commitment towards work tasks. This heightened enthusiasm fosters a positive energy, leading to better results.	• Positive Influence of Motivation on Dedication	High levels of motivation lead to increased dedication and commitment towards work. Motivation fills employees with enthusiasm and positive energy, resulting in heightened dedication.
Moreover, personal experiences indicate a steady growth in dedication over time, driven by a growing passion to contribute meaningfully to organizational goals. This dedication fuels a commitment to excellence and a proactive pursuit of personal and professional growth. Overall, the consensus reflects a clear recognition of the pivotal role of motivation in fostering dedication and driving success within the workplace.	• Personal Growth and Commitment	Personal experience of dedication towards work steadily increasing over time due to growing passion and commitment to organizational goals. Motivation fuels a desire to contribute meaningfully, strive for excellence, and exceed expectations.
	• Universal Agreement on the Relationship	Consensus among respondents that motivation positively impacts dedication towards work. Strong affirmation of the assertion that motivation enhances dedication.

Interpretation: The above question and results suggest that motivation plays a crucial role in shaping individuals' dedication towards work, leading to enhanced performance, continuous improvement, and a commitment to excellence. The responses consistently indicate a strong association between motivation and dedication towards work. This suggests that individuals perceive motivation as a driving force behind their commitment and enthusiasm for their tasks and responsibilities. Participants express those high levels of motivation result in increased enthusiasm, commitment, and ultimately, better performance. This implies that motivation serves as a catalyst for improved work outcomes, as individuals are more energized and focused when they are motivated. Personal experiences shared in the responses suggest that dedication towards work tends to increase steadily over time. This indicates a developmental process wherein individuals become increasingly invested in their work, driven by a growing sense of purpose and passion. The responses reflect a commitment to excellence and continuous improvement fuelled by motivation. Participants express a desire to exceed expectations and make a positive impact within their organizations, indicating a proactive approach to personal and professional growth.

Table 6. What makes you satisfied from your work?

Summary of Opinions	Theme	Iteration Keywords/ Phrases
Satisfaction from work is derived from various sources. For many, it comes from the fulfilment of their teaching assignments and interaction with students, providing a sense of purpose and meaning to their profession. Helping students understand difficult topics, witnessing their achievements, and receiving positive feedback contribute significantly to satisfaction. Additionally, recognition and appreciation from colleagues or team members, as well as desirable results and achievements of students, are important sources of satisfaction. For some, intellectual stimulation, and the ability to choose their work also play a crucial role. Ultimately, the happiness and success of students appear to be central to the satisfaction derived from work, reflecting the intrinsic rewards of teaching, and positively impacting others' lives.	• **Impact and Achievement**	Sense of achievement from desirable results, achievements of students, and intellectual stimulation. Making students understand difficult topics and seeing their happy faces.
	• **Connection and Recognition**	Sense of belongingness to the organization. Positive feedback, rewards, and recognition from students, team members, and consumers. A small word of appreciation or a smile from colleagues or team.
	• **Student Success and Engagement**	Satisfaction and confidence derived from students' success and active interest in the topic. Results obtained from students and their engagement in learning.
	• **Purpose and Meaning**	Teaching assignment and involvement with students providing maximum satisfaction and a sense of purpose to the profession. Happiness of children (students) as a teacher.

Interpretation: The above question and results highlight the multifaceted nature of job satisfaction, encompassing factors such as recognition, purpose, impact, support, autonomy, and student outcomes. It emphasizes the intrinsic motivation and fulfilment derived from meaningful work and positive contributions to students and the organization. The individual finds satisfaction in receiving rewards, recognition, positive feedback, and appreciation from both their team and students. This highlights the importance of acknowledgment and validation in their work environment. Engaging in teaching and interacting with students provides the individual with a deep sense of purpose and meaning in their profession. They derive satisfaction from their teaching assignment and involvement with students, suggesting a strong intrinsic motivation in their role. Witnessing students' understanding of difficult topics, achieving desirable results, and observing the happiness and satisfaction of students and their own children serve as sources of satisfaction. This indicates a sense of fulfilment derived from making a positive impact and achieving tangible outcomes. Feeling a sense of belongingness to the organization and experiencing positive attitudes from colleagues contribute to job satisfaction. This suggests the importance of a supportive work environment and positive relationship with peers. Intellectual stimulation and having the opportunity to engage in work of choice contribute to satisfaction. This indicates a preference for autonomy and intellectual challenge in their work. The satisfaction and confidence of students are paramount, as indicated by the individual's emphasis on students' understanding, engagement, and happiness. This underscores a student-centric approach to teaching and a deep investment in student success.

Table 7. Mention a few things that you think are important for job satisfaction.

Summary of Opinions	Theme	Iteration Keywords/ Phrases
Based on the responses provided, several factors contribute to job satisfaction. These include aspects such as a positive work environment, clear targets, fair compensation, opportunities for growth, work-life balance, and recognition and appreciation for efforts. Autonomy, flexibility, meaningful work, and career advancement opportunities also play crucial roles in fostering satisfaction. Additionally, acknowledgment of efforts, feedback, mutual respect, and trust between employees and employers are highlighted as important contributors to job satisfaction. Ultimately, factors that promote mental peace, such as a supportive work environment and adequate family time, are essential for overall satisfaction. Recognition in the form of bonuses or rewards is also mentioned as a significant aspect of job satisfaction.	• **Work Environment and Atmosphere**	Cordial atmosphere Positive work environment Mutual respect and trust Cooperation among employees
	• **Job Characteristics and Fulfilment**	Meaningful work Learning opportunities Autonomy and flexibility Satisfaction Acknowledgment of efforts Skillset and motivation
	• **Compensation and Recognition**	Proper pay scale Fair compensation Recognition and appreciation Rewards and bonuses Fair appraisal
	• **Work-Life Balance**	Work-life balance Family time Mental peace
	• **Career Growth and Development**	Career growth opportunities Freedom to take decisions Dedication towards work and organization Time management

Interpretation: The above question and results highlight the multifaceted nature of job satisfaction, which encompasses both intrinsic and extrinsic factors, as well as the importance of organizational culture and work-life balance in shaping employee well-being and engagement. The emphasis on a cordial work atmosphere, mutual respect, and cooperation suggests that employees prioritize a supportive and harmonious workplace. This indicates that interpersonal dynamics and organizational culture play significant roles in fostering job satisfaction. The focus on meaningful work, opportunities for learning, and acknowledgment of efforts highlights the importance of intrinsic motivators. Employees seek roles that align with their values and provide opportunities for personal and professional growth. Recognition and appreciation serve as powerful tools for reinforcing positive behaviour and boosting morale. The repeated mention of work-life balance, mental peace, and family time underscores the importance of holistic well-being. Employees value flexibility in their schedules and opportunities to recharge outside of work, indicating a desire for a balanced lifestyle. Fair compensation, along with opportunities for career growth and advancement, are seen as crucial factors in job satisfaction. Employees want to feel financially valued for their contributions and seek opportunities for professional development and progression within the organization. The desire for freedom to make decisions and mutual respect between employees and employers suggests a preference for a level of autonomy in the workplace. Trust and respect are essential for fostering a sense of ownership and empowerment among employees.

Table 8. How do you think greater involvement in your work will give you more job satisfaction or make you satisfied with your job?

Summary of Opinions	Theme	Iteration Keywords/ Phrases
The consensus among respondents is that greater involvement in work leads to increased job satisfaction. They believe that deep engagement in tasks, variety in job responsibilities, and appreciation for their efforts contribute significantly to their overall satisfaction with their job. Some emphasize the importance of interest and dedication in fostering involvement, while others see involvement itself as a driver of interest and dedication in the job. Respondents also note that satisfaction stems from feeling valued and recognized in their roles, as well as from the sense of meaning and achievement derived from their contributions to the organization. However, there are a few dissenting opinions, with some expressing uncertainty regarding the direct correlation between involvement and job satisfaction. Overall, most respondents perceive greater involvement as essential for enhancing job satisfaction and deriving fulfilment from their work.	• **Positive Relationship between Involvement and Satisfaction**	In-depth involvement leads to greater satisfaction with the job. More involvement results in long-term satisfaction. Greater involvement provides happiness and a sense of achievement, contributing to overall satisfaction.
	• **Enhanced Skills and Meaningful Contribution**	Greater involvement enriches skills and provides a sense of meaning as part of the organization, fostering satisfaction. Involvement helps derive happiness and a sense of achievement from the job.
	• **Interest and Dedication**	While involvement is important, it is also influenced by interest and dedication in the job.
	• **Recognition and Appreciation**	Appreciation and recognition for involvement contribute to satisfaction.

Interpretation: The above question and result highlight the significance of involvement in enhancing job satisfaction and the various factors that contribute to individuals' perceptions of satisfaction in their work. Respondents perceive that deep involvement in their work leads to increased job satisfaction. They believe that actively engaging in tasks, taking on diverse responsibilities, and being appreciated for their efforts contribute significantly to their overall satisfaction with their job. While some respondents emphasize the importance of interest and dedication in fostering involvement, others view involvement itself as a driver of interest and dedication in the job. This suggests a reciprocal relationship between involvement and intrinsic motivation. Respondents highlight the importance of feeling valued and recognized in their roles. Appreciation for their efforts and contributions enhances their sense of satisfaction and motivates them to engage more deeply in their work. Satisfaction stems from the sense of meaning and achievement derived from contributing to the organization. Greater involvement provides individuals with a sense of purpose and fulfilment, as they feel that they are making meaningful contributions to the organization's goals. While many respondents perceive a positive correlation between involvement and job satisfaction, there are a few dissenting opinions. Some express uncertainty regarding the direct relationship between involvement and satisfaction, suggesting that individual perceptions may vary.

Table 9. Do you think commitment towards the organization identification and motivation are responsible for employee satisfaction?

Summary of Opinions	Theme	Iteration Keywords/ Phrases
Many respondents believe that commitment towards organizational identification and motivation play significant roles in employee satisfaction. They acknowledge the importance of dedication to the organization and staying motivated in contributing to its success. Some emphasize the need for active listening and compassion from management to further enhance satisfaction. However, there are also nuances in opinions, with one respondent suggesting that individual goals and aspirations also influence satisfaction levels. Overall, while commitment and motivation are recognized as key factors in fostering employee satisfaction, the role of management support and alignment with individual aspirations is also considered important.	• **Commitment and Satisfaction**	Commitment towards organization identification Belief in long-term benefits of organizational loyalty Perception that commitment contributes to satisfaction
	• **Management's Role**	Importance of active listening and compassion from management Recognition of management's influence on satisfaction
	• **Individual Factors**	Recognition that satisfaction also depends on individual goals and aspirations
	• **Affirmative Responses**	Responses affirming the relationship between commitment, motivation, and satisfaction without further elaboration

Interpretation: The above question and results underscore the multifaceted nature of employee satisfaction, with commitment, motivation, management support, and individual aspirations all playing significant roles in shaping employees' experiences and perceptions of satisfaction in the workplace. Respondents acknowledge that commitment towards organizational identification and motivation are significant factors influencing employee satisfaction. They recognize the importance of feeling connected to the organization and being motivated to contribute to its success in fostering satisfaction among employees. Some respondents emphasize the role of management in enhancing employee satisfaction by being active listeners and showing compassion towards employees. They suggest that management support and understanding contribute to a positive work environment and increased satisfaction among employees. Respondents highlight the benefits of long-term commitment to one organization for employee satisfaction. They suggest that staying dedicated to the organization over time fosters a sense of stability and fulfilment, contributing to overall satisfaction in the workplace. However, one respondent suggests that while commitment and motivation are important, individual goals and aspirations also play a role in determining satisfaction levels. This perspective suggests that satisfaction may vary depending on how well an individual's goals align with their work and organizational values.

5. FINDINGS

The findings drawn from the analysis and interpretation of the information gathered from the respondents are listed below.

Dimensions of Employee Engagement: According to the research, employee engagement is a complex concept that includes elements like satisfaction, motivation, communication, commitment, and alignment with company objectives. To enhance employee performance and well-being and to cultivate an engaged culture, effective employee engagement methods should consider these different elements.

Difficulties and Inconsistencies: Although there are some cases of strong organizational identification, there are also some obvious difficulties, like job dissatisfaction and inconsistent engagement initiatives. These difficulties are made worse by elements like poor identification efforts and low job satisfaction.

Alignment with Organizational Goals: Elements like a passion for one's work, adaptability to change, and alignment with the organization's values and goals are what motivate people to identify with their organizations. Establishing a workplace culture that is inclusive, encouraging, and places a high value on goal alignment, recognition, and efficient communication is essential to developing employee engagement and commitment.

Significance of Intrinsic Motivation: Individuals' commitment to work is shaped by their intrinsic motivation, which results in improved performance, ongoing development, and a pursuit of greatness. Workers view motivation as the engine that propels their dedication to and excitement for their jobs and duties.

Impact of Job Satisfaction: Organizational identity and employee engagement are strongly correlated with job satisfaction. Employee satisfaction increases the likelihood that they will be involved, dedicated, and eager to take part in organizational initiatives that foster collaboration and teamwork.

Management Support and acknowledgment: Promoting job happiness and organizational identity requires management support, acknowledgment, and rewards for work. Recognizing employees' efforts and contributions makes them feel more satisfied and encourages them to put more effort into their work.

6. DISCUSSION

Employee engagement is influenced by various factors like motivation, commitment, and alignment with organizational goals, while job satisfaction is shaped by intrinsic and extrinsic factors such as recognition, purpose, and work-life balance.

Different elements such as motivation, dedication, and alignment with organizational goals impact employee engagement, whereas work-life balance, recognition, and purpose shape extrinsic and intrinsic factors that affect job satisfaction. Employees who feel a sense of belonging to their job exhibit pride and loyalty, making organizational identity an important factor. Since engagement and commitment are strongly related, it is essential to have a supportive workplace culture and efficient management-employee communication. Engagement and happiness are known to be significantly influenced by motivation, with intrinsic elements like meaningful work and recognition serving as critical catalysts. Furthermore, participation in duties and a sense of worth are important factors in job happiness. The support of management and personal goals also affect how satisfied people are. Stability is facilitated by long-term commitment, but it is crucial to match individual objectives with company principles.

Overall, increasing engagement and happiness necessitates a comprehensive approach that tackles intrinsic motivators, fosters organizational coherence, and assures supporting management practices. With this knowledge, educational institutions may establish a setting that promotes both organizational success and employee well-being.

7. CONCLUSION

In summary, this study clarifies the crucial relationship that exists between job satisfaction and employee engagement in educational sector of Delhi NCR. A descriptive study that combined qualitative methods has examined many aspects of employee engagement and how it affects job satisfaction. The results highlight the significance of elements including management support, organizational identification, motivation, and commitment in promoting worker engagement and raising job satisfaction. It is evident that happy people are more likely to be interested in their work, which improves student results and organizational effectiveness.

8. LIMITATIONS OF THE STUDY

The limitation of the study is that the time of the study was of short span which acted as a limitation to the study. If there was more time, we could have conducted two to three more interviews and identified more iterations As, we have conducted only one round of interview and came out with few iterations, this acted as our limitation. Additionally, the subjective nature of data collection through surveys and interviews could introduce response bias and may not fully capture the complexity of employee engagement and job satisfaction. The reliance on Interpretative Phenomenological Analysis (IPA) as a qualitative analysis tool also carries the risk of researcher bias and varying interpretations.

9. MANAGERIAL IMPLICATIONS

The research paper's conclusions have numerous managerial implications for educational institutions. First, given the complexity of employee engagement and work satisfaction, managers ought to implement all-encompassing tactics that consider factors like motivation, dedication, and goal alignment. This could entail putting recognition programs into place, encouraging a healthy work environment, and offering chances for advancement within the profession. Furthermore, the understanding of how organizational identification influences employee commitment and loyalty emphasizes how crucial it is for managers to foster a feeling of community and alignment with the organization's values. In this context, it is imperative to have opportunities for resilience-building throughout times of change, supportive leadership, and effective communication.

Moreover, recognizing the significance of motivation in augmenting worker commitment emphasizes the necessity of offering purposeful work, independence, and chances for individual development to cultivate a feeling of direction and enthusiasm among staff members. In summary, managers ought to endeavour to establish a work environment that is inclusive, supportive, and places a high priority on the well-being, engagement, and contentment of employees. This will ultimately result in enhanced organizational performance and success.

10. FUTURE SCOPE

In the future, educational establishments ought to give precedence to tactics that foster an engaged culture, acknowledging the internal and external factors that propel worker contentment. Institutions can cultivate a workforce that is not only engaged but also satisfied by prioritizing effective communication and management practices, creating supportive environments, and matching individual interests with organizational goals. These actions will ultimately improve teaching quality, student success, and overall institutional effectiveness. Carrying out longitudinal research may shed light on the ways in which these constructs change over time and pinpoint variables affecting long-term patterns of pleasure and engagement. Furthermore, comparisons between other educational establishments or geographical areas may highlight differences in the efficacy of interaction tactics. Examining the effects of actions, like leadership efforts or training programs, on employee satisfaction and engagement may also provide useful information for improving the business. Additionally, examining how new developments in technology or developing trends like remote work are influencing employee experiences in the education sector may offer insightful information for modifying engagement tactics in response to evolving workplaces.

REFERENCES

Aghdasi, S., Kiāmanesh, A., & Ebrahim, A. N. (2011). Emotional Intelligence and Organizational Commitment: Testing the mediatory role of occupational stress and job satisfaction. *Procedia: Social and Behavioral Sciences*, 29, 1965–1976. DOI:10.1016/j.sbspro.2011.11.447

Ajila, C. O., & Abiola, A. (2004). Influence of rewards on workers performance in an organization. *Journal of Social Sciences*, 8(1), 7–12. DOI:10.1080/0971892 3.2004.11892397

Allen, N. J., & Meyer, J. P. (1990). Organizational Socialization Tactics: A Longitudinal Analysis of Links to Newcomers' Commitment and Role Orientation. *Academy of Management Journal*, 33(4), 847–858. DOI:10.2307/256294

Armstrong, M. (1999). *A Handbook of Human Resource Management practice*. https://ci.nii.ac.jp/ncid/BA83417636

Armstrong, M. (2010). *Armstrong's essential human resource management practice: A Guide to People Management*. Kogan Page Publishers.

Ashforth, B. E., & Mael, F. A. (1989). Social Identity Theory and the organization. *Academy of Management Review*, 14(1), 20–39. DOI:10.2307/258189

Awais, M., Malik, M. S., & Qaisar, A. (2015). A Review: The Job Satisfaction Act as Mediator between Spiritual Intelligence and Organizational Commitment. *International Review of Management and Marketing*, 5(4), 203–210. https://dergipark .org.tr/en/download/article-file/366720

Baron, R. A., & Greenberg, J. (1990). *Behavior in organizations: Understanding and Managing the Human Side of Work*. Allyn & Bacon.

Bartels, J., Pruyn, A. T., De Jong, M. D., & Joustra, I. (2006). Multiple organizational identification levels and the impact of perceived external prestige and communication climate. *Journal of Organizational Behavior*, 28(2), 173–190. DOI:10.1002/job.420

Biswas, S., & Bhatnagar, J. (2013). Mediator Analysis of employee engagement: Role of perceived organizational support, P-O fit, organizational commitment and job satisfaction. *Vikalpa*, 38(1), 27–40. DOI:10.1177/0256090920130103

Brief, A. P., & Weiss, H. M. (2002). Organizational behavior: Affect in the workplace. *Annual Review of Psychology*, 53(1), 279–307. DOI:10.1146/annurev. psych.53.100901.135156 PMID:11752487

Choi, K. (2006). A Structural Relationship analysis of hotel employees' turn-over intention. *Asia Pacific Journal of Tourism Research*, 11(4), 321–337. DOI:10.1080/10941660600931150

Chung, E. (2013). *The relationship of training and organizational commitment in One Korean organization*. https://conservancy.umn.edu/handle/11299/162440

Cole, M. S., & Bruch, H. (2006). Organizational identity strength, identification, and commitment and their relationships to turnover intention: Does organizational hierarchy matter? *Journal of Organizational Behavior*, 27(5), 585–605. DOI:10.1002/job.378

De Menezes, L. M. (2012). Job satisfaction and quality management: An empirical analysis. *International Journal of Operations & Production Management*, 32(3), 308–328. DOI:10.1108/01443571211212592

Dutton, J. E., Dukerich, J. M., & Harquail, C. V. (1994). Organizational images and member identification. *Administrative Science Quarterly*, 39(2), 239. DOI:10.2307/2393235

Edwards, M. J. A., & Peccei, R. (2007). Organizational identification: Development and testing of a conceptually grounded measure. *European Journal of Work and Organizational Psychology*, 16(1), 25–57. DOI:10.1080/13594320601088195

Fernandez, C. P. (2007). Employee engagement. *Journal of Public Health Management and Practice*, 13(5), 524–526. DOI:10.1097/01.PHH.0000285207.63835.50 PMID:17762699

Giroux, C. (1960). The Motivation to work, by F. Herzberg, B. Mausner and B.-C. Snyderman, John Wiley & Sons, New York, John Wiley & Sons, 1959. *Relations Industrielles*, 15(2), 275. DOI:10.7202/1022040ar

Harpaz, I. (1990). The importance of work Goals: An international perspective. *Journal of International Business Studies*, 21(1), 75–93. DOI:10.1057/palgrave.jibs.8490328

Herzberg, F. (2023, April 4). *One more time: How do you motivate employees?* Harvard Business Review. https://hbr.org/2003/01/one-more-time-how-do-you-motivate-employees

Hochschild, A. R. (1990). Ideology and emotion management: A perspective and path for future research. In Kemper, T. D. (Ed.), *Research agendas in the sociology of emotions* (pp. 117–142). State University of New York Press.

Hsu, S., & Wang, Y. (2008). The development and empirical validation of the Employee Satisfaction Index model. *Total Quality Management & Business Excellence*, 19(4), 353–366. DOI:10.1080/14783360701595052

Judge, T. A., Thoresen, C. J., Bono, J. E., & Patton, G. K. (2001). The job satisfaction–job performance relationship: A qualitative and quantitative review. *Psychological Bulletin*, 127(3), 376–407. DOI:10.1037/0033-2909.127.3.376 PMID:11393302

Kahn, W. A. (1990). Psychological Conditions of Personal Engagement and Disengagement at Work. *Academy of Management Journal*, 33(4), 692–724. DOI:10.2307/256287

Karanika-Murray, M., Duncan, N. G., Pontes, H. M., & Griffiths, M. D. (2015). Organizational identification, work engagement, and job satisfaction. *Journal of Managerial Psychology*, 30(8), 1019–1033. DOI:10.1108/JMP-11-2013-0359

Kreitner, R. (1995).. . *Management.*

Lee, Y., Jungheon, N., Park, D., & Lee, K. A. (2006). What factors influence customer-oriented prosocial behavior of customer-contact employees? *Journal of Services Marketing*, 20(4), 251–264. DOI:10.1108/08876040610674599

Messner, W. (2013). Effect of organizational culture on employee commitment in the Indian IT services sourcing industry. *Journal of Indian Business Research*, 5(2), 76–100. DOI:10.1108/17554191311320764

Meyer, J. P., & Allen, N. J. (1991). A three-component conceptualization of organizational commitment. *Human Resource Management Review*, 1(1), 61–89. DOI:10.1016/1053-4822(91)90011-Z

Mobley, W. H. (1982). *Employee turnover: causes consequences & control.*

Mowday, R. T., Steers, R. M., & Porter, L. W. (1979). The measurement of organizational commitment. *Journal of Vocational Behavior*, 14(2), 224–247. DOI:10.1016/0001-8791(79)90072-1

Muthuveloo, R., & Rose, R. C. (2005). Typology of organisational commitment. *American Journal of Applied Sciences*, 2(6), 1078–1081. DOI:10.3844/ajassp.2005.1078.1081

Price, J. L. (1977). *The study of Turnover.* Iowa State Press.

Rameshkumar, M. (2020). Employee engagement as an antecedent of organizational commitment – A study on Indian seafaring officers. *The Asian journal of shipping and logistics*, 36(3): 105-112.

Robbins, S. P., & Judge, T. (2007). *Organizational behavior*. Prentice Hall.

Saks, A. M. (2006). Antecedents and consequences of employee engagement. *Journal of Managerial Psychology*, 21(6), 600–619. DOI:10.1108/02683940610690169

Salanova, M., Nieto, S. A., & Peíró, J. M. (2005). Linking organizational resources and work engagement to employee performance and customer loyalty: The mediation of service climate. *The Journal of Applied Psychology*, 90(6), 1217–1227. DOI:10.1037/0021-9010.90.6.1217 PMID:16316275

Skaalvik, E. M., & Skaalvik, S. (2011). Teacher job satisfaction and motivation to leave the teaching profession: Relations with school context, feeling of belonging, and emotional exhaustion. *Teaching and Teacher Education*, 27(6), 1029–1038. DOI:10.1016/j.tate.2011.04.001

Skinner, B. (1974). *About behaviorism*. Vintage.

Sow, M. (2015). Relationship Between Organizational Commitment and Turnover Intentions Among Healthcare Internal Auditors. *Walden University Scholar Works*. https://scholarworks.waldenu.edu/cgi/viewcontent.cgi?article=2351&context=dissertations

Tyler, T. R., & Blader, S. L. (2001). Identity and cooperative behavior in groups. *Group Processes & Intergroup Relations*, 4(3), 207–226. DOI:10.1177/1368430201004003003

Ugwu, F. O., Onyishi, I. E., & Rodríguez-Sánchez, A. (2014). Linking organizational trust with employee engagement: The role of psychological empowerment. *Personnel Review*, 43(3), 377–400. DOI:10.1108/PR-11-2012-0198

Van Dijk, R., & Van Dick, R. (2009). Navigating organizational change: Change leaders, employee resistance and work-based identities. *Journal of Change Management*, 9(2), 143–163. DOI:10.1080/14697010902879087

Van Knippenberg, D., Van Dick, R., & Tavares, S. M. (2005). Social Identity and Social Exchange: Identification, Support, and Withdrawal from the Job. *Social Science Research Network*. https://papers.ssrn.com/sol3/Delivery.cfm/8497.pdf?abstractid=960618&mirid=1&type=2

Yang, J. B. (2008). Effect of newcomer socialisation on organisational commitment, job satisfaction, and turnover intention in the hotel industry. *Service Industries Journal*, 28(4), 429–443. DOI:10.1080/02642060801917430

Chapter 6
Navigating the New Norm:
Exploring Work–Life Balance With Evolving Leadership Styles in the Post–COVID–19 Era

S. Raksithaa
Christ University, India

Ginu George
https://orcid.org/0000-0001-5611-6174
Westford University College, India

ABSTRACT

This paper aims to explore and understand employees' subjective experiences and perceptions regarding work-life balance in the context of evolving leadership styles post-COVID-19. It also examines the coping mechanisms and strategies employees and organizations employ to navigate work-life balance challenges in the changed work landscape. Finally, this paper examines the changes in remote work in the context of WLB and various types of leadership in the post-pandemic scenario. The Boolean search was employed, and. keywords relevant to Work-life Balance and Leadership were utilized to find the papers for further analysis. The results state that leaders understand and cooperate with employees during this transition period. They prioritize employees' well-being and flexibility in the work schedule. Leaders follow a mix of servant and transformational leadership styles to lead the employees. The study also highlights the coping mechanisms and the workplace changes that navigate the employees' work-life balance.

DOI: 10.4018/979-8-3693-4412-5.ch006

INTRODUCTION

Managing work and prioritizing personal commitments concern many employees in this fast-paced world. Their well-being is the need of the hour, including psychological, mental, and physical health (Yusuf et al., 2020). Work-Life Balance (WLB) denotes balancing paid work and commitments away from paid work. A gallop in the Work-From-Home (WFH) scenario has depleted the WLB of the employees, leading to less time for their private lives. When a work-life imbalance exists, there is a contradiction between work and life roles, leading to conflict and stress. Poor WLB leads to negative stress, which, in turn, leads to health issues like cholesterol and blood pressure and psychological problems like substance abuse and addiction, stress, and anxiety (Filippi et al., 2022). WLB refers to the capacity of the individual to handle the work and non-work commitments. It is a dynamic state, and people will reap either of the two outcomes: conflict or enrichment (Wong et al., 2023).

The leadership style is vital in determining an organization's output quality and work engagement. A wide range of leadership styles exists, from transformational to laissez-faire. It determines the success rate of the organization. Exemplary leaders focus on doing the right things than doing things right (Gemeda & Lee, 2020). Leadership is the ability to decide on a list of tasks and persuade others to do the tasks. Most organizations have failed because they failed to adopt the right leadership style. The employees of these organizations need to be adequately controlled by their management, which leads to low employee motivation and low productivity; thus, the employees become uncooperative. Leaders adopt leadership styles based on the organization's situation (Mirzani, 2023).

COVID-19 has changed people's lives and the functioning of organizations. On-site work has become more of WFH even after the pandemic, when the hybrid work model is still in existence, and people have begun to work overtime, thus reducing their family time and not prioritizing their commitments. The WFH has increased mental burnout and isolation, leading to work burnout and stress (Irawanto et al., 2021). The people in leadership should understand the employees' needs, especially when they suffer from COVID-19, either emotionally or psychologically, and extend their support. Leaders should permit flexible working and be more empathetic to their employees, increasing employee performance and motivation (AlMazrouei, 2023).

The study mainly revolves around the theme of WLB and the forms of leadership post-COVID crisis, which drastically changed the organization's functioning. Employees are severely hit during these times and need coping mechanisms to attain organizational goals (Nyfoudi et al., 2024). The leaders serve as the primary motivation for the employees to perform their tasks. Based on this background, the following are the Research Questions (RQs) addressed in the current study.

RQ1. What are the employees' subjective experiences and perceptions regarding work-life balance in the context of evolving leadership styles post-COVID-19?

RQ2. What coping mechanisms and strategies should employees and organizations employ to navigate work-life balance challenges in the changed work landscape?

RQ3. What are all the remote work changes in the context of WLB and various types of leadership in the post-pandemic scenario?

The WLB is the most sought-after concept in the workplace; post-COVID, this topic has gained relative importance. Leaders with different approaches should understand the importance of WLB in the present scenario. Employees may face difficulties being at home all day just by looking at their family, and they would also need some distractions other than work. The remote work transition post-COVID is to be understood by the employees when the workers are changing from the remote work model to the hybrid work model, and the leaders should think from the employee's perspective.

LITERATURE REVIEW

Overview of Work-Life Balance

Individuals can attain WLB by distributing equal time between their professional and personal lives. Employees prefer WFH as they can spend their time with family. However, managers do not encourage it as it may reduce the work-related responsibilities taken by the employees. The perception of WLB varies from individual to individual. It depends upon priorities, life goals, family lives, stages of work, and individual goals, values, and aspirations (Bhumika, 2020). WLB leads to an increase in the employees' productivity, leading to a lower turnover rate, which shows that the employees are happier with their work schedules. Life balance does not depend only on work-life alone. It also depends on the family side's conflicts. Work and personal life should give employees more freedom to upskill to retain their jobs in the market. The more leisure time they get, the more involved they are in upskilling, which is required to sustain their career and bring better opportunities for them within the organization (Bhende et al., 2020).

The WLB was given importance by reducing working hours, and the employees felt the utmost positivity and motivation to work in the organization, leading to good relationships with the clients. Even without their manager's intervention, they can deal with their clients calmly, resolve their issues, and do their work on time due to reduced stress. Reduced working hours have led to a decrease in workers' burnout. Due to reduced work time, the workers can also spend time with their kids without any work pressure and handle them with the utmost patience. A good WLB can enable the employee to spend time with his friends whenever they call him for a gathering; they can go without hesitation. They can also visit or contact their relatives more often, leading to more understanding. Since now they can meet their friends due to reduced work time, they can vent their problems and seek solutions (Barck-Holst et al., 2020).

During the pandemic period, workers had to work for more time, leading to less work-life balance. Employers expect employees to be online at all times. Though the employees found WFH to be a cost- and time-saving, the atmosphere in the home-based workspace environment was unsuitable due to the prevalence of noise and disturbance as the climate is not organized and requires reorganization of the environment, so the kids in the home can also carry out their school work and the parents can also look into their workplace (Shirmohammadi et al., 2022).

LEADERSHIP STYLES AND IMPACT ON EMPLOYEE WELL-BEING

Servant Leadership

The servant leadership style focuses more on employee well-being. It focuses on the growth and development of the employees, which in turn enhances the efficiency of the employee's performance (Eva et al., 2019). This leadership style is more inclined towards positively affecting the employees' well-being. The approachable nature of leaders and the cultivation of a motivational environment improve employee satisfaction (Quinteros-Durand et al., 2023). They are knowledgeable, making them approachable to the employees, and possess problem-solving skills. They prioritize the interests of others and behave ethically by being honest, opening up, and treating the employees equally (Paesen et al., 2019).

Laissez-Faire Leadership

In this style, leaders are unavailable when needed, not expressive, and not available to make decisions; thus, they are passive leaders. Under this leadership, the employees with lower learning goal orientation will be lower organizational performers and those with higher learning goal orientation will be high organizational performers and have a chance of getting appraisals (Zhang et al., 2023). It engenders lower mental health among the employees, feeling more depressed. When the leaders are inactive, it vandalizes the organization's reputation, and leaders will leave a wrong impression on the organization (Robert & Vandenberghe, 2022).

Transformational leadership

This style deals with transforming the workforce to comply with the organization's objectives and motivating them to achieve them and should work beyond capacity (Steinmann et al., 2018). Transformational leaders intrinsically motivate the employees, leading to a positive attitude towards the job. They also enhance the quality of relationships, make employees comfortable with their honesty, and deal with organizational issues fairly and ethically, making employees feel less enervated. Employees' contributions are recognized, and the organization's goals and objectives are shared. They know about their employees well, thus making them work in their comfort zone, enriching less stressful work environments (Khan et al., 2020).

Autocratic leadership

In this leadership style, the leaders make all the decisions without consulting the employees. After a decision has been made, the employees are expected to abide by the rules and regulations set up by their leaders. Under this leadership style, absenteeism and a high turnover ratio are the most common scenarios. It has caused behavioral stress among the employees. It triggers negative emotions in the employees, like anger and anxiety. The unfriendly work experience with their leader will give them psychological feelings such as stress and loneliness (Asim et al., 2021).

Democratic leadership

In democratic leadership, the workers are empowered to provide suggestions, and everyone can contribute to the ongoing projects in the organization, where the leaders will make final decisions. Despite being less productive, the workers exhibit good work quality and are treated fairly and duly rewarded, creating a positive work environment that fosters employee well-being and high job satisfaction and morale (Vincent & Baptiste, 2021).

Work Life Balance and Gender difference:

When it comes to WLB, females are worst hit as compared to males as they have to work as well as look after their kids, husband and in-laws. Due to frustration, poor WLB is maintained leading to poor performances in their workplace. Positive WLB is inevitable for women to look after themselves but negative WLB, leads to reduction in their quality of life. Flexibility is the key motivator for them to maintain their WLB as they could do their work with flexibility and also look after their household chores. Husband's support and the organisation's support are the two factors that women required to attain a positive WLB (Uddin, 2021).

They have to look after their families and adopt themselves to the changing workscape. The women who hold higher positions and higher educational qualifications have higher WLBs. The women placed in the organisation's lower hierarchy tend to work for more hours. More the women get old, the more the organisational commitment reduces as they should look after their family. They would prefer more free time to spend quality time with their family (Liu et al., 2021).

WLB exists when there is a perfect balance in the job role and in the home and women can lead a happy life if they attain WLB in their lives. Women should make sure that they are available and resourceful at all times to lead a perfect WLB. Female workers get stressed if they are not adequately paid for their work, despite rendering a quality service. These days, where women and men have to earn for their living, women undergo a huge trauma as they have the pressure to look after their home and also earn for their living. Constant stress in the work place can make them feel that they cannot get up from that fear of getting a healthier WLB, making them feel powerless (Ganapathi et al., 2024).

POST-COVID-19 WORK ENVIRONMENT

Gig economy

The gig economy refers to the working system predominantly known as freelancing, and the post-COVID-19 era saw a spout-up in gig workers. It is a system where companies hire temporary staff based on their skills and qualifications, providing a flexible work environment for their workers without pension or retirement benefits. Their job needs to be secured as they temporarily work for a company that has an unfair agreement. They work in an isolated environment compared to the traditional office setup, creating lower employee well-being. Legal issues like workplace harassment, discrimination, and salary theft cannot be addressed similarly to the employees who work at the offices (Nikoloski et al., 2023).

Hybrid work environment

The work environment is where employees work a part of the week and the remaining time in the office. The employees were hot desking after the COVID period, leading to interaction and socialization amongst the employees when the offices were slowly starting to allow people to come and work on a rotational basis. Though this system has advantages, there is another face of the coin. After the pandemic, companies have focused on creating working spaces without rooftops, increasing non-assigned workspaces, and increasing the need for more seats so employees can work uninterruptedly (Chafi et al., 2021).

The concept of digital watercoolers gained momentum during this period. The employees should be engaged in regular check-ins and virtual team-building sessions. In absenteeism of this concept, team cohesiveness and a sense of belonging do not exist among the team members (Helmold, 2021).

Flexible work arrangements

Flexible work refers to an agreement where the workers can work at whatever time and location they wish to work, giving flexibility to the female as she can look after her child when he is sick and WFH. It improves the work satisfaction and the desire to quit from the job. However, despite these advantages, a list of disadvantages exists. Despite having flexible work and time arrangements, the change in the daily work timings leads to irregular working periods and a high imbalance in family life, leading to stress and workplace loneliness (Cheng et al., 2023).

Hot desking is a concept that permits employees to book their seats in the office beforehand, and on the day, they will work in the place allotted to them. The employees will be able to see their co-workers and interact with them (Bishop, 2022), reducing workplace stress.

Digital nomads also gained momentum during this period as the employees could explore the countries and work while being elsewhere. They are the individuals who would love to travel along with work. Primarily, they are Generation Z or millennials, entitling organizations to attract lots of workers across the globe. If this system is used effectively, these employees can attain WLB (Šímová, 2022).

Theoretical Framework

Hersey-Blanchard Situational Leadership Theory

Paul Hersey and Kenneth Blanchard developed this situational leadership theory. This theory mainly focuses on the fact that the organization is not governed by one type of leadership. They mentioned four leadership style types and the subordinate's readiness and willingness to work.

Telling: The leader will comment, and the subordinates should follow it. This is for people with a low maturity level (M1). They need more motivation, and they need to be more competent and confident.

Selling: The leaders give their ideas and make the subordinates work. They have a moderate maturity level (M2). They are eager to learn despite needing to gain the appropriate skills.

Participating: The leaders make the policy, and the subordinates should implement and follow it. It is more likely that the members should take work than the leaders. The subordinates have moderate, high maturity (M3). They have skills, but they do not take responsibility.

Delegating: The subordinates make decisions, and the leaders are less involved. The subordinates have high maturity (M4). They have high skills and are ready to take on responsibilities (Hersey & Blanchard, 1969).

This theory is related to studying different leadership styles under various situations. Since subordinates will have different capabilities, there is a need to understand the WLB of every individual.

Hersey-Blanchard Situational Leadership Theory, from the perspective of WLB, the subordinates who work under leaders who can sell or delegate the work are more inclined towards the work and are undergoing stress in their workplace. The subordinates who work under the leaders who adopt the delegation style experience more stress than those who work under the leadership of the selling style (Sharma et al., 2020). The higher the stress levels, the lower the WLB (Omilion-Hodges & Ptacek, 2021a). The study concludes that subordinates who work under the selling and delegatory leaders experience less WLB than the other leadership styles.

Leader-Member Exchange (LMX) Theory

The LMX states that managers have different relationships with every subordinate differently. The manager behaves differently with the subordinates with whom he is close, and with others, he behaves the opposite. The subordinate's ingroup is most favored, while the manager least favors out-group subordinates (Omilion-Hodges & Ptacek, 2021b). Due to the above-said scenario, the subordinates will attain different levels of WLB.

The LMX theory, in the context of WLB, states that the managers engage with the ingroup subordinates and get more concessions. They will work more flexibly, gain intrinsic motivation, and gain more trust from the managers. They are more likely to experience high WLB due to the above reasons. However, it is not the same for the out-group subordinates. They will lose motivation, gain low trust from their managers, and get less support. So, these people will experience low WLB and be unsatisfied with their work (Ji et al., 2023).

METHODOLOGY

This research focuses on how various leadership styles affect the WLB of employees post-COVID-19 pandemic. Content analysis methodology was used to source the previous literature research papers were sourced from prominent databases like Sage, Emerald, Taylor and Francis, Springer, Pro Quest, Wiley, Google Scholar, Scopus, and Research Gate. As work-life balance is an emerging research area, more research is being done on this topic. Boolean search was used to find the relevant papers for further analysis. The searches were done with a few keywords like "Work-life balance" AND "leadership styles," "work-life balance" AND "autocratic leadership," "work-life balance" AND "democratic leadership," "Transformational Leadership" AND "post-COVID", "Work-life balance" AND "Remote work" AND" post-COVID', "Work" AND "post-pandemic" AND "coping strategy" was done to understand the availability of current literature and give an idea of where the future scope of research on that particular topic exists. Then, the searches were taken from 2020 till 2024 which deals with the COVID era and after. Then, the papers were scrutinized based on the title's relevance, and only the articles published in Scopus and English were analyzed.

Further, it was reduced based on the abstract and conclusion relating to the study. Then, the papers relevant to the study were analyzed, and their key findings were summarized. Based on the above criteria, 15 articles were taken for further analysis.

FINDINGS AND DISCUSSIONS:

Findings

Employee's experience

The spouse, her family, and the supervisors are the pillars of support for a woman in attaining WLB. A woman can have a better WLB when she has the capacity for resilience and problem-solving instead of being idle. The more they engage in social interactions and seek support, the better their quality of life (Anastasopoulou et al., 2023). The more employees feel that they are organization fit, the more they tend to have WLB (Abdulaziz et al., 2022). The job autonomy for the employees gives them more WLB. Managers should allow employees to choose when, where, and how to submit their work to improve their job autonomy. The more the employees have expertise, the more job autonomy they get (Liu et al., 2023). The employees stated that they have different hobbies, like working out in the gym and swimming, and since all those are available in the companies where they work, it improves motivation and employee engagement. Most employees prefer to spend time with their family and friends as they can interact with them and gain personal recovery, increasing the WLB (Strassburger et al., 2022).

Coping with the changing environment

With the hybrid work model being prevalent recently, the employees do physical crafting, take WFH for a few days, and complete their work while managing it at home. The employees draw a boundary between the work and personal life. After a certain amount of time, they do not work; they look after their household work. They follow a daily routine to ensure they can use the time efficiently and effectively for their professional and personal lives. The employees can connect with their co-workers virtually and interact. Family interactions can also make them feel stress-free and build a good boing between the employees and their close ones (Caringal-Go et al., 2021). Employees can prioritize their tasks to reduce their stress to an extent. The lifestyle model can be adopted, where the lifestyle of work and personal life are not seen as two different aspects. Balance is seen as a component that prioritizes the employee's satisfaction level but has no equilibrium (Perreault & Power, 2021). The employees purposefully distance themselves from the devices to draw boundaries between work and family (Adisa et al., 2022).

Remote work post-COVID

Remote work has been converted into a hybrid model to reduce the impact of COVID-19 on the people. The hybrid work culture will bring many changes, such as technology adoption, employee well-being, health, organizational culture, and various other scenarios (McPhail et al., 2023). The hybrid model will reduce appraisal politics and biased ratings of employees. Upskilling in the field of technology and AI is needed to retain employment. The employees should undergo skill restructuring to cope with the growing technologies (Verma et al., 2022). The teams have started to shift to video-conferencing platforms using asynchronous online platforms, and collaboration tools were emphasized. Cyber security has become a concern as data is stored electronically. The employees' well-being was managed by organizing movie nights, virtual coffee breaks, and book clubs, and the managers had continuous checks on their well-being. To appreciate the work done by the employees, the organizations gave them digital gift cards, leading to a healthy competitive environment amongst the employees (Hopkins & Bardoel, 2023).

The servant leaders focus more on the well-being of the people. They ensure that workers are not compromised upon their WLB, and they do not sacrifice their leisure time. They also keep a tab on the well-being of team members and provide them with psychological safety, WLB, and mental health support. They understand the workers' needs (Minh & Long, 2023) and encourage work-life integration where work and life are balanced based on employee's values and priorities. They provide opportunities for the employees to interact with their teams by having virtual bonding sessions and coffee breaks. They give the employees the flexibility to choose their work environment and assign deadlines for their projects so that the employees will take ownership of the work.

Laissez-faire leaders provide more flexibility, which helps the workers fix their work schedule and environment. However, they will need more guidance and support from the leaders when facing problems. There will be no perfect boundaries between work and personal life as they must work a lot, and work-related confusion exists, leading to burnout. The feeling of isolation and social isolation increases when inadequately supervised. The hybrid work model challenges role ambiguity and confusion, leading to increased burnout and decreased WLB (Desgourdes et al., 2023).

In the post-COVID era, transformational leadership is essential, where employees face psychological issues converting themselves into a new work environment. Leaders should give more emotional support and motivate employees to work. Changed organizational goals are communicated to the employees, who are encouraged to attain them. They cultivate innovation and ensure their employees are upskilled in artificial intelligence (AI) skills and other updated technologies needed for the job by organizing employee training sessions. They lead as an example by having a line between work and personal life (Jones & Schöning, 2021).

The autocratic leadership style is used to decide and manage the crisis. The leader will seek strategies to defend the risk. No employee can question his decisions to mitigate the risk, and they must cooperate with him unquestioningly. Policies like a hybrid work environment and shifting towards using software for virtual collaboration are implemented faster. The followers obey and place the initiatives on time (Du Plessis & Keyter, 2020).

The democratic leaders look into the people's concerns and collectively decide upon further action, like WFH, stress relief programs, and mental health programs. The employees can spill out their problems and get it rectified. They encourage collaboration and motivation amongst the employees, which becomes a pillar of support for them. They arrange training sessions and address employee skill gaps (Gençer & Batırlık, 2022).

DISCUSSION

The secondary data analysis states that the WLB depends upon the support of the family members, especially spouses, children, and managers. They were more comfortable being in their home and spending time with their family, and they could also work without wasting much time commuting (Putri & Amran, 2021). Post-pandemic, organizations are undergoing structural changes, and to relieve stress from work, the employees adopted coping mechanisms like spending time with their family members and friends, drawing boundaries with their work and personal life, and prioritization tasks (Olore et al., 2023). Remote work promotes the use of technology, and employees should be trained and adapted to retain their jobs.

The leaders who follow various leadership styles have also looked into the well-being of the organization and the employees, except the leaders who follow autocratic leadership style. Post-COVID, leaders motivate the subordinates to attain the organizational goals by informing them about the organizational policy changes and prioritizing employee well-being (Lundqvist et al., 2022). The needs of the employees are prioritized, and the leaders are empathetic and considerate of them. Leaders prioritize the employees' well-being and provide flexible work schedules post-COVID (Amrutrao, 2022). Analyzing the leadership styles post-COVID, the organizations have adopted transformational leadership style along with servant leadership style for the smooth functioning of the organization.

The findings show that WLB is a positive attribute, as it allows people to be at home and care for their families. But they were not able to manage both family and their work. When they want to focus on their work, daily responsibilities exist, and since the schooling of the kid and the work of the parents are done in one shelter, this acts as a distraction to work (Diehl et al., 2023); (Sharma, 2023); (Kundu et al., 2022). The coping strategies for the employees are spending time with families and friends and having boundaries with work and family timing (Jurníčková et al., 2024). Due to remote work, employees face health issues like back pain, eye strain, and lack of sleep (Gupta et al., 2024).

Practical Implications

Organizations should prioritize their employees' well-being while facing the transition and devise policies where technological transactions improve work efficiency and achieve goals faster. Organizations should implement policies enhancing their WLB, such as flexible work schedules and organizing programs concerning mental health and well-being (Lorentzon et al., 2023). Feedback mechanisms can be enabled between employees and the company's top management for hassle-free communication. The company should implement reward policies for the employees who practice WLB, and the leaders should be role models to their employees in the organization, motivating them to maintain WLB. Organizational policies should be changed regularly to cater to the needs of the dynamic working environment.

The leaders can better motivate the employees by influencing them to contribute to the company's growth. If they face issues coping with COVID-19 traumas, they should be able to understand and support them during that time. Leaders should understand the needs of their employees and give them time for their personal lives. They should understand the needs of the employees when they are undergoing the trauma of the pandemic changes, like the hybrid work model and fear of losing their jobs due to the emergence of AI.

Limitations and Future Research

The study failed to highlight the recent developments of this emerging topic of study as it is qualitative and more literature-based. This study focuses on the WLB amongst employees with different styles of leadership post-COVID, and obtaining samples from the employees can quantify the study. The above study can also be done in terms of industry and about the generational gaps in how they perceive the WLB under different leadership styles post-pandemic.

CONCLUSION

Work-life balance is one of the most evolving concepts in Organizational Behaviour, and it has gained significance since COVID. The WFH was a boon to many working professionals as they could spend some time with their families and look after their kids. It was a bane for a few, as their employers always expected them to be online, and the employees could barely concentrate on their work as they had to take care of their kids and the household chores. Since the kids were at home, they couldn't focus more on their job. Despite all these, they could socialize with their friends. Despite the border being blurred often, high emphasis was given to drawing a boundary between their work and personal life. Emerging buzzwords like digital nomads, virtual coolers, and hot desking are redefining the work culture in the modern era. The workers are comfortable to work with those leaders who can empathize their situation and changing needs amidst the difficult situation and support them during these dynamic times.

Though different types of leadership exist, they all aim to tackle the challenges thrown by the pandemic. They have managed to be supportive and approachable to their employees, helping them adapt to the new working environment and providing the necessary support during these times. Leaders monitor their team members and help them whenever they are in need. They identified the skills needed in the post-COVID era, notably technology and AI. They are prepared to face the tremendous challenges that the industry throws upon the organization, leaders, and employees.

Scope for further study:

The study gives an overview of the WLB under various leadership styles post COVID- 19 era. The study can be done to measure the WLB under various leadership styles post COVID- 19 era particular industry. Further study can also be done under various countries with this regard of WLB and leadership styles.

Further study:

The employee and the Post-Pandemic Workplace: towards a new, enlightened working environment. (n.d.). Routledge & CRC Press. https://www.routledge.com/The-Employee-and-the-Post-Pandemic-Workplace-Towards-a-New-Enlightened-Working-Environment/Zicari-Gamble/p/book/9781032483627

Handbook of Research on Remote Work and Worker Well-Being in the Post-COVID. . . - Google Books. (n.d.). https://www.google.co.in/books/edition/Handbook_of_Research_on_Remote_Work_and/0e4lEAAAQBAJ?hl=en&gbpv=0

REFERENCES

Abdulaziz, A., Bashir, M., & Alfalih, A. A. (2022). The impact of work-life balance and work overload on teacher's organizational commitment: Do Job Engagement and Perceived Organizational support matter. *Education and Information Technologies*, 27(7), 9641–9663. DOI:10.1007/s10639-022-11013-8

Adisa, T. A., Antonacopoulou, E. P., Beauregard, T. A., Dickmann, M., & Adekoya, O. D. (2022). Exploring the impact of COVID-19 on employees' boundary management and Work–Life balance. *British Journal of Management*, 33(4), 1694–1709. DOI:10.1111/1467-8551.12643

AlMazrouei, H. (2023). The effect of COVID-19 on managerial leadership style within Australian public sector organizations. *Journal of General Management*, 030630702311529. Advance online publication. DOI:10.1177/03063070231152976

Amrutrao, S. (2022). LEADERSHIP STYLE DURING AND POST COVID19 IN CORPORATE: A STUDY OF HUMANITY APPROACH WITH EMPLOYEES. *International Journal of Engineering Technologies and Management Research*, 9(7), 1–7. DOI:10.29121/ijetmr.v9.i7.2022.1189

Anastasopoulou, A., Vraimaki, E., & Trivellas, P. (2023). Recovery for Resilience: The mediating role of Work–Life balance on the quality of life of women employees. *Sustainability (Basel)*, 15(17), 12877. DOI:10.3390/su151712877

Asim, M., Liu, Z., Nadeem, M., Ghani, U., Arshad, M. I., & Xu, Y. (2021). How authoritarian leadership affects employee's helping behavior? The mediating role of rumination and moderating role of psychological ownership. *Frontiers in Psychology*, 12, 667348. Advance online publication. DOI:10.3389/fpsyg.2021.667348 PMID:34552524

Barck-Holst, P., Nilsonne, Å., Åkerstedt, T., & Hellgren, C. (2020). Reduced working hours and work-life balance. *Nordic Social Work Research*, 12(4), 450–463. DOI: 10.1080/2156857X.2020.1839784

Bhende, P., Mekoth, N., Ingalhalli, V., & Reddy, Y. (2020). Quality of work life and Work–Life balance. *Journal of Human Values*, 26(3), 256–265. DOI:10.1177/0971685820939380

Bhumika. (2020). Challenges for work–life balance during COVID-19 induced nationwide lockdown: exploring gender difference in emotional exhaustion in the Indian setting. *Gender in Management: An International Journal*, 35(7/8), 705–718. DOI:10.1108/GM-06-2020-0163

Bishop, C. (n.d.). *What is hot-desking and what are the benefits? - ideas (en-GB).* Ideas (en-GB). https://www.wework.com/en-GB/ideas/workspace-solutions/what-is-hot-desking

Caringal-Go, J. F., Teng-Calleja, M., Bertulfo, D. J., & Manaois, J. O. (2021). Work-life balance crafting during COVID-19: Exploring strategies of telecommuting employees in the Philippines. *Community Work & Family*, 25(1), 112–131. DOI:10.1080/13668803.2021.1956880

Chafi, M. B., Hultberg, A., & Yams, N. B. (2021). Post-Pandemic Office work: Perceived challenges and opportunities for a sustainable work environment. *Sustainability (Basel)*, 14(1), 294. DOI:10.3390/su14010294

Cheng, J., Sun, X., Zhong, Y., & Li, K. (2023). Flexible work arrangements and employees' knowledge sharing in Post-Pandemic era: The roles of workplace loneliness and task interdependence. *Behavioral Sciences (Basel, Switzerland)*, 13(2), 168. DOI:10.3390/bs13020168 PMID:36829396

Desgourdes, C., Hasnaoui, J. A., Umar, M., & González-Feliu, J. (2023). Decoding laissez-faire leadership: An in-depth study on its influence over employee autonomy and well-being at work. *The International Entrepreneurship and Management Journal*. Advance online publication. DOI:10.1007/s11365-023-00927-5

Diehl, D. C., Israel, G. D., Nelson, J. D., & Galindo, S. (2023). Work-Life Balance during the COVID-19 Pandemic: Insights from Extension Professionals. *Scholars Junction, 11*(1). https://scholarsjunction.msstate.edu/jhse/vol11/iss1/6/

Du Plessis, D., & Keyter, C. (2020). Suitable leadership styles for the Covid-19 converged crisis. *Africa Journal of Public Sector Development and Governance*, 3(1), 61–73. DOI:10.55390/ajpsdg.2020.3.1.3

Eva, N., Robin, M., Sendjaya, S., Van Dierendonck, D., & Liden, R. C. (2019). Servant Leadership: A systematic review and call for future research. *The Leadership Quarterly*, 30(1), 111–132. DOI:10.1016/j.leaqua.2018.07.004

Filippi, S., Yerkes, M. A., Bal, M., Hummel, B., & De Wit, J. (2022). (Un)deserving of work-life balance? A cross country investigation of people's attitudes towards work-life balance arrangements for parents and childfree employees. *Community Work & Family*, 27(1), 116–134. DOI:10.1080/13668803.2022.2099247

Ganapathi, P., Aithal, P. S., & Kanchana, D. (2024). Impact of Work-Life Balance and Stress Management on Job Satisfaction among the Working Women in Higher Educational Institutions in Namakkal District. Social Science Research Network. https://doi.org/DOI:10.2139/ssrn.4744545

Gemeda, H. K., & Lee, J. (2020). Leadership styles, work engagement and outcomes among information and communications technology professionals: A cross-national study. *Heliyon*, 6(4), e03699. DOI:10.1016/j.heliyon.2020.e03699 PMID:32280799

Gençer, Y. G., & Batırlık, S. N. (2022). Importance of leadership in managing Post-Pandemic crises. In *Advances in logistics, operations, and management science book series* (pp. 104–122). DOI:10.4018/978-1-6684-5876-1.ch007

Gupta, S., Vasa, S. R., & Sehgal, P. (2024). Mapping the experiences of work-life balance: Implications for the future of work. *Journal of Asia Business Studies*. Advance online publication. DOI:10.1108/JABS-06-2023-0223

Helmold, M. (2021). New work, transformational and virtual leadership. In *Management for professionals*. DOI:10.1007/978-3-030-63315-8

Hersey, P., & Blanchard, K. H. (1969). Management of Organizational BehaviorPrentice-Hall Inc., 1969 (Cloth and Soft cover. Soft cover $3.95). *Academy of Management Journal*, 12(4), 526. DOI:10.5465/amj.1969.19201155

Hopkins, J. L., & Bardoel, A. (2023). The future is hybrid: How organisations are designing and supporting sustainable hybrid work models in Post-Pandemic Australia. *Sustainability (Basel)*, 15(4), 3086. DOI:10.3390/su15043086

Irawanto, D. W., Novianti, K. R., & Roz, K. (2021). Work from Home: Measuring Satisfaction between Work–Life Balance and Work Stress during the COVID-19 Pandemic in Indonesia. *Economies*, 9(3), 96. DOI:10.3390/economies9030096

Ji, H., Zhao, X., & Dang, J. (2023). Relationship between leadership-member exchange (LMX) and flow at work among medical workers during the COVID-19: The mediating role of job crafting. *BMC Psychology*, 11(1), 162. Advance online publication. DOI:10.1186/s40359-023-01194-3 PMID:37198695

Jones, S., & Schöning, M. (2021). Employee Job Satisfaction During Remote Work: The Impact of Transformational Leadership. *Effective Executive, 24*(3), 65–72. https://www.proquest.com/docview/2584571442/fulltextPDF/D86322A2F394374PQ/1?accountid=38885&sourcetype=Scholarly%20Journals

Jurníčková, P., Matulayová, N., Olecká, I., Šlechtová, H., Zatloukal, L., & Jurníček, L. (2024). Home-Office managers should get ready for the "New normal.". *Administrative Sciences*, 14(2), 34. DOI:10.3390/admsci14020034

Khan, H., Rehmat, M., Butt, T. H., Farooqi, S., & Asim, J. (2020). Impact of transformational leadership on work performance, burnout and social loafing: A mediation model. *Future Business Journal*, 6(1), 40. Advance online publication. DOI:10.1186/s43093-020-00043-8

Kundu, S. C., Tuteja, P., & Chahar, P. (2022). COVID-19 challenges and employees' stress: Mediating role of family-life disturbance and work-life imbalance. *Employee Relations*, 44(6), 1318–1337. DOI:10.1108/ER-03-2021-0090

Liu, M., Jeon, J., & Lee, J. Y. (2023). Core job resources to improve employee engagement in China: The role of work-life balance, autonomy and expertise. *Asia Pacific Business Review*, ●●●, 1–25. DOI:10.1080/13602381.2023.2241380

Liu, T., Gao, J., Zhu, M., & Jin, S. (2021). Women's Work-Life Balance in Hospitality: Examining its Impact on Organizational commitment. *Frontiers in Psychology*, 12, 625550. Advance online publication. DOI:10.3389/fpsyg.2021.625550 PMID:33633651

Lorentzon, J., Fotoh, L. E., & Mugwira, T. (2023). *Remote auditing and its impacts on auditors' work and work-life balance: auditors' perceptions and implications.* Accounting Research Journal., DOI:10.1108/ARJ-06-2023-0158

Lundqvist, D., Reineholm, C., Ståhl, C., & Wallo, A. (2022). The impact of leadership on employee well-being: On-site compared to working from home. *BMC Public Health*, 22(1), 2154. Advance online publication. DOI:10.1186/s12889-022-14612-9 PMID:36424558

McPhail, R., Chan, X. W., May, R., & Wilkinson, A. (2023). Post-COVID remote working and its impact on people, productivity, and the planet: An exploratory scoping review. *International Journal of Human Resource Management*, 35(1), 154–182. DOI:10.1080/09585192.2023.2221385

Minh, H. T. P., & Long, N. N. (2023). Adaptive resilience in a post-pandemic era: A case of Vietnamese organizations. *Problems and Perspectives in Management*, 21(3), 219–229. DOI:10.21511/ppm.21(3).2023.17

Mirzani, Y. (2023). A STUDY ON LEADERSHIP STYLES AND ITS IMPACT ON ORGANIZATIONAL SUCCESS. *EPRA International Journal of Economics, Business and Management*, 1–19. DOI:10.36713/epra12138

Nikoloski, D., Najdovska, N. T., Nechkoska, R. P., & Pechijareski, L. (2023). The gig economy in the Post-COVID era. In *Contributions to management science* (pp. 93–117). DOI:10.1007/978-3-031-11065-8_4

Nyfoudi, M., Kwon, B., & Wilkinson, A. (2024). Employee voice in times of crisis: A conceptual framework exploring the role of Human Resource practices and Human Resource system strength. *Human Resource Management*, 63(4), 537–553. Advance online publication. DOI:10.1002/hrm.22214

Olore, A. A., Olawande, T. I., George, T. O., Jegede, A., Egharevba, M. E., & Amoo, E. O. (2023). Understanding coping strategies adults adopted to survive during COVID-19 and Post-COVID-19 pandemic. *Open Access Macedonian Journal of Medical Sciences, 11*(E), 89–95. DOI:10.3889/oamjms.2023.8612

Omilion-Hodges, L. M., & Ptacek, J. K. (2021). What is the Leader–Member Exchange (LMX) Theory? In *New perspectives in organizational communication* (pp. 3–25). DOI:10.1007/978-3-030-68756-4_1

Paesen, H., Wouters, K., & Maesschalck, J. (2019). Servant leaders, ethical followers? The effect of servant leadership on employee deviance. *Leadership and Organization Development Journal*, 40(5), 624–646. DOI:10.1108/LODJ-01-2019-0013

Perreault, M., & Power, N. (2021). Work-life balance as a personal responsibility: The impact on strategies for coping with interrole conflict. *Journal of Occupational Science*, 30(2), 160–174. DOI:10.1080/14427591.2021.1894596

Putri, A., & Amran, A. (2021). Employees' Work-Life Balance Reviewed from work from home aspect during COVID-19 pandemic. *International Journal of Management Science and Information Technology*, 1(1), 30. DOI:10.35870/ijmsit.v1i1.231

Putri, N. K., Melania, M. K. N., Fatmawati, S., & Lim, Y. C. (2023). How does the work-life balance impact stress on primary healthcare workers during the COVID-19 pandemic? *BMC Health Services Research*, 23(1), 730. Advance online publication. DOI:10.1186/s12913-023-09677-0 PMID:37408024

Quinteros-Durand, R., Almanza-Cabe, R. B., Morales-García, W. C., Mamani-Benito, Ó., Sairitupa-Sanchez, L. Z., Puño-Quispe, L., Saintila, J., Saavedra-Sandoval, R., Paredes, A. F., & Ramírez-Coronel, A. A. (2023). Influence of servant leadership on the life satisfaction of basic education teachers: The mediating role of satisfaction with job resources. *Frontiers in Psychology*, 14, 1167074. Advance online publication. DOI:10.3389/fpsyg.2023.1167074 PMID:38023005

Robert, V., & Vandenberghe, C. (2022). Laissez-faire leadership and employee well-being: The contribution of perceived supervisor organizational status. *European Journal of Work and Organizational Psychology*, 31(6), 940–957. DOI:10.1080/1 359432X.2022.2081074

Sharma, A., Sharma, R. B., & Ramawat, R. (2020). THE EFFECT OF LEADERSHIP STYLE AND STRESS OUTCOMES OF ACADEMIC LEADERS. *INTERNATIONAL JOURNAL OF ADVANCED RESEARCH IN ENGINEERING AND TECHNOLOGY (IJARET), 11*(7), 197–207. https://iaeme.com/Home/article_id/IJARET_11_07_021

Sharma, A. S. (2023). Work and life balance post COVID-19. In *Advances in psychology, mental health, and behavioral studies (APMHBS) book series* (pp. 172–186). DOI:10.4018/978-1-6684-8565-1.ch011

Shirmohammadi, M., Au, W. C., & Beigi, M. (2022). Remote work and work-life balance: Lessons learned from the covid-19 pandemic and suggestions for HRD practitioners. *Human Resource Development International*, 25(2), 163–181. DOI: 10.1080/13678868.2022.2047380

Šímová, T. (2022). A research framework for digital nomadism: A bibliometric study. *World Leisure Journal*, 65(2), 175–191. DOI:10.1080/16078055.2022.2134200

Steinmann, B., Klug, H. J. P., & Maier, G. W. (2018). The Path Is the Goal: How Transformational Leaders Enhance Followers' Job Attitudes and Proactive Behavior. *Frontiers in Psychology*, 9, 2338. Advance online publication. DOI:10.3389/fpsyg.2018.02338 PMID:30555375

Strassburger, C., Wachholz, F., Peters, M., Schnitzer, M., & Blank, C. (2022). Organizational leisure benefits – a resource to facilitate employees' work-life balance? *Employee Relations*, 45(3), 585–602. DOI:10.1108/ER-10-2021-0428

Uddin, M. (2021). Addressing work-life balance challenges of working women during COVID-19 in Bangladesh. *International Social Science Journal*, 71(239–240), 7–20. DOI:10.1111/issj.12267 PMID:34230685

Verma, A., Venkatesan, M., Kumar, M., & Verma, J. (2022). The future of work post Covid-19: Key perceived HR implications of hybrid workplaces in India. *Journal of Management Development*, 42(1), 13–28. DOI:10.1108/JMD-11-2021-0304

Vincent, J., & Baptiste, M. (2021). The impact of a democratic leadership style on employee satisfaction, customer satisfaction, and customer loyalty at a midsized nonprofit sport and recreation center. *Global Sport Business Journal, 9*(1), 79–101. http://www.gsbassn.com/Journal/Vol9-1/GSBJ-Vol9-Iss1-Baptisti-pp79-101.pdf

Wong, K., Teh, P., & Chan, A. H. S. (2023). Seeing the Forest and the Trees: A scoping Review of Empirical Research on Work-Life Balance. *Sustainability (Basel)*, 15(4), 2875. DOI:10.3390/su15042875

Yusuf, J., Saitgalina, M., & Chapman, D. W. (2020). Work-life balance and well-being of graduate students. *Journal of Public Affairs Education*, 26(4), 458–483. DOI:10.1080/15236803.2020.1771990

Zhang, J., Wang, Y., & Gao, F. (2023). The dark and bright side of laissez-faire leadership: Does subordinates' goal orientation make a difference? *Frontiers in Psychology*, 14, 1077357. Advance online publication. DOI:10.3389/fpsyg.2023.1077357 PMID:37008876

Chapter 7
Green Human Resource Management in the Textile Industry for Conflict Management

Tanushree Gupta

G.L. Bajaj Group of Institutions, Mathura, India

Hari Prapan Sharma

https://orcid.org/0000-0002-8419-584X

GLA University, Mathura, India

ABSTRACT

GHRM or Green Human Resource Management refers to the use of environmentally friendly as well as environmentally conscious practices across the whole Human Resource Management function. Policies, practices, and systems that encourage green and environmentally sound resource implementation among an organization's staff are called green as well as sustainable practices, respectively. The goal of this work is to show how Human Resource Management can go green without sacrificing effectiveness. The United States, China, and the United Kingdom are among the fastest-developing countries in terms of Green HR laws and practices. The rest of the emerging world is right behind them. Today, sustainable fashion is at the forefront of the textile industry. . McDonagh drafted a green management plan in 1997, but it's unclear when GHRM was first developed. Human resource activities including hiring, orientation, training, promoting, assessing performance, and setting salaries are all part of the plan.

DOI: 10.4018/979-8-3693-4412-5.ch007

1. INTRODUCTION

As a result of the worldwide spread of industrialization, the world's ecosystems are deteriorating, posing serious issues for modern society. This means that businesses need to take the initiative when it comes to environmental management. Moreover, businesses must have a feeling of accountability to the planet including its economic aims. Because it was concerned for the environment, The business has gone green by adopting environmentally friendly practices and creating sustainable products. Therefore, it is necessary to establish an Environmental Management System (EMS). That was discovered that "organizational citizenship behavior for ecology completely links the relationship among strategic management of human resources as well as environmental performance," thereby bridging the gap across Environmental Management as well as Human Resource Management (HRM) (Paillé, et al., 2014). The consistent view numerous scholars have argued that effective HRM practices lead to achieving environmental concert. The interconnectedness of environmental management and HRM has been noted by several other authors. Integrating environmental HRM is a relatively new concept, known as "Green Human Resource Management" (GHRM) (Ren, et al., 2018). Sustainability is a field of study since it integrates environmental considerations with HRM policies and practices. Businesses need to take the initiative to address environmental concerns in the workplace. They must feel an absolute obligation to care for the planet. To reach environmental goals, HRM must implement green policies across a variety of HRM functions (Sathasivam, et al., 2021). Sustainability may be aided by combining environmental management with human resource management.

Figure 1. A General Explanation of GHRM

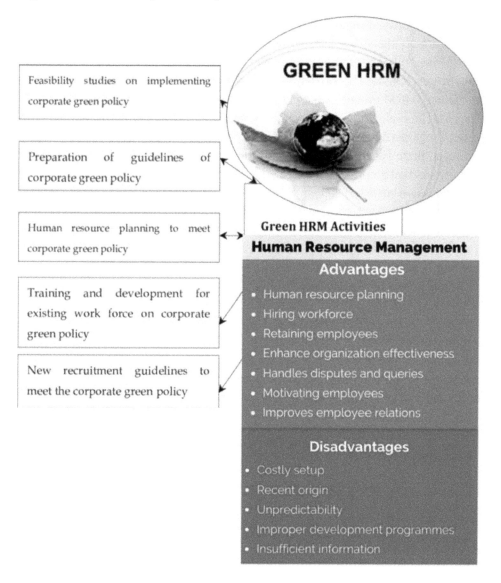

Negative environmental impact may be mitigated by the use of GHRM practices, which foster an upbeat attitude towards the environment among workers. Improved long-term effectiveness is the ultimate aim of GHRM. Employee participation in environmental decision-making, environmental education, and the encouragement of eco-friendly practices are all essential components of GHRM. It raises environmental awareness, converts workers into "green employees," and guarantees their full engagement in achieving organizational goals (Agrawal & Bansal, 2022). All

HRM procedures should be carried out with green initiatives in mind and waste should be minimized for the organization to reach its green aims. There are major holes in the existing literature that need filling. The conceptualizations in the GHRM literature are either too restricted or not founded on academic theory. Disparate GHRM methods with minimal to no overlap have been discovered in theoretical publications. On the flip side, a plethora of theoretical works has uncovered supplementary HRM practices that may aid in the rollout of environmental programs. The terms "recruitment,""performance evaluation,""pay/reward systems,""empowerment/engagement," and "organizational learning" all refer to these processes. However, there is still a need for a unifying theory and empirical confirmation in frameworks that combine a broader range of GHRM practices with GSCM. Some academics and businesspeople have tried to assess where GHRM is at the moment. For example, Renwick et al. highlighted the role of GHRM in HRM by reviewing research articles from 1988-2011 and classifying the relevant material completely. They also discussed the GHRM research agenda and road plan for the future. The need for conceptualization and operationalization of the multiple linked notions is also emphasized by Opatha and Arulrajah, who established a foundational understanding of GHRM (Kodua, et al., 2022). The research published between 2008 and 2017 was analyzed by Ren et al. They paid special attention to the theoretical underpinnings of GHRM and its operational definitions. Recent developments and the numerous GHRM measurement scales were ignored in the aforementioned investigations (Naz, et al., 2023). This study filled such gaps by laying down all of the relevant information on the state of the art in GHRM research. The present study's other distinctive feature is its overview of the existing methods for gauging the idea. Therefore, the current study has concentrated on investigating the many components and measuring instruments of GHRM through a literature review and a variety of empirical experiments. The research review and subsequent attempts to achieve the study's aims are presented in Figure 1.

2. REVIEW OF LITERATURE

Al-Alawnel et al. (2024) examine the direct correlation between green human resource management (GHRM) practices and environmental performance (EP) in Palestinian universities, as well as the intermediary influence of management support (MS) and green organizational culture (GOC) in this correlation. This study presents a theoretical framework and empirical data that demonstrate the relationship between GHRM (Global Human Resource Management), GOC (Global Organizational Culture), MS (Management Strategy), and EP (Employee Performance), specifically in the context of universities. These study findings can be utilized by educational institutions to cultivate an environmentally conscious culture and secure support from high-ranking executives. This strategy encourages the implementation of environmentally sustainable activities and the formulation of initiatives that can have an impact on environmental protection.

Yushi et al. (2024) examine the determinants of implementing Green Human Resource Management techniques that can improve the corporate social performance in the banking industry of Pakistan. The data is gathered from professionals in various banks holding different positions. The utilized methodologies consist of two integrated Multiple Criteria Decision Making (MCDM) methods, namely Interpretive Structural Modeling (ISM) and Decision Making Trial and Evaluation Laboratory (DEMATEL). This research enhances the existing understanding of the components involved by creating a framework that integrates the triple theory approach. This framework will be valuable for effectively implementing GHRM and enhancing Corporate Social Performance. This study provides valuable insights on how companies can improve their social reputation through various GHRM activities. By educating their staff on GHRM practices and fostering a green culture within the organization and society, enterprises can effectively boost their social standing. The study is beneficial for businesses, governments, and industries to enhance their social performance through the implementation of GHRM methods. Tanova, et al., (2022) conducted a systematic analysis of 48 articles to compare the measurement scales used for Green HRM, examine the theoretical frameworks employed in the empirical papers, and identify the nomological network that explains the relationship between Green HRM and its antecedents, outcomes, as well as mediators or moderators. Additionally, address significant concerns pertaining to the present condition of Global Human Resource Management (GHRM) in service companies and suggest potential directions for future investigation. Correia, et al., (2024) aims to determine the implementation of Green Human Resource Management (GHRM) principles through green innovation and its impact on the sustainable performance of healthcare organizations. This study examines how risk management influences the relationship between green innovation, GHRM practices, and sustainable performance. This study examines the links described below using a sample of 400 respondents from both government and non-government hospitals in Pakistan. The PLS-SEM approach is utilized to assess the structural framework of sustainable performance. The findings indicate that the implementation of GHRM practices has a beneficial impact on sustainable performance by promoting green innovation. Moreover, risk management plays a crucial role in mitigating the impact of GHRM practices on green innovation, ultimately leading to improved sustainable performance. Implementing green human resource management (GHRM) methods in an environmentally friendly setting provides valuable guidance for senior executives and policymakers in healthcare companies. It enables the development of a culture of green innovation, which helps reduce risks and enhance sustainable performance.

Iqbal, et al., (2024) investigate the impact of green human resource management (GHRM) practices on employees' environmental commitment (EEC) and organizational citizenship behavior for the environment (OCBE), with harmonious environmental passion (HEP) acting as a mediator. The results indicated that the implementation of GHRM practices had a substantial impact on both employee engagement and organizational citizenship behavior towards the organization. In addition, High Employee Performance (HEP) played a role in partially mediating the connection between Good Human Resource Management (GHRM) practices and Employee Engagement and Organizational Citizenship Behavior (OCBE). This study offers novel insights into the unattended affective processes that explain the connection between GHRM practices and green employee outcomes, using a comprehensive theoretical framework of AET. The statement highlights that the implementation of GHRM practices as a strategic decision can effectively stimulate High Employee Performance (HEP) among employees. This is a crucial factor in shaping employees' environmentally friendly attitudes and behaviors.

Farooq, et al., (2022) utilize Social Cognitive Theory to investigate the correlation between GHRM and green creativity (GC). Furthermore, we analyze the role of green self-efficacy (GSE) as a mediator and green transformational leadership (GTL) as a moderator to offer comprehensive insights into how firms can effectively inspire employees to develop creative solutions for environmental issues. The model is evaluated by examining multi-wave and multi-source data gathered from upscale resorts and hotels. The results validate a direct correlation between GHRM and GC, and also demonstrate that GSE acts as a mediator in the relationship between GHRM and GC. However, there is little evidence to support the idea that GTL has a moderating effect on the indirect impact of GHRM on GC. The results of our research can assist tourism firms in enhancing employees' creativity, thereby facilitating the adoption of environmentally friendly practices and promoting the alignment of these organizations with sustainable development objectives.

Lu, et al., (2023) propose and examine the connections between sustainable HRM practices, employee resilience, job engagement, and employee performance. The empirical findings from a study conducted in China, which involved multiple levels and sources of data, offer supportive evidence for our theoretical framework. The results indicate that implementing sustainable HRM practices has a beneficial impact on employee resilience and promotes a high degree of job engagement among employees. Employee resilience indirectly influences employee performance by affecting job engagement. This study uncovers a sequential mediation process by which sustainable HRM practices positively impact both employee well-being and employee performance, leading to significant theoretical and practical consequences.

Adopting a resource-based perspective (RBV), we examine and clarify HRM's effect on profit margins for small and medium-sized manufacturers in Saudi Arabia. HRM and business strategy already have established connections between human capital with company success (Singh, *et al.*, 2020). Companies that use a resource-based approach consider the potential impact on edge over others and the performance of maximizing the use of important, rare, and difficult-to-imitate strategically valuable assets.(Sharma & Kumar, 2022) Important assets are those that give an organization a long-term competitive edge by making it either difficult for its rivals to replicate its success or prohibitively expensive for them to emulate (Pagan, *et al., 2020*). An organization's competitive edge and high level of performance may be maintained and improved by the use of RBV-based GHRM practices (Hameed, *et al.*, 2022). When included in a company's intricate social structure, human capital often meets the RBV criterion, since it has the potential to improve overall performance and provide the business an edge in the marketplace. The next section is dedicated to hypothesis construction; we employ RBV (Faisal, 2023) to build arguments and offer many hypotheses that may be tested experimentally in future studies, as was mentioned before.

3. ABOUT GHRM

Human resource management that prioritizes environmental sustainability includes measures such as reducing or eliminating pollution and creating artificial environments that mimic the natural world, as depicted in Figure 2. Consequently, a green individual takes into account and acts against these factors. GHRM is more effective in minimizing resource use and throwing away unnecessary items (Ren & Hussain, 2022). To better serve people, communities, and the environment, GHRM entails "policies, practices, and procedures that make staff members of the organization green." Thus, GHRM includes everything associated with sustainable HRM. According to Ren & Hussain, 2022, "Green Human Resource Management" incorporates several eco-friendly practices. Renwick, *et al.*, (2013) discussed the importance of GHRM in HRM by reviewing the research on ability-motivation-opportunity (AMO). Competence, motivation, and opportunity to make ecologically responsible choices are the three most important factors in GHRM (Jiuhua, *et al.*, 2011).

Figure 2. Aim and Essential Elements of GHRM

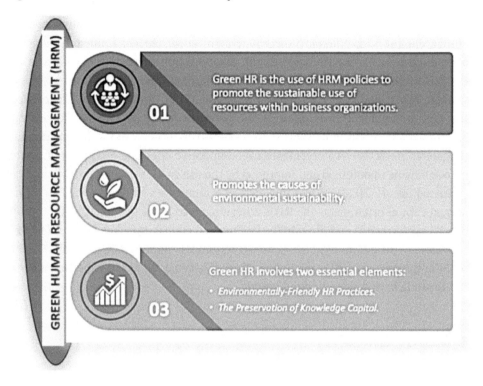

4. THE PRESENT AND FUTURE OF GHRM-WITH RESPECT TO TEXTILE INDUSTRY

Currently, GHRM practices are being used by large corporations, particularly in developed to achieve green organizational goals. By getting employees and businesses involved in green projects, GHRM assures ecological sustainability and boosts competitiveness. For businesses to truly be sustainable, they must fully embrace and implement green practices. Even while GHRM is being adopted by businesses in the developed world, there is still a lack of systematic GHRM-HRM integration in the nations that are developing (Jia, et al., 2018)). In doing so, we can better address environmental and associated problems. Extensive research indicates that applying GHRM can help businesses meet environmental objectives and address related issues.

More studies on Both industrialized and underdeveloped nations require GHRM, with the latter receiving the lion's share of attention because it is there that the majority of large textile-based industrial facilities can be found. To better preserve the natural ecosystem, GHRM practices can assist raise awareness among workers about the need of protecting it. Therefore, sustainability is a major problem that must be solved, and GHRM is the path to making an organization sustainable (Aggarwal & Sharma, 2015). Human resource practices that are more environmentally friendly encourage paperless offices, online job postings, and greener building designs. There has been a rise in environmental preservation consciousness throughout the globe, and governments have responded by passing laws meant to promote long-term environmental sustainability.(Sharma & Chaturvedi 2020) GHRM has grabbed the attention of many experts because it can satisfy environmental concerns while also enabling companies to have a win-win scenario, providing them with an on-going advantage over their competitors. The application of GHRM in this setting is highly promising (Leidner, et al., 2019). GHRM factors common methods and procedures used to achieve an organization's environmental goals are incorporated within GHRM., as depicted in Figure 3.

Figure 3. Green Human Resource Management Models

1. Green Job Analysis & Design: This is a necessary step before GHRM can be put into action. In sustainable job creation and evaluation, businesses must identify the job's purpose, function, and duties in light of the company's green goals (Arulrajah, *et al.*, 2015). Furthermore, environmentally conscious businesses need to develop brand-new roles dedicated to managing the company's environmental impact. Both social as well as technical criteria for a position must be laid out in the position description, with the former focusing on the specifics of the work environment.

2. Green Selection via Recruitment: Many academics contend that green recruiting, as well as selection, underpins a real-world application of GHRM (Tsymbaliuk, *et al.*, 2023). We now explore environmentally responsible hiring practices:

    a. Green Recruitment statistics: The goal of green recruiting for find as well as attract environmentally conscious job seekers to apply for current and future jobs. To truly captivate today's youth, the next step is to use GHRM practices. Employer branding occurs when companies promote their policies via their websites (Abdali, 2019). Internet-based hiring frequently includes questions on the applicant's environmental values and the organization's culture. Job-seekers read this, and if the company seems like a good fit for their ideals and goals, they're more likely to apply for a position there.

    b. Green Selection: Selecting candidates based on their level of green knowledge through a variety of selection methods is known as "green selection". When done right, green recruiting creates a pool of qualified applicants from whom to hire. For environmental progress, green selection is crucial, as indicated by Yusliza, *et al.*, (2019). Selecting environmentally conscious workers up front helps cut down on training expenses. Candidates should be screened to ensure they have an appreciation for the environment and an openness to making beneficial changes. Ali, *et al.*, (2020) state that a green selection procedure guarantees that the candidate is qualified based on the organization's established selection criteria. A candidate's green consciousness and green values may be evaluated with real-world selection techniques.

3. Green Training and Development: A company's success in hiring environmentally conscious workers will shine if it invests in its training. As a result, it is crucial to do a requirements assessment before delivering training. To better prepare workers to apply environmental management practices, "green training" seeks to better equip them with the knowledge and skills necessary to do so. in the place of work (Tang, *et al.*, 2018). As a result, whether or not their work directly involves the environment, the company should give environmentally friendly education to all workers. Training on efficient energy use, trash disposal, and the cultivation of environmentally friendly behaviors should be made available

to all employees, as suggested by Altarawneh, (2016). The company should also implement a system of work rotation. Knowledge management, understanding the environment, and environmental preservation actions are the three components of green training outlined by Shoaih, *et al.*, (2021).

4. Green Performance Management: Green performance management guarantees that all employees work together to ensure that the company's green goals are achieved. Long-term performance is difficult to gauge in its absence (Harvey, *et al.*, 2013). The employee's performance should be evaluated in part according to the company's environmental obligations and rules.(Tarkar, 2022) Thus, workers will feel increased pressure to address environmental concerns and enhance their contribution to the environment. Managers are responsible for communicating the rules and responsibilities of their division or department, as well as setting precise and achievable green goals. Any environmental management goals not met should result in the manager being held responsible.

5. Green Reward System: Green incentives should support the company's environmental goals, as stated by Chaudhary (2019). Green incentives are restricted to enhancing environmental performance.

5. DISCUSSION

A comprehensive literature review was conducted for this investigation of the relevant literature and empirical investigations to investigate the various components and measurement instruments of GHRM. From 2010 to 2024, 37 empirical publications on GHRM were found in the Scopus database. The author used a five-stage approach to find the 37 examined empirical studies, including the selection of the database, the breadth of the search, the criteria used to choose articles, the method used to categorize those articles, including the methods used to generate results. It was found that the criteria, variables, and instruments utilized to assess GHRM vary widely. There is as much divergence among the many definitions as there are academics who have tried to describe it. Consistent with this, variables were found in this study by employing the AMO conceptual framework. The terms "Green recruitment and selection" and "Green training and development" are two ways that "Ability" contributes to building green capabilities (Hameed, *et al.*, 2020). These skills boost imagination and lead to novel approaches to improving environmental performance. The motivation offered by AMO theory entails establishing a suitable evaluation and reward system to promote environmentally responsible actions. As with Green performance management, Green compensation management also boosts productivity in the green sector. Opportunity focuses on the facilitation of Green

Employee empowerment and engagement via the development of chances to improve green behavior (Ahmad, *et al.*, 2021). The morale of workers has been boosted towards environmentally friendly actions thanks to Green Employee Relations. The differences in what makes up GHRM were also highlighted by the study's author. According to the analysis, HRM elements were constrained mostly to HRM acquisition, HRM training, and HRM performance management (Ribeiro, *et al.*, 2022). The research did not find any articles that provided a holistic perspective on the components that contribute to GHRM. Eco-friendly Education and Progress, Conservation-minded hiring and picking, Ethical Methods of Compensation Administration, and Green performance management were found to be the most often employed aspects in the study. Several other crucial elements needed for complete GHRM representation were uncovered in the present investigation. It is important to incorporate the mentioned variables while conducting empirical research concerning GHRM, such as Facilitating Green Relations with employees and Involving Green Staff Members. Likewise, there existed a wide range of options for quantifying GHRM.

6. GHRM ORGANIZATIONAL OUTCOMES

Overall, the AMO(Ability-Motivation-Opportunity) framework is a better fit for studies that examine the organizational results of GHRM practices, whether they employ a global score or focus on certain aspects. The odds of an organization improving its green performance are greater if it equips its workers with the knowledge, resources, and support they need to start caring about the environment and doing something about it (Tsymbaljuk, *et al.*, 2021). Purcell et al. argues that establishing a connection between HRM practices and organizational success relies heavily on the dedication and initiative of employees. Indeed, the authors say that the spread of practices related to specific behaviors increases as employee motivation and commitment to such behaviors increase. When looking at GHRM as a mediator linking green employee behaviors and green organizational performance, selected publications found comparable results (Shoaib, *et al.*, 2021). Incorporating in an identical model the GHRM effects on both green employee behaviors and organizational results for example, demonstrates a close connection between this framework and research addressing GHRM repercussions for both employee and organization-related outcomes, as depicted in Figure 4 and Table 1 shows the benefits of GHRM.

Figure 4. Outcomes of GHRM

Table 1. Benefits of GHRM

BENEFITS	RESULTS	REFERENCE
Individual green values	Using green employee empowerment, Indirectly, GHRM has a substantial impact on OCBE (environmental citizenship behavior in organizations). Worker green empowerment and its positive outcomes and OCBE were further tempered by the fact that people's green values varied.	Shoaih, *et al.*, (2021)
Green behavior	According to structural equation modeling, GHRM does play a moderating function between ethical leadership and environmentally conscious actions in the workplace. The studies also showed that an increase in green behavior caused by ethical leadership through GHRM is amplified when employees have environmental expertise.	(Ahmad, *et al.*, 2021)
Green competency	The scope of GHRM is expansive, including not only the promotion of environmentally responsible conduct but also the development of novel environmental projects by staff members. The investigation confirmed the importance of green concerns and green economic growth in Ukraine but found little evidence of the broad use of GHRM methods.	Tsymbaljuk, *et al.*, (2021)

continued on following page

Table 1. Continued

BENEFITS	RESULTS	REFERENCE
Green Commitment	HRM practices are essential in implementing an environmental strategy that encourages eco-friendly actions on the job. The results can help management and policymakers better understand the part GHRM plays in fostering green workplace cultures and practices.	Ribeiro, *et al.*, (2022)
Company Positive response	Organizational identification acts as a mediator between green HRM and workers' eco-friendly behavior, and both are positively affected by the introduction of green HRM practices in tourist organizations.	Hameed, *et al.*, (2020)

7. CONCLUSIONS, LIMITATIONS, AND FUTURE DIRECTIONS

The current study aids in shedding the way GHRM may be realized, what organizational and employee-related aspects affect how it is carried out, and what organizational and employee-related results arise by systematizing existing information on these topics. Given the abundance of theoretical along with prescriptive papers on GHRM and the monetary and non-monetary resources required for implementation, an analysis of current research accomplishments could prove useful to both academics and practitioners in confirming the results of GHRM methods, and to promote their broad use. This study also helps to identify the causes and effects of GHRM practices as they relate to employees, which is useful for understanding how to get workers interested in green initiatives and how they could affect an organization's green performance. In conclusion, our analysis reveals the following: (1) The bulk of studies using data from underdeveloped countries were published in 2018, and there is also a geographical pattern of studies being released in 2018. (2) Approximately half of the research treats GHRM as a unified concept, whereas the other half takes into account a broader variety of factors. (3) Multifaceted studies frequently investigate issues including instruction and refinement, monitoring and appraisal of performance, salary, and benefits, and personnel choice and placement. (4) While many studies have focused on the impacts of GHRM on organizations, few have examined the impact of GHRM on individual workers. However, there are constraints to this approach. To begin, our qualifying criteria did not include publications written in languages other than English, despite the possibility that such studies might have added significantly to our evaluation. Second, we did not include papers presented at conferences, thus we may have missed some crucial data on ongoing GHRM research and treatments. The crucial features and applications of GHRM are depicted in Figure 5.

Figure 5. Crucial Features and Applications of GHRM

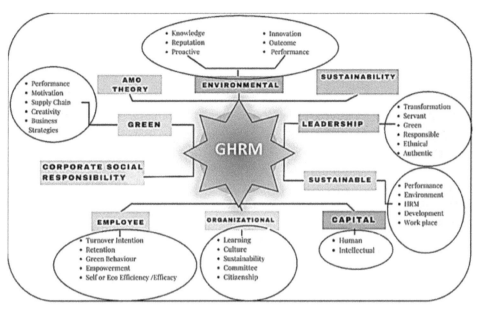

Employee engagement and participation in sustainability forums can contribute to conflict management within GHRM. Implementing a decision-making framework about environmental practices within firms fosters a sense of accountability and dedication among workers. This engagement reduces the likelihood of conflicts arising due to a perception of authority and control, allowing employees to independently improve sustainability initiatives.Furthermore, GHRM facilitates transparent communication channels about the implementation of environmental schemes and practices. Transparent communication involves effectively communicating the purpose and significance of sustainability programs within the firm. Consequently, this resulted in unintentional errors due to the absence of clear guidelines and misunderstandings of signals, resulting to conflicts. However, these conflicts can be minimized by transparency.In addition, GHRM focuses on developing training programs tailored to the specific needs of employees in order to enhance their understanding of environmental issues and acquire new competencies. Training provides employees with guidance on the importance of sustainability in the firm and helps them understand how to incorporate it into their daily life. These individuals have developed the expertise to quickly detect and resolve environmental issues, thereby preventing disputes that may arise from non-compliance or resistance to change. GHRM offers opportunity to establish communication tools to validate stakeholder issues and address grievances connected to environmental concerns. Employees can actively participate in sustainability initiatives by utilizing the available platforms to voice their opinions, address any concerns regarding sustainability processes, and propose potential enhancements. This method will allow organizations to rapidly resolve difficulties and prevent conflicts from escalating into larger challenges. The textile sector improves the sustainable environment and potentially reduces disputes by using GHRM practices such as employee participation, transparent communication, training programs, and feedback mechanisms. Implementing GHRM policies will create a more pleasant corporate environment, as employees will be motivated to contribute not only to the success of the corporation, but also to environmental protection.

To avoid the "organization as a black box" effect, or the inability to understand the contexts and cultures that drive the organization, the current evidence-based literature on GHRM might be enhanced by recognizing and addressing several outstanding difficulties. To begin, researchers and policymakers might benefit from the information that helps place GHRM practices in context, including an examination of their origins and how they affect businesses and individuals. One way to determine which GHRM strategies are best for a given circumstance is to compile data on the features and culture of organizations that employ GHRM. Second, the vast majority of the articles considered for this analysis (except for those belonging to the textile/financial as well as educational industries) got data from for-profit organizations, therefore GHRM practices in nonprofit as well as public contexts are underrepresented. Examining if the current dearth of reliable data results from a lack of dedication to environmental problems or a lack of interest on the part of academics, it would be fascinating to take on these organizations. Organizational initiatives toward greener performance would be better situated with knowledge of the macroeconomic, social, and cultural framework in which they function. That is to say, in the future, scholars may want to investigate the organizational factors that affect GHRM's efficacy but aren't directly tied to it. Despite an enormous amount of descriptive as well as prescriptive publications on GHRM, recent evidence-based research on GHRM determinants and repercussions for individuals and organizations demonstrates the emphasis on certain GHRM aspects, in particular nations and particular sorts of organizations. Such details call for a more in-depth understanding of what GHRM means for both leaders and staff members, the sorts of demands it puts on the organization and the day-to-day activities of employees, and how it meets the requirements and incentives of the entire organization, and the individual. The European Union and the United States-based for-profit business sector might also be affected by these factors. Potential benefits for both academics and professionals from a more robust use of qualitative methodologies to address these issues and, if necessary, to revise the GHRM idea and its application to study and intervention.

REFERENCES

Abdali, M. (2019). The strategic use of digital learning solutions: An HRM perspective (Doctoral dissertation, Auckland University of Technology).

Aggarwal, S., & Sharma, B. (2015). Green HRM: Need of the hour. *International Journal of Management and Social Science Research Review*, 1(8), 63–70.

Agrawal, N., & Bansal, R. (2022). Green HRM: A medium of social responsibility and sustainable development. *International Journal of Innovation and Sustainable Development*, 16(2), 172–185.

Ahmad, S., Islam, T., Sadiq, M., & Kaleem, A. (2021). Promoting green behavior through ethical leadership: A model of green human resource management and environmental knowledge. *Leadership and Organization Development Journal*, 42(4), 531–547.

Al-Alawneh, R., Othman, M., & Zaid, A. A. (2024). Green HRM impact on environmental performance in higher education with mediating roles of management support and green culture. *The International Journal of Organizational Analysis*, 32(6), 1141–1164.

Ali, M. C., Islam, K. A., Chung, S. J., Zayed, N. M., & Afrin, M. (2020). A study of Green Human Resources Management (GHRM) and green creativity for human resources professionals. *International Journal of Business and Management Future*, 4(2), 57–67.

Altarawneh, I. I. (2016). Strategic human resources management and its impact on performance: The case from Saudi Arabia. *International Journal of Business Management and Economic Research*, 7(1).

Arulrajah, A. A., Opatha, H. H. D. N. P., & Nawaratne, N. N. J. (2015). Green human resource management practices. *RE:view*.

Chaudhary, R. (2019). Green human resource management in the Indian automobile industry. *Journal of Global Responsibility*, 10(2), 161–175.

Correia, A. B., Farrukh Shahzad, M., Moleiro Martins, J., & Baheer, R. (2024). Impact of green human resource management towards sustainable performance in the healthcare sector: Role of green innovation and risk management. *Cogent Business & Management*, 11(1), 2374625.

Faisal, S. (2023). Green human resource management—A synthesis. *Sustainability*, 15(3), 2259.

Farooq, R., Zhang, Z., Talwar, S., & Dhir, A. (2022). Do green human resource management and self-efficacy facilitate green creativity? A study of luxury hotels and resorts. *Journal of Sustainable Tourism*, 30(4), 824–845.

Hameed, Z., Khan, I. U., Islam, T., Sheikh, Z., & Naeem, R. M. (2020). Do green HRM practices influence employees' environmental performance? *International Journal of Manpower*, 41(7), 1061–1079.

Hameed, Z., Naeem, R. M., Hassan, M., Naeem, M., Nazim, M., & Maqbool, A. (2022). How GHRM is related to green creativity? A moderated mediation model of green transformational leadership and green perceived organizational support. *International Journal of Manpower*, 43(3), 595–613.

Harvey, G., Williams, K., & Probert, J. (2013). Greening the airline pilot: HRM and the green performance of airlines in the UK. *International Journal of Human Resource Management*, 24(1), 152–166.

Iqbal, R., Shahzad, K., & Chaudhary, R. (2024). Green human resource management practices as a strategic choice for enhancing employees' environmental outcomes: An affective events theory perspective. *International Journal of Manpower*, 45(4), 801–819.

Jia, J., Liu, H., Chin, T., & Hu, D. (2018). The continuous mediating effects of GHRM on employees' green passion via transformational leadership and green creativity. *Sustainability*, 10(9), 3237.

Jiang, Y., Zaman, S. I., Jamil, S., Khan, S. A., & Kun, L. (2024). A triple theory approach to link corporate social performance and green human resource management. *Environment, Development and Sustainability*, 26(6), 15733–15776.

Jiuhua Zhu, C., Thomson, S. B., Hutchings, K., & Cieri, H. D. (2011). Extending the investment development path model to include the human environment factor. *Thunderbird International Business Review*, 53(3), 311–324.

Kodua, L. T., Xiao, Y., Adjei, N. O., Asante, D., Ofosu, B. O., & Amankona, D. (2022). Barriers to green human resources management (GHRM) implementation in developing countries. Evidence from Ghana. *Journal of Cleaner Production*, 340, 130671.

Leidner, S., Baden, D., & Ashleigh, M. J. (2019). Green (environmental) HRM: Aligning ideals with appropriate practices. *Personnel Review*, 48(5), 1169–1185.

Lu, Y., Zhang, M. M., Yang, M. M., & Wang, Y. (2023). Sustainable human resource management practices, employee resilience, and employee outcomes: Toward common good values. *Human Resource Management*, 62(3), 331–353.

Naz, S., Jamshed, S., Nisar, Q. A., & Nasir, N. (2023). Green HRM, psychological green climate and pro-environmental behaviors: An efficacious drive towards environmental performance in China. *Current Psychology (New Brunswick, N.J.)*, 42(2), 1346–1361.

Pagán-Castaño, E., Maseda-Moreno, A., & Santos-Rojo, C. (2020). Wellbeing in work environments. *Journal of Business Research*, 115, 469–474.

Paillé, P., Chen, Y., Boiral, O., & Jin, J. (2014). The impact of human resource management on environmental performance: An employee-level study. *Journal of Business Ethics*, 121, 451–466.

Ren, S., Tang, G., & Jackson, E, S. (2018). Green human resource management research in emergence: A review and future directions. *Asia Pacific Journal of Management*, 35, 769–803.

Ren, Z., & Hussain, R. Y. (2022). A mediated–moderated model for green human resource management: An employee perspective. *Frontiers in Environmental Science*, 10, 973692.

Renwick, D. W., Redman, T., & Maguire, S. (2013). Green human resource management: A review and research agenda. *International Journal of Management Reviews*, 15(1), 1–14.

Ribeiro, N., Gomes, D. R., Ortega, E., Gomes, G. P., & Semedo, A. S. (2022). The impact of green HRM on employees' eco-friendly behavior: The mediator role of organizational identification. *Sustainability*, 14(5), 2897.

Sathasivam, K., Che Hashim, R., & Abu Bakar, R. (2021). Automobile industry managers' views on their roles in environmental sustainability: A qualitative study. *Management of Environmental Quality*, 32(5), 844–862.

Sharma, H. P., & Chaturvedi, A. (2020). The performance of India in the achievement of sustainable development Goals: A way forward. *Int. J. Mod. Agric*, 9, 1496–1505.

Sharma, H. P., & Kumar, K. (2022, October). The Uptake of Environmental Management System by Small and Medium Enterprises (SMEs) in India. []. IOP Publishing.]. *IOP Conference Series. Earth and Environmental Science*, 1084(1), 012015.

Shoaib, M., Abbas, Z., Yousaf, M., Zámečník, R., Ahmed, J., & Saqib, S. (2021). The role of GHRM practices towards organizational commitment: A mediation analysis of green human capital. *Cogent Business & Management*, 8(1), 1870798.

Shoaib, M., Abbas, Z., Yousaf, M., Zámečník, R., Ahmed, J., & Saqib, S. (2021). The role of GHRM practices towards organizational commitment: A mediation analysis of green human capital. *Cogent Business & Management*, 8(1), 1870798.

Singh, S. K., Del Giudice, M., Chierici, R., & Graziano, D. (2020). Green innovation and environmental performance: The role of green transformational leadership and green human resource management. *Technological Forecasting and Social Change*, 150, 119762.

Tang, G., Chen, Y., Jiang, Y., Paillé, P., & Jia, J. (2018). Green human resource management practices: Scale development and validity. *Asia Pacific Journal of Human Resources*, 56(1), 31–55.

Tanova, C., & Bayighomog, S. W. (2022). Green human resource management in service industries: The construct, antecedents, consequences, and outlook. *Service Industries Journal*, 42(5-6), 412–452.

Tarkar, P. (2022). Role of green hospitals in sustainable construction: Benefits, rating systems and constraints. *Materials Today: Proceedings*, 60, 247–252.

Tsymbaliuk, S., Vasylyk, A., & Stoliaruk, K. (2021). Green human resource management: how to implement environmental issues into HR practices. In *E3S Web of Conferences* (Vol. 255, p. 01037). EDP Sciences.

Tsymbaliuk, S., Vasylyk, A., & Stoliaruk, K. (2023). Green recruitment and adaptation practices in GHRM. [). IOP Publishing.]. *IOP Conference Series. Earth and Environmental Science*, 1126(1), 012029.

Yusliza, M. Y., Norazmi, N. A., Jabbour, C. J. C., Fernando, Y., Fawehinmi, O., & Seles, B. M. R. P. (2019). Top management commitment, corporate social responsibility, and green human resource management: A Malaysian study. *Benchmarking*, 26(6), 2051–2078.

Chapter 8
Legal Challenges in Managing Human Resources in the Public Sector

Laura Matjošaityte

Kazimieras Simonavičius University, Lithuania

ABSTRACT

This chapter examines the legal challenges facing the public sector in managing human resources, which can hinder excellent and efficient public administration. The chapter examines the legal challenges most encountered in the public sector due to its specific working conditions and legislative and regulatory requirements, such as ensuring equal opportunities, conflicts of interest, ensuring privacy and confidentiality of public servants, and other legally relevant aspects of human resource management in the civil service.

1. INTRODUCTION

"Public sector organizations (also referred to as authority, governmental, and public administration organizations) refer to organizations and institutions aimed at providing services needed by citizens in societies" (Luoma-aho and Canel, 2016).

Human resources management in the public sector is usually subject to various legal challenges, many of which stem from the sector's unique working conditions and specific legal frameworks.

DOI: 10.4018/979-8-3693-4412-5.ch008

The legal challenges typically relate to recruitment, specific requirements, equal opportunities, non-discrimination, trade union, and strike rights, employee disciplinary liability, whistleblower protection, conflicts of interest, employee privacy, health and safety, and pensions and benefits, which will be the main ones highlighted in the analysis of Lithuania's legal framework in this chapter of the book.

2. LEGAL FRAMEWORK

"The concept of human resource management has gained attention from academics and practitioners alike since it first emerged during the mid-1980s" (Kupur, 2017). Human resource management has received much academic attention in recent decades. For example, Akintoye and Beck (Akintoye et al., 2008). have analysed the politics of public-private partnerships; Ammirato, Felicetti et al. have looked at human resource management in the midst of the fourth industrial revolution; Azzizi, Atlasi et al. (Azizi et al., 2021) have explored innovative human resource strategies during the Covid-19 pandemic; Fahim (Fahim, 2018) has studied the relationship between strategic human resource management and retention of employees; and Fenech, Baguant, and Ivanov have examined the changing role of human resources in the digital transformation era; Huang, Yang et al. (Huang et al., 2023) discuss human resources management using artificial intelligence; Yu, Yuan, Han et al. (Yu et al.,2022) explore the impact of strategic human resources management on organisational resilience; Kapur explores the essence of human recources management; Murray, Duleboh et al. (Murray et al., 2024) and Stone, Deadrick (Stone et al., 2015) analyse the future of human resources management; and Kim, Majeed et al.(Kim et al., 2023) examine whether green human resources management provides a competitive edge; Varga (Varga, 2022) studied the state of human resource management and directions for development in the public sector, Enaifoghe (Enaifoghe et al. 2024) examineted drivers digital transformation drivers and their efficacy in improving public sector human resource management in the digital age. Verma, Kumar, Mittal Gupta, and others 13 analyzed the strategic practices of human resource management. Some authors have limited themselves to a specific area or case study. Bambang (Bambang, 2023), for example, has analyzed the challenges of public administration in managing human resources in the education sector.

As G.S. Batra states, human resources are "the most significant and valuable asset that public administrations manage and on which their performance depends"(Batra, 1996).

Infante (Infante & Darmawan, 2022) argues that "human resources are part of the strategic planning process and is part of the development of organizational policies, planning for the expansion of organizational lines, the process of organizational mergers and acquisitions. Wright and McMahan (Wright & McMahan, 1992) define human resource management as "a planned pattern of human resource allocation and activities that enables a firm to achieve its objectives" (Wright & McMahan, 1992). "They argued that the domain of strategic human resources management encompassed 'the determinants of decisions about human resources practices, the composition of human capital resource pools, the specification of the required human resource behaviors, and the effectiveness of these decisions given various business strategies and/or competitive situations'". Some scholars argue that "human resource management in public administration is a continuous and dynamic process focused on selecting and retaining the best employees, creating the right conditions for their development and their ability to realize their existing competencies while delivering the best value to society in the form of services" (Juknevičienė, 2006).

Given that "the public sector is a sector of the economy comprising a multitude of government organizations, agencies, ministries and public institutions that are responsible for the delivery of basic services and the implementation of policies for the welfare and development of society as a whole" (Ferlie & Osborne, 2002), Afzal et al. argue that "public sector HRM is a way of managing human resources in a hierarchy of activities, which acts as a key driver of the effectiveness and efficiency of public-wide growth and development" (Munna et al., 2023).

However, according to Collings et al. (Collings et al., 2021), "since then, research on strategic HRM has focused on the relationship between HR practices and firm performance (Huselid, 1995), or the effect of these practices on the mediating variables between the two" (Boxall et al., 2016). However, HRM in the public sector has not been extensively analysed in comparative terms with the private sector. Although 'the relevance of HRM today has expanded in this changing era of rapid technological breakthroughs, changing demographics, globalization, and evolving work habits' (Munna et al., 2023).

It is important to note how the legal environment of the Lithuanian public sector differs in this context. First, Lithuania's public governance structure is relatively centralized. This, on the one hand, helps to ensure unity of action. However, it may limit local decision-making.

Another aspect in which the legal environment of the Lithuanian public sector is unique is the rigidity of the legal framework. In Lithuania, public sector activities are regulated by rather strict normative legal acts. In other words, only what is explicitly and expressly provided for in the legislation is allowed. The legislation tries to cover the most critical issues so that, in practice, the legal framework can help find a quick answer if unforeseen circumstances arise. However, it has been noted that the rigidity or inflexibility of the legal framework means that changes are prolonged to materialize. In other words, decisions on changes to the legal framework and implementing new legal frameworks could be faster.

Lithuania also stands out in that the public sector constantly needs reform. Various reforms are required to improve efficiency and transparency and adapt to changing economic and other circumstances and conditions.

Of course, an equally important factor that separates Lithuania is the desire to digitize as many processes as possible. The whole legal environment is therefore geared towards encouraging innovation of all kinds.

However, first and foremost, an appropriate legal framework is needed to ensure that human resources, both in the public and the private sector, are properly managed. This must, of course, be constantly improved and reviewed in due course.

Changes in the legal framework are driven by:

1) economic factors—global economic change, increasing competition, and similar factors are encouraging public sector institutions and organizations to seek more efficient models of human resources management, and the legislator is seeking to ensure job stability and economic balance through the legal framework.

2) Technological change: The rapid changes in technology and innovation that occur daily are rapidly changing the nature of work, and the legislator needs to react swiftly to these evolving trends to implement teleworking, ensure the development of information technology, and protect data.

3) Social change—Demographic changes, such as an aging population and migration, both within and outside the country, lead to greater inclusiveness and diversity in the workforce.

4) International standards and commitments: Lithuania's membership of the European Union and other international organizations requires it, as well as other member states, to align its national legislation with international legislation, standards, and best practices.

Each country has a specific legal framework defining the legal relations between civil servants in the public sector. This framework sets working conditions and requirements and helps shape strategies and practices that adapt to social, economic, and technological change.

However, each country's public management system is different. Not only does the definition of a civil servant vary, but also the functions assigned to the civil service. For example, "in France and Spain, the definition of the civil service is comprehensive, with almost all public sector employees being considered civil servants, while in Denmark, Germany and Italy, some university lecturers and teachers are classified as civil servants, and in Latvia, only those working in central level institutions are considered civil servants" (The Department of Statistics of the Republic of Lithuania information).

Comparisons between countries can also be difficult due to their different demographics. Latvia, for example, has one-third fewer inhabitants than Lithuania. Estonia, on the other hand, has more than twice as many. For this reason, the chapter's author discusses the legal challenges of human resources management in Lithuania, which has 435 public sector bodies (i.e., state and municipal institutions and bodies that have been granted public administration powers under the Law on Public Administration) and 64 046 posts (i.e. the number of approved posts in state and municipal institutions (except for the posts of officers of general affairs and criminal intelligence, and persons whose data are classified under the Law on State and Official Secrets of the Republic of Lithuania) is 55 255 (i.e. the number of approved posts in state and municipal institutions and bodies (except for the posts of officers of general affairs and criminal intelligence, and persons whose data are classified under the Law on State and Official Secrets of the Republic of Lithuania) The Department of Statistics of the Republic of Lithuania information).

Thus, one of the leading legal acts is the Labour Code of the Republic of Lithuania, which regulates labor relations, establishes working conditions and sets out employees' rights and obligations. Using regular amendments to the legislation, the legislator improves it, thus promoting flexibility of working time, granting the right to telework, and guaranteeing the right to reconcile work and private life. The legislator also uses the Labour Code to protect workers' rights and fair wages, encourage organizations to comply with the existing legal framework, and ensure that working conditions are appropriate for employees.

The Law on Public Administration of the Republic of Lithuania is another legislation that regulates public administration institutions' activities and lays down the basic principles and ways of organizing the civil service. Through it, the legislator promotes the efficiency of the public sector and establishes criteria for accountability and performance evaluation.

The Law on Equal Opportunities of the Republic of Lithuania, which lays down the principles of equal opportunities and non-discrimination in the workplace, is also particularly relevant to the public sector. It promotes diversity and ensures equal treatment of all employees, regardless of age, gender, race, or other aspects. Through the law, the legislator strengthens specific legal mechanisms to prevent discrimination at work.

The Law on the Harmonisation of Public and Private Interests in the Civil Service of the Republic of Lithuania also applies to civil service employees.

One of the critical pieces of legislation, the Lithuanian legislator has provided that "the basic principles of civil servants' performance and ethics, the general requirements for admission to the post of civil servant, the recruitment and dismissal of civil servants, the career of civil servants, their responsibilities, social and other guarantees related to the peculiarities of their service, the institutions formulating and implementing civil service policy and their competences" the Law regulates 27 on the Lithuanian Civil Service. On the other hand, although the Civil Service Law is a specific legal act regulating the legal relations between civil servants and the civil service, it does not regulate all the issues arising in the context of the legal relationship between the civil service and the civil service in the public sector. This legislation promotes professional and ethical behavior in the civil service and sets out standards of performance and ethics. It also emphasises career progression and sets out criteria for evaluating and promoting civil servants.

Therefore, the Lithuanian legislator, considering that the Law on the Civil Service does not cover the legal regulation of all issues arising in the course of service provided in Article 2(1) of the Law on the Civil Service of the Republic of Lithuania that "the laws and other legal acts regulating the employment relations and social guarantees shall apply to civil servants in so far as this Law does not regulate their status and social guarantees" (The Department of Statistics of the Republic of Lithuania information). In other words, the particular Civil Service Law is the primary legal act regulating the legal relations of persons employed in the civil service. However, this legal act does not regulate certain aspects of civil servants' work in the civil service. In that case, other legal acts regulating labor relations, such as the Labour Code of the Republic of Lithuania, etc., are used in such cases.

However, while "human resources can be a sustainable source of competitive advantage" (Lim et al., 2017) and "in order to ensure organisational efficiency and competitiveness resulting from human work, continuous development of human resource management is necessary, regardless of whether it is a profit-oriented or non-profit organization" (Varga, 2022). Today, the public sector continues to face human resource management problems, as, for example, a decade ago, when scholars stated that "although public administration employs a relatively large number of well-educated and qualified professionals, an imperfect legal framework still hinders the advancement of public administration" (Juknevičienė, 2006). Moreover, as Radebe argues, "policy makers, in order to achieve public sector efficiency, must take primary responsibility for ensuring that legal norms and standards are in place that enable and do not hinder innovative processes" (Radebe, 2009). Furthermore, according to Osborne and Brown, "understanding the complexity of innovation in public policy design and implementation is essential to the innovation processes of public management" (Osborne & Brown, 2011). Meanwhile, suppose the nation's elected representatives need to gain the necessary knowledge to understand why innovation is needed and that its implementation in public policy-making is complicated. In that case, innovative solutions bypass the legislator and the legislation they pass.

One of the challenges facing the public sector is the need for more legal regulation in specific legislation. In the private sector, for example, the Labour Code is used to deal with particular employment issues, and, in its absence, an analogy is sought; in the case of the civil service, problems that a specific Civil Service Law does not regulate are dealt with based on the provisions of the Labour Code. Only when the Labour Code does not contain a specific labor law norm that directly regulates how to resolve a particular labor dispute, and there are also no norms regulating similar labor relations, is the analogy of the law applied.

Another challenge in the public sector related to regulation is the lengthy process of implementing regulatory change. In other words, while in the private sector, internal policies, descriptions, or procedures can be changed at any time, the process is much more complex in the public sector. It takes incomparably longer due to the vast bureaucratic apparatus. Changes to the legal framework governing the work of public sector bodies require legislative amendments to be initiated, adopted, and implemented. However, suppose the legislator adopts legislative amendments urgently without considering the legal regulation in force in other legislation. In that case, a situation may arise in which the legal regulation in one piece of legislation conflicts with the legal regulation in another. In other words, there will be an incompatibility of legal regulation.

Among other things, the legislator may also worsen the legal position of certain persons on specific issues by amending legislation and introducing new legal regulations. The case of Lithuania well illustrates this. For example, the Civil Service Law has long regulated the leave of public officials such as the Chairman of the High Election Commission of the Republic of Lithuania or permanent deputies, even though they are not civil servants within the meaning of the Law. However, after some time had passed, the legislator changed the long-standing legal regulations without assessing the impact of the legal rules on individual civil servants. It was foreseen that the Labor Code would regulate leave for the Chairperson and the Vice-Chairpersons of the Electoral Commission.

On the one hand, as mentioned above, election commission officials are not civil servants within the meaning of the Civil Service Law and are not subject to many of the guarantees applicable to civil servants. On the other hand, the legislator has created a legitimate expectation on the part of the Electoral Commission officials that their leave will be calculated based on the Civil Service Act. The Labour Code would give this category of persons a shorter annual leave than the Civil Service Law. However, the legislator, considering that public officials had been subjected to the relevant legitimate expectations, once again amended the legal framework, which provided for calculating the leave of election commission officials under the Civil Service Law.

In summary, it can be said that in Lithuania, specific legislation regulating legal relations between civil servants, such as the Civil Service Law, does not cover all issues arising in the civil service. Therefore, it is often necessary to apply general legislation, such as the Labour Code. However, if the Labour Code does not resolve specific labour disputes, analogy must be sought, which may introduce certain ambiguities in interpreting the legal regulation and lead to legal disputes between the parties concerned.

It should also be noted that changes in the legal framework in the Lithuanian public sector could be faster to implement due to the complex bureaucratic structure. Compared to the private sector, where changes can be implemented quickly, changes in public sector legislation require a lengthy process: initiation, adoption, and implementation. This makes it difficult to adapt quickly to new conditions.

Another legal challenge in analysing the Lithuanian legal framework is that amendments to legislation can sometimes be adopted expeditiously without considering the existing legal framework in other legislation. This can result in contradictions between different legal acts, leading to inconsistencies in the legal framework and complicating public sector management.

3. RECRUITING PEOPLE

One of the initiatives to improve public governance set out in the State Progress Strategy "Lithuania 2030" is to make the civil service lean, flexible, professional, accountable, and performance oriented. However, an analysis of the current legal framework shows that more flexibility is needed.

According to Article 33(1) of the Constitution of the Republic of Lithuania, citizens have the right to join the civil service of the Republic of Lithuania on equal terms. This right is linked, among other things, to the right of every person to freely choose his or her employment, enshrined in Article 48 of the Constitution" (Resolutions of the Constitutional Court, 2004, 2007 and 2008). This means that any person holding citizenship of the Republic of Lithuania can apply for the civil service. Still, in legal terms, it does not guarantee that everyone applying for a civil servant's position will obtain it.

"Public administrations are legal entities with different legal forms and have different admission requirements for staff working in their public administration"(-Summary of the State Audit Office's State Audit Report). The Lithuanian legislator has not set uniform requirements for several categories of public administration employees, i.e., civil servants and employees employed under employment contracts in public sector bodies. This means the recruitment requirements for persons applying for the civil servant position are considerably stricter. For example, the requirement to be in a public competition, to have appropriate qualifications, to be loyal to the Republic of Lithuania, to be of the appropriate age, to declare income and assets, etc. In contrast, there is no plethora of admission requirements for the recruitment of employees under an employment contract. This raises questions about whether the legislator is thus creating certain preconditions for non-transparent decisions, nepotism, and other corrupt practices. Moreover, according to the State Audit Office of Lithuania, "the fact that the recruitment process is not subject to a public competition and other requirements and restrictions on the recruitment and performance of civil servants may hurt the quality of their work" "(Summary of the State Audit Office's State Audit Report).

In the public sector, as in many cases in the private sector, vacancies arise through various selections, competitions, etc. In other words, the vacancy cannot be filled by any person, even if he or she meets the highest qualification requirements, has the necessary practical experience, has an excellent knowledge of the legislation, etc. A vacancy may be filled only by competition or, in other cases, provided for in the legislation, such as a staff casualty. This is, in a sense, a challenge, since when a vacancy occurs, it will be vacant for some time, and some of the functions assigned to the former civil servant will be partly delegated to other civil servants who are often less experienced or less familiar with the specifics of the job. In contrast, a vacancy in the private sector can be filled more quickly. An employer in the private sector can announce a selection process at any time, with no requirements, which can take place on the next working day. This is also the position of foreign researchers. For example, Ezeali and Esiagu argue that "that an organisation's efficiency in servicedelivery and its success depends largely on its workforce quality, which wasrecruited into the enterprise through recruitment and selection exercise" (Ezeali & Esiagu, 2010). Adagbabiriand Okolie take the position "that proper selection practices in an organisation's recruitment process will determine who is hired" (Adagbabiri & Okolie, 2020). Adagbabiri and Okolie state that "when competent people are chosen for the task, performance and theproductivity of the enterprise increase thereby leading to its success" (Adagbabiri & Okolie, 2020).

Moreover, the Lithuanian legislator has provided that the competition for civil servant posts shall be organised by those state and municipal institutions and bodies where there are vacant civil servant posts. Only if a public sector body requests it may a body authorised by the Government—the Public Management Agency—carry out the selection. In contrast, selection for a vacancy in a private sector organisation may be organised by the organisation itself or by any other persons engaged. This reduces the time, human and financial resources spent on selection procedures in the private sector.

Another challenge related to the recruitment of individuals is that different unlike in the private sector, in the public sector all procedures for competitions for vacant posts must be clearly and in detail regulated by internal legislation and cannot be amended during the process. However, practice shows that procedural matters are not always adequately regulated in internal legislation and that the legal framework is only sometimes respected. This makes it necessary, in certain circumstances, to annul the results of the call for tenders and to call for a new selection procedure. In contrast, such problems are non-existent or sporadic in the private sector. If a private sector employer has specific selection procedures in place, it is free to change them at any time, to waive part of them, etc. In other words, recruitment in the private sector is much faster, without a lot of bureaucratic apparatus.

Public sector organisations also need some help publicizing the vacancy tender. For example, while a private sector organisation may advertise a selection or a competition in the ways, forms and means of its choice, public sector institutions or organisations have to comply with the statutory requirements for publicising a competition. For example, in Lithuania, the legislator has provided that all competitions for vacancies in public sector bodies, institutions or organisations shall be published in the first instance on the website of the institution responsible for organising competitions in the civil service (the Agency for Public Administration) and on the website of the institution organising the selection, in the Career section. It is recommended that information is additionally published in the media, on social networks, direct search tools, databases, job search portals, sharing information about vacancies in associations of professionals in a particular field, etc. This is well illustrated by the publicity given to the competition for the Director of the State Guaranteed Legal Aid Service. As the competition was organised by the Ministry of Justice of the Republic of Lithuania, the selection was published both on the website of the Ministry of Justice and on the major job search portals. The competition was also distributed to organisations of lawyers.However, in practice, such publicity is the exception to the rule rather than the norm.

Another aspect of recruitment in the public sector is that a vacancy should only be advertised if no civil servant can be transferred to the vacant post through a career move. This means that each public sector body must inform the Public Management Agency electronically, via the Civil Service Information System, of the vacancy and the need for a replacement civil servant before a vacancy is advertised. And only if a vacancy is advertised in the Public Management Agency's information system and no one takes up the opportunity a call for tenders is launched to fill the vacancy. On the one hand, this helps to ensure that a new professional is found quickly and guarantees that the vacancy will remain vacant for a while. On the other hand, it obliges the public-sector body to recruit not the best, most competent person. Still, the person who has expressed a willingness to work for the institution temporarily, and who may not have been particularly interested in the position, jumped at the chance when the opportunity arose.

Public sector bodies and organizations often face legal challenges related to the terms of tenders. While, for example, a private sector organization is free to change the terms of a tender at any time, to terminate the tender, and to reopen it, the legislator imposes stricter requirements on public sector bodies. Public sector bodies or organisations cannot be very flexible in this respect. The requirements for applicants are usually laid down in internal local regulations (job descriptions, regulations, etc.), the amendment of which may not only take a long time but also raise doubts as to whether the position in question is being prepared for a candidate with the appropriate experience. Public sector bodies or organisations cannot be very flexible in this respect. The requirements for applicants are usually laid down in internal local regulations (job descriptions, regulations, etc.), which can be time-consuming to amend, but also can raise doubts as to whether a particular position is being prepared for an applicant with the right experience.

Another challenge facing the public sector in the search for new civil servants is the requirements of the post. In most cases, the relevant requirements for applicants are set out in the job descriptions of civil servants, which are adopted by local legislation adopted by the representatives of the public sector institutions. On the one hand, such requirements may be modified before a new selection of a civil servant is published. On the other hand, if, after a selection has been announced, a highly qualified professional who does not meet at least one of the requirements, for example, a foreign language level below that specified in the requirements, is selected, their candidature will be rejected outright. By contrast, this problem is often avoided in the private sector. For example, if a highly qualified and competent professional participates in a selection procedure published by a private sector legal entity, but needs the knowledge or skills the employer wants, the employer is not prevented from hiring that person anyway. In other words, in the private sector, a successful candidate may not only be a candidate who fully meets the employer's requirements, but may also be a candidate who only partially meets them.

It is also important to note that, unlike in the private sector, in the public sector the qualification requirements for specific categories of officials are laid down not only in local legislation but also in the relevant legislation. However, this is mostly the case for top managers. In some cases, qualification and experience requirements for top managers may also be laid down by law. This means that only applicants who strictly meet the criteria laid down in the law can be recruited to the post. Moreover, these criteria cannot be altered by any other public sector body by means of a local legal act. This requires the adoption of legislative amendments, which is naturally a rather lengthy process. For example, the requirements for the Chairman of the Central Electoral Commission of the Republic of Lithuania, the

Director of the Lithuanian National Radio and Television and other officials are laid down in specific legal acts regulating the activities of institutions. In this case, the adoption of amendments to these legal acts requires going through all the necessary procedures for the adoption of amendments to the legislation in Parliament, obtaining the necessary parliamentary approval, and, finally, the signature of the Head of State on the new legal act or its amendment. However, as such a procedure is usually lengthy, the review of the statutory requirements for top management is very rare. Mostly at the time when the legislation is amended for other reasons. In the meantime, this poses certain legal challenges. For example The requirements for the Director of Lithuanian Radio and Television are laid down in a specific legal act regulating the activities of the national broadcaster - the Law on Lithuanian Radio and Television. The requirements for the post of Director General include a Master's degree and 5 years of managerial experience. However, since the requirements do not include a requirement to have relevant work experience in radio and/or television, the inclusion of such a requirement in the conditions of the competition would be an infringement of the law, which would allow the competition to be declared void. The same applies to the knowledge of a foreign language. A number of public sector institutions participate in various international projects, hold various international discussions and exchange best practices with other countries. In such cases, on the one hand, knowledge of a foreign language is a requirement among the other requirements in the conditions of the competition for the post of Director. On the other hand, if the legislator has not provided for such a requirement in the law, it is not only unreasonable but also unlawful to require applicants to have a working knowledge of one or other foreign language at the relevant level. It would also be contrary to the rule of law and the rule of law

Persons participating in selections announced by both public and private sector institutions or organizations must meet the general requirements for their candidature.

Whereas in the private sector, the requirements for persons applying for vacant posts are set out in the organization's local regulations, in the public sector, some of the requirements are laid down in the legislator's ordinaries. In most cases, the general requirements for a civil servant are laid down at the level of the law. In contrast, specific requirements are laid down in subordinate legislation or individual procedures.

Thus, as can be seen, the Lithuanian legislator has provided in the legal framework a number of safeguards for persons aspiring to the position of a civil servant, as well as a number of obstacles for persons wishing to become one. Recruitment in the private sector is much faster and more flexible. By contrast, those seeking a civil servant's position have to go through a series of lengthy bureaucratic procedures.

Therefore, given that "the current human resources management system in the public sector does not encourage transparent recruitment" (Summary of the State Audit Office's State Audit Report), "the current number of posts in ministries and their subordinate bodies is not based on a realistic (actual) calculation of needs (no optimal number of public sector employees has been identified); the maximum number of posts for civil servants and employees employed under employment contracts and receiving remuneration from the state and municipal budgets and state monetary funds is determined on the basis of the previous year's figures and does not reflect the actual need for posts', as a result of which, according to the State Audit Office, 'there are permanently vacant and unfilled posts at some institutions and a shortage of vacant posts at other institutions, while the total number of public sector employees remains unchanged (only marginally)' (Summary of the State Audit Office's State Audit Report) the Public Management Agency of Lithuania and the National Centre of General Functions 2024 The Human Resource Management System was launched in 2024. By 2026, "the system is expected to include an advanced human resources management component covering selection/hiring and performance evaluation processes, succession and competency management, and other human resources management processes and functions". In addition, "a register of public sector employees will be created, which will enable centralised and automated management of the data needed to meet the needs of public administration, i.e. to ensure systematic decision-making, control and prevention of the management of personnel in the public sector (analysis of the number of posts and their evolution) (National Common Function Centre Press release, 2024).

However, although „citizens have the right to join the civil service of the Republic of Lithuania on equal terms" (Law on the Civil Service of the Republic of Lithuania, Article 33(1) of the Constitution), as the Constitutional Court has pointed out in its case law, such right is not absolute, as "the State cannot and does not undertake to accept every person to work in the public service; the civil service must be qualified and capable of performing the tasks assigned to it; those wishing to become civil servants or officials must, as a general rule, have appropriate education, professional experience and certain personal qualities, and the more senior the post and the more important the field of activity, the higher the requirements for the holder of that post" (Resolutions of the Constitutional Court, 1999, 2007 and 2008).

In this context, the Lithuanian legislator has laid in Article 9(1) of the Law on the Civil Service certain general requirements to be met by all persons seeking the civil service. Such requirements include the obligation to "hold citizenship of the Republic of Lithuania and to be proficient in the official Lithuanian language by the language proficiency categories established by the Government" (Law on the Civil Service of the Republic of Lithuania, Article 1(1)); to "be at least 18 years of age and at least 65 years of age" (Law on the Civil Service of the Republic of

Lithuania, Article 2(2)); to "be of unimpeachable reputation" (Law on the Civil Service of the Republic of Lithuania, Article 3(3)); and to "possess not less than a university degree or a higher collegiate education" (Law on the Civil Service of the Republic of Lithuania, Article 4). This means that a person wishing to take up a position as a civil servant must first meet the general requirements of citizenship, age, reputation, and qualifications laid down in the Law. Private sector organizations are not subject to such stringent requirements. People with foreign or dual nationality can be recruited; in some cases, they may be under 18 or over 65, may not have a university degree, etc.

On the one hand, such a regulation may raise questions about whether a person's right to choose his or her job is being infringed. On the other hand, the right of a person to freely choose his/her work, enshrined in Article 48(1) of the Constitution of the Republic of Lithuania, may be restricted. However, only if "the following conditions are met: it is done by law; the restrictions are necessary in a democratic society to protect the rights and freedoms of others and the values enshrined in the Constitution, as well as constitutionally important objectives; the restrictions do not undermine the nature and essence of the rights and freedoms; and the constitutional principle of proportionality is observed" (Resolutions of the Constitutional Court, 2009, 106, 2019).

However, while the requirements for selection and tendering are sometimes similar in both the public and private sectors, the public sector is distinguished by the imperative requirement to be of good repute. This means that only persons who, in the opinion of the legislator, are of impeccable repute may apply for public service. Persons whose reputation is in doubt may not apply for civil service. In contrast, in the private sector, the various selections and competitions are open to all persons who meet the qualifications, experience, and other requirements for applicants. In other words, there is no obligation in the private sector to recruit exclusively those persons who are of good repute.

In conclusion, it should be noted that in Lithuania, public administration institutions are subject to different requirements for the recruitment process depending on whether the employee is employed as a civil servant or under an employment contract. Civil servants are subject to stricter requirements, including a public competition, qualifications, loyalty to the State, age limits, etc. This raises the issue of possible non-transparent decisions and nepotism.

It should also be noted that the different requirements may have a negative impact on the quality of work performed by public sector employees. Higher requirements for some civil servants performing service functions may be excessive in relation to the nature of their work, while staff performing core activities may face lower qualification requirements.

In addition, the fact that vacancies in the public sector cannot be filled quickly, even if candidates meet high standards, poses a challenge. This makes it difficult to attract new professionals quickly, as strict selection procedures and competitions must be followed.

It should be noted that the publication of public sector tenders is regulated by law and requires information to be published on defined platforms. This limits the flexibility of the public sector to attract candidates compared to the private sector.

Another challenge that Lithuanian public sector institutions may face is that before a vacancy is advertised, it must be checked whether there is any possibility of transferring the incumbent through rotation. This may limit the institutions' ability to select the best suitable candidate.

Although the Constitution of the Republic of Lithuania guarantees the right to enter the civil service on equal terms, in practice this does not always mean that every candidate will have the opportunity to take up the desired position. Civil service requirements can be high and make it difficult to recruit candidates.

In law, public sector selection procedures must be detailed in internal regulations and cannot be changed during the process. However, these procedural issues are not always adequately regulated or followed. This may lead to the need to invalidate competitions and to call for new selections.

4. REQUIREMENT OF GOOD REPUTE

The Constitutional Court has stated that "the constitutional purpose of the civil service and the special tasks assigned to the civil service imply that a citizen who enters the civil service may and must be subject to certain general requirements - the general conditions for entry into the civil service - which, if not fulfilled, will preclude a person from becoming a public servant" (Resolution of the Constitutional Court, 2008).

One of these conditions is that you must be of good repute, which according to Fombrun, is a "collective representation of past actions and results" (Ayubayeva et al., 2020). Therefore, without exception, all persons applying for a civil servant's position or already in a civil servant's position must be subject to an integrity check. To this end, the Lithuanian legislator has provided that a person applying to become a civil servant must complete a declaration in a form approved by the Government, which shall contain information on his or her compliance with the requirements of good repute' (Article 5(4) of the Civil Service Law). This means that if a person applying for a relevant post in the civil service does not fill in such a form and declare that he or she is of good repute, he or she is not eligible to participate in the selection process for a vacant civil servant post. In contrast, the private sector is much less likely to be asked to complete such a questionnaire. Moreover, the fact that a person is not of good repute does not mean that he or she will be barred from selection for a particular position. Finally, even if a person is recruited as a person of good repute and his/her reputation deteriorates during the employment relationship, this does not mean that the employment relationship will always end.

In the public sector, however, the situation is quite different. It is worth noting that whether or not a person meets the requirements of good repute must be assessed at the time of recruitment to the civil service. The authority that has recruited the civil servant must monitor and assess, by lawful means and methods, on an ongoing basis whether the civil servant in post meets the requirements of good repute. However, if "it is established that a person applying to become a civil servant has concealed or misrepresented his or her compliance with the requirements of good repute, he or she shall not be admitted to the post of a civil servant, and if these circumstances are established after the civil servant has been admitted to the post, he or she shall be dismissed from his or her post as a civil servant" (Article 5(4) of the Civil Service Law). In other words, the Lithuanian legislator considers that one of the most important prerequisites for the possession of the legal status of a civil servant is the principle of impeccable reputation (conduct). However, the disappearance of this prerequisite constitutes a serious ground for terminating the legal relationship with the person. This is because "only persons loyal to the State and whose loyalty and trustworthiness to the State are beyond doubt may work in public institutions" (Resolution of the Constitutional Court, 1998). Moreover, as the European Court of Human Rights has pointed out in its case law, "the requirement of loyalty to the State is an intrinsic condition of employment in the public service, which is presupposed by the State's responsibility for the defense and protection of the general interest" (Judgment of the European Court of Human Rights, 2004).

This is essentially because "the public sector guarantees that fundamental requirements are addressed and that citizens have access to important services regardless of their socioeconomic level through publichospitals, schools, public transit systems, and law enforcement organizations" (Dal et al., 2019). However, to avoid various legal interpretations as to when a person applying for civil service is considered to be of good repute and when he/she is not, the Lithuanian legislator has established in the Law on the Civil Service an exhaustive list of grounds for not being considered of good repute. In other words, the legislator presumes that any person seeking civil service shall be considered to be of good repute if he or she fulfills the criteria laid down by the legislator in the Civil Service Law. This is also in line with the case law of the Lithuanian Administrative Courts, which provides that "in accordance with the constitutional principles of the rule of law and legal certainty, it is neither possible nor tolerable for a situation to arise in which the interpretation of one of the most important human values, namely, an irreproachable reputation, in the field of public administration, would not be precisely defined at the level of the law, that is to say, that the interpretation of such a value would be left to the discretion of the entity of the public administration, depending on certain, albeit rather significant, circumstances" (Order of the Supreme Administrative Court, 2014). It is also consistent with "the constitutional principle of the rule of law, which obliges the legislator to establish a legal framework that enables the subjects of legal relations to know what the law requires of them in order to be able to direct their conduct in accordance with the law" (Press release of the Supreme Administrative Court, 2022). In other words, the legislator prescribes in advance for each person applying for a post as a civil servant the requirements he or she must meet in order to be appointed to a post as a civil servant. This enables the person applying for a particular post to prepare.

The current version of the Civil Service Law sets out 7 grounds for being deemed not to be of good repute. One of the most important criteria for judging a person's good reputation is the commission of a criminal offense, i.e., an act contrary to the law.

In Article 5(2) of the Law on the Civil Service, the legislator states that a person "who has been convicted, by the procedure laid down by law, of committing a very serious offence and 10 years have not elapsed since the completion of the sentence, or who has been convicted of committing a serious offence and 8 years have not elapsed since the completion of the sentence, or convicted of a petty offence and sentenced to 4 years or convicted of a non-serious offence and sentenced to 3 years" (Law on the Civil Service) shall not be considered to be of good repute. In the light of this construction of the legal provision, it is clear that the legislator considers any person convicted and found guilty of a criminal offence to be not of good repute. In legal terms, there is no distinction between whether a person has committed a very serious, serious or minor offence under the Criminal Code of the Republic of Lithuania.

Depending on the seriousness of the offence, the period during which a person is not considered to be of good repute varies. For example, if a person has committed a criminal offense that is not very dangerous for society and is included in the list of minor offenses under criminal law, then he or she will be considered to be of good repute three years after the actual completion of the sentence. In contrast, if, for example, a serious criminal offence has been committed which has caused serious damage to society, the person is not considered to be of good repute until 8 years after the completion of the sentence. In other words, in the case of a very serious offence, the time limit is twice as long. However, it is important to note that the 8-year period does not start from the beginning of the trial or the delivery of the judgment but from the date of the actual serving of the sentence. In other words, the earlier a person serves the sentence imposed by the court, the theoretically sooner he or she will be considered good repute.

The Lithuanian legislator has also provided in Article 5(2) that a person shall not be considered to be of good repute if he or she "has been convicted in accordance with the procedure laid down by the law of a criminal offence committed in the public service and in the public interest, and three years have not elapsed since the completion of his or her sentence" (Law on the Civil Service). Thus, the legislator takes the position that a person is not of good repute if he or she has not only committed a criminal offence, but also a criminal offence with lesser negative consequences in legal terms. However, the period during which a person is considered to be of good repute is the same as for a minor offence: three years.

As a person may be exempted from criminal liability under the legal regulation in force in Lithuania, the legislator has also dealt with the reputational issues of such persons in the Civil Service Law. Article 5(2)(3) of the Civil Service provides, that a person is not considered to be of good repute if he or she has been "discharged from criminal liability for a very serious offence in accordance with the procedure laid down by law and four years have not elapsed since the date of discharge from criminal liability, or if he or she has been discharged from criminal liability for the commission of a serious offence (with the exception of the following exemptions from criminal liability, where the person or the offence has ceased to be serious) and 3 years have not elapsed since the date of his or her release from criminal liability, or he or she has been discharged from criminal liability for the commission of a minor offence (except for the discharge from criminal liability, where the person or the offence has ceased to be serious or where the offence is minor) and two years have not elapsed since the date of release from criminal liability or the period of surety has not expired, or has been released from criminal liability for the commission of a low-level crime or a misdemeanour committed in the interests of the civil service or the public interest (with the exception of the release from criminal liability where the person or the offence has ceased to be serious or where the offence is minor) and one year has not elapsed since the date of release from criminal liability or the period of the surety has not expired" (Law on the Civil Service). In other words, whether a person has been convicted of a minor, serious, or very serious crime or misdemeanor, whether he or she has served the sentence imposed on him or her, or whether he or she has been exempted from serving the sentence imposed on him or her, he or she is still not considered to be of good repute. However, in the present case, when comparing persons employed in the public service who have committed criminal offenses and have served their sentences with persons whose sentences have been suspended, it is evident that for the latter, the period of time during which they are considered to be of good repute is half as short. For example, suppose a civil servant has been found guilty of a very serious crime and has been exempted from criminal liability. In that case, he or she will not be considered to be of good repute for a period of four years following the date of his or her dismissal from criminal liability. In other words, he will not be entitled to work in the civil service for four years. In contrast, if a person has committed a legally minor offense and has been released from criminal liability, he or she will already be considered to be of good repute one year later.

The Lithuanian legislator has also provided in the Civil Service Law that civil servants, or persons aspiring to become civil servants, shall not be considered to be of good repute if they have been dismissed from the civil service for serious misconduct in the course of their service and if "three years have not elapsed from the date of their dismissal or from the date on which they were declared to have committed a serious misconduct in office" (Article 5(2)(4) of the Civil Service Act). In this case, in order to find that a person is not of good reputation, it is necessary to assess whether the infringement committed by the person concerned was serious in a legal sense. Therefore, in order to avoid any interpretation, the legislator should clearly define in the legislation and the internal regulations of the public administration what constitutes a serious infringement. Otherwise, if the legal framework is not clear, there is a risk that different decisions will be taken in similar factual circumstances.

Any person, whether aspiring or incumbent, is also not considered to be of good reputation if he or she has been dismissed from his or her previous position or has lost "the right to engage in a particular activity for failure to comply with the requirement of good repute laid down in any other law or for violation of the standards of conduct/ethics" (Article 5(2)(5) of the Law on State Service). This means that the legislator recognizes that other legal acts can and do provide a completely different definition of good repute and requirements for persons of good repute. On the one hand, the legislator has the right to decide what requirements of good repute are to be laid down in each legal act governing a specific legal relationship. On the other hand, it is doubtful whether such inconsistency in the legal framework does not undermine the fundamental principle of the rule of law. Finally, from a legal point of view, it is questionable that the legislator equates 'non-compliance with the requirement of good repute laid down in other laws' with the absence of good repute within the meaning of the Law on Civil Service. This is all the more so as specific legislation may unduly narrow the scope of persons not considered to be of good repute. It is also not clear what the legislator meant when it stated that a person is not considered to be of good reputation if he or she has lost the right to pursue the activity in question. A person may lose the right to engage in the activity in question either voluntarily, through his own fault, or due to circumstances beyond his control, the actions of third parties, or force majeure. This suggests that a lack of legal clarity in practice may give rise to legal disputes.

The Lithuanian legislator also provides that persons who have been excluded from appointed or elected office in accordance with the procedure laid down by law as having broken their oath to the State or as members of a banned organization shall not be eligible to work in the civil service or to aspire to it. Thus, the legislator provides that only after 3 years have elapsed since a person was removed from office or membership of a proscribed organisation will he be considered good repute.

However, when analyzing the legal regulation of Civil Service Law, some doubts arise when a person is found to have broken his oath in accordance with the procedure laid down by the legislation. Still, he is not removed from the office he is appointed to or elected to, but the legal relationship is terminated by the person's own will, i.e. the person who has broken the oath. In such a case, all the prerequisites for considering the person to be of shame are present, but the person is considered to be of good repute in a legal formal sense, since there has been no act of removal from office. Given the above, the legislator should, in its view, bring more clarity to the legal framework to avoid situations of doubt and legal ambiguity.

In addition, the legislator provides that persons who have been members of banned organizations and whose membership of such organizations has been delayed for 3 years are not eligible to apply for, or work in, the civil service. In such a case, the public sector body must lay down in its internal regulations the specific procedures for verifying who, when, and how a person's membership in a criminal organization will end, etc.

Thus, as can be seen, the Lithuanian legislator has provided in the Law on Civil Service a rather broad and exhaustive list of grounds on which a person is not considered to be of good repute. However, unlike other legislation, the legislator has not provided in the Civil Service Law that persons who abuse alcohol, narcotic drugs, or psychotropic substances and persons who have been imposed an administrative fine for certain offenses in accordance with the procedure laid down by the legislation shall not be considered to be persons of impeccable reputation. This, in turn, raises doubts as to whether the legislator has not unduly broadened in the Civil Service Law the circle of persons considered to be of good repute.

Looking at the legal framework, it is clear that most cases are not of an evaluative nature, where the decision-maker can determine whether or not a person is of good repute. However, the fact that the Law on the Civil Service lays down one set of requirements for good reputation and the other set of requirements for good repute in other legislation reveals inconsistencies in the legal framework and raises doubts as to its conformity with the rule of law.

Finally, it is worth noting that, in the face of national threats, it is proposed to add to the requirements of impeccable reputation of civil servants the clause that "a civil servant shall not be considered to be of impeccable reputation if he/she is engaged or has been engaged in any other activity, or if he/she has any contacts, or if there are any other circumstances or facts relating to the person, that would lead to the assumption that the service of the person would be incompatible with the interests of national security of the Republic of Lithuania if no more than three years have elapsed from the date on which the end of these activities, contacts, circumstances" (Explanatory note to the Law on the Civil Service). In order to avoid uncertainty in the legal regulation, the proposed amendments to the Law on the Civil Service provide that "activities that are incompatible with the national security interests of the Republic of Lithuania shall include the clandestine co-operation of persons with the law-enforcement, law-enforcement and security services of the Russian Federation, the Republic of Belarus and/or the People's Republic of China" ((Explanatory note to the Law on the Civil Service).

In summary, it should be noted that the Lithuanian legislator has laid down an exhaustive list of conditions under which a person is not considered to be of good reputation in the Law on the Civil Service. These include crimes and their gravity, dismissal for serious misconduct and other similar cases. However, there is a challenge due to different interpretations of how and when these conditions apply.

The Lithuanian legislator provides that a person is not considered to be of good repute if he or she has committed an offence. Still, the period during which the repute is unacceptable varies according to the gravity of the offence. This raises the issue of subjectivity in assessing when a person's reputation can be considered restored. Meanwhile, the legislator must ensure that the legal system is predictable and that individuals can know what requirements they must meet to become a public servant. This requires legislation to be clear, consistent and not open to different interpretations.

In addition, different assessments of reputational requirements can lead to legal disputes, especially if individuals feel they have been unfairly assessed or dismissed. In this case, ensuring the legal framework is as clear and comprehensible as possible is essential.

At the same time, it should be noted that the legislator must ensure that the criteria for the assessment of reputation are consistent and clear throughout the legal system, so as not to undermine the rule of law. Inconsistencies in legislation, which can hinder the effective application of the law and public administration processes, should be avoided.

5. ENSURING EQUAL OPPORTUNITIES

Over the last three decades, several researchers have studied discrimination in its many forms and manifestations. As Khan states, "the research has revealed that human resource management practices play a critical role in shaping the extent of discrimination that occurs within an organisation as they influence the access that women employees have to opportunities within the workplace viz-training, fair performance appraisals, career advancement, equal rewards and developmental assignments" (Khan et al., 2019). As a result, both the International Labour Organisation and other international organisations have adopted a wide range of anti-discrimination and equal opportunities legislation. Equal opportunities mean the realization of human rights enshrined in national and international human and civil rights instruments regardless of gender, race, nationality, origin, religion, beliefs and opinions, age, sexual orientation, etc., in other words, non-discrimination" (Resolutions of the Constitutional Court, 1997, 1998).

Article 21(1) of the Charter of Fundamental Rights of the European Union, "Prohibition of discrimination", states that "any discrimination based on any ground such as a person's sex, race, color, national or social origin, genetic features, language, religion or belief, political or other opinions, membership of a national minority, property, birth, disability, age, sexual orientation, gender, religion or belief, political or other opinions, religion, belief, political opinion, or any other opinion, or on the basis of the person's" (Charter of Fundamental Rights, 2010).

The prohibition of discrimination is also enshrined in several other international instruments, including Article 26 of the International Covenant on Civil and Political Rights, Article 2(2) of the International Covenant on Economic, Social and Cultural Rights, Article 2(2) of the International Labour Organisation Convention No. 111 concerning discrimination (employment and occupation), Article 1, Article 14 of the European Convention on Human Rights, Article 21 of the Charter of Fundamental Rights of the European Union, and Article 14(1)(a) of Directive 2006/54/EC, which provides that discrimination in respect of access to employment, self-employment or occupation is prohibited, including in the selection criteria and the conditions for admission, for all activities and at all stages of a career, including promotion.

National legislation, such as the constitution, the Labour Code, laws, and by-laws, also prohibits discrimination on various grounds.

The Constitutional Court of the Republic of Lithuania has repeatedly stated that the principle of equality of persons, enshrined in Article 29 of the Constitution, implies the requirement that "the fundamental rights and duties of the law should be established for all equally; This principle implies the right of a person to be treated equally with others, obliges the same facts to be treated in the same way and prohibits the arbitrary treatment of substantially identical facts in a different way; the constitutional principle of equality of persons would be violated if certain persons or groups of persons were treated differently, even though there were no differences of such a nature and extent between them as to justify the unequal treatment on objective grounds" (Resolutions of the Constitutional Court 2013, 2017, 2020); in assessing whether it is justified to impose a different legal regime, it is necessary to take into account the specific legal circumstances; in particular, the differences in the legal situation of the persons and objects subject to the different legal regime must be assessed (Resolution of the Constitutional Court, 2015, 2018, 2020).

This is why public sector bodies must also refer to and comply with the provisions of international and national law prohibiting discrimination in all its forms, ways, and means. However, it is important to note that it is not sufficient for the authorities to merely state declaratively that they comply with international and national law. Every public sector body must adopt internal legislation that sets out rules to ensure that public sector employees have equal access to equal working conditions, training, practical work experience, and benefits, regardless of sex, race, language, origin and other aspects, prohibiting discrimination of any kind, and establishing effective policies to prevent discrimination in the workplace. Failure to do so may violate not only equality but also the rule of law, which is inherent in the principle.

At the same time, it is very important to note that public sector bodies must not only ensure equal opportunities for all employees but must also take the necessary legal measures to ensure that employees comply with such measures in relation to each other and avoid any action that has the appearance of discrimination. In other words, equal opportunities must be real, not merely declarative and inoperative.

On the other hand, it is important that "the measures laid down by law and applied must be proportionate to the aim pursued, and the rights of the individual must not be restricted beyond what is necessary to attain the legitimate aim, which is of general importance and which has a legitimate and universally applicable and constitutionally justified purpose" (Resolution of the Constitutional Court 2013, 2019, 2020). Otherwise, the principle of proportionality, one of the elements of the rule of law and one of the conditions for limiting the exercise of a person's rights and freedoms may be violated.

It is also essential that a public sector institution or organisation should set out very clearly and specifically in its local legislation, policies, or descriptions what constitutes equal rights for civil servants and, conversely, what actions by civil servants may amount to a breach and what liability each civil servant may incur for violating the established procedure. This would be in line with the position of the Constitutional Court of the Republic of Lithuania that "the requirements laid down in legislation must be based on provisions of a general nature (legal norms and principles) which are capable of being applied to all the envisaged subjects of the relevant legal relations; the subjects of the legal relations must be aware of what the law requires from them; legal regulation of social relations must respect the requirements of natural justice, including, among other things, the need to ensure the equality of persons before the law, the courts and public authorities or officials, etc." (Resolution of the Constitutional Court, 2004, 2006, 2010).

The Constitutional Court has also repeatedly stated that "differentiated legal regulation applied to certain groups of persons having the same characteristics, provided that it pursues positive, socially significant objectives, or that the imposition of certain restrictions or conditions is related to the peculiarities of the regulated social relations, does not in itself constitute discrimination" (Resolution of the Constitutional Court, 2006, 2014, 2020).

However, as some researchers argue, "women still experience discrimination in terms of unequal pay, fewer training and advancement opportunities, biased performance appraisals, less developmental assignments" (Pater et al., 2010; Diaz & Sanchez, 2011; Tlaiss & Dirani, 2015; Manisha & Singh, 2016; Khuong & Chi, 2017). Hochschild and Bielby teigia, kad "women are discriminated against in human resources management practices because their employers hold a belief that they give more priority to their family commitments and show negligent attitude towards their work" (Hoschschild & Machung, 1992; Bielby, 1992). Also is stated, that "it has been witnessed that women face gender-biased work environments whether covert or overt not only in developing nations, but also the developed nations as well" (Khan et al., 2019). Be to, "even when the participation of women in labour force increased, but it has been witnessed that long-standing stereotypes and cultural practices continue to dominate our societies even today and has its spill over effects across the workplaces as well." (Lens, 2003; . Roscigno et al., 2007). Often, the fact that civil servants are subject to an age limit is one indicator of discrimination. For example, the Lithuanian legislator has stipulated in the Law on the Civil Service that persons may work in the civil service between the ages of 18 and 65. However, such regulation is not recognized as discriminatory.

Among the classic forms of discrimination, "by far one of the most widespread is the gender and the age ones (Ardeleanu & Josan, 2011).

First, it is important to note that the prohibition of discrimination on grounds of age is a general principle of the European Union and is enshrined in Article 21 of the Charter of Fundamental Rights. As the Constitutional Court of the Republic of Lithuania has noted in its ruling, "the content and scope of application of this principle are defined by Directive 2000/78/EC, Article 6(1) of which also provides for an exception to this principle: the Member States may provide that a difference in treatment on grounds of age does not constitute discrimination if, under national law, it is objectively and adequately justified by a legitimate aim, including legitimate objectives in the field of employment policy, the labor market and vocational training, and if that aim is pursued by appropriate and necessary means" (Resolution of the Constitutional Court, 2021). In other words, "legislation which sets the maximum age of employment at the end of a career at the same time as the retirement age is not considered to be discriminatory on the grounds of age, as it is justified by the objectives of employment and the desire to attract more young people to the labor market" (Resolution of the Constitutional Court, 2021). It is, therefore, for the national courts to determine whether the specific conditions have been met in each case and „whether the measures adopted contribute to the intended employment objectives (Judgments of the Court of Justice, 2009, 2010).

As discrimination can take many forms, ways, and means and can sometimes be difficult to spot or detect, public sector organizations must provide specialized awareness-raising training for their staff.

In addition, in every case, the public sector body must take legal measures to ensure that any public servant who discovers discrimination or any public servant against whom discriminatory acts have been committed is not subjected to harassment or other hostile treatment. In addition, policies or procedures should provide for the shortest possible time limits for complaints and for the adoption of appropriate decisions to allow for the most expeditious and effective possible response to potential discrimination cases.

Equally important, of course, is that organizations in the public sector have clear policies and procedures in place to prevent discrimination and ensure equal opportunities.

Therefore, Public sector bodies must ensure that their activities and human resources management comply with national and international legal requirements and respect the principles of equal opportunities and non-discrimination, including all civil servants regardless of gender, race, religion, age, or other characteristics.

In conclusion, it should be noted that, despite the legal framework, long-standing stereotypes and cultural practices, such as discrimination against and attitudes towards women in the workplace, persist and impact the working environment. This shows that legal changes and reforms do not always fundamentally change societal attitudes and working practices.

Although the prohibition of age discrimination is enshrined in European Union law, certain national laws, such as age restrictions in the civil service, can be seen as discriminatory if not objectively justified. Such laws must be proportionate and consistent with legitimate objectives relating to the achievement of labour market policy and vocational training objectives.

Where institutions lack clear procedures and arrangements for recognizing and responding to discrimination, and where there is a lack of sufficiently clear definitions of responsibilities and sanctions for discrimination, practical methods, and training must be implemented to raise employee awareness and deal with complaints promptly and efficiently.

It should also be noted that legislation on discrimination and equal opportunities must be proportionate and not violate the principle of proportionality, an essential part of the rule of law. This means that any restrictions on legal measures must be necessary and appropriate to achieve legitimate aims and stay within what is required.

Legal regulations must also be clear and understandable so that all actors in the legal relationship know what is required of them and can easily identify cases of discrimination and their consequences.

6. MANAGING CONFLICTS OF INTEREST

To ensure the primacy of the public interest, persons working in the public service must conduct themselves in a way that leaves no doubt that a conflict of interest exists (Press release of the Supreme Administrative Court, 2022).

A conflict of interests, as provided for in Article 2(2) of the Law of the Republic of Lithuania on the Harmonisation of Public and Private Interests in the Civil Service, is a situation where "the declaring person, in the course of the performance of his/her official duties or the carrying out of an official assignment, is required to take or to participate in the taking of a decision or the carrying out of an assignment, which is also related to his/her private interests" (Law on Coordination of Public and Private Interests in the Civil Service, 1997). In science, a conflict of interest is defined as „situations in which the judgment of an individual may be unduly influenced (consciously or not) by a secondary interest, such as the opportunity to derive personal benefit" (Traversy, 2021).

However, clear and specific legal regulation is necessary to ensure that civil servants and public officials in the public sector are not placed in a situation of conflict of interest and that there is not even the appearance of a conflict of interest. At the same time, „managing conflicts of interest is a means for preventing corruption and increasing public transparency, efficiency, accountability, and trust" (Bagher, 2022).

Therefore, the Lithuanian legislator, considering that the public sector employs thousands of civil servants who may be confronted with potential conflicts of interest daily, and to prevent possible risks, has adopted the Law on the Harmonisation of Public and Private Interests in the Civil Service. This law defines what constitutes a conflict of interest, what duties persons in the civil service are required to perform, what restrictions apply to persons who hold office and who have left the service of the State, etc.

However, applying the legislator's legal framework to public and private interests often poses specific legal challenges. For example, the Lithuanian legislator has provided in the Law on the Harmonisation of Public and Private Interests in the Civil Service that "the heads of state and municipal institutions and bodies and other public sector entities where declarants are employed, or persons authorized by them, shall inform persons elected, admitted and appointed to office, and persons who are obliged to declare their private interests on other grounds (a person with the status of a declarant), of their obligation to submit a declaration" (Law on Coordination of Public and Private Interests in the Civil Service). However, the legislator does not specify how a person who has to declare a private interest is to be informed. Since the head of the public administration has such a duty, it is accordingly for the head of the public administration to lay down in local legislation the specific procedures for the proper notification of persons. Otherwise, human error in the late notification of the obligation to declare interests may lead to adverse legal consequences, as provided for by the legislation, for a person who should have declared a private interest but did not.

There may also be some challenges to the disclosure of private interests. The Lithuanian legislator has provided in the Law on the Harmonisation of Public and Private Interests in the Civil Service that persons working in the civil service must declare their private interests when submitting declarations of private interests (Article 4 of the Law). Article 10(1) of the Law provides that the data of the declarations shall be made public, except for certain exceptions. However, if a civil servant chooses the wrong classification row when completing an electronic statement of private interests, their declaration is kept private due to human error. In this case, on the one hand, the civil servant may be considered to have fulfilled his obligation to declare his private interests. On the other hand, the declaration of private interests will not be made public, which may raise doubts about fulfilling the legislator's intention and compliance with the mandatory requirements.

The cooling-off period is another legal challenge related to aligning public and private interests in the civil service. Article 15 of the Law on the Harmonisation of Public and Private Interests in the Civil Service provides that "a person who, while holding a position referred to in the law, during the last one year of his/her employment in that position, has directly drafted, discussed or adopted decisions relating to the supervision or control of the activities of a legal entity (regardless of its legal form and ownership), or decisions whereby funds from the state or municipal budgets and monetary funds of the Republic of Lithuania were allocated to such a legal entity, or any other decisions relating to assets, may not hold a post in such a legal entity for one year after leaving that position." Articles 16 and 17 of the Law prohibit concluding transactions and representing natural and legal persons.

On the one hand, from a formal point of view, the legislator imposes certain restrictions on the work of all those who have held senior positions. On the other hand, in practice, there are problems with the application of the legal framework, where the "cooling-off" period for individuals is much more extended than one year or where a cooling-off period is applied in some instances, even though it is not foreseen for this category of persons. This is well illustrated by the case of a former Minister of the Interior who wished to be reinstated as a judge but was informed that he was subject to a cooling-off period of an unspecified duration. As a result, the time limit for restoring the judge's status was ultimately missed.

In conclusion, the legal challenges in Lithuania related to the alignment of public and private interests in the civil service include problems related to the lack of clarity of the legal framework. This may lead to situations where civil servants fail to declare their interests promptly and where the opacity and inaccuracies in the declaration system raise doubts about compliance with the provisions of the law. It is, therefore, necessary to improve the legal framework and its application practices to ensure transparency and fairness in balancing public and private interests.

7. ENSURING PRIVACY AND CONFIDENTIALITY

In the public sector, individuals applying for and holding a civil service post transmit much information about themselves, known as personal data, to public sector bodies. As a general rule, public sector bodies process personal data such as the name, surname, nationality, personal identification number, date of birth, declared place of residence, series, number, photograph, signature, social security number, civil servant's certificate number, personal file, employment contracts, if any, and their annexes; dates of commencement and expiry of the post; grounds for the termination of the legal relationship; details of social security contributions, other taxes; current account number, telephone number, email address and other information. Details of education and qualifications, details of holidays and missions, details of promotions and penalties, work tools and equipment issued, and other data the civil servant provides to the public administration body (Decision of the Central Electoral Commission, 2019).

Thus, it can be seen that public administration entities process an extensive range of personal data, which may include sensitive data such as personal health. On the one hand, many of these data are necessary for the public administration entity to fill in many internal documents and to provide other authorities with information on the civil servant's entry into service and other aspects of the service. On the other hand, due to the large sample of data, it may be difficult for a public administration entity to manage all personal data and to ensure adequate protection and confidentiality of the civil servant.

Public administrations face legal challenges in managing data to ensure civil servants' privacy and confidentiality. The direct application of the General Data Protection Regulation (GDPR) in 2018 has led to increased obligations for public administrations to protect personal data. This includes ensuring employees' data is processed lawfully, fairly, and transparently. In addition, public sector bodies should put in place appropriate technical and organizational measures to protect civil servants' data against unauthorized access or use.

It is a significant legal challenge for a public administration entity to process civil servants' data. Therefore, it is necessary to draw up personal data processing rules, descriptions, and other localized procedural documents that set out what personal data are collected and for what purpose, where they are stored, etc.

However, another legal challenge often faced by public administrations is protecting the personal data of public sector civil servants and the public's right to know. Therefore, every time these two legal values intersect, deciding which takes priority over the other is necessary. For example, all public sector entities must publish the average salaries of employees in the same position on their websites. However, in rare cases, a single person may hold a particular position in a public sector body. In this case, indicating this employee's salary in the salary table and indicating in the institution's structure that only one person holds the relevant position will lead to the disclosure of personal data. In such a case, the average monthly salary of the staff member who is the sole holder of the post in question shall only be published with his consent.

Situations related to monitoring civil servants through electronic communication also pose specific legal challenges. On the one hand, a public administration entity may monitor the activities of a civil servant in cyberspace based on a reasonable suspicion of a possible illegal act. On the other hand, even though the means of work provided to a civil servant by a public administration body must be used exclusively for official purposes and needs and not for personal use, the civil servant's right to privacy must be guaranteed. However, in each case, depending on the individual situation and circumstances, it must be decided where the threshold is reached where the civil servant's right to privacy is infringed.

The Grand Chamber of the ECtHR also heard a similar dispute in 2016, when in the Barbulescu case, the applicant claimed that "he was dismissed from a private company for using the company's internet network during working hours, in violation of internal rules which prohibited the personal use of the company's computers. His employer monitored his communications on a Yahoo Messenger account, which he was asked to create to respond to customer queries. Records produced in the national proceedings showed that he had clearly private communications with other individuals" (Notice on data protection from the State Data Protection Inspectorate). In this case, the ECtHR found that "the national courts did not establish whether the applicant had been informed in advance by his employer of the possibility that his correspondence via Yahoo Messenger might be monitored, nor did they take into account the fact that he had not been informed of the nature or extent of the monitoring, or of the degree of the intrusion into his private life and correspondence" (Notice on data protection from the State Data Protection Inspectorate). The ECtHR also noted that the national courts "did not establish, firstly, the specific reasons justifying the use of surveillance measures; secondly, whether the employer could have used measures which would have been less intrusive on the applicant's private life and correspondence; and thirdly, whether the correspondence could have been accessed without the applicant's knowledge" (Notice on data protection from the State Data Protection Inspectorate). It was therefore held that "the national authorities did not provide sufficient protection for the applicant's right to respect for his private life and correspondence and consequently failed to strike a fair balance between the competing interests" (Notice on data protection from the State Data Protection Inspectorate). In other words, public sector bodies must ensure that any on-site monitoring of civil servants complies with legal requirements and does not violate their privacy rights.

Public sector institutions also publish information on their websites about civil servants going on sabbatical or parental leave, which raises legal questions.

In conclusion, there are numerous legal challenges related to the privacy and confidentiality of public officials in the public sector. Optimal legal regulation and continuous compliance monitoring with the legal framework can help address some of them.

In summary, public sector institutions in Lithuania face various legal challenges related to the protection and privacy of the personal data of public servants. Due to the large and sensitive volume of information, authorities must ensure that strict legal requirements process personal data, as the General Data Protection Regulation foresaw. It is also essential to consider the resolution of legal dilemmas, such as the publication of data on public sector employees and the application of monitoring measures. Optimal legal regulation, clear procedural documents, and continuous compliance monitoring with the legal regulations can help address these challenges and ensure data protection and employees' privacy.

8. SOCIAL GUARANTEES

The State provides social guarantees to every person working in the public sector, regardless of the type of post they hold. These usually include additional annual leave, sickness benefits, compulsory health insurance, pension insurance, sickness and maternity insurance, unemployment insurance, access to various refresher courses and training, the possibility of working a four-day week if a minor child under three, bereavement support, etc. However, as the legal framework in this area is subject to frequent changes, public sector institutions must constantly monitor and comply with changing legislation on working conditions, remuneration, leave, and other aspects of civil servants.

It is clear from an analysis of the existing legal framework that not all public sector officials enjoy the same social guarantees. For example, the Chairman of the Central Electoral Commission of the Republic of Lithuania, the Ombudsman of the Seimas of the Republic of Lithuania, and other heads of public sector institutions receive severance pay of two months' average monthly salary upon the end of their term of office. The Ombudsman for Academic Ethics, a public official appointed for a term of office of the same duration and bears no less responsibility, does not have this type of social guarantee.

Another legal challenge public officials face in senior positions in the public sector is the calculation of leave. Currently, no single legal regulation requires all public sector officials to take leave by a specific legal act. As a result, some public sector civil servants have their leave calculated by the Civil Service Law and others by the Labour Code. The different applications of the legal framework result in one category of civil servants being granted more leave days than another. In other words, from a legal point of view, some civil servants are privileged to a certain extent.

From a legal point of view, there are also situations where, for example, civil servants working for the Central Electoral Commission of the Republic of Lithuania receive a salary for working on holidays or days off and for working on business trips at weekends. At the same time, the head of this public sector institution is not granted social guarantees of this type.

In summary, the social guarantees provided to people working in the Lithuanian public sector are unique and often depend on specific duties and institutions. Despite widely accepted social guarantees such as additional leave, sickness benefits, health and pension insurance, and opportunities for professional development, the legal framework in this area is frequently changing, and public sector institutions must continuously update their practices. These legal challenges underline the need for a clear, consistent, and fair legal framework to ensure that all public servants enjoy the same social guarantees, regardless of their position or institution.

CONCLUSION

1. In Lithuania, the legal acts regulating the legal relations of civil servants, such as the Law on Civil Service, do not cover all the issues arising for civil servants, which often leads to the application of general legal acts, such as the Labour Code, or to the search for analogies, which may lead to uncertainties in the legal regulation and disputes. In addition, changes to the legal framework in the public sector are slow due to the bureaucratic structure, so changes to legislation in the public sector often take longer than in the private sector.

2. In Lithuania, the recruitment process for public administration faces several problems. Applicants for civil servant positions face stricter requirements, which can lead to non-transparent decisions and nepotism. At the same time, those recruited to the civil service on a contract basis may be underqualified.

3. Age limits in national legislation on civil service employment must be proportionate and justified to avoid discrimination.

4. The large and sensitive volume of personal data and the requirements of the General Data Protection Regulation pose challenges to ensuring adequate data protection and confidentiality. In addition, legal dilemmas also arise in the context of electronic surveillance of civil servants, where an appropriate balance has to be struck between surveillance for official purposes and the protection of personal privacy.

REFERENCES

Adagbabiri, M. M., & Okolie, U. C. (2020). Human Resource Management Practices and OrganizationalPerformance: An Empirical Study of Oil and Gas Industry in Nigeria. *RUDN Journal of Public Administration.*, 7(1), 53–69. DOI:10.22363/2312-8313-2020-7-1-53-69

Ardeleanu, A. M., & Josan, I. J. (2011). Equal opportunities in the public and private sector. Management, Learning Management~, 291.

Ayubayeva, S., Tynyshbayeva, A., & Kussainova, L. (2020). Public Service Efficiency: An Innovative Method for Assessing Public Sector Reputation. *The Innovation Journal, 27*(3), 1-20.

Fombrun, , C. JGardberg, N.ASever, , J.M. (2000). The Reputation Quotient: A Multi-stakeholder Measure of Corporate Reputation. *Journal of Brand Management*, 7, 241–255.

Azizi, M. R., Atlasi, R., Ziapour, A., Abbas, J., & Naemi, R. (2021). Innovative human resource management strategies during the COVID-19 pandemic: A systematic narrative review approach. *Heliyon*, 7(6), e07233. DOI:10.1016/j.heliyon.2021. e07233 PMID:34124399

Bagher, A. (2022). Managing Conflicts of Interest in the Public Sector. *Public Law Studies Quarterly*, 52(1), 297–321.

Bambang, I. (2023). Public Administration Challenges in Human Resource Management in the Education Sector. *Indo-MathEdu Intellectuals Journal.*, 4(2), 1349–1361. DOI:10.54373/imeij.v4i2.359

Batra, G. S. (1996). Human resource auditing as a tool for valuation: interface and emerging practices.

Bielby, D. D. (1992). Commitment to Work and Family. *Annual Review of Sociology*, 18(1), 281–302. DOI:10.1146/annurev.so.18.080192.001433

Boxall, P., Guthrie, J. P., & Paauwe, J. (2016). Progressing our understanding of the mediating variables linking HRM, employee well-being and organizational performance. *Human Resource Management Journal*, 26, 103–111. DOI:10.1111/1748-8583.12104

Collings, D. G., McMackin, J., Nyberg, A. J., & Wright, P. M. (2021). Strategic Human Resource Management and COVID-19: Emerging Challenges and Research Opportunities. *Journal of Management Studies*, 58(5), 1378–1382. DOI:10.1111/joms.12695

Dal Mas, F., Massaro, M., Lombardi, R., & Garlatti, A. (2019). From output to outcome measures in the public sector: A structured literature review. *The International Journal of Organizational Analysis*, ahead-of-print(ahead-of-print). Advance online publication. DOI:10.1108/IJOA-09-2018-1523

Decision No Sp-73 of the Central Electoral Commission of the Republic of Lithuania, dated 7 February 2019, approved the description of the procedure for processing personal data at the Central Electoral Commission.

Diaz, M. A., & Sanchez, R. (2011). Gender and Potential Wage in Europe: A Stochastic Frontier Approach. *International Journal of Manpower*, 32(4), 410–425. DOI:10.1108/01437721111148531

Enaifoghe, A., Ndebele, N. C., Durokifa, A., & Thusi, X. (2024). Drivers of Digital Transformation and Their Efficacy in Public Sector Human Resource Management. In *Digital Transformation in Public Sector Human Resource Management* (pp. 39–59). IGI Global.

European Union. (2010). Charter of Fundamental Rights of the European Union. In Official Journal of the European Union C83 (Vol. 53, p. 380).

Explanatory note to the Law of the Republic of Lithuania on the Civil Service No XIVP-3786- XIVP-3791.

Ezeali, B. O., & Esiagu, N. L. (2010). *Public Personnel Management*. Book Point Ltd.

Fahim, M. G. A. (2018). Strategic human resource management and public employee retention. *Review of Economics and Political Science*, 3(2), 20–39. DOI:10.1108/REPS-07-2018-002

Ferlie, E., & Osborne, S. P. (2002). *New Public Management: Current Trends and Future Prospects* (McLaughlin, K., Ed.). Routledge.

Hoschschild, A., & Machung, A. (1989). *The Second Shift: Working Parents and the Revolution at Home*. Viking.

Huang, X., Yang, F., Zheng, J., Feng, C., & Zhang, L. (2023). *Personalized human resource management via HR analytics and artificial intelligence: Theory and implications*. Asia Pacific Management Review.

Huselid, M. A. (1995). The impact of human resource management practices on turnover, productivity, and corporate financial performance. *Academy of Management Journal*, 38(3), 635–672. DOI:10.2307/256741

Infante, A., & Darmawan, D. (2022). Gender equality: women's involvement in human resource management practices. Journal of Social Science Studies (JOS3), 2(1), 27-30.

Judgment of 12 January 2010 in Case C-341/08 Petersen, paragraph 53;

Judgment of 18 November 2010 in Joined Cases C-250/09 and C-268/09 Georgiev, paragraph 68.

Judgment of the Court of Justice of the European Union of 10 March 2009 in Case C-169/07 Hartlauer, paragraph 55;

Judgment of the European Court of Human Rights of 27 July 2004 in the case of Sidabras and Džiautas v. Lithuania. Application No. 55480/00 and 59330/00), para. 57.

Juknevičienė, V. (2006). Challenges of the time for human resource management in public administration. *Economy and Management: Actualities and Perspectives.*, 1(6), 96–102.

Khan, A., Rainayee, A., & Gull, I. A. (2019). Women Discrimination in HRM Practices: A Review of Literature. International Journal of Management. *Technology and Engineering*, 9(1), 1846–1856.

Khuong, M. N., & Chi, N. T. (2017). Effects of Corporate Glass Ceiling Factors on Female Employees' Organizational Commitment. *Journal of Advanced Management Science*, 5(4), 255–263. DOI:10.18178/joams.5.4.255-263

Kim, T. T., Kim, W. G., Majeed, S., & Haldorai, K. (2023). Does green human resource management lead to a green competitive advantage? A sequential mediation model with three mediators. *International Journal of Hospitality Management*, 111, 111. DOI:10.1016/j.ijhm.2023.103486

Kupur, R. (2017), Human Resource Management – Structure and Roles. No. 3. International Journal of Professional Studies.

Law on Coordination of Public and Private Interests in the Republic of Lithuania Civil Service, Valstybės žinios, 1997-07-16, No. 67-1659.

Law on the Adjustment of Public and Private Interests in the Civil Service, Valstybės žinios, 1997-07-16, Nr. 67-1659.

Law on the Civil Service of the Republic of Lithuania, Valstybės žinios, 30-07-1999, No 66-2130.

Lens. (2003). Reading Between the Lines: Analysing the Supreme Court's view on gender. *Social Science Review,1*(77). 25-50.

Lim, S., Wang, T. K., & Lee, S.-Y. (2017). Shedding New Light on Strategic Human Resource Management: The Impact of Human Resource Management Practices and Human Resources on the Perception of Federal Agency Mission Accomplishment. *Public Personnel Management*, 46(2), 91–1187. DOI:10.1177/0091026017704440

Luoma-aho, V., & Canel, M.-J. (2016). Public Sector Reputation. In Carroll, C. E. (Ed.), *SAGE Encyclopedia of Corporate Reputation* (pp. 597–600).

Manisha, & Singh, R.K. (2016). Problems Faced by Working Women in the Banking Sector. *International Journal of Emerging Research in Management &Technology, 5*(2).

Munna, A. S., Tholibon, D. A., Cantafio, G., & Nasiruddin, U. (2023). Changes of Public Sector Human Resource Management (HRM). *International Journal of Educational Administration, Management, and Leadership*, 65-78.

Murray, B., Dulebohn, J., Stone, D., & Lukaszewski, K. (2024). *The Future of Human Resource Management*. Vol. Research in Human Resource Management.

Notice on data protection from the State Data Protection Inspectorate.

Order of the Supreme Administrative Court of Lithuania of 2 July 2014, TAR, 10-07-2014, No 10106.

Osborne, S. P., & Brown, L. (2011). Innovation, Public Policy and Public Services Delivery in The UK: The Word That Would Be King? *Public Administration*, 89(4), 1335–1350. DOI:10.1111/j.1467-9299.2011.01932.x

Pater, D. E., Annelies, I., Vianen, E. M. V., & Bechtoldt, M. N. (2010). Gender Differences in Job Challenge: A Matter of Task Allocation. *Gender, Work and Organization*, 17(4), 433–453. DOI:10.1111/j.1468-0432.2009.00477.x

Press release of the Supreme Administrative Court of Lithuania of 9 February 2022.

Radebe, T. (2009). The Strategic Value of Innovation in the Public Sector. Ideas that Work: The Public Sector. *The Innovation Journal*, 1(1), 10–14.

Resolution of the Constitutional Court of the Republic of Lithuania. Valstybės žinios, 2007-08-18, No. 90-3580.

Resolution of the Constitutional Court of the Republic of Lithuania. TAR, 18-02-2020, No. 3538.

Resolution of the Constitutional Court of the Republic of Lithuania. TAR, 19-09-2019, No 14836.

Resolution of the Constitutional Court of the Republic of Lithuania. Valstybės žinios, 10-03-1999, No. 23-666.

Resolution of the Constitutional Court of the Republic of Lithuania of 1 July 2013. Valstybės žinios, 2013-10-01, No. 103-5079;

Resolution of the Constitutional Court of the Republic of Lithuania of 11 December 2009. Valstybės žinios, 2009-12-15, No. 148-6632;

Resolution of the Constitutional Court of the Republic of Lithuania of 11 November 1998. Valstybės žinios, 18-11-1998, No. 100-2791.

Resolution of the Constitutional Court of the Republic of Lithuania of 11 September 2020. TAR, 11-09-2020, No 19129.

Resolution of the Constitutional Court of the Republic of Lithuania of 12 February 2021. TAR, 12/02/2021, No. 2775.

Resolution of the Constitutional Court of the Republic of Lithuania of 13 December 2004. Valstybės žinios, 18-12-2004, No 181-6708;

Resolution of the Constitutional Court of the Republic of Lithuania of 16 January 2006. Valstybės žinios, 19 January 2006, No 7-254;

Resolution of the Constitutional Court of the Republic of Lithuania of 17 February 2016. TAR, 17-02-2016, No. 2985.

Resolution of the Constitutional Court of the Republic of Lithuania of 19 December 2018. TAR, 19-12-2018, No 20843.

Resolution of the Constitutional Court of the Republic of Lithuania of 22 February 2013. Valstybės žinios, 2013-02-28, No. 22-1068;

Resolution of the Constitutional Court of the Republic of Lithuania of 22 January 2008. Valstybės žinios, 24-01-2008, No. 10-350.

Resolution of the Constitutional Court of the Republic of Lithuania of 22 March 2010. Valstybės žinios, 25-03-2010, No 34-1620.

Resolution of the Constitutional Court of the Republic of Lithuania of 22 September 2015.

Resolution of the Constitutional Court of the Republic of Lithuania of 25 January 2017. TAR, 25-01-2017, No. 1416.

Resolution of the Constitutional Court of the Republic of Lithuania of 3 July 2014. TAR, 3-07-03-2014, No. 9761;

Resolution of the Constitutional Court of the Republic of Lithuania of 31 May 2006. Valstybės žinios, 2006-06-03, No. 62-2283;

Resolution of the Constitutional Court of the Republic of Lithuania of 6 May 1997. Valstybės žinios, 1997-05-09, No. 40-977;

Resolution of the Constitutional Court of the Republic of Lithuania of 8 July 2020. TAR, 9-07-09-2020, No 15246.

Resolution of the Constitutional Court of the Republic of Lithuania of 8 November 2019. TAR, 8-11-2019, No. 17963.

Roscigno, V. J., Gracia, L. M., & Bobbitt-Zeher, D. (2007). Social Closure and Processes of Race/ Sex/ Employmentdiscrimination. *The Annals of the American Academy of Political and Social Science*, 6(9), 16–48. DOI:10.1177/0002716206294898

Stone, D. L., & Deadrick, D. L. (2015). Challenges and opportunities affecting the future of human resource management. *Human Resource Management Review*, 25(2), 139–145. DOI:10.1016/j.hrmr.2015.01.003

Summary of the State Audit Office's State Audit Report "Human Resource Management in Public Administration Institutions (summarised results of the audits of the three ministries' areas of governance)," 13-02-2017, No VA_P-10-1-1.

Tlaiss, H. A., & Dirani, K. M. (2015). Women and training: An empirical investigation in the Arab Middle East. *Human Resource Development International*, 1–21. DOI:10.1080/13678868.2015.1050315

Traversy, G., Barnieh, L., Akl, E. A., Allan, G. M., Brouwers, M., Ganache, I., Grundy, Q., Guyatt, G. H., Kelsall, D., Leng, G., Moore, A., Persaud, N., Schünemann, H. J., Straus, S., Thombs, B. D., Rodin, R., & Tonelli, M. (2021). Managing conflicts of interest in the development of health guidelines. *Canadian Medical Association Journal*, 193(2), 49–54. DOI:10.1503/cmaj.200651 PMID:33431547

Varga, A. (2022). State and development directions for human resources management in the public sector. Acta Academiae Beregsasiensis. Economics. 115-122.

Verma, P., Kumar, V., Mittal, A., Gupta, P., & Hsu, S. C. (2022). Addressing strategic human resource management practices for TQM: The case of an Indian tire manufacturing company. *The TQM Journal*, 34(1), 29–69. DOI:10.1108/TQM-02-2021-0037

Wright, P. M., & McMahan, G. C. (1992). Theoretical perspectives for strategic human resource management. *Journal of Management*, 18(2), 295–320. DOI:10.1177/014920639201800205

Yu, J., Yuan, L., Han, G., Li, H., & Li, P. (2022). A Study of the Impact of Strategic Human Resource Management on Organizational Resilience. *Behavioral Sciences (Basel, Switzerland)*, 12(12), 508. DOI:10.3390/bs12120508 PMID:36546991

Chapter 9
Examining Human Resource Management With the Bibliometric Analysis Method

Cem Angin
Ordu University, Turkey

ABSTRACT

Human resources management refers to the organizational and managerial activities covering the processes of recruitment, training, development and adaptation of personnel, which is one of the most basic needs of an organization, to the objectives of the organization. Human resources management, which symbolizes a break from the classical understanding of personnel management, first emerged in the private sector and then spread to public administration. For both the private and public sectors, the human element is now of "strategic" importance. This importance has been a development that has brought human resource management to the forefront today. This study focuses on the bibliometric analysis of studies in the field of human resource management. The study will present a multidimensional analysis of the studies conducted in the field of human resource management in the world. In this context, the study aims both to guide academics and researchers who will work in this field and to open the door to new studies by revealing the shortcomings and gaps in this field.

DOI: 10.4018/979-8-3693-4412-5.ch009

INTRODUCTION

Management consists of various elements such as purpose, organization, people, equipment, financial resources, service, plan, coordination (Chalekian, 2013, p. 1-2). Among these elements, the human element is the most active and important one in terms of management (Sarma, 2009: 3). Because humans are the primary actors who ensure the realization of the production of goods and services, guiding the organization towards its defined goals by effectively utilizing financial resources and tools. The fact that humans are so crucial for organizations has led to a growing interest in the field, formerly known as personnel management but now referred to as human resource management, with each passing day.

In light of this importance, the study focuses on both research conducted in the field of human resource management worldwide and the transformation of human resource management in conjunction with global economic developments and technological innovations. In other words, the aim of this study: To evaluate the latest situation of the studies on human resource management through the literature and to clarify the subject with current developments and information. The study aims to serve as a guide for researchers and academics interested in this field. This section, in alignment with the main theme of the book, is designed to fill a significant gap by addressing the extent to which economic developments and technological innovations are reflected in research on human resource management. Methodologically, this study will utilize bibliometric analysis, one of the qualitative research methods, to investigate and analyze the place, importance, and status of human resources management, which is of great significance for both the public and private sectors.

1. WHAT IS BIBLIOMETRIC ANALYSIS? WHY IS IT IMPORTANT?

Bibliometric analysis is "an analytical method used to obtain formal and quantitative data on the current state of a particular field, facilitating the monitoring of academic trends through visualization software" (Dirik et al., 2023, p. 168). It is a popular and widely used method for research and the analysis of scientific data (Naveen, Satish, Debmalya et al., 2021, p.285). The numerous benefits of bibliometric analysis have made it a frequently employed method today. Some of its useful aspects include its interdisciplinary applicability, its utility in both scientific and applied fields, and its ability to provide information about the productivity of institutions, universities, researchers, and academics worldwide. Additionally, it makes large volumes of scientific data more comprehensible through processing, visualization, and simple mathematical formulas. Bibliometric analysis also offers up-to-date information and provides a holistic perspective (Ellegaard & A. Wallin, 2015, p. 1809). Furthermore, it serves as a guide for researchers and academics interested in a specific field of study and opens the door to new research by resolving many questions.

In this study, 385 studies indexed in the Social Science Citation Index (SSCI) in the field of human resource management were identified using the Web of Science database, one of the richest interdisciplinary databases in the world. This was done with the aid of the artificial intelligence-supported R program, which offers researchers opportunities for data analysis, visualization, and mathematical calculations. The dataset obtained in this study will help address several important questions: Who are the authors who have contributed the most in the field of human resource management? Which countries, universities, and journals are prominent in this field? What are the most cited studies, the journals that publish the most studies, and the most frequently used keywords? What is the distribution of studies on human resource management worldwide over the years?

2. HISTORICAL EVOLUTION: FROM PERSONNEL MANAGEMENT TO HUMAN RESOURCE MANAGEMENT

Personnel management emerged as part of the mass production processes that took place during the Industrial Revolution. The employment of large numbers of people in large factories and the research conducted to achieve maximum output with minimal input in the shortest time highlighted the need to address personnel management separately (Dessler, 2020, p. 13-14). From a scientific perspective, personnel management emerged from the recognition that managing personnel in an organization is a distinct managerial process. It involves the processes of planning, organizing, coordinating, and supervising the human elements within an organization (Kaya & Taş, 2015, p. 22). In this regard, personnel management is a more technical, classical management function that includes recruitment, personal rights, and the financial and legal affairs related to employees (Eryılmaz, 2016, p. 295).

From the second half of the 18th century onwards, the Industrial Revolution transformed small-scale and scattered production into mass production through large factories. Mass production required both machines and the manpower to operate them. Consequently, the early period of the Industrial Revolution was marked by a significant need for manpower. In response to this need, employment offices were established in the early 1900s. As personnel management became recognized as a distinct branch within the management process, these employment offices gradually evolved into personnel management departments (Kaufman, 2014, p. 3-4).

Personnel management encompasses the general practices related to specific functions such as recruitment, selection, training, compensation, promotion, and turnover (Pinnington et al., 2007, p. 3). Alongside personnel management, scientific studies have been conducted over time to enhance the efficiency and effectiveness of employees. The advancements in production methods following the Industrial Revolution underscored the necessity of scientific research to develop efficient and effective production units. For instance, Frederick Winslow Taylor developed the theory of scientific management during this period. Throughout his career, Taylor investigated how to achieve greater efficiency in the production departments of enterprises and formulated the scientific management theory based on his findings. This theory emphasizes precise and standardized rules for the workplace and tasks, the division of labor into departments, the identification and training of talented employees according to job requirements, and a wage policy based on productivity.

Since the 1930s, personnel management has been influenced by various fields. For instance, contrary to Taylor's scientific management theory, which considered humans as machines, thinkers such as Elton Mayo and Abraham Maslow emphasized the importance of human psychology in the management process. They argued that humans should not be seen as machines. The discovery of the contributions of human psychology to productivity and efficiency in management has increased interest in personnel management and diversified and developed the research in this field. As indicated by various theories proposed since the early management theorists, significant contributions have been made to the understanding and practice of personnel management (Rotich, 2015, p. 61).

After the Second World War, with the emergence of the welfare state, employment management and social assistance activities were integrated under the broad term "personnel management" (Ahammad, 2017, p. 414). In the 1960s and 1970s, new personnel techniques were developed based on theories from the social sciences, such as motivation and organizational behavior theories, due to the evolution of employment and employment relations. As a result of these developments, there was a transformation from personnel management to "human resource management" (HRM) in the 1980s. The concept was first used in the United States and later adopted worldwide. HRM emerged from the conceptual, empirical, and practical intersection of various disciplines, including psychology, sociology, economics, and management/organizational sciences (Ferris et al., 2004, p. 231).

The changes and transformations in management practices since the Industrial Revolution have also been reflected in personnel management. This transformation has generally been one from personnel management to HRM (Torrington et al., 2008, p. 11). Especially with the impact of globalization, the competitive global environment has brought information and the people who produce it to the forefront for businesses. Human resources have become the main factor in producing knowledge, leveraging it for the benefit of businesses and thus providing a competitive edge (Eryılmaz, 2016, p. 293). Therefore, today, the success of businesses in increasingly competitive conditions depends on continually strengthening, making more efficient, and enhancing the effectiveness of their human resources.

Since the 1980s, the concept of HRM has become widespread, replacing that of personnel management (Legge, 1995, p. 63). Unlike personnel management, HRM is based on the understanding that people are a resource for an organization. It is defined as a strategic and coherent approach to managing an organization's employees, who contribute to the organization's achievement of its goals (Armstrong, 2006, p. 3-4). In this respect, HRM aims to promote a human-centered approach in the workplace, to train and develop individuals, and to ensure that their knowledge is effectively utilized by businesses (Eryılmaz, 2016, p. 293).

Although the concepts of personnel management and HRM may seem similar, they differ completely in scope. While personnel management operates only as a technical department related to the personnel of an organization, HRM is integrated with the strategies and other departments of the organization, views people as a resource in achieving organizational goals, and, therefore, addresses much more than personnel management (Erdil, 1996, p. 64). Personnel management assumes a passive role in the management areas of an organization in terms of authority and duties. HRM, on the other hand, adopts an approach that identifies the most productive human resources for the organization, defines them in the best way, and empowers them by fostering employees who are open to change, development, and desire (Yıldız, 2022a, p. 206). While personnel management has a limited function, HRM has broader functions and contents as it includes various strategies and approaches (Bach, 2005, p. 3). In other words, HRM focuses on human elements in management but does not approach them from a single narrow perspective. Accordingly, it encompasses recruitment, remuneration, training, performance evaluation, occupational health and safety, and career management, or, in short, all processes related to employees (Yıldız, 2022b, p. 298). In contrast to classical personnel management, which considers employees as passive elements, HRM considers employees as a source of equity and enables them to contribute to the organization in the most efficient way by increasing their organizational commitment (Margaret & Winters, 1993, p. 23-24). While personnel management views people as cost elements, HRM regards them as capital and essential inputs for the business.

As can be seen, at the core of the changes and transformations occurring since the Industrial Revolution is the question of how to make people more productive for the organization for which they work. The transformation from personnel management to HRM essentially consists of developing and diversifying the factors and methods that increase this efficiency. This ongoing transformation process encompasses new approaches such as intellectual capital management, strategic HRM, and sustainable HRM.

3. OBJECTIVES, IMPORTANCE, AND FUNCTIONS OF HUMAN RESOURCE MANAGEMENT

The primary goal of HRM is to ensure the most efficient utilization of human resources, enabling an organization to achieve its core objectives and enhance profitability as well as productivity. Simultaneously, HRM aims to achieve several key objectives: aligning organizational goals with employee goals, adapting human resources to organizational needs, formulating employment policies that align with organizational strategies, and fostering an environment that enhances employee performance (Doğanoğlu, 2001, p. 175). Furthermore, HRM strives to cultivate and leverage a skilled and motivated workforce, enhance employee morale through improved working conditions, and incentivize employees through both monetary and non-monetary rewards (Adhav, 2017, p. 36).

In order to demonstrate the importance of HRM, it is first necessary to clarify what roles it plays for organizations. HRM increases the performance and productivity of the organization by increasing the satisfaction and capabilities of employees (Kabene et al., 2006, p. 8). HRM plays a pivotal role in increasing employees' organizational commitment and job satisfaction. It achieves this by fostering a participatory work environment that values employees' input, ensuring fair management practices and compensation, enhancing career advancement opportunities, and bolstering motivation levels.

HRM makes the organization's human resources ready for the needs of the day. In other words, it attracts new and qualified workers to the organization in accordance with the needs of the day. In this respect, it identifies the most suitable and productive people for the organization and hires them. It deals with the needs and wishes of existing staff, offers incentives to improve their performance and capacity, provides new rights, prepares training programs, finds solutions to problems between the organization and the staff, and ensures harmony in the workplace.

HRM also plays a crucial role in identifying strategic deficiencies within organizations and facilitating information management (Soliman & Spooner, 2000, p. 345). It conducts necessary business analyses for the organization, takes proactive measures to maintain a competitive edge, and harmonizes business operations with evolving conditions by developing innovative approaches aligned with strategic objectives and ensuring their effective implementation. This strategic approach enhances the competitiveness of the organization.

It enables the organization to achieve strategic goals by directing, training, and supporting employees. Moreover, it enables the organization to gain a competitive advantage and to maintain that advantage. As can be seen, HRM, which has an extremely important place for organizations today, has many functions for the success and continuation of an organization.

HRM encompasses a range of activities related to employees, who are the foundational elements of an organization. In terms of the functions of HRM, we can outline the key areas as follows:

- Staff selection, recruitment, and placement: HRM primarily plans and executes the recruitment processes of an organization. It also identifies the most suitable and productive employees for the organization and ensures that they settle into the organization smoothly.
- Staff training and development: HRM carries out various activities to ensure that the personnel placed in jobs remain the most suitable for the business by providing training and development and increasing their skills and knowledge.
- Performance management and evaluation: The measurement of the physical and intellectual labor of an organization's employees, determined through a process by which the organization collects information about how well employees do their jobs, is called performance management and evaluation (Waxin & Bateman, 2009, p. 496). In general, HRM carries out activities related to the processes of evaluating the performance of employees, providing feedback, improving their performance, and rewarding them.
- Salary and benefits management: HRM carries out basic activities such as determining a fair and satisfactory salary policy for employees, establishing certain rights such as social benefits and compensation, and developing performance-based reward systems.
- Occupational health and safety management: Occupational health and safety has become extremely important for businesses due to its impact on increasing organizational performance. As work-related illnesses and injuries are on the rise and health costs are very high, businesses are implementing important regulations on occupational health and safety (Boyd, 2003). In this context, HRM carries out activities such as establishing occupational health and safety policies, improving working conditions, organizing training sessions on occupational health and safety, and minimizing potential risks by inspecting the working environment.
- Ensuring motivation and job satisfaction: The success of an organization in achieving its mission and vision is based on highly motivated, loyal, and qualified personnel focused on achieving organizational goals (Jovanović &

Božilović, 2017, p. 97). In this respect, HRM maximizes job satisfaction, motivation, and creativity by meeting the needs of employees on the one hand and increasing the quality of their relationship with work on the other.

- Employee relations management: Creating positive relationships between employees in a workplace, both among themselves and between employees and managers, is called employee relations management. HRM is responsible for managing the relations between employees by ensuring that communication channels between employees remain open, resolving existing conflicts, and anticipating potential risks.
- Employee resignation and retirement management: HRM is responsible for managing resignations, retirement, and severance processes, as well as conducting severance interviews and overseeing retirement plans.

Thus, it is evident that HRM has many fields of activity and essential tasks. Thanks to these basic fields of activity and tasks, organizations achieve their goals, increase their financial power, obtain a competitive advantage, increase their productivity, ensure organizational commitment by motivating their employees, and maximize their knowledge and skills.

4. TECHNOLOGICAL DEVELOPMENTS AND HUMAN RESOURCES MANAGEMENT

Human resources management has experienced many transformations from past to present depending on economic developments and technological innovations, and has reached today by adapting itself to the conditions and requirements of the day. This management approach, which was expressed as personnel management at the turn of the century and then transformed into human resources management, today includes many paradigms such as strategic perspective, sustainability and ecology.

Personnel management, which refers to an older concept and management approach, focuses on specific functions such as recruitment, remuneration, promotion and termination. However, this approach has become inadequate for organizations over time and a transition to a more current paradigm, human resource management, has occurred. Human resource management refers to an understanding that covers broader managerial processes that do not have a single purpose for organizations. Human resource management is the knowledge of the process of using and managing the labor power of employees in accordance with the objectives of the organization (Ayman Güler, 2020: 27). Today, this knowledge is vitally important for organizations. Because with this knowledge, businesses can benefit from the time and labor of employees to the highest degree in order to achieve their goals. Again, with this knowledge, businesses take a step forward in the competitive environment (Lundy, 2006: 687). For this reason, the issue of human resources and human resources management is one of the most prominent and important issues for organizations.

The classical HRM, with its short-term, operational, and support service roles, has entered a new phase of transformation due to economic developments and technological innovations. New paradigms such as strategic HRM, sustainable HRM, green HRM, and electronic HRM reflect this transformation. Strategic HRM (SHRM) emerged first, focusing on developing long-term strategies to determine organizational performance, create and sustain competitive advantages, and align HR policies with business strategies. SHRM involves functions and objectives such as revenue growth, competitive advantage, long-term growth, developing and implementing HR policies aligned with business strategies, improving job performance, and fostering innovation and flexibility (Truss & Gratton, 1994, p. 665).

Sustainable HRM aims to ensure employment, individual responsibility, and a suitable work-life balance between employers and employees (Zaugg, Blum, & Thom, 2001, p. 3-4). It promotes a balance between respect for the workforce, employers, employees, and society, integrating core principles like fairness, equality, and transparency with profitability and employee welfare (Järlström, Saru, & Vanhala, 2016, p. 703).

As a complementary approach, sustainable HRM has evolved into green HRM, which refers to ecological-friendly practices and global and environmental concerns, introducing the term "green" into HRM. Green HRM expands the role of sustainable HRM by incorporating ecological plans and policies into HR practices, aiming for an environmentally conscious, resource-efficient, socially responsible, and sustainable development-focused organization (Shah, Dubey, Shashikant, Renwick, & Misra, 2023, p. 32). For example, green HRM fosters environmental awareness through eco-friendly employee preferences, encourages minimal use of paper, electricity, and water at workplaces, and promotes video conferencing over travel to minimize environmental impact.

Today, the transformation in human resources management has moved to a completely different dimension with the impact of technological developments. Technological developments added to the process of globalization have also affected human resources management, and forms of personnel employment, ways and methods of doing business, and employee profiles have changed. For example, as an extension of this situation, the concept of electronic human resources has gained a place in the literature. Human resources management now carries out its duties by utilizing electronic media, the internet and the technological opportunities it offers. Again, many organizations have created electronic human resources (EHRM) platforms for receiving applications, evaluating them, collecting and storing information and using this information when necessary.

Basic HR functions such as recruitment, training and development, performance evaluation, career planning, and compensation have largely shifted to electronic platforms due to technological advancements and infrastructure (Yılmazer, 2020, p. 268). This shift facilitates business processes and problem-solving, creating a faster, more efficient, effective, and competitive work environment. Accelerated recruitment processes enable businesses to quickly access necessary skills and manage job processes more effectively (İnkaBlog, 2024).

Technological innovations offer benefits such as rapid and effective recruitment, strategic decision-making, flexible and remote working models, cost reduction, increased savings, competitive advantage, and less bureaucratic management. However, there are challenges as well, such as the high cost and time required to establish technological infrastructure, and potential resistance from employees towards technological changes due to security concerns or reluctance. Organizations must closely follow technological advancements and adapt to remain competitive, achieve strategic goals, and engage in innovative activities. Technological innovations enhance information accessibility, allowing everyone to access information previously exclusive to management (Kossek, 1987, p. 77).

Today, technological developments impact employment types and numbers. For instance, artificial intelligence (AI) can replace humans in many areas, which is expected to affect employment figures in the future. Similarly, technological advancements lead to new employment types such as part-time, flexible, or home office work, resulting in emerging trends in HRM. The close involvement of technology with humanity is the result of a historical process and accumulation. The term "Industry 5.0" or "5th Industrial Revolution" is used to describe the latest point humanity has reached economically and technologically. Humanity has reached this point through four major phases:

- The 1st Industrial Revolution (Industry 1.0), covering 1760-1830, marked by the evolution from manual labor to machine power.
- The 2nd Industrial Revolution (Industry 2.0), from 1840-1870, which utilized electrical technologies in addition to machine power.
- The 3rd Industrial Revolution (Industry 3.0), starting in the 1970s, characterized by the shift from mechanical and electronic technologies to digital technologies, influenced by two world wars and the 1929 Great Depression.
- The 4th Industrial Revolution (Industry 4.0), initiated in 2011 with the concept of "Industry 4.0," involves automation and the integration of smart machines into the production process.
- The 5th Industrial Revolution (Industry 5.0), introduced in 2021 by the European Council, emphasizes a sustainable, human-centered, and resilient

industrial approach, focusing on employee well-being rather than mere profit and growth (European Commission, 2022).

As seen, mechanical machines-initiated Industry 1.0 in the 18th century, electrical energy and motors-initiated Industry 2.0 in the 19th century, and computer and internet technologies-initiated Industry 3.0 in the 20th century (Rana & Sharma, 2019, p. 176). Thus, humanity's economic and technological evolution is ongoing, with the world moving towards a new transformation process. Although Industry 4.0 was first introduced as a technology project in Germany in 2011, it has been adopted by countries seeking industrial transformation based on technology. Industry 4.0 encompasses the latest technological developments enabling the integration of humans, smart machines, production lines, and processes across organizations (Alexa, Pîslaru, & Avasilcai, 2022, p. 222).

The effects of Industry 4.0 on HRM can be summarized as follows (Yılmaz & Yılmaz, 2023, p. 17):

- Changes in how employees perform their tasks
- Changes in overall workplace experiences and work processes
- Emergence of new types of relationships within and outside organizations
- Differentiation in job descriptions and required competencies for existing professions
- The rise of new professions or the complete execution of some tasks without human involvement

With Industry 4.0, the importance of skilled human resources in fields like computing, information technology, robotics, and AI increases, leading to higher demand for these professions. The integration of smart and autonomous robots and AI in production processes introduces a new type of workforce—robotic workers—while reducing the demand for human labor. This shift offers significant advantages for employers but presents considerable disadvantages for workers, such as lower social rights or reduced salaries. Consequently, economic innovations and technological advancements have completely transformed the goals, working methods, and priorities of HRM.

In 2021, the European Commission introduced the "Industry 5.0" report as a new phase of economic and social transformation. According to the report (European Commission, 2022), Industry 5.0 envisions the industry leading digital and green transformations, presenting a vision that enhances the role and contribution of industry to society, focusing on well-being rather than just productivity. Industry 5.0 emphasizes using new technologies to ensure well-being, complementing Industry 4.0 with a sustainable, human-centered, and resilient industrial approach (Carayannis

& Joanna Morawska, 2022). The emergence of Industry 5.0 is driven by the need to address societal challenges such as resource conservation, climate change, and social stability, using AI and digital technologies in a human-centered manner.

As evident, the latest scientific and technological advancements, such as those described by "Industry 4.0" or "Industry 5.0," highlight the significance of IT, AI, the internet, and smart robots in HRM. The reality that HRM is most affected by these elements stems from their integration into business processes, leading to reduced human labor and changing core job qualities (Bayraktar & Ataç, 2018, p. 338). Therefore, Industry 5.0 adopts an approach that emphasizes human welfare and balances technology and human elements.

Finally, not only companies but also governments must adapt to technological transformations. Technology offers significant opportunities in global competition, and countries that keep pace with technological and economic developments, invest in them, create public policies, and develop human resources accordingly will gain a competitive advantage and rank among the top globally.

5. METHOD

Bibliometric analysis method was used in the study. In this direction, studies in the field of human resource management were examined by bibliometric analysis method.

5.1. The Aim of the Research

The study aims to present a bibliometric analysis of studies related to human resource management in the light of quantitative data. In this context, the study aims to guide academics and researchers who will conduct work in this field, as well as to identify gaps and deficiencies in this area to pave the way for new research.

5.2. Data and Analysis

Between 1980 and 2024, 385 studies on HRM published in journals indexed by the Social Sciences Citation Index (SSCI) in the Web of Science database were identified. A bibliometric analysis of these 385 studies was conducted using the R program, designed for artificial intelligence-supported data analysis and statistical calculations. As illustrated in Figure 1, these 385 studies were authored by 966 individuals, with only 59 being single-authored. The studies were published across 115 journals and included a total of 1378 keywords. These works received an annual average of 40 citations. Additionally, there was an average annual increase of 3% in the number of studies published in this field.

Figure 1. Main İnformation

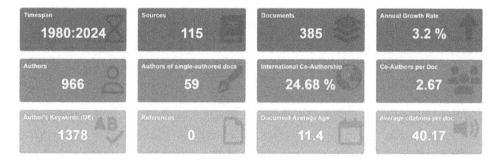

6. FINDINGS

Under this heading, the findings derived from the basic data of the study are presented. Additionally, several important questions are clarified, such as: Who are the authors contributing the most to the field? Which journals publish the most articles in the field of Human Resource Management (HRM) and which articles receive the most citations? What are the most frequently used keywords in the articles? In which years has the most research been conducted in the HRM field? Which countries produce more studies in this area?

Figure 2. Annual Scientific Production

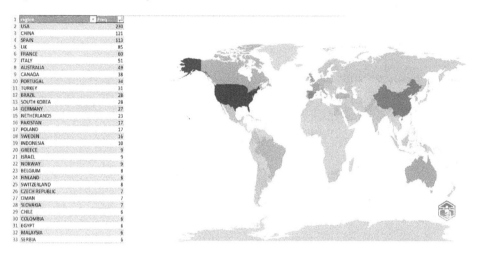

Figure 2 shows the annual studies on HRM. Examining the graph, it is apparent that the numbers of studies conducted in this field from 1980 to 2024 follow a fluctuating pattern, without a consistent increase each year. The fewest studies on HRM were conducted between 1982 and 1984, while the most studies were conducted in 2023 on an annual basis. Excluding the year 2004, fewer than 10 studies were published annually in this field until 2009. Since 2009, there has been a significant increase in the number of publications.

Figure 3. Average Citations Per Year

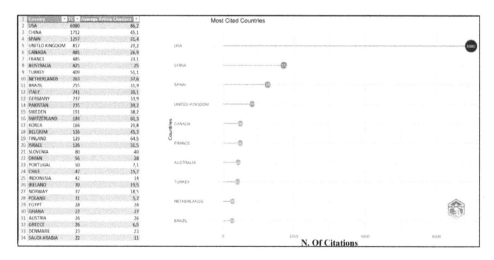

Figure 3 presents the average number of citations per year. According to this figure, the lowest number of citations occurred in 1988, while the highest number occurred in 2006. The numbers of citations of these studies have fluctuated over the years. Except for the years 1993, 1995, 2001, 2006, 2009, 2016, 2019, and 2023, the annual average remained below 5 citations.

Figure 4. Most Relevant Sources

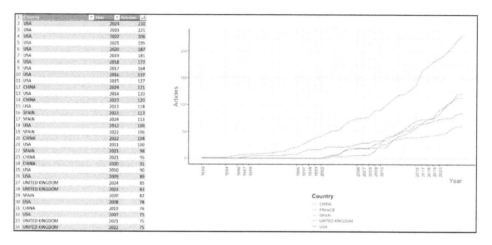

Figure 4 provides information on the most relevant sources on HRM in the Web of Science database. The source with the highest number of studies on the subject is the International Journal of Human Resource Management with 49 relevant publications. It is followed by the International Journal of Contemporary Hospitality Management with 22 publications. In third place is the International Journal of Manpower with 15 publications.

Figure 5. Core Sources by Bradford's Law

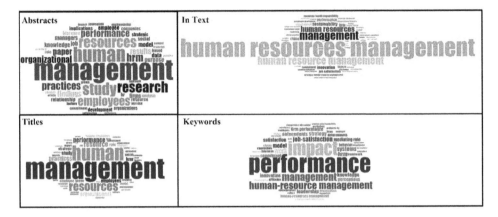

Figure 5 shows the sources of HRM-related literature according to Bradford's law. Bradford's law is a model first created by Samuel Bradford in 1934 to determine the most fundamental scientific journals on a given topic. This law offers a measure to determine which journals are the main sources of reference on a topic being researched (Summers, 1983, p. 103). In this sense, Bradford's law defines a quantitative relationship between journals and the studies they publish (Wilkinson, 1972, p. 122). This law is a guide of sorts as it shows researchers which sources they should turn to. According to Bradford's law, the five most prominent sources in the field of HRM are as follows: International Journal of Human Resource Management, International Journal of Contemporary Hospitality Management, International Journal of Manpower, Sage Open, and Human Resource Management. According to Bradford's law, these sources are the major reference works for individuals conducting research in the field of HRM or preparing new publications.

Figure 6. Sources' Production over Time

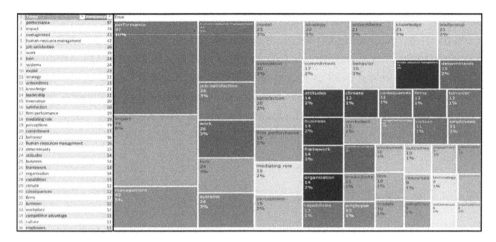

Figure 6 highlights the scientific output of the most referenced sources on HRM by years. As seen in this figure, the highest numbers of publications on HRM were published in the International Journal of Human Resource Management, followed by the International Journal of Contemporary Hospitality Management and the International Journal of Manpower. Another conclusion from Figure 6 is that while there was not much increase in the number of studies published in this field until 1998, a significant increase has been observed in studies on the subject since the 2000s.

Figure 7. Most Relevant Authors

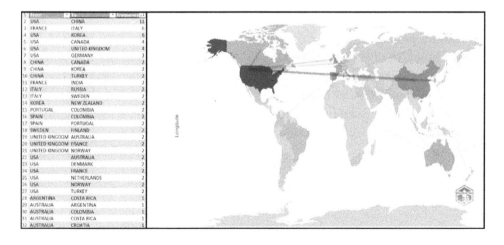

Figure 7 shows the most relevant and most frequently cited authors in the field of HRM. Accordingly, authors such as David E. Bowen, H. Kong, W. J. Rothwell, G. R. Ferris, and A. Fischer are among the most published and cited academics in the field of HRM. According to Google Scholar records as of May 17, 2024, David E. Bowen's study titled "The Service Organization: Human Resources Management Is Crucial" has received 1448 citations, his "HRM and Service Fairness: How Being Fair with Employees Spills Over to Customers" has garnered 600 citations, and his "Understanding HRM-Firm Performance Linkages: The Role of the 'Strength' of the HRM System" has been cited 5035 times. Together, these works have been cited more than 7000 times in total.

Figure 8. Most Relevant Affiliations

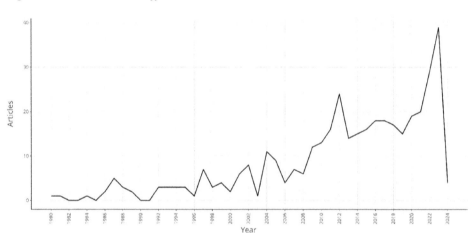

Figure 8 provides a graph of universities' publications in the field of HRM. The University of São Paulo ranks first with 11 studies, the University of California ranks second with 9 studies, and Hong Kong University of Science and Technology and the University of Cádiz rank third with 8 studies each. As can be seen from this figure, many universities in different parts of the world have made significant contributions to the field of HRM.

Figure 9. Corresponding Author's Countries

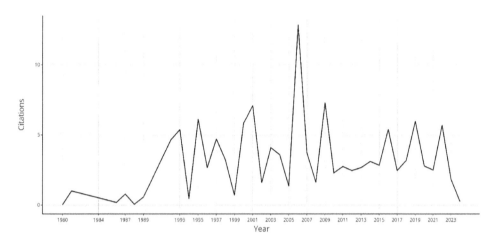

Figure 9 presents information about the countries of the authors who have published the most studies on HRM. According to this information, the USA leads with the highest number of publications on HRM, totaling 81 studies. It is followed by Spain with 40, China with 38, the UK with 28, and France with 21 studies. Additionally, the graph illustrates the intra-country (SCP) and inter-country (MCP) collaboration indices of these publications. Of the 81 studies published in the USA as the top-ranking country, 61 were written solely by authors from the USA, while 17 were co-authored with authors outside the country. The countries with the highest rates of international collaboration for HRM publications are the USA, China, France, Australia, Spain, and the UK.

Figure 10. Countries' Scientific Production

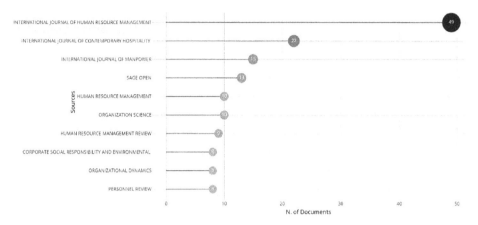

Figure 10 portrays the scientific output on HRM by country. The darker colors on the map indicate the countries where the numbers of publications are higher. Accordingly, the highest numbers of scientific studies in the field of HRM have been conducted in the USA, followed by China, Spain, the UK, and France. Furthermore, it can be concluded from this figure that HRM is a subject of interest and study in all regions of the world, including Asia, Europe, and the Americas.

Figure 11. Most Cited Countries

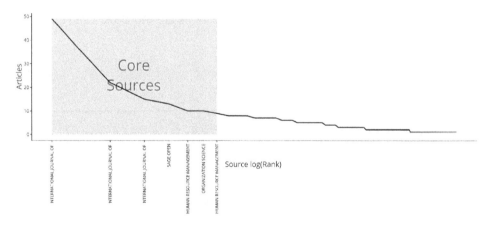

Figure 11 shows the countries with the highest numbers of citations in HRM and numbers of studies by years. According to this figure, the USA ranks first with 6980 citations, followed by China with 1712 citations, Spain with 1257 citations, the UK with 817 citations, and Canada and France with 485 citations each. This figure reveals the clear superiority of the USA in terms of numbers of citations.

Figure 12. Countries' Production Over Time

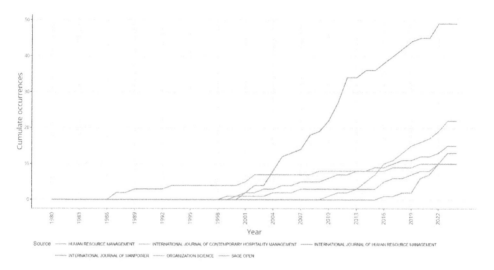

Figure 12 provides information about the scientific output of countries over time. From 1980 to 1996, there was a general horizontal trend in HRM; therefore, smaller numbers of studies were published. Since 1996, there has been a significant increase in the number of studies in general. In the last 10 years, from 2015 to 2024, the USA has had the highest numbers of publications in the field of HRM. China and Spain followed in second and third place, respectively. The year 2017 saw the highest increase compared to the previous year, with 27 studies published

Figure 13. Word Analysis

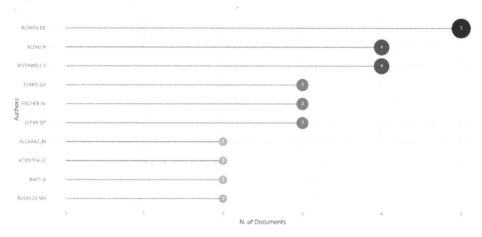

Figure 13 shows the most frequently used words in the abstracts, full texts, titles, and keywords of the studies. Word analysis provides concise information about the topic of a study, its overarching framework, and the problem it addresses. Additionally, word analysis allows for the examination of the most commonly used terms in a research field and transforms the text data into identifiers in the form of word clouds, also known as tag clouds (Patil et al., 2023, p. 14). It also helps researchers, indexers, and search engines find relevant studies, allowing these studies to reach more people and receive more citations, while also aiding researchers in seeing the gaps in the field and carrying out new studies (Baiyegunhi et al., 2022, p. 9-10).

Based on Figure 13, the most frequently used words in the abstracts of studies conducted in the field of HRM are as follows: "management," "human," "study," "resources," "research," "employees," "HRM," "practices," "performance," and "organization." The most frequently used words in the titles of the studies are as follows: "management," "human," "resources," "resource," "performance," and "employees." The most commonly used words in general are as follows: "human resources management," "management," "human resources," "sustainability," "innovation," "performance," and "job satisfaction." Finally, the following words were used most often in the keywords of the studies: "performance," "impact," "management," "human resource management," "job satisfaction," and "strategy." In general, the proportional distribution of the most frequently used words in the studies is as follows: "performance" (10%), "impact" (8%), "management" (5%), "human resource management" (5%), "job satisfaction" (3%), "work" (3%), "HRM" (3%), "systems" (3%), "model" (2%), and "strategy" (2%).

Figure 14. Countries' Collaboration World Map

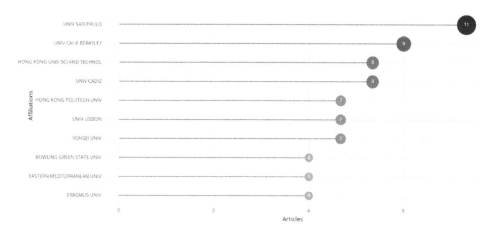

Figure 14 shows the collaboration between countries in publications on HRM. Darker colors indicate higher numbers of publications, while lines depict cooperation between countries. From this figure, it can be inferred that countries with a higher number of publications in this field tend to be more cooperative with each other. For instance, the USA and China exhibit a cooperative trend. Furthermore, the figure indicates that countries such as the USA, China, France, Italy, and the UK engage in more intensive cooperation in studies related to HRM.

CONCLUSION

HRM has emerged in response to the transformative changes in various domains such as technology, trade, production, consumption, and management, coupled with the heightened competitive landscape ushered in by globalization. The intensified competition has prompted organizations to engage in strategic planning, foresee potential future changes, enhance organizational effectiveness, and seek more information. This shift in focus heralded the evolution from personnel management to HRM, particularly towards the latter part of the 1970s. HRM encompasses approaches and sets of practices that address not only employer-employee relationships but also related actions, decisions, and issues within organizations (Ferris et al., 2004, p. 235).

In this study, the current landscape of HRM-related research worldwide has been illuminated using up-to-date data. The study has aimed to provide guidance for researchers and academics interested in this field. Utilizing the bibliometric analysis method, the study has addressed several significant questions and uncovered important insights. The key findings and conclusions derived from the study may be summarized as follows:

Studies in the field of HRM have seen a gradual increase, particularly since the 2000s. While the USA maintains a clear lead in research on this subject, HRM continues to garner significant attention worldwide, with research and articles being published across the globe. The USA stands out as the country with the highest numbers of publications, citations, and international collaborations in HRM, followed by countries such as China, Spain, and the UK. Additionally, this study observed that countries such as the USA, China, France, Italy, and the UK, which boast the highest numbers of publications, engage in more intensive cooperation in studies within this field.

This study has highlighted contributions to the subject of HRM from various regions worldwide and from different universities. Notably, the International Journal of Human Resource Management, International Journal of Contemporary Hospitality Management, and International Journal of Manpower emerged as the sources with the highest numbers of publications in this field. These journals serve as primary resources for individuals interested in new studies or research on HRM. Notably, authors such as David E. Bowen, H. Kong, W. J. Rothwell, G. R. Ferris, and A. Fischer are among the most published and cited academics in the field of HRM. Additionally, the universities with the highest numbers of publications in this field include the University of São Paulo, the University of California, Hong Kong University of Science and Technology, and the University of Cádiz. In terms of common themes, the most frequently used words in HRM studies include "management," "human," "study," "resources," "research," "employees," "HRM," "practices," "performance," and "organization." These terms reflect the central focus and areas of interest within the field of HRM.

REFERENCES

Adhav, A. (2017). Human Resource Management: Objectives And Functions. *International Journal of Advance and Applied Research*, 4(3), 35–37.

Ahammad, T. (2017). Personnel Management to Human Resource Management (HRM): How HRM Functions? *Journal of Modern Accounting and Auditing*, 13(9), 412–420. DOI:10.17265/1548-6583/2017.09.004

Alexa, L., Pîslaru, M., & Avasilcai, S. (2022). *From Industry 4.0 to Industry 5.0: An Overview of European Union Enterprises. A. Draghici, & L. Ivascu içinde, Sustainability and Innovation in Manufacturing Enterprises*. Springer.

Armstrong, M. (2006). *A Handbook of Human Resource Management Practice*. Kogan Page Publishers.

Ayman Güler, B. (2020). *Kamu Personeli: Sistem ve Yönetim*. İmge Kitabevi.

Bach, S. (2005). *Personnel Management*. Blackwell Publishing.

Baiyegunhi, T., Baiyegunhi, C., & Pharoe, B. (2022). Global Research Trends on Shale Gas from 2010–2020 Using a Bibliometric Approach. *Sustainability (Basel)*, 14(6), 1–22. DOI:10.3390/su14063461

Bayraktar, O., & Ataç, C. (2018). *The Effects of Industry 4.0 on Human Resources Management. E. Yıldırım, & H. Çeştepe içinde, Globalization, Institutions and Socio-Economic Performance*. Peter Lang.

Boas, T., & Gans-Morse, J. (2009). Haziran). Neoliberalism: From New Liberal Philosophy to Anti-Liberal Slogan. *Studies in Comparative International Development*, 44(2), 137–161. DOI:10.1007/s12116-009-9040-5

Boyd, C. (2003). *Human Resource Management and Occupational Health and Safety*. Routledge. DOI:10.4324/9780203428061_chapter_1

Carayannis, E., & Joanna Morawska, J. (2022). The Futures of Europe: Society 5.0 and Industry 5.0 as Driving Forces of Future Universities. *Journal of the Knowledge Economy*, 13(4), 3445–3471. DOI:10.1007/s13132-021-00854-2

Chalekian, P. (2013). POSDCORB: Core Patterns of Administration. *Proceedings of the 20th Conference on Pattern Languages of Programs*, (s. 1-20).

Dessler, G. (2020). *Human Resource Management*. Pearson.

Dirik, D., Eryılmaz, İ., & Erhan, T. (2023). Post-Truth Kavramı Üzerine Yapılan Çalışmaların VOSviewer ile Bibliyometrik Analizi. Sosyal Mucit Academic Review, 4(2), s. 164- 188. https://dergipark.org.tr/tr/download/article-file/3036932 (Acces Date: 12.01.2024)

Doğanoğlu, F. (2001). Küreselleşme ve İnsan Kaynakları Yönetimi. Öneri Dergisi, 4(16), s. 173- 181. DOI:10.14783/maruoneri.728734

Ellegaard, O., & Wallin, A. (2015). The Bibliometric Analysis of Scholarly Production: How? *Scientometrics*, 105(3), 1809–1831. DOI:10.1007/s11192-015-1645-z PMID:26594073

Erdil, O. (1996). Personelden İnsan Kaynakları Yönetimi Perspektifine. Öneri Dergisi, 1(4), 61- 65. https://dergipark.org.tr/tr/download/article-file/1025642 (Acces Date: 05.05.2024).

Eryılmaz, B. (2016). Kamu Yönetimi: Düşünceler, Yapılar, Fonksiyonlar ve Politikalar. Kocaeli: Umuttepe Yayınları.

European Commission. (2022). Industry 5.0. https://research-and-innovation.ec .europa.eu/: https://research-and-innovation.ec.europa.eu/research-area/industrial-research-and-innovation/industry-50_en#why-industry-50 (Acces Date: 05.07.2024).

Ferris, G., Hall, A., Todd, R., & Martocchio, J. (2004). Theoretical Development in the Field of Human Resources Management: Issues and Challenges for the Future. *Organizational Analysis*, 12(3), 231–254.

İnkaBlog. (2024). İnsan Kaynakları Süreçlerinde Dijital Dönüşüm ve Teknolojinin Rolü. https://blog.inkaik.com/insan-kaynaklari-sureclerinde-dijital-donusum-ve -teknolojinin-rolu/. (Access On: 22.05.2024)

Järlström, M., Saru, E., & Vanhala, S. (2016). Sustainable Human Resource Management with Salience of Stakeholders: A Top Management Perspective. *Journal of Business Ethics*, 152(3), 703–724. DOI:10.1007/s10551-016-3310-8

Jovanović, G., & Božilović, S. (2017). The Influence of Management of Human Resources on Motivation and Job Satisfaction. Ekonomika - Journal for Economic Theory and Practice and Social Issues, 63(1), s. 97-110. https://www.ceeol.com/ search/viewpdf?id=199986 (Access On: 22.05.2024)

Kabene, S., Orchard, C., Howard, J., Soriano, M., & Leduc, R. (2006). The Importance of Human Resources Management in Health Care: A Global Context. *Human Resources for Health*, 4(20), 1–17. DOI:10.1186/1478-4491-4-20 PMID:16872531

Kaufman, B. (2014). The Historical Development of American HRM Broadly Viewed. *Human Resource Management Review*, 24(3), 196–218. DOI:10.1016/j. hrmr.2014.03.003

Kaya, E., & Taş, İ. (2015). Personel Yönetimi İnsan Kaynakları Yönetimi Ayrımı. Kahramanmaraş Sütçü İmam Üniversitesi İktisadi ve İdari Bilimler Fakültesi Dergisi, 5(1), s. 21- 28. http://iibfdergisi.ksu.edu.tr/tr/download/article-file/107732 (Acces Date: 18.01.2024)

Kossek, E. (1987). Human Resources Management Innovation. *Human Resource Management*, 26(1), 71–92. DOI:10.1002/hrm.3930260105

Legge, K. (1995). *Human Resource Management: Rhetorics and Realities*. Macmillan Press. DOI:10.1007/978-1-349-24156-9

Lundy, O. (2006). From Personnel Management to Strategic Human Resource Management. *International Journal of Human Resource Management*, 5(3), 687–720. DOI:10.1080/09585199400000054

Margaret, P., & Winters, K. (1993). *İnsan Kaynakları*. Rota Yayınevi.

Naveen, D., Satish, K., Debmalya, M., Nitesh, P., & Weng Marc, L. (2021). How to Conduct a Bibliometric Analysis: An Overview and Guidelines. *Journal of Business Research*, 133, 285–296. DOI:10.1016/j.jbusres.2021.04.070

Öncer, A. (2019). Örgütlerde Yeşil İnsan Kaynakları Yönetimi Uygulamaları: Teorik Bir İnceleme. İş ve İnsan Dergisi, 6(2), s. 199-208. DOI:10.18394/iid.552555

Patil, R., Kumar, S., Rani, R., Agrawal, P., & Pippal, S. (2023). A Bibliometric and Word Cloud Analysis on the Role of the Internet of Things in Agricultural Plant Disease Detection. *Applied System Innovation*, 6(1), 2–17. DOI:10.3390/asi6010027

Pinnington, A., Macklin, R., & Campbell, T. (2007). *Human Resource Management: Ethics and Employment*. Oxford University Press. DOI:10.1093/oso/9780199203789.001.0001

Prins, P., Beirendonck, L., Vos, A., & Segers, J. (2014). Sustainable HRM: Bridging Theory and Practice Through the 'Respect Openness Continuity (ROC)' Model. *Management Review*, 25(4), 263–284.

Rana, G., & Sharma, R. (2019). Emerging human resource management practices in Industry 4.0. *Strategic HR Review*, 18(4), 176–181. DOI:10.1108/SHR-01-2019-0003

Rotich, K. (2015). History, Evolution and Development Of Human Resource Management: A Contemporary Perspective. *Global Journal of Human Resource Management*, 3(3), 58–73.

Sarma, A. (2009). Personnel and Human Resource Management. Mubai: Himalaya Publish House.

Shah, P., Dubey, R., Shashikant, R., Renwick, D., & Misra, S. (2023). Green Human Resource Management: A Comprehensive Investigation Using Bibliometric Analysis. *Corporate Social Responsibility and Environmental Management*, 31(1), 31–53. DOI:10.1002/csr.2589

Soliman, F., & Spooner, K. (2000). Strategies for Implementing Knowledge Management: Role of Human Resources Management. *Journal of Knowledge Management*, 4(4), 337–351. DOI:10.1108/13673270010379894

Summers, E. (1983). Bradford's Law and the Retrieval of Reading Research Journal Literature. *Reading Research Quarterly*, 19(1), 102–109. DOI:10.2307/747340

Torrington, D., Hall, L., & Taylor, S. (2008). *Human Resource Management*. Pearson.

Truss, C., & Gratton, L. (1994). Strategic Human Resource Management: A Conceptual Approach. *International Journal of Human Resource Management*, 5(3), 663–686. DOI:10.1080/09585199400000053

Waxin, M., & Bateman, R. (2009). Public Sector Human Resource Management Reform Across Countries: From Performance Appraisal to Performance Steering? *European Journal of International Management*, 3(4), 495–511. DOI:10.1504/EJIM.2009.028852

Wilkinson, E. (1972). The Ambiguity of Bradford's Law. *The Journal of Documentation*, 28(2), 122–130. DOI:10.1108/eb026534

Yıldız, D. (2022a). *Kademe Azaltma (Delayering). İ. Çevik Tekin içinde, Yenilikçi İnsan Kaynakları Uygulamaları ve Örgütsel İnovasyon: Teori, Örnek Olay ve Öneriler*. Nobel.

Yıldız, D. (2022b). *Sosyal Sorumluluk. İ. Çevik Tekin içinde, Güncel ve Teknolojik Gelişmeler Işığında İnsan Kaynakları Yönetimi*. Nobel.

Yılmaz, C., & Yılmaz, T. (2023). Endüstri 4.0'ın İnsan Kaynakları Yönetimine Etkisi: İKY 4.0. *Emek ve Toplum*, 12(32), 11–28. DOI:10.31199/hakisderg.1214130

Yılmazer, A. (2020). *İnsan Kaynakları Yöneitmi ve Örnk Olaylar*. Seçkin Yayıncılık.

Zaugg, R., Blum, A., & Thom, N. (2001). *Sustainability in Human Resource Management*. University of Berne Press.

Chapter 10
E–Training in HRM Context:
A Bibliometric Approach

Sunil Kumar
https://orcid.org/0000-0002-2362-1972
Shoolini University, India

Dushyanth Kumar
https://orcid.org/0000-0002-9483-9274
Lovely Professional University, India

ABSTRACT

E-training refers to virtual, web-based training programs. Organizations are increasingly adopting e-training tools and methods for human resource management (HRM). This study aims to describe the role of e-training and its tools in the learning and development of employees across organizations. Data were collected from the SCOPUS database, identifying 80 publications on e-training through keyword searches. Performance analysis was conducted using bibliometric methods, identifying relevant sources, authors, and countries, along with thematic and factorial evolution. Various problems, challenges, tools, and technologies were identified based on the literature. This study aims to guide and assist learning and development practitioners, scholars, and HR managers in understanding the significance of e-training methods and tools in HRM.

DOI: 10.4018/979-8-3693-4412-5.ch010

INTRODUCTION

Innovations in the field of Science and Technology are not only contributing for the welfare of the mankind, but also for the modernization and advancement in the field. Electronic training, which is virtual training (with the aid of internet) makes environment friendly and during disruptions e-training is the only method to enhance technical and soft skills of employees. Every organization has to ensure that this earth remains a good place to live in. Organisations must train their workforces to develop specialized technical knowledge and soft skills to adapt to changing conditions and boost Organisational effectiveness (Rao, 2009). Electronic training, often referred to as e-training or online training, involves the use of digital resources and technology to deliver educational content remotely.

Benefits of electronic training include flexibility, scalability, cost-effectiveness, and accessibility (Kumar and Kumar, 2023). However, successful implementation requires careful planning, effective instructional design, and consideration of learners' needs and preferences. Additionally, ensuring reliable internet connectivity and providing technical support are crucial for a positive e-training experience (Garg and Sharma, 2020).

Electronic training methods encompass a wide range of approaches and techniques for delivering educational content using digital technology. Each electronic training method has its advantages and limitations, and the most effective approach will depend on factors such as the nature of the content, the needs of the learners, and the available technology infrastructure. Effective implementation requires careful planning, clear learning objectives, and ongoing evaluation and refinement (Sife et al., 2007).

The use of electronic training, also known as e-training or online training, has become increasingly prevalent in various industries and educational settings. Here are several key ways in which electronic training is utilized:

1. **Employee Training and Development:** Many organizations use electronic training to onboard new employees in term of virtual onboarding (Hunt II, 2023), provide ongoing professional development, and deliver compliance training. This allows employees to access training materials at their convenience, regardless of their location, and often includes interactive modules, quizzes, and assessments to enhance learning outcomes.

2. **Education and Academia:** Educational institutions, from K-12 schools to universities, have integrated electronic training into their curriculum delivery methods. Online courses, virtual classrooms, and educational software platforms enable educators to reach a broader audience, provide flexible learning opportunities, and supplement traditional classroom instruction (Liu et al. 2020).

3. **Skills Training and Certification:** Electronic training is commonly used to develop specific skills and obtain certifications in fields such as information technology, healthcare, project management, and professional development. Online courses, simulations, and virtual labs allow learners to gain practical experience and demonstrate proficiency in their chosen areas (Aldrich, 2009).

4. **Continuing Education and Lifelong Learning:** Electronic training platforms offer a convenient way for professionals to pursue continuing education credits, enhance their knowledge, and stay current with industry trends (Weggen and Urdan, 2000). Online courses, webinars, and self-paced modules cater to learners' schedules and preferences, enabling lifelong learning opportunities.

5. **Remote Work and Distributed Teams:** With the rise of remote work and distributed teams, electronic training facilitates collaboration, communication, and skill development among geographically dispersed employees. Virtual meetings, webinars, and online collaboration tools support ongoing training and knowledge sharing across remote locations (Greenhalgh et al. 2024).

6. **Customer and Partner Training:** Organizations use electronic training to educate customers, partners, and stakeholders on product features, best practices, and support resources (Yazdani et al., 2023). Online tutorials, knowledge bases, and self-service portals empower users to troubleshoot issues, maximize product usage, and become advocates for the brand.

7. **Healthcare and Medical Training:** Electronic training is employed in healthcare settings to train medical professionals, students, and support staff on clinical procedures, patient safety protocols, and compliance requirements. Simulations, virtual reality (VR) simulations, and e-learning modules simulate realistic scenarios and enhance learning outcomes in a safe environment (Burnett and Goldhaber-Fiebert, 2024).

8. **Government and Military Training:** Government agencies and military organizations utilize electronic training to train personnel on a wide range of topics, including cybersecurity, emergency response, military tactics, and leadership skills. Online courses, simulations, and scenario-based training prepare individuals for real-world challenges and operational readiness (Kumar and Kumar, 2023).

Overall, the use of electronic training offers numerous benefits, including flexibility, scalability, cost-effectiveness, and accessibility. By leveraging digital technology and innovative instructional design, organizations can create engaging learning experiences that empower individuals to acquire new skills, advance their careers, and achieve their learning goals.

The e-training raises awareness of the fact that every change typically has a positive side as well as being at least the norm. If participants have problem-solving attitudes while facing disruptive situations, their enhanced agility and resilience will suit them to thrive through crises. The e-Training is a digital method of training with the aid of the internet to impart soft skills and behavioural changes, which ultimately enhances agility and resilience in workforces. Computers through the internet are aiding in solving problems, various online exercises and practices. In e-training, Audio-Video methods are used to teach soft skills and knowledge (Rao, 2009). E-Training empowers the modern-age workforce for their self-performance management (Zareie and Navimipour, 2020).

The e-Training methods are:

- Synchronous e-Training [Live audio-video-communication between trainer and trainees]
- Asynchronous e-Training [Delayed time communication, e.g., e-mail, discussion forum, etc.]
- Computer-Based Training- CBT [Preloaded e-courses which are made available on Laptops/Desktop Computers]
- Web-Based Training –WBT [Trainees will learn by accessing the Web]
- Simulation e-Training [Highly interactive, e.g., graphics, audio, and video are used to show similar kinds of situations]
- Game-Based e-Training
- Blended e-Training [synchronous and asynchronous methods]
- Mobile e-Training
- Social Media e-Training

The brief about e-Training methods is as follows:

Synchronous Training: Any learning that occurs when both the trainer and the trainee are present simultaneously is called synchronous training. For instance, synchronous learning occurred when we were in school and regularly attended classes (Granda *et al.*, 2015). The synchronous training promotes the real-time discussion, can create cross-team collaboration and it is a time-sensitive training.

Asynchronous training is when employees access their training coursework without the guidance of a trainer and catch up on their own. As a result, they can access the data at any time and from any place (Prapti, 2023). The following are the advantages of asynchronous training:

- *More reliable outcomes:* With formal instruction, everyone picks up the same skills in the same manner.
- *Improved retention:* That is because it leads itself. As a result, the trainees do not go on to the next subject until they have a firm grasp of the previous one.
- *Every year, save money:* Similarly, employees do not need to nag management when they can complete their training independently.
- *On-demand responses:* The majority of people go to their manager first when they have questions.
- *Encourages hybrid work:* One of the interventions to promote hybrid work management.

Computer-Based Training (CBT) is the process and means of delivering e-Training programmes using a networked or personal computer. Online, web-based, mobile, remote learning, and synchronous and asynchronous are all possible. CBT can teach various subjects but is particularly effective when teaching specific skills and knowledge (Bedwell and Salas, 2010).

Web-based training is also known as internet-based training (IBT); online learning, often known as e-Training, gives employees the freedom to learn whenever and wherever they want, offering unmatched flexibility. WBT can be offered as self-paced learning, instructor-led virtual training, or a combination through a blended learning environment (Khan, 2001; Driscoll and Tomiak, 2000).

Simulation training is the process of creating a realistic learning environment that resembles real-world tasks and situations. Trainees can use real information and skills through actual, hands-on exercises, reading theory books, and attending lectures. Because it takes into account a range of learning methods chosen by various learners, this sort of training is incredibly effective. Simulator-based training considers the demands of kinesthetic learners who prefer hands-on activities because not everyone learns visually or audibly. Simulation-based training is an efficient and highly effective way to teach trainees important skills. It offers the finest means for companies to gauge how well their trainees use their knowledge and make judgement calls (Kincaid *et al.*, 2003; Ward *et al.*, 2006; Fraser *et al.*, 2012).

Game-based Training: Using games and other interactive activities, game-based training teaches trainees new skills and information. Instructors can keep trainees motivated and interested throughout training by making learning more pleasant. Game-based training can take many forms, and the particular games and exercises employed will change depending on the program's objectives and the learner group (Kapp, 2012; Dahalan *et al.*, 2023).

Blended Training: Blended Training combines e-Training and in-person training (traditional training). Due to the pandemic, several firms have recently switched to blended training. Blended learning, often known as blended training, combines the best aspects of traditional face-to-face training with online learning. Blended training enhances learning by allowing for greater flexibility and accessibility and maximising the benefits of both learning styles (Ma *et al.*, 2022; Haftador *et al.*,2023).

Mobile e-Training: Training Programs or content provided or accessed using a mobile device are called mobile training. When a learner or employee is not in a set or predetermined place, the goal of mobile training is to transmit knowledge content to them. (Dahri *et al.*, 2022).

Social Media e-Training: social media serves as a digital portrait of a person by collecting online-catalogued images, phrases, situations, and interactions. Employees should use social media in a way that considers both their level of platform experience and their pertinent professional abilities. Veterans of the workplace for twenty years will not approach social media like a recent graduate who is a digital native may. In order to ensure that every employee receives basic social media training, incorporate in the organisation policy that every employee needs to know about social media access. At least once a year, or after a social media disaster, the company should review its social media policy to make sure it is current and functioning as intended (Susanti *et al.*, 2022; López-Torres *et al.*, 2022; Herman *et al.*,2022).

In the context of large organizations, Learning Management Systems (LMS), Massive Open Online Courses (MOOCs), Virtual Instructor-Led Training (VILT), and Custom E-learning Solutions are more suitable. On the other hand, for Small and Medium Enterprises (SMEs), Off-the-Shelf E-learning Courses, Microlearning, Blended Learning, and Social Learning Platforms are suitable for imparting learning to employees. E-learning approaches vary considerably throughout the business, public, and non-governmental sectors, each tailored to individual demands and goals. In the commercial world, advanced LMSs, MOOCs, and custom solutions prioritize scalability, ROI, and engagement. The public sector stresses accessibility, standardization, and compliance through technologies like Moodle, Blackboard, and virtual classrooms. NGOs seek flexibility, cost-effectiveness, and localized content, and they typically use open-source LMS, mobile learning, and social learning platforms. Best practices in all sectors include connecting e-learning with company goals, making it accessible, fostering continuous learning, and using data to improve.

The present study will help to understand the theoretical and historical aspects of e-training, the problems and challenges associated with implementation of e-training and tools and methods of e-training adopted by organizations. Moreover, the e-training is explored in form of quantitative evidences regarding contributors, sources and thematic evolution.

THEORETICAL BACKGROUND OF STUDY

The theoretical foundation for this study is distributive cognition and conservation of resources theory (Hobfoll, 1989). Distributive Cognition, proposed by Edwin Hutchins in 1995, views cognitive processes as spread across individuals, tools, and the environment. Key concepts include distributed intelligence, which posits that intelligence spans people, tools, and artifacts, rather than being confined to the individual brain. Cognitive artifacts, such as notepads and smartphones, are tools that enhance cognitive abilities. Additionally, scaffolding in e-training refers to the external support provided by teachers, computer programs, or other aids to help individuals tackle complex tasks. While conservation of resources is significant concept in organizational management of stress and burnout. E-training tools and artifacts leads the learners to develop cognitive abilities and conserve the scare organizational resources. There are multiple benefits of training and learning at individual and organizational level.

Workplace training, which includes team collaboration and regular programs, enhances employee adaptability and resilience (Katayama & Bennett, 1999; Sambrook, 2005). It fosters inner abilities and positive psychological changes (Maheshwari & Vohra, 2018). With technological advancements, training has shifted to digital formats, empowering employees through e-training (Nagy, 2005; Zareie & Navimipour, 2020).

E-Training, accelerated by technology and the COVID-19 pandemic, offers flexible learning and often incorporates gamification to enhance engagement (Alfaqiri et al., 2022). Training positively impacts performance, though its effectiveness varies with employee commitment and competence (Pramono & Prahiawan, 2022). Effective programs address skill gaps, enhancing organizational success and productivity (Igudia, 2022; Raja & Kumar, 2016).

Organizations must establish training policies to enhance skills and productivity. Training supports skill development, change implementation, and new work norms (Maheshwari & Vohra, 2018). Evaluating training effectiveness ensures alignment with organizational goals and continuous improvement (Isaacs et al., 2021; Sitzmann & Weinhardt, 2017). A well-trained workforce is essential for growth and adaptability (Owoyemi et al., 2011; Sandamali et al., 2018).

Additionally, green HR practices emphasize training for sustainable behaviors (Veerasamy et al., 2023). Continuous investment in training is crucial for developing competencies, supporting strategies, and fostering a resilient organizational culture (Sudhakar & Basariya, 2017; Prasad, 2016; Sitzmann & Weinhardt, 2018).

E-Training is a virtual method for teaching technical and soft skills and making necessary behavioral adjustments, enhancing workforce agility and resilience to technological changes. This innovative approach uses technological tools to save money and time, update information, and develop green organizations (Agariya & Singh, 2012; Granda et al., 2015). It addresses the high costs and inflexibility of offline training (Mohsin & Sulaiman, 2013) and boosts employee self-efficacy and technical capabilities (Tan & Rasdi, 2017).

E-Training delivers knowledge through online or intranet distance learning, enhancing employee performance (Amara & Atia, 2016; Ramayah et al., 2012). It suits adult learners who are independent and mature and is popular for its flexibility, accessibility, and cost-effectiveness (Rosenberg, 2006). Constructs impacting e-Training include trainee experience, outcomes, and quality dimensions. Platforms like Zoom, Google Meet, Teams, Webex, and Gotowebinar are used for e-training sessions, helping employees acquire technical and soft skills flexibly. Enterprise social media (ESM) is also used to enhance employee collaboration and agility (Pitafi et al., 2020).

E-Training positively impacts organizational development, performance, competence, and commitment (Sudhakar & Basariya, 2017; Sandamali et al., 2018; Owoyemi et al., 2011). Factors favoring e-Training systems include ease of use, utility, compatibility, and social impact (Al-Fraihat et al., 2020). Consistent e-Training platforms provide essential tools and knowledge during technological changes, as seen in sectors like agri-food adopting e-Training for sustainable practices (Marinagi et al., 2019). Technologies like gamification, virtual reality, augmented reality, and AI enhance e-Training delivery (Fertig et al., 2019; Kaizer et al., 2020).

Problems and Challenges of E-Training

- *Technical Issues:* E-Training depends heavily on technology, and issues like poor internet connectivity, software glitches, and hardware failures can disrupt learning (Agariya & Singh, 2012).
- *Lack of Engagement:* Engaging trainees in a virtual environment can be difficult. Without the physical presence of instructors or peers, learners may feel isolated and less motivated (Alfaqiri et al., 2022).
- *Limited Interaction:* The absence of face-to-face interaction can hinder the development of soft skills and limit opportunities for collaborative learning and networking (Ramayah et al., 2012).
- *Varied Technological Proficiency:* Differences in employees' technological skills can affect the effectiveness of e-training. Those less comfortable with technology may struggle, leading to inconsistent learning outcomes (Tan & Rasdi, 2017).
- *Quality of Content:* Maintaining the quality and relevance of e-training content is essential. Outdated or poorly designed materials can reduce training effectiveness (Sambrook, 2005).

- *Assessment and Feedback:* Evaluating the effectiveness of e-training and providing timely feedback is more challenging compared to traditional training methods (Sitzmann & Weinhardt, 2017).
- *Security Concerns:* E-Training platforms can be vulnerable to cyber threats, risking the security of sensitive company information and personal data (Abanda Maga et al., 2019).
- *Adaptability and Customization:* Creating e-training programs that can be easily adapted and customized for different employees and departments is a complex task (Pramono & Prahiawan, 2022).
- *Resistance to Change:* Employees may resist switching from traditional training methods to e-training due to comfort with established practices and doubts about digital learning's effectiveness (Owoyemi et al., 2011).
- *Cost of Implementation:* Although e-training can be cost-effective over time, the initial expenses for technology, content development, and platform maintenance can be high (Sudhakar & Basariya, 2017).

Addressing these challenges requires a strategic approach, including investing in robust technological infrastructure, designing engaging and interactive content, supporting employees with varying tech skills, and regularly updating and evaluating training programs to ensure their effectiveness.

Modern Tools and Technologies in Training

- *Gamification:* Gamification in employee training is becoming more popular but still lacks specific, science-based guidelines for implementation. Armstrong and Landers (2018) have explained the scientific basis for gamification in web-based employee training. Incorporating game elements into training can significantly boost learner engagement and motivation (Larson, 2020). Effective design is crucial for the success of gamified training. Current trends suggest that incorporating virtual reality, augmented reality, and simulators can further enhance training experiences. However, challenges like resistance to change, demographic concerns, and ethical issues impede its broader adoption (Santos et al., 2021). Game-based learning proves to be more engaging and immersive. Gamified training programs are addressing the industry's demand for innovative methods to improve learning outcomes (Kulkarni et al., 2022).
- *Augmented Reality, Virtual Reality and Mixed Reality:*Daling & Schlittmeier (2024) discuss the impact of mixed reality (MR)-based training on performance in manual assembly tasks, addressing industrial needs and effects. Mixed reality, comprising augmented reality (AR) and virtual real-

ity (VR), holds promise for training purposes (Lee et al., 2021). However, current research in this field yields varied outcomes due to differences in hardware, tasks, and methodologies. AR-based training significantly enhances performance, while VR-based training generally matches the effectiveness of traditional methods. Although MR-based training is not consistently superior, it often parallels the effectiveness of traditional training, with potential enhancements through integrating AR and VR. Wider adoption faces challenges such as organizational resistance, demographic concerns, and ethical considerations. In sectors like surgery and military training, MR technologies offer immersive, secure training environments, particularly beneficial where traditional training methods are impractical (Amorim, 2013). According to Kaplan (2021), extended reality (XR), encompassing AR, VR, and MR, proves as effective as traditional training methods across diverse domains, especially in scenarios involving risks or high costs.

- *Artificial Intelligence and Machine Learning:* AI has become a prominent technology in the 21st century (Bordegoni and Ferrise, 2023). Upadhyay and Khandelwal (2019) examine AI-based training, emphasizing its role in personalized and adaptive learning to enhance training effectiveness across various industries. Maity (2019) explores AI's application in industrial maintenance, utilizing technologies such as digital twins and the metaverse to enhance knowledge acquisition and skill development. Lane et al. (2005) and Fiok et al. (2022) review explainable AI (XAI), stressing its significance in addressing the risks associated with AI's opaque decision-making processes, particularly in educational contexts. Additionally, Paranjape et al. (2019) discuss the integration of AI into medical education, advocating for a curriculum framework aimed at equipping healthcare professionals with AI skills to improve clinical decision-making and healthcare outcomes.

- *Learning Management System:* Wu (2024) explores the adoption of learning management systems (LMS) in the EU and China, identifying popular platforms and highlighting regional differences in digital education strategies. Similarly, Prestoza (2024) investigates how Filipino public-school teachers use Google Classroom within blended learning frameworks, noting its benefits and the challenges posed by connectivity issues. Gupta et al. (2024) discusses the integration of Web 3.0 technologies and AI in distance education during the COVID-19 pandemic, proposing frameworks to enhance global knowledge sharing and educational accessibility while addressing the persistent challenges of technology integration in teaching and learning processes.

- Overall, numerous microlearning and simulation platforms have been developed by organizations for the training and development of their employees.

Advancing technology is creating many opportunities for learners and trainers to interact and learn remotely.

Role of E-Training in Human Resource Management (HRM)

- *Skill Development and Enhancement:* E-Training is vital for developing and improving both technical and soft skills among employees, facilitating ongoing learning and skill updates essential for today's dynamic work environment (Zareie & Navimipour, 2020).
- *Flexibility and Accessibility:* E-Training offers flexible and accessible learning opportunities, enabling employees to access training materials at any time and from any location, which is especially advantageous for remote workers or those with irregular schedules (Alfaqiri et al., 2022).
- *Cost-Effectiveness:* By eliminating the need for physical classrooms, travel, and printed materials, e-training significantly reduces training costs for organizations, making it a cost-effective solution for large-scale training initiatives (Mohsin & Sulaiman, 2013).
- *Personalized Learning:* E-Training platforms often use adaptive learning technologies to tailor content to individual learning styles and paces, enhancing the effectiveness and engagement of the learning process (Pramono & Prahiawan, 2022).
- *Tracking and Analytics:* These platforms provide robust tracking and analytics features, allowing HR departments to monitor employee progress, evaluate training effectiveness, and identify areas for improvement (Sitzmann & Weinhardt, 2017).
- *Compliance and Standardization:* E-Training ensures that all employees receive consistent and standardized training, which is essential for meeting industry regulations and organizational standards (Ramayah et al., 2012).
- *Support for Organizational Change:* E-Training facilitates organizational change by quickly disseminating new policies, procedures, and cultural shifts to the workforce, aiding in smooth transitions (Maheshwari & Vohra, 2018).
- *Employee Engagement and Retention:* Interactive and gamified e-training programs can boost employee motivation and satisfaction, leading to higher retention rates (Alfaqiri et al., 2022).
- *Sustainability Initiatives:* E-Training supports green HRM practices by minimizing the environmental impact associated with traditional training methods, such as paper use and travel.
- *Global Reach:* E-Training enables organizations to deliver training to a geographically dispersed workforce, ensuring uniform quality of training for all employees regardless of location (Marinagi et al., 2019).

Incorporating e-training into HRM strategies helps organizations cultivate a skilled, adaptable, and engaged workforce while optimizing resources and aligning with strategic goals.

Method

The data was downloaded from SCOPUS database. In total 80 documents were identified for further analysis. The main information of data is given below in the Table 1. Bibliometrix package in R Language is used for analysis purpose. The Sources, authors, countries, citations, conceptual and thematic evolution of E-training was analysed to study the concept of E-training in contemporary organization. The performance analysis and science mapping tools used in the study, which are the most used tools in bibliometric analysis across the fields (Donthu et al., 2021).

The SCOPUS database is beneficial for bibliometric analysis due to its extensive coverage of peer-reviewed literature across various disciplines and its provision of high-quality data. Additionally, SCOPUS offers advanced analytics tools for comprehensive citation analysis, h-index computation, and visualization of research trends and collaborations.

Table 1. Main Information of Data used for Bibliometric Analysis

Description	Results
Timespan	1974:2024
Sources (Journals, Books, etc)	70
Documents	80
Document Average Age	8.45
Average citations per doc	6.338
References	1489
Document Contents	
Keywords Plus (ID)	794
Author's Keywords (DE)	285
Authors	
Authors	277
Authors of single-authored docs	12
Authors Collaboration	
Single-authored docs	12
Co-Authors per Doc	3.8
International co-authorships %	6.25

continued on following page

Table 1. Continued

Description	Results
Document Types	
Article	36
Book chapter	2
Conference paper	40
Note	1
Review	1

Source: SCOPUS Database

Bibliometric Analysis

Annual Scientific Production: The results show significant positive growth in publications from 2009 onward. In 2019, the highest number of articles, 10, were published. This may be attributed to the pandemic and work-from-home conditions faced during this period. Post-pandemic, a consistent growth is observed in the literature on e-training. The growth of literature on e-training was slow during the initial years, but now it seems to be gaining pace, with increasing interest from scholars in this area (see Figure 1).

Figure 1. Annual Scientific Production

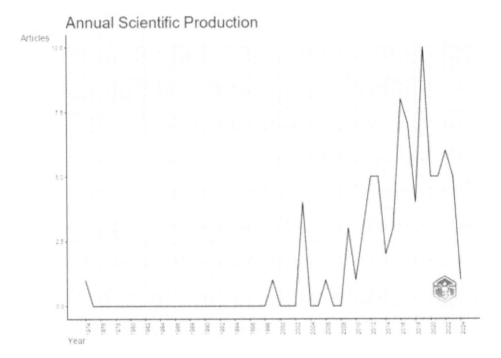

Three Field Plot: In the three-field plot, 'keywords' are mapped to 'authors' and 'authors' are mapped to 'countries'. Terms like 'e-training' and 'e-learning' appear to be more frequently used by authors publishing from the USA. Chinese authors dominate the publication sphere in terms like 'items', 'equipment', 'interactive', and 'electronic training'. This dominance may be attributed to the delivery, measurement, and involvement of trainees in electronic training. The authors also discussed artifacts used in e-training in terms of training aids. Information technology emerges as a major keyword used by many authors (see Figure 2).

Figure 2. Three Field Plot (Keyword, Authors, Countries)

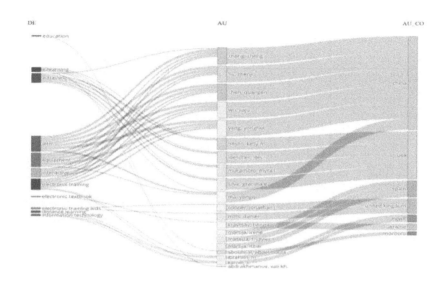

Performance Analysis: The performance analysis of the research topic focuses on relevant sources, authors, affiliations, and countries. The majority of literature on e-training and learning is published in the proceedings of conferences and workshops. The Institute of Computer Applications leads with 12 publications, followed by the University of Arizona with 9 publications. In terms of average citations per article, the USA ranks first, followed by the UK. The contribution of authors to this field of study is illustrated in Figure 3.

Table 2. Sources, Authors, Affiliations, and Countries

Sources		Affiliation		Countries		
Sources	*Articles*	*Affiliation*	*Articles*	*Country*	*Tc*	*Citations*
CEUR Workshop Proceedings	6	Institute of computer application	12	USA	128	11.6
Lecture Notes in Networks and Systems	3	University of Arizona	9	United Kingdom	51	25.5
Proceedings 2018 Chinese Automation Congress, CAC 2018	3	Center for autism and related disorders	6	Iran	19	4.8
Advances in intelligent systems and computing	2	XI'AN Jiaotong university	6	Spain	11	11
15th international conference of technology, learning and teaching of electronics, TAEE 2022 - proceedings	1	Hefei University	5	China	10	1.4

continued on following page

Table 2. Continued

Sources		Affiliation		Countries		
Sources	Articles	Affiliation	Articles	Country	Tc	Citations
2010 international conference on networking and digital society, ICNDS 2010	1	Nizhny Novgorod State Pedagogical University Named After Kozma Minin (Minin University)	5	Malaysia	9	4.5
2015 7th Computer Science and Electronic Engineering Conference, CEEK 2015 - Conference Proceedings	1	Oak Ridge Associated Universities	5	Ukraine	4	2
2016 13th International Scientific-Technical Conference on Actual Problems of Electronic Instrument Engineering, APEIE 2016 - Proceedings	1	Tashkent State Dental Institute	5	Poland	2	2
2016 IEEE 5th forum strategic partnership of universities and enterprises of Hi-tech branches, science. education. innovations 2016	1	Thomas Jefferson University	5	Morocco	1	1

Source: SCOPUS

Figure 3. Authors Production Over Time

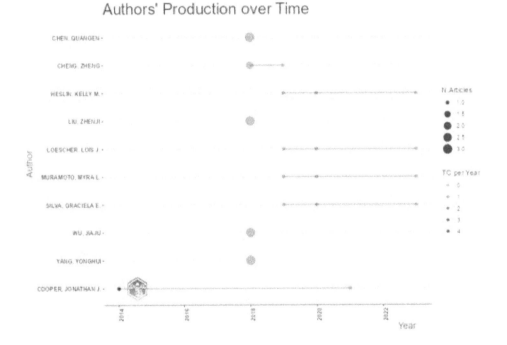

Trend Topics: The "Trend Topics" in Figure 4 visualizes the frequency of various e-training and learning terms in publications from 2003 to 2021. The Y-axis lists terms like "students," "learning systems," and "curricula," while the X-axis shows the timeline. Bubble sizes represent term frequencies, with larger bubbles indicating higher occurrences. The position of each bubble along the timeline reflects the years when terms were frequently mentioned, with terms such as "e-learning" and "education" peaking around 2015-2017.

Key observations reveal consistent mentions of terms like "students," "learning systems," and "curricula," with a noticeable increase in recent years, indicating sustained interest. Terms like "e-learning," "education," and "teaching" show a significant rise around 2015-2017, highlighting a peak in research. The term "internet" peaked earlier around 2003 but declined in later years, suggesting a shift in focus or terminology. Other terms, such as "electronics," "engineering education," and "personnel training," show increasing relevance over time. The chart provides insights into evolving research trends and the emergence of key topics in the field of e-training and learning.

Figure 4. Trend Topics

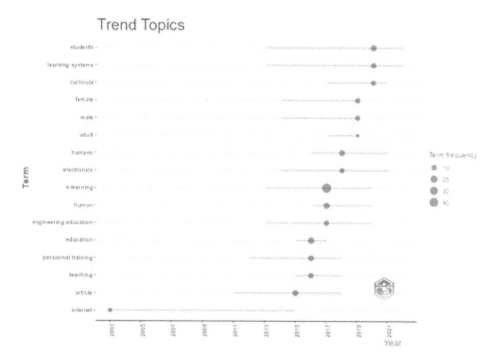

Thematic Analysis: Figure 5 maps various themes related to e-training and learning based on their development degree (density) and relevance degree (centrality), dividing them into four quadrants. The top right quadrant, Motor Themes, contains themes that are both well-developed and central to the research field, such as "human," "education," "article," "e-learning," "personnel training," and "engineering education." The top left quadrant, Niche Themes, includes well-developed but less central themes like "animal welfare," "reward," "animal behavior," "education computing," "application programs," "electronic textbooks," "electronic training," "IETM," and "equipment trainings." The bottom right quadrant, Basic Themes, consists of central but underdeveloped themes such as "students," "learning systems," "educational resource," "training," "female," and "male." The bottom left quadrant, Emerging or Declining Themes, features themes that are neither well-developed nor central, including "information use," "e-training," "information systems," and "optimization."

Key observations from Figure 5 indicate that Motor Themes like "human," "education," "e-learning," and "engineering education" are critical areas of focus, being both highly relevant and well-developed. Niche Themes like "animal welfare," "education computing," and "electronic training" are specialized but not central to the main research agenda, suggesting their importance to specific subfields. Basic Themes such as "students," "learning systems," and "educational resource" are crucial but require further development, pointing to potential areas for future research. Emerging or Declining Themes like "information use," "e-training," and "optimization" may be new and emerging or possibly declining in relevance, highlighting areas needing more investigation to determine their future trajectory. Overall, Figure 5 provides a comprehensive view of the e-training and learning research landscape, emphasizing which themes are central and well-developed and which are emerging or underdeveloped yet significant.

Figure 5. Thematic Mapping of E-Training

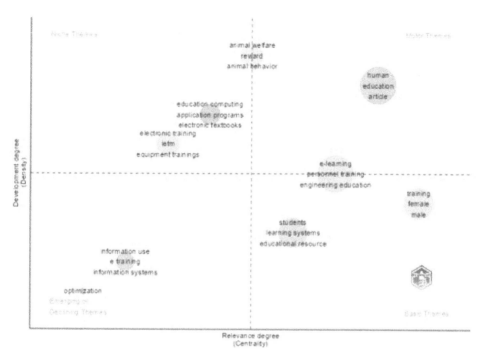

Thematic Evolution: The thematic evolution shows the transformation of specific themes related to education and training across three distinct time periods: 1974-2015, 2016-2019, and 2020-2024. In the first period (1974-2015), prevalent themes include educational environment, electronic training, information technology, e-learning, personnel training, education, articles, and learning. The educational environment consistently appears in all periods, signifying ongoing interest in educational contexts. Electronic training evolves into e-learning, highlighting the increasing importance of online education.

During the 2016-2019 period, new themes such as IETM (Interactive Electronic Technical Manuals), female, and training systems emerge, indicating a diversification from previous themes. Information technology branches into more specialized areas like education and the educational environment, while personnel training transitions into training systems. E-learning remains a significant theme, expanding from its earlier presence.

In the latest period (2020-2024), themes continue to evolve. Learning remains a core theme, now complemented by a new focus on human aspects, underscoring a growing emphasis on human-centered approaches. E-learning continues to be crucial, and a new theme, engineering education, emerges, highlighting a specialized focus in educational trends.

Overall, the Figure 6 effectively captures the dynamic nature of thematic evolution in education and training. It illustrates the continuity of certain themes like e-learning and the educational environment while highlighting the emergence of new areas such as human aspects and engineering education, reflecting broader trends and shifts in focus over time.

Figure 6. Thematic Mapping of E-Training

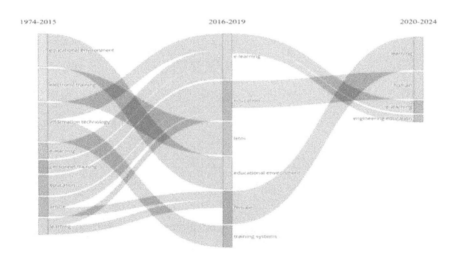

Factorial Analysis: Figure 7 illustrates the relationships between various terms in the context of e-training and learning, plotted based on their co-occurrence in the literature. The X-axis likely represents centrality or relevance, indicating how central a term is within the research field, while the Y-axis likely represents density or development, indicating how developed or specialized a term is within its cluster. The terms are grouped into clusters represented by shaded areas, highlighting thematic areas within the research field. The placement and size of each cluster indicate the degree of centrality and development of that theme.

Key observations reveal that the top right cluster, containing terms like "computer-assisted instruction," "clinical competence," and "in-service training," represents highly specialized and well-developed themes related to instructional methods and professional development. The bottom right cluster, with terms like "controlled study," "randomized controlled trial," and "human experiment," focuses on empirical research and experimental studies. The top left cluster, including terms like "information and communication technologies," "teaching," and "economics," represents broader, interdisciplinary themes related to technology integration in education. The central cluster, with terms like "education," "medical education," and "internet," represents core themes central to e-training and learning, covering general education topics and common research methodologies. This thematic map provides a visual representation of the research landscape, highlighting areas of central importance, specialized research, and interdisciplinary connections

Figure 7. Factorial Analysis of E-Training

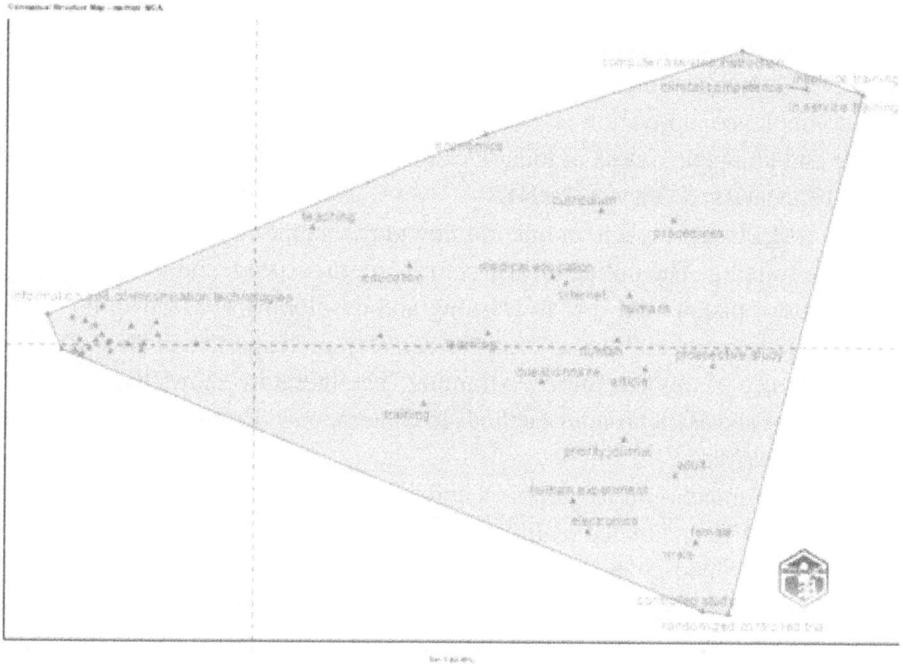

DISCUSSION

Organizations today face a pressing need to maintain agility and resilience in their workforce, driven by the dynamic nature of the business environment. E-Training methods have emerged as critical tools in achieving these objectives, noted for their unique ability to adapt and respond swiftly to changing circumstances. This paradigm shift towards digital learning has garnered significant attention from management scholars, highlighting its potential to enhance organizational effectiveness and employee performance (Sun et al., 2008; Zhao & Namasivayam, 2009). Research identified the pivotal role of e-Training in developing workforce, particularly in sectors where technical expertise and adaptability are paramount for operational success during disruptions (Strother, 2002; Holsapple & Lee-Post, 2006).

Effective implementation of e-Training not only improves job-specific skills but also fosters a culture of continuous learning and adaptation within organizations. This approach is crucial for translating acquired knowledge into tangible job performance improvements, surpassing traditional metrics of training success such as mere satisfaction (Rowold, 2007). Furthermore, studies highlight the intrinsic link between perceived usefulness of e-Training, learner engagement, and organizational outcomes, emphasizing its role in achieving strategic goals and enhancing workforce capabilities (Roca et al., 2006; Wang et al., 2007). By leveraging digital tools effectively, organizations can not only enhance their operational resilience but also bolster employee motivation and engagement, thereby ensuring sustained performance and competitiveness in today's challenging business landscape (Al-Hila et al., 2017; Kabassi & Virvou, 2004).

The artifacts and tools in online training play a significant role in the effectiveness of e-training. The online infrastructure, internet speed, and facilities built by organizations play a vital role in learning and development. Meanwhile, training content and trainers' abilities in terms of delivery and expertise in the area impact the experience of trainees during e-training. The literature shows the presence of synchronous and asynchronous methods in contemporary organizations to train and develop employees.

The major impetus is on equipment and interactions, although modern technologies like AR, VR, and mixed reality are being integrated with e-training tools. Both government and non-government organizations are deploying e-training tools with AR, VR, and gamification. The study shows that e-learning and training are dominating the education sector. Most educational institutions are incorporating online tools into their systems for the learning and development of students.

CONCLUSION

A profound transformation has occurred in e-training and learning, particularly during and after the COVID-19 pandemic, marked by a significant increase in literature focusing on the development and application of e-training tools. The education and healthcare industries are at the forefront of research and utilization of these tools, while other sectors are also increasingly adopting modern training and development methods. The USA and China dominate the production of research in e-training. Contemporary research on e-training is primarily driven by empirical and experimental studies. Organizations are progressively adopting and implementing e-training tools for human resource development, with technologies like AI influencing processes from recruitment to retirement. E-training has become a critical component of organizational practices and will continue to be an integral part of human resource management.

REFERENCES:

Abanda Maga, M. F., Kala Kamdjoug, J. R., Fosso Wamba, S., & Nitcheu Tcheuffa, P. C. (2019). Factors affecting adoption and use of e-learning by business employees in Cameroon. In *New Knowledge in Information Systems and Technologies* (Vol. 3, pp. 216–226). Springer International Publishing. DOI:10.1007/978-3-030-16187-3_21

Agariya, A. K., & Singh, D. (2012). e-Learning quality: Scale development and validation in Indian context. *Knowledge Management & E-Learning*, 4(4), 500–517.

Al-Fraihat, D., Joy, M., & Sinclair, J. (2020). Evaluating E-learning systems success: An empirical study. *Computers in Human Behavior*, 102, 67–86. DOI:10.1016/j.chb.2019.08.004

Al-Hila, A. A., Alhelou, E., Al Shobaki, M. J., & Abu Naser, S. S. (2017). The impact of applying the dimensions of IT governance in improving e-training-case study of the ministry of telecommunications and information technology in gaza governorates. *International Journal of Engineering and Information Systems*, 1(7), 194–219.

Aldrich, C. (2009). *Learning online with games, simulations, and virtual worlds: Strategies for online instruction* (Vol. 11). John Wiley & Sons.

Alfaqiri, A. S., Mat Noor, S. F., & Sahari, N. (2022). Framework for Gamification of Online Training Platforms for Employee Engagement Enhancement. *International journal of interactive mobile technologies, 16*(6).

Amara, N. B., & Atia, L. (2016). E-training and its role in human resources development. *Global journal of human resource management, 4*(1), 1-12.

Amorim, J. A., Matos, C., Cuperschmid, A. R., Gustavsson, P. M., & Pozzer, C. T. (2013). Augmented reality and mixed reality technologies: Enhancing training and mission preparation with simulations. In *NATO Modelling and Simulation Group (MSG) Annual Conference 2013 (MSG-111), 2013.*

Armstrong, M. B., & Landers, R. N. (2018). Gamification of employee training and development. *International Journal of Training and Development*, 22(2), 162–169. DOI:10.1111/ijtd.12124

Bedwell, W. L., & Salas, E. (2010). Computer-based training: Capitalizing on lessons learned. *International Journal of Training and Development*, 14(3), 239–249. DOI:10.1111/j.1468-2419.2010.00355.x

Bordegoni, M., & Ferrise, F. (2023). Exploring the intersection of metaverse, digital twins, and artificial intelligence in training and maintenance. *Journal of Computing and Information Science in Engineering*, 23(6), 060806. DOI:10.1115/1.4062455

Burnett, G. W., & Goldhaber-Fiebert, S. N. (2024). The role of simulation training in patients' safety in anaesthesia and perioperative medicine. *BJA Education*, 24(1), 7–12. DOI:10.1016/j.bjae.2023.10.002 PMID:38495746

Dahalan, F., Alias, N., & Shaharom, M. S. N. (2023). Gamification and game based learning for vocational education and training: A systematic literature review. *Education and Information Technologies*, ●●●, 1–39. PMID:36688221

Dahri, N. A., Vighio, M. S., Alismaiel, O. A., & Al-Rahmi, W. M. (2022). Assessing the Impact of Mobile-Based Training on Teachers' Achievement and Usage Attitude. *International Journal of Interactive Mobile Technologies*, 16(9).

Daling, L. M., & Schlittmeier, S. J. (2024). Effects of augmented reality-, virtual reality-, and mixed reality–based training on objective performance measures and subjective evaluations in manual assembly tasks: A scoping review. *Human Factors*, 66(2), 589–626. DOI:10.1177/00187208221105135 PMID:35635107

Donthu, N., Kumar, S., Mukherjee, D., Pandey, N., & Lim, W. M. (2021). How to conduct a bibliometric analysis: An overview and guidelines. *Journal of Business Research*, 133, 285–296. DOI:10.1016/j.jbusres.2021.04.070

Driscoll, M. and Tomiak, G.R., 2000. Web-based training: Using technology to design adult learning experiences. https://doi.org/DOI:10.1002/pfi.4140390316

Fertig, T., Schütz, A. E., Weber, K., & Müller, N. H. (2019). Measuring the impact of e-learning platforms on information security awareness. In *Learning and Collaboration Technologies. Designing Learning Experiences: 6th International Conference, LCT 2019, Held as Part of the 21st HCI International Conference, HCII 2019, Orlando, FL, USA, July 26–31, 2019* [Springer International Publishing.]. *Proceedings*, 21(Part I), 26–37.

Fiok, K., Farahani, F. V., Karwowski, W., & Ahram, T. (2022). Explainable artificial intelligence for education and training. *The Journal of Defense Modeling and Simulation*, 19(2), 133–144. DOI:10.1177/15485129211028651

Fraser, K., Ma, I., Teteris, E., Baxter, H., Wright, B., & McLaughlin, K. (2012). Emotion, cognitive load and learning outcomes during simulation training. *Medical Education*, 46(11), 1055–1062. DOI:10.1111/j.1365-2923.2012.04355.x PMID:23078682

Garg, S., & Sharma, S. (2020). User satisfaction and continuance intention for using e-training: A structural equation model. *Vision (Basel)*, 24(4), 441–451. DOI:10.1177/0972262920926827

Granda, J. C., Nuño, P., García, D. F., & Suárez, F. J. (2015). Autonomic platform for synchronous e-training in dispersed organizations. *Journal of Network and Systems Management*, 23(1), 183–209. DOI:10.1007/s10922-013-9290-4

Greenhalgh, T., Payne, R., Hemmings, N., Leach, H., Hanson, I., Khan, A., Miller, L., Ladds, E., Clarke, A., Shaw, S. E., Dakin, F., Wieringa, S., Rybczynska-Bunt, S., Faulkner, S. D., Byng, R., Kalin, A., Moore, L., Wherton, J., Husain, L., & Rosen, R. (2024). Training needs for staff providing remote services in general practice: A mixed-methods study. *The British Journal of General Practice*, 74(738), e17–e26. DOI:10.3399/BJGP.2023.0251 PMID:38154935

Gupta, A. K., Aggarwal, V., Sharma, V., & Naved, M. (2024). Education 4.0 and Web 3.0 Technologies Application for enhancement of distance learning management Systems in the Post–COVID-19 ERa. In *The Role of Sustainability and Artificial Intelligence in Education Improvement* (pp. 66-86). Chapman and Hall/CRC.

Haftador, A. M., Tehranineshat, B., Keshtkaran, Z., & Mohebbi, Z. (2023). A study of the effects of blended learning on university students' critical thinking: A systematic review. *Journal of Education and Health Promotion*, 12(1), 12. DOI:10.4103/jehp.jehp_665_22 PMID:37288404

Herman, H., Riadi, I., Abdurrachman, F. I., & Lonang, S. (2022). Training on how to use social media Wisely and Ethically. *ABDIMAS: Journal Pengabdian Masyarakat*, 5(2), 2653–2662.

Hobfoll, S. E. (1989). Conservation of resources: A new attempt at conceptualizing stress. *The American Psychologist*, 44(3), 513–524. DOI:10.1037/0003-066X.44.3.513 PMID:2648906

Holsapple, C. W., & Lee-Post, A. (2006). Defining, assessing, and promoting e-learning success: An information systems perspective. *Decision Sciences Journal of Innovative Education*, 4(1), 67–85. DOI:10.1111/j.1540-4609.2006.00102.x

Hunt, J. A., II. (2023). *Virtual Onboarding Within Geographically Separated Organizations* (Doctoral dissertation, Trident University International).

Igudia, P. O. (2022). Employee training and development, and organisational performance: A study of small-scale manufacturing firms in Nigeria. *American Journal of Economics and Business Management*, 5(5), 38–54.

Isaacs, A. J., Lwendo, S. B., & Kazondovi, C. (2021). The Effectiveness of In-service Training Programmes in Public Sector Organizations. *The Namibia CPD Journal for Educators*, 6(1), 100–156. DOI:10.32642/ncpdje.v6i1.1554

Kabassi, K., & Virvou, M. (2004). Personalised adult e-training on computer use based on multiple attribute decision making. *Interacting with Computers*, 16(1), 115–132. DOI:10.1016/j.intcom.2003.11.006

Kaizer, B. M., Sanches da Silva, C. E., Zerbini, T., & Paiva, A. P. (2020). E-learning training in work corporations: A review on instructional planning. *European Journal of Training and Development*, 44(8/9), 761–781. DOI:10.1108/EJTD-03-2020-0042

Kaplan, A. D., Cruit, J., Endsley, M., Beers, S. M., Sawyer, B. D., & Hancock, P. A. (2021). The effects of virtual reality, augmented reality, and mixed reality as training enhancement methods: A meta-analysis. *Human Factors*, 63(4), 706–726. DOI:10.1177/0018720820904229 PMID:32091937

Kapp, K. M. (2012). *The gamification of learning and instruction: game-based methods and strategies for training and education.* John Wiley & Sons.

Katayama, H., & Bennett, D. (1999). Agility, adaptability and leanness: A comparison of concepts and a study of practice. *International Journal of Production Economics*, 60, 43–51. DOI:10.1016/S0925-5273(98)00129-7

Khan, B. H. (2001). *A framework for e-learning.* LTI magazine.

Kincaid, J. P., Hamilton, R., Tarr, R. W., & Sangani, H. 2003. Simulation in education and training. *Applied System Simulation: Methodologies and Applications*, pp.437-456.

Kulkarni, P., Gokhale, P., Satish, Y. M., & Tigadi, B. (2022). An empirical study on the impact of learning theory on gamification-based training programs. *Organizational Management Journal*, 19(5), 170–188. DOI:10.1108/OMJ-04-2021-1232

Kumar, S., & Kumar, A. D. (2023). E-training impact on trainee experience and self-assessment. *Journal of Workplace Learning*, 35(7), 599–612. DOI:10.1108/JWL-02-2022-0023

Lane, H. C., Core, M. G., Van Lent, M., Solomon, S., & Gomboc, D. (2005, July). Explainable Artificial Intelligence for Training and Tutoring. In *AIED* (pp. 762-764).

Larson, K. (2020). Serious games and gamification in the corporate training environment: A literature review. *TechTrends*, 64(2), 319–328. DOI:10.1007/s11528-019-00446-7

Lee, G. K., Moshrefi, S., Fuertes, V., Veeravagu, L., Nazerali, R., & Lin, S. J. (2021). What is your reality? Virtual, augmented, and mixed reality in plastic surgery training, education, and practice. *Plastic and Reconstructive Surgery*, 147(2), 505–511. DOI:10.1097/PRS.0000000000007595 PMID:33235047

Liu, Z. Y., Lomovtseva, N., & Korobeynikova, E. (2020). Online learning platforms: Reconstructing modern higher education. [iJET]. *International Journal of Emerging Technologies in Learning*, 15(13), 4–21. DOI:10.3991/ijet.v15i13.14645

López-Torres, E., Carril-Merino, M. T., Miguel-Revilla, D., Verdú, M. J., & De La Calle-Carracedo, M. (2022). Twitter in initial teacher training: Interaction with social media as a source of teacher professional development for social studies prospective educators. *Sustainability (Basel)*, 14(23), 16134. DOI:10.3390/su142316134

Ma, G., Yang, R., Minneyfield, A., Gu, X., Gan, Y., Li, L., Liu, S., Jiang, W., Lai, W., & Wu, Y. (2022). A practical analysis of blended training efficacy on organizational outcomes. *Industrial and Commercial Training*, 54(4), 637–646. DOI:10.1108/ICT-12-2021-0085

Maheshwari, S., & Vohra, V. (2018). Role of training and development practices in implementing change. *International Journal of Learning and Change*, 10(2), 131–162. DOI:10.1504/IJLC.2018.090911

Maity, S. (2019). Identifying opportunities for artificial intelligence in the evolution of training and development practices. *Journal of Management Development*, 38(8), 651–663. DOI:10.1108/JMD-03-2019-0069

Marinagi, C., Trivelllas, P., Kofakis, P., Tsouflas, G. T., & Rekleitis, P. (2019). E-Training on green logistics in the agri-food sector. *Scientific Papers. Series Management, Economic, Engineering in Agriculture and Rural Development*, 19(2), 249–256.

Mohsin, M., & Sulaiman, R. (2013). A study on e-training adoption for higher learning institutions. *International Journal of Asian Social Science*, 3(9), 2006–2018.

Nagy, A. (2005). The impact of e-learning. In *E-Content: Technologies and perspectives for the European Market* (pp. 79–96). Springer Berlin Heidelberg. DOI:10.1007/3-540-26387-X_4

Owoyemi, O., Oyelere, M., Elegbede, T., & Gbajumo-Sheriff, M. (2011). Enhancing workforce' commitment to organisation through training. *International Journal of Business and Management*, 6(7), 280–286.

Paranjape, K., Schinkel, M., Panday, R. N., Car, J., & Nanayakkara, P. (2019). Introducing artificial intelligence training in medical education. *JMIR Medical Education*, 5(2), e16048. DOI:10.2196/16048 PMID:31793895

Pitafi, A. H., Rasheed, M. I., Kanwal, S., & Ren, M. (2020). Employee agility and enterprise social media: The Role of IT proficiency and work expertise. *Technology in Society*, 63, 101333. DOI:10.1016/j.techsoc.2020.101333

Pramono, A. C., & Prahiawan, W. (2022). Effect of training on employee performance with competence and commitment as intervening. *Aptisi Transactions on Management*, 6(2), 142–150.

Prapti, N. "ASYNCHRONOUS E-TRAINING AND COACHING TO INDONESIAN PARENTS: NATURALISTIC STRATEGIES TO SUPPORT LANGUAGE DEVELOPMENT OF CHILDREN WITH SOCIAL-COMMUNICATION DELAYS" (2023). Theses and Dissertations--Early Childhood, Special Education, and Counselor Education. 134. https://uknowledge.uky.edu/edsrc_etds/134

Prasad, S. (2016). Training and Post Training Evaluation for Employee Effectiveness: An Empirical Study on Supermarket in India. *Arabian J Bus Manag Review S*, 1(2). Advance online publication. DOI:10.4172/2223-5833.S1-006

Prestoza, M. J. (2024). Assessing remote learning's feasibility: A comprehensive analysis of Philippine public-school teachers' use of learning management systems and blended learning approaches. *Journal of Research. Policy & Practice of Teachers and Teacher Education*, 14(1), 21–27.

Raja, D. V. A. J., & Kumar, R. A. R. (2016). A Study on Effectiveness of Training and Development in Ashok Leyland all over India. *Journal of Management*, 3(1), 1–12.

Ramayah, T., Ahmad, N. H., & Hong, T. S. (2012). An assessment of e-training effectiveness in multinational companies in Malaysia. *Journal of Educational Technology & Society*, 15(2), 125–137.

Rao, P. S. (2009). *Personnel and human resource management (Book)*. Himalaya Publishing House.

Roca, J. C., Chiu, C. M., & Martínez, F. J. (2006). Understanding e-learning continuance intention: An extension of the Technology Acceptance Model. *International Journal of Human-Computer Studies*, 64(8), 683–696. DOI:10.1016/j.ijhcs.2006.01.003

Rosenberg, J. (2006). *A framework for conferencing with the session initiation protocol (SIP)* (No. rfc4353).

Rowold, J. (2007). The impact of personality on training-related aspects of motivation: Test of a longitudinal model. *Human Resource Development Quarterly*, 18(1), 9–31. DOI:10.1002/hrdq.1190

Sambrook, S. (2005). Factors influencing the context and process of work-related learning: Synthesizing findings from two research projects. *Human Resource Development International*, 8(1), 101–119. DOI:10.1080/1367886052000342591

Sandamali, J. G. P., Padmasiri, M. D., Mahalekamge, W. G. S., & Mendis, M. V. S. (2018). The relationship between training and development and employee performance of executive level employees in apparel organizations. *International Invention of Scientific Journal*, 2(1), 12–17.

Santos, S. A., Trevisan, L. N., Veloso, E. F. R., & Treff, M. A. (2021). Gamification in training and development processes: Perception on effectiveness and results. *Revista de Gestão*, 28(2), 133–146. DOI:10.1108/REGE-12-2019-0132

Sife, A., Lwoga, E., & Sanga, C. (2007). New technologies for teaching and learning: Challenges for higher learning institutions in developing countries. *International journal of education and development using ICT, 3*(2), 57-67.

Sitzmann, T., & Weinhardt, J. M. (2018). Training engagement theory: A multilevel perspective on the effectiveness of work-related training. *Journal of Management*, 44(2), 732–756. DOI:10.1177/0149206315574596

Strother, J. B. (2002). An assessment of the effectiveness of e-learning in corporate training programs. *International Review of Research in Open and Distance Learning*, 3(1). Advance online publication. DOI:10.19173/irrodl.v3i1.83

Sudhakar, R., & Basariya, S. R. (2017). Perspectives and the factors influencing effectiveness of training and development on employees' performance. *International Journal of Civil Engineering and Technology*, 8(9), 135–141.

Sun, P. C., Tsai, R. J., Finger, G., Chen, Y. Y., & Yeh, D. (2008). What drives a successful e-Learning? An empirical investigation of the critical factors influencing learner satisfaction. *Computers & Education*, 50(4), 1183–1202. DOI:10.1016/j.compedu.2006.11.007

Susanti, D., Dwihantoro, P., Sandy, F., & Muliawanti, L. (2022). Social media for social movement: A social media training for Turun Tangan Organization. *Community Empowerment*, 7(8), 1429–1436. DOI:10.31603/ce.7673

Tan, Y. Y., & Mohd Rasdi, R. (2017). Antecedents of Employees' E-training Participation in a Malaysian Private Company. *Pertanika Journal of Social Science & Humanities*, 25(2).

Upadhyay, A. K., & Khandelwal, K. (2019). Artificial intelligence-based training learning from application. *Development and Learning in Organizations*, 33(2), 20–23. DOI:10.1108/DLO-05-2018-0058

Veerasamy, U., Joseph, M. S., & Parayitam, S. (2023). Green human resource management and employee green behaviour: participation and involvement, and training and development as moderators. *South Asian Journal of Human Resources Management*, 23220937221144361.

Wang, Y. S., Wang, H. Y., & Shee, D. Y. (2007). Measuring e-learning systems success in an organizational context: Scale development and validation. *Computers in Human Behavior*, 23(4), 1792–1808. DOI:10.1016/j.chb.2005.10.006

Ward, P., Williams, A.M. and Hancock, P.A., 2006. Simulation for Performance and Training.

Weggen, C. C., & Urdan, T. A. (2000). Corporate e-learning: Exploring a new frontier. *WR Hambrecht and Co.*www. wrhambrecht. com/research/coverage/elearning/ idir explore. html

Wu, J.European University. (2024). E-Learning Management Systems in Higher Education: Features of the Application at a Chinese vs. European University. *Journal of the Knowledge Economy*, 1–31. DOI:10.1007/s13132-024-02159-6

Yazdani, M., Pamucar, D., Erdmann, A., & Toro-Dupouy, L. (2023). Resilient sustainable investment in digital education technology: A stakeholder-centric decision support model under uncertainty. *Technological Forecasting and Social Change*, 188, 122282. DOI:10.1016/j.techfore.2022.122282

Zareie, B., & Jafari Navimipour, N. (2020). A model to determine the factors. affecting satisfaction employees in e-learning systems. *Journal of Development & Evolution Management*, 1398(special issue), 187–197.

Zhao, X., & Namasivayam, K. (2009). Posttraining self-efficacy, job involvement, and training effectiveness in the hospitality industry. *Journal of Human Resources in Hospitality & Tourism*, 8(2), 137–152. DOI:10.1080/15332840802269767

Chapter 11
Harmonizing Stakeholder Synergy for Operational Excellence:
Navigating Through Monte Carlo Simulation With a Case Study of Sabiha Gökçen Airport

Kübra Nur Cingöz
Gaziantep University, Turkey

Vildan Durmaz
Eskisehir Technical University, Turkey

ABSTRACT

The surge in airline transportation since the early 2000s, buoyed by incentives like fuel discounts and landing-stopover benefits, has necessitated the expansion of existing airports for sustainable growth. Sabiha Gökçen Airport, experiencing rapid air traffic escalation since 2014, grapples with substantial waiting queues for both aircraft and passengers. Addressing these challenges requires effective stakeholder communication and collaboration. This study underscores the pivotal role of communication in mitigating issues arising from escalating aircraft traffic at Sabiha Gökçen Airport, emphasizing that sustainable growth cannot be attained amidst prolonged waiting times. The study interrogates the extent to which increased capacity influences operational productivity and explores strategies for leveraging enhanced capacity through effective stakeholder collaboration

DOI: 10.4018/979-8-3693-4412-5.ch011

INTRODUCTION

Airports are complex structures that provide residents and businesses with access to air transport services. Airports host numerous companies and organizations in their service chain. These organizations operating at the airport collaborate to provide air travel services to their consumers in a trouble-free, safe and secure manner.

In Turkey, especially in airports located in major cities, consists of this several stakeholders. Sabiha Gökçen Airport, which will be considered in this regulation, consists of various stakeholders as the second airport in the country with the highest aircraft and passenger traffic. Sabiha Gökçen Airport, which was opened in 2001 within the body of Airport Operation and Aeronautical Industries Inc. (HEAS) affiliated to the Undersecretariat of Defense Industries was leased by Sabiha Gökçen International Airport Investment, Construction and Management Inc. (ISG) for 20 years and became a private enterprise. Currently, the airport authority operates under HEAS and the terminal management section operates within the body of ISG. Sabiha Gökçen airport serves the relatively medium body and low-cost airline companies, as well as serving few flag carrier companies. Aside from that, it hosts many businesses (Terminal tenants, ground handling companies, maintenance companies, etc.), Sabiha Gökçen airport served approximately 35 million passengers in 2019 (DHMI, 2010).

Sabiha Gökçen Airport has faced an increasing demand with the transfer of Atatürk Airport to Istanbul Airport. When evaluated in this that, it is an indisputable fact that the Sabiha Gökçen airport should be used more efficiently and increasing capacity. It is possible to use the Monte Carlo simulation in calculations to increase efficiency and capacity at Sabiha Gökçen Airport.

Monte Carlo Simulation, which is a method used in calculating productivity in many fields is based on predicting the expected situation by using current data instead of past data in order to predict future events (Şener and Şener, 2019: 296).

Within the scope of the study, the negative effects of the problems caused by ineffective stakeholder communication at Sabiha Gökçen Airport on operational efficiency have been emphasized. In order to end the inefficiency caused by this ineffective communication, what stakeholders do efficient communication has been examined. The effect of effective communication between stakeholders on operational efficiency for sustainable growth at Sabiha Gökçen Airport has been analysed using Monte Carlo Simulation, and even more, efficient availability of capacity is questioned.

1. LITERATURE REVIEW

Although there are not many sources written about airport stakeholder theory in Turkey, it is possible to reach enough sources in the international literature. Compared to the stakeholder theory, it is possible to reach more sources in the domestic literature on Monte Carlo simulation, while there is a relatively domestic resource problem in the sources that examine airports with this technique. The resources used in the study are shown in Table 1.

Table 1. Literature Review

A. Haghighat	Monte Carlo Methods for Particle Transport	2020	The historical development of Monte Carlo Simulation and the use of Simulation in Mathematics-Physics been explained. In the field of mathematics, the efficiency of the simulation was examined by making normal distribution and sine cosine sampling. Frequency and serial correlation tests have been used to test randomness.
C.Şener, U. Şener	Stock Price Predictions with Monte Carlo Simulation	2019	A comparison has been made Turkish and American stock markets in TL and USD using the Monte Carlo Simulation method, with reference to airline stocks. At the same time, the study presents a different approach about the effects of USD exchange rate fluctuations to the Turkish stock market.
DHMI (STATE AIRPORTS AUTHORITY)	Statistical Data for 2019	2019	The State Airports Authority is also responsible for the management of the airport and navigation services in our country. DHMI publishes data on the number of flights, passengers and freight on its website every year.
HEAS	HEAS, 2019 Annual Report	2019	The aircraft traffic and the number of passengers of the Airport Operation and Aeronautical Industries Inc. from 2014 to 2019 are given comparatively. In addition, Slot planning and stakeholder cooperation were mentioned to increase operational efficiency.
ICAO (INTERNATİONAL CİVİL AVİATİON ORGANİSATİON)	Annex 14 VOL 1	2018	Annex 14, published by ICAO, contains information that Air Traffic Controllers need to know, especially about aerodrome control.
GMR, Hyderabad İnternational airport	Effectivecollaboration and cooperation among airport stakeholders	2016	It was emphasized that the sum of communication and coordination forms cooperation. It was emphasized which stakeholders should come together to increase the runway capacity, which stakeholders are important for improvement in ground services, and the results of effective communication were tabulated.
N.A Mohd Isa, N. Abdul Hamid T.P.Leong	A Stakeholder Analysis of theKlia2 Airport Terminal Project	2016	Within the scope of the project, the aims and targets of the airport stakeholders have been emphasized, and the roles played by the stakeholders from the construction phase of the Klia2 airport terminal project to the completion and operation. The importance of communication between stakeholders was mentioned in the project and It has been tried to achieve optimum satisfaction in the project. With this project, it has been emphasized that the communication between stakeholders at the airports to be built in the future should start before the project.
Munich Airport	MunichAirportAnnual Report	2012	The importance of cooperation between stakeholders in the operation of the airport was highlighted in the light of the statistical data (passengers, freight, etc.) of 2012 regarding Munich Airport.
A.T. Wells S.B. Young	Airportplanning&management,	2011	In the book, not only the historical processes of airports are handled but also the airside (airspace-air traffic) and landside (Terminal, security, etc.) are examined in detail. In addition, the economic effects of airports are emphasized. Planning, capacity and delays were examined with their causes and consequences.

continued on following page

Table 1. Continued

R.E. Freeman J.S. Harrison A.C. Wicks B. Parmar S. De Colle	StakeholderTheory: The State of the Art	2010	Stakeholder theory is emphasized, which stakeholders are in this structure and the importance of stakeholders in the structure.
D. Schaar L.Sherry	Analysis of Airport Stakeholders	2010	This article analysed the public role of airports and analysed the importance of the airport for stakeholders. It detailed the roles of stakeholders at the airport in the operation of airports.
C. Kanghwa	From operational efficiency to financial efficiency, The Asian Journal on Quality	2010	Kanghwa focused on the concepts of operational efficiency, market efficiency and financial efficiency in this study. He made efficiency calculations with various methods to measure performance efficiency.
B. Kurt, D.W. Heerman	Monte Carlo Simulation in Statistical Physics, Fifth Edition	2010	In addition to the theoretical explanation of Monte Carlo Simulation, its usage areas in practice are emphasized. In addition, the energy landscape has been studied with Monte Carlo random numbers.
T. Oum C. Yu	Airport Performance: A Summary of the 2003 ATRS Global Airport Benchmarking Report	2003	The 2003 ATRS Global Airport Comparison Report presents results on a variety of measures of airport productivity and efficiency, unit costs and cost competitiveness, and financial performance for up to 90 airports of various sizes and forms of ownership in North America, Europe and Asia Pacific. The purpose of this article is to provide a summary of airports' productivity and efficiency performance and to explore the relationships between efficiency measures and airport features and management strategies to better understand the observed differences in airport performance.
R. Mitchell B. Agle D. Wood	Toward a Theory of Stakeholder Identification and Salience: Defining the Principle of Who and What Really Counts.	1997	The general definition of the stakeholders was made and who the stakeholders were or who should be were evaluated from different perspectives. It has been presented with various theories which one is stronger and dominant among the stakeholders.

Using the resources given in Table 1, responses to the questions put forward in the study were queried.

1.1. Economic effects of the airport

Airports are known as large structures consisting of various stakeholders. Although there are various definitions of the airport, the most well-known definition is the definition made by the International Civil Aviation Organization (ICAO). An airport is defined as the area where aircraft are used for landing, taking off and moving on land or water (including buildings, facilities and equipment) (ICAO, 2018:VOL I:2).

As can be understood from the definition, while airports can be an area allocated on land, they can be in an area allocated on the sea. At the same time, the airport has multiple structures consisting of various buildings, facilities and equipment.

Airports support the growth of the regional economy in terms of serving many companies within their own structure and creating a new commercial formation in its vicinity.

Figure 1. Economic Relationship Between the Airport and its Region

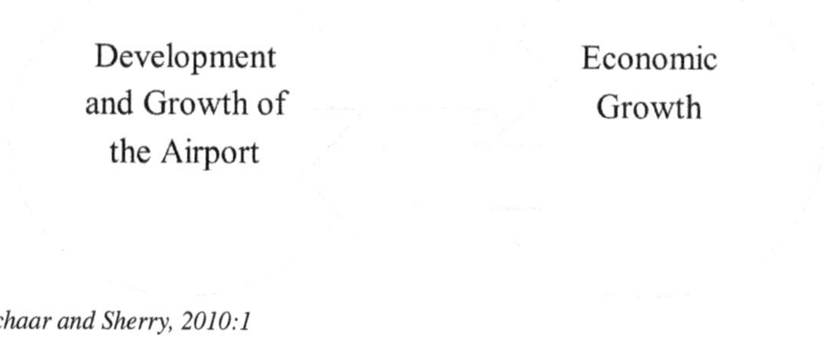

Development
and Growth of
the Airport

Economic
Growth

Source: Schaar and Sherry, 2010:1

As can be understood from Figure 1, while the airports develop the region where they are established economically, the economic growth also provides the further development of the airport. The existence of an airport in a region will cause many businesses to contribute to the region, as it hosts many stakeholders.

It is well understood that a manageable and efficient transport system is essential element for the economy of any region. Transport, by definition, enables people and goods to move between communities. This movement induces to commerce between markets, which in turn generates jobs, earnings and overall economic benefit for a community's inhabitants (Wells and Young, 2011: 360).

1.2. Airport stakeholders

It is possible to see the presence of stakeholders in many organizations as well as in airports. Stakeholders; It is possible to characterize as individuals, groups, institutions-organizations, societies and even the natural environment itself. It is obvious that the main goal of the stakeholders within the Organization is to increase their own gains. Because what matters to the stakeholders is the benefit that is ultimately achieved (Mitchell at al, 1997: 855-856).

The main reason for stakeholders to come together is to increase profits with the strength arising from togetherness.

According to a more basic definition, stakeholder theory is that customers, suppliers, employees, financiers (shareholders, bondholders, banks, etc.), Communities and managers come together to form value, trade together and interact to make a profit (Freeman at al, 2010:23).

Airports consist of various stakeholders that contribute directly and indirectly to the economy of the region where they are located.

There is cooperation and interest in stakeholder theory. It is the case that customers, suppliers, employees, financiers (shareholders, bondholders, banks, etc.), Communities and managers come together to form value, trade together and interact to generate profits (Freeman at al, 2010:23).

Activities are carried out with many stakeholders in an airport from the construction phase to the operation phase. It is possible to see the relationships between these stakeholders and them in Table: 2.

Table 2. Airport Stakeholders in Turkey

AIRLINES	National and International Airlines (National Flag Carrier, Lowcost, Charter), Cargo Flights
PASSENGERS	Arriving and Departing Passengers, Transit Passengers, Arrivals for the Purpose of Greeting
GENERAL AVIATION	Business and Personel Travels, Law Enforcement, Medical Transport, Search and Resque, Aerial Firefighting, Flight Academy and Agricultural Aviation,
AFFECTED BY AIRPORT OPERATIONS	Residing Nearby the Airport
NON GOVERMENTS ORGANIZATION	NGOs such as Environmental Organizations, Pro-Aviation Associations etc.
PUBLIC UTILITIES	SHGM (Directorate General of Civil Aviation)
	DHMI (General Directorate Of State Airports Authority)
	Goverment and Local Goverments
AIRPORT AUTHORITIES	DHMI [(All airports except Sabiha Gökcen, (HEAS), Istanbul (IGA), Gazipasa (TAV), Zafer (ICTAS), Zonguldak (Zonguldak Aviation), Aydın (THY), Selçuk (THY), Eskisehir Hasan Polatkan (ESTU), Hezarfen (Hazarfen)]
AIRPORT PARTNERS	Major Partner of the Airport Terminal Building (DHMI, TAV, ISG, IGA, ICTAS, ZONGULDAK AVIATION, YDA)
INVESTORS AND BOND HOLDERS	Businesses Making Minor Investments in the Airport Assets
CONCESSIONAIRES	Those Who Rent Space at the Airport Terminal Building (Duty Free, Banks, Rent a Car etc.)
ACTIVITIES CARRIED OUT AT THE AIRPORT	Business, Trade, Tourism, Art, Sports Organizations and Activities at the Airport
EMPLOYEES	Direct Employees of the Airports Organization and Employees of Companies Operating at the Airport
GRAND SERVICES PROVIDERS	Fuel Providers, Parking Services, Apron Passanger Transfer etc.
TRANSPORTATION PROVIDERS	Commercial Ground Transportation from Airport to City/Residential

Source: Prepared by the author

1.3. Communication Between Airport Stakeholders

Future-proof solutions and sustainable development can only be achieved through continuous dialogue with all stakeholders. Therefore, it is necessary to enter into a continuous communication process with stakeholders not only within the organization but also at local, regional, national and international levels. Detailed analysis of the stakeholder base should be done through structured interviews with internal contacts representing each target group (Munich Airport, 2012:66).

Large airport infrastructure projects often involve multiple stakeholders such as air navigation providers, Airlines, regulators, passengers, local communities and Airport Operators. New projects can form a conflict of interest between different stakeholder groups because different groups naturally have different interests and views (GMR, 2016:1). However, it is undoubtedly a fact that the interests of all airport stakeholders will increase with the strengthening of cooperation between stakeholders and meeting on common ground.

Table 3. Stakeholders' Expectations from the Airport

Passengers	- Move passengers quickly and comfortably - Provide performance on time - Get access to low fees
Airlines and General Aviation	- Provide performance on time - Provide low operating cost - Ensure the safety of operations - Access high efficiency
Those Affected by Airport Activities	- Maximize economic impact - Maximize the number of goals served and the frequency of those services - Minimize noise and emissions
Civil Society Organizations	-Ensure the safety of employees -Ensure the safety of passengers -Minimize negative environmental impact
Regulatory and Supervisory Institutions	- Maximize economic impact - Maximize the number of goals served and the frequency of those services - Minimize the noise - Make sure airports can meet the growth - Keep airports to standards - Ensure the safety, security and efficiency of operations

continued on following page

Table 3. Continued

Airport Terminal Management	- Increase revenue and manage costs - Increase the number of passengers - Find deals for new locations and increase service frequency - Maximize non-aviation revenues - Maximize customer satisfaction - Ensure environmental sustainability - Increase your competitive advantage - Provide performance on time
Service Providers	- Maximize traffic volumes - Minimize wages paid

Source: Prepared by the author, using the work in Schaar and Sherry, 2010:9

As can be understood from Table 3, the expectations of the stakeholders from the airport may be common at certain points or they may be different in some areas. The important thing is to be able to meet common goals and increase productivity with effective cooperation. Nevertheless, increasing the runway capacity highlighted within the scope of the study and minimizing the landing-take-off waiting of the aircraft emerges as the common expectations of passengers, airlines, general aviation, regulatory and supervisory institutions and terminal management.

Stakeholder collaboration at the airport is a process where groups with similar or different perspectives can exchange views and seek solutions that go beyond their own visions of what is possible. Collaboration goes beyond people (passively or actively) participating in this process (GMR, 2016:1)

Collaboration between stakeholders at airports is very important for all stakeholders. Increasing the operation and efficiency of the airport is undoubtedly possible with strong communication between stakeholders. The development of this communication will pave the way for different common benefit projects to take place at airports.

Figure 2. Shared Value Scheme

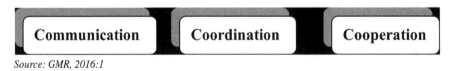

Source: GMR, 2016:1

As seen in Figure 2, the existence of effective communication prepares the ground for coordination between stakeholders. The result of this leads to cooperation between stakeholders and stakeholder interests increase.

1.4. Operational efficiency

Operational efficiency is the process formed by bringing together the right person process and technology combination to increase the productivity of any business operation by reducing the cost of routine operations to the desired level (Kanghwa, 2010:138).

As can be understood from the definition, operational efficiency can be defined as the ratio between the inputs and outputs of the organization to run a business. The higher the output costs than the input costs, the higher the productivity.

Airports provide a wide variety of services to passengers, carriers, airlines and many other organizations, including runway services, apron services, loading and unloading, passenger services, concessions, office rental, parking, etc.

The airport industry consists of diverse stakeholders and heterogeneous. Because of this heterogeneous structure and diversity of stakeholders, measuring and comparing the performance of airports is a challenging process (Isa at al, 2016:2). In some airports, most of the airport service activities are carried out directly by the airport operator, while in some, many services such as terminal management are offered to airlines and independent companies through tenders. The extent of an airport operator's direct involvement in various activities at the airport affects the cost and revenue structure of each airport (Oum and Yu, 2003:4).

Sabiha Gökçen Airport service activities were not entirely carried out by the owner, HEAŞ, but rented to various stakeholders such as İSG. In addition, the number of stakeholders is increasing with a wide variety of airline companies and affiliates. Coordination between stakeholders is very important in increasing operational efficiency due to stakeholder diversity and the heterogeneous structure at Sabiha Gökçen airport.

The aircraft traffic of Sabiha Gökçen Airport has experienced a rapid increase after 2014. There has been a noticeable increase in the number of passengers with the increasing aircraft traffic.

Figure 3. Sabiha Gökçen Airport Aircraft Traffic between 2014-2019

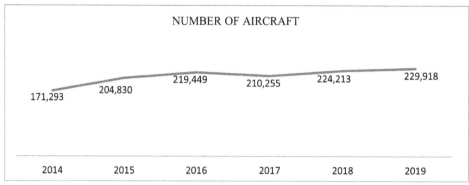

Source: DHMI, 2010

While the traffic at Sabiha Gökçen Airport increased between 2014 and 2016, it is seen in Figure 2 that there was a slight decrease between the previous year and the year 2017. Later in 2017, the momentum of growth continued with the construction of 2 rapid exit taxiways at Sabiha Gökçen Airport.

Figure 4. Sabiha Gökçen Airport Passenger Traffic Between 2014-2019

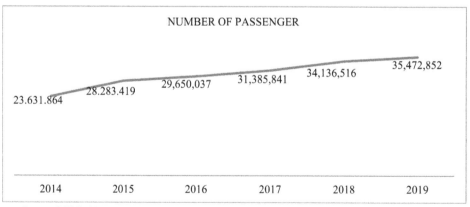

Source: DHMI, 2010

Although it is seen in Figure 2 and Figure 3 that both aircraft traffic and the number of passengers increased until 2017, it is difficult to say that this increase is sustainable and efficient.It is known that it is very difficult for stakeholders to carry out the service operationally, as there were intense flights waiting in the relevant years. As will be mentioned in the conclusion of the study, achieving sustainable growth through systematic stakeholder communication instead of continuous and inefficient growth will be the main point in increasing operational efficiency.

2.5. Economic Perspectives of HR

In the contemporary competitive landscape of the aviation industry, airports are incessantly driven to augment their operational efficiency, a strategic imperative aimed at mitigating costs, elevating customer satisfaction levels, and securing a competitive advantage (Li & Li, 2021). A pivotal avenue toward achieving this objective resides in the realm of human resource (HR) management efficacy (Ariyawansa & Aponso, 2016). Effective stewardship of human capital resources enables businesses including airports to methodically harness their workforce potential, ensuring alignment with requisite skills and qualifications requisite for proficient task execution (Konrad & Deckop, 2001). Furthermore, judicious investments in employee training and development engender heightened productivity and job contentment, thereby engendering an overarching enhancement in operational efficiency (Kucharčíková & Míčiak, 2018). Additionally, the ramifications of astute HR management transcend mere operational augmentation, extending to fiscal benefits such as the mitigation of turnover-related expenses, absenteeism, as well as curtailing recruitment and training outlays (Mohammed, 2019). Moreover, strategic alignment of HR practices with organizational objectives facilitates the optimization of workforce dynamics, fostering heightened employee engagement and concomitant operational efficacy (González, 2004). This concerted effort towards HR optimization culminates in tangible benefits for airport operations, evidenced by improved service quality, diminished waiting periods, and enriched passenger experiences (Karami et al., 2004). In summation, the economic underpinnings of HR management airport operational efficiency underscore the imperative of adept human capital stewardship as a linchpin strategy for cultivating competitiveness, cost containment, and overarching organizational prosperity within the aviation milieu (Kucharčíková & Míčiak, 2018).

Moreover, the operational efficiency of Sabiha Gökçen Airport exerts significant economic impacts on human resources management. As one of the key pillars of organizational success, operational efficiency directly influences the utilization and management of human capital within the airport. A finely tuned operational framework ensures that human resources are deployed optimally, with employees possessing the requisite skills and qualifications to fulfill their roles efficiently. This alignment between operational efficiency and HR management translates into tangible economic benefits. Firstly, it reduces costs associated with workforce inefficiencies, such as turnover, absenteeism, and redundant training expenditures. Secondly, it enhances productivity and job satisfaction among employees, thereby fostering a more conducive work environment and reducing labor-related expenses in the long term. Furthermore, the efficient operation of Sabiha Gökçen Airport elevates its competitive standing within the aviation industry, attracting passengers and airline partners alike, which in turn stimulates economic activity in the region. Ultimately, by intertwining operational efficiency with HR management practices, Sabiha Gökçen Airport not only optimizes its internal operations but also contributes positively to the broader economic landscape, reinforcing its role as a vital economic engine in the aviation sector.

3. MATERIALS AND METHODS

In this study, in which is about the Investigation of the effect of cooperation between Stakeholders on Operational Efficiency, Sabiha Gökçen Airport, where single runway operations are carried out, has been examined. Monte Carlo simulation has been used to analyze single runway operations at Sabiha Gökçen Airport.

3.1. Research Data

The data used within the scope of the study consists of daily actual peak hour flight traffic numbers at Sabiha Gökçen Airport on July 2018 and August 2019 and DHMI 2018 aircraft traffic statistics. The reason for choosing the 2-month date range covering the July – August period in 2018 and 2019, which we take as the base year, is due to the fact that it is the period in which the busiest number of aircraft traffic occurs at Sabiha Gökçen airport

At Sabiha Gökçen Airport, as a result of the requests from airline companies to increase capacity, a cooperation group with stakeholders was established, and as a result of the studies and capacity increasing measures taken, the runway capacity was increased to $20 + 20 = 34$ as of the summer 2016 tariff period. With the completion of the construction of two new fast exit taxiways in 2017, runway occupancy times have reduced and the capacity has increased. Hourly runway capacity has been determined by DHMI as $24 + 24 = 40$ to be valid as of the summer 2017 tariff period. Thus, it is aimed that hourly flight capacity can be managed flexibly according to the weight of landing traffic or take-off traffic (HEAS, 2019:34).

Here, determining the Slot (the highest number of aircraft traffic that can be carried out at an airport in a 1-hour period) as $24 + 24 = 40$ means the following. It is the determination of the total hourly capacity as 40, provided that any of the take-off or landing aircraft traffic does not exceed 24. If the departure traffic is determined to be 24, the highest number that the landing traffic will reach is 16.

In the study, aeroplane traffic data occurring during peak hours are based on actual aeroplane traffic data. The numbers of landing and taking off are taken from real data and have been computed as follows. The data were compiled from the aircraft traffic occurring in peak time zones on July2018 and August 2019. The reason why July and August are chosen is that the summer months are the most active period.

3.2. Research Methodology

Monte Carlo Simulation modelling was used in this study, which is based on the efficient use of Sabiha Gökçen airport.

The Monte Carlo simulation method was first developed in 1945 by two Mathematicians John Von Neumann and Stanislaw Ulam and Physicist Nicholas Metropolis. The simulation was named Monte Carlo Simulation, inspired by the Monte Carlo gambling centre by Nicholas Metropolis, as the basis of the simulation is based on random numbers (Haghighat, 2020:2).

Monte Carlo Simulation is a simulation system in which random numbers, whether simple or complex, are at the heart of the system. The success of a Monte Carlo Simulation and the accuracy of its results largely depends on the quality of the random numbers generated (Kurt and Heerman, 2010:77).

Two points were emphasized while defining Monte Carlo Simulation. The first of these is that Monte Carlo Simulation is a system consisting of random numbers. These random numbers range from 0 to 1. The second point we encounter is that the quality of the random numbers produced in the simulation directly affects the result of the simulation. Since the data used will be shaped according to a random number, these numbers shape the result.

In this study, daily actual peak hour aircraft traffic numbers between July– August 2018 were used in order to measure the runway capacity and the impact of the multiplier effect on other stakeholders at Sabiha Gökçen Airport with the Monte Carlo simulation method. The aforementioned data appear as two different data as real traffic data and data generated using Monte Carlo Simulation. Generating random numbers through Monte Carlo Simulation is the beginning of the simulation.

6 and 8 knots separations were used within the scope of the study. 6 and 8 knots (NM or Knot) separations are as shown in Figure 5.In Figure 5, the distances between lines in the Instrument Approach System (ILS) are 1 NM.In the 6 NM separation, if the second landing traffic is at 6 NM when the traffic in front comes to the touchdown zone, the departure traffic is allowed to enter the runway when the landing traffic passes the runway starting point.In the 8 NM separation, if the second landing traffic is at 8 NM when the first landing traffic passes the runway starting point, departing traffic is allowed to enter the runway.

Figure 5. Sabiha Gökçen Airport Instrument Landing System (ILS) Line

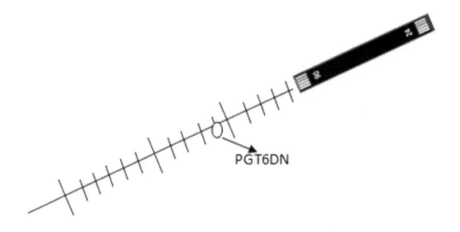

In the study, based on real data, 95% mid-body (M = Medium) and 5% Large body (H= Heavy) aircraft traffics were used as data. The length of the ILS line we used in Monte Carlo Simulation modelling was taken as 15 NM as it is in reality, and the average speeds of aircraft traffic on the ILS line are close to the average of the real data, 160 knots for the large body (H) traffic and medium body (M) traffic. It was taken as 140 knots.

The runway vacating times of the landing aircraft used in the simulation assumed that 30% of the aircraft vacate the runway within 30-40 seconds, 40% within 40-50 seconds and 20% within 50-60 seconds. Runway occupations for departing aircraft are 75 seconds for mid-body aircraft and 100 seconds for large body aircraft. The runway vacating times of the landing-take off aircraft traffic are included in the Monte Carlo Simulation according to the real-time runway occupancy times in July and August 2018.

4. RESULT AND DISCUSSION

The number of aircraft traffic at the Sabiha Gökçen Airport between July2018 and August 2018, the runway occupancy of the landing-take-off aircraft, the vacated rapid exit taxiways, the runway usedand the approach speed of the landing aircraft are given in Table 4 and Table 5.

In Table 4 and Table 5, the speeds of the landing and departing aircraft and the wind speed are given in NM (Nautical Mile-Nautical Miles).Monte Carlo Simulation was formed by taking the runway occupation times in Table 4 and Table 5 into consideration. In addition,Table 4 and Table 5 are valuable in showing how efficient "T" and "U" rapid exit taxiways are at leaving the runway.

Table 4. Peak Hour Landing-Departing Aircraft Traffics of Sabiha Gökçen Airport 24 Runway

LANDING AIRCRAFT

Call sign	4NM		2NM		Wind (Direction/ NM)	Touch Down Zone Time	Vacated Taxiway	Vacated Time	Runway Occupation Time
	Time	Speed (NM)	Time	Speed (NM)					
								0	
X_LAND1	15:07:53	150	15:08:48	135	210/06	15:09:40	U	34	15:10:14
X_LAND2	15:10:59	180	15:11:44	153	210/06	15:12:30	U	39	15:13:09
X_LAND3	15:14:11	165	15:14:58	153	210/06	15:15:42	U	38	15:16:20
X_LAND4	15:16:42	151	15:17:40	150	210/06	15:18:20	U	36	15:18:56
X_LAND5	15:19:45	178	15:20:32	151	210/06	15:21:23	U	33	15:21:56
X_LAND6	15:22:43	186	15:23:25	160	210/06	15:24:15	H	60	15:25:15
X_LAND7	15:26:40	176	15:24:24	143	210/06	15:28:40	U	35	15:29:15
X_LAND8	15:26:47	180	15:29:46	145	210/06	15:30:35	H	45	15:31:20
X_LAND9	15:31:15	165	15:32:15	134	210/06	15:33:04	U	41	15:33:45
					210/06			0	
X_LAND10	15:44:12	180	15:44:59	150	210/06	15:45:49	U	39	15:46:28
X_LAND11	15:46:30	150	15:47:25	140	210/06	15:48:14	U	42	15:48:56
X_LAND12	15:53:30	145	15:54:22	145	210/06	15:55:10	U	38	15:55:48

DEPARTING AIRCRAFT

Call sign	Runway Entering Time	First Landing		Wind (Direction/ NM)	Rolling Time	First Landing NM	Departing Time	Runway Occupation Time
		Call sign	NM					
X_DEPART1	15:06:40	X_LAND1	7	210/05	15:07:25	4,5	15:08:04	84

continued on following page

Table 4. Continued

LANDING AIRCRAFT

Call sign	4NM Time	Speed (NM)	2NM Time	Speed (NM)	Wind (Direction/NM)	Touch Down Zone Time	Vacated Taxiway	Vacated Time	Runway Occupation Time
$X_{DEPART2}$	15:09:50	X_{LAND2}	7,5	210/05	15:10:19	3	15:10:59	69	
$X_{DEPART3}$	15:12:53	X_{LAND3}	7,5	210/05	15:13:29	6	15:14:05	72	
$X_{DEPART4}$	15:16:06	X_{LAND4}	5,5	210/05	15:16:29	3,5	15:17:37	81	
$X_{DEPART5}$	15:18:35	X_{LAND5}	7,5	210/05	15:19:07	6	15:19:59	84	
$X_{DEPART6}$	15:21:36	X_{LAND6}	8	210/05	15:22:16	5,5	15:22:50	84	
$X_{DEPART7}$	15:26:40	X_{LAND7}	6	210/05	15:27:18	1,5	15:27:56	76	
$X_{DEPART8}$	15:28:45	X_{LAND8}	5,5	210/05	15:29:20	3	15:29:59	74	
				210/05				0	
				210/05				0	
$X_{DEPART9}$	15:43:18	X_{LAND10}	6,5	210/05	15:44:00	3,5	15:44:20	62	
$X_{DEPART10}$	15:46:06	X_{LAND11}	5,5	210/05	15:46:42	4	15:47:15	69	
$X_{DEPART11}$	15:52:49	X_{LAND12}	6	210/05	15:53:30	3,5	15:54:10	81	
								0	

Table 6. Average Runway Occupations for the Runway 24 at Sabiha Gökçen Airport

LANDING OCCUPATION TIME VACATING VIA "U" TAXIWAY	LANDING OCCUPATION TIME VACATING VIA "H" TAXIWAY	AVERAGE	DEPARTING OCCUPATION TIME
38 SECONDS	52 SECONDS	40 SECONDS	76 SECONDS

Table 7. Average Runway Occupations for the Runway 06 at Sabiha Gökçen Airport

LANDING OCCUPATION TIME VACATING VIA "T" TAXIWAY	LANDING OCCUPATION TIME VACATING VIA "F" TAXIWAY	AVERAGE	DEPARTING OCCUPATION TIME
43 SECONDS	53 SECONDS	45 SECONDS	75 SECONDS

In Table 6, the average runway occupation time of vacating aircraft from the "U" taxiway is 38 seconds. The average runway occupation time of vacating aircraft from the "H" taxiway is 52 seconds.The average runway occupancy of aircraft departing from runway 24 is 76 seconds. While the rate of vacating the "U" taxiway of the aircraft is 83%, the rate of vacating the "H" taxiway is 17%.When Table 7 is examined, the average runway occupation time of vacating aircraft from the "T" taxiway is 40 seconds. The average runway occupancy of vacating aircraft from the "F" taxiway is 53 seconds.The average runway occupancy of aircraft taking off from runway 06 is 76 seconds. While the active runway is 06, the rate of vacating the runway from the "T" taxiway is 79%, while the rate of vacating the "F" taxiway is 21%. In the mixed traffic assessment, it is seen that rapid exit taxiways form 9 seconds less runway occupancy per aircraft.

Before "F" and "T" taxiways were opened, 8 NM separation was applied. When the Monte Carlo Simulation is played 50 times using the 8NM separation criteria, it is seen that a total of 35 aircraft, 17 landings and 18 departing per hour, can perform landing and departing operations from Sabiha Gökçen Airport.

After the "F" and "T" taxiways were opened, the separations decreased to 6 NM. When the Monte Carlo Simulation is played 50 times using the 6 NM separation criterion, it is seen that a total of 45 aircraft, 23 landings and 22 departing per hour, can perform landing and departing operations from Sabiha Gökçen Airport.

According to Monte Carlo Simulation, it is seen that the total hourly aircraft traffic has increased from 35 to 45 with the activation of the "T" taxiway for runway 06 and the "U" taxiway for runway 24. The opening of "U" and "T" taxiways has led to an increase of 29% in the runway capacity.

Figure 6. Sabiha Gökçen Airport Runway 06/24 and Rapid Exit Taxi Routes

4.1. Research limitations

In the study, Sabiha Gökçen airport was chosen instead of all airports that implement a single runway operation. In the study, the hours which are expressed as peak hours and when domestic and international lines are busy were preferred. The reason why the relevant hours are preferred is due to the fact that the measurement of the capacity is healthier in time zones where the arrival and departure traffic will form traffic to each other. The study was carried out using the Monte Carlo simulation in the simulation environment. The operating performances of the tower and approach controllers, the reaction times of the pilots, meteorological conditions are the factors affecting the capacity in the real traffic environment and these factors are excluded from the scope of the study.

5. CONCLUSION

Airline companies prefer to fly at productive hours. These hours are between 03:00-06: 00 GMT and 15:00-17:00 GMT for domestic flights, and between 07:00-10:00 GMT and 18:00-20:00 GMT for international flights. Before the "F" and "T" rapid exit taxiways were opened at Sabiha Gökçen Airport, it was observed that there were heavy waits of more than 1 hour at the relevant times between 2014 – 2017.While these intense waits increased the costs for the airline companies from the stakeholders, it was a waste of time for the passengers. For the airport terminal operator, the inability of the aircraft to depart or land on time caused the congestion in the terminal building. In addition, the heavy waits were causing stress and tension on the Air Traffic Controllers and Pilots. All these negativities are important in terms of showing what kind of negatives ineffective communication between stakeholders forms.

As a result of effective communication between stakeholders, DHMI, HEAS, ISG and Airlines, the opening of the "F" and "T" taxiways has led to a 29% increase in runway capacity, resulting in more flights during peak hours and fewer holdings for airlines. In addition, passenger waiting has decreased and passenger satisfaction has increased. When evaluated in terms of landing aircraft, there were 9 seconds less runway occupation per aircraft on average.

Efficient use of airports and sustainable capacity are of great importance for airline companies. Cooperation between stakeholders must be operated continuously for sustainable growth at airports. This cooperation between stakeholders will enable the efficient use of scarce resources such as runways and taxiways owned by airports.

At Sabiha Gökçen Airport, effective communication and cooperation between the major stakeholders of the airport, airlines, the aerodrome authority, terminal operator and air traffic management, has brought the airport, which has been used inefficiently for many years, almost to the highest level of operational efficiency.

At the airport, airlines have commenced using the most efficient flight hours at the optimum level, and the waiting times of airline companies and passengers have been reduced to a minimum. As a result of effective cooperation, the taxi times of the aircraft (the time between the aircraft being pushed back from the parking area and the departure) did not exceed 30 minutes, and a sustainable traffic flow was achieved.

The stress and workloads of Air Traffic Controllers and Pilots decreased significantly with the reduced waiting times. Although the increase in the hourly slot capacity of 2 rapid exit taxiways from 32 to 40 traffic, which was opened as a result of effective cooperation at Sabiha Gökçen Airport, increased the operational efficiency a lot; As seen in Monte Carlo Simulation, it seems possible to increase the hourly traffic capacity to 45 traffic. If the number of traffic reaches 45 per peak hour, it will increase the existing slot capacity by 12%. At airports such as Sabiha Gökçen Airport where single-runway operation is carried out and capacity is difficult to increase, 12% capacity will cause serious increases in traffic and passenger numbers. In order to catch the number of 45 aircraft per hour given in Monte Carlo Simulation, especially Pilots and Air Traffic Controllers responsible for the execution of the current operation should not bend the rules. Pilots must comply with the speed constraints given on the approach line as much as possible, Air Traffic controllers working in the approach should not stretch the 6 NM separation, and the Tower Air Traffic Controllers must tell each departing aircraft the conditional entry instructions (behind landing aircraft line up and wait behind) to raise awareness.

REFERENCES

DHMI. (2010). DHMI. DHMI Statistical Data, https://www.dhmi.gov.tr/istatistik .aspx [Retrieved date: 26-October -2010]. Ariyawansa, C. M., & Aponso, A. C. (2016, May). Review on state of art data mining and machine learning techniques for intelligent Airport systems. In *2016 2nd International Conference on Information Management (ICIM)* (pp. 134-138). IEEE.

DHMI. (2010). DHMI. DHMI Statistical Data, https://www.dhmi.gov.tr/istatistik .aspx [Retrieved date: 26-October -2010].

Freeman, R. E., Harrison, J. S., Wicks, A. C., Parmar, B., & De Colle, S. (2010). Stakeholder Theory: The State of the Art. *The Academy of Management Annals*, 3(1), 403–445.

GMR. (2016). *Hyderabad International Airport, Aciasiapac, Haghighat, A. (2020). Monte Carlo methods for particle transport. Raton.* Crc Press.

HEAŞ. (2019). HEAŞ 2019 Activity Report. https://www.sgairport.com/media/ default/docs/pdf/Mali/Faaliyet-Raporu-2019.pdf [Retrieved date: 21-November - 2020] https://fdocuments.in/document/effective-collaboration-and-cooperation -among-airport-effective-collaboration.html?page=1 [Retrieved date: 20-October -2020]

ICAO. (2005). *Annex II: Rules of the Air*. International Civil Aviation Organization press.

Isa, N. A. M., Hamid, N. A., & Leong, T. P. (2016). A stakeholder analysis of the Klia2 Airport Terminal Project. *Environment-Behaviour Proceedings Journal*, 1(3), 281–289. DOI:10.21834/e-bpj.v1i3.372

Kanghwa, C. (2010). From operational efficiency to financial efficiency. *The Asian Journal on Quality*, 11(2), 137–145. DOI:10.1108/15982681011075943

Karami, A., Analoui, F., & Cusworth, J. (2004). Strategic human resource management and resource-based approach: The evidence from the British manufacturing industry. *Management Research News*, 27(6), 50–68. DOI:10.1108/01409170410784202

Kurt, B. and Heerman, D.W. (2010). *Monte Carlo Simulation in Statistical Physics*, Berlin: Springer company

Ming-jun, L. I., & Xiang-dong, L. I. (2021). Research on Factors Affecting Green Airport Development Based on Scale Analysis. [). IOP Publishing.]. *IOP Conference Series. Earth and Environmental Science*, 647(1), 012148.

Mitchell, R., Agle, B., & Wood, D. (1997). Toward a theory of stakeholder identification and salience: Defining the principle of who and what really gounts. *Academy of Management Review*, 22(4), 853–886. DOI:10.2307/259247

Munich Airport. (2012). Munich Airport Annual Report, https://www.munich-airport.com/_b/000000000000000001983421bb593a8d51/ib2012-en.pdf [Retrieved date: 20-October -2020]

Oum, T. H. and Yu, C. (2004). *Airport Performance: A Summary of the 2003 ATRS Global Airport Benchmarking Report* (No. 1425-2016-118401).

Schaar, D., & Sherry, L. (2010, May). Analysis of airport stakeholders. *In 2010 Integrated Communications, Navigation, and Surveillance Conference Proceedings* (pp. J4-1). IEEE.

Şener, C. and Şener, U. (2019). Monte Carlo Simülasyonu İle Hisse Senedi Fiyat Tahminleri [Stock Price Predictions using Monte Carlo Simulation], *Beykoz Akademi Dergisi,* [Beykoz Academy] 7(2), 294-306.

Wells, A. T., & Young, S. B. (2011). *Airport Planning &Management*. McGraw-Hill Companies.

Chapter 12
Disruptive Innovations in Human Resource Management:
Creating Sustainable Human Asset Management in the Fourth Industrial Revolution

B. Anthony Brown
https://orcid.org/0000-0001-7709-1164
Independent Researcher, USA

Keri L. Heitner
https://orcid.org/0000-0003-2851-5682
Walden University, USA

ABSTRACT

The theories and practices comprising modern human resource management (HRM) boast an extensive evolution and continue to evolve. Fayolism by Henri Fayol (1841-1925), Taylorism by Frederic Winslow Taylor (1857-1915), bureaucracy by Maximilian Weber (1864-1920), leadership styles and change management by Kurt Lewin (1890-1947), theory X and theory Y by Douglas McGregor (1906-1964), the hierarchy of needs by Abraham Maslow (1908-1970), need theory by David Clarence McClelland (1917- 1988), and motivation-hygiene theory by Frederick Herzberg (1923-2000) precipitated and consolidated HRM as known today. Although fundamental to present-day HRM, globally, the HRM tenets hewed in the three previous industrial revolutions remain largely misaligned with sustainable human asset management (sHAM). Given the preceding, the question is whether organizational

DOI: 10.4018/979-8-3693-4412-5.ch012

leaders can use disruptive innovation to (a) enable sustainable human asset management while (b) maximizing efficiency and production to achieve organizational sustainability in the impending fourth industrial revolution.

INTRODUCTION

The advent of the COVID-19 pandemic considerably altered traditional human resource management (HRM) practices globally (B. A. Brown & Heitner, 2022; Eightfold AI, 2022). The COVID-19 pandemic rendered some traditional human resource management practices nearly obsolete, particularly when managers with neither training nor experience were sent home to manage employees working remotely (B. A. Brown & Heitner, 2022). The pandemic emphasized the need for integrating disruptive innovations with traditional human resource management and precipitated a revamping of conventional change management theories and concepts applicable to pre-COVID-19 organizational restructuring processes (B. A. Brown & Heitner, 2023a). The pandemic also widened the global skills gap by creating an accelerated growing deficit for science, engineering, technology, and math (STEM) graduates as the fourth industrial revolution progresses (B. A. Brown & Heitner, 2024; Eightfold AI, 2022).

Additionally, the United Nations called for global organizational sustainability via its 17 sustainable development goals by 2030 (Agarwal et al., 2021; B. A. Brown & Heitner, 2023b; United Nations, n.d.-a, n.d.-b). Pertinent to this chapter, sustainable development goal 8 target 2 dictates *achieving higher levels of economic productivity through diversification, technological upgrading, and innovation, including through a focus on high-value added and labor-intensive sectors* (United Nations, n.d.-a). Incorporating disruptive innovations in HRM and achieving sustainable development goal 8 target 2 simultaneously will require implementing disruptive innovations that globally, many present and prospective employees, including HRM officers, are neither familiar with nor trained to use (B. A. Brown & Heitner, 2022, 2024; Buchholz, 2023).

This chapter contains a systematic literature review to synthesize the existing literature on creating sustainable human asset management in the fourth industrial revolution. In the chapter, we incorporate information from books, surveys, peer-reviewed articles, scholarly articles, government reports, and other sources relevant to creating sHAM in the fourth industrial revolution. The purpose of this chapter is to review the benefits and challenges of integrating disruptive technology into current and traditional HRM to create sHAM and any differences that exist by geographic location (the United States or international), industry sector, and organization size. The question that guides this systematic literature review is whether organizational leaders can use disruptive innovation to (a) enable sustainable human asset management while (b) maximizing efficiency and production to achieve organizational sustainability in the impending fourth industrial revolution.

REVIEW OF THE LITERATURE AND LITERATURE SEARCH STRATEGY

The theories and practices comprising modern human resource management (HRM) boast an extensive evolution and continue to evolve. Despite being credited for the inaugural appearance of the term *human resource* in the book *The Distribution of Wealth* (Commons, 1893), the works of many pioneers preceded the works and writings of Commons (1893). During the first industrial revolution (circa 1760 to the 1840s), HRM pioneers, such as Adam Smith (1723-1790), Robert Owen (1771-1858), and Charles Babbage (1791-1871), made revolutionary contributions to the evolution of HRM (Aungsuroch et al., 2021; Hatcher, 2013; Prendergast, 2021; Simkin, 2016).

Heralded as the founder of modern economics (History.com Editors, 2023) and father of the first industrial revolution (Werhane, 2000), Adam Smith introduced his *division of labor* theory in his 1776 book *The Wealth of Nations* (Aungsuroch et al., 2021; Smith, 1964; Szmigin & Rutherford, 2013). The concept of division of labor ushered in the fundamental HRM tenor of production efficiency denoted by delegating a specific task to a designated employee – where that designated employee was assessed and determined to be best suited for said task (Smith, 1964).

In the prime of the British first industrial revolution, Robert Owen, a Welsh textile manufacturer in Scotland, was the forerunner of socialism, communitarianism, and the cooperative movement (Dowd, 2024; Hatcher, 2013; Owen, 1857). Additionally, Owen received copious acknowledgment for his stints as an entrepreneur and industrialist, pioneering work as a trade union activist, and contributions made to feminism in New Lanark, Scotland (Aungsuroch et al., 2021; Dowd, 2024; Owen, 1857; Simkin, 2016). However, one of his most extraordinary credits was pioneering modern personnel management (Aungsuroch et al., 2021; Osai et al., 2009). During the era of the first industrial revolution, the working conditions at New Lanark Scotland's factories epitomized the worst of workplace conditions (Aungsuroch et al., 2021). Employers deemed machinery more critical than employees, and children as young as 5 worked 13 hours per day, six days per week, like their adult counterparts (Aungsuroch et al., 2021; Hatcher, 2013).

In 1817, Robert Owen coined the term *8 hours' labor, 8 hours' recreation, and 8 hours' rest* (citation). The successful implementation of Owen's innovative proposal significantly reduced workplace abuse and employee burnout (Aungsuroch et al.,

2021; Owen, 1857). Post the successful acceptance of Owen's 1817 revolutionary *8 hours' labor, 8 hours' recreation, and 8 hours' rest* proclamation in New Lanark, Scotland, more than a century elapsed (and after the second industrial revolution spanning 1870-1914) before the U.S. factory workforce experienced adjusted work hours (Aungsuroch et al., 2021; Sahadi, 2023). In 1926, the American auto manufacturer Henry Ford formulated a modified version of Owen's innovation and introduced the 5-day, 40-hour work week in the United States (Aungsuroch et al., 2021; Sahadi, 2023).

British mathematician Charles Babbage was most recognized as the father of modern computing because of his 1821 invention of the *Difference Engine* to compile mathematical tables (Charles Babbage Institute, 2024; Prendergast, 2021). However, during the British first industrial revolution, Babbage made a fundamental contribution to Adam Smith's theory on the division of labor in the book *On the Economy of Machinery and Manufactures* (Babbage, 1832; Friedland, 2024). Babbage concluded and added that employees would complete any assigned task solely based on their inherent (and only) skill set (Aungsuroch et al., 2021; Babbage, 1832). According to Babbage, management can reduce labor costs by assigning higher-skilled jobs to higher-paid workers and lower-skilled jobs to lower-paid workers (Aungsuroch et al., 2021; Babbage, 1832).

Recognized as the founder of the modern (personnel) management method, french mining engineer and executive Henri Fayol (1841-1925) developed and introduced Fayolism in the book *General and Industrial Management* (Fayol, 1949). Fayolism comprises five primary elements (or functions) and 14 management principles deemed common to all organizations (Aungsuroch et al., 2021; Brunsson, 2008; Dickson & John, 2022; Fayol, 1949). Despite the contentions that Fayolism does not qualify as human resource management (Aungsuroch et al., 2021; Mind Tools Content Team, 2024), Fayol's five primary elements of management and 14 management principles are still in use today. Modern HR practitioners cannot ignore Fayolism's contributions to the genesis of human resource development (Aungsuroch et al., 2021; Brunsson, 2008). Notably, while Adam Smith's division of labor heads the 14 management principles, equity is listed as the 11th principle, indicating the early recognition of the importance of employee equity (Aungsuroch et al., 2021; Dickson & John, 2022; Fayol, 1949).

Adam Smith, Robert Owen, Charles Babbage (first industrial revolution), and Henri Fayol (second industrial revolution) provided the launch pad for advancing human resource development. Following on the heels of the predecessors mentioned above, Australian George Elton Mayo (1880-1949), dubbed the progenitor of human relations management, was revered for his 1920s Hawthorne studies (Britannica, 2024; Mayo, 1933). Coming out of the Chicago Hawthorne Western Electric Company experiments in the late 1920s, Mayo (1933) concluded that relations between employers and employees should not be mechanistic but humanistic. Mayo further concluded (from the Hawthorne experiments) that factors such as workplace illumination, social conditions, and employee relationship with supervisors positively affected employee productivity, quality of work, and efficiency and eclipsed financial incentives as an economic factor (Mayo, 1933; Menon, 2016). Mayo (post the 1870-1914 second industrial revolution but before the 1950s start of the third industrial revolution) was also pivotal in establishing the human relations movement (Menon, 2016).

Fayolism by Henri Fayol (1841-1925), Taylorism by Frederic Winslow Taylor (1857-1915), bureaucracy by Maximilian Weber (1864-1920), leadership styles and change management by Kurt Lewin (1890-1947), theory X and theory Y by Douglas McGregor (1906-1964), the hierarchy of needs by Abraham Maslow (1908-1970), need theory by David Clarence McClelland (1917- 1988), and motivation-hygiene theory by Frederick Herzberg (1923-2000) precipitated and congealed HRM as known today. Subsequently, HRM metamorphosized into a multifaceted process that has cycled through many application modes, often based on the type of organization. Based on the work of the progenitors, HRM consolidated to a holistic process comprising recruitment, selection, onboarding, compensating and benefits management; training and development; engagement; performance appraisal; resolving employee concerns, disputes, or conflicts; and developing policies and strategies to retain employees (Aungsuroch et al., 2021; Cheng & Hackett, 2021; Maryville University, 2024).

The literature search process involved conducting searches of key terms and assessing the references associated with the results. The key search terms included but were not limited to *disruptive innovation, fourth industrial revolution, large language model, generative artificial intelligence, generative AI, machine learning, ChatGPT, sustainability, human resource management, sustainable human resource management, pre-employment assessment, talent acquisition, employee onboarding, training and development, learning and development, performance appraisal, performance evaluation, performance management, performance development, diversity, equity, inclusion, and United Nations 17 sustainable development goals.*

CASE DESCRIPTION

The works of all the aforementioned theorists who bolstered and expedited HRM spanned the circa 1760 to the 1840s first industrial revolution, 1870 to 1914 second industrial revolution, and the 1950 to 2000 third industrial revolution (Aungsuroch et al., 2021; Brunsson, 2008; Dickson & John, 2022). Notwithstanding the theorists' fundamental contributions to present-day HRM, globally, the HRM tenets hewed in the three previous industrial revolutions remain largely misaligned with sHAM required in today's fourth industrial revolution. For this chapter, we define sHAM as the amalgamation of relevant disruptive innovation with conventional HRM practices to equitably recruit and sustainably manage personnel to achieve long-term social, ecological, and economic goals while mitigating adverse outcomes. Given the preceding, the fourth industrial revolution will require organizational leaders to amalgamate disruptive innovation with conventional HRM to enable sHAM and maximize efficiency and production to achieve organizational sustainability.

A disruptive innovation is not always denoted by the cataclysmic emergence of radical, state-of-the-art, groundbreaking, or cutting-edge technology but can be an imperceptibly evolving technology where the now emerging version gradually and permanently eclipses the older versions (B. A. Brown & Heitner, 2022; Christensen, 1997; Si & Chen, 2020). With generative artificial Intelligence (AI) applications precipitously evolving to aid in materializing what was once perceived as science fiction (Harney & Collings, 2021), AI as a *hyper-disruptive innovation* is now prevalent in the HRM fraternity (Budhwar et al., 2022). We adopt the European Commission's definition of artificial intelligence for this chapter. Article 3(1) of the European Union Artificial Intelligence Act (EU AI Act) states that an

AI system means a machine-based system designed to operate with varying levels of autonomy, that may exhibit adaptiveness after deployment and that, for explicit or implicit objectives, infers, from the input it receives, how to generate outputs such as predictions, content, recommendations, or decisions that can influence physical or virtual environments. (Nahra et al., 2024, p. 1).

In this chapter, the primary mention of an AI system will be machine learning, a subfield of generative artificial intelligence, which is a mechanical, automated, or digital device or software designed to impersonate intelligent human behavior (Agouridis, 2021; S. Brown, 2021; IBM, n.d.-b, n.d.-a).

Common Applications and Benefits of Integrating Machine Learning as a Disruptive Innovation in HRM to Create sHAM

Reductions in overhead costs from (a) improved time and process efficiencies, (b) reduction of human staffing, and (c) better decision-making on compensation and benefits are predominantly the default (first response) organizational benefits analogous with integrating disruptive innovations with conventional HRM (Agouridis, 2021, 2023; Maurer, 2024a; Sharma, 2023; Siocon, 2023). While cost reductions emanating from HRM improve profit (the corporate bottom line), sHAM is more pivotal to the achievement of organizational sustainability as sHAM encompasses

(a) the triple bottom line, which comprises the incorporation of the elements of people, planet, and profit, (B. A. Brown & Heitner, 2023b; Elkington, 2004; Slaper & Hall, 2011) and (b) the United Nation's sustainable development goal 8 target 2 (B. A. Brown & Heitner, 2023b; United Nations, n.d.-a). Thus, we establish that creating and implementing sHAM allows for attracting and *equitably* hiring diverse, qualified candidates from under-represented (deemed previously inaccessible) pools of potential applicants, and including these hires as organizational ambassadors is integral to the foundation of sHAM.

As the disruptive innovations propelling the fourth industrial revolution continuously direct today's labor biosphere (B. A. Brown & Heitner, 2023a, 2024), corporate HR staff employ machine learning AI pre-employment assessment, talent acquisition, and talent management software to attain competitive advantage and cost reduction (Buchholz, 2023; Murad, 2023; Sharma, 2023) - essentially optimizing the alignment between human assets and corporate goals (Dhawan, 2023). However, organizational leaders employing these disruptive innovations for attaining organizational agility and cost efficiency can also use said disruptive innovations for equitable hiring (Abrams, 2024), continuous (objective) employee performance evaluation (Maurer, 2024b), and benefits management, which stimulates sustainable employee satisfaction and well-being (BambooHR, 2023). In a January 2024 survey of 2,366 HR respondents representing organizations of all sizes in a multiplicity of industries across the United States conducted by the Society for Human Resource Management ([SHRM], 2024), approximately 60% indicated optimism concerning the potential for the effective use of AI at their organization (Maurer, 2024b). Fifty-six percent were optimistic about the potential for AI to improve workplace and employee collaboration (Maurer, 2024b). The following sections highlight some benefits and common usages of integrating machine learning with conventional HRM.

Recruiting, Interviewing, and Hiring

In said January 2024 survey of 2,366 HR respondents in the United States, 64% indicated that recruiting, interviewing, and hiring were the primary uses of machine learning in HRM (Maurer, 2024b). Corporate leaders and staff in recruiting agencies employ machine learning HRM recruitment tools and talent intelligence platforms as the preliminary tool for screening incoming job applications - a process claimed to select *efficiently* applicants who meet the recruiters' requirements (Agouridis, 2021, 2023; Murad, 2023; Sharma, 2023; York, 2024). Examples of popular machine learning HRM recruitment systems and talent intelligence platforms include but are not limited to LinkedIn Insight, Talent Insight, Eightfold, Workday Talent Management, Indeed, Pymetrics, ClickUp, Turing, Findem, Talenture, Talenteer, Recrut.AI, Fetcher, and Paradox (6sense, 2024; Eightfold AI, 2022; indeed, 2024;

Linkedin, 2024; Paradox, 2024; York, 2024). HR officers in multinational corporations such as Colgate-Palmolive, PwC, Boston Consulting Group, and food group conglomerate KraftHeinz employ Pymetrics' talent acquisition and management AI software (Murad, 2023; Pymetrics, n.d.).

Machine learning HRM recruitment systems and talent intelligence platform developers such as the New York-based firm Pymetrics stand by their (hyper-disruptive innovation) tool (Murad, 2023; Pymetrics, n.d.), which they dub as a soft skills machine learning HRM and talent intelligence platform incorporating data-driven behavioral insights and appraised AI to create a more efficient, effective, and fair hiring process across the talent lifespan or employees. Most interesting is that while Pymetrics boasts multiple multinational corporations as clients, the Pymetrics AI software is ranked 36th with a 0.39% market share in the pre-employment assessment category. Kaggle, boasting 11.21%, AON with 11.09%, and Pearson VUE, with 8.22% market share, comprise the top three generative AI software in the pre-employment assessment category (6sense, 2024). Paradox, another United States-based machine learning HRM software provider, retains clients such as fast food giant McDonald's, Nestlé (the world's largest food & beverage company), Unilever, HP Inc. (formerly part of Hewlett Packard) 3M, Pfizer, USAA Investment Services Company, Denny's (restaurant chain), Lowe's (home improvement store chain), and Dollar General (Paradox, 2024).

Learning and Development

Conventional employee training and development is grounded in the concept of developing employees' skill sets based on the requirements of a specific organizational task (van Vulpen, 2023). Training sessions are often sporadic, organizational interposition of (quasi-coordinated) instruction-based events intended to develop employees' job-relevant knowledge and skills to improve corporate performance (Dachner et al., 2021). In contrast, learning and development is a systematic approach designed by corporate HR to holistically advance and augment employees' inherent skill sets, knowledge, and competency (van Vulpen, 2023). The all-inclusive umbrella of employee learning and development is aimed at empowering employees, thus leading to improved employee work performance (van Vulpen, 2023).

Post-hiring, employee development is crucial to sHAM (Allianz Care, 2023; Richards, 2020). The results of the January 2024 survey of 2,366 HR respondents in the United States indicated that 43% of the respondents selected employee learning and development (as part of talent management) as the second most popular use of machine learning in HRM (Maurer, 2024b; SHRM, 2024). While employee learning and development is integral to sHAM, the authors note that recruitment agencies (head hunters) only perform talent acquisitions and will likely only need a talent intelligence platform to serve their clients' needs. However, manufacturing, goods, and service-providing corporations will elect to acquire a machine learning HRM suite with learning and development capabilities to best serve their (individual corporate) HRM needs.

Performance Management

In all organizations, objective performance management is momentous in creating sHAM (Agarwal et al., 2021; Aungsuroch et al., 2021). According to Maurer (2024b), the findings of the January 2024 survey of 2,366 HR respondents in the United States indicated that 25% of the respondents selected performance management as the third most common use of machine learning in HRM. We will reiterate that recruitment agencies specializing only in talent acquisitions need a talent intelligence platform and do not require a machine learning HRM tool with performance management capability to satisfy clients' requirements. However, manufacturing, goods, and service-providing corporations (especially multinational corporations) will elect to acquire a machine learning HRM platform with performance management functions.

Other Applications of Machine Learning in HRM

Onboarding, computing (supposedly equitable) market remuneration packages, productivity monitoring, succession planning, and decisions on promotion and termination comprise the other common uses of machine learning in conventional HRM (Agouridis, 2021, 2023; Maurer, 2024b). While some organizational leaders aim to integrate machine learning into their traditional HRM, the primary thrust (apparently) embodies achieving increased efficiencies in the HRM department, leading to a reduction in departmental operating costs (Agouridis, 2021, 2023), versus focusing on creating sHAM, which leads to a more holistic improvement of psychosocial safety climate and organizational sustainability (B. A. Brown, 2020; Richards, 2020).

Application of Machine Learning in Learning in Other Nations

On January 30, 2020, the Director General of the World Health Organization inveterated the 2019 pandemic caused by the rapid global spread of Coronavirus 2 (SARS-CoV-2) as a public health emergency of international concern (United Nations, 2020). February 2020 marked the commencement of the first global, mass, synchronous, spontaneous organizational exodus when globally, organizational leaders sent employees home to work remotely (B. A. Brown & Heitner, 2022). The advent of the COVID-19 pandemic would have accelerated the use of machine learning HRM tools (Sharma, 2023), considering that of 1 in every 4 surveyed HR respondents, 66.7% confirmed that their organization started incorporating machine learning in HRM in the last year leading up to the January 2024 survey (Maurer, 2024b). Maurer (2024b) neither disclosed (a) which organizations the HR respondents represented, (b) if the HR respondents worked for multinational corporations, nor whether the organizations were private or government enterprises. However, Maurer reported that 38% of surveyed organizations were extra-large organizations (> 5,000 employees), while 27% were large organizations (500-4,999 employees). The remaining HR respondents comprised medium and small organizations.

MNCs such as Colgate-Palmolive, PwC, KraftHeinz, McDonald's, Nestlé Unilever, HP Inc, and 3M are large and extra-large corporations with thousands of employees globally. The aforementioned multinational corporations incorporating Pymetrics or Paradox machine learning HRM software (Paradox, 2024; Pymetrics, n.d.) in their respective private operations would have introduced and extended the novelty of machine learning HRM systems wherever they operate globally. We posit that leaders of multinational corporations would rely on machine learning HRM tools to streamline their global HRM activities to attain a competitive advantage and cost reductions (Murad, 2023; Sharma, 2023), especially during and post the COVID-19 pandemic. The scope of this chapter does not allow for the in-depth delineation of the adaptation of machine learning HRM platforms per country, by specific industries in specific countries, or by the public or private sector.

Challenges with Creating and Implementing sHAM

We distinguish between (a) the inherent (technological, security) and external (organizational, managerial) concerns arising from integrating AI and machine learning with traditional HRM (to create sHAM), which will be discussed in later sections of this chapter, and (b) the challenges or barriers to creating and implementing sHAM, mentioned in this section. Multiple reasons exist for corporate leadership not integrating AI as disruptive innovation with traditional HRM. Forty-two percent of surveyed HR respondents indicated ignorance regarding what AI tools would help or best suit their organization; 41% cited inadequate time, finances, and labor force to maintain AI algorithms, while 40% deem AI void of human touch (Maurer, 2024b; Murad, 2023; Sharma, 2023; SHRM, 2024). Another 33% remain unclear of AI's benefit to HRM, and 29% have trepidation regarding AI eliminating candidates during the candidate's resume prescreening phase (Maurer, 2024b; Murad, 2023; Sharma, 2023; SHRM, 2024).

Furthermore, 25% of respondents admitted that they do not know where to start, 25% remain confident that AI is less accurate and reliable compared to their employees, and 21% cited that their organization has insufficient data volume to inform AI algorithms (SHRM, 2024). Twenty-one percent highlighted a dearth of transparency regarding the AI decision-making process (SHRM, 2024. At the same time, 20% fear that AI will exacerbate bias patterns by virtue of the innate algorithms because machine learning (as a subfield of AI) operates on pattern recognition and *learns* from past data (SHRM, 2024).

Governance of Generative AI (Machine Learning) as a Form of Disruptive Innovation in HRM

The adverse consequences of AI usage are well documented, as mentioned in this chapter's *Technology Concerns* section. Aside from AI's unprecedented utility and potential, the lack of regulations allows for unfettered generative AI usage (EU Artificial Intelligence Act, 2024; European Commission, 2024; Molaiepour, 2024). Subsequently, governments and public and private corporations will gravitate toward generative AI usage to indicate their desire for technical advancement (Bahrke & Regnier, 2023).

The European Union Artificial Intelligence Act is the first and only inclusive horizontal legal framework (regulation) by a significant regulator anywhere (EU Artificial Intelligence Act, 2024; Molaiepour, 2024; Nahra et al., 2024). Adopted on March 13, 2024, by the European Union Parliament, the European Union Artificial Intelligence Act provides European Union-wide rules designed to govern AI usage regarding data quality, transparency, human oversight, and accountability (Nahra et al., 2024). The EU AI Act assigns applications of AI to various risk categories, namely, unacceptable risk, high risk, limited risk, and minimal risk (European Commission, 2024; Molaiepour, 2024; Nahra et al., 2024).

AI machine learning systems are classified as high-risk if used to scan curriculum vitae (CV) and rank job applicants in recruitment procedures to determine access to European Union jobs (EU Artificial Intelligence Act, 2024; European Commission, 2024; Nahra et al., 2024). Consequently, the EU subjects such high-risk AI systems to strict obligations before and after marketing, and failing to comply with all requisite pre-marketing compulsions will result in fines of up to 35 million euros or 7% of global annual revenue, whichever is higher (European Commission, 2024; Nahra et al., 2024).

Technology Components

A surfeit of current and emerging disruptive innovations propagates the acceleration of the labor biosphere through the fourth industrial revolution and continuously changes how modern people live and work(B. A. Brown & Heitner, 2022, 2024). Current leading (and emerging) disruptive digital and technological innovations synonymous with the fourth industrial revolution include generative AI, machine learning, deep learning, and large language models such as ChatGPT, Google Gemini AI, and Chatsonic built with generative AI (Drapkin, 2024; Google, n.d.; IBM, n.d.-a, n.d.-b). Other relevant and notable disruptive innovations include but are not limited to virtual and augmented reality, the Internet of Things (IoT), cloud computing, blockchain, big data analytics, quantum computing, user interface and user experience (UI/UX), cognitive robotics, and intelligent automation (B. A. Brown & Heitner, 2022; Economic Commission for Latin America and the Caribbean [ECLAC], 2022; Elias, 2023; Gill & Kaur, 2023; Maisiri et al., 2019; Mhlanga, 2022; TeamLease EDTECH, n.d.; Vaishya et al., 2020).

Despite the prevalence of ChatGPT as the most prominent generative AI for written script production, critical limitations of ChatGPT are its inability to provide current and real-time responses and the production of racial and gender-biased AI-driven responses (Helsinger, 2024; Murad, 2023; Sharma, 2023; Yin et al., 2024). This limitation stems from the developers building the system upon the GPT-3.5 and GPT-4 platforms and training GPT to generate responses using data up to and including the year 2021 (Garg, 2023) and also to use pattern recognition as part of its modus operandi (Agouridis, 2023; DiBenedetto, 2024; SHRM, 2024). However, more than 30 alternatives to ChatGPT currently exist, with the leading alternative being Chatsonic, built on full GPT-4 and incorporating Google Knowledge Graph (Garg, 2023). Subsequently, Chatsonic generates hyper-relevant and trending content on any given topic and excels in areas where ChatGPT (built on GPT-3.5 and GPT-4) falters (Garg, 2023). Google's AI named Gemini (Google, n.d.), formerly Bard, is also one of the leading AI platforms that rivals and outperforms ChatGPT in some user experiences (Drapkin, 2024).

Technology Concerns

Breach of employee data privacy, cybersecurity threats, and data risk accounted for 40% of surveyed HR respondents' concerns with integrating machine learning with traditional HRM (IBM, n.d.-b; Marr, 2024; Murad, 2023; Sharma, 2023; Wolford, 2018). Additionally, 13% of surveyed HR respondents cited a lack of transparency in ML's decision-making process regarding matters including but not limited to the elimination of suitably qualified applicants during resume prescreening, hiring, selection, and automated employee termination – practices that could generate diversity, equity, inclusion (DEI), and gender bias issues (IBM, n.d.-b, n.d.-a; Marr, 2024; Murad, 2023; Sharma, 2023; Wolford, 2018). Another concern is that many generative AI designers, like OpenAI, create their AI tool using an open-source platform, and an open-source generative AI such as OpenAI's ChatGPT can be modified or nefariously used by anyone to outfit specific needs. Of even graver concern is that on its own, ChatGPT's building block GPT-3.5 learns and exponentially regurgitates racial and gender bias (Helsinger, 2024, 2024; Lund & Wang, 2023; Penn Today, 2023).

In a recent Bloomberg investigation (DiBenedetto, 2024; Yin et al., 2024), ChatGPT's foundation platform GPT-3.5 exhibited blatant racial biases when tested for job recruiting. After using GPT-3.5 to conduct multiple simulated resume sorting scenarios involving 1,000 equally qualified resumes, GPT-3.5 not only repeatedly *awarded* certain jobs to a specific gender but also repeatedly awarded certain jobs to a particular race because the Bloomberg investigators assigned demographically distinct surnames – surnames synonymous with either Asian, Black, Hispanic or White ethnicity (DiBenedetto, 2024; Helsinger, 2024; Yin et al., 2024). Being a subfield of AI, machine learning operates on pattern recognition, learns from past data, and makes predictions based on said learning (Agouridis, 2021). Pattern recognition and learning from past data is the hyper-incubator for AI repeating or exacerbating patterns of bias (SHRM, 2024).

The matter of machine learning exacerbating patterns of bias (SHRM, 2024) will increase exponentially, leading to a sustained decline in the quality and reliability of output and, most prominently, increased bias associated with diversity, equity, and inclusion (DiBenedetto, 2024). The expected hyper-elevation of exacerbating patterns of bias is due to the monolith, incestuous construction pattern associated with AI's evolution (DiBenedetto, 2024). According to DiBenedetto (2024), ongoing AI development is consanguineous as AI designers no longer train the foundation constructs using previous and other AI models instead of human inputs.

Management and Organizational Concerns

Approximately 70% of organizations encountered at least one challenge when using AI to augment HR undertakings (SHRM, 2024). In said January 2024 survey of HR respondents across the United States, approximately 60% were optimistic concerning the potential for the effective use of AI at their organization, while 56% were optimistic about the potential for AI to improve workplace and employee collaboration (SHRM, 2024). However, approximately 24% of surveyed HR respondents noted concern that AI would lead to job displacement (Maurer, 2024b). Beyond perceived job insecurities driven by the adoption of ML, lies the resistance from line staff and executive management. Resistance from senior leadership and line employees (due to lack of trust) is synonymous with all forms of organizational change endeavors (B. A. Brown & Heitner, 2023a). Thus, creating and implementing sHAM will undoubtedly propagate resistance to change – like any other organizational change process (B. A. Brown & Heitner, 2023a; Srivastava & Agrawal, 2020). Surveyed HR respondents indicated that 21% of their line employees and 15% of their corporate executives admit resistance to or lack of trust in AI tools (SHRM, 2024). Executive leadership's acceptance of organizational change ventures is paramount to the success of organizational change management as their acceptance will set the tone for line staff acceptance (B. A. Brown & Heitner, 2023a), especially regarding trusting machine learning with their employee data.

Preventing privacy breaches associated with the security of data processed using machine learning HRM platforms mandates the protection of employees' data, respect for employees' privacy, and managing how machine learning uses employee data (to cause or prevent discrimination, gender bias, and identity theft) in any organization (Agouridis, 2021; Marr, 2024). Regarding the privacy of data used by machine learning tools, 40% of said surveyed HR respondents indicated concern about the security and privacy of employee data used by machine learning tools (SHRM, 2024). Machine learning tools based on their algorithms could cause breaches of the Health Insurance Portability and Accountability Act, the California Consumer Privacy Act, or the European Union General Data Protection Regulation (GDPR) designed to protect consumer privacy. While similar and different in some ways, the regulations (a) combat the numerous data breaches associated with inadequately demarcated access controls and privacy management, (b) require specific and explicit consent from (European) consumers for the use of their personal data and (c) give (Californian) residents the right to know when and how their information is being collected and sold, as well as the ability to opt-out (Agouridis, 2021; IBM, n.d.-b; Marr, 2024; Wolford, 2018).

Additionally, employee privacy violations include using AI tools to predict employee turnover by analyzing employee social media activity (Agouridis, 2021). Using AI in such a manner could constitute a breach of the California Consumer Privacy Act, the European Union GDPR, or other ethical standards and best practices (Agouridis, 2021). Other management and organizational concerns include but are not limited to resume exclusion during prescreening, gender and racial biases arising from innate machine learning algorithms, civil lawsuits arising from AI wrongful termination, and biased performance appraisals (Guerin, 2024; Murad, 2023; Scopelliti, 2019; Sharma, 2023; SHRM, 2024). Racial and gender biases propagated during prescreening will be further discussed in the following section.

CURRENT CHALLENGES FACING THE ORGANIZATION

As the fourth industrial revolution progresses, integrating AI's machine learning as a hyper-disruptive innovation with orthodox HRM progresses at near hypersonic speed (Siocon, 2023). The positive outcome is the creation of sHAM, intended to enable HR officers to leverage machine learning and algorithms to allay gender and racial biases in recruitment, create a sustainable equilibrium of diversity, equality, and inclusion, streamline HR and corporate work processes, improve learning and development, provide objective performance management, develop and enhance workplace psychosocial safety climate, improve analysis and decision-making processes, and subsequently aid in achieving the United Nation's sustainable development goal 8 target 2 (Abrams, 2024; BambooHR, 2023; B. A. Brown & Heitner, 2023b; Maurer, 2024b; Siocon, 2023; United Nations, n.d.-a; van Vulpen, 2023). However, current limitations and vulnerabilities have given some organization leadership much cause for concern, especially given the documented cases of machine learning HRM platforms repeatedly producing the reciprocal of expected outcomes (Dastin, 2018, 2022; IBM, n.d.-b; Murad, 2023; Sharma, 2023; Siocon, 2023).

With corporations as the end user of machine learning tools (though some corporations develop their own machine learning tool which produces equally devastating results), the genesis of their machine learning HRM challenges lies in the lack of resources to properly audit AI algorithms (SHRM, 2024) or simply a failure to audit and train the algorithms post-acquisition or building of the machine learning HRM tool (Bahrke & Regnier, 2023). The fundamental problems then extend into machine learning from past behavior (thus becoming rogue) and precipitate actions such as eliminating candidates' resumes based on content without consideration for context (Murad, 2023; Sharma, 2023; SHRM, 2024).

Machine Learning HRM Systems Eliminating Potentially Valuable Candidates During Resume Prescreening

Some corporate HRM officers and staff in recruiting agencies employ machine learning HRM platforms as the preliminary tool for screening incoming job applications - a process claimed to *efficiently* select applicants who meet the recruiters' requirements – while eliminating applicants who do not meet the said requirements (Agouridis, 2021, 2023; Murad, 2023; Sharma, 2023; York, 2024). Resume rejection by machine learning HRM tools during prescreening is based on ML's algorithm, which makes decisions based on content, not context, and subsequently eliminates applicants' resumes (Murad, 2023; Sharma, 2023). Consequently, the resumes of potential candidates who could have made vital or even groundbreaking contributions to an organization are jettisoned even before the applicants receive an interview with a human being (Murad, 2023; Sharma, 2023).

Gender Biased and Racial Discriminatory Decisions by Machine Learning HRM Platforms During Resume Prescreening and Recruiting

The prototypical algorithm problems then extend into discrimination based on documented instances of job positions being awarded based on machine learning-promulgated gender bias or racial profiling (Murad, 2023). Machine learning HRM tools have exhibited gender bias by favoring men over women, as highlighted at Amazon (Dastin, 2018, 2022; IBM, n.d.-b; Murad, 2023). Amazon's machine learning gender bias debacle dates back to 2015 when Amazon's talent iML HRM platform favored men over women (Dastin, 2018, 2022). According to Dastin (2018, 2022), the machine learning algorithm *taught itself that male candidates were preferable and penalized resumes that contained the word women.* For example, when the word *women* appeared, as in *women's chess club captain,* the machine learning HRM tool authoritatively downgraded said resumes (Dastin, 2018, 2022). Additionally, Amazon's machine learning HRM downgraded two resumes because the applicants' resume content indicated the applicants graduated from prominent all-women's-colleges (Dastin, 2018, 2022). Owing to machine learning's innate incestuous construct, which propagates hyper-elevation of exacerbating patterns of bias based on pattern recognition and learning from past data (DiBenedetto, 2024; SHRM, 2024), the use of machine learning in HRM recruiting continues to produce gender-biased and racially discriminating decisions (DiBenedetto, 2024; Helsinger, 2024; Yin et al., 2024).

The recent Bloomberg investigation involving OpenAI's ChatGPT simulated screening of 1,000 equally qualified resumes highlighted that when tested for job recruiting, ChatGPT's foundation platform GPT-3.5 (the version most widely used for building machine learning systems), exhibited irrefutable racial and gender biases (DiBenedetto, 2024; Yin et al., 2024). Leveraging voter and census data to ensure a 90% accuracy in demographic representation, the Bloomberg investigative team produced 1,000 equally qualified, contrived resumes with names predominantly correlated with specific ethnic or racial groups (Yin et al., 2024). The Bloomberg team submitted the 1,000 equally qualified resumes to OpenAI's GPT for ranking via 1,000 simulations for various job postings, isolating names as the primary variable to assess bias. Yin et al. (2024) repeated the experiment for job postings (HR business partner, senior software engineer, retail manager, and financial analyst), featuring names principally related to White, Black, Asian, and Hispanic ethnic or racial groups, while men and women represented the gender variables, to systematically appraise GPT's bias across the elected job sectors, ethnicity, race, and gender (Yin et al., 2024).

Using GPT-3.5 for 1,000 simulated sorting of the 1,000 equally qualified resumes, GPT-3.5 repeatedly and consistently awarded specific jobs to the same race - predicated on the Bloomberg investigators' assigning demographically distinct names synonymous with either Asian, Black, Hispanic, or White ethnicity (DiBenedetto, 2024; Helsinger, 2024; Yin et al., 2024). Additionally, GPT-3.5 repeatedly and consistently *awards* particular job(s) to the same specific gender(s) (Helsinger, 2024; Yin et al., 2024). Beyond racial discrimination alone, gender and racial biases varied depending on the job role. For example, regarding HR positions, a field customarily dominated by women, GPT-3.5 consistently favorably ranked names affiliated with Hispanic women above women of other races and men of all races (Helsinger, 2024; Yin et al., 2024). GPT-3.5 systematically ranked resumes such that Black Americans (based on assigned demographically distinct names) were remarkably disadvantaged for jobs such as financial analyst and software engineer and, holistically, less likely to be ranked as top candidates (Helsinger, 2024; Yin et al., 2024). With GPT-3.5 propagating such flagrant racial and gender-biased results (based on its inherent characteristics of incestuous DNA, pattern recognition, and earning from past data), global organizational leadership must be resolutely concerned about organizational DEI and achieving the United Nation's sustainable development goal 8 target 2 (Abrams, 2024; B. A. Brown & Heitner, 2023b).

SOLUTIONS AND RECOMMENDATIONS

Corporate leadership encounters many challenges with integrating AI and machine learning as a hyper-disruptive innovation with traditional HRM and managing the use and subsequent output of machine learning in HRM (IBM, n.d.-b; Murad, 2023; Sharma, 2023). Incorporating disruptive innovations in HRM to create sHAM and achieving sustainable development goal 8 target 2 simultaneously will require implementing disruptive innovations that globally, many present and prospective employees, including HRM officers, are neither familiar with nor trained to use (B. A. Brown & Heitner, 2022, 2024; Buchholz, 2023). However, the incorporation should not be ad-hoc or for the sake of positive publicity to show that the organization is on board with the latest DEI trends. However, we would be remiss not to suggest recommendations for the safe adoption, deployment, and ethical governance and management of machine learning before commenting on the benefits of integrating machine learning with orthodox HRM to create sHAM. Having reviewed the disastrous outcomes of the 1,000 simulated rankings of 1,000 resumes using GPT-3.5, we noted the obvious that building sHAM must, at a minimum, start with (a) establishing a functional ethics committee (Marr, 2024) along with a robust framework for machine learning deployment and management and (b) *building* a bias-free machine learning system using sufficient and uncontaminated data (DiBenedetto, 2024; Helsinger, 2024; Yin et al., 2024).

Installation of Ethics Committee and Framework for Governance and Management of own Machine Learning Tool(s)

The EU AI ACT classifies the use of machine learning HRM systems to rank applicants' CVs in recruitment procedures as a high-risk undertaking because the machine learning ranking process infringes on the rights of European citizens' access to jobs (EU Artificial Intelligence Act, 2024; European Commission, 2024; Nahra et al., 2024). The EU mandates that said high-risk machine learning systems must comply with specific criteria before and after marketing (European Commission, 2024; Nahra et al., 2024). Subsequently, we strongly recommend that every corporation desirous of integrating AI, specifically machine learning with HRM, install a functional ethics committee (Marr, 2024) and a robust framework for machine learning deployment and management. The purpose of the committee and corresponding framework is to (a) ensure that the machine learning system must comply with specific criteria before and after the acquisition, (b) regularly audit the machine learning's algorithm, (c) assess real-world cases of other organization's machine learning pitfalls, (d) reprogram the algorithm on an as-needed basis and (e) document all audit findings, corrective actions, programming, maintenance, and dataset used to test or train the algorithm to process CV's or other HRM activities (Bahrke & Regnier, 2023; Crispin, 2021; European Commission, 2024; Marr, 2024).

The purpose of the committee and the corresponding framework stated in the previous paragraph now becomes exceptionally relevant when analyzed alongside OpenAI's response to the failed 1,000-simulated ranking exercise of 1,000 resumes using their GPT-3.5. When contacted by the Bloomberg investigators (Yin et al., 2024), OpenAI's spokesperson's response to the findings was that the use of GPT models *out-of-the-box* may not precisely reflect real-world applications by businesses (Helsinger, 2024; Yin et al., 2024). The OpenAI spokesperson underscored that many end users apply additional measures to assuage bias, such as removing names from resumes before processing resumes (Helsinger, 2024; Yin et al., 2024). The response from OpenAI also reinforces the need for superior governance and legal framework, especially the likes of the EU AI Act – which stipulates that high-risk machine learning systems, such as GPT-3.5 machine learning curriculum vitae evaluation systems, must comply with specific criteria before and after being marked (European Commission, 2024; Nahra et al., 2024).

Before acquiring and deploying machine learning in HRM, HR officers must acquaint themselves with the EU AI ACT to (a) at least inform themselves of the pros and cons of machine learning in HRM, (b) learn the importance of safeguarding employees' data processed by ML, and (c) especially prevent adverse consequences to DEI, particularly racial and gender bias (Bahrke & Regnier, 2023; European Commission, 2024). Globally, the EU AI Act is the first and only all-encompassing operational regulation on the development and use of AI, designed and established to safeguard the rights and safety of European citizens (Bahrke & Regnier, 2023; EU Artificial Intelligence Act, 2024; European Commission, 2024). As no other legal frameworks exist, public and private corporate leadership and HR officers must (with requisite permission where necessary) use the EU AI Act as a template to develop and establish their pertinent ethics committee and framework. For example, the 2016 European Union GDPR requires persons to give unambiguous and affirmative consent before their (personal) data are collected and processed (Agouridis, 2021; IBM, n.d.-b; Marr, 2024; Wolford, 2018). The GDPR is the world's strictest privacy and security law (Wolford, 2018). It applies globally, including to foreigners who do business with European nations, corporations, and citizens, making the GDPR the global gold standard for protecting citizens' privacy (Wolford, 2018). After the 2016 enforcement of the EU GDPR came the 2018 California Consumer Privacy Act (Agouridis, 2021). We make the point that, similarly, the EU AI Act could soon become a global gold standard like the GDPR (EU Artificial Intelligence Act, 2024).

Provide Sufficient Pristine Dataset to Inform Machine Learning Algorithms

Output or machine learning-derived decisions depend on the quality and quantity of the input dataset (IBM, n.d.-b). Insufficient and flawed dataset input guarantees 100% flawed AI-driven decisions, thus negating the benefits machine learning could potentially convey to HRM (IBM, n.d.-b; Marr, 2024). Users must provide the machine learning system with substantial quantities of pristine data for the machine learning system to best function in its inherent pattern recognition autonomous self-teaching mode and refine its algorithms while learning from the uncorrupted input data (IBM, n.d.-b; Marr, 2024). To guarantee optimum bias-free machine learning-driven decisions in HRM, machine learning system users must promptly provide accurate, consistent, relevant, unique (not duplicated) datasets (Marr, 2024).

Aside from the importance of immaculate datasets, Machine learning users must provide a substantial quantity of flawless data to inform the algorithm (IBM, n.d.-b). Twenty-one percent of surveyed HR respondents indicated that their organization had insufficient data to inform the machine learning algorithm, resulting in the organization's inability to leverage and benefit from integrating machine learning with HRM (SHRM, 2024). HR officers must ensure sufficient faultless data to inform the machine learning algorithm, as insufficient data could cause the machine learning

HRM system to produce a perfectly logical algorithm that is wholly erroneous or ambiguous (IBM, n.d.-b).

Leveraging Machine Learning in HRM (sHAM) to Attract, Develop, and Retain Human Assets; Promote Diversity, Equity, and Inclusion; and Improve Organizational Sustainability

Forming the ethics committee, creating the framework for governing corporate machine learning usage, and providing a sufficient dataset to inform the machine learning algorithms are essential but just the beginning. Post leveraging machine learning (with an authentic thrust) to hiring DEI candidates, HR officers must extend the integration of machine learning with traditional HRM to encompass generating job postings and related descriptions that reflect the organization's inclination towards DEI, learning and development, performance management, and other sHAM activities create high psychosocial climate work environments.

Generating Job Postings and Related Descriptions Punctuated for Diversity, Equity, and Inclusion

We posit that an organization's first impression regarding its appetite for DEI is reflected in the job posting content and its related description when advertising a vacancy. When seeking new recruits, HR officers must advertise vacancies using appropriate language in their job postings and descriptions to showcase the organization's DEI proclivity. Maurer (2024b) cited that 42% of surveyed HR respondents use AI to customize job postings, while 65% use AI to help create job descriptions. Thus, to attract under-represented or minority candidates, HR officers must leverage the disruptive innovation element of sHAM to create job postings and associated descriptions punctuated for diversity, equity, and inclusion – rather than exclusion.

Reorienting Recruiting, Interviewing, and Hiring Machine Learning HRM Systems Towards Diversity, Equity, and Inclusion Hiring to Mitigate Bias

A benefit of machine learning HRM and talent intelligence platforms is eliminating the onerous administrative aspects of candidate sourcing and reviewing or screening applicant resumes (Sharma, 2023). Employing job resources (such as machine learning HRM tools) to reduce job demands (tedious administrative aspects of candidate sourcing and reviewing or screening applicant resumes) reduces job strain and aids in creating high psychosocial safety climate work environments (B. A. Brown, 2020). Regarding attracting and *equitably* hiring *diverse*, qualified candidates from under-represented (deemed previously inaccessible) pools of potential applicants, 69% of HR officers cite DEI as a top priority, while 31% of HR officers struggle to attract diverse talent (Eightfold AI, 2022). Thus, we recommend that HR Officers must, though carefully, engage and leverage machine learning to augment orthodox HRM and create sHAM to improve their probabilities of capturing and retaining diverse talent.

According to Maurer (2024b), 33% of surveyed HR respondents use machine learning HRM systems to automate candidate searches, review or screen applicant resumes, or communicate with applicants during the interview process. However, the primary concern is that many corporations and recruiting agencies alike employ machine learning HRM tools as the preliminary screening tool for incoming job applications - a tool that sorts and ranks applicants' resumes and CVs based on the machine learning algorithm (Murad, 2023; Sharma, 2023). The concern shared by 29% of 2,366 surveyed HR respondents is that the resumes and CVs of potential candidates or employees who could have made crucial or even revolutionary con-tributions to organizational sustainability are excluded even before the applicants receive an interview with a human being (Murad, 2023; Sharma, 2023; SHRM, 2024). We refer to the Bloomberg experiment (Yin et al., 2024), which highlighted GPT-3.5 (as the nucleus of ChatGPT, the most popular AI platform marginalizing Black women and men during a machine learning resume screening exercise. Subsequently, HR Officers must ensure that machine learning HRM systems have substantial quantities of faultless data for the machine learning system to provide race and gender-bias-free ML-driven HRM decisions (IBM, n.d.-b; Marr, 2024), decisions that epitomize DEI and sHAM.

Designing Tailored and Targeted Learning and Development Programs

We established that employee learning and development is a systematic ap-proach designed by corporate HR to holistically advance and augment employees' inherent skill sets, knowledge, and competency (van Vulpen, 2023). Learning and development as a process is a tenet of sHAM and highlights two components of the triple bottom line (B. A. Brown & Heitner, 2023b; Elkington, 2004). Competencies and skill sets differ across employees, thus requiring varied types and intensities of development, for example, upskilling or reskilling (B. A. Brown & Heitner, 2024). Presently, 49% of surveyed HR respondents use machine learning to recommend or create personalized opportunities for their workforces, 19% use AI to upskill or reskill their staff, and 45% employ AI to monitor employees' learning progress (Maurer, 2024b; SHRM, 2024). Using the tenets of sHAM, HR officers must develop and deliver customized learning and development programs for individual employees (Maurer, 2024b).

Furthermore, scholars, practitioners, employees, and (particularly) prospective employees now ponder whether AI as a disruptive innovation will eventually eclipse the human decision-making element of HRM talent acquisition and performance management (Murad, 2023; Sharma, 2023). The advent of sHAM can potentially reduce the HR (and organizational-wide) labor force, thus precipitating and accelerating the erosion of human decision-making in conventional HRM (Maurer, 2024a; Zinkula & Mok, 2024). According to Maurer (2024a) and Mok and Zikula (2024), corporate-wide AI adoption will most affect white-collared workers. Subsequently, HR officers must leverage sHAM protocols to provide reskilling and upskilling under learning and development to allay job insecurities (Maurer, 2024a). Employee learning and development is a lifelong symbiotic venture for both the employee and the organization; thus, HR officers must leverage machine learning in sHAM to empower the *people* or employees, which ideally leads to improved employee work performance and translates to increased *profits* or corporate sustainability (van Vulpen, 2023).

Conducting Objective Performance Management

Employee performance management is a shared task among HR officers and supervisors (B. A. Brown, 2020; Qin et al., 2023). Objective employee performance evaluation (review, assessment, or appraisal) is an integral aspect of performance management, which is pivotal to sHAM (Agarwal et al., 2021; Aungsuroch et al., 2021). Subsequently, the respective supervisors must conduct objective performance evaluations of their subordinates as part of performance management in sHAM (Agarwal et al., 2021; Aungsuroch et al., 2021). In a recent study of machine learning versus human managers conducting employee appraisals, employees voted machine learning to be both fairer and more accurate, that is, more objective in evaluating their performance than the average human manager (Qin et al., 2023). Thus, supervisors must embrace sHAM because objective performance evaluations drive employee satisfaction and promote employee well-being (Agarwal et al., 2021; Aungsuroch et al., 2021). Subjective or biased performance evaluations are a form of employee bullying that precipitates toxic workplace environments that neither embody and propagate sHAM nor lead to organizational sustainability (Johnson, 2019). Furthermore, there are copious records of legal actions against supervisors using employee performance evaluations associated with conventional HRM as a form of employee bullying (Guerin, 2024; Scopelliti, 2019; Yadegar, Minoofar & Soleymani LLP, 2024).

In the realms of sHAM, objective goal setting and employee feedback are crucial elements of performance management (Maurer, 2024b; SHRM, 2024). Regarding objective goal setting and feedback as components of performance management, 57% of surveyed HR respondents used machine learning to assist managers in providing more comprehensive or actionable feedback to their employees, and 46% used machine learning to enable employee goal setting (Maurer, 2024b; SHRM, 2024). Supervisors and managers must enforce sHAM to experience benefits such as increased efficiency from the reduction in the labor-intensive aspects of the performance evaluations, goal setting and processing of employee feedback, and holistic improvement in performance management (Maurer, 2024b).

CONCLUSION

The question that guided this systematic literature review is whether organizational leaders can use disruptive innovation to (a) enable sustainable human asset management while (b) maximizing efficiency and production to achieve organizational sustainability in the impending fourth industrial revolution. We unequivocally concluded that organizational leaders can leverage disruptive innovation, particularly machine learning, to (a) enable sustainable human asset management, (b) maximize efficiency and production to achieve organizational sustainability in the impending fourth industrial revolution, and (c) eventually eclipse inefficient pre-fourth industrial revolution HR technologies. Pre-fourth industrial revolution HR technologies, such as human resources information systems (HRIS) and applicant tracking systems, proved helpful for record-keeping, automation, and compliance (Eightfold AI, 2022; Hmoud & Várallyai, 2019). However, with the fourth industrial revolution, the ever-widening global skills gap, the COVID-19 pandemic, and the need to achieve the United Nation's sustainable development goal 8 target 2 (Abrams, 2024; B. A. Brown & Heitner, 2022, 2023b, 2023a, 2024), HRM conditions became increasingly challenging.

Record-keeping and applicant tracking systems were not designed to assimilate and process candidates' potential and subsequently inform future-focused workforce strategies and needs (Eightfold AI, 2022; Hmoud & Várallyai, 2019). Subsequently, in the corporate hyper-competition to source, hire, and retain superior talent, corporate leaders and HRM officers must decide and uncover what talent is capable of now and which skills they need to guarantee sustainability – their ability to succeed today and tomorrow without disenfranchising the needs of the future generation (Eightfold AI, 2022; Hmoud & Várallyai, 2019; United Nations, n.d.-a, n.d.-b). Thus, machine learning HRM and talent intelligence platforms incorporating machine learning or deep learning to gain competitive advantage became compellingly necessary to deliver these insights on sourcing, hiring, and retaining superior talent (Eightfold AI, 2022; Hmoud & Várallyai, 2019).

Integrating machine learning with legacy HRM is for creating benefits that include but are not limited to (a) supporting and streamlining HRM by removing the arduous and repetitive parts of HRM-related activities, (b) gaining maximum access to once-hard-to-reach and under-represented pools of diverse potential hires, (c) mitigating racial and gender bias while promoting DEI by creating an unbiased recruitment and hiring process to sort equally qualified CV's uniformly for a given job posting (Agouridis, 2021; B. A. Brown, 2020; Eightfold AI, 2022; Guerin, 2024; IBM, n.d.-b; Qin et al., 2023; SHRM, 2024). Additional and equally essential benefits are empowering employees through learning and development, creating more engaged employees, improving workplace psychosocial safety climate through machine learning-aided objective performance management, and (g) creating organizational and environmental sustainability per the United Nations' sustainable development goal 8 target 2 (Agouridis, 2021; B. A. Brown, 2020; Eightfold AI, 2022; Guerin, 2024; IBM, n.d.-b; Qin et al., 2023; SHRM, 2024).

While we highly recommend the integration of disruptive innovation with orthodox HRM to create sHAM for the diversity of perceived and actual benefits, we conclude that the governance and cautious use of AI, machine learning, and deep learning in HRM sustains sHAM success. In the opening paragraph of our recommendations and solutions section and the two sub-sections immediately below said opening paragraph, we highlighted and emphasized that machine learning tools (specifically referencing those built on (GPT-3.5) are not plug-and-play. OpenAI's representative highlighted that a ChatGPT built on GPT-3.5, right out of the box, is prone to generating erroneous ML-driven decisions and requires modification(s) to input data before use (Dastin, 2018, 2022; Helsinger, 2024; Yin et al., 2024). Consequently, integrating machine learning with legacy HRM to create sHAM is not the invention of a wonder drug or magic potion to replace interaction between human beings but rather the use of machine learning systems to refine orthodox HRM while maximizing efficiency and production to achieve organizational sustainability (Agouridis, 2021; Murad, 2023; Sharma, 2023).

The November 30, 2022, inaugural debut of OpenAI's generative AI technology ChatGPT (Alser & Waisberg, 2023; Qadir, 2023) created an unprecedented stir in nearly every industry at all levels. Instantaneously, ChatGPT gained colossal recognition and acceptance as the pioneer generative AI for written script production (Baidoo-Anu & Owusu Ansah, 2023; Qadir, 2023; Rahman & Watanobe, 2023). The release of ChatGPT propagated an all-out AI developers' war, as within the first year of release, there were more than 30 alternatives to ChatGPT, many built on GPT-3.5, ChatGPT's nucleus and chassis (Garg, 2023). According to Maurer (2024a), the industries that are most likely affected by machine learning include business and legal services, financial services, marketing, writing and editing, graphic design, computer programming, and HR. We posit that machine learning will affect HR the most. For example, not every organization will have a legal or marketing department. Still, nearly all organizations (including legal and marketing corporations) will have an HRM department, which explains the hyper-absorption of AI and machine learning in almost all facets of HRM. Despite the unparalleled acceptance of machine learning due to its perceived and actual potential in HRM departments (in virtually all industries), machine learning, as a hyper-disruptive innovation, has critical disadvantages (Crispin, 2021; Dastin, 2018, 2022; Helsinger, 2024; Yin et al., 2024). Such critical disadvantages left unchecked not only have the potential to but have produced racial and gender-biased machine learning-driven decisions deemed excruciatingly damaging to DEI (Crispin, 2021; Dastin, 2018, 2022; Helsinger, 2024; Yin et al., 2024).

Synonymous with all industrial revolution periods, solving real-world problems with technological advancements subsequently created even more significant real-world problems using said technological advancement. For example, technological advancement over the first three industrial revolutions spiked a hyper-greed for corporate wealth, giving rise to climate change, food insecurities, and near irreparable damage to global water and air quality issues, requiring the intervention of the United Nations 17 sustainable development goal (B. A. Brown & Heitner, 2023b). In this fourth industrial revolution, while sHAM has immense potential to solve a plethora of problems associated with traditional HRM, some HRM AI-driven tools generated biased decisions that were not conducive to promoting DEI. Subsequently, some prospective recruits cognizant of the biases affiliated with machine learning HRM systems and talent intelligence platforms found solution(s) to satisfy machine learning prescreening processes and ultimately defeat the machine learning HRM or talent intelligence platforms' algorithms (Egan, 2024).

Final Round AI uses the posted job descriptions and company details to create AI-generated cover letters and resumes - even deep fake resumes if desired (Final Round AI, n.d.). To augment sHAM, HRM officers must scan cover letters, CVs, and resumes with software such as GPTZero to determine if the author is human, AI, or a mix of both (Egan, 2024; GPTZero, 2023). Candid but factual, we submitted the first 4,918 characters of this chapter to GPTZero. The GPTZero results read that *we are highly confident this text is entirely human... probability breakdown is 97% human, 0% mixed, 3% AI* (GPTZero, 2023). The trial version used was available online at https://gptzero.me/ without downloading, only accepted 5,000 characters, and checked across five dimensions, namely ChatGPT (using GPT-3.5), GPT-4, Llama2 (developed for Facebook), human, and AI+human (GPTZero, 2023). As a disclaimer, our impromptu use of GPTZero was not to proclaim or promote its accuracy, and the only artificial interference was the use of software for citation management and correcting grammar and tenses.

Final Round AI is also equipped with *Interview Copilot*, an onscreen AI assistant that helps interviewees ace interviews (Final Round AI, n.d.; Sharma, 2023). *Interview Copilot* provides the interviewee with real-time AI-driven transcription and contextual assistance through responses and prompts based on questions the interviewer asks during a virtual interview (Final Round AI, n.d.). *Interview Copilot* allows interviewees to appear exceptionally prepared as interviewees can deliver responses without stuttering, fumbling, or using mid-sentence words and sounds like *uh, um, well, er, you know,* as they collect their thoughts and prepare a response (Sharma, 2023). According to Final Round AI (n.d.), *Interview Copilot* does not require downloading and supports all popular virtual meeting platforms, including but not limited to Google Meet, Microsoft Teams, Zoom, and WebEx (Final Round AI, n.d.). We found Final Round AI's statement mind-bending and detected a (new for us) spatial leap with generative AI. Typically, the downloaded and dedicated platforms (Google Meet, Microsoft Teams, Zoom, and WebEx, in this instance) would support Final Round AI (as an add-on that does not require downloading). In this case, Final Round AI (as an add-on) supports the downloaded and dedicated platforms. The unprecedented rise in actions and counteractions driven by AI, machine learning, and deep learning in sHAM reinforces (a) the need for regulations such as the EUAI Act, (b) why the EU AI Act classifies machine learning resume screening, specifically the use of talent intelligence platforms as high-risk, and why the EU AI Act enforces stipulations that talent intelligence platforms must comply with before and after marketing (Bahrke & Regnier, 2023; EU Artificial Intelligence Act, 2024; Nahra et al., 2024).

In closing, we also acknowledge the infinite need for human input when deploying sHAM, not sHAM replacing humans. Even if sHAM ultimately becomes capable of replacing humans, this should not happen because human intervention and interaction are fundamental prerequisites of any labor force required to drive a sustainable organization (Agouridis, 2021). Every HR officer, corporate manager, supervisor, recruiting agency, and anyone using machine learning platforms in sHAM to manage employees must acquaint themselves with the benefits and potentials of machine learning, especially with its critical shortcomings regarding employees (and potential hires). Subsequently, organizational leaders can use disruptive innovation to (a) enable sustainable human asset management while (b) maximizing efficiency and production to achieve organizational sustainability in the impending fourth industrial revolution. However, sHAM's success depends on managing the risks posed by integrating machine learning with orthodox. Users must, at a minimum, exhibit due regard for the EU AI ACT (Bahrke & Regnier, 2023; EU Artificial

Intelligence Act, 2024; Nahra et al., 2024) and ensure that technology is combined with corporate HRM, not in lieu of it (Agouridis, 2021).

REFERENCES

Abrams, Z. (2024). Addressing equity and ethics in artificial intelligence. *American Pstchological Asociation*, 55(3), 1.

Agarwal, V., Mathiyazhagan, K., Malhotra, S., & Saikouk, T. (2021). Analysis of challenges in sustainable human resource management due to disruptions by Industry 4.0: An emerging economy perspective. *International Journal of Manpower*, 43(2), 513–541. DOI:10.1108/IJM-03-2021-0192

Agouridis, A. (2021, September 2). *All you need to know about AI and machine learning in HR*. https://www.jobylon.com/blog/all-you-need-to-know-about-ai-and-machine-learning-in-hr

Agouridis, A. (2023, February 9). *How AI is transforming the world of recruitment*. https://www.jobylon.com/blog/how-ai-is-transforming-the-world-of-recruitment

Allianz Care. (2023). *Sustainable global HRM practices*. Allianzcare.Com. https://www.allianzcare.com/en/employers/business-hub/hr-blogs/sustainable-global-hrm-practices.html

Alser, M., & Waisberg, E. (2023). Concerns with the usage of ChatGPT in academia and medicine: A viewpoint. *American Journal of Medicine Open*, 9, 2. DOI:10.1016/j.ajmo.2023.100036 PMID:39035060

Artificial Intelligence Act, E. U. (2024). *EU Artificial Intelligence Act | Up-to-date developments and analyses of the EU AI Act*. https://artificialintelligenceact.eu/

Aungsuroch, Y., Gunawan, J., & Fisher, M. L. (2021). *Redesigning the nursing and human resource partnership: A model for the new normal era*. Springer Nature.

Babbage, C. (1832). *On the economy of machinery and manufactures* (2nd ed.). Charles Knight. DOI:10.5479/sil.975430.39088015716483

Bahrke, J., & Regnier, T. (2023, December 14). *Artificial intelligence – Q&As* [Text]. European Commission - European Commission. https://ec.europa.eu/commission/presscorner/detail/en/qanda_21_1683

Baidoo-Anu, D., & Owusu Ansah, L. (2023). Education in the era of generative artificial intelligence (ai): Understanding the potential benefits of ChatGPT in promoting teaching and learning. *Journal of AI*, 7(1), 1. DOI:10.61969/jai.1337500

Bamboo, H. R. (2023). *Performance management software*. https://www.bamboohr.com/hr-software/performance-management

Britannica, T. E. of E. (2024, February 14). *Elton Mayo*. https://www.britannica.com/biography/Elton-Mayo

Brown, B. A. (2020). *Evaluating Expert Opinions for Reducing Voluntary Employee Absenteeism in Trinidad and Tobago* [Ph.D., Walden University]. http://search.proquest.com/pqdtglobal/docview/2447561234/abstract/1A8116E743549EAPQ/1

Brown, B. A., & Heitner, K. L. (2022). Worker response to the rapid changes caused by disruptive innovation: Managing a remote workforce without any training or preparation. In Hynes, R., Aquino, C., & Hauer, J. (Eds.), *Multidisciplinary approach to diversity and inclusion in the COVID-19-era workplace* (pp. 189–205). IGI Global., DOI:10.4018/978-1-7998-8827-7.ch011

Brown, B. A., & Heitner, K. L. (2023a). Obstacles and resistance to organizational change in the new post-COVID-19 environment. In Belias, D., Rossidis, I., Papademetriou, C., Masouras, A., & Anastasiadou, S. (Eds.), *Managing successful and ethical organizational change* (pp. 167–195). IGI Global., DOI:10.4018/979-8-3693-0235-4.ch008

Brown, B. A., & Heitner, K. L. (2023b). Organizational transformation: The way to Sustainability. In De Moraes, A. (Ed.), *Strategic management and international business policies for maintaining competitive advantage* (pp. 34–75). IGI Global., DOI:10.4018/978-1-6684-6845-6.ch003

Brown, B. A., & Heitner, K. L. (2024). International business staffing challenges and the growing global skills gap in the post-COVID environment: A Latin American and Caribbean perspective. In Christiansen, B., & Even, A. M. (Eds.), *Advancing student employability through higher education* (pp. 199–219). IGI Global., DOI:10.4018/979-8-3693-0517-1.ch011

Brown, S. (2021, April 21). *Machine learning, explained*. https://mitsloan.mit.edu/ideas-made-to-matter/machine-learning-explained

Brunsson, K. H. (2008). Some effects of Fayolism. *International Studies of Management & Organization*, 38(1), 30–47. DOI:10.2753/IMO0020-8825380102

Buchholz, L. (2023, December 15). *93% of HR managers use AI tools to reduce costs, report finds*. UNLEASH. https://www.unleash.ai/artificial-intelligence/93-of-hr-managers-use-ai-tools-to-reduce-costs-report-finds/

Budhwar, P., Malik, A., De Silva, M. T. T., & Thevisuthan, P. (2022). Artificial intelligence – challenges and opportunities for international HRM: A review and research agenda. *International Journal of Human Resource Management*, 33(6), 1065–1097. DOI:10.1080/09585192.2022.2035161

Charles Babbage Institute. (2024). *Who was Charles Babbage?* College of Science and Engineering. https://cse.umn.edu/cbi/who-was-charles-babbage

Cheng, M. M., & Hackett, R. D. (2021). A critical review of algorithms in HRM: Definition, theory, and practice. *Human Resource Management Review*, 31(1), 100698. DOI:10.1016/j.hrmr.2019.100698

Christensen, C. M. (1997). *The innovator's dilemma: When new technologies cause great firms to fail.* Harvard Business Review Press.

Crispin, J. (2021, July 5). Welcome to dystopia: Getting fired from your job as an Amazon worker by an app. *The Guardian.* https://www.theguardian.com/commentisfree/2021/jul/05/amazon-worker-fired-app-dystopia

Dachner, A. M., Ellingson, J. E., Noe, R. A., & Saxton, B. M. (2021). The future of employee development. *Human Resource Management Review*, 31(2), 14. DOI:10.1016/j.hrmr.2019.100732

Dastin, J. (2018, October 10). *Insight—Amazon scraps secret AI recruiting tool that showed bias against women.* https://www.reuters.com/article/idUSKCN1MK0AG/

Dastin, J. (2022). Amazon scraps secret AI recruiting tool that showed bias against women. In *Ethics of data and analytics.* Auerbach Publications. DOI:10.1201/9781003278290-44

Dhawan, A. (2023, March 20). *Evolution of HRM (human resource development).* https://datatrained.com/post/evolution-of-hrm/

DiBenedetto, C. (2024, March 8). *AI shows clear racial bias when used for job recruiting, new tests reveal.* Mashable. https://mashable.com/article/openai-chatgpt-racial-bias-in-recruiting

Dickson, C. N., & John, A. J. (2022). Public administration: Theory and practice in Nigeria. In Iba, O. J., Dickson, C. N., & John, A. J. (Eds.), *Public administration: Theory and practice in Nigeria* (pp. 84–96). CHANANPRINTS.

Dowd, D. F. (2024, February 17). *Robert Owen.* https://www.britannica.com/biography/Robert-Owen

Drapkin, A. (2024, March 13). Google Gemini vs ChatGPT: Which AI chatbot wins in 2024? *Tech.Co.* https://tech.co/news/google-bard-vs-chatgpt

Economic Commission for Latin America and the Caribbean. (2022). *A digital path for sustainable development in Latin America and the Caribbean.* https://repositorio.cepal.org/handle/11362/48461

Egan, J. (2024, March 18). *How to spot AI-generated lies on a resume*. https://www
.shrm.org/topics-tools/news/technology/how-to-spot-ai-generated-lies-on-a-resume

Eightfold, A. I. (2022). *The future of work: Intelligent by design*. https://eightfold
.ai/wp-content/uploads/2022_Talent_Survey.pdf

Elias, G. (2023, March 17). *Common issues with ChatGPT and how to mitigate
them*. https://skimai.com/common-issues-with-chatgpt/

Elkington, J. (2004). Enter the triple bottom line. In *The triple bottom line: Does it
all add up?* (1st ed.). Routledge.

European Commission. (2024, March 6). *AI Act | Shaping Europe's digital future*.
https://digital-strategy.ec.europa.eu/en/policies/regulatory-framework-ai

Fayol, H. (1949). *General and industrial management*. Pitman.

Final Round, A. I. (n.d.). *Final Round AI: Interview Copilot*. Retrieved April 17,
2024, from https://www.finalroundai.com/

Friedland, R. (2024). Lorraine Daston. Rules: A short history of what we live by.
Administrative Science Quarterly, 00018392241227435(2), NP34–NP36. Advance
online publication. DOI:10.1177/00018392241227435

Garg, S. (2023, June 25). *ChatGPT alternatives that will blow your mind in 2023*.
The Writesonic Blog - Making Content Your Superpower. https://writesonic.com/
blog/chatgpt-alternatives/

Gill, S. S., & Kaur, R. (2023). ChatGPT: Vision and challenges. *Internet of Things
and Cyber-Physical Systems*, 3, 262–271. DOI:10.1016/j.iotcps.2023.05.004

Google. (n.d.). *Gemini—Chat to supercharge your ideas*. Gemini. Retrieved April
15, 2024, from https://gemini.google.com

GPTZero. (2023). *GPTZero*. GPTZero. https://gptzero.me/

Guerin, L. (2024). *Avoid legal trouble when giving performance evaluations*. https://
www.nolo.com/legal-encyclopedia/avoid-legal-trouble-when-giving-performance
-evaluations.html

Harney, B., & Collings, D. (2021). Navigating the shifting landscapes of HRM. *Human
Resource Management Review*, 31(4), 100824. DOI:10.1016/j.hrmr.2021.100824

Hatcher, T. (2013). Robert Owen: A historiographic study of a pioneer of human
resource development. *European Journal of Training and Development*, 37(4),
414–431. DOI:10.1108/03090591311319799

Helsinger, L. (2024, March 11). *1,000 equally-qualified resumes, different names. Guess which ones gpt 3.5 place at the top and bottom ranks?*https://www.linkedin.com/pulse/1000-equally-qualified-resumes-different-names-guess-which-helsinger-x4gac/

History.com Editors. (2023, March 27). *Industrial revolution: Definition, inventions & dates.* HISTORY. https://www.history.com/topics/industrial-revolution/industrial-revolution

Hmoud, B., & Várallyai, L. (2019). *Will artificial intelligence take over human resources recruitment and selection?*

IBM. (n.d.-a). *What is artificial intelligence (AI)?* Retrieved April 2, 2024, from https://www.ibm.com/topics/artificial-intelligence

IBM. (n.d.-b). *What Is machine learning (ML)?* Retrieved April 2, 2024, from https://www.ibm.com/topics/machine-learning

indeed. (2024). *Job Search | Indeed.* https://www.indeed.com/?from=social_share

Johnson, S. L. (2019). Workplace bullying, biased behaviours and performance review in the nursing profession: A qualitative study. *Journal of Clinical Nursing*, 28(9–10), 1528–1537. DOI:10.1111/jocn.14758 PMID:30588721

Linkedin. (2024). *Best Talent Intelligence Software | Products | LinkedIn.* https://www.linkedin.com/products/categories/talent-intelligence-software

Lund, B. D., & Wang, T. (2023). Chatting about ChatGPT: How may AI and GPT impact academia and libraries? *Library Hi Tech News*, 40(3), 26–29. DOI:10.1108/LHTN-01-2023-0009

Maisiri, W., Darwish, H., & van Dyk, L. (2019). An investigation of Industry 4.0 skills requirements. *South African Journal of Industrial Engineering*, 30(3), 90–105. DOI:10.7166/30-3-2230

Marr, B. (2024, January 12). *The biggest challenges and pitfalls of data-driven, AI-enabled HR.* Forbes. https://www.forbes.com/sites/bernardmarr/2024/01/12/the-biggest-challenges-and-pitfalls-of-data-driven-ai-enabled-hr/

Maryville University. (2024). The importance of human resource management in the modern workplace. *Maryville University Online.* https://online.maryville.edu/online-bachelors-degrees/human-resource-management/resources/what-is-human-resource-management/

Maurer, R. (2024a, February 1). *White-collar workers to be most impacted by GenAI.* https://www.shrm.org/topics-tools/news/technology/white-collar-workers -most-impacted-by-genai

Maurer, R. (2024b, February 15). *AI adoption in HR is growing.* https://www.shrm .org/topics-tools/news/technology/ai-adoption-hr-is-growing

Mayo, G. E. (1933). *The human problems of an industrial civilization.* Macmillan and Company.

Menon, S. (2016). *George Elton Mayo: The father of human resource management & his Hawthorne Studies.* https://www.linkedin.com/pulse/george-elton-mayothe -father-human-resource-management-sarita-menon/

Mhlanga, D. (2022). The role of artificial intelligence and machine learning amid the COVID-19 pandemic: What lessons are we learning on 4IR and the sustainable development goals. *International Journal of Environmental Research and Public Health*, 19(3), 1879. DOI:10.3390/ijerph19031879 PMID:35162901

Mind Tools Content Team. (2024). *Henri Fayol's five functions of management.* https://cdn.jwplayer.com/previews/QpuUregs-5WSyalpf

Molaiepour, S. (2024, February 1). *EU AI Act: What HR teams need to know.* https:// www.jobylon.com/blog/eu-ai-act-what-hr-teams-need-to-know

Murad, A. (2023). *The computers rejecting your job application.* Pocket. https:// getpocket.com/explore/item/the-computers-rejecting-your-job-application

Nahra, K. J., Evers, A., Jessani, A. J., Braun, M., Vallery, A., & Benizri, I. (2024, March 14). *The European Parliament adopts the AI Act.* https://www.wilmerhale .com/en/insights/blogs/wilmerhale-privacy-and-cybersecurity-law/20240314-the -european-parliament-adopts-the-ai-act

Osai, O., Eleanya, L., Gabriel, J., & Okene, N. (2009). Jethro as the Patriarch of Administration and Management: An Analysis of His Works. *Journal of Social Sciences*, 18(3), 157–162. DOI:10.1080/09718923.2009.11892677

Owen, R. (1857). *The life of Robert Owen written by himself: With selections from his writings and correspondence.* Effingham Wilson.

Paradox. (2024). *AI Recruiting—Paradox.* https://www.paradox.ai/demo/ai-recruiting

Penn Today. (2023, June 16). *AI could transform social science research.* Penn To-day. https://penntoday.upenn.edu/news/ai-could-transform-social-science-research

Prendergast, R. (2021). Charles Babbage's economy of knowledge. In *Information and the history of philosophy*. Routledge. DOI:10.4324/9781351130752-19

Pymetrics. (n.d.). *Pymetrics*. Retrieved January 22, 2024, from https://www.pymetrics.ai/

Qadir, J. (2023). Engineering education in the era of ChatGPT: Promise and pitfalls of generative AI for education. *2023 IEEE Global Engineering Education Conference (EDUCON)*, 1–9. https://doi.org/DOI:10.1109/EDUCON54358.2023.10125121

Qin, S., Jia, N., Luo, X., Liao, C., & Huang, Z. (2023). Perceived fairness of human managers compared with artificial intelligence in employee performance evaluation. *Journal of Management Information Systems*, 40(4), 1039–1070. DOI:10.1080/07421222.2023.2267316

Rahman, M. M., & Watanobe, Y. (2023). ChatGPT for education and research: Opportunities, threats, and strategies. *Applied Sciences (Basel, Switzerland)*, 13(9), 9. Advance online publication. DOI:10.3390/app13095783

Richards, J. (2020). Putting employees at the centre of sustainable HRM: A review, map and research agenda. *Employee Relations*, 44(3), 533–554. DOI:10.1108/ER-01-2019-0037

Sahadi, J. (2023, September 9). *Why do we work 9 to 5? The history of the eight-hour workday*. CNN. https://www.cnn.com/2023/09/09/success/work-culture-9-to-5-curious-consumer/index.html

Scopelliti, V. (2019, June 12). Performance management vs bullying: Where's the line? *WISE Workplace*. https://www.wiseworkplace.com.au/2019/06/performance-management-vs-bullying-wheres-the-line/

6. sense. (2024). *Pymetrics—Market share, competitor insights in pre-employment assessment*. 6sense. https://www.6sense.com/tech/pre-employment-assessment/pymetrics-market-share

Sharma, N. (2023, December 26). The computers rejecting your job application. *ISHIR | Software Development India*. https://www.ishir.com/blog/106625/the-computers-rejecting-your-job-application.htm

Si, S., & Chen, H. (2020). A literature review of disruptive innovation: What it is, how it works and where it goes. *Journal of Engineering and Technology Management*, 56, 101568. DOI:10.1016/j.jengtecman.2020.101568

Simkin, J. (2016). *Robert Owen*. Spartacus Educational. https://spartacus-educational.com/IRowen.htm

Siocon, G. (2023, November 20). *Ways AI is changing HR departments*. Business News Daily. https://www.businessnewsdaily.com/how-ai-is-changing-hr

Slaper, T. F., & Hall, T. J. (2011). *The triple bottom line: What is it and how does it work?*https://www.ibrc.indiana.edu/ibr/2011/spring/article2.html

Smith, A. (1964). *The wealth of nations*. Dutton.

Society for Human Resource Management. (2024). *2024 talent trends survey findings: Artificial intelligence in HR*. SHRM's Voice of Work Research Panel. https://shrm-res.cloudinary.com/image/upload/AI/2024-Talent-Trends-Survey_Artificial-Intelligence-Findings.pdf

Srivastava, S., & Agrawal, S. (2020). Resistance to change and turnover intention: A moderated mediation model of burnout and perceived organizational support. *Journal of Organizational Change Management*, 33(7), 1431–1447. DOI:10.1108/JOCM-02-2020-0063

Szmigin, I., & Rutherford, R. (2013). Shared value and the impartial spectator test. *Journal of Business Ethics*, 114(1), 171–182. DOI:10.1007/s10551-012-1335-1

TeamLease EDTECH. (n.d.). *What is causing the skill gap in India?* Retrieved May 16, 2023, from https://www.teamleaseedtech.com/blog/what-is-causing-the-skill-gap-in-india.html

UN. (n.d.-a). *#Envision2030: 17 goals to transform the world for persons with disabilities*. https://www.un.org/development/desa/disabilities/envision2030.html

UN. (n.d.-b). *The 17 goals | sustainable development*. https://sdgs.un.org/goals

United Nations. (2020, February 12). *Covid-19 public health emergency of international concern (PHEIC) global research and innovation forum*. https://www.who.int/publications/m/item/covid-19-public-health-emergency-of-international-concern-(pheic)-global-research-and-innovation-forum

Vaishya, R., Javaid, M., Khan, I. H., & Haleem, A. (2020). Artificial intelligence (AI) applications for COVID-19 pandemic. *Diabetes & Metabolic Syndrome*, 14(4), 337–339. DOI:10.1016/j.dsx.2020.04.012 PMID:32305024

van Vulpen, E. (2023, December 15). Learning and development. *AIHR*. https://www.aihr.com/blog/learning-and-development/

Werhane, P. H. (2000). Business ethics and the origins of contemporary capitalism: Economics and ethics in the work of Adam Smith and Herbert Spencer. *Journal of Business Ethics*, 24(3), 185–198. DOI:10.1023/A:1005937623890

Wolford, B. (2018, November 7). *What is GDPR, the EU's new data protection law?* GDPR.Eu. https://gdpr.eu/what-is-gdpr/

Yadegar, Minoofar & Soleymani LLP. (2024). Retaliation in performance evaluations. *Yadegar, Minoofar & Soleymani, LLP*. https://www.ymsllp.com/blog/2023/09/retaliation-in-performance-evaluations/

Yin, L., Alba, D., & Nicoletti, L. (2024, March 7). OpenAI's GPT Is a recruiter's dream tool. Tests show there's racial bias. *Bloomberg.Com*. https://www.bloomberg.com/graphics/2024-openai-gpt-hiring-racial-discrimination/

York, A. (2024, February 13). *10 best AI recruitment tools for hiring teams in 2024.* ClickUp. https://clickup.com/blog/ai-tools-for-recruitment/

Zinkula, J., & Mok, A. (2024, March 6). *ChatGPT may be coming for our jobs. Here are the 10 roles that AI is most likely to replace.* Business Insider. https://www.businessinsider.com/chatgpt-jobs-at-risk-replacement-artificial-intelligence-ai-labor-trends-2023-02

KEY TERMS AND DEFINITIONS

Disruptive Innovation: An imperceptibly evolving technology where the now emerging version gradually and permanently eclipses the older versions.

Fourth Industrial Revolution: The current and developing biosphere in which disruptive technologies and trends such as generative artificial intelligence, machine learning, virtual and augmented reality, the Internet of Things, cloud computing, blockchain, big data analytics, quantum computing, user interface and user experience, cognitive robotics, and intelligent automation are changing the way modern people live and work.

Generative Artificial Intelligence: A machine-based system designed to operate with varying levels of autonomy that may exhibit adaptiveness after deployment and that, for explicit or implicit objectives, infers, from the input it receives, how to generate outputs such as predictions, content, recommendations, or decisions that can influence physical or virtual environments.

Human Resource Management: A holistic process comprising recruitment, selection, onboarding, compensating and benefits management; training and development; engagement; performance appraisal; resolving employee concerns, disputes, or conflicts; and developing policies and strategies to retain employees.

Learning and Development: A systematic approach designed by corporate HR to holistically advance and augment employees' inherent skill sets, knowledge, and competency. The comprehensive nature of employee learning aims to empower the employees, leading to improved work performance.

Machine Learning: The subfield of artificial intelligence is recognized as the competency of a mechanical apparatus to imitate intelligent human behavior.

Sustainable Human Resource Management: The amalgamation of relevant disruptive innovation with conventional HRM practices to equitably recruit and sustainably manage personnel to achieve long-term social, ecological, and economic goals while mitigating adverse outcomes.

Training and Development: A sporadic, organizational interposition of quasi-coordinated instruction-based events intended to develop employees' job-relevant knowledge and skills for the solitary aim of improving corporate performance. Conventional employee training and development is grounded in developing employees' skill sets based on the requirements of a specific organizational task.

Chapter 13
Big Data Analytics in Human Resources Management With Qualitative Insights

Hüseyin Özgür Erol
Isparta Uygulamalı Bilimler Üniversitesi, Turkey

Ahmet Yildirim
https://orcid.org/0000-0002-1208-071X
Süleyman Demirel University, Turkey

ABSTRACT

This study investigates how human resource employees experience the big data phenomenon in the recruitment function of human resource management and how their perceptions of the phenomenon have evolved. This study also examines how big data will affect organizational and human resource management and how it can be improved in other functions of human resources. In this exploratory study, which comprehensively addresses the big data phenomenon in human resources management, the phenomenological design approach, one of the qualitative research methods, was applied to test the research questions and a semi-structured interview form was used for research data.

DOI: 10.4018/979-8-3693-4412-5.ch013

1. INTRODUCTION

Today's human resources management has a responsibility beyond its basic function of "selecting" and "recruiting" the human value needed by the organization. While human resources management does the necessary work to retain the talents within the organization, it also reaches and attracts people with the required skills and competencies that companies need from the unemployed labour market. Moreover, in the current period, the existence of global developments such as Industry 4.0 (Kagermann, et al., 2013) and Society 5.0 (Fukuyama, 2018) has led to changes in the structure of the workforce and the way of doing business. Within the scope of these developments and changes, improving organizational performance and gaining competitive advantage organizations depend on effective human resources management (Armstrong & Taylor, 2014, p.5). Human resource management uses digital technologies to increase organizational performance and competitive advantage, to carry out its activities more proactively, to retain employees, and to bring highly competent human value from the labour market to the organization.

It is understood from the research in the literature that the perspective of digital human resources management is that all activities of the management take place in the transformation of information technologies with a focus on the organization and people, and thus a radical change in the way of doing business (Ruël, et al., 2004, p.370 ; Strohmeier & Kabst, 2014, p.334; Rajalakshmi & Gomath, 2016, p.176). Since this digital transformation in human resources involves a transformational structure that includes the reorientation, reorganization, and strategic management of data and information management (Strohmeier & Kabst, 2014, p.334), it has also increased the interest in data science and analytical studies in management (Angrave at al., 2016; van der Togt & Rasmussen, 2017; Minbaeva, 2018; Kim, et al., 2021; Margherita, 2022). In this context, this increasing interest in the use of big data analytics in HR management has paved the way for different studies in the literature. For example, in the literature, Davenport, at al., (2010) evaluated the activities carried out in human resources within the scope of six different talent analytics, while Nocker & Sena, (2019, p.15) concluded that analysis methods (predictive, network, and sensory analysis) to be carried out with employee data would help in planning supportive measures for HR activities. Moreover, (Sadath, 2013, p.154) in his study tried to understand the potential impact of data mining techniques on the knowledge management strategy for automated intelligent decisions from employee databases for predicting employee performance. In addition, there are different empirical studies in the literature to measure the impact of big data-based decision-making models on business and organizational performance (McAfee & Brynjolfsson, 2012; Ji-fan Ren, et al., 2017). Fu, et al., (2022, p.263) unlike the studies in the literature, which try to explain the role of HR analysts in analysis methods by addressing their interpretation skills. When the research in the literature is examined, it is understood that almost all of them touch upon the concept of "big data", which is an extension of Industry 4.0 and includes unstructured data, and how it contributes to the HR structure. However, there is no study on how this technology is perceived by human resources employees.

Big data technology helps HR processes to solve business challenges and generate useful insights from data collection and analysis (Angrave at al., 2016). This benefit that big data technology offers to HR management brings to mind the question of "how big data technology benefits the recruitment process of human resources" and how big data affects the way HR employees do business in this process. The limited number of studies on big data and HR analytics in the literature (Erb, 2016; Micic & Radosavac, 2018; Zhang, 2019; Xie, 2020; Zhu, 2020; Zhang, et.al, 2021; Margherita, 2022) makes it difficult to understand how the phenomenon benefits human resource management. Moreover, the fact that big data technology acts in an integrated manner with other functions of Industry 4.0 (cloud computing, cyber security, artificial intelligence, etc.), enabling to obtain meaningful and valuable information from structured and unstructured data from the digital environment, as well as providing advantages in creating predictions for the future, raises the curiosity of how big data can affect organizational performance and which functions of human resources management, and how it can be improved in management.

In this study, the authors aim to make an exploratory contribution to the literature by determining how the big data phenomenon is perceived by human resource employees and how they experience the phenomenon in the recruitment process, which is a function of human resource management. In addition, the study seeks to understand and explore how big data will affect organizational performance and human resource management and how it can be improved in other functions of human resources. For these purposes, a phenomenological design approach, which is one of the qualitative research methods, was adopted, and in-depth interviews were conducted with HR employees of large and semi-structured enterprises operating in Turkey through a semi-structured interview form. As a matter of fact, the main contribution of this study is to define and reveal the effects of big data analytics applications on the recruitment process in digital human resources, and the perceptions and thoughts of those working in the field of human resources in the business world. In addition, the research offers a new perspective for future research and practitioners with an integrative review by including the thoughts of HR professionals on how the big data phenomenon can be improved in human resources functions.

2. LITERATURE REVIEW

2.1. Big Data

It is accepted that studies on the concept of big data, which emerged as an ingredient of the information age with digitalization, emerged in the late 20th and early 21st centuries (Mashey, 1999; Laney, 2001). As of 2011, the notion of big data, which has become very popular among IT communities and researchers and whose popularity has accelerated day by day with increasing momentum after 2018 (Sütçü & Aytekin, 2018, p.165), brings to mind the question "What is big data?" When the definitions in the literature are examined, the notion of big data can be generally defined as a term that enables and defines the management and analysis of highly valuable information through technologies that require advanced techniques that enable the capture, storage and distribution of high-volume, high-speed, complex and variable data (Laney, 2001; Mills, et al., 2012; Liu, et al., 2014; Gandomi & Haider, 2015). Although there are different views on the notion of big data in the literature, there is a common understanding that the notion has five basic elements (Zang & Ye, 2015; Ma & Jiang, 2013). These elements:

The first one is volume. Volume refers to the size of the data. Definitions of big data volumes are relative and vary according to factors such as time or data type. In other words, it refers to the collection of different amounts and sizes of data from various sources (O'Leary, 2013). For example, every day, e-commerce, social media, Google search engine searches, and the obtaining of major volumes of data such as audio, photos, and video connected to many other sensors are useful in describing the volume factor of big data (Lee, 2017).

The second one is Variety. Variety refers to using multiple types of data to analyze a situation or case. The millions of devices generating a constant stream of data in the IoT (Internet of Things) not only generate large amounts of data, but also different types of data for different situations (O'Leary, 2013). At the present time with the developing technologies, unstructured and semi-structured data can be analyzed by using NoSQL structure and can be processed, analyzed and directed by data mining methods such as Hadoop, Google file systems, MabReduce and similar techniques (Bayrakçı & Albayrak, 2019).

The third one is velocity. Velocity refers to big data obtain from a flood of data rather than a systematic flow of data. Data should be processed and analyzed at the instantaneous rate at which they are acquired (Zikopoulos, et al., 2012). The speed element of big data is compelling because the analytics that come with streaming data need to make sense of and act on the data in real time (Russom, 2011). Otherwise, the massive proliferation of data will become a huge burden to solve problems, and big data that is not handled effectively will diminish in value over time.

The fourth one is value. Value refers to big data is usually characterized by low value density. In other words, the data received in the original form usually has a low value relative to its volume. However, large volumes of such data can be analyzed to extract high-value information (Gandomi & Haider, 2015). Thus, since the intensity and value of data are relative, sometimes a small amount of detail data can have a very large impact (Zang & Ye, 2015).

The last one is veracity. Veracity refers to the dimension that expresses the inherent unreliability of big data (Owais & Hussein, 2016). For example, customer sentiment on social media is an inherently ambiguous data set because it requires human judgment. However, it still contains valuable information. Therefore, the need to deal with imprecise data, the use of tools and analytical methods developed for the management and mining of data is another aspect aimed at determining the veracity of the data.

Analytical methods realized by taking into account the dimensions of big data are seen as a technology that enables accessing information of very high value from terabytes of low-value datasets or, in some cases, vital information, as stated in (Fisher, et al. (2012). Moreover, in order to interpret human digital footprints, analytical methods are applied to handle the diversity of big data in order that obtained workable, predictive and descriptive results (Loebbecke & Picot, 2015; Mikalef, et al., 2017). This means harnessing the power of data to make better decisions and accurate predictions from big data technology. Therefore, big data is used in areas such as e-commerce, politics, education, health, science and technology, security and business sectors (Lodefalk, 2013). In addition, big data analytics not only affects disciplines such as statistics, computing and information technologies, but also affects fields such as social sciences and business management with emerging technologies and innovations in industry 4.0 (Reinse, et al., 2017). Big data analytics, which is used in many different fields, provides added value to organizations and business sectors, such as efficient resource management and control, high transparency, adaptability to changes, streamlining business processes (Chen et al., 2012), productivity, growth and innovation, as well as making better decisions and accurate predictions, thus becoming an important determinant of competitiveness (Vassakis et al., 2018). In addition, big data analytics provides information about risk management activities and helps businesses to detect errors, deviations and irregularities in data management and continuous audit processes (Ramamoort, et al., 2017; Tekbaş, 2019). Moreover, it facilitates the detection of fraud and accounting risks in real time (Satyanarayana, 2015, p.118-119). In addition to these advantages, it provides cost and time savings and enables competitive advantage (Pala, 2021, p.46) and operational efficiency, creating an increase in organizational performance through more pro-active use of functional data. Big data studies within the scope of data analytics and data management contribute to the development of new business models and provide an advantage in employment generation (Ji-fan Ren, et al., 2017; De Mauro, et al., 2018). Finally, the use and analysis of high volumes of complex and variable data in scientific research enables new experimental and analytical research to be conducted and developed (Altunışık, 2015).

When working with large datasets, there can be some disadvantages as well as advantages (Oğuzlar, 2003). Therefore, the result of a big data application that does not overcome the difficulties that may arise due to disadvantages when working with big data will most likely end in failure (Özdemir & Sağıroğlu, 2018). Accordingly, data with a highly heterogeneous structure should be reduced, cleaned and transformed to be included in the analysis. This complicates the task of data mining and makes it difficult to analyze rapidly flowing data in real time (Chen, et al., 2014). At the same time, challenges can arise in the privacy and security of open access data, including access control and authentication, secure data management, infrastructure security and security of distributed systems (ENISA, 2015, p.17). This leads to misuse of data, which can lead to organizations or individuals being harmed by malicious hackers (Cukier & Mayer-Schoenberger, 2013). In addition, the fact that big data consists of voluminous, complex and variable data flowing at high speed brings along the uncertainties and inconsistencies that will occur in the data (Özdemir & Sağıroğlu, 2018). This leads to poor data quality and jeopardizes the validity of the data. How to benefit from big data analytics, what kind of human resources will be needed in this direction, what kind of competencies the workforce should have, how the workforce should be trained within the scope of developing and changing technologies constitute other problems encountered (Çiğdem & Seyrek, 2015). In order to explore how big data analytics, which has the above characteristics, advantages and disadvantages, is evaluated in the context of HRM, the next section will present and discuss a theoretical perspective of big data analytics in digital HRM through a literature review.

2.2. Big Data Analytics in Human Resources Management

Big data technology is recognized as a natural component of Industry 4.0 (Kagermann, et al., 2013). Developments in Industry 4.0 are reshaping everyday life and affecting the human-work life relationship on a large scale. Therefore, the information, predictions and analysis capability obtained by analyzing data fed from various sources also affect human resources management (Erb, 2016). Employee selection, which constitutes one of the main tasks of human resource management, constitutes a critical situation for any organization that wants to use the human factor to gain competitive advantage (Palmer & Winters, 1993, s.25; Vranova, 2012; Calp, 2016). Accordingly, HR management can achieve this goal by investing in the human factor and new developments in technology to give the organization a competitive advantage

(Martinez-Gil, 2021, p.1). In addition, the understanding of digital human resources discipline uses technology not only as a tool to recruit competent workforce, but also to change the work environment, to motivate employees, to make them more collaborative and less confrontational, and to make them capable of doing work by creating higher work productivity and satisfaction (Micic ve Radosavac, 2017). Therefore, it is necessary for human resources to take part in digital transformation and to handle digital technologies and data science-based achievements more effectively. This is a critical input to understand the importance of analytical work based on big data sources and to make smarter decisions in employee selection, HR strategy and organizational strategies (Küsbeci, 2021).

Human resources management, which is in a continuous transformation within the scope of technological innovations, should see big data analytics and big data-based technologies as a strategic part of the next step of digital transformation (Aguinis & O'Boyle, 2014; Hamilton & Sodeman, 2020; Li, 2021). HR managers have the opportunity to use structured and unstructured data through big data analytics to increase the competencies of selected candidates, measure their performance, to measure their performance and effectiveness within the company and to evaluate employees without prejudice (Dong, et al., 2014). In this way, information that can help eliminate unconscious prejudices that may occur both in the employees within the organization and in the recruitment process can be created (Mammadova & Jabrayilova, 2016). Moreover, the use of automated calculation methods with big data analytics and the creation of a prediction model (Mishra, et al., 2016) enables easier monitoring of operational business conduct, as well as increasing the effectiveness of the recruitment process within the scope of business models that may emerge in the future (Chien & Chen, 2008). For this reason, human resources management can benefit from the meticulous use of big data technology in strategic decisions and the recruitment process.

HR management, which constitutes one of the most important building blocks of organizations in the current period, ensures that the business has the power to get ahead in market competition with a strong talent team (Zhang, 2019). While the employees who carry out business activities in the organization undertake a very important task in terms of the sustainability of the business, the knowledge and skills of the employees should be continuously improved to increase the productivity of the employees and ensure effective business processes (Mammadova & Jabrayilova, 2016). In this direction, as Fink & Sturman, (2017) state, the use of big data technology in human resources helps to improve the job capacities of employees by creating a personalized training plan in the training and development process and to understand job requirements and main job content. Thus, organizations benefit from training and development management studies carried out with big data and have the opportunity to calculate the costs and returns of training investments (Shen, 2015).

In this context, it is seen that most of the big data studies carried out within the framework of human resources have developed within the framework of talent analytics. While (Davenport, at al., 2010) state that talent analytics activities carried out in human resources take place in six different ways, they also point out that these analytical studies bring advantages such as providing a competitive advantage to organizations, making employee performance more efficient, increasing employee motivation and commitment, and saving costs that may occur in talent management. In another big data-based talent analytics study in the literature, it is argued that employee data analysis methods (predictive, network, sensory analysis) help plan supportive measures for factors such as performance, retention, planning, turnover rate, engagement and recruitment (Nocker & Sena, 2019, p.15). Thus, big data analytics methods contribute to organizations as a management revolution (McAfee & Brynjolfsson, 2012) in improving organizational performance by providing advantages such as retaining employees, increasing their motivation, ensuring their loyalty, and optimizing their performance. In addition, since individual performance affects overall organizational performance, collecting and analyzing data that can be used to measure workforce engagement and design the support that employees need in their work can improve individual performance and thus positively affect organizational performance. In studies measuring the impact of data-driven decision-making models on business and organizational performance (McAfee & Brynjolfsson, 2012; Ji-fan Ren, et al., 2017), it is thought that organizations using big data technology in the same sector perform 5% more efficiently than their competitors who do not use this technology and provide a competitive advantage to the organization. Unlike the studies in the literature, this study has an exploratory nature by determining how human resources management employees make sense of the big data phenomenon in the digital world based on their thoughts, how they benefit from this phenomenon in the recruitment process, and how big data analytics applications can be developed in human resources activities.

3. METHODOLOGY

Qualitative research methods are a process that starts with theoretical perspectives and their interpretation and aims to examine a phenomenon or concept in depth from the perspective of individuals and to reveal the relevant social structures and processes (Yıldırım & Şimşek, 2005). Accordingly, in order to better understand and interpret the exploratory nature of the study and the experiences related to the phenomenon, the phenomenological design, which is a philosophical research approach (Van Manen, 2007; Creswell, 2013; Patton, 2014) that refers to the understanding, interpretation and perception of a person or persons based on their lived experiences (Merleau-Ponty,

2012), was used. From this point of view, it is seen that the phenomenon or concept to be explored corresponds to "big data analytics experience" and the people to be examined correspond to "human resource management employees", and answers are sought to the main research question "how does human resource management experience big data analytics in the digital age?" and the sub-research questions (1) how do human resource management employees define the phenomenon of big data? (2) How do human resource management employees benefit from big data and analytics in the recruitment process? (3) According to human resource employees, how can big data analytics be improved in HR management? In addition, in order to realize research and data collection processes more effectively, it is important to plan all stages of the research in detail in order to realize the process more effectively. In this direction, the "seven stages of interviewing" work plan in Brinkmann and Kvale's (2018, p.40-41) "Doing interviews" book was utilized.

3.1. Participant Profile and Data Collection

Patton (2014) discussed the process of determining the sample size in qualitative research as research in pursuit of breadth and depth. He defined accessing more superficial information from a large number of participants as breadth-seeking research while accessing information from a small group through in-depth interviews as depth-seeking research. He also emphasized that "there is no rule for determining sample size" for qualitative research (Patton, 2014, p.244). (Creswell (2013), stated that the number of participants in phenomenological research could vary between three and twenty-five. In addition, in qualitative research, the sample size takes into account the relationship with the subject rather than the representation of the sample, and for this reason, researchers prefer the non-probability sampling method (Neuman, 2006, p.220). However, the non-probability sampling method also has various sub-techniques in terms of suitability and access to the subject matter, and in this study, the participants were reached by using the snowball sampling technique (Yazıcıoğlu & Erdoğan, 2004, p. 45). The size of the participant group was shaped during the research as the data related to the study reached saturation (Glaser, 1978, p.36; Charmaz, 2006, p.113-115.). In line with these definitions, the sample group was selected from different industries, sectors and organizational environments in Turkey, and in-depth interviews were conducted with 10 HR participants engaged in analytical work, taking into account the above-mentioned principles of depth, easy accessibility and volunteerism. Table-1 summarizes the socio-demographic characteristics of the participants in terms of the sectors they work in and the length of their work experience.

Table 1. Socio-Demographic characteristics of participants

Participant	Level of Responsibility	Sector	Experience	Gender
P1	HR manager	Textile	10	F
P2	HR Specialist	Engineering	4	M
P3	Recruitment Specialist	Holding/Tourism	3	M
P4	Recruitment Specialist	Professional Service	2	M
P5	Recruitment Specialist	ICT	2	F
P6	Recruitment Specialist	Professional Service	2	F
P7	HR Specialist	Automotive	1	M
P8	HR Performance and Talent Management Manager	Manufacturing	5	F
P9	Recruitment Specialist	Logistic	5	M
P10	Talent Recruitment Account Manager	ICT	19	M

Within the scope of Brinkmann and Kvale's (2018, p.40-41) "Seven Stages of Interviewing" work plan, interview questions were categorized into themes and sub-themes, and the interview form was designed. It is aimed to determine how human resources employees perceive the big data analytics phenomenon, what their positive and negative perspectives are towards the phenomenon regarding their perceptions, and the potential effects on HR management. In addition, a semi-structured interview form was prepared to obtain data in order to determine how they benefit from this phenomenon and how it can be developed, and three main topics and sub-topics determined according to these topics were created:

1. Big Data Awareness
   - Big Data Perception
   - Positive and Negative Ways
   - The Impact of Big Data on Human Resources
2. Big Data Experience and Utilization
   - Data Collection and Analysis
   - Factors Affecting the Work Done
3. Developing Big Data Analytics
   - Human Resources Operations
   - Factors Affecting Organizational Performance

In line with the data collection methods in qualitative research, in-depth interviews were conducted with 10 participants through semi-structured interview forms using the online data collection method (Stirling, 2016, p.68). Interviews conducted with semi-structured interview forms allow the researcher to change the order of questions in line with the research and to ask more questions in line with the answers they receive, as well as encouraging research depth and vitality (Doody & Noonan, 2013, p.30). Therefore, the interviews conducted during the research were conducted under the supervision of the researchers, and the dynamism and depth of the research were ensured by following the insights that emerged during the interviews with the participants and fine-tuning the questions at the time of data collection (Pratt, et al., 2020).

3.2. Research Process

After the audio recordings of the in-depth interviews conducted in line with Brinkmann and Kvale's (2018, p.40-41) "seven stages of interviewing" research plan were created as a written text, they were analyzed descriptively within the scope of Miles and Huberman's (1994, p.10-12) data analysis model. In this research model, as Creswell (2016, p.195) points out, data analysis can be carried out simultaneously with the other parts of the development of the qualitative study (data collection, data reduction, data presentation and visualization of results). In the process of data reduction, the coding method was used to make the qualitative data more easily understandable and to transform the raw data into a more manageable form in a more straightforward sense. As part of the presentation of the data, the data was made more visualized by organizing, compressing, and combining the data in order to evaluate the findings of the reduced data in a more analytical way. After the reduction process, which was carried out simultaneously with the data collection, the results started to become analytically clearer with the visualized data. The final stage is to bring together the results obtained in the data analysis process to form a whole (Miles & Huberman, 1994, p.10-12).

Considering Creswell's (2016, p.202) suggestion to use a qualitative software program to analyze the data obtained in qualitative research, MAXQDA Analytics Pro 2020 program was used in the research process to reduce and present the data and visualize the results. In order to reveal the experiential expressions in the interviews with the participants, initial coding was created by reading the written texts in detail, and the conceptual and competence power of the initial codes, which is the purpose of focused coding, was determined by reviewing the most frequently encountered codes (Charmaz, 2015, p.182; Elnur, 2022, p.46). The codes created by a comparative reading of the interview records and the initial codes were brought together under themes and sub-themes. The statements obtained from the participant's views were compared with the findings of previous studies and the theme headings were discussed within the scope of big data analytics.

4. RESULTS

The focus of this study is on the awareness of big data analytics, its utilization in the recruitment process and its development in HR activities, and the data obtained from in-depth interviews are discussed below. In line with the research, it has been understood that HR managers are aware of the big data phenomenon and suggestions on how they benefit from this phenomenon and how it can be improved in other HR activities have been determined.

Big Data Awareness

In the study, firstly, participant views on big data awareness were analyzed. In this direction, the data on how the perception of big data awareness is shaped, what are the positive and negative aspects of big data, and how big data affects human resources management processes were analyzed. The hierarchical theme-sub-theme relationship of the themes to be examined in this section is shown in Figure 1.

Figure 1. Big data awareness hierarchical theme-subtheme section model

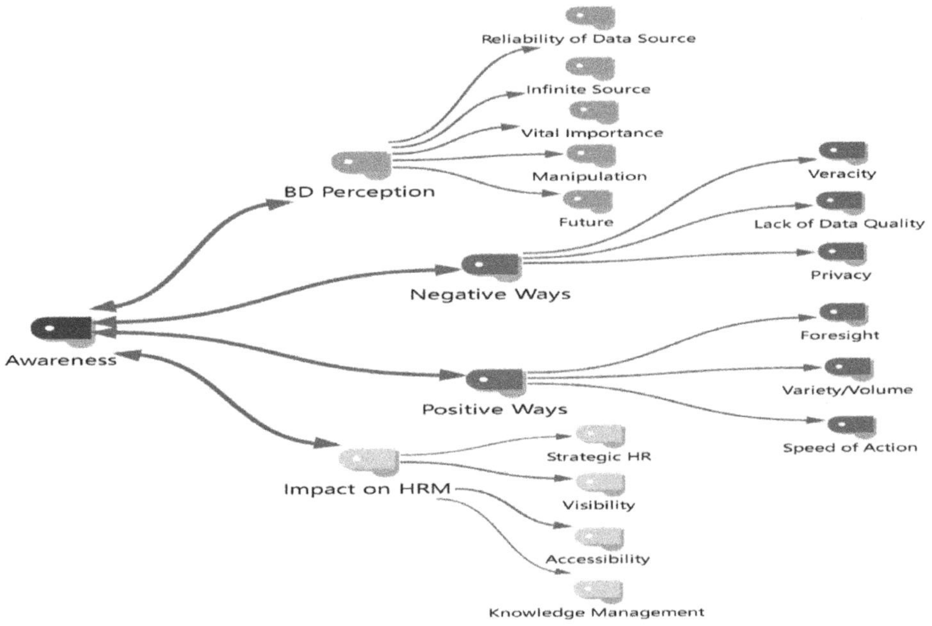

Big Data Perception Aspects

By asking the participants what they think about big data and what this phenomenon means to them, it was tried to understand how the perception of big data is shaped. When the responses have been analyzed, it is seen that big data is characterized as an "infinite resource" and contradicts the *"data is the new oil"* (Humby, 2006) analogy in the literature in terms of infinity/limitlessness and substitutability.

"I come from a generation that used to go to libraries. Now information is at my fingertips and it's like an endless source, you can access all kinds of information in seconds..." (P1)

Another expression that shapes the perception of big data is *"reliability of the data source"*. It is understood that the reliability of the data depends on the source of the data and that increasing the volume and variety of data, along with the use of initial data in algorithmic learning, will ensure the reliability of the data.

"...I think context is important. Because where the data is calculated, who calculates it, where they get this data, validity and reliability change according to these"(P5)

Participants also emphasized that the big data phenomenon contains data that can *"manipulate"* people in terms of the trustworthiness of the data source. The reason for such a perception is that a large number of data such as "cultural, ethnic, health, personal preferences, daily life" belonging to people are in the digital environment and these data constitute the *"digital footprints"* of people. Therefore, it is understood that it causes *"desire manipulation"* (Andrejevic, 2011, p.618; Janssen, et al., 2017, p.200) due to the formation of demand for analyzing people's habits and predicting their future needs.

"We're trying to take advantage of any program, for example, do you want us to access your contacts, do you want us to access your photos, we get all these things all the time and they're all collecting data about us. So technologically it is impossible to cover your tracks. Big data means to me an environment, a technology where our digital footprint is constantly present. It especially affects our choices, what we make, and how we make them, so it can manipulate them." (P8)

Regarding the perception of big data, participants characterized this phenomenon as *"future" and "vital importance"*. Participants see big data as "the vanguard of a massive transformation (P4)" and describe it as a *"treasure"* (P10). It is also understood that they are aware that the opportunities offered by big data are valuable to be used effectively for the smooth execution of the work done and that it has an indispensable place in today's business world.

"At the end of the day, for my colleagues whose job is to bring a new employee to the company, this big data is of vital importance and using it effectively is very, very valuable, in terms of ensuring that the work is done smoothly." (P7)

Positive and Negative Aspects of Big Data Technology

The answers given by the participants about the positive and negative aspects of big data were analyzed.

Negative Ways

Participants point out that the high volume and diversity of big data help perform effective analysis. However, they negatively evaluate that it makes necessary to question the *"veracity"* of the data if people do not fill in their data clearly or provide false information, which is associated with a *"lack of data quality."* The veracity dimension is related to the extent to which the information derived from big data is reliable.

"I mean, it will produce much better results, much better profiles than the analysis that people do on their own. However, in some cases, there are sections of the profile that the person has omitted to fill in, jobs they have done, etc., or some people do not enter their certificates, which can also be overlooked, and in this respect, poor quality data prevents us from obtaining real or accurate results. Therefore, it may cause us to miss a very good employee." (P6)

In a technology that includes unstructured data sets such as big data, it is known that a security vulnerability that may arise from the information infrastructure or unconsciousness of people creates a danger such as not ensuring the confidentiality of the data. When the answers given in this direction were analyzed, it was seen that the expression *"data privacy"* was evaluated negatively by the participants due to reasons such as the storage of big data in cloud-based technologies in distributed clusters with open access, inadequate security measures and insufficient awareness of the people.

"The negative part is that it creates a data privacy gap for me. This puts us at a bit of a disadvantage, because it is very difficult to ensure data privacy in a digital environment, and I think that the inability to take cyber security measures or the lack of IT infrastructure creates a major security gap in the inability to ensure data privacy."(P3)

"All of the applications we use provide data terms of use. They are so long texts that it is not possible for a person, someone who is not equipped in this field, to read them and say yes, I give these permissions with peace of mind. Therefore, we do not know what will happen or what will come, this is the scary aspect." (P8)

Positive Aspects

It is understood that the participants positively evaluated the "volume and variety" expression of big data because it relieves organizations, improves the quality of work, reaches the ideal profile, produces an objective and subjective result, and provides ease of movement. The volume and variety dimensions help human resources to make more objective decisions and increase the "speed of action" in any given situation by accessing high-value information through data processing and analysis technologies.

"In any situation, action needs to be taken quickly, we need data to produce useful information, and big data allows us to act quickly with data fed from various sources, which we call voluminous, and in this way, I think it relieves organizations." (P10)

Participants explained the creation of prediction models and taking action in situations such as identifying the people to be recruited, what kind of jobs and what kind of working environment the candidates want to work in, organizational development, performance gap, and training and development gap with the expression "creating foresight" and it was understood that they evaluated big data positively.

"Positively, by creating foresight, if that person has a training deficit or any other situation, you can take action to eliminate it."(P2)

"When we collect CVs of many employees, collect their information and store it in a certain source and analyze them, we can have a certain idea about what kind of jobs people have, how they work, what their working conditions are, etc." (P4)

The stages of learning from data or transforming data into information through analysis performed within the framework of big data analytics algorithms are about making sense of and evaluating data. Accordingly, big data analytics is used to overcome uncertainties and predict future events. Therefore, it is understood that predictive modeling and validation analyses created within the framework of big data analytics are useful in preventing uncertainties, preventing future mishaps and creating insights to get to know employees and to learn what they want.

Impact of Big Data on Human Resources Management

Participants believe that big data is in constant flow through social media and cloud-based technologies, increasing the interaction between the job market and the labor market. Therefore, it is understood that big data provides "accessibility" to highly competent people and information in the labor market in a time- and space-independent manner.

"We reach more people, so I can say it is a very valuable area for us. The biggest advantage is that it has filtering features, so we find and place the most competent candidate there through filters. This gives us speed and increases our accessibility."(P9)

"I have good data, including past CV data, which creates a candidate pool for me and it is a nice feeling to have thousands of people's CVs in my hands. I can reach those people whenever I want."(P10)

According to the findings, it is understood that big data influences situations such as persuading the management, having a voice in the management, and making itself accepted by other departments with the expressions of "HR strategy" and "visibility". In addition, it is also included in the participant's opinions that it provides a competitive advantage by emphasizing the ability to execute business strategies such as managing data, talent acquisition and talent retention more effectively.

"It makes us more visible. We have the chance to go to the management with the results of the analysis by saying to them, this many competitors have private health insurance and I have lost this many people because of this situation. Among the people I offered this year, let's say, 35 people refused because I don't have private health insurance, or my premium rate is too low, or this is the number of candidates who gave up on us because they don't get a net salary. So you are talking with data, you have data and you show who these people are." (P10)

Respondents believe that big data enables more operational "knowledge management" and more effective transfer of information between departments and even between other companies in the market. In addition, it is understood that big data acts as a bridge between companies and employees in terms of information transfer and helps management to develop corporate culture, identify and attract the best talents to the organization, as well as to create a reward system to retain talents and provide a competitive advantage.

"Of course, in other channels, you also transfer information within other departments, including HR, for example, you make benchmarks with other companies. This is also a source of data. This can lead to excellence in the more operational execution of your other processes. So it doesn't just stop at recruitment." (P7)

Big Data Experience and Exploitation

In this section of the study, participant views on the big data technology experience are analyzed. In this direction data on how human resources management employees benefit from the big data phenomenon, how their workload and work are affected, and the data collection process are analyzed. The hierarchical theme-sub-theme section model for utilizing big data is presented in Figure 2.

Figure 2. Big data experience and utilization hierarchical theme sub-theme model

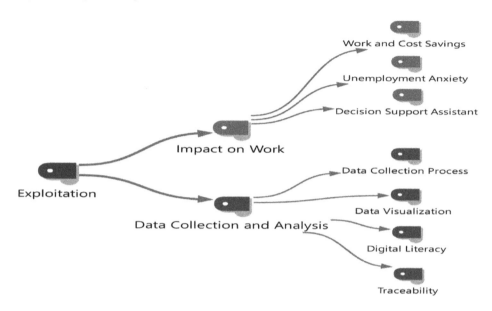

Factors Affecting the Work

When the findings were analyzed, it was understood that the participants achieved *"savings"* in workload, time, cost and effort with big data technology. HR management can benefit from big data analytics to lighten its workload and save cost and time by automating stages of the recruitment process, such as advertising, candidate search and screening, candidate matching, and candidate classification (Martinez-Gil, 2021, p.3), and thus, it can work more effectively and efficiently with less effort.

"The recruitment process, as you know, is a very long and tedious process that saves both the recruiter and the candidates time by creating a shortlist for us and we can prevent the costs that may occur in the open position by being able to close the position gap very quickly."(P4)

It is seen that the answers of the participants to the question of how big data technology affects your job are gathered in the expressions of *"unemployment anxiety"* and the participants have two different opinions on this expression. The views of the participants are as follows;

"But if we don't develop our business, it can cause anxiety, fear/anxiety of losing our business. The biggest concern for me is that when we do not turn to the field of informatics in our own field, many of us are worried that we will fall into that group of lost professions. As I mentioned before, if the person does not develop himself/herself towards information technology for the digital environment, he/she may have problems in process management and the biggest problem is of course losing our job."(P3)

"As for how it affects your job, there are situations such as losing our job or developing a business, which is very frequently discussed today, but I have not seen such a specific decrease or increase. I do not think we will lose our job. Here, I think we can use both HR and information technologies together with more business development or training we will receive in this field, that is, we can improve ourselves in this field by starting to think analytically." (P6)

Some of the participants think that there will not be a job loss based on big data technology in Turkey or any other country, but with the presence of artificial intelligence algorithms that will be created through this technology in the near future, HR employees who do not develop themselves in information technologies and cannot interpret the analysis results correctly will be unemployed. Other participants stated that they will not lose their jobs due to factors such as artificial intelligence's lack of human emotions, business development, and gaining analytical skills through the training received, and they think that this situation is an opportunity to improve themselves.

Participants utilize big data analytics as a *"decision support assistant"*. In this way, they stated that they conducted the interviews with the information they obtained, that the process progressed with a more objective perspective and that objectivity was ensured in line with the data obtained from the candidates. It is also emphasized that another reason for using big data technology as a "decision support assistant" is that it is important to conduct interviews because algorithms cannot measure emotions, behaviors and skills such as persuasiveness.

"The analytical process is completely driven by the candidate, that is, it is driven by the data they share with us. Here, data only increase our relevance and affects our decision-making attitude as you mentioned in the question. Other than that, data cannot affect my decisions much because there should be a human interaction yes, let's make use of the data and let them help us in a situation such as assisting, but I think there should also be a human interaction." (P9)

"I think human interaction should not be cut down here. Okay, big data does a candidate search for us, it allows us to reach candidates with the desired characteristics, but we need to know whether the candidate can adapt to the organization or not, or in some niche jobs, for example, a sales specialist needs to have high persuasiveness. Yes, his CV is very good, but the candidate cannot speak or has no persuasion skills. I don't think that big data can figure this out. I think there should be human interaction and human thoughts here."(P6)

Big Data Analytics: Data Collection and Analysis Process

In light of the information obtained from the participants, it is seen that they carry out the *"data collection process"* about potential talents in the labor market through digital career platforms that provide comprehensive information about candidates and enable interactive accessibility between the labor market and the organization. In this process, cloud-based systems and analysis tools (Google Cloud, Casandra, HBase, Docker, Hadoop, Sparks) are found to be useful as they facilitate the way of doing business in data transfer and allow past and current advertisements and CVs to be stored together. Thus, visualizing who applied for which positions, identifying the areas where the data is stored and providing ease of access to the data from anywhere at any time reveals the importance and critical skill of the data collection process with big data technology.

"All CVs, postings, and qualifications from the past are all in our data, we have all the data right now. When we go back, I can see which advertisements we have opened, what we have done, and which roles have changed. When a new position is opened, I analyze whether qualified candidates can be reached from there. In other words, we evaluate the actions we have taken in the past in current actions."(P10)

"As HR, we do more recruitment through Kariyer.net" (P1)

"These platforms, such as Casandra, HBase, etc. have started to emerge. Especially in the field of human resources and because it collects and analyzes data from such platforms, it is very valuable for HR professionals to access this data. As in the example I just gave, we can store and analyze data from platforms such as Kariyer.net and LinkedIn directly through these technologies."(P2)

It is known that big data is a technology that produces more effective results in *"data visualization"* such as graphics, tables, pictures and animations. In this direction, the participants have stated that big data analytics offers more effective data visualization in the recruitment process and helps to persuade the organizational management and HR management by increasing the level of perception and understanding with the possibility of instant viewing.

"I find it much more effective in terms of analytics, after uploading certain data, I find it more useful to use programs that we can get faster results rather than using a simpler program to make inferences about them, because it visualizes the data more effectively, thus increasing our level of understanding and perception."(P8)

Although big data technology offers effective data visualization for the participants, the findings also show that "digital literacy", known as "the ability to survive in the digital age" by Eshet (2004), is a must-have skill for HR professionals.

"Of course, the person doing the work here who has a very big task, the ability to interpret the data, which we call digital literacy, has become very important in recent times. At this point, the person must have the ability to both use these technologies to analyze the data and to interpret that data."(P7)

The ability of HR professionals to access, manage, evaluate, create, and analyze information in the digital environment, as well as to select and use the right platforms is the foundation of digital literacy in the Society 5.0 era.

Since big data refers to the combination of all structured, semi-structured, and unstructured data, the analysis of this data can identify people's repetitive behaviors. In this case, it is understood from the findings that the participants drew attention to the element of *"traceability"*. With the participants' perception of *"traceability"*, it is understood that in addition to forming predictions that information can be obtained about candidates without ever contacting them, prejudices may also be formed and a security vulnerability in the information technology infrastructure may result in the leakage of all information belonging to the company and its employees and subsequently a follow-up may be carried out by malicious hackers. It is also seen that this situation raises various issues related to privacy, ethics, and legality within HR.

"But it will also increase the traceability of the employee. Here, if we can monitor every move they make, we have enough data that we can draw the personality characteristics of people. This may be a bit of an intervention in people's personal spaces. We may reach prejudices about them without realizing it."(P2)

"...Yes, employee tracking is very important for HR, but if there is a security gap after installing these systems, these data may fall into the hands of malicious people and unexpected results may occur." (P1)

"Even if I don't know that person at all, I have graphs where I can evaluate their personal characteristics, and this applies to people who work inside. I can see why the graph has fallen or risen over the years. I mean, I can have information about an employee without talking to him/her thanks to the storage and analysis tools we use."(P10)

Development of Big Data in HR

In this part of the study, the views of the participants on the development of big data analytics in human resources and its evaluation in terms of organizational performance were examined. In this direction, data on how big data analytics can affect organizational performance, how it will contribute to human resources management, and which HR functions it will affect will be analyzed. The findings on the development of big data analytics in HR are shown in Figure 3 as a hierarchical code-subcode model.

Figure 3. Hierarchical Theme Sub-theme Model for the Theme of Big Data Development in Human Resources9

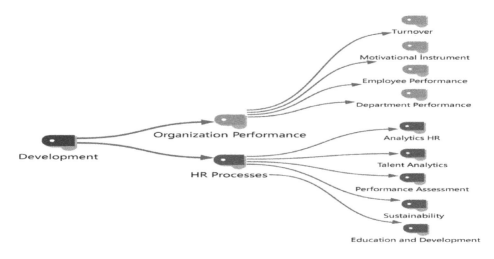

Factors Affecting Organizational Performance

As mentioned before, big data provides human resources management with easy access to information and people. Participants think that this leads to an increase in the *"turnover rate"*. Participants stated that the circulation in employee turnover is due to easy accessibility and high salary offers from start-up companies, which are the new generation entrepreneurship model. In this direction, it is understood from the findings that the fact that new-generation entrepreneurship models are based on data and data science has increased the importance of data scientists and algorithm developers in the labor market and new-generation jobs have emerged.

"Actually, of course, this was also the case for us in the past years. In this process, we were able to look at turnover rates. We were able to analyze whether turnover was high or not, why did he come a year ago and why did he leave, etc. However, our sector is very different now, maybe if you do this in the retail sector or the manufacturing sector, you will get a very different result, but this is not valid for our sector now due to the growth of start-ups established in the technology sector (Getir, Trendyol, and Yemek Sepeti) and very aggressive price policies. Because our turnover rates are completely based on developers and they are looking at the salary they receive and this leads to increased circulation with easy accessibility."(P10)

Participants working outside the technology sector acknowledged that there is a circulation in the *"turnover rate"* due to the war for talent, but thought that this situation should be addressed with a more proactive approach with big data technology and that the necessary solutions can be developed to reduce the turnover rate. In this direction, it can be stated that the solutions to be created with big data analytics can help reduce employee turnover and increase organizational performance and productivity.

> *"For example, as we talked about at the beginning, I think it would be very nice to use it to calculate and predict the person's turnover time. For example, what time does he get up in the morning, what time does he leave work, how many meetings did he attend, did he attend a meeting during lunch break, is there dissatisfaction with his work or is he dissatisfied with his salary, etc. It is necessary to collect data in different areas and think about what can be done to reduce that rate in the turnover data next year."(P5)*

It is seen in the findings that organizational performance is directly proportional to *"employee performance,"* that it is necessary to analyze how the recruited employees will contribute to organizational performance, and that big data analytics can be used in this context. 360 performance appraisal, performance prediction analyses, retrospective training data of employees, and similar applications to monitor employee performance and forward-looking forecasts with big data analytics that need to be done to increase employee performance will contribute to increasing the performance of the organization.

> *"We can now do studies that go as far as predicting performance. In other words, there are studies we conduct in the field of HR analytics and performance on certain factors, how the curve has progressed over the past performance data of current employees, how competencies have changed over the years, how the training received at work have contributed to this, what the seniority periods of employees are. Forward-looking predictions based on retrospective data obtained within the scope of big data are one of the biggest areas that affect organizational performance."(P8)*

It is understood from the answers given by the participants that big data analytics should be used as a "motivational tool" to increase the performance of employees and that this situation is very critical. It is necessary to consider various data to understand the satisfaction levels of employees within the organization. In this direction, big data analytics can be used to analyze various other data such as organizational satisfaction surveys, social media, interviews, interactive ratings, etc. to create predictive models and improve employee motivation.

"At the end of the day, what we want to achieve, and what every human being wants to achieve is to be happy. So, yes, maybe money, yes, but for people who see that money as a tool, to achieve happiness, you have to make that person visible there, it is possible with data. These can be small touches, you can increase their motivation. With motivation, the performance of that person increases, and in direct proportion, that is, if the performance of the person increases, the performance of the organization increases in any case. This is all done through close monitoring and this can be done with big data. With this tracking you get from big data, very simple things can be done by adding human emotions."(P1)

When the answers given by the participants are examined, it is seen that the dimension of *"department performance"* also affects organizational performance and the analyses to be carried out with big data analytics contribute to the identification of candidates with a profile suitable for the organizational culture with the artificial intelligence algorithm created by reducing the error rate of human resources management. In addition, it is seen in the findings that Chatbot applications, which are the result of combining big data analytics and artificial intelligence systems, provide convenience to human resources management by fulfilling the role of the operational workforce of human resources management. Moreover, it is understood from the participant responses that instead of the studies such as the year's performance, analysis of employees' career planning, and reward analyses, which already exist in human resources management and are now seen as reactive studies, more proactive analyses, in other words, predicting the future based on past data, should be carried out.

"There are chatbots, for example, in HR, especially corporate companies use them. They are created by making use of big data. Those chatbots are created by making use of big data and they are the windows that were opened before, which mailings are the most common in HR, what kind of requests are made by employees you are chatting as if there is a human being in front of you, you ask, for example, "Can I get my payroll?" and he sends you a link to where you can get the payroll or sends you the payroll directly. You say, "I want to upload my "Minimum Living Allowance" document, they send you the "Minimum Living Allowance" form and explain how to upload it. This makes people's work easier because it fulfills the operational workforce of an HR person."(P5)

4.3.2. Human Resources Processes

When the responses of some of the participants are analyzed, it is seen that they draw attention to the concept of *"Analytical HR"*. From my participant statements, it is understood that HR metrics are created based on data science for all activities in HR functions. Therefore, HRM is no longer an intuitive management perception where only the information of the organization and its employees is stored and simple analysis methods are performed. Thus, human resources management becomes a management that increases the level of perception in the decisions to be taken by the organizational management with big data analytics, can predict the future with past and current data, and take action by creating the necessary plans.

"...training, orientation, wages and benefits, recruitment, coaching, business partnership, collecting and analyzing data from various sources and taking action accordingly makes a great contribution in this managerial area, so we can talk about an analytical HR here."(P7)

Participant views suggest that the way of recruitment should become more analytical and a *"talent analytics"* phenomenon should be adopted. From the participant statements, it is understood that they focus more on recruitment, retention and workforce forecasting in talent analytics managed with big data, and in this way, competent candidates who can adopt the organizational culture are attracted to the advice in order to ensure a peaceful environment in the organization. Moreover, it is also seen in the findings that talent analytics managed with big data provides an advantage in obtaining superior talents against rival companies in the market and facilitates the management of operational business processes in recruitment and subsequent stages (orientation, employee follow-up, etc.).

"From top to bottom, what is a recruiter's job is to go through the CVs of job applicants in detail. They take care of personal affairs. This is where big data is already very useful. We can be more analytical in this area and shorten the processes, but at the moment we only use it to reach more candidates, minimize various stages and post-employment orientation and candidate follow-up. I think talent analytics can be realized by taking this situation further, or actions can be taken to attract and retain talent with other prediction models." (P2)

Participants' responses that big data analytics are utilized in applications for *"performance appraisal"* activities and that they should be improved are noteworthy. Big data analytics is known to contribute to more accurate performance evaluation by analyzing diverse and large amounts of employee data. Thus, the use of big data analytics in performance appraisal by evaluating different perspectives helps the organization reveal the hidden talents and skills of employees. In addition, grouping the highest-performing employees within the organization with big data analytics enables the organization to determine the best profile to eliminate the employment gap that the organization may need in the future (Sadath, 2013, p.154).

"Actually, it can also be used in this way, for example, let's say we are going to hire employees for a department, we can make recruitment based on the performance data of the employees in the department we are going to hire. In other words, we can create what is desired for a job from the performances of the individuals working in that department, filter accordingly, and reach the appropriate candidate. Of course, we have never used big data in that respect, I am speaking purely hypothetically here."(P3)

It is seen in the findings that big data analytics should also be developed in the process of *"training and development management"*. It is understood that the use of big data analytics in training and development management will contribute to the creation of appropriate training and development programs as well as the identification of employees' strengths and weaknesses. Therefore, big data analytics enables employees to track the processes and results of targeted training and development programs more effectively, provide appropriate training portraits, and provide feedback to make training and development management more effective.

"In training and development, I think it can be used in analytical situations such as a prediction or a definite result in determining how an employee can access training or what kind of training they need, such as this training is needed, the employee should receive this training."(P4)

"I think that with the same logic in education management, big data can be analyzed and something can be done about how to improve processes and in this way, it will always save us both our effort and our time."(P6)

It is seen that the participants mentioned the concept of *"sustainability"* in their statements. While it is stated that the mission of human resources is sustainability, it is understood from the findings obtained that this sustainability is to increase the quality of repetitive work stages and to ensure that the processes reach optimum efficiency by ensuring that the work runs smoothly. It is understood that the creation of more effective and sustainable use of data sources for more objective analysis and follow-up affects the way of doing business from a strategic perspective to human resources management.

"I think that we need to spread analytics to all areas of the HR unit and ensure its sustainability in all areas, and I think it will contribute more in this way."(P9)

"Monitoring certain metrics from data sources in certain units to a certain extent to make more regular, more sustainable, more effective, and more objective analyzes provides serious resources for the studies to be carried out within the scope of HR and this is a serious contribution."(P8)

5. DISCUSSION

In this study, big data technology is critical for human resource management. Although our findings are similar to the existing literature, this study aims to provide new information to the literature on how HR management's perception of big data is shaped, how this perception is defined by HR employees and its impact on HR, and how big data technology can contribute to HR management and explain how they benefit from big data analytics. In line with the sub-themes under the themes of awareness, utilization and development, it is understood that big data technology is perceived and defined differently by HR units than the existing definition in the literature (Laney, 2001, p.1; Douglas, 2001, p.6; Mills, et al., 2012; Jianguang & Wei, 2013 ; Liu, et al., 2014, p.12-13; Zang & Ye, 2015, p.42). It has been observed that big data is defined by HR employees as "a phenomenon of vital importance in an environment where all structured and unstructured digital footprints exist, which contains phenomena that can manipulate people and for this reason, the reliability of the source is questioned, which refers to the future and infinity". In addition, although there are researchers who liken big data to "oil" in terms of value creation (Humby, 2006; Mayer-Schönberger & Cukier, 2013; Wilson, 2019), it is revealed in the research findings that the phenomena of these two phenomena are fundamentally different from each other in terms of "infinity" and "substitutability". Moreover, the statements of reality/accuracy, lack of data quality, and data privacy, which constitute the negative aspects of big data within the framework of the positive-negative aspects sub-theme, are similar to the literature (Gahi, et al., 2016; Aktan, 2018), the volume and diversity statement is seen as a reason that makes data quality and reliability difficult in the literature (Chandra, et al., 2017, p.49). However, from the statements of the participants, big data is considered positive as it increases the volume and variety of data, the speed of action in accessing high-value data, and the ideal candidate profile, as well as being useful in generating valuable insights. As a result, with the question on the impact of big data on HR, it is understood that

HR employees are aware of the impact of big data on HR and that this technology serves the purposes of HR.

In the theme of utilizing big data, the findings revealed that the use of this technology in the recruitment process automates some stages of the process (advertisement, candidate search and screening, candidate matching and candidate classification), thus enabling HR management to increase efficiency in the recruitment process, control risks instantly, take precautions against risks and save time, cost and effort in low-value repetitive tasks. Moreover, HR management should spend time on other tasks (e.g., performance appraisal, developing predictive models for training development) that will improve departmental and organizational efficiency by more proactively leveraging the savings opportunity offered by big data analytics. Due to the rapid development of artificial intelligence technologies created with big data analytics and the automation of some business processes by these technologies, HR professionals think that in the near future, if they do not develop themselves towards big data technology and cannot read data correctly, they will be unemployed and will be included in the group of lost professions. It is seen that the concern about being unemployed arises from the fact that HR-related skills have developed and changed in parallel with today's technology. However, it is noteworthy that some participants saw this situation as an opportunity. HR employees need to gain analytical thinking skills for big data technology and develop digital literacy skills to use and interpret information technologies in order to correctly interpret data visualizations generated in analytical results (Eshet, 2004; Bassi, L. (2011), Raging debates in HR analytics., 2011, p.16-17; Nocker & Sena, 2019, p.11). In parallel to this, since big data analytics lacks human senses and cannot measure variables in human nature (such as persuasiveness, speaking skills, etc.), utilizing this technology as a decision support assistant will enable more objective decisions to be made.

Human resource management puts forward strategies to attract and retain talented human value in line with the needs of organizations. Therefore, the increase or decrease in employee turnover is very important for organizational performance. To attract competent candidates in the job market to the organization, collecting comprehensive data about them and then ensuring the traceability of competent candidates attracted to the organization within the framework of privacy, legality, and ethical rules, and creating predictions of situations that can motivate them within the organization will contribute to increasing employee productivity and loyalty. In short, using big data technology as a motivational tool that determines the motivating factors for employees will have an impact on increasing employee performance, thus big data analytics will both increase the efficiency of the HR department and contribute to organizational performance. Moreover, analyzing the performance appraisal and training/development data of all employees in the organization, determining which employees need what kind of training, examining which skills and skill sets the human value that is desired to be attracted to the organization in the past should contain, in other words, the application of "data mining" (Sadath, 2013) will enable talent analytics to be used more effectively. Thus, it is predicted that the inclusion of analytical studies in all functions of HR will ensure the sustainability of big data and serve to increase the visibility of HR employees within the organization.

5.1. Limitations of the Research

The study, which was carried out to determine how big data analytics is perceived by human resources management, how these analytical studies are utilized in the recruitment process, and how they can be improved, have an exploratory nature and has originality since it constitutes a limited area of study in the literature. In addition, during the research process, the snowball sampling method was utilized and 310 people with participant qualifications were reached via LinkedIn. 25 participants filled out the pre-interview form, but 10 participants could be interviewed. The other 15 participants who completed the interview form were contacted afterward, but no feedback was received. Of the interviewees, 65 of those who provided feedback stated that they could not share the information due to company policy, while 45 stated that they could not contribute to the study because they were too busy. The remaining part did not provide any feedback. This shows that big data analytics in HR management is quite new, limited, and not yet fully established. On the other hand, the fact that an online interview was conducted with the participants instead of a face-to-face interview due to COVID-19 pandemic conditions limits the research. At this point, it has been observed that online interviews have a limiting characteristic in terms of establishing the trust relationship between the researcher and the interview participants and observing the gestures and facial expressions of the interview participants due to being limited to the camera field of view. The flexibility of time and space provided by technological means made it easier to schedule interviews, which was experienced as an important advantage. Online interviews facilitated the inclusion of people living in other cities or working in high positions, as well as protecting the health of the researcher and interview participants during the COVID-19 pandemic.

5.2. Implications for Future Research

The limited studies on the concept of big data in the literature and in the field of human resources management in the business world make it difficult to understand this technology. This exploratory study aims to understand how HR employees in organizations evaluate this phenomenon. Although the results we have obtained characterize the big data phenomenon, it does not seem possible to generalize it to all organizations. But future research may show how widely this phenomenon can develop. For example, the fact that the big data phenomenon adopts the use of open source means that it is an unlimited resource. This limitlessness of big data is seen as a technology that not only provides easy access to information but also contains phenomena that can manipulate people. In this way, investigating the psychological and sociological effects of a technology that contains different contrasts on people will contribute to understanding the phenomenon.

Moreover, the technology that allows the use of open source leads to negative consequences such as poor quality of data and thus questioning its authenticity/ authenticity, is the analytical skill that HR employees should have a key skill to prevent this negative situation. How will analytics serving HR's objectives change HR's strategies and culture? In addition, the fact that the storage and analysis tools used in Big Data technology allow the use of open source reveals the risk of data privacy, what kind of measures should be taken to reduce or prevent this risk, and is increasing the level of awareness of organizational employees about data privacy a practice that will reduce the risk? What skills and abilities do HR professionals need to maximize the benefits of big data analytics for HR? Answering questions such as how this situation will affect the career adaptation skills of HR employees will guide the studies to be carried out in the field.

Although the research reveals that the existence of data on all kinds of human values for every job in the labor market, whether they are employees of the organization or not, increases the traceability of people, studies on how the ethical and privacy elements will be shaped and what measures should be taken against this will be important. Finally, big data technology, its proactive approach to reducing employee turnover, its use as a motivational tool to increase employee performance, and the use of analytics in all functions of HR increase organizational effectiveness and competitiveness. But how will the assumptions about the value and position of human beings affect organizational culture and employee engagement when evaluating the new generation of jobs emerging with the rapid advancement of this technology? In this context, further research on the impact of big data on HR and the organization can reveal how the subtleties, challenges, and dynamics of understanding the big data phenomenon will take shape.

6. IMPLICATIONS FOR PRACTICE and CONCLUSION

In the current era, big data analytics is changing the business landscape by creating added value through evidence-based people management, independent of industrialization, with a recognized trend across data-driven businesses, market segments and countries. This study aims to provide a perspective on how big data is defined by the human resources management of organizations, how they benefit from these analytical applications in the recruitment process and how big data analytics can be improved in human resources functions. In this context, the question of how human resources management experiences big data analytics applications within the scope of recruitment process in the digital age has been tried to be answered. Thus, the study revealed how organizations perceive and experience the big data phenomenon in HR management. More importantly, this study reveals the positive and negative consequences of big data in HR from the perspective of HR professionals. As of the results obtained, it was concluded that big data serves the main purpose of HR and provides HR management with a strategic competitive advantage, increases the visibility of HR against management and other departments, and should develop an analytical HR policy to ensure its sustainability. Accordingly, HR management should fulfill the following conditions to carry out the recruitment process and talent management, performance appraisal, and training and development functions more fully and effectively, and to increase their visibility and influence in management. These are;

- Investing in big data storage and analysis tools
- Data-driven strategic HR management
- Create a big data knowledge management team
- Digital literacy skills development
- Adopt a culture of sustainable data.

Therefore, human resource management should change its own ideas, create a complete and effective human resource management system, and optimize the management phenomenon by using big data technology in human resource management. This enables human resources to work more effectively and efficiently, saving time and costs, and can also save human resources the effort they spend on repetitive operational tasks such as the recruitment process. On the other hand, establishing big data information management teams within the scope of human resources management and providing digital literacy skills to human resources employees will contribute to reducing the anxiety of losing a job as it will reveal new job opportunities. The adoption of a sustainable data culture in organizations will contribute to improving the performance of human resources management departments of organizations, and sustainable information management carried out with big data can provide the opportunity to instantly view employees' performance and training development data. Today, increasing organizational performance, departmental productivity, employee performance and motivation, and reducing employee turnover have become directly related to the use of big data analytics technology in human resource management activities.

REFERENCES

Aguinis, H., & O'Boyle, E.Jr. (2014). Star performers in twenty-first century organizations. *Personnel Psychology*, 67(2), 313–350. DOI:10.1111/peps.12054

Aktan, E. (2018). Büyük veri: Uygulama alanları, analitiği ve güvenlik boyutu. *Bilgi Yönetimi*, 1(1), 1–22. DOI:10.33721/by.403010

Altunışık, R. (2015). Büyük Veri: Fırsatlar Kaynağı mı Yoksa Yeni Sorunlar Yumağı mı? Yildiz Social Science Review, 1(1), 45-76. https://dergipark.org.tr/en/pub/yssr/issue/21899/235390

Andrejevic, M. (2011). The work that affective economics does. *Cultural Studies*, 25(4-5), 604–620. DOI:10.1080/09502386.2011.600551

Angrave, D., Charlwood, A., Kirkpatrick, I., Lawrence, M., & Stuart, M. (2016). HR and analytics: Why HR is set to fail the big data challenge. *Human Resource Management Journal*, 26(1), 1–11. DOI:10.1111/1748-8583.12090

Armstrong, M., & Taylor, S. (2014). Armstrong's Handbook of Human Resource Management Practice: US/Philadelphia: Edition 13. Kogan page, E-ISBN 978 0 7494 6965 8.

Bassi, L. (2011). Raging debates in HR analytics. (2011, p.16-17). *People and Strategy*, 34(2), 14–18.

Bayrakçı, S., & Albayrak, M. A. (2019). Büyük Verinin Akademik Çalışmalarda Kullanımı Üzerine Mukayeseli Bir Veri Tabanı Araştırması. AJIT-e. *Bilişim Teknolojileri Online Dergisi*, 10(36), 73–94. DOI:10.5824/1309-1581.2019.1.004.x

Brinkmann, S., & Kvale, S. (2018). Doing interviews. London: (2. ed.) SAGE Publications https://uk.sagepub.com/en-gb/eur/doing-interviews/book244549

Calp, M. H. (2016). İşletmelerde uygulanan insan kaynaklari yönetiminde veritabani kullaniminin önemi. *Gazi Üniversitesi İktisadi ve İdari Bilimler Fakültesi Dergisi*, 18(2), 539–557.

Chandra, S., & Ray, S. ve Goswami, R. T. (2017), Big data security: survey on frameworks and algorithms. 2017 IEEE 7th International Advance Computing Conference (IACC) (pp. 48-54). Hyderabad, İndia: IEEE.

Charmaz, K. (2006). *Constructing grounded theory: A practical guide through qualitative analysis*. SAGE Publications.

Charmaz, K. (2015). *Grounded Theory Configuration* (Hoş, R., Ed. & Trans.). Seçkin Publishing.

Chen, H., Chiang, R. H., & Storey, V. C. (2012). Business intelligence and analytics: From big data to big impact. *Management Information Systems Quarterly*, 36(4), 1165–1188. DOI:10.2307/41703503

Chen, M., Mao, S., Zhang, Y., & Leung, V. C. M. (2014). Big Data Storage. In *Big Data Related Technologies, Challenges and Future Prospects* (pp. 33–49). Springer., DOI:10.1007/978-3-319-06245-7_4

Chien, C. F., & Chen, L. F. (2008). Data mining to improve personnel selection and enhance human capital: A case study in high-technology industry. *Expert Systems with Applications*, 34(1), 280–290. DOI:10.1016/j.eswa.2006.09.003

Çiğdem, Ş., & Seyrek, İ. H. (2015). *İşletmelerde Büyük Veri Uygulamaları: Bir Literatür Taraması. Ulusal Yönetim Bilişim Sistemleri Kongresi.* Ataturk University.

Creswell, J. W. (2013). *Qualitative research methods* (Bütün, L., & Demir, B., Trans.). Siyasal Kitabevi.

Creswell. (2016, p.195). Creswell, J. W. (2016). Research design: Qualitative, quantitative and mixed method approaches. (Translation: Demir, S.). Ankara: (4.edition) Eğiten Kitap.

Cukier, K., & Mayer-Schoenberger, V. (2013). The rise of big data: How it's changing the way we think about the world. *Foreign Affairs*, 92(3), 28–40. https://heinonline.org/HOL/P?h=hein.journals/fora92&i=593

Davenport, T. H., Harris, J. G., & Morison, R. (2010). Analytics at work: Smarter decisions, better results. Boston, Massachusetts: Harvard Business Press. ISBN 978-4221-7769-3.

De Mauro, A., Greco, M., Grimaldi, M., & Ritala, P. (2018). Human resources for Big Data professions: A systematic classification of job roles and required skill sets. *Information Processing & Management*, 54(5), 807–817. DOI:10.1016/j.ipm.2017.05.004

Dong, X. H., Ying, A., & Guo, J. G. (2014). Research on the Application of the Big Data Technology in the Network Recruitment. *Human Resource Development of China*, 18, 37–41.

Doody, O., & Noonan, M. (2013). Preparing and conducting interviews to collect data. *Nurse Researcher*, 20(5), 28–32. DOI:10.7748/nr2013.05.20.5.28.e327 PMID:23687846

Douglas, L. (2001), 3d data management: Controlling data volume, velocity and variety. Gartner. Retrieved. 6.

Elnur, A. (2022). *Kadınların Ve Erkeklerin Tek Başına Seyahat Deneyimlerinin Toplumsal Cinsiyet Bağlamında Analizi. Akdeniz Üniversitesi Sosyal Bilimler Üniversitesi.* Yayınlanmış Dalı Doktora Tezi.

ENISA. (2015). *Big Data Security, "Big Data Security Good Practices and Recommendations on the security of Big Data Systems", European Union: European Union Agency for Network and Information Security.* ENISA.

Erb, B. (2016), Human resources management in the age of big data. In Seminar: Applied Management Diagnostics, 1 (pp. 3-14.). Ulm: Ulm University.

Eshet, Y. (2004). Digital Literacy: A Conceptual Framework for Survival Skills in the Digital era. *Journal of Educational Multimedia and Hypermedia*, 13(1), 93–106.

Fink, A. A., & Sturman, M. C. (2017). HR metrics and talent analytics. In Collings, D. M. (Ed.), *The Oxford handbook of talent management (Chapter: 20)* (pp. 375–390). Oxford University Press.

Fisher, D., DeLine, R., Czerwinski, M., & Drucker, S. (2012). Interactions with big data analytics. interactions, 19(3), 50-59. .DOI:10.1145/2168931.2168943

Fu, N., Keegan, A., & McCartney, S. (2022). The duality of HR analysts' storytelling: Showcasing and curbing. *Human Resource Management Journal*, 33(2), 261–286. DOI:10.1111/1748-8583.12466

Fukuyama, M. (2018). Society 5.0: Aiming for a New Human-Centered Society. *Japan Spotlight*, 27(5), 47–50.

Gahi, Y., Guennoun, M., & Mouftah, H. T. (2016). Big data analytics: Security and privacy challenges. In *2016 IEEE Symposium on Computers and Communication (ISCC)* (pp. 952-957). IEEE. DOI:10.1109/ISCC.2016.7543859

Gandomi, A., & Haider, M. (2015). Beyond the hype: Big data concepts, methods, and analytics. *International Journal of Information Management*, 35(2), 137–144. DOI:10.1016/j.ijinfomgt.2014.10.007

Glaser, B. (1978). *Theoretical sensitivity.* The Sociology Press.

Hamilton, R. H., & Sodeman, W. A. (2020). The questions we ask: Opportunities and challenges for using big data analytics to strategically manage human capital resources. *Business Horizons*, 63(1), 85–95. DOI:10.1016/j.bushor.2019.10.001

Humby, C. (2006). Data is the new Oil! ANA Senior marketer's summit, Kellogg School. https://ana.blogs.com/maestros/2006/11/data_is_the_new.html

Janssen, M., van der Voort, H., & Wahyudi, A. (2017). Factors influencing big data decision-making quality. *Journal of Business Research*, 70, 197–208. DOI:10.1016/j.jbusres.2016.08.007

Jianguang, M., & Wei, J. (2013). The Concept, Characteristics and Application of Big Data. National defense science & technology, 2, 10-17.

Kagermann, H., Wahlster, W., & Helbig, J. (2013). Recommendations for implementing the strategic initiative INDUSTRIE 4.0. Final report of the Industrie, Frankfurt. *Office of the Industry-Science Research Alliance.*, 4(0), 1–82.

Kim, S., Wang, Y., & Boon, C. (2021). Sixty years of research on technology and human resource management: Looking back and looking forward. *Human Resource Management*, 60(1), 229–247. DOI:10.1002/hrm.22049

Küsbeci, P. (2021). Büyük Veri, In İ. Ç. (Editor), Yenilikçi İnsan Kaynakları Uygulamaları ve Örgütsel İnovasyon (4.Bölüm) (pp. 61-78.). İstanbul: Nobel Yayınları, E-ISBN: 978-625-439-437-9.

Laney, D. (2001). 3D data management: Controlling data volume, velocity and variety. . META group research note, 6(70), 1-4.

Lee, I. (2017). Big data: Dimensions, evolution, impacts, and challenges. *Business Horizons*, 60(3), 293–303. DOI:10.1016/j.bushor.2017.01.004

Li, P. (2021). On the application of big data technology in human resource management in the new era. *Journal of Physics: Conference Series*, 1915(4), 1–7. DOI:10.1088/1742-6596/1915/4/042038

Liu, C., Ranjan, R., Yang, C., Zhang, X., Wang, L., & Chen, J. (2014). MuR-DPA: Top-down levelled multi-replica merkle hash tree based secure public auditing for dynamic big data storage on cloud. *IEEE Transactions on Computers*, 64(9), 2609–2622. DOI:10.1109/TC.2014.2375190

Lodefalk, M. (2013). Servicification of manufacturing–evidence from Sweden. *International Journal of Economics and Business Research*, 6(1), 87–113. DOI:10.1504/IJEBR.2013.054855

Loebbecke, C., & Picot, A. (2015). Reflections on societal and business model transformation arising from digitization and big data analytics: A research agenda. *The Journal of Strategic Information Systems*, 24(3), 149–157. DOI:10.1016/j.jsis.2015.08.002

Ma, J. G., & Jiang, W. (2013). The concept, characteristics and application of big data. *Natl. Def. Sci. Technol*, 34, 10–16.

Mammadova, M., & Jabrayilova, Z. (2016). Opportunities and Challenges of Big Data Utilization in the Resolution of Human Resource Management. Problems of information technology, 7(1), 33-40. .DOI:10.25045/jpit.v07.i1.05

Margherita, A. (2022). Human resources analytics: A systematization of research topics and directions for future research. *Human Resource Management Review*, 32(2), 100795. DOI:10.1016/j.hrmr.2020.100795

Martinez-Gil. (2021), Jorge Towards the automation of recruitment processes. e-prints in library & information science, 1-6. http://eprints.rclis.org/42472/

Mashey, J. R. (1999). Big data and the next wave of {InfraStress} problems, solutions, opportunities. In 1999 USENIX annual technical conference. (USENIX ATC 99).

McAfee, A., ve Brynjolfsson, E. (2012). Big Data: The Management Revolution. *Harvard Business Review*, (90), 70–77. PMID:23074865

Merleau-Ponty, M. (2012). *Phenomenology of perception* (Sarıkartal, E., & Hacımuratoğlu, E., Trans.). Ithaki Publications.

Micic, L., & Radosavac, V. (2018). Influence of Information Technology to Human Resources Management: Key Trends in 21st Century. In Hadžikadić, M. A. (Ed.), *Lecture Notes in Networks and Systems* (Vol. 28, pp. 271–281). Springer., DOI:10.1007/978-3-319-71321-2_25

Mikalef, P., Framnes, V. A., Danielsen, F., Krogstie, J., & Olsen, D. (2017). Big data analytics capability: antecedents and business value. Pacific Asia Conference On Information Systems, https://aisel.aisnet.org/pacis2017/136

Miles, M. B., & Huberman, A. M. (1994). *Qualitative data analysis: An expanded sourcebook. sage*. SAGE Publications.

Mills, S., Lucas, S., Irakliotis, L., Rappa, M., Carlson, T., & Perlowitz, B. (2012). *Demystifying big data: a practical guide to transforming the business of government*. TechAmerica Foundation.

Minbaeva, D. (2018). Building credible human capital analytics for organizational competitive advantage. *Human Resource Management*, 57(3), 701–713. DOI:10.1002/hrm.21848

Mishra, S. N., Lama, D. R., & Pal, Y. (2016). Human Resource Predictive Analytics (HRPA) for HR management in organizations. *International Journal of Scientific & Technology Research*, 5(5), 33–35.

Morales, H. A. H. (2018). Mayer-Schönberger, V. & Cukier, K.(2013). Big Data. La revolución de los datos masivos. Clivajes. *Revista de Ciencias Sociales*, (9), 189–189. DOI:10.25009/clivajes-rcs.v0i9.2536

Neuman, W. L. (2006). *Social Research Methods: Qualitative and Quantitative Approaches*. Pearson.

Nocker, M., & Sena, V. (2019). Big data and human resources management: The rise of talent analytics. *Social Sciences (Basel, Switzerland)*, 8(10), 1–19. DOI:10.3390/socsci8100273

O'Leary, D. E. (2013). Artificial intelligence and big data. *IEEE Intelligent Systems*, 28(2), 96–99. DOI:10.1109/MIS.2013.39

Oğuzlar, A. (2003). Veri ön işleme. *Erciyes Üniversitesi İktisadi ve İdari Bilimler Fakültesi Dergisi*, (21), 67–76.

Owais, S. S., & Hussein, N. S. (2016). Extract five categories CPIVW from the 9V's characteristics of the big data. *International Journal of Advanced Computer Science and Applications*, 7(3), 254–258.

Özdemir, İ., & Sağıroğlu, Ş. (2018). Denetimlerde büyük veri kullanımı ve üzerine bir değerlendirme. *Gazi University Journal of Science Part C: Design and Technology*, 6(2), 470–480. DOI:10.29109/http-gujsc-gazi-edu-tr.347728

Pala, İ. B. (2021). *Kurumsal Büyük Veri Analitiği Yetenekleri Ve Performans İlişkisi: Türkiye İçin Bir Araştırma, İstanbul Teknik Üniversitesi Lisansüstü Eğitim Enstitüsü*. Yayınlanmış Yüksek Lisans Tezi.

Palmer, M., & Winters, K. T. (1993). *Human Resources (Translated into Turkish: Şahiner, D.)*. Rota Publications.

Patton, M. Q. (2014). *Qualitative Research and Evaluation Methods* (Bütün, M., & Demir, S. B., Trans.). Pegem Akademi.

Pratt, M. G., Kaplan, S., & Whittington, R. (2020). Editorial Essay: The Tumult over Transparency: Decoupling Transparency from Replication in establishing trustworthy qualitative research*. *Administrative Science Quarterly*, 65(1), 1–19. DOI:10.1177/0001839219887663

Rajalakshmi, M., & Gomathi, S. (2016). A review on E-HRM: Electronic human resource management. *Indian Journal of Research*, 5(8), 364–379.

Ramamoorti, S., Agarwal, A., & Nijhawan, S. (2016). Big data and continuous monitoring: A synergy whose time has come? *Internal Auditing*, 31(1), 19–26.

Reinsel, D., Gantz, J., & Rydning, J. (2017). Data age 2025: The evolution of data to life-critical. Don't Focus on Big Data, 2.

Ren, J. (2017). Modelling quality dynamics, business value and firm performance in a big data analytics environment. *International Journal of Production Research*, 55(17), 5011–5026. DOI:10.1080/00207543.2016.1154209

Ren, J. (2017). Modelling quality dynamics, business value and firm performance in a big data analytics environment. *International Journal of Production Research*, 55(17), 5011–5026. DOI:10.1080/00207543.2016.1154209

Ruël, H., & Bondarouk, T. ve Looise, J. K. (2004). e-HRM: Innovation or irritation: An explorative empirical study in five large companies on Web-based HRM. Management Revue, 15(3), 364–380. https://www.jstor.org/stable/41783479

Russom, P. (2011). Big data analytics. TDWI best practices report, fourth quarter, 19(4), 1-34.

Sadath, L. (2013). Data Mining: A tool for knowledge management in human resource. *International Journal of Innovative Technology and Exploring Engineering*, 2(6), 154–159.

Satyanarayana, L. V. (2015). A Survey on challenges and advantages in big data. *International Journal of Computer Science and Technology*, 6(2), 115–119.

Shen, H. (2015). Research on enterprise human resources management mode innovation in the age of big data. In *2015 International Conference on Economics, Management, Law and Education*. (pp. 322-325). Paris: Atlantis Press. DOI:10.2991/emle-15.2015.73

Stirling, E. (2016). 'I'm Always on Facebook!': Exploring Facebook as a Mainstream Research Tool and Ethnographic Site. In Snee, H., Hine, C., Morey, Y., Roberts, S., & Watson, H. (Eds.), *Digital Methods for Social Science*. Palgrave Macmillan., DOI:10.1057/9781137453662_4

Strohmeier, S., & Kabst, R. (2014). Configurations of e-HRM–an empirical exploration. *Employee Relations*, 36(4), 333–353. DOI:10.1108/ER-07-2013-0082

Sütçü, C. S. ve Aytekin Ç., (2018). Veri Bilimi. İstanbul: Paloma Kitapları (1.Baskı).

Tekbaş, İ. (2019). *Muhasebenin dijital dönüşümü ve mali mühendislik*. CERES Yayınları.

van der Togt, J., & Rasmussen, T. H. (2017). Toward evidence-based HR. *Journal of Organizational Effectiveness*, 4(2), 127–132. DOI:10.1108/JOEPP-02-2017-0013

Van Manen, M. (2007). Phenomenology of practice. *Phenomenology & Practice*, 1(1), 11–30.

Vassakis, K., Petrakis, E., & Kopanakis, I. (2018). Big Data Analytics: Applications, Prospects and Challenges. In G. M. In: Skourletopoulos, Mobile Big Data. Lecture Notes on Data Engineering and Communications Technologies, vol 10. (pp. 3-20). Springer.

Vranova, S. (2012). Identifying the specifics of motivating different groups of employees. *GSTF Journal on Business Review*, 2(2), 98–104.

Wilson, E. (2019). Disrupting dark web supply chains to protect precious data. *Computer Fraud & Security*, 2019(4), 6–9. DOI:10.1016/S1361-3723(19)30039-9

Xie, Z. (2020), Research on Enterprise Human Resource Management Under the Background of Big Data. In 2020 International Conference on Intelligent Transportation, Big Data & Smart City (ICITBS), (pp. pp.600-604, IEEE.). DOI:10.1109/ICITBS49701.2020.00132

Yazıcıoğlu, Y., & Erdoğan, S. (2004). *SPSS Uygulamalı Bilimsel Araştırma Yöntemleri*. Detay Yayıncılık.

Yıldırım, A., & Şimşek, H. (2005), Sosyal bilimlerde nitel araştırma yöntemleri. Ankara: Seçkin Yayıncılık (5. Baskı).

Zang, S. Y., & Ye, M. L. (2015). Human Resource Management in the Era of Big Data. *Journal of Human Resource and Sustainability Studies*, 3(1), 41–45. DOI:10.4236/jhrss.2015.31006

Zhang, H. (2019). Reflections on innovation of human resource management in the era of big data. 8th International Conference on Education and Management in 2018 (ICEM 2018), 75 (pp. 518-520.). China: Atlantis Press.

Zhang, Y., Xu, S., Zhang, L., & Yang, M. (2021). Big data and human resource management research: An integrative review and new directions for future research. *Journal of Business Research*, 133, 34–50. DOI:10.1016/j.jbusres.2021.04.019

Zhu, W. (2020). Reconstruction of human resource management under big data and artificial intelligence. *Journal of Physics: Conference Series*, 1533(4), 1–6. DOI:10.1088/1742-6596/1533/4/042016

Zikopoulos, P., Deroos, D., Parasuraman, K., Deutsch, T., Giles, J., & Corrigan, D. (2012). *Harness the power of big data The IBM big data platform*. McGraw Hill Professional.

Chapter 14
Integrating Robotics Into the HRM Framework:
Challenges and Opportunities

Jaspreet Kaur
https://orcid.org/0000-0002-3587-6841
Chandigarh University, Mohali, India

ABSTRACT

The burgeoning adoption of robotics in Human Resource Management (HRM) offers a double-edged sword. Automation by robots unlocks a plethora of opportunities, streamlining HR processes and enabling strategic pursuits. However, this integration presents significant challenges that demand attention. Job displacement due to automation, the emergence of skill gaps, ethical concerns surrounding data privacy and algorithmic bias, and potential employee resistance all pose hurdles to successful implementation. This study delves into these challenges and proposes solutions for a smooth transition towards a robotics-infused HRM framework, ensuring organizations reap the benefits of this technological revolution.

INTRODUCTION

The incorporation of robotics is becoming more widespread in the constantly shifting landscape of human resource management (HRM), which is constantly going through changes. In a time when businesses are working to improve their human resource management systems in terms of efficiency, effectiveness, and innovation, robotics presents a viable option for transformation. Nevertheless, this integration has its own unique set of obstacles and opportunities, which human resource professionals are need to effectively traverse.

DOI: 10.4018/979-8-3693-4412-5.ch014

AN OVERVIEW OF ROBOTICS IN HUMAN RESOURCE MANAGEMENT

When it comes to human resource management (HRM), the incorporation of robotics involves the utilisation of many modern technologies, such as artificial intelligence (AI), robotic process automation (RPA), and others, in order to streamline HR procedures. Several aspects of human resource management (HRM) have the potential to be revolutionised by robotics. These aspects include recruitment and onboarding, performance management, and employee engagement. The recruitment process is one of the key areas in which robots is making great progress for advancement. The process by which businesses locate and choose talent is being revolutionised by technologies such as chatbots for initial candidate contacts, automated resume screening, and candidate matching algorithms driven by artificial intelligence. Utilising robotics in the recruiting process allows human resources departments to improve the overall candidate experience, lower the amount of prejudice that occurs during the hiring process, and increase the efficiency of candidate screening (Aripin et al., 2024).

Additionally, robotics is an essential component of the onboarding procedures utilised. New hires can be guided through the orientation process by virtual assistants powered by artificial intelligence (AI), which can also answer their questions and give pertinent information about the policies and procedures of the organisation. This not only speeds up the process of onboarding new employees, but it also guarantees that all new workers receive information in the same manner for the same reason (Basu et al., 2023).

An further domain that is suitable for the incorporation of robotics is performance management. Analytics systems that are powered by artificial intelligence are able to examine huge volumes of employee data in order to provide insights into performance trends, suggest areas for improvement, and even anticipate future performance trends. It is possible for human resources departments to devote more time to strategic objectives, such as talent development and succession planning, if they automate certain components of performance review. The use of robotics can also be beneficial to initiatives to increase employee engagement and retention. Chatbots and virtual agents have the potential to improve employee satisfaction by facilitating the collecting of real-time input, conducting pulse surveys, and providing personalised recommendations all at the same time. Organisations have the ability to cultivate a culture of continuous improvement and engagement by utilising robotics to improve communication and feedback processesas depicted in figure 1 below (Budhwar et al., 2022).

Figure 1. Impact of Robotics in HRM

```
+---------------------+
|      Robots         |
+---------------------+
        ^          ^              ^
        |          |              |
   Efficiency  Safety   Data Analysis
        |          |              |
        v          v              v
+---------------------+
| Job Displacement    |
+---------------------+
        |
        v
+---------------------+
| Skill Obsolescence  |
+---------------------+
        |
        v
+---------------------+
| Ethical Concerns    | (e.g., control, bias)
+---------------------+
        |
        v
+---------------------+
| Reskilling &        |
| Upskilling          |
+---------------------+
        |
        v
+---------------------+
| Human-Robot         |
| Collaboration       |
+---------------------+
        |
        v
+---------------------+
| Focus on Human      |
| Skills (Creativity, |
| Empathy)            |
+---------------------+
```

IMPORTANCE OF UNDERSTANDING CHALLENGES

The incorporation of robots into human resource management (HRM) presents organisations with a number of issues that they need to handle, despite the fact that it presents a multitude of opportunities. The potential for human labour to be displaced is one of the key issues currently being raised. Many people are concerned that particular jobs may become obsolete as a result of robotics' ability to automate repetitive operations. This could result in increased unemployment and workforce dislocation. Moreover, the ethical implications of robotics in human resource management are not something that can be ignored. Regarding data privacy, algorithmic bias, and the ethical application of artificial intelligence algorithms, there are a lot of questions. It is necessary for human resource experts to wrestle with these ethical conundrums in order to guarantee that the incorporation of robots is in accordance with the values of the organisation and that it respects the rights of employees (Dhatterwal et al., 2024).

In addition to this, the complexity of putting robotics ideas into action presents a substantial obstacle. On the route to effective deployment, organisations confront a multitude of challenges, ranging from the selection of appropriate technology partners to the incorporation of robotics into pre-existing human resource management systems. When it comes to human resource management (HRM), resistance to change from employees and organisational inertia might further hamper the adoption of robotics (Kaur, 2024).

THE EXISTENCE OF OPPORTUNITIES FOR INNOVATION

Despite the difficulties, the use of robotics into human resource management gives chances for innovation and growth that are unmatched by any other. Through the automation of regular processes, human resources departments are able to divert their attention to strategic projects that contribute to the organization's overall value. For instance, human resource professionals have the ability to devote more time to the cultivation of talent, the training of employees, and the establishment of organisational culture. Additionally, robotics makes it possible for human resources departments to make decisions based on data-driven insights as well. A more in-depth understanding of workforce dynamics, the identification of talent gaps, and the anticipation of future HR needs are all things that can be accomplished by organisations through the analysis of huge amounts of employee data. This strategy, which is powered by data, gives human resource professionals the ability to make decisions that are more informed and ultimately benefit the organisation as presented in figure 2 below (Fregnan et al., 2020).

Figure 2. Advantages of Robotics in HRM

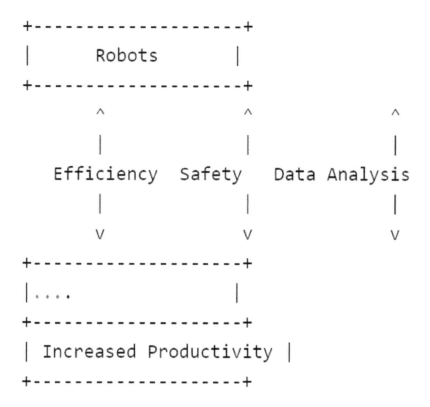

In addition, robotics improves the experience of working for an organisation by facilitating personalised interactions and streamlining different processes. The use of chatbots and virtual assistants enables employees to receive quick support, whether it be in the form of answering questions pertaining to human resources or providing assistance with administrative duties. This not only increases the level of satisfaction experienced by workers, but it also frees up human resources to concentrate on initiatives that are more strategic. A paradigm shift in the way that organisations manage their human capital has occurred as a result of the use of robotics into human resource management. Within their operations, human resources departments have the potential to improve their efficiency, effectiveness, and innovativeness by utilising robotics technologies. However, this integration is accompanied by its own unique set of difficulties, such as worries about the loss of jobs, ethical problems, and the complexity of the implementation process (Gärtner & Kern, 2021).

The prospects for innovation and advancement are enormous, despite the fact that these challenges exist. Automation of regular operations, utilisation of data-driven insights, and improvement of the employee experience are all ways in which organisations can benefit from adopting robotics. It is possible for human resource professionals to successfully negotiate the integration of robotics into HRM frameworks, which will ultimately drive organisational success in the digital age. This is possible if they have a sophisticated grasp of both the problems and the potential (Kaur, 2024).

CHALLENGES OF INTEGRATING ROBOTICS INTO HRM

When it comes to Human Resource Management (HRM), the use of robotics gives a multitude of potential for optimising operations and improving productivity. On the other hand, this integration is accompanied by a plethora of issues that organisations need to address in order to guarantee the successful acceptance and implementation of those challenges. In this in-depth investigation, the study looks into the different issues that are associated with incorporating robotics into human resource management (HRM) and examine techniques that can be utilised to effectively manage these challenges as presented in figure 3 below:

Figure 3. Challenges of Integrating Robotics into HRM

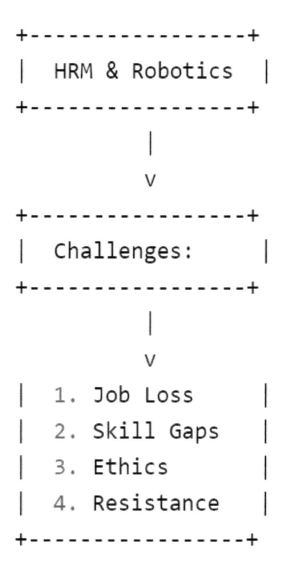

1.Job Displacement:

The introduction of robotics into human resource management raises a number of serious concerns, one of the most significant of which being the possibility of job displacement. Considering that robotics technologies are automating operations that are repetitive and normal, there is a concern that certain roles may become obsolete, which might result in more unemployment and a reorganisation of the workforce. This has the potential to have significant repercussions on the organisational structure of the workforce as well as the morale of the workforce. Proactive strategies are required to be implemented by organisations in order to offset the negative consequences of job displacement. Retraining and improving the skills of workers whose jobs are at risk of becoming automated is one strategy that can be taken. Organisations have the ability to equip their staff with the skills necessary to operate and maintain robotics systems by investing in training and development programmes. This enables employees to move into new jobs within the organisation (Gunathunge & Lakmal, 2019).

In addition, organisations have the ability to investigate alternate employment arrangements, such as job sharing or flexible work arrangements, in order to keep competent individuals whose jobs may be affected by automation. In addition, the cultivation of a culture that encourages continuous learning and adaptation can provide individuals with the ability to embrace change and prosper in a workplace that is becoming increasingly automated (Gärtner & Kern, 2021).

2.Skill Requirements:

Employees are required to acquire new skills in order to properly operate and maintain robots technology, which implies a shift in the skill requirements that are required for the integration of robotics into human resource management. The identification of these new skill sets is absolutely necessary in order to guarantee a seamless transition to a more automated human resources landscape. It is necessary for human resource professionals to work together with technology specialists in order to evaluate the skill gaps that exist within their organisations and to devise specific training and development programmes in order to fill these gaps. It is possible that this will require the provision of technical training on robotics technology, in addition to the cultivation of soft skills such as critical thinking, problem-solving competencies, and flexibility. To further ensure that employees have access to the most recent information and expertise in robotics technology, organisations can complement their internal training initiatives with external resources like as online courses, seminars, and certification programmes. These resources can be leveraged by organisations (Haubold et al., 2020).

3. Ethical Considerations:

When it comes to the incorporation of robotics into human resource management (HRM), there are a number of ethical concerns that need to be taken into account. These concerns include privacy, data security, and algorithmic bias. As human resources departments continue to collect and analyse large volumes of employee data, there is a growing worry over the ethical implications of how this data is handled and secured. It is imperative that organisations establish transparent ethical rules and regulatory frameworks that regulate the utilisation of robotics technologies in human resource management in order to solve these problems (Kaur, 2024). To do this, it may be necessary to implement stringent data privacy policies, encryption mechanisms, and access controls in order to adequately protect sensitive employee information. Additionally, organisations need to be careful in recognising and eliminating algorithmic bias in HR processes that are driven by artificial intelligence. In order to accomplish this, it is necessary to perform regular audits in order to identify and address any biases that may emerge, as well as to continuously monitor and evaluate algorithms in order to guarantee fairness and transparency in decision-making (Kambur & Yildirim, 2023).

4.Employee Resistance:

The opposition of employees is yet another key obstacle that companies have to overcome in order to successfully integrate robotics into human resource management. Fears about job security, worries about job relocation, or apprehensions about the influence that automation will have on their work lives are all possible sources of resistance. It is imperative that organisations prioritise effective change management methods in order to overcome resistance from their workforce. The adoption of robotics technologies may include open and honest communication regarding the reasons for doing so, as well as the possible benefits that these technologies may bring to employees and the organisation as a whole (Knod Jr et al., 1984).

Furthermore, integrating employees in the decision-making process and asking their views and input can assist develop a sense of ownership and buy-in for the changes that are being implemented for the organisation. Providing employees with opportunities for training and skill development can also help relieve concerns about job displacement and enable workers to adapt to the changing technology landscape (Libert et al., 2020).

COST AND IMPLEMENTATION CHALLENGES

When it comes to human resource management (HRM), organisations who are interested in integrating robotics face considerable problems due to the cost and logistical challenges associated with the introduction of robotics. The path to effective deployment is fraught with several challenges for organisations, ranging from the selection of appropriate technology partners to the incorporation of robotics into preexisting human resource management systems. It is necessary for organisations to do exhaustive cost-benefit assessments in order to evaluate the return on investment (ROI) of robotics technology in order to take action against these difficulties. In order to accomplish this, it is necessary to compare the initial expenses of implementation with the long-term advantages, which may include increased productivity, less errors, and enhanced decision-making (Liboni et al., 2019).

In addition, businesses have the opportunity to investigate several options for the integration of robotics that are both cost-effective and flexible. These options include cloud-based robotics platforms, open-source software, and modular robotics systems that allow for scalability and adaptability. In addition, forming partnerships with seasoned technology providers and making use of their expertise can assist in streamlining the implementation process and reducing the likelihood of potential dangers (Mohamed et al., 2022).

In nutshell, the incorporation of robotics into human resource management (HRM) presents organisations with a variety of benefits as well as obstacles. Organisations are able to successfully navigate the complexities of robotics integration and reap the benefits of a more efficient and innovative human resource management landscape if they address issues such as job displacement, skill requirements, ethical considerations, employee resistance, and challenges related to cost and implementation (Vrontis et al., 2022).

OPPORTUNITIES OF INTEGRATING ROBOTICS INTO HRM

Organisations that are looking to improve their HR operations in terms of efficiency, productivity, and creativity have a multitude of opportunities available to them as a result of the incorporation of robotics into Human Resource Management (HRM). In addition to enabling data-driven decision-making and automating repetitive operations, robotics technologies offer a multitude of benefits that have the potential to revolutionise the landscape of human resource management. In this in-depth investigation, we look into the numerous opportunities that can be gained by incorporating robotics into human resource management (HRM), and we analyse the ways in which organisations may make use of these opportunities to propel their success (Molitor & Renkema, 2022).

1.Efficiency and Productivity

The incorporation of robotics into human resource management presents a number of significant potential, one of the most important of which is the development of efficiency and productivity (Stanley & Aggarwal, 2019). Robotics technologies, such as robotic process automation (RPA) and algorithms driven by artificial intelligence, have the ability to automate operations that are repetitive and time-consuming. This enables human resource experts to devote their attention to more strategic endeavours. Routine administrative operations, such as data input, file management, and scheduling, can be automated with the use of robotic process automation (RPA). This enables human resource professionals to devote their time and resources to jobs that require human judgement and creativity. Robotics technologies have the potential to dramatically boost the efficiency of human resource management activities, ultimately leading to the success of an organisation. This is accomplished by streamlining processes and reducing automatic errors (Ogbeibu et al., 2024).

2. Data-Driven Decision Making:

The ability to make decisions based on data-driven insights is yet another appealing possibility that is given by the incorporation of robotics into human resource management. Robotics technologies make it possible for businesses to gather, analyse, and interpret huge volumes of personnel data. This provides organisations with significant insights into the dynamics of their workforce, trends in performance, and talent gaps. For example, analytics tools that are powered by artificial intelligence may analyse data on employee performance in order to uncover high-potential talent, foresee risks associated with employee attrition, and optimise workforce planning methods. In a similar vein, data analytics has the potential to enhance recruiting procedures by locating sources of top talent, evaluating the efficiency of recruitment channels, and refining candidate selection criteria (Kaur, 2024).

If human resource professionals are able to leverage the power of data analytics, they will be able to make decisions that are better informed, which will ultimately promote organisational success and boost the overall effectiveness of HRM procedures (Moniz, 2013).

3.Enhanced Candidate Experience:

The use of robotics technologies presents a potential to improve the candidate experience throughout the entire process of human resource recruiting. Personalised and easily available communication can be provided to candidates through the use of chatbots and virtual assistants. These communication tools can answer candidates' questions, provide status updates, and direct candidates through the application process. Chatbots, for instance, can provide candidates with assistance in filling out application forms, scheduling interviews, and providing information about the culture and values of the organisation. Technologies that utilise robots have the potential to improve the candidate experience, raise candidate happiness, and enhance the employer brand. This is accomplished by providing help and guidance in real time (Ogbeibu et al., 2024).

Furthermore, robotics technologies make it possible for businesses to automate routine administrative activities such as screening resumes and sourcing prospects. This frees up human resource workers to concentrate on developing meaningful relationships with candidates and developing a great experience for the recruitment process (Omer, 2018).

4.24/7 Accessibility:

When it comes to human resource management, one of the most significant benefits of incorporating robotics is the capacity to offer employees HR help around the clock. Through the use of chatbots, virtual assistants, and self-service portals, robotics systems are able to provide accessibility around the clock. This enables employees to access human resources information and help anytime they require it, regardless of the time zone or region they are travelling from. Employees, for instance, have the ability to use chatbots outside of regular office hours to make requests for time off, check pay stubs, and enrol in benefit programmes. This level of accessibility not only increases the level of happiness that employees feel, but it also improves efficiency by decreasing the reliance on manual HR processes and increasing the amount of autonomy that employees have. In addition, organisations are able to provide help to employees who are working remotely or in different geographical regions, which ensures that HR support is provided in a timely and uniform manner across the whole workforce (Pan & Froese, 2023).

AUGMENTED HUMAN CAPABILITIES

One of the most potentially game-changing opportunities presented by the use of robots into human resource management is the way in which it may enhance human talents. Robotics technologies enable businesses to realise the full potential of their human capital by automating routine operations and freeing up time for human resource experts to concentrate on activities that have a greater value. For instance, human resource professionals have the ability to spend more time to strategic initiatives such as talent development, succession planning, and the formation of organisational culture, which in turn drives innovation and growth within the organisation. Furthermore, robotics technologies have the potential to contribute to the enhancement of human decision-making by delivering data-driven insights and predictive analytics that may be utilised to guide HR policies and initiatives. A workforce that is more nimble and adaptive, and that is suited to prosper in an increasingly complex and competitive business environment, can be created by organisations through the utilisation of robotics to complement human capabilities (Pattali, 2022).

In conclusion, the incorporation of robotics into human resource management (HRM) gives a multitude of options for businesses to improve the effectiveness, productivity, and creativity of their HR procedures. Technologies that utilise robots offer a multitude of advantages that can contribute to the success of an organisation. These advantages include the automation of monotonous operations, the facilitation of data-driven decision-making, and the enhancement of the applicant experience. Organisations have the ability to revolutionise their human resource management methods and position themselves for long-term success in the digital age if they embrace these opportunities and successfully leverage robotics technologies (Rastogi & Sharma, 2022).

CONCLUSION AND FUTURE DIRECTIONS

In conclusion, the incorporation of robotics into the framework of human resource management (HRM) brings a considerable number of opportunities as well as obstacles for organisations. Throughout the entirety of this chapter, the study has investigated the myriad of components that comprise this integration, scrutinising the ramifications that it has for both companies and employees. From the challenges of job displacement, skill requirements, ethical considerations, employee resistance, and cost and implementation barriers to the opportunities of efficiency and productivity gains, data-driven decision-making, enhanced candidate experience, 24/7 accessibility, and augmented human capabilities, it is evident that robotics has the potential to reshape the landscape of human resource management practices through the use of robotics.

The difficulties that are connected with incorporating robotics into human resource management cannot be overstated. The phenomenon of job displacement, for example, gives rise to worries over the future of work and the necessity of developing measures to efficiently manage transitions in the workforce. As a result of the increasing automation of ordinary jobs by robotics technologies, there is a growing necessity for personnel to acquire new skill sets in order to run and maintain these computers. Furthermore, in order to guarantee that the implementation of robots is in accordance with ethical norms and social values, it is necessary to pay close attention to ethical aspects such as privacy, data security, and algorithmic bias. Employee resistance, which is frequently fuelled by worries of job loss or job displacement, provides additional obstacles to the successful integration of robotics, the relevance of which is highlighted by the fact that effective change management strategies are essential. In conclusion, the difficulties in terms of both cost and implementation that are linked with the adoption of robotics bring to light the necessity of meticulous preparation and investment in order to guarantee a smooth transition.

On the other hand, despite these limitations, there are enormous opportunity for businesses to improve their human resource management processes by utilising robotic system. It is impossible to ignore the possibility of higher levels of efficiency and productivity that could be achieved through the automation of jobs that are repetitive. The use of robotics helps human resource professionals to devote their attention to strategic initiatives and value-added tasks that contribute to the overall performance of the organisation. This is accomplished by freeing up their time from routine chores. Furthermore, robotics makes it possible to collect and analyse large volumes of data, which in turn makes it easier to make decisions based on the data collected. This method, which is driven by data, improves recruiting, performance management, and workforce planning, which in turn enables organisations to make decisions that are informed and in line with their business objectives with greater efficiency. Robotics technologies, such as chatbots and virtual assistants, provide an enhanced candidate experience, which further increases the ability of organisations to recruit and retain top talent in a labour market that is very competitive. Additionally, the accessibility benefits of round-the-clock human resources support that are provided by robotics systems ensure that employees have access to HR services and information whenever and wherever they need it, which in turn increases overall employee happiness and engagement. Furthermore, robots has the potential to enhance human talents by automating ordinary jobs. This enables workers to concentrate on creative and difficult problem-solving, which in turn increases their level of job satisfaction and fulfilment.

Taking a look into the future, there are a number of potential future possibilities for research and practice in the subject of integrating robotics into human resource management. The first thing that has to be done is more research to determine the long-term effects that the adoption of robotics will have on the workforce. These effects will include the creation of new jobs, the development of new skills, and the performance of organisations. It is possible to gain significant insights into the changing nature of work and the role that human resource management plays in navigating these changes through longitudinal studies that track the adoption journeys of robotics on the part of organisations. Furthermore, research that focuses on the ethical implications of the integration of robots, such as privacy, data security, and algorithmic fairness, can provide valuable insights that can be used to inspire the formulation of rules and legislation that will ensure the adoption of robotics in a responsible manner. Furthermore, research that investigate the efficacy of various change management strategies in tackling employee resistance to the integration of robotics can provide organisations that are beginning this path with valuable insights that can be put into practice.

From a pragmatic point of view, organisations need to design comprehensive plans for the integration of robotics that are in line with their larger human resource management goals and the culture of the organisation. The investment in employee training and development programmes is one example of this. These programmes are designed to provide workers with the skills they need to succeed in a workplace that is enhanced by robotics. In addition, organisations have a responsibility to prioritise ethical issues throughout the entire process of adopting robots. This will ensure that there is openness, justice, and accountability in the utilisation of robotics technologies. Furthermore, the cultivation of a culture that encourages transparency and collaboration can assist in the reduction of employee resistance, as well as the development of a sense of ownership and participation among workers.

In conclusion, the incorporation of robotics within the framework of human resource management (HRM) represents a transformative potential for organisations to optimise their workforce management processes. Organisations have the ability to improve their efficiency, productivity, and decision-making in human resource management (HRM) by tackling the issues connected with the deployment of robotics and capitalising on the opportunities it brings. This can be accomplished while also supporting the well-being and growth of their workforce. Organisations have the ability to leverage the potential of robotics to create innovation and success in the digital age if they plan carefully, make investments, and work together.

REFERENCES

Aripin, Z., Matriadi, F., & Ermeila, S. (2024, February). OPTIMIZATION OF WORKER WORK ENVIRONMENT, ROBOTS, AND MARKETING STRATEGY: THE IMPACT OF DIGITAL-BASED SPATIOTEMPORAL DYNAMICS ON HUMAN RESOURCE MANAGEMENT (HRM). In Journal of Jabar Economic Society Networking Forum (Vol. 1, No. 3, pp. 33-49).

Basu, S., Majumdar, B., Mukherjee, K., Munjal, S., & Palaksha, C. (2023). Artificial intelligence–HRM interactions and outcomes: A systematic review and causal configurational explanation. *Human Resource Management Review*, 33(1), 100893. DOI:10.1016/j.hrmr.2022.100893

Budhwar, P., Malik, A., De Silva, M. T., & Thevisuthan, P. (2022). Artificial intelligence–challenges and opportunities for international HRM: A review and research agenda. *International Journal of Human Resource Management*, 33(6), 1065–1097. DOI:10.1080/09585192.2022.2035161

Dhatterwal, J. S., Kaswan, K. S., Pathak, J. P., & Balusamy, B. (2024). Robotics in Production and Its Impact on HR Functions. In The Role of HR in the Transforming Workplace (pp. 10-31). Productivity Press.

Fregnan, E., Ivaldi, S., & Scaratti, G. (2020). Hrm 4.0 and new managerial competences profile: The comau case. *Frontiers in Psychology*, 11, 578251. DOI:10.3389/fpsyg.2020.578251 PMID:33329228

Gärtner, C., & Kern, D. (2021). Smart HRM in 2030: Conversational HR, Connected Robotics, and Controlled Analytics. Managing Work in the Digital Economy: Challenges, Strategies and Practices for the Next Decade, 203-221.

Gunathunge, K. L. N. K., & Lakmal, K. G. P. (2019). *Industrial Revolution 4.0 and the future of HRM*. Contemporary Innovation in Management.

Haubold, A. K., Obst, L., & Bielefeldt, F. (2020). Introducing service robotics in inpatient geriatric care—A qualitative systematic review from a human resources perspective. Gruppe. Interaktion. Organisation. [GIO]. *Zeitschrift Für Angewandte Organisationspsychologie*, 51(3), 259–271.

Kambur, E., & Yildirim, T. (2023). From traditional to smart human resources management. *International Journal of Manpower*, 44(3), 422–452. DOI:10.1108/IJM-10-2021-0622

Kaur, J. (2024). AI-Augmented Medicine: Exploring the Role of Advanced AI Alongside Medical Professionals. In Advances in Computational Intelligence for the Healthcare Industry 4.0 (pp. 139-159). IGI Global.

Kaur, J. (2024). Revolutionizing Healthcare: Synergizing Cloud Robotics and Artificial Intelligence for Enhanced Patient Care. In Shaping the Future of Automation With Cloud-Enhanced Robotics (pp. 272-287). IGI Global.

Kaur, J. (2024). Robotics Rx: A Prescription for the Future of Healthcare. In Applications of Virtual and Augmented Reality for Health and Wellbeing (pp. 217-238). IGI Global. DOI:10.4018/979-8-3693-1123-3.ch012

Kaur, J. (2024). Smart Solutions for Health: Computational Intelligence Reshaping the Industry 4.0 Healthcare Paradigm. In Advances in Computational Intelligence for the Healthcare Industry 4.0 (pp. 194-211). IGI Global.

Knod, E. M.Jr, Wall, J. L., Daniels, J. P., Shane, H. M., & Wernimont, T. A. (1984). Robotics: Challenges for the human resources manager. *Business Horizons*, 27(2), 38–46. DOI:10.1016/0007-6813(84)90007-7

Libert, K., Mosconi, E., & Cadieux, N. (2020). Human-machine interaction and human resource management perspective for collaborative robotics implementation and adoption.

Liboni, L. B., Cezarino, L. O., Jabbour, C. J. C., Oliveira, B. G., & Stefanelli, N. O. (2019). Smart industry and the pathways to HRM 4.0: Implications for SCM. *Supply Chain Management*, 24(1), 124–146. DOI:10.1108/SCM-03-2018-0150

Mohamed, S. A., Mahmoud, M. A., Mahdi, M. N., & Mostafa, S. A. (2022). Improving efficiency and effectiveness of robotic process automation in human resource management. *Sustainability (Basel)*, 14(7), 3920. DOI:10.3390/su14073920

Molitor, M., & Renkema, M. (2022). Human-robot collaboration in a smart industry context: Does hrm matter? In *Smart Industry–Better Management* (pp. 105–123). Emerald Publishing Limited. DOI:10.1108/S1877-636120220000028008

Moniz, A. B. (2013). Organisational challenges of human–robot interaction systems in industry: human resources implications. In *Human resource management and technological challenges* (pp. 123–131). Springer International Publishing.

Ogbeibu, S., Emelifeonwu, J., Pereira, V., Oseghale, R., Gaskin, J., Sivarajah, U., & Gunasekaran, A. (2024). Demystifying the roles of organisational smart technology, artificial intelligence, robotics and algorithms capability: A strategy for green human resource management and environmental sustainability. *Business Strategy and the Environment*, 33(2), 369–388. DOI:10.1002/bse.3495

Omer, S. K. (2018). ORGANIZATION ROBOTS; TREND TO POST-HUMAN RESOURCES MANAGEMENT (POST-HRM). Journal of process management and new technologies, 6(1).

Pan, Y., & Froese, F. J. (2023). An interdisciplinary review of AI and HRM: Challenges and future directions. *Human Resource Management Review*, 33(1), 100924. DOI:10.1016/j.hrmr.2022.100924

Pattali, S. (2022). ROLE OF ARTIFICIAL INTELLIGENCE IN HRM. *International Journal of Early Childhood Special Education*, 14(5).

Rastogi, S., & Sharma, P. (2022). Revisiting Artificial Intelligence in HRM. SJCC Management Research Review, 110-128.

Stanley, D. S., & Aggarwal, V. (2019). Impact of disruptive technology on human resource management practices. *International Journal of Business Continuity and Risk Management*, 9(4), 350–361. DOI:10.1504/IJBCRM.2019.102608

Vrontis, D., Christofi, M., Pereira, V., Tarba, S., Makrides, A., & Trichina, E. (2022). Artificial intelligence, robotics, advanced technologies and human resource management: A systematic review. *International Journal of Human Resource Management*, 33(6), 1237–1266. DOI:10.1080/09585192.2020.1871398

Chapter 15
The Gig Economy:
Economic Innovations and Technological Advancements in Human Resource Management

Mohammad Badruddoza Talukder
https://orcid.org/0000-0001-7788-2732
International University of Business Agriculture and Technology, Bangladesh

Sharmin Akter Chowdhury
International University of Business Agriculture and Technology, Bangladesh

Musfiqur Rahoman Khan
Daffodil Institute of IT, Bangladesh

ABSTRACT

Technological developments and economic breakthroughs are propelling the gig economy, revolutionizing human resource management. Significant economic shifts include decentralized workplaces, flexible work arrangements, freelancing, and dynamic pricing patterns. The administration of gig workers is made more accessible by technological improvements, including digital HR tools, AI-driven recruitment, and virtual collaboration platforms. Considering these shifts, strategic workforce planning, regulatory compliance, and initiatives to engage and retain gig workers are imperative. HR departments must adjust to a diverse workforce by promoting inclusivity striking a balance between stability and flexibility. Technology-enabled integration of gig workers improves productivity and job satisfaction. To manage a diversified and regionally distributed workforce, businesses must adopt these advances to enhance their HR procedures. This flexibility is essential to keeping a competitive advantage in the changing labour market, where the gig economy is becoming increasingly important.

DOI: 10.4018/979-8-3693-4412-5.ch015

INTRODUCTION

Due to the rise of the gig economy in the twenty-first century, the typical characteristics of labour are experiencing a significant alteration. The absence of solid roles, the presence of freelance work, and the use of short-term contracts are some of the characteristics that P. A. Jain (2024) identifies regarding this phenomenon. This transformation is being driven by economic innovations and quick technological developments, both of which have played a vital part in changing human resource management, according to Hassan (2023). Both of these factors have been a driving force behind this transition. Following Joshi et al. (2024), examples of this tendency include using digital platforms such as Uber, Upwork, and TaskRabbit. In addition to providing workers with unprecedented flexibility and autonomy, these platforms allow employers to access a diverse talent pool readily available on demand. More widespread cultural developments, such as an increased preference for a work-life balance and the demand for a range of working experiences, are reflected in the rise of the gig economy (Tug & Basar, 2023). Kumar et al. (2024) state that the gig economy reflects these broader cultural shifts. This shift has not only been made feasible but has also been accelerated due to the growth of technology. As of April 2024, these three technologies—data analytics, machine learning, and artificial intelligence (AI)—have evolved into components of necessary contemporary human resource management methods. In the year 2024, Abdul Rani and Co. Through the provision of real-time performance tracking, the support of dynamic workforce management, and the connection of employment prospects with available positions, these technologies enhance the efficiency of the recruitment process. For example, Systems powered by artificial intelligence can sift through enormous amounts of data to determine which candidates best fit for particular activities.

Machine learning algorithms can also anticipate labour patterns and improve scheduling (Khosroeva et al., 2024). On the other hand, several significant problems are associated with the gig economy. According to Vernyuy (2024), gig work generally lacks the security and privileges typically associated with full-time employment. Gig work is also known as the gig economy. The advantages included under this category include retirement plans and health insurance, amongst other things.

Consequently, concerns have been expressed about the feasibility and fairness of the gig economy, which has led to requests for new legislative frameworks to protect workers in the gig economy. These concerns have been brought about at the same time. There are also concerns about privacy and algorithmic bias that arise as a result of the reliance on technology and data. These issues must be addressed to ensure all employees are treated equitably (Kaushik, 2024; Badruddoza et al., 2024)).

To quote Nair et al. (2024), to provide a comprehensive analysis of the gig economy's impact on contemporary labour markets, this study aims to investigate both the advantages and difficulties presented by the gig economy. The examination of case studies and empirical data will provide insights into how businesses can strategically manage this changing landscape, as well as how policymakers can establish frameworks that promote a gig economy that is both fair and sustainable (Oladipo et al., 2024: Mohammad et al., 2024b). The examination of case studies and empirical data will provide these insights. Auguste et al. (2023) state that, in the end, it is necessary to understand these relationships to maximize the positive features of the gig economy and minimize the negative aspects. This is the case to maximize the gig economy's positive aspects.

LITERATURE REVIEW

Theoretical Overview

Much research has been conducted on the gig economy, particularly regarding its influence on labour markets, the incorporation of technology into human resource management, and the socioeconomic ramifications (Shah & Sarif, 2023). Meijerink and Keegan (2019) note that numerous scholars have brought attention to the revolutionary potential of the gig economy, which is powered by digital platforms that make it possible to work flexibly and on demand. As a result of these platforms, which make use of developments in artificial intelligence (AI) and machine learning, the organization and management of work have undergone substantial transformations, resulting in the creation of new opportunities for both organizations and employees (Behl et al., 2022; Mohammad et al., 2024a). The benefits of working freelance are the subject of a sizeable amount of published research. Gig workers can determine their schedules and select activities that match their skills well, leading to increased job satisfaction (Joshi et al., 2024). Flexibility and autonomy are two aspects that are frequently listed as advantages of gig employment. In addition, businesses reap the benefits of decreased labour costs and the capacity to scale their workforce in response to fluctuations in demand rapidly (Gusai et al., 2022).

On the other hand, there is a substantial amount of controversy over the disadvantages of the gig economy. Several academics contend that gig work frequently does not provide the same security and benefits typically associated with full-time employment. These benefits include health insurance, retirement plans, and paid leave (Zalizko et al., 2022). Gig workers can experience stress and financial instability due to this precariousness. In addition, worries over the possibility of exploitation and the deterioration of labour standards in the gig economy brought to light the necessity of establishing solid legislative frameworks to safeguard workers' rights (Vu & Nguyen, 2024).

Incorporating technology into human resource practices is yet another important field of research. Okolo et al. (2023) state that artificial intelligence and machine learning revolutionize recruitment, performance monitoring, and labour management. These technologies improve the efficiency and accuracy of matching people to positions, forecasting labour needs, and optimizing task allocation (Li, 2023; Mohammad et al., 2023). It is also possible to maximize task allocation. That said, there are also problems related to algorithmic bias and privacy concerns, which can lead to unjust treatment and discrimination (Huđek & Širec, 2023). There are a variety of regulatory solutions to the gig economy around the world, which reflects the various approaches to striking a balance between innovation and worker protection. According to Huang et al.'s 2020 research, comparative assessments imply that effective regulation should assure equitable salaries, employment stability, and access to benefits without restricting the flexibility and innovation that are characteristic of gig work. In a nutshell, the research that has been done on the gig economy unearths a complicated terrain that is filled with both potential and challenges. Technological improvements and economic innovations have made the emergence of flexible, on-demand labour possible. Yet, these developments have also brought about significant concerns concerning the rights of workers and the regulatory frameworks that govern them (Talukder, 2024). The findings of this review highlight the importance of doing ongoing research and developing flexible rules to guarantee that the gig economy will grow in a way that benefits both individuals and enterprises.

Introduction to the Gig Economy

The gig economy, which is also known as the "on-demand," "sharing," or "freelance" economy, is a substantial departure from traditional employment arrangements. It has the potential to drastically disrupt the way individuals work and how businesses function (Talukder, 2021). Short-term contracts, freelance employment, and autonomous, on-demand labour are the defining characteristics of the gig economy, which is primarily made possible by digital platforms and technical developments (Talukder, Kumar, Kaiser, et al., 2024). In recent years, this developing economic paradigm has garnered much attention, and it has been altering labour markets and questioning conventional concepts of work (Flanagan, 2017). Throughout history, the gig economy may trace its origins to various transitory or project-based job arrangements. According to Özbilgin et al. (2024), the modern manifestation of this phenomenon has been boosted by the widespread availability of digital technology and the Internet.

Digital platforms such as Uber, Airbnb, Upwork, and TaskRabbit have facilitated gig labour and connected independent contractors with individuals or organizations that require particular services or tasks (Talukder & Kumar, 2024). According to Talukder (2024), these platforms create a marketplace where individuals can sell their skills or services flexibly and frequently temporarily. According to Talukder et al. (2023), the gig economy is characterized by its emphasis on flexibility and autonomy, one of its distinguishing characteristics. Gig workers, in contrast to those who pursue regular full-time employment, can choose when, where, and how much they work. According to Talukder et al. (2023), this flexibility highly appeals to many individuals, including freelancers and independent contractors, students, retirees, and those seeking additional money. According to Das et al. (2024), many people find that gig labour provides them with the opportunity to improve their work-life balance, pursue initiatives that they are passionate about, or supplement other sources of income. The expansion of the gig economy has been significantly fueled by technological advancements, which have played a significant role. For example, artificial intelligence (AI), machine learning, and advanced data analytics have enabled digital platforms to match people with jobs, optimize pricing and scheduling, and provide real-time performance monitoring (Liu et al., 2023; Kumar et al., 2024). For instance, artificial intelligence systems can evaluate enormous volumes of data to match freelance writers with suitable writing projects or connect drivers with passengers based on location and demand trends (Duggan et al., 2021). With these technologies, the scalability and accessibility of gig work have been significantly increased, resulting in new opportunities for enterprises and individuals (Gusai et al., 2022). There are a variety of difficulties and uncertainties associated with the gig economy, even though it has many benefits. According to Song and Jo (2023), one of the most significant issues is the absence of job stability and perks usually associated with traditional employment.

In many cases, gig workers are not eligible for benefits such as health insurance, retirement plans, paid leave, or any other perks offered to full-time employees. Gig workers can be vulnerable to revenue swings, economic downturns, and unanticipated expenses due to the lack of financial security they afford themselves. Not only that, but the classification of gig workers as independent contractors rather than employees creates problems regarding labour rights, salary protections, and access to social safety nets (Ncamane, 2023).

In addition, the gig economy has inspired discussions over the deterioration of labour standards and the possibility of exploitation (Jeon et al., 2021). Some opponents have argued that gig workers are exposed to unpredictable working conditions, poor wages, and little bargaining power (Barrios et al., 2022). Concerns regarding income inequality and the rising divide between those who benefit from the gig economy and those who do not are raised due to this. It is common for regulatory frameworks to have difficulty keeping up with the rapid expansion of the gig economy. This results in uncertainty and ambiguity surrounding the legal rights and duties of platform firms and gig workers (Shibata, 2020).

There has been a significant shift in how individuals work and businesses function in the 21st century, and this shift is represented by the gig economy (1921). Through the provision of flexibility, autonomy, and access to a global talent marketplace, the gig economy has transformed the conventional employment models that have existed for a long time. This has resulted in the creation of new opportunities for both individuals and businesses. On the other hand, it also presents substantial issues regarding job security, benefits, labour rights, and regulatory frameworks (Puspitarini & Basit, 2020). As the gig economy continues to develop, it is vital to do an in-depth analysis of its impact and investigate potential solutions to guarantee that it is inclusive, equitable, and sustainable for all parties involved (Prassl, 2018).

DIGITAL PLATFORMS AND GIG WORK

According to Dunn (2020), digital platforms have profoundly altered employment patterns and contributed to the gig economy's growth. This has resulted in a revolution in the organization and performance of labour. According to Alacovska et al. (2024), this chapter examines the significant role that digital platforms play in supporting gig employment and the impact of these platforms on the labour market and workforce dynamics.

The Rise of Digital Platforms

The gig economy has become increasingly dependent on digital platforms like Uber, Airbnb, Upwork, and TaskRabbit. These platforms offer online marketplaces where individuals can offer their skills or services flexibly and frequently transitory (Waldkirch et al., 2021). These platforms connect gig workers directly with clients and customers through the Internet and mobile technologies. This makes transactions more accessible and allows labour to be completed remotely or on demand (Churchill & Craig, 2019).

Critical Characteristics of Digital Platforms

Digital platforms share several key characteristics that make them well-suited for gig work:

- **Accessibility**: Digital platforms are accessible to a broad spectrum of persons, making it possible for anyone with an internet connection and relevant talents to participate in the gig economy (Straughan & Bissell, 2022).
- **Flexibility**: Gig workers can select when, where, and how much they work, which gives them superior control over their schedules and the ability to maintain a healthy work-life balance.
- **Algorithms for Matching**: Gig workers are matched with jobs based on their talents, availability, and location through sophisticated algorithms and data analytics (Kaushik, 2024). This ensures that services are delivered in a timely and efficient manner.
- **Rating and Review Systems**: Digital platforms frequently feature rating and review systems that enable customers and employees to submit feedback on their experiences. This helps cultivate trust and accountability within the platform's ecosystem (Ahamad Nawawi et al., 2023).

Impact on Employment Patterns

It is becoming increasingly difficult to differentiate between traditional full-time employment and gig work due to the expansion of digital platforms, which has dramatically impacted employment patterns. As a principal source of income, many people utilize employment in the gig economy. On the other hand, other people utilize gig labour as a means of supplementing their current jobs or pursuing initiatives that they are passionate about (Mironova et al., 2022).

Worker Flexibility and Autonomy

According to Joshi et al. (2024), one of the most significant benefits of digital platforms is the freedom and liberty they provide to gig workers through online platforms. In contrast to standard employment agreements, gig workers can determine their schedules, select the projects they wish to work on and choose the clients they would like to engage with. People who value having control over when, where, and how they work will likely find this flexibility appealing (Qiu et al., 2023). Freelancers, independent contractors, students, and retirees are some individuals who appreciate this flexibility.

Challenges and Concerns

Although there are numerous advantages to using digital platforms for gig labour, there are also several serious issues and concerns that need to be addressed:

- **Job insecurity**: Job insecurity is a common problem among gig workers, as they frequently do not receive the benefits and job security typically associated with full-time employment. These advantages include health insurance, retirement plans, and paid leave. According to Tug and Basar (2023), this exposes individuals to the risk of experiencing income and economic uncertainty swings.
- **Regulatory Uncertainty**: The designation of gig workers as independent contractors rather than employees raises problems regarding labour rights, wage protections, and access to social safety nets. This regulatory uncertainty has to be addressed. It is common for regulatory regimes to have difficulty keeping up with the rapid expansion of the gig economy. This results in uncertainty and ambiguity surrounding the legal rights and duties of gig workers and platform firms (Hajiheydari & Delgosha, 2024).
- **Algorithmic prejudice and Discrimination**: There are worries regarding the possibility of algorithmic prejudice and discrimination inside digital platforms. Automated algorithms may perpetuate existing inequities and biases in employment (Dedema & Rosenbaum, 2024).

Economic Impact of the Gig Economy

According to Joshi et al. (2024), the gig economy, characterized by jobs that are performed on a freelance basis and short-term contracts, has radically transformed the economic landscape by changing traditional employment arrangements and company models. This chapter investigates the financial repercussions of the gig economy and its consequences on various stakeholders, such as enterprises, workers, and the economy (Auguste et al., 2023). By providing businesses with increased flexibility in managing their workers, the gig economy has contributed to its expansion (April, 2024). As a result of the ability to rapidly scale up or down in response to variable demand, businesses can reduce the overhead expenditures involved with keeping a full-time workforce. Because of this flexibility, companies can quickly adjust to shifting market conditions and have access to a comprehensive workforce pool that possesses specialized talents when required (Li, 2023). In addition, the gig economy has resulted in the addition of new employment options as well as innovation potential. Individuals have been given the ability to monetize their skills and talents through digital platforms and online marketplaces, which has resulted in the development of new industries and business models (Endress, 2024). According to Najiha and Herman (2024), freelancers, independent contractors, and gig workers have emerged as significant contributors to the economy, as they are the primary drivers of innovation and entrepreneurship in various industries.

According to Hassan (2023), the gig economy allows businesses to realize considerable cost savings compared to traditional employment models. Companies can cut the labour costs, overhead expenses, and administrative difficulties involved with hiring and managing full-time employees by utilizing freelance workers and independent contractors (V. Jain & Rani, 2024). In addition, firms can avoid making long-term obligations such as salary, benefits, and retirement plans, which results in more financial flexibility and agility. Workers have more control over their work schedules and careers because the gig economy offers them greater flexibility and autonomy. Freelancers can select when, where, and how much they work, enabling them to pursue numerous revenue sources, balance their personal and professional obligations, and investigate various employment alternatives. According to Kim et al. (2023), this flexibility appeals to many individuals, including retirees, students, freelancers, and professionals looking to augment their income.

Nevertheless, the gig economy also raises issues regarding the unequal distribution of income and the lack of job security. Gig workers commonly lack the job stability, benefits, and protections typically provided to traditional full-time employees. These benefits and protections include health insurance, retirement plans, and unemployment benefits. In addition, gig work is frequently characterized by unpredictability in income streams, irregular work hours, and restricted access to social safety nets, which can result in financial instability and economic vulnerability for certain workers (Huđek & Širec, 2023). There have been issues in terms of regulation brought about by the rapid rise of the gig economy, as well as questions regarding the rights and protections of workers. There have been discussions regarding the entitlement of gig workers to minimum wages, overtime pay, and other benefits due to the designation of gig workers as independent contractors rather than employees. According to Khan and Saqib (2024), policymakers are currently wrestling with the issue of how to update existing labour laws and regulatory frameworks to guarantee that gig workers are provided essential safeguards and rights in the context of the growing economy.

AI and Automation in Gig Work

The gig economy, comprised of temporary, flexible jobs and frequently made feasible by digital platforms, has been severely impacted by artificial intelligence (AI) and robotics (Tug & Basar, 2023). These technological advancements are causing a shift in how gig work is organized, managed, and carried out. Consequently, this alters the opportunities and difficulties available to employees and companies (Braganza et al., 2022). (Spencer, 2024) This chapter examines the roles that artificial intelligence (AI) and technology play in the gig economy, with a particular emphasis on how these factors influence the management of workers, the quality of jobs, and the future of work.

How Can AI Help Match Workers With Gigs?

One of the most significant ways artificial intelligence affects gig labour is by making it more straightforward for workers to identify employment opportunities. An extensive amount of data, including worker profiles, task needs, and user reviews, is analyzed by sophisticated algorithms to facilitate a more streamlined assignment process (Nimmagadda et al., 2024). This guarantees that workers are offered positions that are a better fit for their abilities and preferences, contributing to increased levels of happiness and productivity within the workforce. Examples of ride-sharing businesses that use artificial intelligence include Uber and Lyft, which connect drivers with passengers based on factors like geography, traffic, and driver availability, among other considerations (Bankole Popoola, 2024).

Task Management and Scheduling Can Be Automated

According to Mabungela (2023), automation is a game-changer in the gig economy since it considerably improves job administration and scheduling. Complex scheduling requirements are expertly managed by automated systems, which consider the availability of workers, the urgency of the operation, and the proximity of places. By doing so, employers can cut administrative expenses, and gig workers can enjoy more consistent and adaptable work schedules. According to Tyson and Zysman (2022), platforms such as TaskRabbit and Upwork use automation to allocate assignments and manage workflows, guaranteeing that operations run smoothly and efficiently.

Getting More Done and Improving Performance

Tools powered by artificial intelligence are increasingly being utilized to monitor and enhance the work of gig workers. By providing feedback and analyzing data in real time, these tools enable workers to improve their level of productivity and the quality of service they give (Sureth, 2024). Artificial intelligence is used by delivery services such as DoorDash and Postmates to monitor arrival times, determine the most efficient routes, and provide feedback to couriers regarding their performance. According to Sodiya et al. (2024), through this loop of continuous input, workers can enhance their skills and become more proficient at what they do.

Making Sure There is Fairness and Openness

Artificial intelligence (AI) and technology have the potential to play a significant role in promoting justice and transparency in the gig work industry. The use of these technologies helps to speed operations, reduce the impact of human bias, and ensure that workers are compensated fairly. By way of illustration, automated dispute settlement solutions can handle arguments between employees and customers fairly and impartially by utilizing predetermined criteria and data. Another factor that contributes to the maintenance of responsibility and confidence in gig platforms is the presence of rating and review systems that are both clear and understandable (Özbilgin et al., 2024).

Problems and Moral Points to Think

There are a lot of positive aspects to integrating artificial intelligence and robotics in gig labour, but there are also some negative aspects and ethical concerns to consider. The possibility that people would lose their jobs due to automating routine tasks is a significant cause for concern. This leads me to wonder whether or not some gig jobs will continue to exist in the long run, as well as whether or not workers will need to acquire new skills to work in new roles. According to Adeola Olusola Ajayi-Nifise et al. (2024), data-based algorithms can also result in privacy and surveillance issues. This is because the behaviours of gig workers are continuously monitored and analyzed.

Consider the possibility of algorithmic prejudice as another social issue to consider. AI systems can potentially promote prejudices and injustice, which can be detrimental to some groups of workers if they are not constructed with care. To mitigate these threats, it is of the utmost importance to guarantee that artificial intelligence and automation tools are developed and utilized equitably and incorporate all individuals (Wu & Huang, 2024).

What Does the Future Hold?

The use of artificial intelligence and robotics in gig labour is anticipated to continue to advance and become more integrated. Artificial intelligence (AI) systems are expected to become more innovative and better manage complex occupations as technology advances. This will provide us with more information about how workers interact with one another. According to Singh and Bisen (2023), this will not only make gig platforms more effective and scalable, but it will also make new opportunities available to workers as well as enterprises.

It is crucial, however, to establish a balance between making the most of technology to your benefit and maintaining the human element of self-employment. (Shafik & Lakshmi, 2024) Policymakers, platform owners, and other interested parties must collaborate to formulate regulations that safeguard workers' rights, guarantee that they are adequately paid, and stimulate the adoption of long-term employment practices.

RECOMMENDATIONS

1. **Develop Comprehensive Job Descriptions and Clear Expectations**: Make sure that gig work job listings are accurate and comprehensive, defining the project's parameters (i.e., necessary skills, deadlines, and performance standards). This lessens misconceptions and draws in the proper talent.
2. **Leverage Digital Platforms and Technologies**: To find a large skill pool, use niche gig economy sites like Fiverr, Freelancer, and Upwork. Invest in hiring technologies that use AI to match candidates, conduct computerized skill evaluations, and facilitate effective communication.
3. **Create a Strong Employer Brand**: Establish a solid reputation as a dependable and appealing gig employer. Emphasize the advantages of working for your organization, such as competitive salary, fascinating tasks, and chances for career advancement. Promote your brand by utilizing professional networks and social media.
4. **Implement a Rigorous Vetting Process**: Create a comprehensive screening procedure that involves examining references, completing video interviews, and evaluating portfolios. Use review sites and ranking systems to evaluate the dependability and calibre of possible gig workers.
5. **Foster Long-term Relationships with Top Gig Workers**: Create a network of productive freelancers by staying in touch and providing repeat work. To ensure that your best gig workers feel appreciated and are more likely to select your tasks, consider developing a preferred freelancer program.
6. **Ensure Fair and Timely Compensation**: Repay gig workers promptly and equitably. Pay policies that are open, honest, and competitive draw in top personnel and foster loyalty. Bonuses should be given out for achieving great work or meeting deadlines.
7. **Provide Clear Guidelines and Support**: Provide gig workers with the tools and assistance they require to be successful. Assign a point of contact for inquiries or problems, give access to the needed resources, and establish clear instructions.

Frequent check-ins may guarantee that workers feel supported and that projects remain on course.

8. **Facilitate Seamless Integration with Full-time Teams**: Establishing open lines of communication and including gig workers in team processes will help to foster productive collaboration between gig workers and full-time staff. To preserve transparency and coordinate efforts, use project management software.

9. **Focus on Diversity and Inclusion**: Make an effort to increase the diversity of your gig workforce by contacting marginalized groups and ensuring your hiring procedure is inclusive. A varied gig workforce can improve innovation and problem-solving by bringing a range of viewpoints and talents.

10. **Stay Informed about Legal and Regulatory Requirements**: Stay informed about the most recent laws and regulations in your area about gig employment. Ensure labour regulations are followed to avoid legal trouble and give gig workers a fair workplace. This entails knowing tax responsibilities, job classification, and any necessary benefits.

11. **Offer Training and Development Opportunities**: Give your gig workers access to training and opportunities for upskilling as an investment in their professional development. This raises the calibre of the work produced, fosters loyalty, and motivates gig workers to select their projects over others.

12. **Collect and Act on Feedback**: Get input from gig workers regularly regarding their experience working for your business. Make adjustments to your hiring and management procedures based on this feedback. To keep the working relationship positive, any problems must be addressed quickly.

13. **Adapt to Technological Advancements**: Keep up with technological developments affecting the gig economy. Adopt technologies that increase the effectiveness of managing gig workers overall, expedite administrative processes, and boost distant communication.

By following these suggestions, businesses may attract top-tier gig workers and build enduring, fruitful partnerships by optimizing their talent acquisition tactics in the gig economy.

Figure 1. Conceptual Model

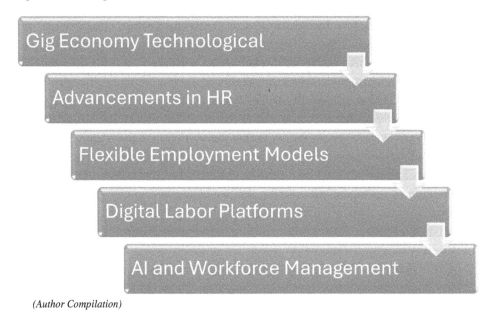

(Author Compilation)

CONCLUSION

Finding talent is a dynamic and ever-changing business challenge in the gig economy. New methods of finding, hiring, and managing personnel are required as the gig economy grows. To draw in and keep top gig workers, businesses must embrace digital platforms, use cutting-edge technologies, and create all-encompassing strategies. Creating a great employer brand, defining job roles clearly, and offering equitable pay is crucial to winning over gig workers' confidence and loyalty. In addition, cultivating enduring connections and smoothly assimilating freelancers into permanent teams can improve output and cooperation.

It is essential to stay current on legal and regulatory changes to ensure compliance, safeguard the business, and ensure the safety of gig workers. The gig labour may be strengthened further by emphasizing diversity and inclusion, providing training opportunities, and aggressively seeking feedback. Businesses that innovate and adapt will be better positioned to attract top personnel and experience long-term success as technology breakthroughs continue influencing the gig economy. By implementing these best practices, businesses may successfully negotiate the challenges of hiring in the gig economy and maintain a competitive advantage in a labour market that is evolving quickly.

REFERENCES

Abdul Rani, A. A., Muda, R., Hanif, A., & Abd Rashid, A. (2024). Enhancing Consumer and Family Economic Well-Being in ASEAN: The Role of Technological Advancement and Institutional Quality in Navigating the Informal Economy. *Malaysian Journal of Consumer and Family Economics*, 32(1), 480–514. DOI:10.60016/majcafe.v32.19

Ajayi-Nifise, A. O., Odeyemi, O., Mhlongo, N. Z., Falaiye, T., Elufioye, O. A., Awonuga, K. F., & Nwankwo, E. E. (2024). The future of accounting: Predictions on automation and AI integration. *International Journal of Science and Research Archive*, 11(1), 2063–2071. DOI:10.30574/ijsra.2024.11.1.0275

Ahamad Nawawi, N. H., Ramli, R., Khalid, N., & Abdul Rashid, S. F. (2023). Understanding The Presence of the Gig Economy in Malaysia. *Malaysian Journal of Consumer and Family Economics*, 31(1), 274–293. DOI:10.60016/majcafe.v31.11

Alacovska, A., Bucher, E., & Fieseler, C. (2024). A Relational Work Perspective on the Gig Economy: Doing Creative Work on Digital Labour Platforms. *Work, Employment and Society*, 38(1), 161–179. DOI:10.1177/09500170221103146

April, K. (2024). Precarious Work in the Gig Economy: Diversity, Race and Indigeneity Lenses. In Meliou, E., Vassilopoulou, J., & Ozbilgin, M. F. (Eds.), *Diversity and Precarious Work During Socioeconomic Upheaval* (1st ed., pp. 137–162). Cambridge University Press., DOI:10.1017/9781108933070.008

Auguste, D., Roll, S., & Despard, M. (2023). Democratizing the Economy or Introducing Economic Risk? Gig Work During the COVID-19 Pandemic. *Work and Occupations*, 07308884231202032, 07308884231202032. Advance online publication. DOI:10.1177/07308884231202032

Badruddoza Talukder, M., Kumar, S., Misra, L. I., & Firoj Kabir, . (2024). Determining the role of eco-tourism service quality, tourist satisfaction, and destination loyalty: A case study of Kuakata beach. *Acta Scientiarum Polonorum. Administratio Locorum*, 23(1), 133–151. DOI:10.31648/aspal.9275

Popoola, B. (2024). *AI AND AUTOMATION*. Unpublished. DOI:10.13140/RG.2.2.15359.21929

Barrios, J. M., Hochberg, Y. V., & Yi, H. (2022). Launching with a parachute: The gig economy and new business formation. *Journal of Financial Economics*, 144(1), 22–43. DOI:10.1016/j.jfineco.2021.12.011

Behl, A., Rajagopal, K., Sheorey, P., & Mahendra, A. (2022). Barriers to entry of gig workers in the gig platforms: Exploring the dark side of the gig economy. *Aslib Journal of Information Management*, 74(5), 818–839. DOI:10.1108/AJIM-08-2021-0235

Beretta, G. (2021). The New Rules for Reporting by Sharing and Gig Economy Platforms Under the OECD and EU Initiatives. *EC Tax Review*, 30(1), 31–38. DOI:10.54648/ECTA2021004

Braganza, A., Chen, W., Canhoto, A., & Sap, S. (2022). Gigification, job engagement and satisfaction: The moderating role of AI enabled system automation in operations management. *Production Planning and Control*, 33(16), 1534–1547. DOI:10.1080/09537287.2021.1882692

Churchill, B., & Craig, L. (2019). Gender in the gig economy: Men and women using digital platforms to secure work in Australia. *Journal of Sociology (Melbourne, Vic.)*, 55(4), 741–761. DOI:10.1177/1440783319894060

Das, I. R., Talukder, M. B., & Kumar, S. (2024). Implication of Artificial Intelligence in Hospitality Marketing. In Kumar, S., Talukder, M. B., & Pego, A. (Eds.), *Advances in Hospitality, Tourism, and the Services Industry* (pp. 291–310). IGI Global., DOI:10.4018/979-8-3693-1978-9.ch014

Dedema, M., & Rosenbaum, H. (2024). Socio-technical issues in the platform-mediated gig economy: A systematic literature review: An Annual Review of Information Science and Technology (ARIST) paper. *Journal of the Association for Information Science and Technology*, 75(3), 344–374. DOI:10.1002/asi.24868

Duggan, J., McDonnell, A., Sherman, U., & Carbery, R. (2021). *Work in the Gig Economy: A Research Overview* (1st ed.). Routledge., DOI:10.4324/9780429351488

Dunn, M. (2020). Making gigs work: Digital platforms, job quality and worker motivations. *New Technology, Work and Employment*, 35(2), 232–249. DOI:10.1111/ntwe.12167

Endress, T. (2024). Disruption and the Gig Economy: What's Next? In Endress, T., & Badir, Y. F. (Eds.), *Business and Management in Asia: Disruption and Change* (pp. 109–122). Springer Nature Singapore., DOI:10.1007/978-981-99-9371-0_7

Sodiya, E. O., Umoga, U. J., Amoo, O. O., & Atadoga, A. (2024). AI-driven warehouse automation: A comprehensive review of systems. *GSC Advanced Research and Reviews*, 18(2), 272–282. DOI:10.30574/gscarr.2024.18.2.0063

Flanagan, F. (2017). Symposium on work in the 'gig' economy: Introduction. *Economic and Labour Relations Review*, 28(3), 378–381. DOI:10.1177/1035304617724302

Gusai, O. P., Rani, A., & Yadav, P. (2022). Digital Industrial Revolution 4.0 and Sustaining Gig Economy: Challenges and Opportunities Ahead. In Gupta, A., Tewary, T., & Gopalakrishnan, B. N. (Eds.), *Sustainability in the Gig Economy* (pp. 187–198). Springer Nature Singapore., DOI:10.1007/978-981-16-8406-7_14

Hajiheydari, N., & Delgosha, M. S. (2024). Investigating engagement and burnout of gig-workers in the age of algorithms: An empirical study in digital labor platforms. *Information Technology & People*. Advance online publication. DOI:10.1108/ITP-11-2022-0873

Hassan, R. (2023). *Work Arrangements in the Informal Sector and Gig Economy/Digital Platform Economy in Egypt*. Unpublished. DOI:10.13140/RG.2.2.24113.19041

Huang, N., Burtch, G., Hong, Y., & Pavlou, P. A. (2020). Unemployment and Worker Participation in the Gig Economy: Evidence from an Online Labor Market. *Information Systems Research*, 31(2), 431–448. DOI:10.1287/isre.2019.0896

Huđek, I., & Širec, K. (2023). The terminology and the concept of the gig economy. *Ekonomski Pregled*, 74(1), 34–58. DOI:10.32910/ep.74.1.2

Jain, P. A. (2024). The Gig Economy: Disruption, Innovation, and Economic Evolution. *Educational Administration: Theory and Practice*, 5133–5140. DOI:10.53555/kuey.v30i5.3755

Jain, V., & Rani, A. (2024). Labor Market Trends in the Gig Economy: Implications for Workers and Employers. *International Journal for Research Publication and Seminar*, 15(2), 50–54. DOI:10.36676/jrps.v15.i2.08

Jeon, S., Liu, H., & Ostrovsky, Y. (2021). Measuring the gig economy in Canada using administrative data. *The Canadian Journal of Economics. Revue Canadienne d'Economique*, 54(4), 1638–1666. DOI:10.1111/caje.12558

Joshi, A., Jain, S., & Gupta, P. K. (2024). Challenges and impact of the gig economy. *Sustainable Economies*, 2(2), 96. DOI:10.62617/se.v2i2.96

Kaushik, A. (2024). Comprehensive Impact of On-Demand Platforms: Examining the Gig Economy \'s Influence on Specialized Professionals, Work-Life Balance, and Gig Workers\' Perspectives. *International Journal for Research in Applied Science and Engineering Technology*, 12(1), 552–559. DOI:10.22214/ijraset.2024.58005

Khan, M., & Saqib, Z. (2024). Emerging Voice Mechanisms in Asian Gig Economies: Implications for Gig Workers' Work and Life. In Chan, X. W., Shang, S., & Lu, L. (Eds.), *Work-Life Research in the Asia-Pacific* (pp. 47–76). Springer Nature Switzerland., DOI:10.1007/978-3-031-52795-1_3

Khosroeva, N. I., Mamsurova, L. G., Kuchieva, I. Kh., Begieva, A. Sh., & Bekmur-zaeva, Z. Kh. (2024). Problems of Human Resource Management of the Innovation Economy. In Sergi, B. S., Popkova, E. G., Ostrovskaya, A. A., Chursin, A. A., & Ragulina, Y. V. (Eds.), *Ecological Footprint of the Modern Economy and the Ways to Reduce It* (pp. 279–283). Springer Nature Switzerland., DOI:10.1007/978-3-031-49711-7_47

Kim, M.-S., Oh, J., Sim, J., Yun, B.-Y., & Yoon, J.-H. (2023). Association between exposure to violence, job stress and depressive symptoms among gig economy workers in Korea. *Annals of Occupational and Environmental Medicine*, 35, e43. DOI:10.35371/aoem.2023.35.e43 PMID:38029274

Kumar, S., Talukder, M. B., & Kaiser, F. (2024). Artificial Intelligence in Business: Negative Social Impacts. In *Demystifying the Dark Side of AI in Business* (pp. 81-97). IGI Global. https://doi.org/DOI:10.4018/979-8-3693-0724-3.ch005

Kumar, S., Talukder, M. B., & Pego, A. (Eds.). (2024). *Utilizing Smart Technology and AI in Hybrid Tourism and Hospitality*. IGI Global., DOI:10.4018/979-8-3693-1978-9

Kumar, S., Talukder, M. B., Kabir, F., & Kaiser, F. (2024). Challenges and Sustainability of Green Finance in the Tourism Industry: Evidence from Bangladesh. In Taneja, S., Kumar, P., Grima, S., Ozen, E., & Sood, K. (Eds.), (pp. 97–111). Advances in Finance, Accounting, and Economics. IGI Global., DOI:10.4018/979-8-3693-1388-6.ch006

Li, S. (2023). The Gig Economy and Labour Market Dynamics. *Advances in Economics. Management and Political Sciences*, 61(1), 275–281. DOI:10.54254/2754-1169/61/20231285

Liu, K., Feng, Z., & Zhang, Q. (2023). Examining the role of digitalization and gig economy in achieving a low carbon society: An empirical study across nations. *Frontiers in Environmental Science*, 11, 1197708. DOI:10.3389/fenvs.2023.1197708

Mabungela, M. (2023). Artificial Intelligence (AI) and Automation in the World of Work: A Threat to Employees? *Research in Social Sciences and Technology*, 8(4), 135–146. DOI:10.46303/ressat.2023.37

Meijerink, J., & Keegan, A. (2019). Conceptualizing human resource management in the gig economy: Toward a platform ecosystem perspective. *Journal of Managerial Psychology*, 34(4), 214–232. DOI:10.1108/JMP-07-2018-0277

Mironova, S. M., Kozhemyakin, D. V., & Ponomarchenko, A. E. (2022). Adaptation of the legal regulation of labor, civil, tax relations to the gig economy. *Law Enforcement Review*, 6(4), 314–329. DOI:10.52468/2542-1514.2022.6(4).314-329

Mohammad Badruddoza Talukder. Firoj Kabir, K. M., & Das, I. R. (2023). Emerging Concepts of Artificial Intelligence in the Hotel Industry: A Conceptual Paper. *International Journal of Research Publication and Reviews, Vol 4, no*, pp 1765-1769. https://doi.org/https://doi.org/10.55248/gengpi.4.923.92451

Mohammad Badruddoza Talukder. Sanjeev Kumar, I. R. Das. (2024a). Implications of Blockchain Technology- Based Cryptocurrency in the cloud for the Hospitality Industry. In *Emerging Trends in Cloud Computing Analytics, Scalability, and Service Models* (p. 19). DOI:10.4018/979-8-3693-0900-1.ch018

Mohammad Badruddoza Talukder. Sanjeev Kumar, I. R. Das. (2024b). Perspectives of Digital Marketing for the Restaurant Industry. In *Advancements in Socialized and Digital Media Communications* (p. 17). DOI:10.4018/979-8-3693-0855-4.ch009

Nair, A. J., Manohar, S., & Chaudhry, R. (2024). Role of Knowledge Management in Enhancing the Effectiveness of the Gig Economy. In Ordóñez De Pablos, P., Almunawar, M. N., & Anshari, M. (Eds.), (pp. 161–175). Advances in Finance, Accounting, and Economics. IGI Global., DOI:10.4018/979-8-3693-1942-0.ch009

Najiha, I., & Herman, S. (2024). Factors Affecting the Gig Economy of Labor Productivity in Ride Hailing Services. *Digital Economics Review*, 1(1). Advance online publication. DOI:10.58968/der.v1i1.474

Ncamane, N. (2023). Digital platform workers and the conundrum of the definition of an 'employee' in the era of the Fourth Industrial Revolution. *South African Mercantile Law Journal*, 35(1), 1–26. DOI:10.47348/SAMLJ/v35/i1a1

Nimmagadda, B., Vangaveti, Y., Aaluri, S., Mallikarjuna Rao, Ch., & Singh, B. (2024). An Analytical study on Navigating Sustainability Challenges and Opportunities in the era of AI and the Gig Economy. *MATEC Web of Conferences, 392*, 01044. DOI:10.1051/matecconf/202439201044

Okolo, C. V., Wen, J., & Susaeta, A. (2023). Maximizing natural resource rent economics: The role of human capital development, financial sector development, and open-trade economies in driving technological innovation. *Environmental Science and Pollution Research International*, 31(3), 4453–4477. DOI:10.1007/s11356-023-31373-z PMID:38103137

Oladipo Olugbenga Adekoya, Adedayo Adefemi, Olawe Alaba Tula, Nwabueze Kelvin Nwaobia, & Joachim Osheyor Gidiagba. (2024). Technological innovations in the LNG sector: A review: Assessing recent advancements and their impact on LNG production, transportation and usage. *World Journal of Advanced Research and Reviews, 21*(1), 040–057. DOI:10.30574/wjarr.2024.21.1.2685

Özbilgin, M. F., Gundogdu, N., & Akalin, J. (2024). Artificial Intelligence, the Gig Economy, and Precarity. In Meliou, E., Vassilopoulou, J., & Ozbilgin, M. F. (Eds.), *Diversity and Precarious Work During Socioeconomic Upheaval* (1st ed., pp. 284–305). Cambridge University Press., DOI:10.1017/9781108933070.014

Prassl, J. (2018). *Humans as a Service: The Promise and Perils of Work in the Gig Economy* (1st ed.). Oxford University PressOxford., DOI:10.1093/oso/9780198797012.001.0001

Puspitarini, R. C., & Basit, A. (2020). Race to the Bottom: An Introduction to Gig Economy based on Moral Economy in Islam Perspective. *POLITEA*, 3(2), 167. DOI:10.21043/politea.v3i2.8331

Qiu, J. L., Hong, R., & Badger, A. (2023). Auditing Gig Work Platforms: Fairwork's Research, Advocacy, and Impact. *Singapore Labour Journal*, 02(01), 22–38. DOI:10.1142/S281103152300013X

Shafik, W., & Lakshmi, D. (2024). Explainable AI (EXAI) for Smart Healthcare Automation. In Prabhakar, P. K. (Ed.), (pp. 289–316). Advances in Bioinformatics and Biomedical Engineering. IGI Global., DOI:10.4018/979-8-3693-4439-2.ch012

Shah, S. Q., & Sarif, S. M. (2023). Exploring the Economic Dimensions of Human Resource Management: A Systematic Literature Review. *International Journal of Business and Economic Affairs*, 8(3). Advance online publication. DOI:10.24088/IJBEA-2023-830012

Shibata, S. (2020). Gig Work and the Discourse of Autonomy: Fictitious Freedom in Japan's Digital Economy. *New Political Economy*, 25(4), 535–551. DOI:10.1080/13563467.2019.1613351

Singh, R., & Bisen, G. K. (2023). Job Related Uncertainty in the age of Artificial Intelligence and Gig Economy. *COMMERCE RESEARCH REVIEW*, 1(1), 85–100. DOI:10.21844/crr.v1i01.1107

Song, L., & Jo, S. J. (2023). How job crafting behaviors influence the innovative behavior of knowledge workers in the gig economy: Based on the organismic integration theory. *Frontiers in Psychology*, 14, 1228881. DOI:10.3389/fpsyg.2023.1228881 PMID:37731880

Spencer, D. A. (2024). AI, automation and the lightening of work. *AI & Society*. Advance online publication. DOI:10.1007/s00146-024-01959-3

Straughan, E. R., & Bissell, D. (2022). Curious encounters: The social consolations of digital platform work in the gig economy. *Urban Geography*, 43(9), 1309–1327. DOI:10.1080/02723638.2021.1927324

Sureth, A. M. (2024). *Venturing Into Uncharted Territory – Exploring the Psychological Implications of AI-Driven Automation for Employees*. DOI:10.18452/28643

Talukder, M. B. (2021). An assessment of the roles of the social network in the development of the Tourism Industry in Bangladesh. *International Journal of Business, Law, and Education*, 2(3), 85–93. DOI:10.56442/ijble.v2i3.21

Talukder, M. B. (2024). Implementing Artificial Intelligence and Virtual Experiences in Hospitality. In Manohar, S., Mittal, A., Raju, S., & Nair, A. J. (Eds.), *Advances in Hospitality, Tourism, and the Services Industry* (pp. 145–160). IGI Global., DOI:10.4018/979-8-3693-2019-8.ch009

Talukder, M. B., & Kumar, S. (2024). The Development of ChatGPT and Its Implications for the Future of Customer Service in the Hospitality Industry. In Derbali, A. M. S. (Ed.), (pp. 100–126). Advances in Information Security, Privacy, and Ethics. IGI Global., DOI:10.4018/979-8-3693-1511-8.ch005

Talukder, M. B., Kabir, F., Muhsina, K., & Das, I. R. (2023). Emerging Concepts of Artificial Intelligence in the Hotel Industry: A Conceptual Paper. *International Journal of Research Publication and Reviews*, 4(9), 1765–1769. DOI:10.55248/gengpi.4.923.92451

Talukder, M. B., Kumar, S., & Das, I. R. (2024). Perspectives of Digital Marketing for the Restaurant Industry. In Erol, G., & Kuyucu, M. (Eds.), (pp. 118–134). Advances in Media, Entertainment, and the Arts. IGI Global., DOI:10.4018/979-8-3693-0855-4.ch009

Talukder, M. B., Kumar, S., Kaiser, F., & Mia, Md. N. (2024). Pilgrimage Creative Tourism: A Gateway to Sustainable Development Goals in Bangladesh. In M. Hamdan, M. Anshari, N. Ahmad, & E. Ali (Eds.), *Advances in Public Policy and Administration* (pp. 285–300). IGI Global. DOI:10.4018/979-8-3693-1742-6.ch016

Torma, C. Heloisa Brenha Ribeiro, & Cuéllar, L. V. (2022). *Democracy at no workplace: The voice of gig economy workers and its implications for corporate governance*. DOI:10.13140/RG.2.2.28583.62886

Tug, M. A., & Basar, P. (2023). FUTURE OF THE GIG ECONOMY. *Pressacademia*, 1, 1. Advance online publication. DOI:10.17261/Pressacademia.2023.1796

Tyson, L. D., & Zysman, J. (2022). Automation, AI & Work. *Daedalus*, 151(2), 256–271. DOI:10.1162/daed_a_01914

Vernyuy, A. (2024). Impact of Technological Advancements on Human Existence. *International Journal of Philosophy*, 3(2), 54–66. DOI:10.47941/ijp.1874

Vu, A. N., & Nguyen, D. L. (2024). The gig economy: The precariat in a climate precarious world. *World Development Perspectives*, 34, 100596. DOI:10.1016/j.wdp.2024.100596

Waldkirch, M., Bucher, E., Schou, P. K., & Grünwald, E. (2021). Controlled by the algorithm, coached by the crowd – how HRM activities take shape on digital work platforms in the gig economy. *International Journal of Human Resource Management*, 32(12), 2643–2682. DOI:10.1080/09585192.2021.1914129

Wu, D., & Huang, J. L. (2024). Gig work and gig workers: An integrative review and agenda for future research. *Journal of Organizational Behavior*, job.2775. DOI:10.1002/job.2775

Zalizko, V. D., Dobrowolski, R. H., Cherniak, A. M., Artemov, V. Y., & Nowak, D. V. (2022). Gig-economy as a safety gradient for sustainable development of the mining industry. *Naukovyi Visnyk Natsionalnoho Hirnychoho Universytetu*, 4(4), 170–175. DOI:10.33271/nvngu/2022-4/170

Chapter 16
Artificial Intelligence in Human Resource Management Training

Alev Orhan
Sivas Cumhuriyet Üniversitesi, Turkey

Salim Kurnaz
https://orcid.org/0000-0002-8060-5151
Kazimiera Simonaviaus University, Lithuania

ABSTRACT

The objective of this study is to conduct a bibliometric analysis of the keyword network, numerical distribution by years, citation network of the most frequently cited publications, most active researchers, most active journals, countries and institutions of the studies published in the field of human resource management education between 1990 and May 1, 2024 in the WOS database. Furthermore, the objectives of the studies examined in the research are analysed in order to identify the trends of research in the field of artificial intelligence in human resources management and the remaining gaps in the research area. In the study, the criterion sampling method, one of the purposive sampling methods, was selected. The research is a descriptive content analysis study employing qualitative research methods. The R Programming Language "biblioshiny" package program was employed in the analysis of the data collected for the initial objective of the study, while MAXQDA 2020 (20.4.0) was utilized in the second stage.

DOI: 10.4018/979-8-3693-4412-5.ch016

INTRODUCTİON

The term "human resources" is defined as the achievement of optimal results for both employees and the organization as a whole (Storey, 1995). Every organization, regardless of its size, requires human capital to fulfill its objectives. Human resources encompass the personnel employed by the organization to fulfill their daily tasks (Qahtani ve Alsmairat, 2023).

The objective of human resource management is to identify and utilise the potential resources available in individuals (Sinambela, 2021). The field of human resource management is founded upon a series of strategic initiatives, including the provision of human resource management, talent management, succession management, industrial relations, and multiculturalism. These initiatives are distinct from the traditional functions of human resource management, which include the selection, training, assignment of responsibilities, and administration of compensation (Pourrashidi, Mehranpour, & Nick, 2017). In order to manage human resources effectively, it is necessary to employ a range of motivational techniques. These should be used to activate employees' sense of belonging to the organization, to ensure that employees receive appropriate training, and to provide opportunities for employee development (Storey, 1995). In order to achieve optimal performance from employees in a company or organization, it is of the utmost importance for human resource management to take the initial steps in the selection of the potential workforce, the maintenance of said workforce, the development of said workforce, the evaluation of said workforce, and the management of employee relations (Sukardi, Herminingsih, Djumarno, & Kasmir, 2021).

The effective management of human resources is of critical importance within the context of the modern workplace. It is anticipated that companies will ensure long-term growth as a result of the high level of utilisation of their personnel's talents (Al-Kassem, 2021). Consequently, organisations implement human resources training programmes with the objective of enhancing the competencies of their personnel. The objective of human resources training is to equip employees with the requisite skills to meet the demands of an ever-changing world, developments in the sector, technological and environmental changes (Al-Kassem, 2021). Education is defined as the process of effecting a desired change in an individual's behaviour through their own experience and with the intention of influencing their actions (Ertürk, 2017). It is therefore of the utmost importance to ascertain the current level of knowledge of the individuals in question at the inception of the study. Training should be initiated with a clear understanding of the participants' existing knowledge base and the information they require. The design of an educational programme should be aligned with the desired outcome, taking into account the level of preparedness of the individuals involved. In establishing the training objectives, it is imperative to ensure that the desired outcomes for the participants are explicitly delineated, quantifiable, realistic, and oriented towards observable behavioural changes. The second stage of the training process involves the creation of the content that will be utilized to achieve the previously outlined objectives. It is now necessary to structure the content in a systematic manner, providing information pertinent to the participants' needs. Emphasis should be placed on interdisciplinary data, contextualising information within real-world scenarios, and incorporating up-to-date knowledge and technologies. The third stage of the training process, as previously outlined, entails the implementation of training, otherwise known as training situations. Training situations should be designed in alignment with the established objectives and the characteristics of the participants, in order to ensure the most effective and beneficial training experience for all involved. In training situations, it is of the utmost importance to adopt a participant-centred approach, utilising methods and techniques that are tailored to the specific needs and preferences of the individuals involved. It is equally important to consider how training can be conducted in such a way as to ensure effective time management. The ultimate phase of the training programme is the phase of measurement and evaluation. It is of the utmost importance to plan in a manner that allows for the accurate measurement of the training objectives, as this is a fundamental aspect of any training programme. An effective assessment and evaluation tool should be reliable, objective, and impartial in order to ensure the accuracy and fairness of the results. It is recommended that the process include the utilisation of alternative methodologies for the measurement and evaluation of outcomes. The measurement tool should be capable of providing transparency and facilitating accurate data analysis. It is the primary duty of the human resources management department to ensure that employees receive the necessary training to fulfil their roles effectively, in line with identified requirements and with a view to enhancing the overall competence of the workforce.

In the current era of rapid technological advancement, there has been a notable transformation in the roles and responsibilities of human resource management (Kliestik, 2015). Following this alteration and metamorphosis, the parameters of human resource management, including efficacy, productivity, and cost-effectiveness, were established, and an effort was made to enhance the quality of human resource management (Bileviciene, Bileviciute, & Parazinskaite, 2015). It can be posited that the most fundamental effect in enhancing this quality is the implementation of artificial intelligence and digital transformation in human resources management. In an effort to enhance the quality of human resource management, countries and organizations are striving to develop innovative services and establish rigorous quality standards in this nascent field (Kambur & Yildirim, 2023).

The 21st-century global economy has further increased the importance of the ability to innovate in the face of a highly dynamic market where competitive positions are constantly evolving (Stank et al., 2019). Artificial intelligence (AI) is a technology that is widely used and is the driving force behind all changes in the way we approach life (Jain, Chopra, & Sharma, 2023). The application of artificial intelligence within the domain of information technology has the potential to enhance business performance and facilitate the execution of more complex tasks by machines (Kelly et al., 2019). The integration of information technologies into business operations has been demonstrated to yield positive outcomes, particularly in the areas of customer acquisition and partner collaboration (Lauterbach, 2019).

Artificial intelligence (AI) is a technology that has emerged in recent years and has the capacity to emulate the functions of the human brain. It is now a pervasive force in all sectors of science and business, particularly in the domain of human resources (Kambur & Yildirim, 2023). Artificial intelligence is currently one of the most rapidly developing computer technologies, with a great deal of attention being paid to it in recent times (Wiljer & Hakim, 2019). A review of numerous studies reveals the significance of AI in human resource management. These studies indicate that companies should utilize AI to enhance their human resources (Jain, Chopra, & Sharma, 2023). Artificial intelligence can facilitate positive contributions to the recruitment process. These include the formulation of recruitment strategies and policy interventions, the improvement of the effective recruitment process, the recruitment of qualified talent, and the development of a competitive and sustainable environment (Nawaz, 2019).

The application of artificial intelligence in the domains of recruitment, training, performance appraisal, and engagement, which are the primary responsibilities of human resource management, should be regarded as a revolutionary shift in the field (Jain, 2018). The advent of digital transformation in human resources management has led to a reduction in the workload of employees. It is estimated that the use of artificial intelligence in human resources management has reduced the workload rate by approximately 69% (Varma, Dawkins, & Chaudhuri, 2023).

The application of artificial intelligence in human resources management enables the strengthening of personnel communication, the making of universal activities applicable, and the processes of recruitment and professional development of personnel (Kambur & Yildirim, 2023). In recent times, the organisation of training programmes in human resources management online, in accordance with the principles of lifelong learning, has enhanced the impact value of such training. The use of machine programming and intelligent systems in educational settings has become increasingly prevalent, with studies indicating that these technologies enhance the quality of education (Kemendi, Michelberger, & Mesjasz-Lech, 2022).

Artificial intelligence (AI) is being used in human resources management for a number of purposes, including recruitment, employee development, and performance management.In recruitment, AI can be used to identify individual job requirements. This allows companies to find the right candidates for the roles they have available.In employee development, AI can provide just-in-time, specialized training. This helps employees to develop their skills in a way that is relevant to their roles.Finally, in performance management, AI can be used to prepare a holistic performance picture. This allows companies to evaluate their employees against each other (Tabor-Błażewicz, 2023). The objective of human resources management programmes is to facilitate adaptation to technological advances and changing conditions (Al-Kassem, 2021). This is due to the fact that the rate of change is considerable and the trajectory of business is more uncertain (Gascó, Llopis, Reyes González, 2004). It is therefore incumbent upon human resources managers to remain abreast of developments in the wider world. The business-oriented use of technologies has resulted in the advent of a novel order, designated as Web 2.0 (Rodríguez-Sánchez, Montero-Navarro & Gallego-Losada, 2019). The advent of new technologies and artificial intelligence has led to the development of innovative performance evaluation systems in the field of human resources management. The utilisation of artificial intelligence, big data inputs, neural network systems and machine learning methods has enabled the collection and reflection of employee performance data in wage and reward structures (Arora & Mittal, 2024). Furthermore, the application of artificial intelligence in the field of human resources management has been most prevalent in the recruitment process. For example, job simulation techniques have been employed extensively in the recruitment process. In job simulation techniques, candidates are required to perform exercises that replicate situations related to the position they will occupy. Their behavioural patterns are then determined according to the problems they may encounter at work (Rodríguez-Sánchez, Montero-Navarro & Gallego-Losada, 2019). The use of AI-supported human resources enables the prediction of future workforce trends in the context of the complexities of the modern workforce. This, in turn, facilitates the development of data-driven strategies (Nyathani, 2023).

The field of study pertaining to the application of artificial intelligence in the domain of human resource management is, as a consequence of the dynamic changes resulting from the use of new technologies, a constantly growing and developing field of study (Tabor-Błażewicz, 2023). The critical role of AI in the global economy has prompted numerous global companies, including Amazon, Tesla Motors, Microsoft, Baidu, Google, IBM, Facebook, and Nvidia, to increase their investments in AI on a daily basis (Bibi, 2019).

It is imperative that human resource practitioners embrace the potential of AI applications and training, as the failure to incorporate AI into human resource management functions can have a profoundly negative impact on the overall growth of organizations (Alvi, 2019). The utilization of AI in human resource management should address the advantages and concerns associated with the interactions between humans and machines in the workplace (Bibi, 2019). Although AI presents certain challenges, it is more often the case that the benefits outweigh the harms (Leszkiewicz et al., 2022).

Artificial intelligence (AI) is employed in a multitude of fields, including finance, agriculture, health, manufacturing, production, sales, e-commerce, and human resource management. Its implementation has the potential to transform people's daily lives, as it enables machines to perform tasks that previously required human intelligence (Jain, Chopra, & Sharma, 2023).

The profound effects of the post-Covid-19 economic downturn have compelled a fundamental restructuring of the traditional business landscape (Angielsky, Copus, Madzik & Falat, 2024). New Vantage Partners (2017). In a recent statement, executives from numerous prominent American corporations have asserted that artificial intelligence will exert a considerable influence on the business landscape in the immediate future (Jarrahi, 2018). It can be seen that there are a number of economic challenges associated with the use of artificial intelligence programs in human resources management for small and medium-sized enterprises. These include the costs and maintenance required, as well as the training of staff and managers. In addition Firstly, the utilisation of artificial intelligence (AI) programmes in human resources management for small and medium-sized enterprises (SMEs) presents economic challenges in terms of cost, maintenance, staff and manager training, and working time. However, in the long term, these challenges can be overcome, enabling the development of intelligent and personalised human resources management services and increased competitiveness (Huo, Qi & Wang, 2024). The five most significant aspects of human resources management are leader development, training and knowledge creation, the empowerment of staff, an understanding of employee characteristics and cost management. At this juncture, a primary objective is to regulate expenditure and augment revenue streams. The sub-levels of achieving this are improvement of targets, increase of productivity and assurance of customer satisfaction (Enz & Siguaw, 2000). The implementation of performance reports supported by artificial intelligence in the field of human resources management has the potential to enhance the company's overall potential, particularly in terms of employee motivation and professional development (Huo, Qi & Wang, 2024).

The application of artificial intelligence-supported technologies has been demonstrated to result in cost savings, enhanced workplace efficiency, and improved employee productivity (Jain, Chopra, and Sharma, 2023). In this manner, corporations may persevere by enhancing their operational efficacy.

In light of the aforementioned considerations, the growing interest in digital technology and its expanding range of applications has prompted a re-evaluation of the ethical principles that should guide its use. Although there is considerable divergence of opinion regarding the ethical implications of artificial intelligence, each field of application develops its own criteria for evaluating the ethical principles involved in the use of AI.

It is imperative that ethical frameworks and guidelines be established to guide the responsible deployment of AI technologies in human resource management (Gulliford and Dixon, 2019). As the utilization of AI in human resource management expands, organizations are confronted with a series of ethical challenges, including those pertaining to bias, privacy, transparency, ensuring fairness in algorithmic decision-making, and the protection of employee data (Sposato, 2024).

A plethora of guidelines have been developed in the field of social sciences pertaining to the ethical considerations of artificial intelligence. For instance, Fjeld, Achten, Hilligoss, Nagy, and Srikumar (2020) developed a significant ethical guideline within the context of specific themes within the social sciences. The AI ethical guideline is comprised of eight chapters, each with a distinct heading. These include: privacy, accountability, safety and security, transparency and accountability, fairness and non-discrimination, human control of technology, professional responsibility, and the promotion of human values (Fjeld, Achten, Hilligoss, Nagy, & Srikumar, 2020). Artificial intelligence (AI) should be transparent in its decision-making processes, be fair without perpetuating prejudices and discrimination in society, benefit humanity rather than harm it, and protect data privacy. These ethical principles can be considered to be fundamental to the ethical conduct of AI.

One of the most fundamental ethical principles where AI will make a difference is cybersecurity. Artificial intelligence is capable of analyzing vast quantities of data and detecting irregularities. This is of great significance in the detection of malicious behavior. Concurrently, there are potential risks associated with the use of artificial intelligence, including the possibility of data leaks, the protection of personal data, and model theft (González, Moreno, Román, Fernández, & Pérez, 2024). The advent of artificial intelligence has introduced a new dimension to our lives, one that is both promising and potentially risky. At this juncture, scholars are investigating the intended applications, advantages, disadvantages, and integration of artificial intelligence into domains aligned with their respective areas of expertise. The objective of this research is to elucidate the trajectory of research on artificial intelligence in human resources management.

PURPOSE OF THE RESEARCH

The objective of this study is to conduct a bibliometric analysis of the keyword network, numerical distribution by years, citation network of the most frequently cited publications, most active researchers, most active journals, countries and institutions of the studies published in the field of human resource management education between 1990 and May 1, 2024 in the WOS database. Another objective of this research is to conduct a bibliometric analysis of studies employing artificial intelligence in human resource management education, with a focus on demographic characteristics. Furthermore, the objectives of the studies examined in the research are analysed in order to identify the trends of research in the field of artificial intelligence in human resources management and the remaining gaps in the research area. This situation will prove to be an invaluable source of information for future researchers, providing a clear direction for those who will work in this field. Additionally, the objective is to facilitate interdisciplinary studies by analyzing the objectives of the studies. One of the objectives of this study is to analyze the methodologies employed in the various studies.

METHOD

This research employs a descriptive content analysis methodology to determine the demographic characteristics of studies published in the field of human resource management education and artificial intelligence in human resource management education. This is done within the framework of bibliometric parameters, with a particular focus on examining the characteristics of studies in which artificial intelligence is used in human resource management education regarding the purpose and methods. Descriptive content analysis is a form of qualitative analysis that summarizes the information in the texts in the data set by categorizing them as codes and themes (Shelley, 1984).

Creating the Record

The data utilized in this research were obtained from the WOS database, which is produced by Clarivate Analytics. One of the purposive sampling methods, criterion sampling, was employed to ascertain the data. In this context, the initial step was to restrict the screening process to the years 1990 and 2024 and to include the following terms: human resources management training, artificial intelligence, CHATGPT, machine learning, AI, generative AI, natural language processing, and NLP. The second criterion was also established by including all languages and all fields. In accordance with the predetermined criteria, the stages of creating a data set were followed, resulting in the inclusion of 1,000 studies in the field of human resources management education and 46 studies in the field of artificial intelligence in human resources management education in the research. The research revealed that these studies underwent a transformation in terms of bibliometric parameters throughout the process.

Data Collection Tools

For the initial objective of the study, document analysis was deemed the most appropriate data collection method. With regard to the second objective, a publication review form was developed by the researcher. The initial section of the publication review form is devoted to the purpose of the studies. The form also includes criteria for the methodology of the studies. The aforementioned criteria encompass the methodology employed in the studies, the manner of sample selection, the data collection instruments utilized, the analytical techniques employed in the data analysis, and the recommendations formulated.

Data Analysis

The first objective of the study was achieved through the use of bibliometric analysis. The "R" programming language and the "Biblioshiny" package program were employed in the analysis of the data set (Aria & Cuccurullo, 2017). In the second stage of the study, 46 studies on the use of artificial intelligence in human resources education were subjected to content analysis using a publication review form developed by the researcher in accordance with the research questions. The data set was initially designated as S1, S2, S3, and so forth. The research data were subjected to analysis using the MAXQDA 2020 (20.4.0) program, with the identification of themes and codes.

FINDINGS

This study presents findings related to a bibliometric analysis of studies on human resource management education. With regard to the initial issue under investigation, the research studies conducted within the field of human resource management education are subjected to analysis within the context of bibliometric parameters. A quantitative analysis of the temporal distribution of articles published in the field of "HRM Education" has been conducted and presented in Figure 1.

Figure 1. Presents a Numerical Distribution of Articles Published in the Field of "HRM Education" by Year

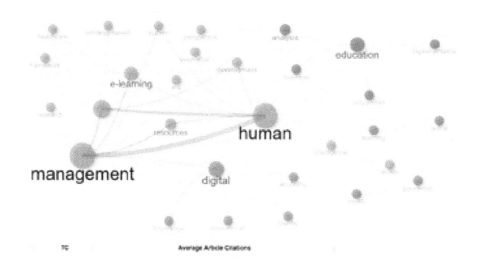

Upon examination of Figure 1, it can be concluded that the greatest number of articles published in the field of HRM Education was published in 2017 (106 articles), followed by 2016 (99 articles), 2020 (80 articles), 2019 (75 articles), and 2018 (66 articles), respectively. It was determined that there were no studies on HRM education in 1992, 1993, 1996, and 2004. The growing corpus of articles can be attributed to the growing recognition of the importance of human resources management education for companies. In light of the intensifying competition in the labour market, it has become imperative for companies to enhance the competencies of their personnel. This situation was also identified in the studies conducted by Danvila-del-Valle, Estévez-Mendoza & Lara (2019) and Rodríguez-Sánchez, Montero-Navarro & Gallego-Losada (2019). A keyword analysis of articles published in the field of HRM Education is presented in Figure 2.

Figure 2. Presents a List of the Most Frequently used Keywords in Articles Published in the Field of "HRM Education."

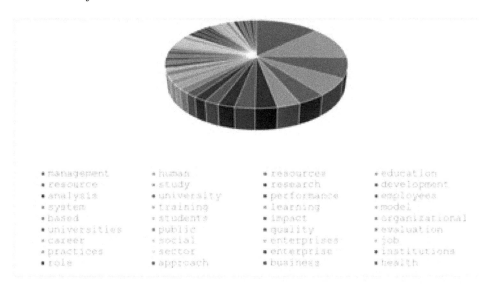

• management	• human	• resources	• education
• resource	• study	• research	• development
• analysis	• university	• performance	• employees
• system	• training	• learning	• model
• based	• students	• impact	• organizational
• universities	• public	• quality	• evaluation
• career	• social	• enterprises	• job
• practices	• sector	• enterprise	• institutions
• role	• approach	• business	• health

Figure 2 illustrates that a total of 2,168 distinct keywords were utilized in 1,000 articles. Upon analysis of keywords with a frequency of 50% or greater, the most prevalent keywords were identified as "management," with 386 articles, "human," with 359 articles, "resources," with 222 articles, "education," with 184 articles, and "study," with 103 articles.The predominance of keywords such as "management," "human," "resource," and "education" can be attributed to their status as the fundamental elements and priorities within the field. The journals that published the most articles in the field of HRM Education were analyzed and presented in Figure 3.

Figure 3. Depicts the Number of Journals that have Published at least 10 Articles in the Field of "HRM Education."

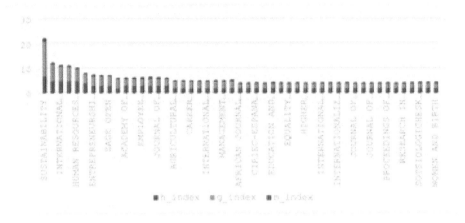

Figure 3 illustrates that there are 51 journals with two or more indexes in the field of human resource management education. Among the journals under consideration, "Sustainability" has the highest index value, with 14 index values. "Journal Of Chinese Human Resources Management" has 7 index values, while "International Journal Of Educational Management" and "Sa Journal Of Human Resource Management" have 6 index values. The esteemed reputation and rigorous standards associated with these academic journals may serve as a significant draw for researchers, particularly given the prominent role these standards play in the advancement of academic careers. This can be attributed to the fact that they are acknowledged as pioneering journals in this field, having played an instrumental role in advancing academic discourse. The articles published in the field of HRM Education examined and presented effective institutions in Figure 4.

Figure 4. Depicts the Institutions that have been Active within the Scope of the Articles Published in the Field of "HRM Education."

- UNIV JINAN
- UNIV ECON BRATISLAVA
- BUCHAREST UNIV ECON STUDIES
- MATEJ BEL UNIV BANSKA BYSTRICA
- XIAN INT UNIV
- UNIV SAO PAULO
- MACEWAN UNIV

Figure 4 illustrates that the most prolific institution in the field of human resource management education is the University of Jinan, with 31 published articles. The next most prolific institutions are "Univ Econ Bratislava" with 22 publications, "Bucharest Univ Econ Studies" with 17 publications, "Matej Bel Univ Banska Bystrica and Xıan Int Univ" with 14 publications, and "Univ Sao Paulo" with 13 publications. The University of Jinan is a well-established institution of higher education in the People's Republic of China. It was established in 1958 and is situated in the city of the same name in the eastern province of Shandong. The university provides a diverse range of academic programmes across all three levels of education (undergraduate, graduate and doctoral), with a particular emphasis placed upon the field of human resource management. The university has established a multitude of collaborative partnerships with both the private sector and public institutions. Bucharest University of Economic Studies represents a dynamic and well-established educational establishment, originally founded in Slovakia in 1959. In a comparable manner, the institution provides undergraduate, postgraduate and doctoral programmes in the field of human resource management. A key factor contributing to the effectiveness of these institutions is their reputation as leaders in human resources management, enabling students to gain access to the latest training techniques. In the context of the published articles on the subject of human resource management education, the authors who have been most active in this field were analyzed and presented in Figure 5.

Figure 5. Authors Active in the Articles Published in the Field of "HRM Education"

• MOUSA M	• JANKELOVA N	• JONIAKOVA Z	• LYSKOVA I
• SMEREK L	• VETRAKOVA M	• WANG J	• RUGGUNAN S
• STACHOVA K	• GU X	• WANG H	• WANG L
• ZHANG J	• ZHANG Y	• ALTINAY Z	• ASFAHANI AM
• BAJENARU L	• BAPORIKAR N	• BENSON L	• BLSTAKOVA J
• HAN CHUNHUA HC	• ILIC M	• LI Y	• LI YULONG LY
• LISSPERS J	• LIU Y	• PROCHAZKOVA K	• RANKOVIC M
• MUNHAAP P	• SPRTOVA H	• SPRTOVA M	• SVEJDAROVA E
• VARSHAVSKAYA KY			

Figure 5 illustrates that the most prolific researcher is "Mousa M," with eight published articles. The next author, Jankelova N, Joniakova Z, lyskova I, Smerek L, Vetrakova M, and Wang J, has published five articles. Figure 6 presents a visual representation of the countries that have been most active in publishing articles in the field of human resource management education.

Figure 6. Depicts the Countries that have been Most Prolific in Publishing Articles on the Subject of Human Resource Management Education.

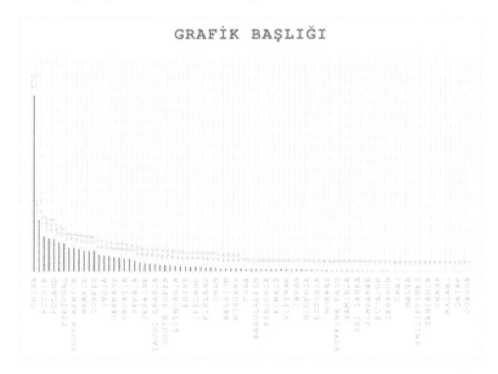

GRAFİK BAŞLIĞI

Figure 6 shows that the country with the highest number of publications is "China" with 578 articles. The next most prolific countries are the United States of America, with 171 articles, Russia, with 116 articles, Romania, with 109 articles, and Poland, with 108 articles. The accelerated economic expansion witnessed in countries such as China, the United States, Russia, and Poland has been propelled by the advent of the Industrial Revolution and the subsequent technological advancements. This has resulted in substantial advancements within the labour market, accompanied by an intensified emphasis on the domain of human resources. One of the prerequisites for enhancing production is the expansion of personnel competence and the stimulation of personnel motivation. It is anticipated that these countries will be identified as the most effective from this perspective. In their 2019 study, Danvila-del-Valle, Estévez-Mendoza and Lara identified the USA and China as the countries with the highest number of publications in the field of human resource management. Figure 7 presents a network of countries that are active in terms of articles published in the field of human resource management education.

Figure 7. Depicts the Networks between Countries that have Published Articles in the Field of "HRM Education."

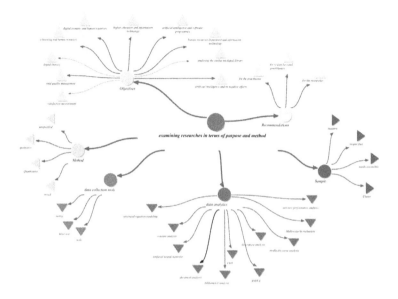

Upon examination of Figure 7, it becomes evident that the country exhibiting the most collaboration in the field of "HRM Education" is China, which has the highest number of publications. China cooperates with the USA, Australia, Malaysia, Bangladesh and Brazil. Furthermore, it was determined that there is a degree of collaboration between Hungary, Slovakia, and Romania; Egypt and Saudi Arabia; Canada and Iran; Kuwait and the United Arab Emirates; Mexico; Russia and the Czech Republic.

The United States of America and the People's Republic of China are the two countries with the largest economies in the world. A significant number of areas have been identified in which major corporations in these countries are engaged in collaborative activities. It is foreseen that this development will lead to the conclusion of a multitude of research projects within the domain of human resources management. In the context of the partnership between Bangladesh and Brazil, it is evident that both countries are classified under the category of developing countries. Consequently, it is possible that the challenges or opportunities facing companies in the fields of economics and human resources may be similar. Once these variables have been assessed in combination, the predicted results can be discerned. This is contingent on the assumption that the countries engaged in collaboration possess economic structures that are analogous in nature.

Findings on Bibliometric Analysis of Studies Using Artificial Intelligence in Human Resource Management Education

With regard to the second research problem, the analysis of studies employing artificial intelligence in human resource management education within the framework of bibliometric parameters is included. The distribution of articles published in the field of artificial intelligence in human resource management education according to year is presented in Figure 8.

Figure 8. Presents a Numerical Distribution of Articles Published in the Field of "Artificial Intelligence in HRM Education" by Year

A quantitative analysis of the temporal distribution of articles published in the field of artificial intelligence in human resource management education reveals that the highest number of articles was published in 2023 (8 articles). The following years were also represented in the corpus: 2022 (7 articles), 2016 (5 articles), 2013-2018-2019-2020 (3 articles). In 2009 and 2010, a comprehensive search of the literature revealed that no studies had been conducted on the topic of "Artificial Intelligence in HRM Training." The exponential growth in research on artificial intelligence (AI) in human resources management can be attributed to several factors, including the ability to expeditiously analyse large data sets in order to utilise their insights in a fair and objective decision-making process; to personalise training and enhance performance by identifying and addressing individual needs; to streamline recruitment procedures by using automated assessment tools and algorithms to evaluate candidates; and to realise cost savings by automating tasks and eliminating redundancies. Frequently used keywords in articles published in the field of Artificial Intelligence in HRM Education were analyzed and presented in Figure 9.

Figure 9. Presents a List of the Most Frequently used Keywords in Articles Published in the Field of "Artificial Intelligence in HRM Education."

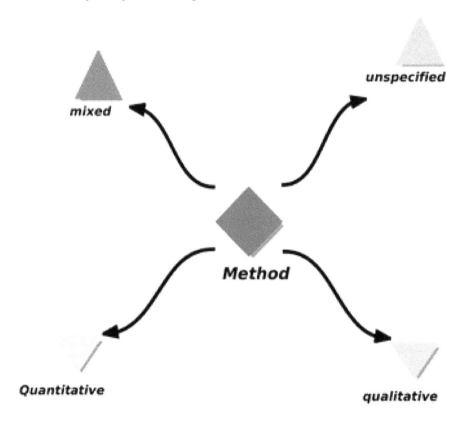

Figure 9 illustrates that a total of 52 distinct keywords were utilized in 46 articles. Upon analysis of keywords with three or more terms, the most prevalent keywords were identified as "management," with 16 articles, "human," with 14 articles, "digital and education," with 10 articles, and "e-learning and resources," with nine articles. Keywords utilized in conjunction with one another in the published articles pertaining to the field of artificial intelligence in human resource management education were subjected to analysis and presented in Figure 10.

Figure 10. Presents a List of Keywords that have been used in Conjunction with one another in Articles Published within the Field of "Artificial Intelligence in HRM Training."

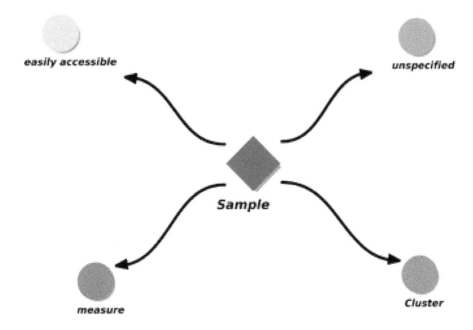

Figure 10 illustrates the co-occurrence of various terms related to the field of artificial intelligence in human resource management education. These include management, human resources, e-learning, development, innovation, the digital age, business analysis, e-learning online, digital knowledge, and educational economy trends. Additionally, intelligence review, covid, and pandemic are also observed in the same context. Figure 11 presents the indices of journals and authors engaged in publishing research in the field of artificial intelligence in human resource management education.

Figure 11. Presents an Index of Journals and Authors Publishing in the Field of Artificial Intelligence in HRM Education

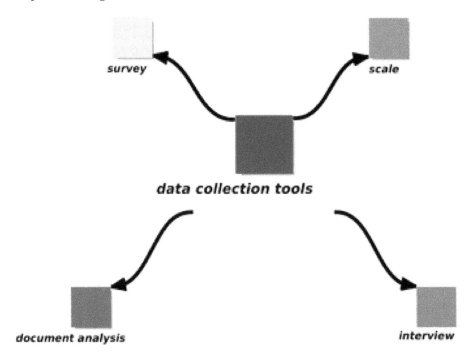

Upon examination of Figure 11, it becomes evident that the h and g index values of 23 journals publishing in the field of artificial intelligence in human resource management education are 1, while the m index values fluctuate. The journals with an M index value of 0.5 were identified as the International Journal of Stem Education, the Journal of Computers in Education, and the Journal of Innovation and Knowledge. It was determined that 67 authors published in the field of "Artificial Intelligence in HRM Education". A total of 67 authors were identified as having published in the field of "Artificial Intelligence in HRM Education." A comparison of the h-index values of the authors revealed that Bajenaru L, Smeureanu I, and Uymaz AO had an h-index value of 2, while the other authors had an h-index value of 1. Figure 12 illustrates the collaborative networks of authors engaged in the publication of research in the field of artificial intelligence in human resource management education.

Figure 12. Depicts the Relationship Networks of Authors who have Published in the Field of Artificial Intelligence in HRM Education

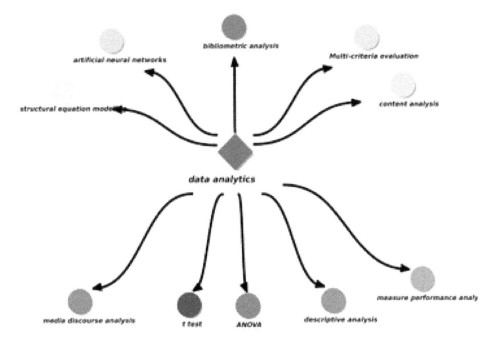

Upon examination of Figure 12, it becomes evident that there are study groups related to the field of artificial intelligence in human resource management education. It is also apparent that Zmazek V. and Kobal D., Balog A. and Bajenaru I., Freng X. and Cavallaro F., Butov G. and Abramov V., Benson I. and Enstrom R., and Bocatto have collaborated. Figure 13 illustrates the active journals and authors within the scope of articles published in the field of artificial intelligence in human resource management education.

Figure 13. Presents a List of Journals and Authors who have Published Articles in the Field of Artificial Intelligence in HRM Education

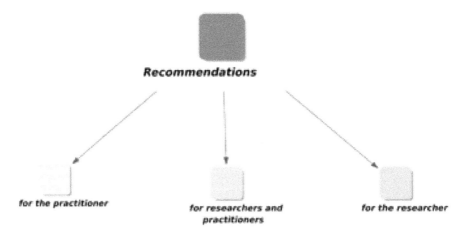

Recommendations

for the practitioner

for researchers and practitioners

for the researcher

Upon analysis of Figure 13, it can be determined that the most prolific journals within the scope of articles published in the field of artificial intelligence in human resource management education are as follows: COMPUT EDUC with 48 articles, Comput Hum Behav with 37 articles, Mıs Quart with 23 articles, J Appl Psychol with 22 articles, and Pers Psychol with 14 articles.

Figure 14. Presents a List of Institutions that have been Active within the Scope of Articles Published in the Field of Artificial Intelligence in HRM Education

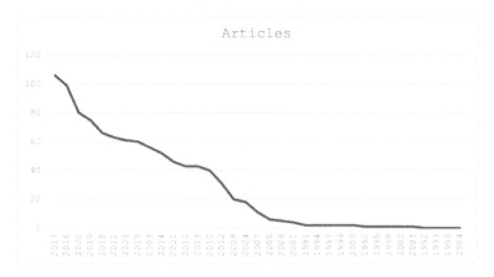

Upon examination of Figure 14, it can be determined that the most effective institution in the field of artificial intelligence in human resource management education is the "Alanya Alaaddin Keykubat University and University of Economics Bratislava," with nine articles. The next most prolific institutions are Bucharest University of Economic Studies (7 articles), University of Tiranë (5 articles), California State University, Long Beach, Macewan University, and National Institute of Research and Development in Informatics and Yunnan University (4 articles each). Figure 15 presents a map of countries engaged in the field of artificial intelligence in HRM education.

Figure 15. Depicts the Countries that are Currently Engaged in the Field of Artificial Intelligence in HRM Education

Figure 15 illustrates that the country with the greatest number of publications is China, with 182 articles. This is followed by Romania, with 156 articles, Russia, with 120 articles, and Turkey, with 60 articles.

The observation that China is the country with the highest number of published articles can be attributed to the fact that China is the world leader in terms of expenditure on artificial intelligence technologies. China's economic growth has provided a conducive environment for the expansion of large corporations, which have subsequently made substantial investments in research and development activities, particularly in the domain of artificial intelligence as it pertains to human resources management. The Romanian state is situated among those countries which are at an early phase of development in the domain of information technology. With the funds it has received from the European Union, it is engaged in the creation of significant research projects in the field of artificial intelligence. The Russian Federation has established the development of artificial intelligence (AI) as a national research priority and is providing substantial support for research and development in the field of AI. Turkey has, conversely, witnessed significant advancements in the realms of artificial intelligence and sophisticated technologies, with a marked inclination towards research and development activities within these domainsIt can be reasonably deduced that the countries with the highest number of publications, namely China, Romania, Russia and Turkey, afford the greatest importance to technological innovation and demonstrate a commitment to fostering international collaboration in this field. It can be reasonably inferred that the countries with the highest number of publications, namely China, Romania, Russia and Turkey, are those that accord the greatest importance to technological innovation and demonstrate a commitment to fostering international collaboration in this field. Furthermore, it seems probable that these countries also support research in this field at the state level, which could account for their high publication rates.

FINDINGS ON THE OBJECTIVES AND METHODS OF STUDIES USING ARTIFICIAL INTELLIGENCE IN HUMAN RESOURCE MANAGEMENT EDUCATION

The findings related to the second sub-problem of the study were formed in accordance with the stated purpose of the research, the research design, the sample, the data collection tools, the data analysis, and the recommendations. The themes and codes identified in the findings are presented in Figure 16, which also outlines the aims and methods of the studies.

Figure 16. Presents a Hierarchical Code-Subcode Model Regarding the Aims and Methods of the Studies, with the Code Section Serving as the Basis for this Model

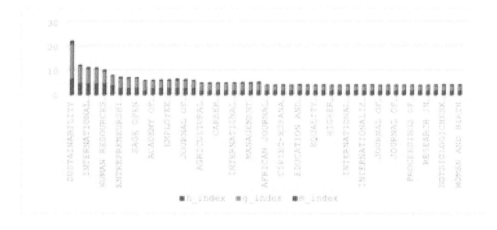

Upon examination of Figure 16, the subthemes pertaining to the examination of research in terms of purpose and method are evaluated in six categories: "Objectives," "Method," "Sample," "Data Collection Tools," "Data Analytics," and "Recommendations." A hierarchical code-subcode model was employed to analyze each category. The themes and codes identified in the findings are presented in Figure 17, which also indicates the purposes of the studies.

Figure 17. Hierarchical Code Sub-Code Model Regarding the Objectives of the Studies (Code Section Based)

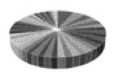

- UNIV JINAN
- UNIV ECON BRATISLAVA
- BUCHAREST UNIV ECON STUDIES
- MATEJ BEL UNIV BANSKA BYSTRICA
- XIAN INT UNIV
- UNIV SAO PAULO
- MACEWAN UNIV

In Figure 17, the sub-theme *"Objectives"* is comprised of the following codes: *"artificial intelligence and its negative effects", "digital literacy", "analysing the studies on digital library", "artificial intelligence and software programmes", "total quality management", "total quality management", "digital economy and human resources", "higher education and information technology", "human resources department and information technology"*. A review of the 46 studies analyzed revealed that the majority of studies focused on the effectiveness of e-learning as a method for preparing human resources (S3, S4, S6, S17, S20, S32, S37, S38, S41, S44, S45). In addition, studies on improving information technology in higher education predominate (S1, S10, S11, S13, S22, S23, S24, S27, S31, S35, S39). Upon examination of both issues, it becomes evident that they are unified by their common objective of integrating technology with education and offering qualified distance education. Furthermore, studies have been conducted on the digital economy and human resources, investigating the impact of the digital economy on human resources management and the global trends associated with the digital economy (S5, S8, S18, S34, S42, S46, S30). The subsequent research topic was identified as artificial intelligence and software programs. The integration of artificial intelligence and human resources management has been attempted, and software programs have been developed to facilitate this integration. It is generally used in the health sector, but has also been used to expand companies' portfolios. Furthermore, they have developed software programs that utilize artificial intelligence to facilitate self-assessments among personnel, enabling them to follow the training provided in human resources management, personnel tracking systems, and development stages. The objective of the studies was to ascertain the purpose of these programs and their efficacy in the process (S15, S7, S25, S28, S40, S30). Additionally, three studies in the field of human resources management and information technologies address the provision of training to enhance the technological competencies of personnel and the evaluation of the effectiveness of such training (Q33, Q36, Q43). A total of two studies on total quality management were identified. The objective of these studies was to obtain opinions on total quality management practices in distance education (T14, T19). Two studies were conducted on the negative effects of artificial intelligence. One examined the impact of AI-supported human resources management on employees, while the other explored the implications of artificial intelligence on general education and academia. Qualitative research was employed as the research method (S29, S44). Two studies were conducted on the creation of digital libraries, and the results of these studies were subjected to bibliometric analysis (S2, S45). The themes and codes identified in the findings are presented in Figure 18, which also includes a description of the methods employed in the studies.

Figure 18. Hierarchical Code Sub-Code Regarding the Methods of the Studies (Code Section Based)

In Figure 18, the sub-theme "Method" is comprised of the following codes: "unspecified," "mixed," "quantitative," and "qualitative." A comprehensive examination of the studies revealed that 23 of them lacked sufficient information regarding the methodology employed. It is notable that two studies in the sample employed a mixed design. The researchers provided a comprehensive rationale for their preference for the mixed method in their articles (Q6, Q36). A total of 14 studies were designed and justified quantitatively (Q7, Q18, Q19, Q9, Q24, Q25, Q27, Q30, Q3, Q10, Q13). Fourteen studies were designed and justified quantitatively (Q43, Q22, Q39), while seven studies were designed and justified qualitatively (Q29, Q44, Q28, Q14, Q5, Q31, Q46). The themes and codes identified in the findings of the samples of the studies are presented in Figure 19.

Figure 19. Hierarchical (Code Section Based) Code Subcode Hierarchy for the Study Samples

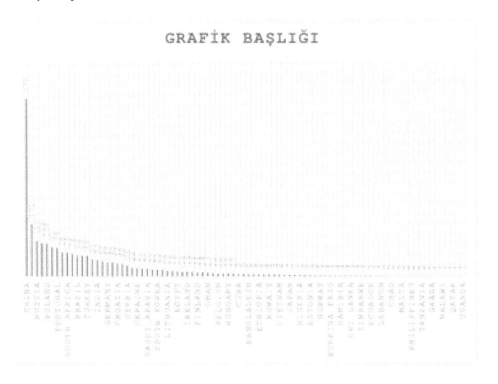

In Figure 19, the sub-theme "Sample" is comprised of the following codes: "unspecified," "measure," "cluster," and "easily accessible." The studies were subjected to a comprehensive analysis, during which it was determined that 40 studies lacked sufficient information regarding the selection of their samples. It was determined that the cluster sampling method was employed in one of the studies (Q 39) and the criterion sampling method was utilized in one of the studies (Q 6). The analysis revealed that the convenience sampling method (S9, S30, S1, S3) was employed in four of the studies under examination. In the majority of the studies examined, the study group was formed and the sample selection method was not explicitly stated. The themes and codes identified in the data collection tools of the studies are presented in Figure 20.

Figure 20. Hierarchical (Code Section Based) Hierarchical Code Sub-Code Regarding the Data Collection Tools of the Studies

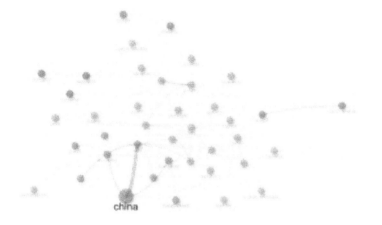

In Figure 20, the sub-theme "Data collection tools" is comprised of the following codes: In Figure 20, the sub-theme "Data collection tools" is comprised of the codes "interview," "survey," and "scale" and *"document analysis"*. A total of six studies employed a pre-existing scale (S10, S30, S7, S23, S41, S43), three studies utilized interviews (S29, S44, S31), and the remaining 37 studies employed questionnaire and document analysis methods. The majority of studies employ the survey method, as evidenced by the data. The themes and codes identified in the data analysis of the studies are presented in Figure 21.

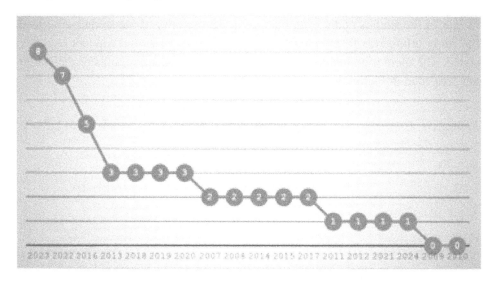

In Figure 21, the sub-theme *"Data analytics"* is comprised of the following codes: *"document analysis", "descriptive analysis", "structural equation modeling", "media discourse analysis", "Multi-criteria evaluation", "ANOVA", "t test", "measure performance analysis", "content analysis", "pre-test - post-test", "reliability coefficient", "artificial neural networks", "bibliometric analysis".* A total of 5 studies were identified that employed the document analysis design (S18, S19, S28, S27, S35, S46), 4 studies that used the structural equation modeling design (S6, S2, S38, S45), 4 studies that employed the structural equation modeling design (S9, S30, S39, S22), 1 study that used the media discourse analysis design (S40), and 1 study that employed the Multi-criteria evaluation design (S17). With Multi-criteria evaluation (S17), four studies employed ANOVA (S43, S20, S8, S25), seven utilized t test (S36, S4, S12, S16, S21, S37, S7), one study employed measure performance analysis (S41), and nine studies employed content analysis (S5, S6, S14, S28, S29, S31, S36, S44, S46), 3 used pre-test - post-test (S3, S26, S42), 2 used reliability coefficient (S13, S32), 3 used artificial neural networks (S10, S1, S24), 4 used bibliometric analysis (S15, S11, S23, S34). The themes and codes identified in the findings are presented in Figure 22 alongside the recommendations of the studies.

Figure 22. Hierarchical Code Sub-Code Regarding the Recommendations of the Studies (Code Section Based)

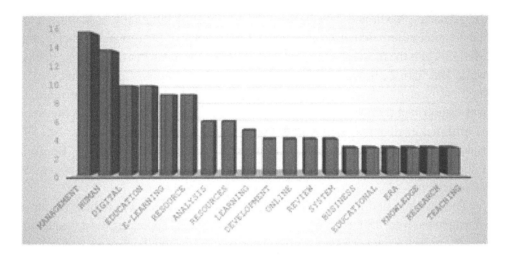

In Figure 22, the sub-theme *"Recommendations"* is comprised of the following codes: *"for researchers and practitioners"*, *"for the practitioner"*, *"for the researcher"*. *In the analyzed studies, four studies (S1, S6, S11, S14) made recommendations* for researchers and practitioners, *four studies (S2, S10, S19, S41) made recommendations* for the practitioner, *and one study (S21) made recommendations* for the researcher.

CONCLUSION

A review of the WoS database revealed that there were 1,000 studies in the field of human resource management between 1990 and 2024. Of these, 46 were related to the application of artificial intelligence in human resource management. A quantitative analysis of the literature in the field of educational research on human resources management revealed that the highest number of publications was observed in 2017 (106 articles). Similarly, in the category of artificial intelligence in human resources management, the highest number of publications was observed in 2023 (8 articles). The results indicated that there has been a notable increase in the number of studies on human resources management and artificial intelligence in human resources management. In recent years, there has been a notable increase in interest in artificial intelligence, with the technology being rapidly integrated into various scientific disciplines. This phenomenon is also evident in the field of human resources management. Artificial intelligence is a highly utilized tool in the realm of recruitment processes. In particular, it is employed in the establishment of recruitment criteria and the assurance of transparency in the process. Furthermore, it is employed in the development of training programs designed to enhance the personal growth and development of personnel. Additionally, it is utilized in the creation of individualized programs. The findings of the research indicate that MOUSA M is the most effective author in the field of human resource management, while Bajenaru L, Smeureanu I, and Uymaz AO are the most prolific authors in the field of artificial intelligence in human resource management. Furthermore, it was established that working groups had been established by authors in the field of artificial intelligence in human resources management. Zmazek, V., Kobal, D., Balog, A., Bajenaru, I., Freng, X., Cavallaro, F., Butov, G., Abramov, V., Benson, I., Enstrom, R., and Bocatto, in the field of artificial intelligence in human resources management.

The research findings indicate that 2,168 keywords related to human resource management were utilized, with the term "management" appearing most frequently in 386 articles. A total of 52 keywords related to artificial intelligence were identified in the context of human resources management. The most prevalent keyword was "management." In examining the functions of human resources, it is evident that recruitment and placement, the preparation of programs to enhance the knowledge and skills of the staff, and the management of the aforementioned processes are of paramount importance. Furthermore, the improvement of communication skills among employees, the organization's relations with the union and other institutions, and the preparation of strategic reports on human resources are also crucial. Consequently, it can be reasonably assumed that the most frequently utilized keyword in this context is "management." Given that the objective of the deployment of artificial intelligence in the field of human resources management is to automate the management of human resources, oversee social media platforms, and develop bespoke programmes for both individuals and institutions, it is anticipated that the most sought-after keyword will be management. Concurrently, it was established that these studies were published in 51 distinct journals. The most efficacious journal was "Sustainability" in the field of human resource management, and "Comput Educ" with 48 articles in the field of artificial intelligence in human resource management. Sustainability is an open access journal that covers a wide range of topics related to sustainability, including the environment, culture, the economy, social sustainability, and multidisciplinary studies on sustainability. Comput Educ has a high impact factor in the field of educational technology, as well as the function of a journal that publishes the use of computers and technology in education and new approaches. The findings of the research indicate that the journals Sustainability and Comput Educ were found to be the most effective in terms of their impact on the field of study. This can be attributed to the fact that they cover a wide range of subjects, have a high impact factor, and are open access journals.

The research findings indicate that China is the most prolific country in terms of research output in the field of human resource management, with 578 studies in this area and 182 studies in the field of artificial intelligence in human resource management. The analysis revealed that the most impactful institutions in the field of human resources management are the University of Jinan with 31 articles, the Alaaddin Keykubat University with 9 studies, and the University of Economics Bratislava with 9 studies. The University of Jinan is a public university located in Shandong province, China. The University of Jinan offers a range of academic programs, including those in engineering, science, management, and economics. Alaaddin Keykubat University is a public institution of higher education situated in Alanya, Turkey. The university comprises a number of faculties, including the Faculty of Engineering, the Faculty of Education, the Faculty of Economics and Administrative Sciences, the Faculty of Health Sciences, and the Faculty of Tourism. The university is a recognized institution of higher learning in the field of business management, situated in Bratislava, the capital of Slovakia. The university comprises the following faculties: the Faculty of Business Administration, the Faculty of International Relations, the Faculty of Economics and Finance, and the Faculty of Information Technology. The most effective institutions, as identified by the study, were Univ Jinan, Univ Alaaddin Keykubat Univ, and Univ Econ Bratislava. This effectiveness can be attributed to their extensive international collaborations with numerous other universities and research institutions.

The findings of the research indicate that the primary objective of the studies conducted in the field of artificial intelligence in human resources management is to design training programs in the form of e-learning and online learning, and to determine the effectiveness of this training. The preference for online learning over traditional education is based on the fact that it does not impose limitations in terms of space and time. In online learning, the training is typically recorded and can be viewed repeatedly by the participants, which allows employees to progress at their own pace. Furthermore, the implementation of online learning has the potential to reduce the financial burden associated with travel and accommodation costs for participants. This reduction in costs is a key advantage of online learning, contributing to its growing popularity in comparison to traditional education. In light of the numerous advantages associated with online learning, it is particularly suited to the field of human resource management, as well as to all other disciplines.

A body of research has been conducted on the effectiveness of information technology in higher education, and recommendations that may be important for higher education have been put forward. Some of the studies are related to the digital economy and its implications for human resources management, global trends and developments in this field. Some studies have attempted to integrate artificial intelligence and software programs into the domain of human resources management. The objective of the studies was to evaluate the purposes of software programs and their effectiveness in the process. The programs may be utilized to identify potential candidates. In particular, it is ensured that job advertisements, which often receive hundreds of applications, are scanned in a timely and accurate manner within the framework of the specified criteria. Software programs are employed to ascertain the training requirements of personnel and to develop individualized training programs. In the case of certain inherently dangerous and critical tasks, the use of simulation programs, virtual reality, and augmented reality technologies can be employed. Furthermore, software programs are employed to monitor and provide feedback on the performance of personnel. In some studies, the efficacy of training programs designed to enhance technological competencies among personnel has been evaluated. Some studies have investigated the potential negative consequences of artificial intelligence in the field of human resource management. It has been demonstrated that the deployment of artificial intelligence in recruitment processes without the requisite training may result in suboptimal decision-making. A number of studies have been conducted on the potential security issues that may arise in the context of working with large datasets and managing personal data through the use of artificial intelligence. Some studies have indicated that the frequent use of artificial intelligence may have a negative impact on human relations.

It was determined that approximately half of the studies examined did not mention the research design. Furthermore, it was determined that approximately half of the studies whose method was specified were created with a quantitative research design. A paucity of qualitative studies was identified among the analyzed data. Nevertheless, it is of paramount importance to employ a qualitative research design in the field of human resources. Qualitative research is an effective method for examining events and phenomena in depth. In the field of human resources management, in-depth qualitative research can be employed to investigate factors such as staff motivation, satisfaction levels, and stress factors. This research can then be used to develop solutions for the problem sources identified. Qualitative research methods can be employed to ascertain personnel's views on management, career planning, and needs. Furthermore, the organization can be evaluated from the personnel's perspective. The research findings indicate that the mixed method was employed in only three of the studies. A mixed method is a research design that employs a combination of quantitative and qualitative research approaches. In mixed methods, quantitative data are subjected to in-depth examination, while qualitative data are either examined in conjunction with quantitative data or supported by quantitative data. In this instance, the reliability of the studies is enhanced by the use of diverse data collection tools, methods, and analysis techniques. In light of the aforementioned considerations, it is imperative to prioritize the mixed method in the field of human resource management.

In the majority of the studies examined, it was determined that the study group was formed and the sample selection method was not mentioned. The rationale behind the selection of working groups is not always made clear. The failure to specify the sample selection results in a lack of clarity regarding the extent to which the sample aligns with the research objectives. This situation calls into question the validity and reliability of the research and raises concerns about the transparency of the research process.

The analyses employed in the reviewed studies encompass document analysis, descriptive analysis, structural equation modeling, media discourse analysis, multi-criteria evaluation, ANOVA, t-test, measure performance analysis, content analysis, pre-test-post-test, reliability coefficient, and artificial neural networks. It was determined that a bibliometric analysis was conducted.

The recommendations derived from the reviewed studies are divided into three stages. The following recommendations are provided for practitioners, researchers, and those engaged in both practitioner and research roles. A review of the literature revealed a paucity of suggestions for researchers. Nevertheless, the recommendations for researchers presented in the articles are of significant value in guiding future research endeavors. Furthermore, the programme provides an opportunity for those with specialist expertise to gain experience in a similar field.

The results of this study can be utilized to inform subsequent research and analysis conducted by educational institutions and business enterprises, respectively. This approach will facilitate the implementation of more effective artificial intelligence solutions within the field of human resources management. In consideration of the conclusions drawn from the research, it is recommended that professionals in the domain of human resources receive further training and develop enhanced knowledge regarding the subject of artificial intelligence. Moreover, it has been demonstrated that artificial intelligence is predominantly utilised within the domain of human resources, particularly in the context of recruitment and the design of tailored training programmes. Furthermore, it has been noted that there is a paucity of empirical studies in the existing literature on this topic, despite a predominant theoretical approach. Given the paucity of empirical research evaluating the efficacy of software applications designed for the utilisation of artificial intelligence in human resources management, it is recommended that further studies be conducted.

REFERENCES

Al-Kassem, A. H. (2021). Significance of human resources training and development on organizational achievement. *PalArch's Journal of Archaeology of Egypt/Egyptology, 18*(7), 693-707.

Alvi, D. A. (2019, January 20). Pakistan's place in artificial intelligence and omputing. *The Nation*. Retrieved from https://nation.com.pk/20-Jan-2019/pakistan-splace-in-artificial-intelligence-and-computing

Angielsky, M., Copus, L., Madzik, P., & Falat, L. (2024). Navigating the human element: Unveiling insights into workforce dynamics in supply chain automation through smart bibliometric analysis.

Aria, M., & Cuccurullo, C. (2017). bibliometrix: An R-tool for comprehensive science mapping analysis. *Journal of Informetrics*, 11(4), 959–975. DOI:10.1016/j.joi.2017.08.007

Arora, M., & Mittal, A. (2024). Employees' change in perception when artificial intelligence integrates with human resource management: A mediating role of AI-tech trust. *Benchmarking*. Advance online publication. DOI:10.1108/BIJ-11-2023-0795

Bibi, M. (2019). Execution of artificial intelligence approach in human resource management functions: Benefits and challenges in Pakistan. *Sarhad Journal of Management Sciences*, 5(1), 113–124. DOI:10.31529/sjms.2018.5.1.8

Bilevičienė, T., Bilevičiūtė, E., & Parazinskaitė, G. (2015). Innovative trends in human resources management. *Economics & Sociology (Ternopil)*, 8(4), 94–109. DOI:10.14254/2071-789X.2015/8-4/7

Danvila-del-Valle, I., Estévez-Mendoza, C., & Lara, F. J. (2019). Human resources training: A bibliometric analysis. *Journal of Business Research*, 101, 627–636. DOI:10.1016/j.jbusres.2019.02.026

Enz, C. A., & Siguaw, J. A. (2000). Best practices in human resources. *The Cornell Hotel and Restaurant Administration Quarterly*, 41(1), 48–61. DOI:10.1177/001088040004100123

Ertürk, S. (2017). *Eğitimde 'program' geliştirme*. Edge Akademi.

Fjeld, J., Achten, N., Hilligoss, H., Nagy, A., & Srikumar, M. (2020). Principled artificial intelligence: Mapping consensus in ethical and rights-based approaches to principles for AI. *Berkman Klein Center Research Publication* (2020-1). DOI:10.2139/ssrn.3518482

Gascó, J. L., Llopis, J., & González, M. R. (2004). İnsan kaynaklarının eğitiminde bilgi teknolojisinin kullanımı: Bir e-öğrenme vaka çalışması. *Avrupa Endüstriyel Eğitim Dergisi*, 28(5), 370–382.

González, A. L., Moreno, M., Román, A. C. M., Fernández, Y. H., & Pérez, N. C. (2024). Ethics in artificial intelligence: An approach to cybersecurity. *Inteligencia Artificial*, 27(73), 38–54. DOI:10.4114/intartif.vol27iss73pp38-54

Gulliford, F., & Dixon, A. P. (2019). AI: The HR revolution. *Strategic HR Review*, 18(2), 52–55. DOI:10.1108/SHR-12-2018-0104

Huo, X., Qi, M., & Wang, S. (2024). The application of electronic human resource management systems (e-HRM) in HR management. *Advances in Economics and Management Research*, 10(1), 316–316. DOI:10.56028/aemr.10.1.316.2024

Jain, D. (2018). Human resource management and artificial intelligence. *International Journal of Management and Social Sciences Research*, 7(3), 56–59.

Jain, E., Chopra, T., & Sharma, S. K. (2023, February). Reinventing human resource management in the era of artificial intelligence. In *ICASDMBW 2022: Proceedings of the International Conference on Application of AI and Statistical Decision Making for the Business World, ICASDMBW 2022,16-17 December 2022,Rukmini Devi Institute of Advanced Studies,Delhi, India* (Vol. 86). European Alliance for Innovation. DOI:10.4108/eai.16-12-2022.2326241

Jarrahi, M. H. (2018). Artificial intelligence and the future of work: Human-AI symbiosis in organizational decision making. *Business Horizons*, 61(4), 577–586. DOI:10.1016/j.bushor.2018.03.007

Kambur, E., & Yildirim, T. (2023). From traditional to smart human resources management. *International Journal of Manpower*, 44(3), 422–452. DOI:10.1108/IJM-10-2021-0622

Kelly, C. J., Karthikesalingam, A., Suleyman, M., Corrado, G., & King, D. (2019). Key challenges for delivering clinical impact with artificial intelligence. *BMC Medicine*, 17(195), 1–9. DOI:10.1186/s12916-019-1426-2 PMID:31665002

Kemendi, Á., Michelberger, P., & Mesjasz-Lech, A. (2022). Industry 4.0 and 5.0–organizational and competency challenges of enterprises. *Polish Journal of Management Studies*, 26(2), 209–232. DOI:10.17512/pjms.2022.26.2.13

Kliestik, T. (2015). Future evolutions of human resource management. In *Globalization and its socio-economic consequences,22th International Scientific Conference* (Vol. I & II, pp. 604-607). Zilina: University of Zilina.

Lauterbach, A. (2019). Artificial intelligence and policy: Quo vadis? *Digital Policy. Regulation & Governance*, 21(3), 238–263. DOI:10.1108/DPRG-09-2018-0054

Leszkiewicz, A., Hormann, T., & Krafft, M. (2022). Smart business and the social value of AI. In *Smart Industry–Better Management* (pp. 19–34). Emerald Publishing Limited., DOI:10.1108/S1877-636120220000028004

Nawaz, N. (2019). Artificial intelligence interchange human intervention in the recruitment process in Indian software industry. *International Journal of Advanced Trends in Computer Science and Engineering*, 8(4), 1433–1442. DOI:10.30534/ijatcse/2019/62842019

Nyathani, R. (2023). AI-Driven HR analytics: Unleashing the power of HR data management. *Journal of Technology and Systems*, 5(2), 15–26. DOI:10.47941/jts.1513

Pourrashidi, R., Mehranpour, M., & Nick, M. F. (2017). Human resources management: Challenges and solutions. *Helix*, 8, 998–1001.

Qahtani, E. H. A., & Alsmairat, M. A. (2023). Assisting artificial intelligence adoption drivers in human resources management: A mediation model. *Acta Logistica*, 10(1), 141–150. DOI:10.22306/al.v10i1.371

Rodríguez-Sánchez, J. L., Montero-Navarro, A., & Gallego-Losada, R. (2019). The opportunity presented by technological innovation to attract valuable human resources. *Sustainability (Basel)*, 11(20), 5785. DOI:10.3390/su11205785

Shelley, M., & Krippendorff, K. (1984). Content analysis: An introduction to its methodology (by K. Krippendorff). *Journal of the American Statistical Association*, 79(385), 240–240. DOI:10.2307/2288384

Sinambela, L. P. (2021). *Human resource management: Building a solid work team to improve performance*. Earth Literacy.

Sposato, M. (2024). Editorial. *Strategic HR Review*, 23(1), 40–42. DOI:10.1108/SHR-02-2024-204

Stank, T., Esper, T., Goldsby Thomas, J., Zinn, W., & Autry, C. (2019). Toward a digitally dominant paradigm for twenty-first century supply chain scholarship. *International Journal of Physical Distribution & Logistics Management*, 49(10), 956–971. DOI:10.1108/IJPDLM-03-2019-0076

Storey, J. (1995). *Human resource management: A critical text*. Routledge.

Sukardi, S., Herminingsih, A., Djumarno, D., & Kasmir, K. (2021). Effect of human resource management practices to maturity knowledge management. [JDM]. *Jurnal Doktor Manajemen*, 4(1), 14–29. DOI:10.22441/jdm.v4i1.12103

Tabor-Błażewicz, J. (2023). Artificial intelligence adoption in human resources management. In Hajdas, M. (Ed.), *Game changers in management* (pp. 30–43). Publishing House of Wroclaw University of Economics and Business., DOI:10.15611/2023.10.9.02

Varma, A., Dawkins, C., & Chaudhuri, K. (2023). Artificial intelligence and people management: A critical assessment through the ethical lens. *Human Resource Management Review*, 33(1), 100923. DOI:10.1016/j.hrmr.2022.100923

Wiljer, D., & Hakim, Z. (2019). Developing an artificial intelligence–enabled health care practice: Rewiring health care professions for better care. *Journal of Medical Imaging and Radiation Sciences*, 50(4), 8–14. DOI:10.1016/j.jmir.2019.09.010 PMID:31791914

Compilation of References

6. sense. (2024). *Pymetrics—Market share, competitor insights in pre-employment assessment*. 6sense. https://www.6sense.com/tech/pre-employment-assessment/pymetrics-market-share

Abanda Maga, M. F., Kala Kamdjoug, J. R., Fosso Wamba, S., & Nitcheu Tcheuffa, P. C. (2019). Factors affecting adoption and use of e-learning by business employees in Cameroon. In *New Knowledge in Information Systems and Technologies* (Vol. 3, pp. 216–226). Springer International Publishing. DOI:10.1007/978-3-030-16187-3_21

Abdali, M. (2019). The strategic use of digital learning solutions: An HRM perspective (Doctoral dissertation, Auckland University of Technology).

Abdul Rani, A. A., Muda, R., Hanif, A., & Abd Rashid, A. (2024). Enhancing Consumer and Family Economic Well-Being in ASEAN: The Role of Technological Advancement and Institutional Quality in Navigating the Informal Economy. *Malaysian Journal of Consumer and Family Economics*, 32(1), 480–514. DOI:10.60016/majcafe.v32.19

Abdulaziz, A., Bashir, M., & Alfalih, A. A. (2022). The impact of work-life balance and work overload on teacher's organizational commitment: Do Job Engagement and Perceived Organizational support matter. *Education and Information Technologies*, 27(7), 9641–9663. DOI:10.1007/s10639-022-11013-8

Abrams, Z. (2024). Addressing equity and ethics in artificial intelligence. *American Pstchological Asociation*, 55(3), 1.

Acciarini, C., Boccardelli, P., & Vitale, M. (2021). Resilient companies in the time of Covid-19 pandemic: A case study approach. *Journal of Entrepreneurship and Public Policy*, 10(3), 336–351. DOI:10.1108/JEPP-03-2021-0021

Adagbabiri, M. M., & Okolie, U. C. (2020). Human Resource Management Practices and OrganizationalPerformance: An Empirical Study of Oil and Gas Industry in Nigeria. *RUDN Journal of Public Administration.*, 7(1), 53–69. DOI:10.22363/2312-8313-2020-7-1-53-69

Adhav, A. (2017). Human Resource Management: Objectives And Functions. *International Journal of Advance and Applied Research*, 4(3), 35–37.

Adisa, T. A., Antonacopoulou, E. P., Beauregard, T. A., Dickmann, M., & Adekoya, O. D. (2022). Exploring the impact of COVID-19 on employees' boundary management and Work–Life balance. *British Journal of Management*, 33(4), 1694–1709. DOI:10.1111/1467-8551.12643

Agariya, A. K., & Singh, D. (2012). e-Learning quality: Scale development and validation in Indian context. *Knowledge Management & E-Learning*, 4(4), 500–517.

Agarwal, V., Mathiyazhagan, K., Malhotra, S., & Saikouk, T. (2021). Analysis of challenges in sustainable human resource management due to disruptions by Industry 4.0: An emerging economy perspective. *International Journal of Manpower*, 43(2), 513–541. DOI:10.1108/IJM-03-2021-0192

Aggarwal, S., & Sharma, B. (2015). Green HRM: Need of the hour. *International Journal of Management and Social Science Research Review*, 1(8), 63–70.

Aggarwal, V., & Sharon, S. D. (2017). Digital human resource management. *Gyan Management Journal*, 11(2), 23–27.

Aghdasi, S., Kiāmanesh, A., & Ebrahim, A. N. (2011). Emotional Intelligence and Organizational Commitment: Testing the mediatory role of occupational stress and job satisfaction. *Procedia: Social and Behavioral Sciences*, 29, 1965–1976. DOI:10.1016/j.sbspro.2011.11.447

Agouridis, A. (2021, September 2). *All you need to know about AI and machine learning in HR.* https://www.jobylon.com/blog/all-you-need-to-know-about-ai-and-machine-learning-in-hr

Agouridis, A. (2023, February 9). *How AI is transforming the world of recruitment.* https://www.jobylon.com/blog/how-ai-is-transforming-the-world-of-recruitment

Agrawal, S., De Smet, A., Lacroix, S., & Reich, A. (2020). To emerge stronger from the COVID-19 crisis, companies should start reskilling their workforces now. *McKinsey Insights*, 2.

Agrawal, N., & Bansal, R. (2022). Green HRM: A medium of social responsibility and sustainable development. *International Journal of Innovation and Sustainable Development*, 16(2), 172–185.

Aguinis, H., & Burgi-Tian, J. (2021). Measuring performance during crises and beyond: The Performance Promoter Score. *Business Horizons*, 64(1), 149–160. DOI:10.1016/j.bushor.2020.09.001 PMID:32981944

Aguinis, H., & O'Boyle, E.Jr. (2014). Star performers in twenty-first century organizations. *Personnel Psychology*, 67(2), 313–350. DOI:10.1111/peps.12054

Ahamad Nawawi, N. H., Ramli, R., Khalid, N., & Abdul Rashid, S. F. (2023). Understanding The Presence of the Gig Economy in Malaysia. *Malaysian Journal of Consumer and Family Economics*, 31(1), 274–293. DOI:10.60016/majcafe.v31.11

Ahammad, T. (2017). Personnel Management to Human Resource Management (HRM): How HRM Functions? *Journal of Modern Accounting and Auditing*, 13(9), 412–420. DOI:10.17265/1548-6583/2017.09.004

Ahmad, S., Islam, T., Sadiq, M., & Kaleem, A. (2021). Promoting green behavior through ethical leadership: A model of green human resource management and environmental knowledge. *Leadership and Organization Development Journal*, 42(4), 531–547.

Aitken-Fox, E., Coffey, J., Dayaram, K., Fitzgerald, S., Gupta, C., McKenna, S., & Wei Tian, A. (2020). The impact of Covid-19 on human resource management: avoiding generalisations. *LSE Business Review*.

Ajayi-Nifise, A. O., Odeyemi, O., Mhlongo, N. Z., Falaiye, T., Elufioye, O. A., Awonuga, K. F., & Nwankwo, E. E. (2024). The future of accounting: Predictions on automation and AI integration. *International Journal of Science and Research Archive*, 11(1), 2063–2071. DOI:10.30574/ijsra.2024.11.1.0275

Ajila, C. O., & Abiola, A. (2004). Influence of rewards on workers performance in an organization. *Journal of Social Sciences*, 8(1), 7–12. DOI:10.1080/0971892 3.2004.11892397

Aksu, B. Ç., & Doğan, A. (2021). Çevresel sürdürülebilirlik ve insan kaynakları yönetimi fonksiyonlarının yeşil İKY bağlamında değerlendirilmesi. *Aksaray Üniversitesi İktisadi ve İdari Bilimler Fakültesi Dergisi*, 13(3), 137–148. DOI:10.52791/aksarayiibd.947200

Aktan, E. (2018). Büyük veri: Uygulama alanları, analitiği ve güvenlik boyutu. *Bilgi Yönetimi*, 1(1), 1–22. DOI:10.33721/by.403010

Alacovska, A., Bucher, E., & Fieseler, C. (2024). A Relational Work Perspective on the Gig Economy: Doing Creative Work on Digital Labour Platforms. *Work, Employment and Society*, 38(1), 161–179. DOI:10.1177/09500170221103146

Al-Alawneh, R., Othman, M., & Zaid, A. A. (2024). Green HRM impact on environmental performance in higher education with mediating roles of management support and green culture. *The International Journal of Organizational Analysis*, 32(6), 1141–1164.

Aldrich, C. (2009). *Learning online with games, simulations, and virtual worlds: Strategies for online instruction* (Vol. 11). John Wiley & Sons.

Alexa, L., Pîslaru, M., & Avasilcai, S. (2022). *From Industry 4.0 to Industry 5.0: An Overview of European Union Enterprises. A. Draghici, & L. Ivascu içinde, Sustainability and Innovation in Manufacturing Enterprises*. Springer.

Alfaqiri, A. S., Mat Noor, S. F., & Sahari, N. (2022). Framework for Gamification of Online Training Platforms for Employee Engagement Enhancement. *International journal of interactive mobile technologies, 16*(6).

Al-Fraihat, D., Joy, M., & Sinclair, J. (2020). Evaluating E-learning systems success: An empirical study. *Computers in Human Behavior*, 102, 67–86. DOI:10.1016/j.chb.2019.08.004

Al-Hila, A. A., Alhelou, E., Al Shobaki, M. J., & Abu Naser, S. S. (2017). The impact of applying the dimensions of IT governance in improving e-training-case study of the ministry of telecommunications and information technology in gaza governorates. *International Journal of Engineering and Information Systems*, 1(7), 194–219.

Ali, M. C., Islam, K. A., Chung, S. J., Zayed, N. M., & Afrin, M. (2020). A study of Green Human Resources Management (GHRM) and green creativity for human resources professionals. *International Journal of Business and Management Future*, 4(2), 57–67.

Alkan, A. D. (2022). The effects of COVID-19 on human resource management in aviation companies: the case of Europe. In *Digitalization and the Impacts of COVID-19 on the Aviation Industry* (pp. 225–242). IGI Global. DOI:10.4018/978-1-6684-2319-6.ch012

Al-Kassem, A. H. (2021). Significance of human resources training and development on organizational achievement. *PalArch's Journal of Archaeology of Egypt/ Egyptology, 18*(7), 693-707.

Allen, N. J., & Meyer, J. P. (1990). Organizational Socialization Tactics: A Longitudinal Analysis of Links to Newcomers' Commitment and Role Orientation. *Academy of Management Journal*, 33(4), 847–858. DOI:10.2307/256294

Allianz Care. (2023). *Sustainable global HRM practices*. Allianzcare.Com. https://www.allianzcare.com/en/employers/business-hub/hr-blogs/sustainable-global-hrm-practices.html

AlMazrouei, H. (2023). The effect of COVID-19 on managerial leadership style within Australian public sector organizations. *Journal of General Management*, 030630702311529. Advance online publication. DOI:10.1177/03063070231152976

Alser, M., & Waisberg, E. (2023). Concerns with the usage of ChatGPT in academia and medicine: A viewpoint. *American Journal of Medicine Open*, 9, 2. DOI:10.1016/j.ajmo.2023.100036 PMID:39035060

Altarawneh, I. I. (2016). Strategic human resources management and its impact on performance: The case from Saudi Arabia. *International Journal of Business Management and Economic Research*, 7(1).

Altunışık, R. (2015). Büyük Veri: Fırsatlar Kaynağı mı Yoksa Yeni Sorunlar Yumağı mı? Yildiz Social Science Review, 1(1), 45-76. https://dergipark.org.tr/en/pub/yssr/issue/21899/235390

Alvi, D. A. (2019, January 20). Pakistan's place in artificial intelligence and omputing. *The Nation*. Retrieved from https://nation.com.pk/20-Jan-2019/pakistan-splace-in-artificial-intelligence-and-computing

Amara, N. B., & Atia, L. (2016). E-training and its role in human resources development. *Global journal of human resource management, 4*(1), 1-12.

Amorim, J. A., Matos, C., Cuperschmid, A. R., Gustavsson, P. M., & Pozzer, C. T. (2013). Augmented reality and mixed reality technologies: Enhancing training and mission preparation with simulations. In *NATO Modelling and Simulation Group (MSG) Annual Conference 2013 (MSG-111), 2013*.

Amrutrao, S. (2022). LEADERSHIP STYLE DURING AND POST COVID19 IN CORPORATE: A STUDY OF HUMANITY APPROACH WITH EMPLOYEES. *International Journal of Engineering Technologies and Management Research*, 9(7), 1–7. DOI:10.29121/ijetmr.v9.i7.2022.1189

Anastasopoulou, A., Vraimaki, E., & Trivellas, P. (2023). Recovery for Resilience: The mediating role of Work–Life balance on the quality of life of women employees. *Sustainability (Basel)*, 15(17), 12877. DOI:10.3390/su151712877

Andrejevic, M. (2011). The work that affective economics does. *Cultural Studies*, 25(4-5), 604–620. DOI:10.1080/09502386.2011.600551

Angielsky, M., Copus, L., Madzik, P., & Falat, L. (2024). Navigating the human element: Unveiling insights into workforce dynamics in supply chain automation through smart bibliometric analysis.

Angrave, D., Charlwood, A., Kirkpatrick, I., Lawrence, M., & Stuart, M. (2016). HR and analytics: Why HR is set to fail the big data challenge. *Human Resource Management Journal*, 26(1), 1–11. DOI:10.1111/1748-8583.12090

April, K. (2024). Precarious Work in the Gig Economy: Diversity, Race and Indigeneity Lenses. In Meliou, E., Vassilopoulou, J., & Ozbilgin, M. F. (Eds.), *Diversity and Precarious Work During Socioeconomic Upheaval* (1st ed., pp. 137–162). Cambridge University Press., DOI:10.1017/9781108933070.008

Ardeleanu, A. M., & Josan, I. J. (2011). Equal opportunities in the public and private sector. Management, Learning Management~, 291.

Aria, M., & Cuccurullo, C. (2017). bibliometrix: An R-tool for comprehensive science mapping analysis. *Journal of Informetrics*, 11(4), 959–975. DOI:10.1016/j.joi.2017.08.007

Aripin, Z., Matriadi, F., & Ermeila, S. (2024, February). OPTIMIZATION OF WORKER WORK ENVIRONMENT, ROBOTS, AND MARKETING STRATEGY: THE IMPACT OF DIGITAL-BASED SPATIOTEMPORAL DYNAMICS ON HUMAN RESOURCE MANAGEMENT (HRM). In Journal of Jabar Economic Society Networking Forum (Vol. 1, No. 3, pp. 33-49).

Armstrong, M. (1999). *A Handbook of Human Resource Management practice*. https://ci.nii.ac.jp/ncid/BA83417636

Armstrong, M., & Taylor, S. (2014). Armstrong's Handbook of Human Resource Management Practice: US/Philadelphia: Edition 13. Kogan page, E-ISBN 978 0 7494 6965 8.

Armstrong, M. (2006). *A Handbook of Human Resource Management Practice*. Kogan Page Publishers.

Armstrong, M. (2010). *Armstrong's essential human resource management practice: A Guide to People Management*. Kogan Page Publishers.

Armstrong, M. B., & Landers, R. N. (2018). Gamification of employee training and development. *International Journal of Training and Development*, 22(2), 162–169. DOI:10.1111/ijtd.12124

Armstrong, M., & Taylor, S. (2006). *Human resource management practice* (10th ed.). Distributed Computing., DOI:10.1002/9781118802717

Arora, M., & Mittal, A. (2024). Employees' change in perception when artificial intelligence integrates with human resource management: A mediating role of AI-tech trust. *Benchmarking*. Advance online publication. DOI:10.1108/BIJ-11-2023-0795

Artificial Intelligence Act, E. U. (2024). *EU Artificial Intelligence Act | Up-to-date developments and analyses of the EU AI Act.* https://artificialintelligenceact.eu/

Arulrajah, A. A., Opatha, H. H. D. N. P., & Nawaratne, N. N. J. (2015). Green human resource management practices. *RE:view*.

Ashforth, B. E., & Mael, F. A. (1989). Social Identity Theory and the organization. *Academy of Management Review*, 14(1), 20–39. DOI:10.2307/258189

Asim, M., Liu, Z., Nadeem, M., Ghani, U., Arshad, M. I., & Xu, Y. (2021). How authoritarian leadership affects employee's helping behavior? The mediating role of rumination and moderating role of psychological ownership. *Frontiers in Psychology*, 12, 667348. Advance online publication. DOI:10.3389/fpsyg.2021.667348 PMID:34552524

Auguste, D., Roll, S., & Despard, M. (2023). Democratizing the Economy or Introducing Economic Risk? Gig Work During the COVID-19 Pandemic. *Work and Occupations*, 07308884231202032, 07308884231202032. Advance online publication. DOI:10.1177/07308884231202032

Aungsuroch, Y., Gunawan, J., & Fisher, M. L. (2021). *Redesigning the nursing and human resource partnership: A model for the new normal era.* Springer Nature.

Awais, M., Malik, M. S., & Qaisar, A. (2015). A Review: The Job Satisfaction Act as Mediator between Spiritual Intelligence and Organizational Commitment. *International Review of Management and Marketing*, 5(4), 203–210. https://dergipark.org.tr/en/download/article-file/366720

Ayman Güler, B. (2020). *Kamu Personeli: Sistem ve Yönetim.* İmge Kitabevi.

Ayubayeva, S., Tynyshbayeva, A., & Kussainova, L. (2020). Public Service Efficiency: An Innovative Method for Assessing Public Sector Reputation. *The Innovation Journal, 27*(3), 1-20.

Azizi, M. R., Atlasi, R., Ziapour, A., Abbas, J., & Naemi, R. (2021). Innovative human resource management strategies during the COVID-19 pandemic: A systematic narrative review approach. *Heliyon*, 7(6), e07233. DOI:10.1016/j.heliyon.2021.e07233 PMID:34124399

Babbage, C. (1832). *On the economy of machinery and manufactures* (2nd ed.). Charles Knight. DOI:10.5479/sil.975430.39088015716483

Bach, S. (2005). *Personnel Management*. Blackwell Publishing.

Badruddoza Talukder, M., Kumar, S., Misra, L. I., & Firoj Kabir, . (2024). Determining the role of eco-tourism service quality, tourist satisfaction, and destination loyalty: A case study of Kuakata beach. *Acta Scientiarum Polonorum. Administratio Locorum*, 23(1), 133–151. DOI:10.31648/aspal.9275

Bagher, A. (2022). Managing Conflicts of Interest in the Public Sector. *Public Law Studies Quarterly*, 52(1), 297–321.

Bahrke, J., & Regnier, T. (2023, December 14). *Artificial intelligence – Q&As* [Text]. European Commission - European Commission. https://ec.europa.eu/commission/presscorner/detail/en/qanda_21_1683

Baïdoo-Anu, D., & Owusu Ansah, L. (2023). Education in the era of generative artificial intelligence (ai): Understanding the potential benefits of ChatGPT in promoting teaching and learning. *Journal of AI*, 7(1), 1. DOI:10.61969/jai.1337500

Baiyegunhi, T., Baiyegunhi, C., & Pharoe, B. (2022). Global Research Trends on Shale Gas from 2010–2020 Using a Bibliometric Approach. *Sustainability (Basel)*, 14(6), 1–22. DOI:10.3390/su14063461

Bajer, J. (2017). Digital transformation needs the human touch. *Strategic HR Review*, 16(2), 91–92. DOI:10.1108/SHR-02-2017-0011

Balakrishnan, R., & Das, S. (2020). How do firms reorganize to implement digital transformation? *Strategic Change*, 29(5), 531–541. DOI:10.1002/jsc.2362

Bambang, I. (2023). Public Administration Challenges in Human Resource Management in the Education Sector. *Indo-MathEdu Intellectuals Journal.*, 4(2), 1349–1361. DOI:10.54373/imeij.v4i2.359

Bamboo, H. R. (2023). *Performance management software*. https://www.bamboohr.com/hr-software/performance-management

Barck-Holst, P., Nilsonne, Å., Åkerstedt, T., & Hellgren, C. (2020). Reduced working hours and work-life balance. *Nordic Social Work Research*, 12(4), 450–463. DOI:10.1080/2156857X.2020.1839784

Barney, J. (1991). Firm Resources and Sustained Competitive Advantage. *Journal of Management*, 17(1), 99–121. DOI:10.1177/014920639101700108

Baron, R. A., & Greenberg, J. (1990). *Behavior in organizations: Understanding and Managing the Human Side of Work.* Allyn & Bacon.

Barrios, J. M., Hochberg, Y. V., & Yi, H. (2022). Launching with a parachute: The gig economy and new business formation. *Journal of Financial Economics*, 144(1), 22–43. DOI:10.1016/j.jfineco.2021.12.011

Barro, R. J., Ursúa, J. F., & Weng, J. (2020). *The coronavirus and the great influenza pandemic: Lessons from the "Spanish flu" for the coronavirus's potential effects on mortality and economic activity* (No. w26866). National Bureau of Economic Research.

Bartels, J., Pruyn, A. T., De Jong, M. D., & Joustra, I. (2006). Multiple organizational identification levels and the impact of perceived external prestige and communication climate. *Journal of Organizational Behavior*, 28(2), 173–190. DOI:10.1002/job.420

Bassi, L. (2011). Raging debates in HR analytics. (2011, p.16-17). *People and Strategy*, 34(2), 14–18.

Basu, S., Majumdar, B., Mukherjee, K., Munjal, S., & Palaksha, C. (2023). Artificial intelligence–HRM interactions and outcomes: A systematic review and causal configurational explanation. *Human Resource Management Review*, 33(1), 100893. DOI:10.1016/j.hrmr.2022.100893

Batra, G. S. (1996). Human resource auditing as a tool for valuation: interface and emerging practices.

Bayrakçı, S., & Albayrak, M. A. (2019). Büyük Verinin Akademik Çalışmalarda Kullanımı Üzerine Mukayeseli Bir Veri Tabanı Araştırması. AJIT-e. *Bilişim Teknolojileri Online Dergisi*, 10(36), 73–94. DOI:10.5824/1309-1581.2019.1.004.x

Bayraktar, O., & Ataç, C. (2018). *The Effects of Industry 4.0 on Human Resources Management. E. Yıldırım, & H. Çeştepe içinde, Globalization, Institutions and Socio-Economic Performance.* Peter Lang.

Bedwell, W. L., & Salas, E. (2010). Computer-based training: Capitalizing on lessons learned. *International Journal of Training and Development*, 14(3), 239–249. DOI:10.1111/j.1468-2419.2010.00355.x

Behl, A., Rajagopal, K., Sheorey, P., & Mahendra, A. (2022). Barriers to entry of gig workers in the gig platforms: Exploring the dark side of the gig economy. *Aslib Journal of Information Management*, 74(5), 818–839. DOI:10.1108/AJIM-08-2021-0235

Beretta, G. (2021). The New Rules for Reporting by Sharing and Gig Economy Platforms Under the OECD and EU Initiatives. *EC Tax Review*, 30(1), 31–38. DOI:10.54648/ECTA2021004

Best, S. J., Krueger, B. S., & Ladewig, J. (2006). Privacy in the information age. *Public Opinion Quarterly*, 70(3), 375–401. DOI:10.1093/poq/nfl018

Bharadwaj, A., El Sawy, O., Pavlou, P., & Venkatraman, N. (2013). Digital business strategy: Toward the next generation of insights. *Management Information Systems Quarterly*, 37(2), 471–482. DOI:10.25300/MISQ/2013/37:2.3

Bhende, P., Mekoth, N., Ingalhalli, V., & Reddy, Y. (2020). Quality of work life and Work–Life balance. *Journal of Human Values*, 26(3), 256–265. DOI:10.1177/0971685820939380

Bhumika. (2020). Challenges for work–life balance during COVID-19 induced nationwide lockdown: exploring gender difference in emotional exhaustion in the Indian setting. *Gender in Management: An International Journal, 35*(7/8), 705–718. DOI:10.1108/GM-06-2020-0163

Bibi, M. (2019). Execution of artificial intelligence approach in human resource management functions: Benefits and challenges in Pakistan. *Sarhad Journal of Management Sciences*, 5(1), 113–124. DOI:10.31529/sjms.2018.5.1.8

Bielby, D. D. (1992). Commitment to Work and Family. *Annual Review of Sociology*, 18(1), 281–302. DOI:10.1146/annurev.so.18.080192.001433

Biesalski, E. (2003). Knowledge management and e-human resource management, Available at: https://www.kde.cs.uni-kassel.de/wpcontent/uploads/ws/LLWA03/fgwm/Resources/FGWM03_08_Ernst_Biesalski.pdf. [Accessed: 13 April 2024].

Bilevičienė, T., Bilevičiūtė, E., & Parazinskaitė, G. (2015). Innovative trends in human resources management. *Economics & Sociology (Ternopil)*, 8(4), 94–109. DOI:10.14254/2071-789X.2015/8-4/7

Bishop, C. (n.d.). *What is hot-desking and what are the benefits? - ideas (en-GB)*. Ideas (en-GB). https://www.wework.com/en-GB/ideas/workspace-solutions/what-is-hot-desking

Biswas, S., & Bhatnagar, J. (2013). Mediator Analysis of employee engagement: Role of perceived organizational support, P-O fit, organizational commitment and job satisfaction. *Vikalpa*, 38(1), 27–40. DOI:10.1177/0256090920130103

Boas, T., & Gans-Morse, J. (2009). Haziran). Neoliberalism: From New Liberal Philosophy to Anti-Liberal Slogan. *Studies in Comparative International Development*, 44(2), 137–161. DOI:10.1007/s12116-009-9040-5

Boje, D., Burnes, B., & Hassard, J. (2012). *The Routledge companion to organizational change*. Routledge. DOI:10.4324/9780203810279

Bordegoni, M., & Ferrise, F. (2023). Exploring the intersection of metaverse, digital twins, and artificial intelligence in training and maintenance. *Journal of Computing and Information Science in Engineering*, 23(6), 060806. DOI:10.1115/1.4062455

Boxall, P., Guthrie, J. P., & Paauwe, J. (2016). Progressing our understanding of the mediating variables linking HRM, employee well-being and organizational performance. *Human Resource Management Journal*, 26, 103–111. DOI:10.1111/1748-8583.12104

Boyd, C. (2003). *Human Resource Management and Occupational Health and Safety*. Routledge. DOI:10.4324/9780203428061_chapter_1

Braganza, A., Chen, W., Canhoto, A., & Sap, S. (2022). Gigification, job engagement and satisfaction: The moderating role of AI enabled system automation in operations management. *Production Planning and Control*, 33(16), 1534–1547. DOI:10.108 0/09537287.2021.1882692

Bratianu, C., & Bejinaru, R. (2021). COVID-19 induced emergent knowledge strategies. *Knowledge and Process Management*, 28(1), 11–17. DOI:10.1002/kpm.1656

Brega, C., Briones, S., Javornik, J., León, M., & Yerkes, M. (2023). Flexible work arrangements for work-life balance: A cross-national policy evaluation from a capabilities perspective. *The International Journal of Sociology and Social Policy*, 43(13/14), 278–294. DOI:10.1108/IJSSP-03-2023-0077

Brief, A. P., & Weiss, H. M. (2002). Organizational behavior: Affect in the workplace. *Annual Review of Psychology*, 53(1), 279–307. DOI:10.1146/annurev.psych.53.100901.135156 PMID:11752487

Brinkmann, S., & Kvale, S. (2018). Doing interviews. London: (2. ed.) SAGE Publications https://uk.sagepub.com/en-gb/eur/doing-interviews/book244549

Britannica, T. E. of E. (2024, February 14). *Elton Mayo*. https://www.britannica.com/biography/Elton-Mayo

Brown, B. A. (2020). *Evaluating Expert Opinions for Reducing Voluntary Employee Absenteeism in Trinidad and Tobago* [Ph.D., Walden University]. http://search.proquest.com/pqdtglobal/docview/2447561234/abstract/1A8116E743549EAPQ/1

Brown, S. (2021, April 21). *Machine learning, explained.* https://mitsloan.mit.edu/ideas-made-to-matter/machine-learning-explained

Brown, B. A., & Heitner, K. L. (2022). Worker response to the rapid changes caused by disruptive innovation: Managing a remote workforce without any training or preparation. In Hynes, R., Aquino, C., & Hauer, J. (Eds.), *Multidisciplinary approach to diversity and inclusion in the COVID-19-era workplace* (pp. 189–205). IGI Global., DOI:10.4018/978-1-7998-8827-7.ch011

Brown, B. A., & Heitner, K. L. (2023a). Obstacles and resistance to organizational change in the new post-COVID-19 environment. In Belias, D., Rossidis, I., Papademetriou, C., Masouras, A., & Anastasiadou, S. (Eds.), *Managing successful and ethical organizational change* (pp. 167–195). IGI Global., DOI:10.4018/979-8-3693-0235-4.ch008

Brown, B. A., & Heitner, K. L. (2023b). Organizational transformation: The way to Sustainability. In De Moraes, A. (Ed.), *Strategic management and international business policies for maintaining competitive advantage* (pp. 34–75). IGI Global., DOI:10.4018/978-1-6684-6845-6.ch003

Brown, B. A., & Heitner, K. L. (2024). International business staffing challenges and the growing global skills gap in the post-COVID environment: A Latin American and Caribbean perspective. In Christiansen, B., & Even, A. M. (Eds.), *Advancing student employability through higher education* (pp. 199–219). IGI Global., DOI:10.4018/979-8-3693-0517-1.ch011

Brunsson, K. H. (2008). Some effects of Fayolism. *International Studies of Management & Organization*, 38(1), 30–47. DOI:10.2753/IMO0020-8825380102

Buchholz, L. (2023, December 15). *93% of HR managers use AI tools to reduce costs, report finds.* UNLEASH. https://www.unleash.ai/artificial-intelligence/93-of-hr-managers-use-ai-tools-to-reduce-costs-report-finds/

Budhwar, P., Malik, A., De Silva, M. T. T., & Thevisuthan, P. (2022). Artificial intelligence – challenges and opportunities for international HRM: A review and research agenda. *International Journal of Human Resource Management*, 33(6), 1065–1097. DOI:10.1080/09585192.2022.2035161

Burchardt, C., & Maisch, B. (2019). Digitalization needs a cultural change–examples of applying Agility and Open Innovation to drive the digital transformation. *Procedia CIRP*, 84, 112–117. DOI:10.1016/j.procir.2019.05.009

Burnett, G. W., & Goldhaber-Fiebert, S. N. (2024). The role of simulation training in patients' safety in anaesthesia and perioperative medicine. *BJA Education*, 24(1), 7–12. DOI:10.1016/j.bjae.2023.10.002 PMID:38495746

Bye, A. (2023). Future needs of human reliability analysis: The interaction between new technology, crew roles and performance. *Safety Science*, 158, 105962. DOI:10.1016/j.ssci.2022.105962

Cahyono, A. S., Tuhuteru, L., Julina, S., Suherlan, S., & Ausat, A. M. A. (2023). Building a Generation of Qualified Leaders: Leadership Education Strategies in Schools. *Journal of Education*, 5(4), 12974–12979. https://jonedu.org/index.php/joe/article/view/2289

Calp, M. H. (2016). İşletmelerde uygulanan insan kaynaklari yönetiminde veritabani kullaniminin önemi. *Gazi Üniversitesi İktisadi ve İdari Bilimler Fakültesi Dergisi*, 18(2), 539–557.

Carayannis, E., & Joanna Morawska, J. (2022). The Futures of Europe: Society 5.0 and Industry 5.0 as Driving Forces of Future Universities. *Journal of the Knowledge Economy*, 13(4), 3445–3471. DOI:10.1007/s13132-021-00854-2

Caringal-Go, J. F., Teng-Calleja, M., Bertulfo, D. J., & Manaois, J. O. (2021). Work-life balance crafting during COVID-19: Exploring strategies of telecommuting employees in the Philippines. *Community Work & Family*, 25(1), 112–131. DOI:10.1080/13668803.2021.1956880

Carlson, D. S., Grzywacz, J. G., & Michele Kacmar, K. (2010). The relationship of schedule flexibility and outcomes via the work-family interface. *Journal of Managerial Psychology*, 25(4), 330–355. DOI:10.1108/02683941011035278

Carnevale, J. B., & Hatak, I. (2020). Employee adjustment and well-being in the era of COVID-19: Implications for human resource management. *Journal of Business Research*, 116, 183–187. DOI:10.1016/j.jbusres.2020.05.037 PMID:32501303

Castells, M. (2010). *The rise of the network society. (Information age. economy, society and culture, 1.).* Wiley-Blackwell.

Chafi, M. B., Hultberg, A., & Yams, N. B. (2021). Post-Pandemic Office work: Perceived challenges and opportunities for a sustainable work environment. *Sustainability (Basel)*, 14(1), 294. DOI:10.3390/su14010294

Chalekian, P. (2013). POSDCORB: Core Patterns of Administration. *Proceedings of the 20th Conference on Pattern Languages of Programs*, (s. 1-20).

Chandra, S., & Ray, S. ve Goswami, R. T. (2017), Big data security: survey on frameworks and algorithms. 2017 IEEE 7th International Advance Computing Conference (IACC) (pp. 48-54). Hyderabad, İndia: IEEE.

Charles Babbage Institute. (2024). *Who was Charles Babbage?* College of Science and Engineering. https://cse.umn.edu/cbi/who-was-charles-babbage

Charmaz, K. (2006). *Constructing grounded theory: A practical guide through qualitative analysis*. SAGE Publications.

Charmaz, K. (2015). *Grounded Theory Configuration* (Hoş, R., Ed. & Trans.). Seçkin Publishing.

Chaudhary, R. (2019). Green human resource management in the Indian automobile industry. *Journal of Global Responsibility*, 10(2), 161–175.

Chaudhuri, S., Arora, R., & Roy, P. (2020). Work–life balance policies and organisational outcomes – a review of literature from the Indian context. *Industrial and Commercial Training*, 52(3), 155–170. DOI:10.1108/ICT-01-2019-0003

Cheng, J., Sun, X., Zhong, Y., & Li, K. (2023). Flexible work arrangements and employees' knowledge sharing in Post-Pandemic era: The roles of workplace loneliness and task interdependence. *Behavioral Sciences (Basel, Switzerland)*, 13(2), 168. DOI:10.3390/bs13020168 PMID:36829396

Cheng, M. M., & Hackett, R. D. (2021). A critical review of algorithms in HRM: Definition, theory, and practice. *Human Resource Management Review*, 31(1), 100698. DOI:10.1016/j.hrmr.2019.100698

Cheng, Z., Nielsen, I., & Cutler, H. (2019). Perceived job quality, work-life interference and intention to stay. *International Journal of Manpower*, 40(1), 17–35. DOI:10.1108/IJM-08-2017-0208

Chen, H., Chiang, R. H., & Storey, V. C. (2012). Business intelligence and analytics: From big data to big impact. *Management Information Systems Quarterly*, 36(4), 1165–1188. DOI:10.2307/41703503

Chen, M., Mao, S., Zhang, Y., & Leung, V. C. M. (2014). Big Data Storage. In *Big Data Related Technologies, Challenges and Future Prospects* (pp. 33–49). Springer., DOI:10.1007/978-3-319-06245-7_4

Cherian, J., & Jacob, J. (2012). A study of green HR practices and its effective implementation in the organization: A review. *International Journal of Business and Management*, 7(21), 25–33. DOI:10.5539/ijbm.v7n21p25

Chien, C. F., & Chen, L. F. (2008). Data mining to improve personnel selection and enhance human capital: A case study in high-technology industry. *Expert Systems with Applications*, 34(1), 280–290. DOI:10.1016/j.eswa.2006.09.003

Choi, K. (2006). A Structural Relationship analysis of hotel employees' turnover intention. *Asia Pacific Journal of Tourism Research*, 11(4), 321–337. DOI:10.1080/10941660600931150

Christensen, C. M. (1997). *The innovator's dilemma: When new technologies cause great firms to fail*. Harvard Business Review Press.

Chung, E. (2013). *The relationship of training and organizational commitment in One Korean organization*. https://conservancy.umn.edu/handle/11299/162440

Churchill, B., & Craig, L. (2019). Gender in the gig economy: Men and women using digital platforms to secure work in Australia. *Journal of Sociology (Melbourne, Vic.)*, 55(4), 741–761. DOI:10.1177/1440783319894060

Chytiri, A. P. (2019). Human resource managers' role in the digital era. *Journal of Economics and Business*, 69(1-2), 62–72.

Cichosz, M., Wallenburg, C. M., & Knemeyer, A. M. (2020). Digital transformation at logistics service providers: Barriers, success factors and leading practices. *International Journal of Logistics Management*, 31(2), 209–238. DOI:10.1108/IJLM-08-2019-0229

Çiğdem, Ş., & Seyrek, İ. H. (2015). *İşletmelerde Büyük Veri Uygulamaları: Bir Literatür Taraması. Ulusal Yönetim Bilişim Sistemleri Kongresi*. Ataturk University.

Cole, M. S., & Bruch, H. (2006). Organizational identity strength, identification, and commitment and their relationships to turnover intention: Does organizational hierarchy matter? *Journal of Organizational Behavior*, 27(5), 585–605. DOI:10.1002/job.378

Collings, D. G., McMackin, J., Nyberg, A. J., & Wright, P. M. (2021). Strategic Human Resource Management and COVID-19: Emerging Challenges and Research Opportunities. *Journal of Management Studies*, 58(5), 1378–1382. DOI:10.1111/joms.12695

Coronavirus Resource Center. (2020). Johns Hopkins University & Medicine. Retrieved on 22th March 2024 from https://coronavirus.jhu.edu/map.html

Correia, A. B., Farrukh Shahzad, M., Moleiro Martins, J., & Baheer, R. (2024). Impact of green human resource management towards sustainable performance in the healthcare sector: Role of green innovation and risk management. *Cogent Business & Management*, 11(1), 2374625.

Cortellazzo, L., Bruni, E., & Zampieri, R. (2019). The role of leadership in a digitalized world: A review. *Frontiers in Psychology*, 10, 1–21. DOI:10.3389/fpsyg.2019.01938 PMID:31507494

Creswell. (2016, p.195). Creswell, J. W. (2016). Research design: Qualitative, quantitative and mixed method approaches. (Translation: Demir, S.). Ankara: (4.edition) Eğiten Kitap.

Creswell, J. W. (2013). *Qualitative research methods* (Bütün, L., & Demir, B., Trans.). Siyasal Kitabevi.

Crispin, J. (2021, July 5). Welcome to dystopia: Getting fired from your job as an Amazon worker by an app. *The Guardian*. https://www.theguardian.com/commentisfree/2021/jul/05/amazon-worker-fired-app-dystopia

Cukier, K., & Mayer-Schoenberger, V. (2013). The rise of big data: How it's changing the way we think about the world. *Foreign Affairs*, 92(3), 28–40. https://heinonline.org/HOL/P?h=hein.journals/fora92&i=593

Dachner, A. M., Ellingson, J. E., Noe, R. A., & Saxton, B. M. (2021). The future of employee development. *Human Resource Management Review*, 31(2), 14. DOI:10.1016/j.hrmr.2019.100732

Dahalan, F., Alias, N., & Shaharom, M. S. N. (2023). Gamification and game based learning for vocational education and training: A systematic literature review. *Education and Information Technologies*, ●●●, 1–39. PMID:36688221

Dahlbom, P., Siikanen, N., Sajasalo, P., & Jarvenpää, M. (2019). Big data and HR analytics in the digital era. *Baltic Journal of Management*, 8(2), 221–234. DOI:10.1108/BJM-11-2018-0393

Dahri, N. A., Vighio, M. S., Alismaiel, O. A., & Al-Rahmi, W. M. (2022). Assessing the Impact of Mobile-Based Training on Teachers' Achievement and Usage Attitude. *International Journal of Interactive Mobile Technologies*, 16(9).

Dal Mas, F., Massaro, M., Lombardi, R., & Garlatti, A. (2019). From output to outcome measures in the public sector: A structured literature review. *The International Journal of Organizational Analysis*, ahead-of-print(ahead-of-print). Advance online publication. DOI:10.1108/IJOA-09-2018-1523

Daling, L. M., & Schlittmeier, S. J. (2024). Effects of augmented reality-, virtual reality-, and mixed reality–based training on objective performance measures and subjective evaluations in manual assembly tasks: A scoping review. *Human Factors*, 66(2), 589–626. DOI:10.1177/00187208221105135 PMID:35635107

Danvila-del-Valle, I., Estévez-Mendoza, C., & Lara, F. J. (2019). Human resources training: A bibliometric analysis. *Journal of Business Research*, 101, 627–636. DOI:10.1016/j.jbusres.2019.02.026

Das, I. R., Talukder, M. B., & Kumar, S. (2024). Implication of Artificial Intelligence in Hospitality Marketing. In Kumar, S., Talukder, M. B., & Pego, A. (Eds.), *Advances in Hospitality, Tourism, and the Services Industry* (pp. 291–310). IGI Global., DOI:10.4018/979-8-3693-1978-9.ch014

Das, S. C., & Singh, R. K. (2016). Green HRM and organizational sustainability: An empirical review. *Kegees Journal of Social Science*, 8(1), 227–236.

Dastin, J. (2018, October 10). *Insight—Amazon scraps secret AI recruiting tool that showed bias against women*. https://www.reuters.com/article/idUSKCN1MK0AG/

Dastin, J. (2022). Amazon scraps secret AI recruiting tool that showed bias against women. In *Ethics of data and analytics*. Auerbach Publications. DOI:10.1201/9781003278290-44

Davenport, T. H., Harris, J. G., & Morison, R. (2010). Analytics at work: Smarter decisions, better results. Boston, Massachusetts: Harvard Business Press. ISBN 978-4221-7769-3.

De Mauro, A., Greco, M., Grimaldi, M., & Ritala, P. (2018). Human resources for Big Data professions: A systematic classification of job roles and required skill sets. *Information Processing & Management*, 54(5), 807–817. DOI:10.1016/j.ipm.2017.05.004

De Menezes, L. M. (2012). Job satisfaction and quality management: An empirical analysis. *International Journal of Operations & Production Management*, 32(3), 308–328. DOI:10.1108/01443571211212592

Decision No Sp-73 of the Central Electoral Commission of the Republic of Lithuania, dated 7 February 2019, approved the description of the procedure for processing personal data at the Central Electoral Commission.

Dedema, M., & Rosenbaum, H. (2024). Socio-technical issues in the platform-mediated gig economy: A systematic literature review: An Annual Review of Information Science and Technology (ARIST) paper. *Journal of the Association for Information Science and Technology*, 75(3), 344–374. DOI:10.1002/asi.24868

Deloitte. (2021). https://www2.deloitte.com/ua/en/pages/about-deloitte/press -releases/gx-2021-global-human-capital-trends-report.html.[Accessed: 13 April 2024].

Desgourdes, C., Hasnaoui, J. A., Umar, M., & González-Feliu, J. (2023). Decoding laissez-faire leadership: An in-depth study on its influence over employee autonomy and well-being at work. *The International Entrepreneurship and Management Journal.* Advance online publication. DOI:10.1007/s11365-023-00927-5

Dessler, G. (2020). *Human Resource Management.* Pearson.

Dhatterwal, J. S., Kaswan, K. S., Pathak, J. P., & Balusamy, B. (2024). Robotics in Production and Its Impact on HR Functions. In The Role of HR in the Transforming Workplace (pp. 10-31). Productivity Press.

Dhawan, A. (2023, March 20). *Evolution of HRM (human resource development).* https://datatrained.com/post/evolution-of-hrm/

DHMI. (2010). DHMI. DHMI Statistical Data, https://www.dhmi.gov.tr/istatistik .aspx [Retrieved date: 26-October -2010].

DHMI. (2010). DHMI. DHMI Statistical Data, https://www.dhmi.gov.tr/istatistik .aspx [Retrieved date: 26-October -2010]. Ariyawansa, C. M., & Aponso, A. C. (2016, May). Review on state of art data mining and machine learning techniques for intelligent Airport systems. In *2016 2nd International Conference on Information Management (ICIM)* (pp. 134-138). IEEE.

Diaz, M. A., & Sanchez, R. (2011). Gender and Potential Wage in Europe: A Stochastic FrontierApproach. *International Journal of Manpower*, 32(4), 410–425. DOI:10.1108/01437721111148531

DiBenedetto, C. (2024, March 8). *AI shows clear racial bias when used for job recruiting, new tests reveal.* Mashable. https://mashable.com/article/openai-chatgpt -racial-bias-in-recruiting

Dickson, C. N., & John, A. J. (2022). Public administration: Theory and practice in Nigeria. In Iba, O. J., Dickson, C. N., & John, A. J. (Eds.), *Public administration: Theory and practice in Nigeria* (pp. 84–96). CHANANPRINTS.

Diehl, D. C., Israel, G. D., Nelson, J. D., & Galindo, S. (2023). Work-Life Balance during the COVID-19 Pandemic: Insights from Extension Professionals. *Scholars Junction, 11*(1). https://scholarsjunction.msstate.edu/jhse/vol11/iss1/6/

Dirani, K. M., Abadi, M., Alizadeh, A., Barhate, B., Garza, R. C., Gunasekara, N., Ibrahim, G., & Majzun, Z. (2020). Leadership competencies and the essential role of human resource development in times of crisis: A response to COVID-19 pandemic. *Human Resource Development International*, 23(4), 380–394. DOI:10. 1080/13678868.2020.1780078

Dirik, D., Eryılmaz, İ., & Erhan, T. (2023). Post-Truth Kavramı Üzerine Yapılan Çalışmaların VOSviewer ile Bibliyometrik Analizi. Sosyal Mucit Academic Review, 4(2), s. 164- 188. https://dergipark.org.tr/tr/download/article-file/3036932 (Acces Date: 12.01.2024)

Dissanayake, K. (2020). Encountering COVID-19: Human resource management (HRM) practices in a pandemic crisis. *Colombo Journal of Multi-Disciplinary Research*, 5(1-2), 1–22. DOI:10.4038/cjmr.v5i1-2.52

Doğanoğlu, F. (2001). Küreselleşme ve İnsan Kaynakları Yönetimi. Öneri Dergisi, 4(16), s. 173- 181. DOI:10.14783/maruoneri.728734

Dong, X. H., Ying, A., & Guo, J. G. (2014). Research on the Application of the Big Data Technology in the Network Recruitment. *Human Resource Development of China*, 18, 37–41.

Doody, O., & Noonan, M. (2013). Preparing and conducting interviews to collect data. *Nurse Researcher*, 20(5), 28–32. DOI:10.7748/nr2013.05.20.5.28.e327 PMID:23687846

Douglas, L. (2001), 3d data management: Controlling data volume, velocity and variety. Gartner. Retrieved. 6.

Dowd, D. F. (2024, February 17). *Robert Owen.* https://www.britannica.com/ biography/Robert-Owen

Draghici, A. (2020). Changes and challenges of human systems management during and after the pandemic. *Human Systems Management*, 39(4), 469–472. DOI:10.3233/ HSM-209001

Drapkin, A. (2024, March 13). Google Gemini vs ChatGPT: Which AI chatbot wins in 2024? *Tech.Co.* https://tech.co/news/google-bard-vs-chatgpt

Driscoll, M. and Tomiak, G.R., 2000. Web-based training: Using technology to design adult learning experiences. https://doi.org/DOI:10.1002/pfi.4140390316

Du Plessis, D., & Keyter, C. (2020). Suitable leadership styles for the Covid-19 converged crisis. *Africa Journal of Public Sector Development and Governance*, 3(1), 61–73. DOI:10.55390/ajpsdg.2020.3.1.3

Duggan, J., McDonnell, A., Sherman, U., & Carbery, R. (2021). *Work in the Gig Economy: A Research Overview* (1st ed.). Routledge., DOI:10.4324/9780429351488

Dumont, J., Shen, J., & Deng, X. (2017). Effects of green HRM practices on employee workplace green behavior: The role of psychological green climate and employee green values. *Human Resource Management*, 56(4), 613–627. DOI:10.1002/hrm.21792

Dunnette, M. D. (1976). *Handbook of industrial and organizational psychology*. Rand McNally College Publishing Company.

Dunn, M. (2020). Making gigs work: Digital platforms, job quality and worker motivations. *New Technology, Work and Employment*, 35(2), 232–249. DOI:10.1111/ntwe.12167

Dutton, J. E., Dukerich, J. M., & Harquail, C. V. (1994). Organizational images and member identification. *Administrative Science Quarterly*, 39(2), 239. DOI:10.2307/2393235

Economic Commission for Latin America and the Caribbean. (2022). *A digital path for sustainable development in Latin America and the Caribbean*. https://repositorio.cepal.org/handle/11362/48461

Edelman, D. (2012). The war for digital talent is already here. Available at: https://www.forbes.com/sites/mckinsey/2012/01/23/the-war-for-digital-talent-is-alreadyhere/#6c75189762cb, [Accessed: 14 April 2024].

Edwards, M. J. A., & Peccei, R. (2007). Organizational identification: Development and testing of a conceptually grounded measure. *European Journal of Work and Organizational Psychology*, 16(1), 25–57. DOI:10.1080/13594320601088195

Egan, J. (2024, March 18). *How to spot AI-generated lies on a resume*. https://www.shrm.org/topics-tools/news/technology/how-to-spot-ai-generated-lies-on-a-resume

Eightfold, A. I. (2022). *The future of work: Intelligent by design*. https://eightfold.ai/wp-content/uploads/2022_Talent_Survey.pdf

Elias, G. (2023, March 17). *Common issues with ChatGPT and how to mitigate them*. https://skimai.com/common-issues-with-chatgpt/

Elkington, J. (2004). Enter the triple bottom line. In *The triple bottom line: Does it all add up?* (1st ed.). Routledge.

Ellegaard, O., & Wallin, A. (2015). The Bibliometric Analysis of Scholarly Production: How? *Scientometrics*, 105(3), 1809–1831. DOI:10.1007/s11192-015-1645-z PMID:26594073

Elnur, A. (2022). *Kadınların Ve Erkeklerin Tek Başına Seyahat Deneyimlerinin Toplumsal Cinsiyet Bağlamında Analizi. Akdeniz Üniversitesi Sosyal Bilimler Üniversitesi.* Yayınlanmış Dalı Doktora Tezi.

Enaifoghe, A., Ndebele, N. C., Durokifa, A., & Thusi, X. (2024). Drivers of Digital Transformation and Their Efficacy in Public Sector Human Resource Management. In *Digital Transformation in Public Sector Human Resource Management* (pp. 39–59). IGI Global.

Endress, T. (2024). Disruption and the Gig Economy: What's Next? In Endress, T., & Badir, Y. F. (Eds.), *Business and Management in Asia: Disruption and Change* (pp. 109–122). Springer Nature Singapore., DOI:10.1007/978-981-99-9371-0_7

ENISA. (2015). *Big Data Security, "Big Data Security Good Practices and Recommendations on the security of Big Data Systems", European Union: European Union Agency for Network and Information Security.* ENISA.

Enz, C. A., & Siguaw, J. A. (2000). Best practices in human resources. *The Cornell Hotel and Restaurant Administration Quarterly*, 41(1), 48–61. DOI:10.1177/001088040004100123

Erb, B. (2016), Human resources management in the age of big data. In Seminar: Applied Management Diagnostics, 1 (pp. 3-14.). Ulm: Ulm University.

Erdil, O. (1996). Personelden İnsan Kaynakları Yönetimi Perspektifine. Öneri Dergisi, 1(4), 61- 65. https://dergipark.org.tr/tr/download/article-file/1025642 (Acces Date: 05.05.2024).

Ertürk, S. (2017). *Eğitimde 'program' geliştirme*. Edge Akademi.

Eryılmaz, B. (2016). Kamu Yönetimi: Düşünceler, Yapılar, Fonksiyonlar ve Politikalar. Kocaeli: Umuttepe Yayınları.

Eshet, Y. (2004). Digital Literacy: A Conceptual Framework for Survival Skills in the Digital era. *Journal of Educational Multimedia and Hypermedia*, 13(1), 93–106.

Eurofound. (2021a). Digitisation in the workplace. Publications Office of the European Union, Luxembourg. Available at: https://www.eurofound.europa.eu/sites/default/files/ef_publication/field_ef_document/ef21001en.pdf

European Commission. (2022). Industry 5.0. https://research-and-innovation.ec.europa.eu/: https://research-and-innovation.ec.europa.eu/research-area/industrial-research-and-innovation/industry-50_en#why-industry-50 (Acces Date: 05.07.2024).

European Commission. (2024, March 6). *AI Act | Shaping Europe's digital future.* https://digital-strategy.ec.europa.eu/en/policies/regulatory-framework-ai

European Union. (2010). Charter of Fundamental Rights of the European Union. In Official Journal of the European Union C83 (Vol. 53, p. 380).

Eva, N., Robin, M., Sendjaya, S., Van Dierendonck, D., & Liden, R. C. (2019). Servant Leadership: A systematic review and call for future research. *The Leadership Quarterly*, 30(1), 111–132. DOI:10.1016/j.leaqua.2018.07.004

Explanatory note to the Law of the Republic of Lithuania on the Civil Service No XIVP-3786- XIVP-3791.

Ezeali, B. O., & Esiagu, N. L. (2010). *Public Personnel Management*. Book Point Ltd.

Fahim, M. G. A. (2018). Strategic human resource management and public employee retention. *Review of Economics and Political Science*, 3(2), 20–39. DOI:10.1108/REPS-07-2018-002

Faisal, S. (2023). Green human resource management—A synthesis. *Sustainability*, 15(3), 2259.

Farooq, R., Zhang, Z., Talwar, S., & Dhir, A. (2022). Do green human resource management and self-efficacy facilitate green creativity? A study of luxury hotels and resorts. *Journal of Sustainable Tourism*, 30(4), 824–845.

Fayol, H. (1949). *General and industrial management*. Pitman.

Fenech, R. (2022). Human resource management in a digital era through the lens of next generation human resource managers. *Journal of Management Information and Decision Sciences*, 25(1), 1–10.

Ferlie, E., & Osborne, S. P. (2002). *New Public Management: Current Trends and Future Prospects* (McLaughlin, K., Ed.). Routledge.

Fernandez, C. P. (2007). Employee engagement. *Journal of Public Health Management and Practice*, 13(5), 524–526. DOI:10.1097/01.PHH.0000285207.63835.50 PMID:17762699

Ferris, G., Hall, A., Todd, R., & Martocchio, J. (2004). Theoretical Development in the Field of Human Resources Management: Issues and Challenges for the Future. *Organizational Analysis*, 12(3), 231–254.

Fertig, T., Schütz, A. E., Weber, K., & Müller, N. H. (2019). Measuring the impact of e-learning platforms on information security awareness. In *Learning and Collaboration Technologies. Designing Learning Experiences: 6th International Conference, LCT 2019, Held as Part of the 21st HCI International Conference, HCII 2019, Orlando, FL, USA, July 26–31, 2019* [Springer International Publishing.]. *Proceedings*, 21(Part I), 26–37.

Filippi, S., Yerkes, M. A., Bal, M., Hummel, B., & De Wit, J. (2022). (Un)deserving of work-life balance? A cross country investigation of people's attitudes towards work-life balance arrangements for parents and childfree employees. *Community Work & Family*, 27(1), 116–134. DOI:10.1080/13668803.2022.2099247

Final Round, A. I. (n.d.). *Final Round AI: Interview Copilot*. Retrieved April 17, 2024, from https://www.finalroundai.com/

Fink, A. A., & Sturman, M. C. (2017). HR metrics and talent analytics. In Collings, D. M. (Ed.), *The Oxford handbook of talent management (Chapter: 20)* (pp. 375–390). Oxford University Press.

Fiok, K., Farahani, F. V., Karwowski, W., & Ahram, T. (2022). Explainable artificial intelligence for education and training. *The Journal of Defense Modeling and Simulation*, 19(2), 133–144. DOI:10.1177/15485129211028651

Fisher, D., DeLine, R., Czerwinski, M., & Drucker, S. (2012). Interactions with big data analytics. interactions, 19(3), 50-59. .DOI:10.1145/2168931.2168943

Fitzgerald, M., Kruschwitz, N., Bonnet, D., & Welch, M. (2014). Embracing digital technology: A new strategic imperative. *MIT Sloan Management Review*, 55(2), 1–16.

Fjeld, J., Achten, N., Hilligoss, H., Nagy, A., & Srikumar, M. (2020). Principled artificial intelligence: Mapping consensus in ethical and rights-based approaches to principles for AI. *Berkman Klein Center Research Publication* (2020-1). DOI:10.2139/ssrn.3518482

Flanagan, F. (2017). Symposium on work in the 'gig' economy: Introduction. *Economic and Labour Relations Review*, 28(3), 378–381. DOI:10.1177/1035304617724302

Florijan Barišić, A., Rybacka Barišić, J., & Miloloža, I. (2021). Digital transformation: Challenges for human resources management. [ENTRENOVA]. *ENTerprise REsearch InNOVAtion Conference*, 7(1), 377–387. DOI:10.54820/GTFN9743

Fombrun, , C. JGardberg, N.ASever, , J.M. (2000). The Reputation Quotient: A Multi-stakeholder Measure of Corporate Reputation. *Journal of Brand Management*, 7, 241–255.

Fraser, K., Ma, I., Teteris, E., Baxter, H., Wright, B., & McLaughlin, K. (2012). Emotion, cognitive load and learning outcomes during simulation training. *Medical Education*, 46(11), 1055–1062. DOI:10.1111/j.1365-2923.2012.04355.x PMID:23078682

Freeman, R. E., Harrison, J. S., Wicks, A. C., Parmar, B., & De Colle, S. (2010). Stakeholder Theory: The State of the Art. *The Academy of Management Annals*, 3(1), 403–445.

Fregnan, E., Ivaldi, S., & Scaratti, G. (2020). Hrm 4.0 and new managerial competences profile: The comau case. *Frontiers in Psychology*, 11, 578251. DOI:10.3389/fpsyg.2020.578251 PMID:33329228

Friedland, R. (2024). Lorraine Daston. Rules: A short history of what we live by. *Administrative Science Quarterly*, 00018392241227435(2), NP34–NP36. Advance online publication. DOI:10.1177/00018392241227435

Fukuyama, M. (2018). Society 5.0: Aiming for a New Human-Centered Society. *Japan Spotlight*, 27(5), 47–50.

Fu, N., Keegan, A., & McCartney, S. (2022). The duality of HR analysts' storytelling: Showcasing and curbing. *Human Resource Management Journal*, 33(2), 261–286. DOI:10.1111/1748-8583.12466

Gahi, Y., Guennoun, M., & Mouftah, H. T. (2016). Big data analytics: Security and privacy challenges. In *2016 IEEE Symposium on Computers and Communication (ISCC)* (pp. 952-957). IEEE. DOI:10.1109/ISCC.2016.7543859

Ganapathi, P., Aithal, P. S., & Kanchana, D. (2024). Impact of Work-Life Balance and Stress Management on Job Satisfaction among the Working Women in Higher Educational Institutions in Namakkal District. Social Science Research Network. https://doi.org/DOI:10.2139/ssrn.4744545

Gandomi, A., & Haider, M. (2015). Beyond the hype: Big data concepts, methods, and analytics. *International Journal of Information Management*, 35(2), 137–144. DOI:10.1016/j.ijinfomgt.2014.10.007

Garg, S. (2023, June 25). *ChatGPT alternatives that will blow your mind in 2023*. The Writesonic Blog - Making Content Your Superpower. https://writesonic.com/blog/chatgpt-alternatives/

Garg, S., & Sharma, S. (2020). User satisfaction and continuance intention for using e-training: A structural equation model. *Vision (Basel)*, 24(4), 441–451. DOI:10.1177/0972262920926827

Gärtner, C., & Kern, D. (2021). Smart HRM in 2030: Conversational HR, Connected Robotics, and Controlled Analytics. Managing Work in the Digital Economy: Challenges, Strategies and Practices for the Next Decade, 203-221.

Gascó, J. L., Llopis, J., & González, M. R. (2004). İnsan kaynaklarının eğitiminde bilgi teknolojisinin kullanımı: Bir e-öğrenme vaka çalışması. *Avrupa Endüstriyel Eğitim Dergisi*, 28(5), 370–382.

Gemeda, H. K., & Lee, J. (2020). Leadership styles, work engagement and outcomes among information and communications technology professionals: A cross-national study. *Heliyon*, 6(4), e03699. DOI:10.1016/j.heliyon.2020.e03699 PMID:32280799

Gençer, Y. G., & Batırlık, S. N. (2022). Importance of leadership in managing Post-Pandemic crises. In *Advances in logistics, operations, and management science book series* (pp. 104–122). DOI:10.4018/978-1-6684-5876-1.ch007

Gerten, E., Beckmann, M., & Bellmann, L. (2018). Controlling working crowds: The impact of digitalization on worker autonomy and monitoring across hierarchical levels. Retrieved from: https://edoc.unibas.ch/61490/1/20180307130203_5a9fd4bb4605b.pdf.

Giannikis, S. K., & Mihail, D. M. (2011). Flexible work arrangements in Greece: A study of employee perceptions. *International Journal of Human Resource Management*, 22(2), 417–432. DOI:10.1080/09585192.2011.540163

Gifford, J. (2021). Strategic human resource management. Available at: https://www.cipd.co.uk/knowledge/strategy/hr/strategic-hrm-factsheet#gref [Accessed: 14 April 2024].

Gigauri, I. (2020a). Implications of COVID-19 for human resource management. *International Journal of Economics and Management Studies*, 7(11), 25–33. DOI:10.14445/23939125/IJEMS-V7I11P104

Gigauri, I. (2020b). Effects of Covid-19 on Human Resource Management from the Perspective of Digitalization and Work-life-balance. *International Journal of Innovative Technologies in Economy*, 4(31). Advance online publication. DOI:10.31435/rsglobal_ijite/30092020/7148

Gilch, P. M., & Sieweke, J. (2021). Recruiting digital talent: The strategic role of recruitment in organisations' digital transformation. *German Journal of Human Resource Management*, 35(1), 53–82. DOI:10.1177/2397002220952734

Gill, S. S., & Kaur, R. (2023). ChatGPT: Vision and challenges. *Internet of Things and Cyber-Physical Systems*, 3, 262–271. DOI:10.1016/j.iotcps.2023.05.004

Giorgi, G., Lecca, L. I., Alessa, F., Finstad, G. L., Bondanini, G., Lulli, L. G., & Mucci, N. (2020). COVID-19-related mental health effects in the workplace: A narrative review. *International Journal of Environmental Research and Public Health*, 17(21), 7857. DOI:10.3390/ijerph17217857 PMID:33120930

Giroux, C. (1960). The Motivation to work, by F. Herzberg, B. Mausner and B.-C. Snyderman, John Wiley & Sons, New York, John Wiley & Sons, 1959. *Relations Industrielles*, 15(2), 275. DOI:10.7202/1022040ar

Giurge, L., & Bohns, V. K. (2020). 3 tips to avoid WFH burnout. *Harvard Business Review*.

Glaser, B. (1978). *Theoretical sensitivity*. The Sociology Press.

GMR. (2016). *Hyderabad International Airport, Aciasiapac, Haghighat, A. (2020). Monte Carlo methods for particle transport. Raton*. Crc Press.

Göetz, M., & Jankowska, B. (2020). Adoption of Industry 4.0 Technologies and Company Competitiveness: Case Studies from a Post-Transition Economy. *National Research University Higher School of Economics*, 14(4), 61–78. DOI:10.17323/2500-2597.2020.4.61.78

Gonçalves, S. P., Santos, J. V. D., Silva, I. S., Veloso, A., Brandão, C., & Moura, R. (2021). COVID-19 and people management: The view of human resource managers. *Administrative Sciences*, 11(3), 69. DOI:10.3390/admsci11030069

González, A. L., Moreno, M., Román, A. C. M., Fernández, Y. H., & Pérez, N. C. (2024). Ethics in artificial intelligence: An approach to cybersecurity. *Inteligencia Artificial*, 27(73), 38–54. DOI:10.4114/intartif.vol27iss73pp38-54

Google. (n.d.). *Gemini—Chat to supercharge your ideas*. Gemini. Retrieved April 15, 2024, from https://gemini.google.com

Gorensek, T. & Kohont, A; (2018). Conceptualization of the Digitalization: Opportunities and Challenges for Organizations in the Euro- Meditteranean Area, 11(2). Pp. 94-115.

GPTZero. (2023). *GPTZero*. GPTZero. https://gptzero.me/

Granda, J. C., Nuño, P., García, D. F., & Suárez, F. J. (2015). Autonomic platform for synchronous e-training in dispersed organizations. *Journal of Network and Systems Management*, 23(1), 183–209. DOI:10.1007/s10922-013-9290-4

Green, M. (2020). Recruitment: an introduction Available at: https://www.cipd.ie/newsresources/practical-guidance/factsheets/recruitment#7034 [Accessed: 14 April 2024].

Greenhalgh, T., Payne, R., Hemmings, N., Leach, H., Hanson, I., Khan, A., Miller, L., Ladds, E., Clarke, A., Shaw, S. E., Dakin, F., Wieringa, S., Rybczynska-Bunt, S., Faulkner, S. D., Byng, R., Kalin, A., Moore, L., Wherton, J., Husain, L., & Rosen, R. (2024). Training needs for staff providing remote services in general practice: A mixed-methods study. *The British Journal of General Practice*, 74(738), e17–e26. DOI:10.3399/BJGP.2023.0251 PMID:38154935

Guerin, L. (2024). *Avoid legal trouble when giving performance evaluations*. https://www.nolo.com/legal-encyclopedia/avoid-legal-trouble-when-giving-performance-evaluations.html

Gulliford, F., & Dixon, A. P. (2019). AI: The HR revolution. *Strategic HR Review*, 18(2), 52–55. DOI:10.1108/SHR-12-2018-0104

Gunathunge, K. L. N. K., & Lakmal, K. G. P. (2019). *Industrial Revolution 4.0 and the future of HRM*. Contemporary Innovation in Management.

Gupta, A. K., Aggarwal, V., Sharma, V., & Naved, M. (2024). Education 4.0 and Web 3.0 Technologies Application for enhancement of distance learning management Systems in the Post–COVID-19 ERa. In *The Role of Sustainability and Artificial Intelligence in Education Improvement* (pp. 66-86). Chapman and Hall/CRC.

Gupta, S., Vasa, S. R., & Sehgal, P. (2024). Mapping the experiences of work-life balance: Implications for the future of work. *Journal of Asia Business Studies*. Advance online publication. DOI:10.1108/JABS-06-2023-0223

Gusai, O. P., Rani, A., & Yadav, P. (2022). Digital Industrial Revolution 4.0 and Sustaining Gig Economy: Challenges and Opportunities Ahead. In Gupta, A., Tewary, T., & Gopalakrishnan, B. N. (Eds.), *Sustainability in the Gig Economy* (pp. 187–198). Springer Nature Singapore., DOI:10.1007/978-981-16-8406-7_14

Haddock-Millar, J., Sanyal, C., & Müller-Camen, M. (2016). Green human resource management: A comparative qualitative case study of a United States multinational corporation. *International Journal of Human Resource Management*, 27(2), 192–211. DOI:10.1080/09585192.2015.1052087

Haftador, A. M., Tehranineshat, B., Keshtkaran, Z., & Mohebbi, Z. (2023). A study of the effects of blended learning on university students' critical thinking: A systematic review. *Journal of Education and Health Promotion*, 12(1), 12. DOI:10.4103/jehp.jehp_665_22 PMID:37288404

Hajiheydari, N., & Delgosha, M. S. (2024). Investigating engagement and burnout of gig-workers in the age of algorithms: An empirical study in digital labor platforms. *Information Technology & People*. Advance online publication. DOI:10.1108/ITP-11-2022-0873

Halid, H., Yusoff, Y. M., & Somu, H. (2020). The relationship between digital human resource management and organizational performance, In First ASEAN Business, Environment, and Technology Symposium, Atlantis Press, pp: 96 -99.

Halid, H., Yusoff, Y. M., & Somu, H. (2020). The relationship between digital human resource management and organizational performance. In *First ASEAN Business, Environment, and Technology Symposium (ABEATS 2019)*, 96-99. Atlantis Press. DOI:10.2991/aebmr.k.200514.022

Hameed, Z., Khan, I. U., Islam, T., Sheikh, Z., & Naeem, R. M. (2020). Do green HRM practices influence employees' environmental performance? *International Journal of Manpower*, 41(7), 1061–1079.

Hameed, Z., Naeem, R. M., Hassan, M., Naeem, M., Nazim, M., & Maqbool, A. (2022). How GHRM is related to green creativity? A moderated mediation model of green transformational leadership and green perceived organizational support. *International Journal of Manpower*, 43(3), 595–613.

Hamilton, R. H., & Sodeman, W. A. (2020). The questions we ask: Opportunities and challenges for using big data analytics to strategically manage human capital resources. *Business Horizons*, 63(1), 85–95. DOI:10.1016/j.bushor.2019.10.001

Hamouche, S. (2023). Human resource management and the COVID-19 crisis: Implications, challenges, opportunities, and future organizational directions. *Journal of Management & Organization*, 29(5), 799–814. DOI:10.1017/jmo.2021.15

Harney, B., & Collings, D. (2021). Navigating the shifting landscapes of HRM. *Human Resource Management Review*, 31(4), 100824. DOI:10.1016/j.hrmr.2021.100824

Harpaz, I. (1990). The importance of work Goals: An international perspective. *Journal of International Business Studies*, 21(1), 75–93. DOI:10.1057/palgrave.jibs.8490328

Harvey, G., Williams, K., & Probert, J. (2013). Greening the airline pilot: HRM and the green performance of airlines in the UK. *International Journal of Human Resource Management*, 24(1), 152–166.

Hassan, R. (2023). *Work Arrangements in the Informal Sector and Gig Economy/Digital Platform Economy in Egypt*. Unpublished. DOI:10.13140/RG.2.2.24113.19041

Hatcher, T. (2013). Robert Owen: A historiographic study of a pioneer of human resource development. *European Journal of Training and Development*, 37(4), 414–431. DOI:10.1108/03090591311319799

Haubold, A. K., Obst, L., & Bielefeldt, F. (2020). Introducing service robotics in inpatient geriatric care—A qualitative systematic review from a human resources perspective. Gruppe. Interaktion. Organisation. [GIO]. *Zeitschrift Für Angewandte Organisationspsychologie*, 51(3), 259–271.

HEAŞ. (2019). HEAŞ 2019 Activity Report. https://www.sgairport.com/media/default/docs/pdf/Mali/Faaliyet-Raporu-2019.pdf [Retrieved date: 21-November -2020] https://fdocuments.in/document/effective-collaboration-and-cooperation-among-airport-effective-collaboration.html?page=1 [Retrieved date: 20-October -2020]

Helmold, M. (2021). New work, transformational and virtual leadership. In *Management for professionals*. DOI:10.1007/978-3-030-63315-8

Helsinger, L. (2024, March 11). *1,000 equally-qualified resumes, different names. Guess which ones gpt 3.5 place at the top and bottom ranks?*https://www.linkedin.com/pulse/1000-equally-qualified-resumes-different-names-guess-which-helsinger-x4gac/

Henriette, E., Feki, M., & Boughzala, I. (2016). Digital Transformation Challenges, *Tenth Mediterranean Conference on Information Systems (MCIS)*, Paphos, Cyprus, 33.pp 1-8.

Herman, H., Riadi, I., Abdurrachman, F. I., & Lonang, S. (2022). Training on how to use social media Wisely and Ethically. *ABDIMAS: Journal Pengabdian Masyarakat*, 5(2), 2653–2662.

Hersey, P., & Blanchard, K. H. (1969). Management of Organizational Behavior-Prentice-Hall Inc., 1969 (Cloth and Soft cover. Soft cover $3.95). *Academy of Management Journal*, 12(4), 526. DOI:10.5465/amj.1969.19201155

Herzberg, F. (2023, April 4). *One more time: How do you motivate employees?* Harvard Business Review. https://hbr.org/2003/01/one-more-time-how-do-you-motivate-employees

History.com Editors. (2023, March 27). *Industrial revolution: Definition, inventions & dates*. HISTORY. https://www.history.com/topics/industrial-revolution/industrial-revolution

Hmoud, B., & Várallyai, L. (2019). *Will artificial intelligence take over human resources recruitment and selection?*

Hoberg, P., Krcmar, H., & Welz, B. (2017). Skills for digital transformation Available at: http://www.corporateleaders.com/sitescene/custom/userfiles/file/Research/sapskillsfordigitaltransformation.pdf [Accessed: 10 April 2024].

Hobfoll, S. E. (1989). Conservation of resources: A new attempt at conceptualizing stress. *The American Psychologist*, 44(3), 513–524. DOI:10.1037/0003-066X.44.3.513 PMID:2648906

Hochschild, A. R. (1990). Ideology and emotion management: A perspective and path for future research. In Kemper, T. D. (Ed.), *Research agendas in the sociology of emotions* (pp. 117–142). State University of New York Press.

Hofer, C. W. (1990). *Toward a contingency theory of business strategy*. Physica-Verlag HD. DOI:10.1007/978-3-662-41484-2_7

Holsapple, C. W., & Lee-Post, A. (2006). Defining, assessing, and promoting e-learning success: An information systems perspective. *Decision Sciences Journal of Innovative Education*, 4(1), 67–85. DOI:10.1111/j.1540-4609.2006.00102.x

Hopkins, J. L., & Bardoel, A. (2023). The future is hybrid: How organisations are designing and supporting sustainable hybrid work models in Post-Pandemic Australia. *Sustainability (Basel)*, 15(4), 3086. DOI:10.3390/su15043086

Hoschschild, A., & Machung, A. (1989). *The Second Shift: Working Parents and the Revolution at Home*. Viking.

Hsu, S., & Wang, Y. (2008). The development and empirical validation of the Employee Satisfaction Index model. *Total Quality Management & Business Excellence*, 19(4), 353–366. DOI:10.1080/14783360701595052

Huang, N., Burtch, G., Hong, Y., & Pavlou, P. A. (2020). Unemployment and Worker Participation in the Gig Economy: Evidence from an Online Labor Market. *Information Systems Research*, 31(2), 431–448. DOI:10.1287/isre.2019.0896

Huang, X., Yang, F., Zheng, J., Feng, C., & Zhang, L. (2023). *Personalized human resource management via HR analytics and artificial intelligence: Theory and implications*. Asia Pacific Management Review.

Huđek, I., & Širec, K. (2023). The terminology and the concept of the gig economy. *Ekonomski Pregled*, 74(1), 34–58. DOI:10.32910/ep.74.1.2

Humby, C. (2006). Data is the new Oil! ANA Senior marketer's summit, Kellogg School. https://ana.blogs.com/maestros/2006/11/data_is_the_new.html

Hunt, J. A., II. (2023). *Virtual Onboarding Within Geographically Separated Organizations* (Doctoral dissertation, Trident University International).

Huo, X., Qi, M., & Wang, S. (2024). The application of electronic human resource management systems (e-HRM) in HR management. *Advances in Economics and Management Research*, 10(1), 316–316. DOI:10.56028/aemr.10.1.316.2024

Huselid, M. A. (1995). The impact of human resource management practices on turnover, productivity, and corporate financial performance. *Academy of Management Journal*, 38(3), 635–672. DOI:10.2307/256741

Ibarra, P. (2020). "We've Always Done it that Way" Is Over—WHAT'S NEXT? Public Management, 6-9. Received from: https://gettingbetterallthetime.com/wp-content/uploads/2020/04/Ibarra-Bldg-a-Talent-Centric-Workforce.pdf

IBM. (n.d.-a). *What is artificial intelligence (AI)?* Retrieved April 2, 2024, from https://www.ibm.com/topics/artificial-intelligence

IBM. (n.d.-b). *What Is machine learning (ML)?* Retrieved April 2, 2024, from https://www.ibm.com/topics/machine-learning

ICAO. (2005). *Annex II: Rules of the Air*. International Civil Aviation Organization press.

Iddagoda, A., Hysa, E., Bulińska-Stangrecka, H., & Manta, O. (2021). Green work-life balance and greenwashing the construct of work-life balance: Myth and reality. *Energies*, 14(15), 4556. DOI:10.3390/en14154556

Igudia, P. O. (2022). Employee training and development, and organisational performance: A study of small-scale manufacturing firms in Nigeria. *American Journal of Economics and Business Management*, 5(5), 38–54.

indeed. (2024). *Job Search | Indeed*. https://www.indeed.com/?from=social_share

Infante, A., & Darmawan, D. (2022). Gender equality: women's involvement in human resource management practices. Journal of Social Science Studies (JOS3), 2(1), 27-30.

İnkaBlog. (2024). İnsan Kaynakları Süreçlerinde Dijital Dönüşüm ve Teknolojinin Rolü. https://blog.inkaik.com/insan-kaynaklari-sureclerinde-dijital-donusum-ve-teknolojinin-rolu/. (Access On: 22.05.2024)

Iqbal, R., Shahzad, K., & Chaudhary, R. (2024). Green human resource management practices as a strategic choice for enhancing employees' environmental outcomes: An affective events theory perspective. *International Journal of Manpower*, 45(4), 801–819.

Irawanto, D. W., Novianti, K. R., & Roz, K. (2021). Work from Home: Measuring Satisfaction between Work–Life Balance and Work Stress during the COVID-19 Pandemic in Indonesia. *Economies*, 9(3), 96. DOI:10.3390/economies9030096

Isaacs, A. J., Lwendo, S. B., & Kazondovi, C. (2021). The Effectiveness of In-service Training Programmes in Public Sector Organizations. *The Namibia CPD Journal for Educators*, 6(1), 100–156. DOI:10.32642/ncpdje.v6i1.1554

Isa, N. A. M., Hamid, N. A., & Leong, T. P. (2016). A stakeholder analysis of the Klia2 Airport Terminal Project. *Environment-Behaviour Proceedings Journal*, 1(3), 281–289. DOI:10.21834/e-bpj.v1i3.372

Jain, E., Chopra, T., & Sharma, S. K. (2023, February). Reinventing human resource management in the era of artificial intelligence. In *ICASDMBW 2022: Proceedings of the International Conference on Application of AI and Statistical Decision Making for the Business World, ICASDMBW 2022, 16-17 December 2022, Rukmini Devi Institute of Advanced Studies, Delhi, India* (Vol. 86). European Alliance for Innovation. DOI:10.4108/eai.16-12-2022.2326241

Jain, P. A. (2024). The Gig Economy: Disruption, Innovation, and Economic Evolution. *Educational Administration: Theory and Practice*, 5133–5140. DOI:10.53555/kuey.v30i5.3755

Jain, D. (2018). Human resource management and artificial intelligence. *International Journal of Management and Social Sciences Research*, 7(3), 56–59.

Jain, V., & Rani, A. (2024). Labor Market Trends in the Gig Economy: Implications for Workers and Employers. *International Journal for Research Publication and Seminar*, 15(2), 50–54. DOI:10.36676/jrps.v15.i2.08

Janssen, M., van der Voort, H., & Wahyudi, A. (2017). Factors influencing big data decision-making quality. *Journal of Business Research*, 70, 197–208. DOI:10.1016/j.jbusres.2016.08.007

Järlström, M., Saru, E., & Vanhala, S. (2016). Sustainable Human Resource Management with Salience of Stakeholders: A Top Management Perspective. *Journal of Business Ethics*, 152(3), 703–724. DOI:10.1007/s10551-016-3310-8

Jarrahi, M. H. (2018). Artificial intelligence and the future of work: Human-AI symbiosis in organizational decision making. *Business Horizons*, 61(4), 577–586. DOI:10.1016/j.bushor.2018.03.007

Jeffrey Hill, E., Grzywacz, J. G., Allen, S., Blanchard, V. L., Matz-Costa, C., Shulkin, S., & Pitt-Catsouphes, M. (2008). Defining and conceptualizing workplace flexibility. *Community Work & Family*, 11(2), 149–163. DOI:10.1080/13668800802024678

Jeon, S., Liu, H., & Ostrovsky, Y. (2021). Measuring the gig economy in Canada using administrative data. *The Canadian Journal of Economics. Revue Canadienne d'Economique*, 54(4), 1638–1666. DOI:10.1111/caje.12558

Jia, J., Liu, H., Chin, T., & Hu, D. (2018). The continuous mediating effects of GHRM on employees' green passion via transformational leadership and green creativity. *Sustainability*, 10(9), 3237.

Jianguang, M., & Wei, J. (2013). The Concept, Characteristics and Application of Big Data. National defense science & technology, 2, 10-17.

Jiang, Y., Zaman, S. I., Jamil, S., Khan, S. A., & Kun, L. (2024). A triple theory approach to link corporate social performance and green human resource management. *Environment, Development and Sustainability*, 26(6), 15733–15776.

Ji, H., Zhao, X., & Dang, J. (2023). Relationship between leadership-member exchange (LMX) and flow at work among medical workers during the COVID-19: The mediating role of job crafting. *BMC Psychology*, 11(1), 162. Advance online publication. DOI:10.1186/s40359-023-01194-3 PMID:37198695

Jiuhua Zhu, C., Thomson, S. B., Hutchings, K., & Cieri, H. D. (2011). Extending the investment development path model to include the human environment factor. *Thunderbird International Business Review*, 53(3), 311–324.

Johanna Bath, J. X., & Markulin, V. (2024). Exploring the impact of work arrangements on employee well-being in the post-pandemic workplace: The role of perceived flexibility, work-life balance, and managerial support. International Journal of Business and Applied Social Science, 1-17. DOI:10.33642/ijbass.v10n1p1

Johnson, S. L. (2019). Workplace bullying, biased behaviours and performance review in the nursing profession: A qualitative study. *Journal of Clinical Nursing*, 28(9–10), 1528–1537. DOI:10.1111/jocn.14758 PMID:30588721

Jones, S., & Schöning, M. (2021). Employee Job Satisfaction During Remote Work: The Impact of Transformational Leadership. *Effective Executive, 24*(3), 65–72. https://www.proquest.com/docview/2584571442/fulltextPDF/D86322A2F394374PQ/1?accountid=38885&sourcetype=Scholarly%20Journals

Jones, M., Versace, V., Lyle, D., & Walsh, S. (2021). Return of the unexpected: Rural workforce recruitment and retention in the era of COVID-19. *The Australian Journal of Rural Health*, 29(5), 612–616. DOI:10.1111/ajr.12817 PMID:34672056

Joshi, A., Jain, S., & Gupta, P. K. (2024). Challenges and impact of the gig economy. *Sustainable Economies*, 2(2), 96. DOI:10.62617/se.v2i2.96

Jovanović, G., & Božilović, S. (2017). The Influence of Management of Human Resources on Motivation and Job Satisfaction. Ekonomika - Journal for Economic Theory and Practice and Social Issues, 63(1), s. 97-110. https://www.ceeol.com/search/viewpdf?id=199986 (Access On: 22.05.2024)

Judge, T. A., Thoresen, C. J., Bono, J. E., & Patton, G. K. (2001). The job satisfaction-job performance relationship: A qualitative and quantitative review. *Psychological Bulletin*, 127(3), 376–407. DOI:10.1037/0033-2909.127.3.376 PMID:11393302

Judgment of 12 January 2010 in Case C-341/08 Petersen, paragraph 53;

Judgment of 18 November 2010 in Joined Cases C-250/09 and C-268/09 Georgiev, paragraph 68.

Judgment of the Court of Justice of the European Union of 10 March 2009 in Case C-169/07 Hartlauer, paragraph 55;

Judgment of the European Court of Human Rights of 27 July 2004 in the case of Sidabras and Džiautas v. Lithuania. Application No. 55480/00 and 59330/00), para. 57.

Juknevičienė, V. (2006). Challenges of the time for human resource management in public administration. *Economy and Management: Actualities and Perspectives.*, 1(6), 96–102.

Jurníčková, P., Matulayová, N., Olecká, I., Šlechtová, H., Zatloukal, L., & Jurníček, L. (2024). Home-Office managers should get ready for the "New normal.". *Administrative Sciences*, 14(2), 34. DOI:10.3390/admsci14020034

Kabassi, K., & Virvou, M. (2004). Personalised adult e-training on computer use based on multiple attribute decision making. *Interacting with Computers*, 16(1), 115–132. DOI:10.1016/j.intcom.2003.11.006

Kabene, S., Orchard, C., Howard, J., Soriano, M., & Leduc, R. (2006). The Importance of Human Resources Management in Health Care: A Global Context. *Human Resources for Health*, 4(20), 1–17. DOI:10.1186/1478-4491-4-20 PMID:16872531

Kagermann, H. (2015). Change through digitization - Value creation in the age of Industry 4.0. In *Management of permanent change* (pp. 23–45). Springer Gabler. DOI:10.1007/978-3-658-05014-6_2

Kagermann, H., Wahlster, W., & Helbig, J. (2013). Recommendations for implementing the strategic initiative INDUSTRIE 4.0. Final report of the Industrie, Frankfurt. *Office of the Industry-Science Research Alliance.*, 4(0), 1–82.

Kahn, W. A. (1990). Psychological Conditions of Personal Engagement and Disengagement at Work. *Academy of Management Journal*, 33(4), 692–724. DOI:10.2307/256287

Kaizer, B. M., Sanches da Silva, C. E., Zerbini, T., & Paiva, A. P. (2020). E-learning training in work corporations: A review on instructional planning. *European Journal of Training and Development*, 44(8/9), 761–781. DOI:10.1108/EJTD-03-2020-0042

Kalogiannidis, S. (2021). The Impact of COVID-19 on human resource management practices and future marketing. *International Journal of Industrial Marketing*, 6(1), 43–55. DOI:10.5296/ijim.v6i1.17994

Kambur, E., & Yildirim, T. (2023). From traditional to smart human resources management. *International Journal of Manpower*, 44(3), 422–452. DOI:10.1108/IJM-10-2021-0622

Kanghwa, C. (2010). From operational efficiency to financial efficiency. *The Asian Journal on Quality*, 11(2), 137–145. DOI:10.1108/15982681011075943

Kaplan, A. D., Cruit, J., Endsley, M., Beers, S. M., Sawyer, B. D., & Hancock, P. A. (2021). The effects of virtual reality, augmented reality, and mixed reality as training enhancement methods: A meta-analysis. *Human Factors*, 63(4), 706–726. DOI:10.1177/0018720820904229 PMID:32091937

Kapp, K. M. (2012). *The gamification of learning and instruction: game-based methods and strategies for training and education.* John Wiley & Sons.

Karami, A., Analoui, F., & Cusworth, J. (2004). Strategic human resource management and resource-based approach: The evidence from the British manufacturing industry. *Management Research News*, 27(6), 50–68. DOI:10.1108/01409170410784202

Karanika-Murray, M., Duncan, N. G., Pontes, H. M., & Griffiths, M. D. (2015). Organizational identification, work engagement, and job satisfaction. *Journal of Managerial Psychology*, 30(8), 1019–1033. DOI:10.1108/JMP-11-2013-0359

Katayama, H., & Bennett, D. (1999). Agility, adaptability and leanness: A comparison of concepts and a study of practice. *International Journal of Production Economics*, 60, 43–51. DOI:10.1016/S0925-5273(98)00129-7

Kaufman, B. (2014). The Historical Development of American HRM Broadly Viewed. *Human Resource Management Review*, 24(3), 196–218. DOI:10.1016/j.hrmr.2014.03.003

Kaur, J. (2024). AI-Augmented Medicine: Exploring the Role of Advanced AI Alongside Medical Professionals. In Advances in Computational Intelligence for the Healthcare Industry 4.0 (pp. 139-159). IGI Global.

Kaur, J. (2024). Revolutionizing Healthcare: Synergizing Cloud Robotics and Artificial Intelligence for Enhanced Patient Care. In Shaping the Future of Automation With Cloud-Enhanced Robotics (pp. 272-287). IGI Global.

Kaur, J. (2024). Robotics Rx: A Prescription for the Future of Healthcare. In Applications of Virtual and Augmented Reality for Health and Wellbeing (pp. 217-238). IGI Global. DOI:10.4018/979-8-3693-1123-3.ch012

Kaur, J. (2024). Smart Solutions for Health: Computational Intelligence Reshaping the Industry 4.0 Healthcare Paradigm. In Advances in Computational Intelligence for the Healthcare Industry 4.0 (pp. 194-211). IGI Global.

Kaushik, A. (2024). Comprehensive Impact of On-Demand Platforms: Examining the Gig Economy \'s Influence on Specialized Professionals, Work-Life Balance, and Gig Workers\' Perspectives. *International Journal for Research in Applied Science and Engineering Technology*, 12(1), 552–559. DOI:10.22214/ijraset.2024.58005

Kaya, E., & Taş, İ. (2015). Personel Yönetimi İnsan Kaynakları Yönetimi Ayrımı. Kahramanmaraş Sütçü İmam Üniversitesi İktisadi ve İdari Bilimler Fakültesi Dergisi, 5(1), s. 21- 28. http://iibfdergisi.ksu.edu.tr/tr/download/article-file/107732 (Acces Date: 18.01.2024)

Kelliher, C., Richardson, J., & Boiarintseva, G. (2018). All of work? All of life? Reconceptualising work-life balance for the 21st century. *Human Resource Management Journal*, 29(2), 97–112. DOI:10.1111/1748-8583.12215

Kelly, C. J., Karthikesalingam, A., Suleyman, M., Corrado, G., & King, D. (2019). Key challenges for delivering clinical impact with artificial intelligence. *BMC Medicine*, 17(195), 1–9. DOI:10.1186/s12916-019-1426-2 PMID:31665002

Kemendi, Á., Michelberger, P., & Mesjasz-Lech, A. (2022). Industry 4.0 and 5.0–organizational and competency challenges of enterprises. *Polish Journal of Management Studies*, 26(2), 209–232. DOI:10.17512/pjms.2022.26.2.13

Khan, B. H. (2001). *A framework for e-learning*. LTI magazine.

Khan, A., Rainayee, A., & Gull, I. A. (2019). Women Discrimination in HRM Practices: A Review of Literature. International Journal of Management. *Technology and Engineering*, 9(1), 1846–1856.

Khan, H., Rehmat, M., Butt, T. H., Farooqi, S., & Asim, J. (2020). Impact of transformational leadership on work performance, burnout and social loafing: A mediation model. *Future Business Journal*, 6(1), 40. Advance online publication. DOI:10.1186/s43093-020-00043-8

Khan, I., & Nawaz, A. (2016). The leadership styles and the employees performance: A review. *Gomal University Journal of Research*, 32(2), 144–150.

Khan, M., & Saqib, Z. (2024). Emerging Voice Mechanisms in Asian Gig Economies: Implications for Gig Workers' Work and Life. In Chan, X. W., Shang, S., & Lu, L. (Eds.), *Work-Life Research in the Asia-Pacific* (pp. 47–76). Springer Nature Switzerland., DOI:10.1007/978-3-031-52795-1_3

Khosroeva, N. I., Mamsurova, L. G., Kuchieva, I. Kh., Begieva, A. Sh., & Bekmurzaeva, Z. Kh. (2024). Problems of Human Resource Management of the Innovation Economy. In Sergi, B. S., Popkova, E. G., Ostrovskaya, A. A., Chursin, A. A., & Ragulina, Y. V. (Eds.), *Ecological Footprint of the Modern Economy and the Ways to Reduce It* (pp. 279–283). Springer Nature Switzerland., DOI:10.1007/978-3-031-49711-7_47

Khuong, M. N., & Chi, N. T. (2017). Effects of Corporate Glass Ceiling Factors on Female Employees' Organizational Commitment. *Journal of Advanced Management Science*, 5(4), 255–263. DOI:10.18178/joams.5.4.255-263

Kim, M.-S., Oh, J., Sim, J., Yun, B.-Y., & Yoon, J.-H. (2023). Association between exposure to violence, job stress and depressive symptoms among gig economy workers in Korea. *Annals of Occupational and Environmental Medicine*, 35, e43. DOI:10.35371/aoem.2023.35.e43 PMID:38029274

Kim, S., Wang, Y., & Boon, C. (2021). Sixty years of research on technology and human resource management: Looking back and looking forward. *Human Resource Management*, 60(1), 229–247. DOI:10.1002/hrm.22049

Kim, T. T., Kim, W. G., Majeed, S., & Haldorai, K. (2023). Does green human resource management lead to a green competitive advantage? A sequential mediation model with three mediators. *International Journal of Hospitality Management*, 111, 111. DOI:10.1016/j.ijhm.2023.103486

Kincaid, J. P., Hamilton, R., Tarr, R. W., & Sangani, H. 2003. Simulation in education and training. *Applied System Simulation: Methodologies and Applications*, pp.437-456.

King, D. B., O'Rourke, N., & DeLongis, A. (2014). Social media recruitment and online data collection: A beginner's guide and best practices for reaching low-prevalence and hard-to-reach populations. *Canadian Psychology*, 55(4), 240–248. DOI:10.1037/a0038087

Kiremitci, E. (2023). *İnsan kaynakları yönetiminde Dijital dönüşüm* (Doctoral dissertation, Dokuz Eylul Universitesi (Turkey).

Kirilmaz, S. K. (2020). Digital transformation in human resources management: Investigation of digital hrm practices of businesses. *Research Journal of Business and Management*, 7(3), 188–200. DOI:10.17261/Pressacademia.2020.1282

Kliestik, T. (2015). Future evolutions of human resource management. In *Globalization and its socio-economic consequences, 22th International Scientific Conference* (Vol. I & II, pp. 604-607). Zilina: University of Zilina.

Knod, E. M.Jr, Wall, J. L., Daniels, J. P., Shane, H. M., & Wernimont, T. A. (1984). Robotics: Challenges for the human resources manager. *Business Horizons*, 27(2), 38–46. DOI:10.1016/0007-6813(84)90007-7

Kodua, L. T., Xiao, Y., Adjei, N. O., Asante, D., Ofosu, B. O., & Amankona, D. (2022). Barriers to green human resources management (GHRM) implementation in developing countries. Evidence from Ghana. *Journal of Cleaner Production*, 340, 130671.

Koirala, J., & Acharya, S. (2020). Dimensions of human resource management evolved with the outbreak of COVID-19. *Available atSSRN* 3584092. DOI:10.2139/ssrn.3584092

Kossek, E. (1987). Human Resources Management Innovation. *Human Resource Management*, 26(1), 71–92. DOI:10.1002/hrm.3930260105

Kraus, S., Mahto, R.V. & Walsh, S.T. (2021). "The importance of literature reviews in small business and entrepreneurship research", Journal of Small Business Management, Vol. ahead-of-print, .DOI:10.1080/00472778.2021.1955128

Kreitner, R. (1995)... *Management*.

Kulkarni, P., Gokhale, P., Satish, Y. M., & Tigadi, B. (2022). An empirical study on the impact of learning theory on gamification-based training programs. *Organizational Management Journal*, 19(5), 170–188. DOI:10.1108/OMJ-04-2021-1232

Kumar, S., Talukder, M. B., & Kaiser, F. (2024). Artificial Intelligence in Business: Negative Social Impacts. In *Demystifying the Dark Side of AI in Business* (pp. 81-97). IGI Global. https://doi.org/DOI:10.4018/979-8-3693-0724-3.ch005

Kumar, B. N. (2016). Digital revolution in the mauritian public service: A human resource development perspective in two unrelated companies. *International Journal of Novel Research in Interdisciplinary Studies*, 3(5), 1–10.

Kumar, S., & Kumar, A. D. (2023). E-training impact on trainee experience and self-assessment. *Journal of Workplace Learning*, 35(7), 599–612. DOI:10.1108/JWL-02-2022-0023

Kumar, S., Talukder, M. B., Kabir, F., & Kaiser, F. (2024). Challenges and Sustainability of Green Finance in the Tourism Industry: Evidence from Bangladesh. In Taneja, S., Kumar, P., Grima, S., Ozen, E., & Sood, K. (Eds.), (pp. 97–111). Advances in Finance, Accounting, and Economics. IGI Global., DOI:10.4018/979-8-3693-1388-6.ch006

Kumar, S., Talukder, M. B., & Pego, A. (Eds.). (2024). *Utilizing Smart Technology and AI in Hybrid Tourism and Hospitality*. IGI Global., DOI:10.4018/979-8-3693-1978-9

Kundu, S. C., Tuteja, P., & Chahar, P. (2022). COVID-19 challenges and employees' stress: Mediating role of family-life disturbance and work-life imbalance. *Employee Relations*, 44(6), 1318–1337. DOI:10.1108/ER-03-2021-0090

Kupur, R. (2017), Human Resource Management – Structure and Roles. No. 3. International Journal of Professional Studies.

Kurnaz, S., Rodrigues, A., & Sunar, O. N. (2024). Digitalization in the Public Management: Turkish Public Institutions Example. In *Advancements in Socialized and Digital Media Communications* (pp. 135-150). IGI Global.

Kurt, B. and Heerman, D.W. (2010). *Monte Carlo Simulation in Statistical Physics*, Berlin: Springer company

Küsbecí, P. (2021). Büyük Veri, In İ. Ç. (Editor), Yenilikçi İnsan Kaynakları Uygulamaları ve Örgütsel İnovasyon (4.Bölüm) (pp. 61-78.). İstanbul: Nobel Yayınları, E-ISBN: 978-625-439-437-9.

Kuusisto, M. (2015). Effects of digitalization on organiza¬tions. Master of Science thesis. Tampere university of Technology.

KV, B. M., & Walarine, M. T. (2021). Human Resource Management: Pre-pandemic, Pandemic and beyond. *Recoletos Multidisciplinary Research Journal*, 9(2), 103–114.

Lagowska, U., Sobral, F., & Furtado, L. M. G. P. (2020). Leadership under crises: A research agenda for the post-Covid-19 Era. *BAR - Brazilian Administration Review*, 17(2), e200062. DOI:10.1590/1807-7692bar2020200062

Lane, H. C., Core, M. G., Van Lent, M., Solomon, S., & Gomboc, D. (2005, July). Explainable Artificial Intelligence for Training and Tutoring. In *AIED* (pp. 762-764).

Laney, D. (2001). 3D data management: Controlling data volume, velocity and variety. . META group research note, 6(70), 1-4.

Larson, K. (2020). Serious games and gamification in the corporate training environment: A literature review. *TechTrends*, 64(2), 319–328. DOI:10.1007/s11528-019-00446-7

Lauterbach, A. (2019). Artificial intelligence and policy: Quo vadis? *Digital Policy. Regulation & Governance*, 21(3), 238–263. DOI:10.1108/DPRG-09-2018-0054

Law on Coordination of Public and Private Interests in the Republic of Lithuania Civil Service, Valstybės žinios, 1997-07-16, No. 67-1659.

Law on the Adjustment of Public and Private Interests in the Civil Service, Valstybės žinios, 1997-07-16, Nr. 67-1659.

Law on the Civil Service of the Republic of Lithuania, Valstybės žinios, 30-07-1999, No 66-2130.

Lee, G. K., Moshrefi, S., Fuertes, V., Veeravagu, L., Nazerali, R., & Lin, S. J. (2021). What is your reality? Virtual, augmented, and mixed reality in plastic surgery training, education, and practice. *Plastic and Reconstructive Surgery*, 147(2), 505–511. DOI:10.1097/PRS.0000000000007595 PMID:33235047

Lee, I. (2017). Big data: Dimensions, evolution, impacts, and challenges. *Business Horizons*, 60(3), 293–303. DOI:10.1016/j.bushor.2017.01.004

Lee, Y., Jungheon, N., Park, D., & Lee, K. A. (2006). What factors influence customer-oriented prosocial behavior of customer-contact employees? *Journal of Services Marketing*, 20(4), 251–264. DOI:10.1108/08876040610674599

Legge, K. (1995). *Human Resource Management: Rhetorics and Realities*. Macmillan Press. DOI:10.1007/978-1-349-24156-9

Leidner, S., Baden, D., & Ashleigh, M. J. (2019). Green (environmental) HRM: Aligning ideals with appropriate practices. *Personnel Review*, 48(5), 1169–1185.

Lens. (2003). Reading Between the Lines: Analysing the Supreme Court's view on gender. *Social Science Review,1*(77). 25-50.

Libert, K., Mosconi, E., & Cadieux, N. (2020). Human-machine interaction and human resource management perspective for collaborative robotics implementation and adoption.

Liboni, L. B., Cezarino, L. O., Jabbour, C. J. C., Oliveira, B. G., & Stefanelli, N. O. (2019). Smart industry and the pathways to HRM 4.0: Implications for SCM. *Supply Chain Management*, 24(1), 124–146. DOI:10.1108/SCM-03-2018-0150

Li, J. Y., Sun, R., Tao, W., & Lee, Y. (2021). Employee coping with organizational change in the face of a pandemic: The role of transparent internal communication. *Public Relations Review*, 47(1), 101984. DOI:10.1016/j.pubrev.2020.101984 PMID:36568504

Lim, S., Wang, T. K., & Lee, S.-Y. (2017). Shedding New Light on Strategic Human Resource Management: The Impact of Human Resource Management Practices and Human Resources on the Perception of Federal Agency Mission Accomplishment. *Public Personnel Management*, 46(2), 91–1187. DOI:10.1177/0091026017704440

Linkedin. (2024). *Best Talent Intelligence Software | Products | LinkedIn*. https://www.linkedin.com/products/categories/talent-intelligence-software

Li, P. (2021). On the application of big data technology in human resource management in the new era. *Journal of Physics: Conference Series*, 1915(4), 1–7. DOI:10.1088/1742-6596/1915/4/042038

Li, S. (2023). The Gig Economy and Labour Market Dynamics. *Advances in Economics. Management and Political Sciences*, 61(1), 275–281. DOI:10.54254/2754-1169/61/20231285

Liu, C., Ranjan, R., Yang, C., Zhang, X., Wang, L., & Chen, J. (2014). MuR-DPA: Top-down levelled multi-replica merkle hash tree based secure public auditing for dynamic big data storage on cloud. *IEEE Transactions on Computers*, 64(9), 2609–2622. DOI:10.1109/TC.2014.2375190

Liu, K., Feng, Z., & Zhang, Q. (2023). Examining the role of digitalization and gig economy in achieving a low carbon society: An empirical study across nations. *Frontiers in Environmental Science*, 11, 1197708. DOI:10.3389/fenvs.2023.1197708

Liu, M., Jeon, J., & Lee, J. Y. (2023). Core job resources to improve employee engagement in China: The role of work-life balance, autonomy and expertise. *Asia Pacific Business Review*, ●●●, 1–25. DOI:10.1080/13602381.2023.2241380

Liu, T., Gao, J., Zhu, M., & Jin, S. (2021). Women's Work-Life Balance in Hospitality: Examining its Impact on Organizational commitment. *Frontiers in Psychology*, 12, 625550. Advance online publication. DOI:10.3389/fpsyg.2021.625550 PMID:33633651

Liu, Z. Y., Lomovtseva, N., & Korobeynikova, E. (2020). Online learning platforms: Reconstructing modern higher education. [iJET]. *International Journal of Emerging Technologies in Learning*, 15(13), 4–21. DOI:10.3991/ijet.v15i13.14645

Lodefalk, M. (2013). Servicification of manufacturing–evidence from Sweden. *International Journal of Economics and Business Research*, 6(1), 87–113. DOI:10.1504/IJEBR.2013.054855

Loebbecke, C., & Picot, A. (2015). Reflections on societal and business model transformation arising from digitization and big data analytics: A research agenda. *The Journal of Strategic Information Systems*, 24(3), 149–157. DOI:10.1016/j.jsis.2015.08.002

López-Torres, E., Carril-Merino, M. T., Miguel-Revilla, D., Verdú, M. J., & De La Calle-Carracedo, M. (2022). Twitter in initial teacher training: Interaction with social media as a source of teacher professional development for social studies prospective educators. *Sustainability (Basel)*, 14(23), 16134. DOI:10.3390/su142316134

Lorentzon, J., Fotoh, L. E., & Mugwira, T. (2023). *Remote auditing and its impacts on auditors' work and work-life balance: auditors' perceptions and implications.* Accounting Research Journal., DOI:10.1108/ARJ-06-2023-0158

Lumi, A. (2020). The impact of digitalisation on human resources development. *Prizren Social Science Journal*, 4(3), 39–46. DOI:10.32936/pssj.v4i3.178

Lund, B. D., & Wang, T. (2023). Chatting about ChatGPT: How may AI and GPT impact academia and libraries? *Library Hi Tech News*, 40(3), 26–29. DOI:10.1108/LHTN-01-2023-0009

Lundqvist, D., Reineholm, C., Ståhl, C., & Wallo, A. (2022). The impact of leadership on employee well-being: On-site compared to working from home. *BMC Public Health*, 22(1), 2154. Advance online publication. DOI:10.1186/s12889-022-14612-9 PMID:36424558

Lundy, O. (2006). From Personnel Management to Strategic Human Resource Management. *International Journal of Human Resource Management*, 5(3), 687–720. DOI:10.1080/09585199400000054

Luoma-aho, V., & Canel, M.-J. (2016). Public Sector Reputation. In Carroll, C. E. (Ed.), *SAGE Encyclopedia of Corporate Reputation* (pp. 597–600).

Lu, Y., Zhang, M. M., Yang, M. M., & Wang, Y. (2023). Sustainable human resource management practices, employee resilience, and employee outcomes: Toward common good values. *Human Resource Management*, 62(3), 331–353.

Mabungela, M. (2023). Artificial Intelligence (AI) and Automation in the World of Work: A Threat to Employees? *Research in Social Sciences and Technology*, 8(4), 135–146. DOI:10.46303/ressat.2023.37

Ma, G., Yang, R., Minneyfield, A., Gu, X., Gan, Y., Li, L., Liu, S., Jiang, W., Lai, W., & Wu, Y. (2022). A practical analysis of blended training efficacy on organizational outcomes. *Industrial and Commercial Training*, 54(4), 637–646. DOI:10.1108/ICT-12-2021-0085

Maheshwari, S., & Vohra, V. (2018). Role of training and development practices in implementing change. *International Journal of Learning and Change*, 10(2), 131–162. DOI:10.1504/IJLC.2018.090911

Maisiri, W., Darwish, H., & van Dyk, L. (2019). An investigation of Industry 4.0 skills requirements. *South African Journal of Industrial Engineering*, 30(3), 90–105. DOI:10.7166/30-3-2230

Maity, S. (2019). Identifying opportunities for artificial intelligence in the evolution of training and development practices. *Journal of Management Development*, 38(8), 651–663. DOI:10.1108/JMD-03-2019-0069

Ma, J. G., & Jiang, W. (2013). The concept, characteristics and application of big data. *Natl. Def. Sci. Technol*, 34, 10–16.

Mammadova, M., & Jabrayilova, Z. (2016). Opportunities and Challenges of Big Data Utilization in the Resolution of Human Resource Management. Problems of information technology, 7(1), 33-40. .DOI:10.25045/jpit.v07.i1.05

Mandip, G. (2012). Green HRM: People management commitment to environmental sustainability. *Research Journal of Recent Sciences, ISSN*, 2277, 2502.

Manisha, & Singh, R.K. (2016). Problems Faced by Working Women in the Banking Sector. *International Journal of Emerging Research in Management &Technology*, 5(2).

Margaret, P., & Winters, K. (1993). *İnsan Kaynakları*. Rota Yayınevi.

Margherita, A. (2022). Human resources analytics: A systematization of research topics and directions for future research. *Human Resource Management Review*, 32(2), 100795. DOI:10.1016/j.hrmr.2020.100795

Marinagi, C., Trivelllas, P., Kofakis, P., Tsouflas, G. T., & Rekleitis, P. (2019). E-Training on green logistics in the agri-food sector. *Scientific Papers. Series Management, Economic, Engineering in Agriculture and Rural Development*, 19(2), 249–256.

Marr, B. (2024, January 12). *The biggest challenges and pitfalls of data-driven, AI-enabled HR*. Forbes. https://www.forbes.com/sites/bernardmarr/2024/01/12/the -biggest-challenges-and-pitfalls-of-data-driven-ai-enabled-hr/

Martinez-Gil. (2021), Jorge Towards the automation of recruitment processes. e-prints in library & information science, 1-6. http://eprints.rclis.org/42472/

Maryville University. (2024). The importance of human resource management in the modern workplace. *Maryville University Online*. https://online.maryville.edu/ online-bachelors-degrees/human-resource-management/resources/what-is-human -resource-management/

Mashey, J. R. (1999). Big data and the next wave of {InfraStress} problems, solutions, opportunities. In 1999 USENIX annual technical conference. (USENIX ATC 99).

Maurer, R. (2024a, February 1). *White-collar workers to be most impacted by GenAI*. https://www.shrm.org/topics-tools/news/technology/white-collar-workers -most-impacted-by-genai

Maurer, R. (2024b, February 15). *AI adoption in HR is growing*. https://www.shrm .org/topics-tools/news/technology/ai-adoption-hr-is-growing

Mayo, G. E. (1933). *The human problems of an industrial civilization*. Macmillan and Company.

Mazurchenko, A., & Maršíková, K. (2019). Digitally-powered human resource management: Skills and roles in the digital era. *Acta Informatica Pragensia*, 8(2), 72–87. DOI:10.18267/j.aip.125

McAfee, A., ve Brynjolfsson, E. (2012). Big Data: The Management Revolution. *Harvard Business Review*, (90), 70–77. PMID:23074865

McPhail, R., Chan, X. W., May, R., & Wilkinson, A. (2023). Post-COVID remote working and its impact on people, productivity, and the planet: An exploratory scoping review. *International Journal of Human Resource Management*, 35(1), 154–182. DOI:10.1080/09585192.2023.2221385

Meijerink, J., & Keegan, A. (2019). Conceptualizing human resource management in the gig economy: Toward a platform ecosystem perspective. *Journal of Managerial Psychology*, 34(4), 214–232. DOI:10.1108/JMP-07-2018-0277

Menges, J. I., Tussing, D. V., Wihler, A., & Grant, A. M. (2017). When job performance is all relative: How family motivation energizes effort and compensates for intrinsic motivation. *Academy of Management Journal*, 60(2), 695–719. DOI:10.5465/ amj.2014.0898

Menon, S. (2016). *George Elton Mayo: The father of human resource management & his Hawthorne Studies.* https://www.linkedin.com/pulse/george-elton-mayothe -father-human-resource-management-sarita-menon/

Menzel, S. (2020). *VW-Software-Einheit startet im Juli - Betriebssystem soll bis kommen.* Handelsblatt.

Merleau-Ponty, M. (2012). *Phenomenology of perception* (Sarıkartal, E., & Hacımuratoğlu, E., Trans.). Ithaki Publications.

Messner, W. (2013). Effect of organizational culture on employee commitment in the Indian IT services sourcing industry. *Journal of Indian Business Research*, 5(2), 76–100. DOI:10.1108/17554191311320764

Meyer, J. P., & Allen, N. J. (1991). A three-component conceptualization of organizational commitment. *Human Resource Management Review*, 1(1), 61–89. DOI:10.1016/1053-4822(91)90011-Z

Mgammal, M. H., Mohammed Al-Matari, E., & Bardai, B. (2022). How coronavirus (COVID-19) pandemic thought concern affects employees' work performance: Evidence from real time survey. *Cogent Business & Management*, 9(1), 2064707. Advance online publication. DOI:10.1080/23311975.2022.2064707

Mhlanga, D. (2022). The role of artificial intelligence and machine learning amid the COVID-19 pandemic: What lessons are we learning on 4IR and the sustainable development goals. *International Journal of Environmental Research and Public Health*, 19(3), 1879. DOI:10.3390/ijerph19031879 PMID:35162901

Micic, L., & Radosavac, V. (2018). Influence of Information Technology to Human Resources Management: Key Trends in 21st Century. In Hadžikadić, M. A. (Ed.), *Lecture Notes in Networks and Systems* (Vol. 28, pp. 271–281). Springer., DOI:10.1007/978-3-319-71321-2_25

Micu, A., Capatina, A., Micu, A. E., & Schin, G. (2017). Exploring e-HCM Systems' benefits in organizations from private sector and public administration. *Journal of Promotion Management*, 23(3), 407–418. DOI:10.1080/10496491.2017.1294885

Mikalef, P., Framnes, V. A., Danielsen, F., Krogstie, J., & Olsen, D. (2017). Big data analytics capability: antecedents and business value. Pacific Asia Conference On Information Systems, https://aisel.aisnet.org/pacis2017/136

Miles, M. B., & Huberman, A. M. (1994). *Qualitative data analysis: An expanded sourcebook. sage.* SAGE Publications.

Mills, S., Lucas, S., Irakliotis, L., Rappa, M., Carlson, T., & Perlowitz, B. (2012). *Demystifying big data: a practical guide to transforming the business of government.* TechAmerica Foundation.

Minbaeva, D. (2018). Building credible human capital analytics for organizational competitive advantage. *Human Resource Management,* 57(3), 701–713. DOI:10.1002/hrm.21848

Mind Tools Content Team. (2024). *Henri Fayol's five functions of management.* https://cdn.jwplayer.com/previews/QpuUregs-5WSyalpf

Ming-jun, L. I., & Xiang-dong, L. I. (2021). Research on Factors Affecting Green Airport Development Based on Scale Analysis. [). IOP Publishing.]. *IOP Conference Series. Earth and Environmental Science,* 647(1), 012148.

Minh, H. T. P., & Long, N. N. (2023). Adaptive resilience in a post-pandemic era: A case of Vietnamese organizations. *Problems and Perspectives in Management,* 21(3), 219–229. DOI:10.21511/ppm.21(3).2023.17

Mironova, S. M., Kozhemyakin, D. V., & Ponomarchenko, A. E. (2022). Adaptation of the legal regulation of labor, civil, tax relations to the gig economy. *Law Enforcement Review,* 6(4), 314–329. DOI:10.52468/2542-1514.2022.6(4).314-329

Miroslava, B. (2018). *Challenges Related To The Digital Transformation Of Business Companies.* Innovation Management, Entrepreneurship and Sustainability.

Mirzani, Y. (2023). A STUDY ON LEADERSHIP STYLES AND ITS IMPACT ON ORGANIZATIONAL SUCCESS. *EPRA International Journal of Economics, Business and Management,* 1–19. DOI:10.36713/epra12138

Mishra, P. K. (2013). Job satisfaction. *IOSR Journal Of Humanities And Social Science,* 14(5), 45–54. DOI:10.9790/1959-1454554

Mishra, S. N., Lama, D. R., & Pal, Y. (2016). Human Resource Predictive Analytics (HRPA) for HR management in organizations. *International Journal of Scientific & Technology Research,* 5(5), 33–35.

Mitchell, R., Agle, B., & Wood, D. (1997). Toward a theory of stakeholder identification and salience: Defining the principle of who and what really gounts. *Academy of Management Review,* 22(4), 853–886. DOI:10.2307/259247

Mobley, W. H. (1982). *Employee turnover: causes consequences & control.*

Mohamed, S. A., Mahmoud, M. A., Mahdi, M. N., & Mostafa, S. A. (2022). Improving efficiency and effectiveness of robotic process automation in human resource management. *Sustainability (Basel),* 14(7), 3920. DOI:10.3390/su14073920

Mohammad Badruddoza Talukder. Firoj Kabir, K. M., & Das, I. R. (2023). Emerging Concepts of Artificial Intelligence in the Hotel Industry: A Conceptual Paper. *International Journal of Research Publication and Reviews, Vol 4, no*, pp 1765-1769. https://doi.org/https://doi.org/10.55248/gengpi.4.923.92451

Mohammad Badruddoza Talukder. Sanjeev Kumar, I. R. Das. (2024a). Implications of Blockchain Technology- Based Cryptocurrency in the cloud for the Hospitality Industry. In *Emerging Trends in Cloud Computing Analytics, Scalability, and Service Models* (p. 19). DOI:10.4018/979-8-3693-0900-1.ch018

Mohammad Badruddoza Talukder. Sanjeev Kumar, I. R. Das. (2024b). Perspectives of Digital Marketing for the Restaurant Industry. In *Advancements in Socialized and Digital Media Communications* (p. 17). DOI:10.4018/979-8-3693-0855-4.ch009

Mohsin, M., & Sulaiman, R. (2013). A study on e-training adoption for higher learning institutions. *International Journal of Asian Social Science*, 3(9), 2006–2018.

Molaiepour, S. (2024, February 1). *EU AI Act: What HR teams need to know*. https://www.jobylon.com/blog/eu-ai-act-what-hr-teams-need-to-know

Molitor, M., & Renkema, M. (2022). Human-robot collaboration in a smart industry context: Does hrm matter? In *Smart Industry–Better Management* (pp. 105–123). Emerald Publishing Limited. DOI:10.1108/S1877-636120220000028008

Molotkova, N. V., Makeeva, M. N., & Khazanova, D. L. Digitalized Personnel Management. *European Proceedings of Social and Behavioural Sciences*. DOI:10.15405/epsbs.2019.03.75

Moniz, A. B. (2013). Organisational challenges of human–robot interaction systems in industry: human resources implications. In *Human resource management and technological challenges* (pp. 123–131). Springer International Publishing.

Morales, H. A. H. (2018). Mayer-Schönberger, V. & Cukier, K.(2013). Big Data. La revolución de los datos masivos. Clivajes. *Revista de Ciencias Sociales*, (9), 189–189. DOI:10.25009/clivajes-rcs.v0i9.2536

Mowday, R. T., Steers, R. M., & Porter, L. W. (1979). The measurement of organizational commitment. *Journal of Vocational Behavior*, 14(2), 224–247. DOI:10.1016/0001-8791(79)90072-1

Munich Airport. (2012). Munich Airport Annual Report, https://www.munich-airport.com/_b/0000000000000001983421bb593a8d51/ib2012-en.pdf [Retrieved date: 20-October -2020]

Munna, A. S., Tholibon, D. A., Cantafio, G., & Nasiruddin, U. (2023). Changes of Public Sector Human Resource Management (HRM). *International Journal of Educational Administration, Management, and Leadership*, 65-78.

Murad, A. (2023). *The computers rejecting your job application*. Pocket. https://getpocket.com/explore/item/the-computers-rejecting-your-job-application

Murray, B., Dulebohn, J., Stone, D., & Lukaszewski, K. (2024). *The Future of Human Resource Management*. Vol. Research in Human Resource Management.

Muthuveloo, R., & Rose, R. C. (2005). Typology of organisational commitment. *American Journal of Applied Sciences*, 2(6), 1078–1081. DOI:10.3844/ajassp.2005.1078.1081

Nagel, L. (2020). The influence of the COVID-19 pandemic on the digital transformation of work. *The International Journal of Sociology and Social Policy*, 40(9/10), 861–875. DOI:10.1108/IJSSP-07-2020-0323

Nagy, A. (2005). The impact of e-learning. In *E-Content: Technologies and perspectives for the European Market* (pp. 79–96). Springer Berlin Heidelberg. DOI:10.1007/3-540-26387-X_4

Nahra, K. J., Evers, A., Jessani, A. J., Braun, M., Vallery, A., & Benizri, I. (2024, March 14). *The European Parliament adopts the AI Act*. https://www.wilmerhale.com/en/insights/blogs/wilmerhale-privacy-and-cybersecurity-law/20240314-the-european-parliament-adopts-the-ai-act

Nair, A. J., Manohar, S., & Chaudhry, R. (2024). Role of Knowledge Management in Enhancing the Effectiveness of the Gig Economy. In Ordóñez De Pablos, P., Almunawar, M. N., & Anshari, M. (Eds.), (pp. 161–175). Advances in Finance, Accounting, and Economics. IGI Global., DOI:10.4018/979-8-3693-1942-0.ch009

Najiha, I., & Herman, S. (2024). Factors Affecting the Gig Economy of Labor Productivity in Ride Hailing Services. *Digital Economics Review*, 1(1). Advance online publication. DOI:10.58968/der.v1i1.474

Naveen, D., Satish, K., Debmalya, M., Nitesh, P., & Weng Marc, L. (2021). How to Conduct a Bibliometric Analysis: An Overview and Guidelines. *Journal of Business Research*, 133, 285–296. DOI:10.1016/j.jbusres.2021.04.070

Nawaz, N. (2017). A comprehensive literature review of the digital HR research filed. In Information and Knowledge Management (Vol. 7, No. 4).

Nawaz, N. (2017). A comprehensive literature review of the digital HR research filed. *Information and Knowledge Management* 7(4).

Nawaz, N. (2019). Artificial intelligence interchange human intervention in the recruitment process in Indian software industry. *International Journal of Advanced Trends in Computer Science and Engineering*, 8(4), 1433–1442. DOI:10.30534/ijatcse/2019/62842019

Naz, S., Jamshed, S., Nisar, Q. A., & Nasir, N. (2023). Green HRM, psychological green climate and pro-environmental behaviors: An efficacious drive towards environmental performance in China. *Current Psychology (New Brunswick, N.J.)*, 42(2), 1346–1361.

Ncamane, N. (2023). Digital platform workers and the conundrum of the definition of an 'employee' in the era of the Fourth Industrial Revolution. *South African Mercantile Law Journal*, 35(1), 1–26. DOI:10.47348/SAMLJ/v35/i1a1

Neuman, W. L. (2006). *Social Research Methods: Qualitative and Quantitative Approaches*. Pearson.

Nidhi, B. S. (2023). The impact of flexible work arrangements on work-life balance. *International Journal For Multidisciplinary Research*, 5(3), 3144. Advance online publication. DOI:10.36948/ijfmr.2023.v05i03.3144

Nikoloski, D., Najdovska, N. T., Nechkoska, R. P., & Pechijareski, L. (2023). The gig economy in the Post-COVID era. In *Contributions to management science* (pp. 93–117). DOI:10.1007/978-3-031-11065-8_4

Nimmagadda, B., Vangaveti, Y., Aaluri, S., Mallikarjuna Rao, Ch., & Singh, B. (2024). An Analytical study on Navigating Sustainability Challenges and Opportunities in the era of AI and the Gig Economy. *MATEC Web of Conferences, 392*, 01044. DOI:10.1051/matecconf/202439201044

Nocker, M., & Sena, V. (2019). Big data and human resources management: The rise of talent analytics. *Social Sciences (Basel, Switzerland)*, 8(10), 1–19. DOI:10.3390/socsci8100273

Notice on data protection from the State Data Protection Inspectorate.

Nwugballa, E. A. (2016). Evaluating the relationship between work-family conflict and organisational commitment among rural women health workers in Ebonyi state, Nigeria. *International Journal of Academic Research in Business & Social Sciences*, 6(5). Advance online publication. DOI:10.6007/IJARBSS/v6-i5/2169

Nyanga, T., & Chindanya, A. (2020). Covid 19 pandemic shifting the job satisfaction landscape among employees. *Business Excellence and Management*, 10(5), 168–176. DOI:10.24818/beman/2020.S.I.1-14

Nyathani, R. (2023). AI-Driven HR analytics: Unleashing the power of HR data management. *Journal of Technology and Systems*, 5(2), 15–26. DOI:10.47941/jts.1513

Nyfoudi, M., Kwon, B., & Wilkinson, A. (2024). Employee voice in times of crisis: A conceptual framework exploring the role of Human Resource practices and Human Resource system strength. *Human Resource Management*, 63(4), 537–553. Advance online publication. DOI:10.1002/hrm.22214

O'Donohue, W., & Torugsa, N. (2016). The moderating effect of 'Green' HRM on the association between proactive environmental management and financial performance in small firms. *International Journal of Human Resource Management*, 27(2), 239–261. DOI:10.1080/09585192.2015.1063078

O'Leary, D. E. (2013). Artificial intelligence and big data. *IEEE Intelligent Systems*, 28(2), 96–99. DOI:10.1109/MIS.2013.39

Ogbeibu, S., Emelifeonwu, J., Pereira, V., Oseghale, R., Gaskin, J., Sivarajah, U., & Gunasekaran, A. (2024). Demystifying the roles of organisational smart technology, artificial intelligence, robotics and algorithms capability: A strategy for green human resource management and environmental sustainability. *Business Strategy and the Environment*, 33(2), 369–388. DOI:10.1002/bse.3495

Oğuzlar, A. (2003). Veri ön işleme. *Erciyes Üniversitesi İktisadi ve İdari Bilimler Fakültesi Dergisi*, (21), 67–76.

Okolo, C. V., Wen, J., & Susaeta, A. (2023). Maximizing natural resource rent economics: The role of human capital development, financial sector development, and open-trade economies in driving technological innovation. *Environmental Science and Pollution Research International*, 31(3), 4453–4477. DOI:10.1007/s11356-023-31373-z PMID:38103137

Oladipo Olugbenga Adekoya, Adedayo Adefemi, Olawe Alaba Tula, Nwabueze Kelvin Nwaobia, & Joachim Osheyor Gidiagba. (2024). Technological innovations in the LNG sector: A review: Assessing recent advancements and their impact on LNG production, transportation and usage. *World Journal of Advanced Research and Reviews, 21*(1), 040–057. DOI:10.30574/wjarr.2024.21.1.2685

Olore, A. A., Olawande, T. I., George, T. O., Jegede, A., Egharevba, M. E., & Amoo, E. O. (2023). Understanding coping strategies adults adopted to survive during COVID-19 and Post-COVID-19 pandemic. *Open Access Macedonian Journal of Medical Sciences, 11*(E), 89–95. DOI:10.3889/oamjms.2023.8612

Omer, S. K. (2018). ORGANIZATION ROBOTS; TREND TO POST-HUMAN RESOURCES MANAGEMENT (POST-HRM). Journal of process management and new technologies, 6(1).

Omilion-Hodges, L. M., & Ptacek, J. K. (2021). What is the Leader–Member Exchange (LMX) Theory? In *New perspectives in organizational communication* (pp. 3–25). DOI:10.1007/978-3-030-68756-4_1

Oncer, A. Z. (2019). Örgütlerde yeşil insan kaynakları yönetimi uygulamaları: Teorik bir inceleme. *İş ve İnsan Dergisi, 6*(2), 199-208, .DOI:10.18394/iid.552555

Order of the Supreme Administrative Court of Lithuania of 2 July 2014, TAR, 10-07-2014, No 10106.

Osai, O., Eleanya, L., Gabriel, J., & Okene, N. (2009). Jethro as the Patriarch of Administration and Management: An Analysis of His Works. *Journal of Social Sciences*, 18(3), 157–162. DOI:10.1080/09718923.2009.11892677

Osborne, S. P., & Brown, L. (2011). Innovation, Public Policy and Public Services Delivery in The UK: The Word That Would Be King? *Public Administration*, 89(4), 1335–1350. DOI:10.1111/j.1467-9299.2011.01932.x

Oum, T. H. and Yu, C. (2004). *Airport Performance: A Summary of the 2003 ATRS Global Airport Benchmarking Report* (No. 1425-2016-118401).

Owais, S. S., & Hussein, N. S. (2016). Extract five categories CPIVW from the 9V's characteristics of the big data. *International Journal of Advanced Computer Science and Applications*, 7(3), 254–258.

Owen, R. (1857). *The life of Robert Owen written by himself: With selections from his writings and correspondence*. Effingham Wilson.

Owoyemi, O., Oyelere, M., Elegbede, T., & Gbajumo-Sheriff, M. (2011). Enhancing workforce' commitment to organisation through training. *International Journal of Business and Management*, 6(7), 280–286.

Özdemir, İ., & Sağıroğlu, Ş. (2018). Denetimlerde büyük veri kullanımı ve üzerine bir değerlendirme. *Gazi University Journal of Science Part C: Design and Technology*, 6(2), 470–480. DOI:10.29109/http-gujsc-gazi-edu-tr.347728

Özgen, H., & Yalçın, A. (2017). *İnsan kaynakları yönetimi stratejik bir yaklaşım*. Akademisyen Kitabevi.

Paesen, H., Wouters, K., & Maesschalck, J. (2019). Servant leaders, ethical followers? The effect of servant leadership on employee deviance. *Leadership and Organization Development Journal*, 40(5), 624–646. DOI:10.1108/LODJ-01-2019-0013

Pagán-Castaño, E., Maseda-Moreno, A., & Santos-Rojo, C. (2020). Wellbeing in work environments. *Journal of Business Research*, 115, 469–474.

Paillé, P., Chen, Y., Boiral, O., & Jin, J. (2014). The impact of human resource management on environmental performance: An employee-level study. *Journal of Business Ethics*, 121, 451–466.

Pala, İ. B. (2021). *Kurumsal Büyük Veri Analitiği Yetenekleri Ve Performans İlişkisi: Türkiye İçin Bir Araştırma, İstanbul Teknik Üniversitesi Lisansüstü Eğitim Enstitüsü.* Yayınlanmış Yüksek Lisans Tezi.

Palmer, M., & Winters, K. T. (1993). *Human Resources (Translated into Turkish: Şahiner, D.).* Rota Publications.

Palumbo, R., Manna, R., & Cavallone, M. (2020). Beware of side effects on quality! Investigating the implications of home working on work-life balance in educational services. *The TQM Journal*, 33(4), 915–929. DOI:10.1108/TQM-05-2020-0120

Pandey, N., & Pal, A. (2020). Impact of digital surge during Covid-19 pandemic: A viewpoint on research and practice. *International Journal of Information Management*, 55, 102171. DOI:10.1016/j.ijinfomgt.2020.102171 PMID:32836633

Pandey, S., Viswanathan, V., & Kamboj, P. (2016). Sustainable green HRM – Importance and factors affecting successful implementation in organizations. *International Journal of Research in Management and Business*, 2(3), 11–29.

Pant, B., & Lal, A. (2020). Aarogya Setu App: A tale of the complex challenges of a rights-based regime. May 13, Retrieved March 23, 2024, from https://thewire.in/tech/aarogya-setu-app-challenges-rights-based-regime

Pan, Y., & Froese, F. J. (2023). An interdisciplinary review of AI and HRM: Challenges and future directions. *Human Resource Management Review*, 33(1), 100924. DOI:10.1016/j.hrmr.2022.100924

Paradox. (2024). *AI Recruiting—Paradox.* https://www.paradox.ai/demo/ai-recruiting

Paranjape, K., Schinkel, M., Panday, R. N., Car, J., & Nanayakkara, P. (2019). Introducing artificial intelligence training in medical education. *JMIR Medical Education*, 5(2), e16048. DOI:10.2196/16048 PMID:31793895

Parida, V., Sjödin, D., & Reim, W. (2019). Reviewing literature on digitalization, business model innovation, and sustainable industry: Past achievements and future promises. *Sustainability (Basel)*, 11(2), 391–410. DOI:10.3390/su11020391

Parviainen, P., Tihinen, M., Kääriäinen, J., & Teppola, S. (2017). Tackling the digitalization challenge: How to benefit from digitalization in practice. *International Journal of Information Systems and Project Management*, 5(1), 63–77. DOI:10.12821/ijispm050104

Pater, D. E., Annelies, I., Vianen, E. M. V., & Bechtoldt, M. N. (2010). Gender Differences in Job Challenge: A Matter of Task Allocation. *Gender, Work and Organization*, 17(4), 433–453. DOI:10.1111/j.1468-0432.2009.00477.x

Patil, R., Kumar, S., Rani, R., Agrawal, P., & Pippal, S. (2023). A Bibliometric andWord Cloud Analysis on the Role of the Internet of Things in Agricultural Plant Disease Detection. *Applied System Innovation*, 6(1), 2–17. DOI:10.3390/asi6010027

Pattali, S. (2022). ROLE OF ARTIFICIAL INTELLIGENCE IN HRM. *International Journal of Early Childhood Special Education*, 14(5).

Patton, M. Q. (2014). *Qualitative Research and Evaluation Methods* (Bütün, M., & Demir, S. B., Trans.). Pegem Akademi.

Penn Today. (2023, June 16). *AI could transform social science research*. Penn Today. https://penntoday.upenn.edu/news/ai-could-transform-social-science-research

Perreault, M., & Power, N. (2021). Work-life balance as a personal responsibility: The impact on strategies for coping with interrole conflict. *Journal of Occupational Science*, 30(2), 160–174. DOI:10.1080/14427591.2021.1894596

Peteraf, M. A. (1993). The Cornerstones of Competitive Advantage: A Resource Based–View. *Strategic Management Journal*, 14(3), 179–188. DOI:10.1002/smj.4250140303

Pinnington, A., Macklin, R., & Campbell, T. (2007). *Human Resource Management: Ethics and Employment*. Oxford University Press. DOI:10.1093/oso/9780199203789.001.0001

Pitafi, A. H., Rasheed, M. I., Kanwal, S., & Ren, M. (2020). Employee agility and enterprise social media: The Role of IT proficiency and work expertise. *Technology in Society*, 63, 101333. DOI:10.1016/j.techsoc.2020.101333

Platanou, K. & Mäkelä, K. (2016). HR function at the crossroads of digital disruption. Työn, 1, PP. 19–26.

Plater, Q. C., Frazier, M. D., Talbert, P. Y., Davis, V. H., & Talbert, P. S. (2022). Human resources strategies & lessons learned during the COVID-19 pandemic: A literature review. *Management Dynamics in the Knowledge Economy*, 10(4), 330–342. DOI:10.2478/mdke-2022-0021

Popoola, B. (2024). *AI AND AUTOMATION*. Unpublished. DOI:10.13140/RG.2.2.15359.21929

Pourrashidi, R., Mehranpour, M., & Nick, M. F. (2017). Human resources management: Challenges and solutions. *Helix*, 8, 998–1001.

Pramono, A. C., & Prahiawan, W. (2022). Effect of training on employee performance with competence and commitment as intervening. *Aptisi Transactions on Management*, 6(2), 142–150.

Prapti, N. "ASYNCHRONOUS E-TRAINING AND COACHING TO INDONESIAN PARENTS: NATURALISTIC STRATEGIES TO SUPPORT LANGUAGE DEVELOPMENT OF CHILDREN WITH SOCIAL-COMMUNICATION DELAYS" (2023). Theses and Dissertations--Early Childhood, Special Education, and Counselor Education. 134. https://uknowledge.uky.edu/edsrc_etds/134

Prasad, S. (2016). Training and Post Training Evaluation for Employee Effectiveness: An Empirical Study on Supermarket in India. *Arabian J Bus Manag Review S*, 1(2). Advance online publication. DOI:10.4172/2223-5833.S1-006

Prassl, J. (2018). *Humans as a Service: The Promise and Perils of Work in the Gig Economy* (1st ed.). Oxford University PressOxford., DOI:10.1093/oso/9780198797012.001.0001

Pratt, M. G., Kaplan, S., & Whittington, R. (2020). Editorial Essay: The Tumult over Transparency: Decoupling Transparency from Replication in establishing trustworthy qualitative research*. *Administrative Science Quarterly*, 65(1), 1–19. DOI:10.1177/0001839219887663

Prendergast, R. (2021). Charles Babbage's economy of knowledge. In *Information and the history of philosophy*. Routledge. DOI:10.4324/9781351130752-19

Press release of the Supreme Administrative Court of Lithuania of 9 February 2022.

Prestoza, M. J. (2024). Assessing remote learning's feasibility: A comprehensive analysis of Philippine public-school teachers' use of learning management systems and blended learning approaches. *Journal of Research. Policy & Practice of Teachers and Teacher Education*, 14(1), 21–27.

Price, J. L. (1977). *The study of Turnover*. Iowa State Press.

Primc, K., & Čater, T. (2015). Environmental proactivity and firm performance: A fuzzy-set analysis. *Management Decision*, 53(3), 648–667. DOI:10.1108/MD-05-2014-0288

Prins, P., Beirendonck, L., Vos, A., & Segers, J. (2014). Sustainable HRM: Bridging Theory and Practice Through the 'Respect Openness Continuity (ROC)' Model. *Management Review*, 25(4), 263–284.

Puspitarini, R. C., & Basit, A. (2020). Race to the Bottom: An Introduction to Gig Economy based on Moral Economy in Islam Perspective. *POLITEA*, 3(2), 167. DOI:10.21043/politea.v3i2.8331

Putri, A., & Amran, A. (2021). Employees' Work-Life Balance Reviewed from work from home aspect during COVID-19 pandemic. *International Journal of Management Science and Information Technology*, 1(1), 30. DOI:10.35870/ijmsit.v1i1.231

Putri, N. K., Melania, M. K. N., Fatmawati, S., & Lim, Y. C. (2023). How does the work-life balance impact stress on primary healthcare workers during the COVID-19 pandemic? *BMC Health Services Research*, 23(1), 730. Advance online publication. DOI:10.1186/s12913-023-09677-0 PMID:37408024

Pymetrics. (n.d.). *Pymetrics*. Retrieved January 22, 2024, from https://www.pymetrics.ai/

Qadir, J. (2023). Engineering education in the era of ChatGPT: Promise and pitfalls of generative AI for education. *2023 IEEE Global Engineering Education Conference (EDUCON)*, 1–9. https://doi.org/DOI:10.1109/EDUCON54358.2023.10125121

Qahtani, E. H. A., & Alsmairat, M. A. (2023). Assisting artificial intelligence adoption drivers in human resources management: A mediation model. *Acta Logistica*, 10(1), 141–150. DOI:10.22306/al.v10i1.371

Qin, S., Jia, N., Luo, X., Liao, C., & Huang, Z. (2023). Perceived fairness of human managers compared with artificial intelligence in employee performance evaluation. *Journal of Management Information Systems*, 40(4), 1039–1070. DOI:10.1080/07421222.2023.2267316

Qiu, J. L., Hong, R., & Badger, A. (2023). Auditing Gig Work Platforms: Fairwork's Research, Advocacy, and Impact. *Singapore Labour Journal*, 02(01), 22–38. DOI:10.1142/S281103152300013X

Quinteros-Durand, R., Almanza-Cabe, R. B., Morales-García, W. C., Mamani-Benito, Ó., Sairitupa-Sanchez, L. Z., Puño-Quispe, L., Saintila, J., Saavedra-Sandoval, R., Paredes, A. F., & Ramírez-Coronel, A. A. (2023). Influence of servant leadership on the life satisfaction of basic education teachers: The mediating role of satisfaction with job resources. *Frontiers in Psychology*, 14, 1167074. Advance online publication. DOI:10.3389/fpsyg.2023.1167074 PMID:38023005

Radebe, T. (2009). The Strategic Value of Innovation in the Public Sector. Ideas that Work: The Public Sector. *The Innovation Journal*, 1(1), 10–14.

Rahman, M. M., & Watanobe, Y. (2023). ChatGPT for education and research: Opportunities, threats, and strategies. *Applied Sciences (Basel, Switzerland)*, 13(9), 9. Advance online publication. DOI:10.3390/app13095783

Raja, D. V. A. J., & Kumar, R. A. R. (2016). A Study on Effectiveness of Training and Development in Ashok Leyland all over India. *Journal of Management*, 3(1), 1–12.

Rajalakshmi, M., & Gomathi, S. (2016). A review on E-HRM: Electronic human resource management. *Indian Journal of Research*, 5(8), 364–379.

Ramamoorti, S., Agarwal, A., & Nijhawan, S. (2016). Big data and continuous monitoring: A synergy whose time has come? *Internal Auditing*, 31(1), 19–26.

Ramayah, T., Ahmad, N. H., & Hong, T. S. (2012). An assessment of e-training effectiveness in multinational companies in Malaysia. *Journal of Educational Technology & Society*, 15(2), 125–137.

Rameshkumar, M. (2020). Employee engagement as an antecedent of organizational commitment – A study on Indian seafaring officers. *The Asian journal of shipping and logistics*, 36(3): 105-112.

Rana, G., & Sharma, R. (2019). Emerging human resource management practices in Industry 4.0. *Strategic HR Review*, 18(4), 176–181. DOI:10.1108/SHR-01-2019-0003

Rao, P. S. (2009). *Personnel and human resource management (Book)*. Himalaya Publishing House.

Rasskazova, A., Koroleva, E., & Rasskazov, S. (2019, March). Digital transformation: Statistical evaluation of success factors of an ICO-campaign. []. IOP Publishing.]. *IOP Conference Series. Materials Science and Engineering*, 497(1), 012087. DOI:10.1088/1757-899X/497/1/012087

Rastogi, S., & Sharma, P. (2022). Revisiting Artificial Intelligence in HRM. SJCC Management Research Review, 110-128.

Rehman, S. U., Giordino, D., Zhang, Q., & Alam, G. M. (2023). Twin transitions & industry 4.0: Unpacking the relationship between digital and green factors to determine green competitive advantage. *Technology in Society*, 73, 102227. DOI:10.1016/j.techsoc.2023.102227

Reinsel, D., Gantz, J., & Rydning, J. (2017). Data age 2025: The evolution of data to life-critical. Don't Focus on Big Data, 2.

Ren, J. (2017). Modelling quality dynamics, business value and firm performance in a big data analytics environment. *International Journal of Production Research*, 55(17), 5011–5026. DOI:10.1080/00207543.2016.1154209

Ren, S., Tang, G., & Jackson, E, S. (2018). Green human resource management research in emergence: A review and future directions. *Asia Pacific Journal of Management*, 35, 769–803.

Renwick, D., Redman, T., & Maguire, S. (2008). Green HRM: A review, process model, and research agenda. *University of Sheffield Management School Discussion Paper, 1*(1), 1-46.

Renwick, D. W., Redman, T., & Maguire, S. (2013). Green human resource management: A review and research agenda. *International Journal of Management Reviews*, 15(1), 1–14.

Ren, Z., & Hussain, R. Y. (2022). A mediated–moderated model for green human resource management: An employee perspective. *Frontiers in Environmental Science*, 10, 973692.

Resolution of the Constitutional Court of the Republic of Lithuania of 1 July 2013. Valstybės žinios, 2013-10-01, No. 103-5079;

Resolution of the Constitutional Court of the Republic of Lithuania of 11 December 2009. Valstybės žinios, 2009-12-15, No. 148-6632;

Resolution of the Constitutional Court of the Republic of Lithuania of 11 November 1998. Valstybės žinios, 18-11-1998, No. 100-2791.

Resolution of the Constitutional Court of the Republic of Lithuania of 11 September 2020. TAR, 11-09-2020, No 19129.

Resolution of the Constitutional Court of the Republic of Lithuania of 12 February 2021. TAR, 12/02/2021, No. 2775.

Resolution of the Constitutional Court of the Republic of Lithuania of 13 December 2004. Valstybės žinios, 18-12-2004, No 181-6708;

Resolution of the Constitutional Court of the Republic of Lithuania of 16 January 2006. Valstybės žinios, 19 January 2006, No 7-254;

Resolution of the Constitutional Court of the Republic of Lithuania of 17 February 2016. TAR, 17-02-2016, No. 2985.

Resolution of the Constitutional Court of the Republic of Lithuania of 19 December 2018. TAR, 19-12-2018, No 20843.

Resolution of the Constitutional Court of the Republic of Lithuania of 22 February 2013. Valstybės žinios, 2013-02-28, No. 22-1068;

Resolution of the Constitutional Court of the Republic of Lithuania of 22 January 2008. Valstybės žinios, 24-01-2008, No. 10-350.

Resolution of the Constitutional Court of the Republic of Lithuania of 22 March 2010. Valstybės žinios, 25-03-2010, No 34-1620.

Resolution of the Constitutional Court of the Republic of Lithuania of 22 September 2015.

Resolution of the Constitutional Court of the Republic of Lithuania of 25 January 2017. TAR, 25-01-2017, No. 1416.

Resolution of the Constitutional Court of the Republic of Lithuania of 3 July 2014. TAR, 3-07-03-2014, No. 9761;

Resolution of the Constitutional Court of the Republic of Lithuania of 31 May 2006. Valstybės žinios, 2006-06-03, No. 62-2283;

Resolution of the Constitutional Court of the Republic of Lithuania of 6 May 1997. Valstybės žinios, 1997-05-09, No. 40-977;

Resolution of the Constitutional Court of the Republic of Lithuania of 8 July 2020. TAR, 9-07-09-2020, No 15246.

Resolution of the Constitutional Court of the Republic of Lithuania of 8 November 2019. TAR, 8-11-2019, No. 17963.

Resolution of the Constitutional Court of the Republic of Lithuania. TAR, 18-02-2020, No. 3538.

Resolution of the Constitutional Court of the Republic of Lithuania. TAR, 19-09-2019, No 14836.

Resolution of the Constitutional Court of the Republic of Lithuania. Valstybės žinios, 10-03-1999, No. 23-666.

Resolution of the Constitutional Court of the Republic of Lithuania. Valstybės žinios, 2007-08-18, No. 90-3580.

Ribeiro, N., Gomes, D. R., Ortega, E., Gomes, G. P., & Semedo, A. S. (2022). The impact of green HRM on employees' eco-friendly behavior: The mediator role of organizational identification. *Sustainability*, 14(5), 2897.

Richards, J. (2020). Putting employees at the centre of sustainable HRM: A review, map and research agenda. *Employee Relations*, 44(3), 533–554. DOI:10.1108/ER-01-2019-0037

Robbins, S. P., & Judge, T. (2007). *Organizational behavior*. Prentice Hall.

Robert, V., & Vandenberghe, C. (2022). Laissez-faire leadership and employee well-being: The contribution of perceived supervisor organizational status. *European Journal of Work and Organizational Psychology*, 31(6), 940–957. DOI:10.1080/1359432X.2022.2081074

Roca, J. C., Chiu, C. M., & Martínez, F. J. (2006). Understanding e-learning continuance intention: An extension of the Technology Acceptance Model. *International Journal of Human-Computer Studies*, 64(8), 683–696. DOI:10.1016/j.ijhcs.2006.01.003

Rodgers, C. S. (1992). The flexible workplace: What have we learned? *Human Resource Management*, 31(3), 183–199. DOI:10.1002/hrm.3930310305

Rodríguez-Sánchez, J. L., Montero-Navarro, A., & Gallego-Losada, R. (2019). The opportunity presented by technological innovation to attract valuable human resources. *Sustainability (Basel)*, 11(20), 5785. DOI:10.3390/su11205785

Roscigno, V. J., Gracia, L. M., & Bobbitt-Zeher, D. (2007). Social Closure and Processes of Race/ Sex/ Employmentdiscrimination. *The Annals of the American Academy of Political and Social Science*, 6(9), 16–48. DOI:10.1177/0002716206294898

Rosenberg, J. (2006). *A framework for conferencing with the session initiation protocol (SIP)* (No. rfc4353).

Rotich, K. (2015). History, Evolution and Development Of Human Resource Management: A Contemporary Perspective. *Global Journal of Human Resource Management*, 3(3), 58–73.

Rowold, J. (2007). The impact of personality on training-related aspects of motivation: Test of a longitudinal model. *Human Resource Development Quarterly*, 18(1), 9–31. DOI:10.1002/hrdq.1190

Ruël, H., & Bondarouk, T. ve Looise, J. K. (2004). e-HRM: Innovation or irritation: An explorative empirical study in five large companies on Web-based HRM. Management Revue, 15(3), 364–380. https://www.jstor.org/stable/41783479

Ruël, H., & Van der Kaap, H. (2012). E -HRM usage and value creation. Does a facilitating context matter? *German Journal of Human Resource Management*, 26(3), 260–281. DOI:10.1177/239700221202600304

Russom, P. (2011). Big data analytics. TDWI best practices report, fourth quarter, 19(4), 1-34.

Sadath, L. (2013). Data Mining: A tool for knowledge management in human resource. *International Journal of Innovative Technology and Exploring Engineering*, 2(6), 154–159.

Sahadi, J. (2023, September 9). *Why do we work 9 to 5? The history of the eight-hour workday*. CNN. https://www.cnn.com/2023/09/09/success/work-culture-9-to-5-curious-consumer/index.html

Saks, A. M. (2006). Antecedents and consequences of employee engagement. *Journal of Managerial Psychology*, 21(7), 600–619. DOI:10.1108/02683940610690169

Salanova, M., Nieto, S. A., & Peíró, J. M. (2005). Linking organizational resources and work engagement to employee performance and customer loyalty: The mediation of service climate. *The Journal of Applied Psychology*, 90(6), 1217–1227. DOI:10.1037/0021-9010.90.6.1217 PMID:16316275

Sambrook, S. (2005). Factors influencing the context and process of work-related learning: Synthesizing findings from two research projects. *Human Resource Development International*, 8(1), 101–119. DOI:10.1080/1367886052000342591

Sandamali, J. G. P., Padmasiri, M. D., Mahalekamge, W. G. S., & Mendis, M. V. S. (2018). The relationship between training and development and employee performance of executive level employees in apparel organizations. *International Invention of Scientific Journal*, 2(1), 12–17.

Santos, S. A., Trevisan, L. N., Veloso, E. F. R., & Treff, M. A. (2021). Gamification in training and development processes: Perception on effectiveness and results. *Revista de Gestão*, 28(2), 133–146. DOI:10.1108/REGE-12-2019-0132

Sarma, A. (2009). Personnel and Human Resource Management. Mubai: Himalaya Publish House.

Şaşmaz, E. C. (2022). Dijital dönüşüm sürecinde insan kaynakları yönetimi. *Sosyal, beşeri ve idari bilimler alanında uluslararası araştırmalar VIII*, 239.

Sathasivam, K., Che Hashim, R., & Abu Bakar, R. (2021). Automobile industry managers' views on their roles in environmental sustainability: A qualitative study. *Management of Environmental Quality*, 32(5), 844–862.

Satyanarayana, L. V. (2015). A Survey on challenges and advantages in big data. *International Journal of Computer Science and Technology*, 6(2), 115–119.

Schaar, D., & Sherry, L. (2010, May). Analysis of airport stakeholders. *In 2010 Integrated Communications, Navigation, and Surveillance Conference Proceedings* (pp. J4-1). IEEE.

Schwanholz, J., & Graham, T. (2018). Digital Transformation: New Opportunities and Challenges for Democracy? In Schwanholz J., Graham T., Stoll P. T. (Eds.), Managing Democracy in the Digital Age, pp. 1-7. Springer.

Schwertner, K. (2017). Digital transformation of business. *Trakia Journal of Sciences*, 15(1, Suppl.1), 388–393. DOI:10.15547/tjs.2017.s.01.065

Scoones, I. (2007). Sustainability. *Development in Practice*, 17(4-5), 589–596. DOI:10.1080/09614520701469609

Scopelliti, V. (2019, June 12). Performance management vs bullying: Where's the line? *WISE Workplace*. https://www.wiseworkplace.com.au/2019/06/performance-management-vs-bullying-wheres-the-line/

Sekiguchi, T. & Huber, V. L. (2011). The use of person–organization fit and person–job fit information in making selection decisions', Organizational Behavior and Human Decision Processes, 116(2), pp. 203–216, ScienceDirect. .DOI:10.1016/j.obhdp.2011.04.001

Şener, C. and Şener, U. (2019). Monte Carlo Simülasyonu İle Hisse Senedi Fiyat Tahminleri [Stock Price Predictions using Monte Carlo Simulation], *Beykoz Akademi Dergisi,* [Beykoz Academy] 7(2), 294-306.

Shaffer, M. A., Sebastian Reiche, B., Dimitrova, M., Lazarova, M., Chen, S., Westman, M., & Wurtz, O. (2015). Work- and family-role adjustment of different types of global professionals: Scale development and validation. *Journal of International Business Studies*, 47(2), 113–139. DOI:10.1057/jibs.2015.26

Shafik, W., & Lakshmi, D. (2024). Explainable AI (EXAI) for Smart Healthcare Automation. In Prabhakar, P. K. (Ed.), (pp. 289–316). Advances in Bioinformatics and Biomedical Engineering. IGI Global., DOI:10.4018/979-8-3693-4439-2.ch012

Shah, P., Dubey, R., Shashikant, R., Renwick, D., & Misra, S. (2023). Green Human Resource Management: A Comprehensive Investigation Using Bibliometric Analysis. *Corporate Social Responsibility and Environmental Management*, 31(1), 31–53. DOI:10.1002/csr.2589

Shah, S. Q., & Sarif, S. M. (2023). Exploring the Economic Dimensions of Human Resource Management: A Systematic Literature Review. *International Journal of Business and Economic Affairs*, 8(3). Advance online publication. DOI:10.24088/IJBEA-2023-830012

Sharma, A. S. (2023). Work and life balance post COVID-19. In *Advances in psychology, mental health, and behavioral studies (APMHBS) book series* (pp. 172–186). DOI:10.4018/978-1-6684-8565-1.ch011

Sharma, A., Sharma, R. B., & Ramawat, R. (2020). THE EFFECT OF LEADERSHIP STYLE AND STRESS OUTCOMES OF ACADEMIC LEADERS. *INTERNATIONAL JOURNAL OF ADVANCED RESEARCH IN ENGINEERING AND TECHNOLOGY (IJARET), 11*(7), 197–207. https://iaeme.com/Home/article_id/IJARET_11_07_021

Sharma, N. (2023, December 26). The computers rejecting your job application. *ISHIR | Software Development India.* https://www.ishir.com/blog/106625/the-computers-rejecting-your-job-application.htm

Sharma, H. P., & Chaturvedi, A. (2020). The performance of India in the achievement of sustainable development Goals: A way forward. *Int. J. Mod. Agric*, 9, 1496–1505.

Sharma, H. P., & Kumar, K. (2022, October). The Uptake of Environmental Management System by Small and Medium Enterprises (SMEs) in India. [). IOP Publishing.]. *IOP Conference Series. Earth and Environmental Science*, 1084(1), 012015.

Sharma, R., & Gupta, N. (2015). Green HRM: An innovative approach to environmental sustainability. In *Proceeding of the Twelfth AIMS International Conference on Management,* 2-5.

Sheikh, A. M. (2022). Impact of perceived organizational support on organizational commitment of banking employees: Role of work-life balance. *Journal of Asia Business Studies*, 17(1), 79–99. DOI:10.1108/JABS-02-2021-0071

Shelley, M., & Krippendorff, K. (1984). Content analysis: An introduction to its methodology (by K. Krippendorff). *Journal of the American Statistical Association*, 79(385), 240–240. DOI:10.2307/2288384

Shen, H. (2015). Research on enterprise human resources management mode innovation in the age of big data. In *2015 International Conference on Economics, Management, Law and Education*. (pp. 322-325). Paris: Atlantis Press. DOI:10.2991/emle-15.2015.73

Shibata, S. (2020). Gig Work and the Discourse of Autonomy: Fictitious Freedom in Japan's Digital Economy. *New Political Economy*, 25(4), 535–551. DOI:10.108 0/13563467.2019.1613351

Shirmohammadi, M., Au, W. C., & Beigi, M. (2022). Remote work and work-life balance: Lessons learned from the covid-19 pandemic and suggestions for HRD practitioners. *Human Resource Development International*, 25(2), 163–181. DOI: 10.1080/13678868.2022.2047380

Shoaib, M., Abbas, Z., Yousaf, M., Zámečník, R., Ahmed, J., & Saqib, S. (2021). The role of GHRM practices towards organizational commitment: A mediation analysis of green human capital. *Cogent Business & Management*, 8(1), 1870798.

Sife, A., Lwoga, E., & Sanga, C. (2007). New technologies for teaching and learning: Challenges for higher learning institutions in developing countries. *International journal of education and development using ICT, 3*(2), 57-67.

Simkin, J. (2016). *Robert Owen*. Spartacus Educational. https://spartacus-educational .com/IRowen.htm

Šímová, T. (2022). A research framework for digital nomadism: A bibliometric study. *World Leisure Journal*, 65(2), 175–191. DOI:10.1080/16078055.2022.2134200

Sinambela, L. P. (2021). *Human resource management: Building a solid work team to improve performance*. Earth Literacy.

Singh, R., & Bisen, G. K. (2023). Job Related Uncertainty in the age of Artificial Intelligence and Gig Economy. *COMMERCE RESEARCH REVIEW*, 1(1), 85–100. DOI:10.21844/crr.v1i01.1107

Singh, S. K., Del Giudice, M., Chierici, R., & Graziano, D. (2020). Green innovation and environmental performance: The role of green transformational leadership and green human resource management. *Technological Forecasting and Social Change*, 150, 119762.

Siocon, G. (2023, November 20). *Ways AI is changing HR departments*. Business News Daily. https://www.businessnewsdaily.com/how-ai-is-changing-hr

Sirgy, M. J., & Lee, D. (2017). Work-life balance: An integrative review. *Applied Research in Quality of Life*, 13(1), 229–254. DOI:10.1007/s11482-017-9509-8

Si, S., & Chen, H. (2020). A literature review of disruptive innovation: What it is, how it works and where it goes. *Journal of Engineering and Technology Management*, 56, 101568. DOI:10.1016/j.jengtecman.2020.101568

Sitzmann, T., & Weinhardt, J. M. (2018). Training engagement theory: A multilevel perspective on the effectiveness of work-related training. *Journal of Management*, 44(2), 732–756. DOI:10.1177/0149206315574596

Skaalvik, E. M., & Skaalvik, S. (2011). Teacher job satisfaction and motivation to leave the teaching profession: Relations with school context, feeling of belonging, and emotional exhaustion. *Teaching and Teacher Education*, 27(6), 1029–1038. DOI:10.1016/j.tate.2011.04.001

Skinner, N., Cathcart, A., & Pocock, B. (2016). To ask or not to ask? Investigating workers' flexibility requests and the phenomenon of discontented non-requesters. Labour & Industry: a journal of the social and economic relations of work, 26(2), 103-119. DOI:10.1080/10301763.2016.1157677

Skinner, B. (1974). *About behaviorism*. Vintage.

Slaper, T. F., & Hall, T. J. (2011). *The triple bottom line: What is it and how does it work?* https://www.ibrc.indiana.edu/ibr/2011/spring/article2.html

Smith, A. (1964). *The wealth of nations*. Dutton.

Society for Human Resource Management. (2024). *2024 talent trends survey findings: Artificial intelligence in HR*. SHRM's Voice of Work Research Panel. https://shrm-res.cloudinary.com/image/upload/AI/2024-Talent-Trends-Survey_Artificial-Intelligence-Findings.pdf

Sodiya, E. O., Umoga, U. J., Amoo, O. O., & Atadoga, A. (2024). AI-driven warehouse automation: A comprehensive review of systems. *GSC Advanced Research and Reviews*, 18(2), 272–282. DOI:10.30574/gscarr.2024.18.2.0063

Soliman, F., & Spooner, K. (2000). Strategies for Implementing Knowledge Management: Role of Human Resources Management. *Journal of Knowledge Management*, 4(4), 337–351. DOI:10.1108/13673270010379894

Song, L., & Jo, S. J. (2023). How job crafting behaviors influence the innovative behavior of knowledge workers in the gig economy: Based on the organismic integration theory. *Frontiers in Psychology*, 14, 1228881. DOI:10.3389/fpsyg.2023.1228881 PMID:37731880

Sow, M. (2015). Relationship Between Organizational Commitment and Turnover Intentions Among Healthcare Internal Auditors. *Walden University Scholar Works*. https://scholarworks.waldenu.edu/cgi/viewcontent.cgi?article=2351&context=dissertations

Spencer, D. A. (2024). AI, automation and the lightening of work. *AI & Society*. Advance online publication. DOI:10.1007/s00146-024-01959-3

Sposato, M. (2024). Editorial. *Strategic HR Review*, 23(1), 40–42. DOI:10.1108/SHR-02-2024-204

Srivastava, S. C. (2005). Managing core competence of the organization. *Vikalpa*, 30(4), 49–64. DOI:10.1177/0256090920050405

Srivastava, S., & Agrawal, S. (2020). Resistance to change and turnover intention: A moderated mediation model of burnout and perceived organizational support. *Journal of Organizational Change Management*, 33(7), 1431–1447. DOI:10.1108/JOCM-02-2020-0063

Stank, T., Esper, T., Goldsby Thomas, J., Zinn, W., & Autry, C. (2019). Toward a digitally dominant paradigm for twenty-first century supply chain scholarship. *International Journal of Physical Distribution & Logistics Management*, 49(10), 956–971. DOI:10.1108/IJPDLM-03-2019-0076

Stanley, D. S., & Aggarwal, V. (2019). Impact of disruptive technology on human resource management practices. *International Journal of Business Continuity and Risk Management*, 9(4), 350–361. DOI:10.1504/IJBCRM.2019.102608

Steinmann, B., Klug, H. J. P., & Maier, G. W. (2018). The Path Is the Goal: How Transformational Leaders Enhance Followers' Job Attitudes and Proactive Behavior. *Frontiers in Psychology*, 9, 2338. Advance online publication. DOI:10.3389/fpsyg.2018.02338 PMID:30555375

Stirling, E. (2016). 'I'm Always on Facebook!': Exploring Facebook as a Mainstream Research Tool and Ethnographic Site. In Snee, H., Hine, C., Morey, Y., Roberts, S., & Watson, H. (Eds.), *Digital Methods for Social Science*. Palgrave Macmillan., DOI:10.1057/9781137453662_4

STOA (Scientific Foresight Unit). (2022), AI and digital tools in workplace management and evaluation. An assessment of the EU's legal framework. Available at: https://www.europarl.europa.eu/RegData/etudes/STUD/2022/729516/EPRS_STU(2022)729516_EN.pdf

Stone, D. L., & Deadrick, D. L. (2015). Challenges and opportunities affecting the future of human resource management. *Human Resource Management Review*, 25(2), 139–145. DOI:10.1016/j.hrmr.2015.01.003

Storey, J. (1995). *Human resource management: A critical text*. Routledge.

Strassburger, C., Wachholz, F., Peters, M., Schnitzer, M., & Blank, C. (2022). Organizational leisure benefits – a resource to facilitate employees' work-life balance? *Employee Relations*, 45(3), 585–602. DOI:10.1108/ER-10-2021-0428

Straughan, E. R., & Bissell, D. (2022). Curious encounters: The social consolations of digital platform work in the gig economy. *Urban Geography*, 43(9), 1309–1327. DOI:10.1080/02723638.2021.1927324

Strohmeier, , S. (2020), Digital human resource management: A conceptual clarification. *German Journal of Human Resource Management, 34*(3), pp. 345 -365.

Strohmeier, S., & Kabst, R. (2014). Configurations of e-HRM–an empirical exploration. *Employee Relations*, 36(4), 333–353. DOI:10.1108/ER-07-2013-0082

Strother, J. B. (2002). An assessment of the effectiveness of e-learning in corporate training programs. *International Review of Research in Open and Distance Learning*, 3(1). Advance online publication. DOI:10.19173/irrodl.v3i1.83

Sudhakar, R., & Basariya, S. R. (2017). Perspectives and the factors influencing effectiveness of training and development on employees' performance. *International Journal of Civil Engineering and Technology*, 8(9), 135–141.

Sukardi, S., Herminingsih, A., Djumarno, D., & Kasmir, K. (2021). Effect of human resource management practices to maturity knowledge management. [JDM]. *Jurnal Doktor Manajemen*, 4(1), 14–29. DOI:10.22441/jdm.v4i1.12103

Sukenti, S. (2023). Financial Management Concepts: A Review. [ADMAN]. *Journal of Contemporary Administration and Management*, 1(1), 13–16. DOI:10.61100/adman.v1i1.4

Summary of the State Audit Office's State Audit Report "Human Resource Management in Public Administration Institutions (summarised results of the audits of the three ministries' areas of governance)," 13-02-2017, No VA_P-10-1-1.

Summers, E. (1983). Bradford's Law and the Retrieval of Reading Research Journal Literature. *Reading Research Quarterly*, 19(1), 102–109. DOI:10.2307/747340

Sun, P. C., Tsai, R. J., Finger, G., Chen, Y. Y., & Yeh, D. (2008). What drives a successful e-Learning? An empirical investigation of the critical factors influencing learner satisfaction. *Computers & Education*, 50(4), 1183–1202. DOI:10.1016/j.compedu.2006.11.007

Sureth, A. M. (2024). *Venturing Into Uncharted Territory – Exploring the Psychological Implications of AI-Driven Automation for Employees*. DOI:10.18452/28643

Susanti, D., Dwihantoro, P., Sandy, F., & Muliawanti, L. (2022). Social media for social movement: A social media training for Turun Tangan Organization. *Community Empowerment*, 7(8), 1429–1436. DOI:10.31603/ce.7673

Sütçü, C. S. ve Aytekin Ç., (2018). Veri Bilimi. İstanbul: Paloma Kitapları (1.Baskı).

Szmigin, I., & Rutherford, R. (2013). Shared value and the impartial spectator test. *Journal of Business Ethics*, 114(1), 171–182. DOI:10.1007/s10551-012-1335-1

Tabor-Błażewicz, J. (2023). Artificial intelligence adoption in human resources management. In Hajdas, M. (Ed.), *Game changers in management* (pp. 30–43). Publishing House of Wroclaw University of Economics and Business., DOI:10.15611/2023.10.9.02

Tabrizi, B., Lam, E., Girard, K., & Irvin, V. (2019). Digital transformation is not about technology Available at: https://bluecirclemarketing.com/wpcontent/uploads/2019/07/Digital-Transformation-Is-Not-About-Technology.pdf [Accessed: 10 April 2024].

Talukder, M. B., Kumar, S., Kaiser, F., & Mia, Md. N. (2024). Pilgrimage Creative Tourism: A Gateway to Sustainable Development Goals in Bangladesh. In M. Hamdan, M. Anshari, N. Ahmad, & E. Ali (Eds.), *Advances in Public Policy and Administration* (pp. 285–300). IGI Global. DOI:10.4018/979-8-3693-1742-6.ch016

Talukder, M. B. (2021). An assessment of the roles of the social network in the development of the Tourism Industry in Bangladesh. *International Journal of Business, Law, and Education*, 2(3), 85–93. DOI:10.56442/ijble.v2i3.21

Talukder, M. B., Kabir, F., Muhsina, K., & Das, I. R. (2023). Emerging Concepts of Artificial Intelligence in the Hotel Industry: A Conceptual Paper. *International Journal of Research Publication and Reviews*, 4(9), 1765–1769. DOI:10.55248/gengpi.4.923.92451

Talukder, M. B., & Kumar, S. (2024). The Development of ChatGPT and Its Implications for the Future of Customer Service in the Hospitality Industry. In Derbali, A. M. S. (Ed.), (pp. 100–126). Advances in Information Security, Privacy, and Ethics. IGI Global., DOI:10.4018/979-8-3693-1511-8.ch005

Tang, G., Chen, Y., Jiang, Y., Paillé, P., & Jia, J. (2018). Green human resource management practices: Scale development and validity. *Asia Pacific Journal of Human Resources*, 56(1), 31–55.

Tanova, C., & Bayighomog, S. W. (2022). Green human resource management in service industries: The construct, antecedents, consequences, and outlook. *Service Industries Journal*, 42(5-6), 412–452.

Tan, Y. Y., & Mohd Rasdi, R. (2017). Antecedents of Employees' E-training Participation in a Malaysian Private Company. *Pertanika Journal of Social Science & Humanities*, 25(2).

Tariq, S., Jan, F. A., & Ahmad, M. S. (2016). Green employee empowerment: A systematic literature review on state-of-art in green human resource management. *Quality & Quantity*, 50(1), 237–269. DOI:10.1007/s11135-014-0146-0

Tarkar, P. (2022). Role of green hospitals in sustainable construction: Benefits, rating systems and constraints. *Materials Today: Proceedings*, 60, 247–252.

TeamLease EDTECH. (n.d.). *What is causing the skill gap in India?* Retrieved May 16, 2023, from https://www.teamleaseedtech.com/blog/what-is-causing-the-skill-gap-in-india.html

Tekbaş, İ. (2019). *Muhasebenin dijital dönüşümü ve mali mühendislik.* CERES Yayınları.

ten Brummelhuis, L. L., & Van der Lippe, T. (2010). Effective work-life balance support for various household structures. *Human Resource Management*, 49(2), 173–193. DOI:10.1002/hrm.20340

Tett, R. P., & Meyer, J. P. TETT. (1993). Job satisfaction, organizational commitment, turnover intention, and turnover: Path analyses based on meta-analytic findings. *Personnel Psychology*, 46(2), 259–293. DOI:10.1111/j.1744-6570.1993.tb00874.x

Thite, M. (2019). Electronic/digital HRM: a primer. In Thite, M. (Ed.), *e-HRM: Digital Approaches, Directions & Applications* (pp. 1–21). Routledge.

Tlaiss, H. A., & Dirani, K. M. (2015). Women and training: An empirical investigation in the Arab Middle East. *Human Resource Development International*, 1–21. DOI:10.1080/13678868.2015.1050315

Torma, C. Heloisa Brenha Ribeiro, & Cuéllar, L. V. (2022). *Democracy at no workplace: The voice of gig economy workers and its implications for corporate governance.* DOI:10.13140/RG.2.2.28583.62886

Traversy, G., Barnieh, L., Akl, E. A., Allan, G. M., Brouwers, M., Ganache, I., Grundy, Q., Guyatt, G. H., Kelsall, D., Leng, G., Moore, A., Persaud, N., Schünemann, H. J., Straus, S., Thombs, B. D., Rodin, R., & Tonelli, M. (2021). Managing conflicts of interest in the development of health guidelines. *Canadian Medical Association Journal*, 193(2), 49–54. DOI:10.1503/cmaj.200651 PMID:33431547

Truss, C., & Gratton, L. (1994). Strategic Human Resource Management: A Conceptual Approach. *International Journal of Human Resource Management*, 5(3), 663–686. DOI:10.1080/09585199400000053

Tsymbaliuk, S., Vasylyk, A., & Stoliaruk, K. (2021). Green human resource management: how to implement environmental issues into HR practices. In *E3S Web of Conferences* (Vol. 255, p. 01037). EDP Sciences.

Tsymbaliuk, S., Vasylyk, A., & Stoliaruk, K. (2023). Green recruitment and adaptation practices in GHRM. []. IOP Publishing.]. *IOP Conference Series. Earth and Environmental Science*, 1126(1), 012029.

Tug, M. A., & Basar, P. (2023). FUTURE OF THE GIG ECONOMY. *Pressacademia*, 1, 1. Advance online publication. DOI:10.17261/Pressacademia.2023.1796

Tüm, K. (2014). Kurumsal sürdürülebilirlik ve muhasebeye yansımaları: Sürdürülebilirlik muhasebesi. *Akademik Yaklaşımlar Dergisi, 5*(1).

Turşucular, E. (2023). *Covid-19 salgın döneminde insan kaynakları yönetiminde meydana gelen değişimler ve dijital insan kaynakları yönetiminin artan önemi* (Master's thesis, Trakya Üniversitesi Sosyal Bilimler Enstitüsü).

Tyler, T. R., & Blader, S. L. (2001). Identity and cooperative behavior in groups. *Group Processes & Intergroup Relations*, 4(3), 207–226. DOI:10.1177/1368430201004003003

Tyson, L. D., & Zysman, J. (2022). Automation, AI & Work. *Daedalus*, 151(2), 256–271. DOI:10.1162/daed_a_01914

Uddin, M. (2021). Addressing work-life balance challenges of working women during COVID-19 in Bangladesh. *International Social Science Journal*, 71(239–240), 7–20. DOI:10.1111/issj.12267 PMID:34230685

Ugwu, F. O., Amazue, L. O., & Onyedire, N. G. (2017). Work-family life balance in a Nigerian banking sector setting. *Cogent Psychology*, 4(1), 1290402. DOI:10.1080/23311908.2017.1290402

Ugwu, F. O., Onyishi, I. E., & Rodríguez-Sánchez, A. (2014). Linking organizational trust with employee engagement: The role of psychological empowerment. *Personnel Review*, 43(3), 377–400. DOI:10.1108/PR-11-2012-0198

Ulatowska, R., Wainio, E., & Pierzchała, M. (2023). Digital transformation in HRM of the modern business service sector in Finland and Poland. *Journal of Organizational Change Management*, 36(7), 1180–1192. DOI:10.1108/JOCM-11-2022-0339

UN. (n.d.-a). *#Envision2030: 17 goals to transform the world for persons with disabilities*. https://www.un.org/development/desa/disabilities/envision2030.html

UN. (n.d.-b). *The 17 goals | sustainable development*. https://sdgs.un.org/goals

United Nations. (2020, February 12). *Covid-19 public health emergency of international concern (PHEIC) global research and innovation forum*. https://www.who.int/publications/m/item/covid-19-public-health-emergency-of-international-concern-(pheic)-global-research-and-innovation-forum

Upadhyay, A. K., & Khandelwal, K. (2019). Artificial intelligence-based training learning from application. *Development and Learning in Organizations*, 33(2), 20–23. DOI:10.1108/DLO-05-2018-0058

Uslu, Y. D., & Kedikli, E. (2017). Sürdürülebilirlik kapsamında yeşil insan kaynakları yönetimine genel bir bakış. *Üçüncü Sektör Sosyal Ekonomi, 52*(3), 66-81, DOI:10.15659/3.sektor-sosyal-ekonomi.17.12.694

Vaishya, R., Javaid, M., Khan, I. H., & Haleem, A. (2020). Artificial intelligence (AI) applications for COVID-19 pandemic. *Diabetes & Metabolic Syndrome*, 14(4), 337–339. DOI:10.1016/j.dsx.2020.04.012 PMID:32305024

van der Togt, J., & Rasmussen, T. H. (2017). Toward evidence-based HR. *Journal of Organizational Effectiveness*, 4(2), 127–132. DOI:10.1108/JOEPP-02-2017-0013

Van Dijk, R., & Van Dick, R. (2009). Navigating organizational change: Change leaders, employee resistance and work-based identities. *Journal of Change Management*, 9(2), 143–163. DOI:10.1080/14697010902879087

Van Knippenberg, D., Van Dick, R., & Tavares, S. M. (2005). Social Identity and Social Exchange: Identification, Support, and Withdrawal from the Job. *Social Science Research Network*. https://papers.ssrn.com/sol3/Delivery.cfm/8497.pdf?abstractid=960618&mirid=1&type=2

Van Manen, M. (2007). Phenomenology of practice. *Phenomenology & Practice*, 1(1), 11–30.

van Vulpen, E. (2023, December 15). Learning and development. *AIHR*. https://www.aihr.com/blog/learning-and-development/

Vardarlier, P. (2020). Digital Transformation of Human Resource Management: Digital Applications and Strategic Tools in HRM. In *Digital Business Strategies in Blockchain Ecosystems* (pp. 239–264). Springer. DOI:10.1007/978-3-030-29739-8_11

Varga, A. (2022). State and development directions for human resources management in the public sector. Acta Academiae Beregsasiensis. Economics. 115-122.

Varma, A., Dawkins, C., & Chaudhuri, K. (2023). Artificial intelligence and people management: A critical assessment through the ethical lens. *Human Resource Management Review*, 33(1), 100923. DOI:10.1016/j.hrmr.2022.100923

Vassakis, K., Petrakis, E., & Kopanakis, I. (2018). Big Data Analytics: Applications, Prospects and Challenges. In G. M. In: Skourletopoulos, Mobile Big Data. Lecture Notes on Data Engineering and Communications Technologies, vol 10. (pp. 3-20). Springer.

Veerasamy, U., Joseph, M. S., & Parayitam, S. (2023). Green human resource management and employee green behaviour: participation and involvement, and training and development as moderators. *South Asian Journal of Human Resources Management*, 23220937221144361.

Verma, A., Venkatesan, M., Kumar, M., & Verma, J. (2022). The future of work post Covid-19: Key perceived HR implications of hybrid workplaces in India. *Journal of Management Development*, 42(1), 13–28. DOI:10.1108/JMD-11-2021-0304

Verma, P., Kumar, V., Mittal, A., Gupta, P., & Hsu, S. C. (2022). Addressing strategic human resource management practices for TQM: The case of an Indian tire manufacturing company. *The TQM Journal*, 34(1), 29–69. DOI:10.1108/TQM-02-2021-0037

Vernyuy, A. (2024). Impact of Technological Advancements on Human Existence. *International Journal of Philosophy*, 3(2), 54–66. DOI:10.47941/ijp.1874

Vidas, B. M., & Bubanja, I. (2017). The challenge of going digital. Journal of engineering management and competitiveness (jemc), 7(2), 126-136.

Vincent, J., & Baptiste, M. (2021). The impact of a democratic leadership style on employee satisfaction, customer satisfaction, and customer loyalty at a midsized nonprofit sport and recreation center. *Global Sport Business Journal, 9*(1), 79–101. http://www.gsbassn.com/Journal/Vol9-1/GSBJ-Vol9-Iss1-Baptisti-pp79-101.pdf

Vnoučková, L. (2020). Impact of COVID-19 on human resource management. *RELAIS*, 3(1), 18–21.

Vranova, S. (2012). Identifying the specifics of motivating different groups of employees. *GSTF Journal on Business Review*, 2(2), 98–104.

Vrontis, D., Christofi, M., Pereira, V., Tarba, S., Makrides, A., & Trichina, E. (2022). Artificial intelligence, robotics, advanced technologies and human resource management: A systematic review. *International Journal of Human Resource Management*, 33(6), 1237–1266. DOI:10.1080/09585192.2020.1871398

Vu, A. N., & Nguyen, D. L. (2024). The gig economy: The precariat in a climate precarious world. *World Development Perspectives*, 34, 100596. DOI:10.1016/j.wdp.2024.100596

Waldkirch, M., Bucher, E., Schou, P. K., & Grünwald, E. (2021). Controlled by the algorithm, coached by the crowd – how HRM activities take shape on digital work platforms in the gig economy. *International Journal of Human Resource Management*, 32(12), 2643–2682. DOI:10.1080/09585192.2021.1914129

Wang, D., Cui, L., Vu, T., & Feng, T. (2022). Political capital and MNE responses to institutional voids: The case of Chinese state-owned enterprises in Africa. *Organization Studies*, 43(1), 105–126. DOI:10.1177/0170840620954011

Wang, Y. S., Wang, H. Y., & Shee, D. Y. (2007). Measuring e-learning systems success in an organizational context: Scale development and validation. *Computers in Human Behavior*, 23(4), 1792–1808. DOI:10.1016/j.chb.2005.10.006

Ward, P., Williams, A.M. and Hancock, P.A., 2006. Simulation for Performance and Training.

Waxin, M., & Bateman, R. (2009). Public Sector Human Resource Management Reform Across Countries: From Performance Appraisal to Performance Steering? *European Journal of International Management*, 3(4), 495–511. DOI:10.1504/EJIM.2009.028852

Weggen, C. C., & Urdan, T. A. (2000). Corporate e-learning: Exploring a new frontier. *WR Hambrecht and Co.*www. wrhambrecht. com/research/coverage/elearning/idir explore. html

Welch, C. L., & Welch, D. E. (2012). What do HR managers really do? HR roles on international projects. *MIR. Management International Review*, 52(4), 597–617. DOI:10.1007/s11575-011-0126-8

Wells, A. T., & Young, S. B. (2011). *Airport Planning &Management*. McGraw-Hill Companies.

Werhane, P. H. (2000). Business ethics and the origins of contemporary capitalism: Economics and ethics in the work of Adam Smith and Herbert Spencer. *Journal of Business Ethics*, 24(3), 185–198. DOI:10.1023/A:1005937623890

Whyte, W. H. (1956). *The organization man*. LaFarge Literary Agency.

Wibowo, A., Chen, S. C., Wiangin, U., Ma, Y., & Ruangkanjanases, A. (2020). Customer behavior as an outcome of social media marketing: The role of social media marketing activity and customer experience. *Sustainability (Basel)*, 13(1), 189. DOI:10.3390/su13010189

Wiljer, D., & Hakim, Z. (2019). Developing an artificial intelligence–enabled health care practice: Rewiring health care professions for better care. *Journal of Medical Imaging and Radiation Sciences*, 50(4), 8–14. DOI:10.1016/j.jmir.2019.09.010 PMID:31791914

Wilkinson, E. (1972). The Ambiguity of Bradford's Law. *The Journal of Documentation*, 28(2), 122–130. DOI:10.1108/eb026534

Wilson, E. (2019). Disrupting dark web supply chains to protect precious data. *Computer Fraud & Security*, 2019(4), 6–9. DOI:10.1016/S1361-3723(19)30039-9

Wolford, B. (2018, November 7). *What is GDPR, the EU's new data protection law?* GDPR.Eu. https://gdpr.eu/what-is-gdpr/

Wong, K., Teh, P., & Chan, A. H. S. (2023). Seeing the Forest and the Trees: A scoping Review of Empirical Research on Work-Life Balance. *Sustainability (Basel)*, 15(4), 2875. DOI:10.3390/su15042875

Wright, P. M., Dunford, B. B. & Snell, S. A. (2001). Human resources and the resourcebased view of the firm', Journal of Management, 27(6), pp. 701 - 721. Business Source Ultimate. .DOI:10.1177/014920630102700607

Wright, P. M., & McMahan, G. C. (1992). Theoretical perspectives for strategic human resource management. *Journal of Management*, 18(2), 295–320. DOI:10.1177/014920639201800205

Wu, D., & Huang, J. L. (2024). Gig work and gig workers: An integrative review and agenda for future research. *Journal of Organizational Behavior*, job.2775. DOI:10.1002/job.2775

Wu, J.European University. (2024). E-Learning Management Systems in Higher Education: Features of the Application at a Chinese vs. European University. *Journal of the Knowledge Economy*, ●●●, 1–31. DOI:10.1007/s13132-024-02159-6

Xie, Z. (2020), Research on Enterprise Human Resource Management Under the Background of Big Data. In 2020 International Conference on Intelligent Transportation, Big Data & Smart City (ICITBS), (pp. pp.600-604, IEEE.). DOI:10.1109/ICITBS49701.2020.00132

Xu, M., Dust, S. B., & Liu, S. (2023). COVID-19 and the great resignation: The role of death anxiety, need for meaningful work, and task significance. *The Journal of Applied Psychology*, 108(11), 1790–1811. DOI:10.1037/apl0001102 PMID:37261767

Yadegar, Minoofar & Soleymani LLP. (2024). Retaliation in performance evaluations. *Yadegar, Minoofar & Soleymani, LLP.* https://www.ymsllp.com/blog/2023/09/retaliation-in-performance-evaluations/

Yang, J. B. (2008). Effect of newcomer socialisation on organisational commitment, job satisfaction, and turnover intention in the hotel industry. *Service Industries Journal*, 28(4), 429–443. DOI:10.1080/02642060801917430

Yazdani, M., Pamucar, D., Erdmann, A., & Toro-Dupouy, L. (2023). Resilient sustainable investment in digital education technology: A stakeholder-centric decision support model under uncertainty. *Technological Forecasting and Social Change*, 188, 122282. DOI:10.1016/j.techfore.2022.122282

Yazıcıoğlu, Y., & Erdoğan, S. (2004). *SPSS Uygulamalı Bilimsel Araştırma Yöntemleri*. Detay Yayıncılık.

Yıldırım, A., & Şimşek, H. (2005), Sosyal bilimlerde nitel araştırma yöntemleri. Ankara: Seçkin Yayıncılık (5. Baskı).

Yıldız, D. (2022a). *Kademe Azaltma (Delayering). İ. Çevik Tekin içinde, Yenilikçi İnsan Kaynakları Uygulamaları ve Örgütsel İnovasyon: Teori, Örnek Olay ve Öneriler*. Nobel.

Yıldız, D. (2022b). *Sosyal Sorumluluk. İ. Çevik Tekin içinde, Güncel ve Teknolojik Gelişmeler Işığında İnsan Kaynakları Yönetimi*. Nobel.

Yılmaz, C., & Yılmaz, T. (2023). Endüstri 4.0'ın İnsan Kaynakları Yönetimine Etkisi: İKY 4.0. *Emek ve Toplum*, 12(32), 11–28. DOI:10.31199/hakisderg.1214130

Yılmazer, A. (2020). *İnsan Kaynakları Yöneitmi ve Örnk Olaylar*. Seçkin Yayıncılık.

Yin, L., Alba, D., & Nicoletti, L. (2024, March 7). OpenAI's GPT Is a recruiter's dream tool. Tests show there's racial bias. *Bloomberg.Com*. https://www.bloomberg.com/graphics/2024-openai-gpt-hiring-racial-discrimination/

York, A. (2024, February 13). *10 best AI recruitment tools for hiring teams in 2024*. ClickUp. https://clickup.com/blog/ai-tools-for-recruitment/

Yu, Z., & JInajun, N. (2020). How to achieve HRM digital transformation. available at: https://www.sohu.com/a/400600846_343325

Yu, J., Park, J., & Hyun, S. S. (2021). Impacts of the COVID-19 pandemic on employees' work stress, well-being, mental health, organizational citizenship behavior, and employee-customer identification. *Journal of Hospitality Marketing & Management*, 30(5), 529–548. DOI:10.1080/19368623.2021.1867283

Yu, J., Yuan, L., Han, G., Li, H., & Li, P. (2022). A Study of the Impact of Strategic Human Resource Management on Organizational Resilience. *Behavioral Sciences (Basel, Switzerland)*, 12(12), 508. DOI:10.3390/bs12120508 PMID:36546991

Yusliza, M. Y., Norazmi, N. A., Jabbour, C. J. C., Fernando, Y., Fawehinmi, O., & Seles, B. M. R. P. (2019). Top management commitment, corporate social responsibility, and green human resource management: A Malaysian study. *Benchmarking*, 26(6), 2051–2078.

Yusuf, J., Saitgalina, M., & Chapman, D. W. (2020). Work-life balance and well-being of graduate students. *Journal of Public Affairs Education*, 26(4), 458–483. DOI:10.1080/15236803.2020.1771990

Zainal, N. S., Wider, W., Lajuma, S., Ahmad Khadri, M. W., Taib, N. M., & Joseph, A. (2022). Employee retention in the service industry in Malaysia. *Frontiers in Sociology*, 7, 928951. Advance online publication. DOI:10.3389/fsoc.2022.928951 PMID:35880145

Zalizko, V. D., Dobrowolski, R. H., Cherniak, A. M., Artemov, V. Y., & Nowak, D. V. (2022). Gig-economy as a safety gradient for sustainable development of the mining industry. *Naukovyi Visnyk Natsionalnoho Hirnychoho Universytetu*, 4(4), 170–175. DOI:10.33271/nvngu/2022-4/170

Zang, S. Y., & Ye, M. L. (2015). Human Resource Management in the Era of Big Data. *Journal of Human Resource and Sustainability Studies*, 3(1), 41–45. DOI:10.4236/jhrss.2015.31006

Zareie, B., & Jafari Navimipour, N. (2020). A model to determine the factors. affecting satisfaction employees in e-learning systems. *Journal of Development & Evolution Management*, 1398(special issue), 187–197.

Zaugg, R., Blum, A., & Thom, N. (2001). *Sustainability in Human Resource Management*. University of Berne Press.

Zhang, H. (2019). Reflections on innovation of human resource management in the era of big data. 8th International Conference on Education and Management in 2018 (ICEM 2018), 75 (pp. 518-520.). China: Atlantis Press.

Zhang, J., & Chen, Z. (2023). Exploring Human Resource Management Digital Transformation in the Digital Age. *Journal of the Knowledge Economy*, 1–17.

Zhang, J., Wang, Y., & Gao, F. (2023). The dark and bright side of laissez-faire leadership: Does subordinates' goal orientation make a difference? *Frontiers in Psychology*, 14, 1077357. Advance online publication. DOI:10.3389/fpsyg.2023.1077357 PMID:37008876

Zhang, Y., Xu, S., Zhang, L., & Yang, M. (2021). Big data and human resource management research: An integrative review and new directions for future research. *Journal of Business Research*, 133, 34–50. DOI:10.1016/j.jbusres.2021.04.019

Zhao, X., & Namasivayam, K. (2009). Posttraining self-efficacy, job involvement, and training effectiveness in the hospitality industry. *Journal of Human Resources in Hospitality & Tourism*, 8(2), 137–152. DOI:10.1080/15332840802269767

Zhu, W. (2020). Reconstruction of human resource management under big data and artificial intelligence. *Journal of Physics: Conference Series*, 1533(4), 1–6. DOI:10.1088/1742-6596/1533/4/042016

Zikopoulos, P., Deroos, D., Parasuraman, K., Deutsch, T., Giles, J., & Corrigan, D. (2012). *Harness the power of big data The IBM big data platform*. McGraw Hill Professional.

Zinkula, J., & Mok, A. (2024, March 6). *ChatGPT may be coming for our jobs. Here are the 10 roles that AI is most likely to replace*. Business Insider. https://www.businessinsider.com/chatgpt-jobs-at-risk-replacement-artificial-intelligence-ai-labor-trends-2023-02

Zülch, G., Stock, P., & Schmidt, D. (2012). Analysis of the strain on employees in the retail sector considering work-life balance. *Work (Reading, Mass.)*, 41, 2675–2682. DOI:10.3233/WOR-2012-0510-2675 PMID:22317125

About the Contributors

Salim Kurnaz is an Associate Professor, with 22 years of experience in aviation. He worked as a maintenance technician, quality control technician and maintenance instructor in the Turkish Armed Forces between 1997-2020. He worked at Joint Force Command (JFCBS) Brunssum/ Netherlands between 2010-2013. He received bachelor's degree on Public Management in 2005 and on Aviation Management in 2022 from Anadolu University; master's degree in International Relations from Oklahoma University Oklahoma/USA in 2013 and in Business Management from Malatya Inonu University in 2018. He received his doctorate degree on management Sciences in 2019 from Malatya Inonu University. He continues his studies in the fields of public administration, aviation management, contemporary management systems, strategic management, and behavioral sciences. He is also working as visiting Associate Professor at Kazimiero Simonaviciaus University Vilnius, Lithuania.

Jolanta Bieliauskaitė is a professor and the Rector at Kazimieras Simonavicius University (Lithuania), with an educational background in philosophy and law, and nearly 20 years of experience in higher education. Alongside her passion for legal philosophy and academic ethics, she addresses both the theoretical and practical aspects of human resources management. Her holistic approach combines legal expertise with practical HR strategies, including talent acquisition, employee development, performance management, and fostering a positive organizational culture. She emphasizes ethical and shared leadership, as well as collaborative work environments, which foster improvements in employee engagement and advance the university's strategic goals.

***

Cem Angin is a faculty member at Ordu University, Faculty of Economics and Administrative Sciences, Department of Political Science and Public Administration. In 2009, he completed his undergraduate studies at Uludağ University, Department of Political Science and Public Administration, in 2016 he completed his master's degree at Samsun Ondokuz Mayıs University, and in 2019 he completed his doctorate at Ankara University, Faculty of Political Sciences. He has studies on E-Government, Artificial Intelligence, Administrative Law, Public Administration, Local Governments, Personnel Management.

Vandita Bhaumik is a student at CHRIST University. She has a keen interest in the emerging areas of human resources.

B. Anthony Brown is a Business Strategy and Maritime Consultant specializing in corporate restructuring and change management. His work emphasizes ethical and sustainable organizational transformation, diversity, and inclusion. He earned his Ph.D. in Management With an Emphasis on Leadership and Organizational Change from Walden University in 2020. He has over 30 years in the Maritime Industry, where he served as Captain on passenger and cargo ships, as well as Marine Superintendent, Chief Operations Officer, and Maritime Consultant for land-based maritime corporations.

Sharmin Akter Chowdhury is a distinguished Author, Researcher, and Assistant Professor at the College of Agricultural Sciences at the International University of Business Agriculture and Technology (IUBAT) in Dhaka, Bangladesh. With a robust academic foundation in Agricultural Science, she earned her BSc in Agriculture and MSc in Agronomy from Bangladesh Agricultural University, followed by a PhD from Niigata University, Japan. Dr. Chowdhury has an extensive portfolio of research publications, driven by her passion for advancing agricultural sciences. She has also actively participated in numerous international conferences across the globe, showcasing her dedication to sharing knowledge and fostering global collaboration in her field.

Kübra Cingöz has been working for about 2,5 years as a Research Assistant in Gaziantep University. She completed her master degree in Aviation Management Department and is currently getting her PhD in Kocaeli University.

Vildan Durmaz was born in Eskişehir. She graduated from Anadolu University, Educational Faculty, English Teaching Department in 1988. She had studied as an instructor at Anadolu University, School of Civil Aviation. She had her master degree on Management and Organization and doctorate on Civil Aviation Management at the same university. She has been teaching undergraduate, graduate and PhD courses such as; Air Transportation Management, Airport Management, Airports and Environment, Aviation English at Eskişehir Technical University. She has been attending national and international conferences and studying on the field of management and aviation related to the subject of environmental management systems, airport sustainability, team management, current management applications. She wrote several course and scientific books on strategic management.

Deeksha Gupta Ganguly is an Assistant Professor, School of Business & Management. She is a Post-graduate in Commerce & Management (Human Resource Management & Marketing). She has also cleared UGC NET in Management. Prof. Ganguly has a rich academic & industry experience of 15 plus years and worked for various Educational institutions & universities in Delhi NCR and Chennai. She is very much involved in academic research and has extensively published research papers in various Scopus-indexed academic journals. Her research interest includes sustainability and green behavior in higher education.

Ginu George is passionate about delivering high-quality education and research for over 10 years in the field of human resources management, organisational behaviour, business communication and research methodology for undergraduate and postgraduate students. Holds a PhD in Commerce (HRM & OB) and an MPhil in Commerce (Marketing) from Christ University, Bangalore, India. Dr Ginu have more than 10 Scopus-indexed publications and a prolific record of presenting research papers at international conferences, showcasing a commitment to advancing knowledge." Additionally, Dr Ginu George is currently guiding two Ph.D. scholars, providing mentorship and guidance to the next generation of researchers. Beyond academia, also comes with 3 years of practical experience as HR contributing to employee engagement, and talent acquisition. Through the combined experience as an educator and a practitioner, Dr Ginu aims to bridge the gap between theory and practice, and to contribute to the advancement of knowledge and skills in the field of HR.

Keri L. Heitner is a research psychologist, consultant, and contributing faculty in the PhD in Management Program at Walden University. Her work involves applied research, evaluation, and program development about diversity and inclusion; career advancement and re-entry; service delivery research and development in health, mental health, and the government and nonprofit sectors; and entrepreneurship. She is also a writer, editor, methodologist, and curriculum developer.

Jaspreet Kaur is an accomplished Assistant Professor at the University School of Business, Chandigarh University, Mohali, Punjab, India. With a robust educational background, she has earned an MBA in Hospital Management with a specialization in Human Resource Management (HRM) and a Ph.D. in Business Management. Dr. Kaur's research interests extend to the critical intersection of healthcare and business management. With a focus on healthcare and medicine, her scholarly pursuits delve into areas such as healthcare administration, organizational behavior in healthcare settings, and strategic management in the healthcare industry. Through her research, Dr. Kaur aims to address pressing challenges faced by healthcare organizations and contribute to the development of innovative solutions that enhance patient care and organizational effectiveness.

Dushyanth Kumar is PhD from Lovely Professional University, He has published 10 National and International Research Papers and Book Chapters. His area of expertise is Human Resource Management.

Sunil Kumar, currently an Associate Professor at Faculty of Management Sciences, Shoolini University, possesses extensive academic and research experience. With a background in Business Administration, Sunil's research endeavors span multiple domains, including human resource management, e-training, and the application of artificial intelligence in business. His prolific contributions are evidenced by numerous research papers, book chapters, copyrights, and patents. Dr. Kumar has a knack for teaching with expertise in subjects like HR Analytics, Talent Management, Industrial Psychology, and more. He has also successfully guided PhD students and actively contributes to various academic administrative roles. Dr. Kumar's vast research landscape includes topics like AI-based chatbots in recruitment, e-training impact, and more. His papers have been published in esteemed journals like Journal of Workplace Learning and International Journal of Law and Management. Moreover, he has authored books and edited volumes touching upon themes related to the contemporary business environment. Dr. Sunil has been a dynamic participant in numerous workshops, ranging from data analysis to stress

Alev Orhan is a Doctor of Education (Ed.D.) in the field of Educational Sciences. She completed her master's and doctoral studies in the field of Curriculum and Instruction, and has also studied educational programs, the quality of education, accreditation, artificial intelligence, and medical education.

Vedika Pathania Graduated from Christ University with a degree in BBA in Human Resource Management. With a keen interest in the HR domain, she is dedicated to exploring the dynamic and evolving facets of Human Resource Management.

Raksithaa S Currently pursuing her master's in Commerce since 2023 at Christ(Deemed to be University). She Completed Her Undergraduate Degree From Christ(Deemed to be University) in 2023. She is a budding researcher, and her areas of interest include human resources, education, Artificial Intelligence (AI) and ESG. She has presented papers at various conferences and attended multiple workshops in the field of research.

Deepti Sinha has an overall experience of 22 years and is presently associated with Christ University, as Associate Professor. Her specialization is in Human Resource Management and she has carried out her doctoral work in the area of Quality of Work Life. She is presently on the editorial and review board of a few journals and has published more than 30 research papers in journals of national and international repute and one book. She is certified as Accredited Management Teacher in the area of Organizational Behaviour by All India Management Association, New Delhi.

Mohammad Badruddoza Talukder is an Associate Professor, College of Tourism and Hospitality Management, IUBAT - International University of Business Agriculture and Technology, Dhaka-1230, Bangladesh. He holds PhD in Hotel Management from Lovely Professional University, India. He has been teaching various courses in the Department of Tourism and Hospitality at various universities in Bangladesh since 2008. His research areas include tourism management, hotel management, hospitality management, food & beverage management, and accommodation management, where he has published research papers in well-known journals in Bangladesh and abroad. Mr. Talukder is one of the executive members of the Tourism Educators Association of Bangladesh. He has led training and consulting for a wide range of hospitality organizations in Bangladesh. He just became an honorary facilitator at the Bangladesh Tourism Board's Bangabandhu international tourism and hospitality training institution.

Ronit Varghese is a student at CHRIST University. He has a keen interest in the emerging areas of human resources.

Index

Milton Keynes UK
Ingram Content Group UK Ltd.
UKHW051052270924
448873UK00006B/92

9 798369 344125